AFRICANISMS IN THE GULLAH DIALECT

SOUTHERN CLASSICS SERIES

John G. Sproat and Barbara L. Bellows, General Editors

AFRICANISMS IN THE GULLAH DIALECT

LORENZO D. TURNER

with a new introduction by

Katherine Wyly Mille and
Michael B. Montgomery

UNIVERSITY OF SOUTH CAROLINA PRESS

Published in cooperation with the Institute for Southern Studies and
the South Caroliniana Society of the University of South Carolina

Published in Columbia, South Carolina, by the
University of South Carolina Press
Institute for Southern Studies and the South Caroliniana Society
of the University of South Carolina

Manufactured in the United States of America

06 05 5 4 3 2

Library of Congress Cataloging-in-Publication Data

Turner, Lorenzo Dow.
Africanisms in the Gullah dialect / Lorenzo D. Turner.
p. cm. — (Southern classics series)
Originally published: Chicago : University of Chicago Press, 1949. With new introduction by Katherine Wyly Mille and Michael B. Montgomery.
Includes bibliographical references and index.
ISBN 1-57003-452-4 (pbk. : alk. paper)
1. Sea Islands Creole dialect—Etymology. I. Title. II. Series.
PM7875.G8 T8 2002
427'.9757'08996073—dc21 2002071969

CONTENTS

LIST OF ILLUSTRATIONS

GENERAL EDITORS' PREFACE

Lorenzo Dow Turner was a pioneering scholar in the fullest sense of the term. As the introduction to this new edition of his major work makes clear, his systematic examination of the Gullah dialect among African Americans in the Sea Islands of South Carolina and Georgia opened new vistas in the study of vernacular language for linguists and, by extension, for sociologists and other social scientists. A work essential to understanding the African American experience in all its rich variety, *Africanisms in the Gullah Dialect* eminently deserves designation as a Southern Classic.

Southern Classics returns to general circulation books of importance dealing with the history and culture of the American South. Sponsored by the Institute for Southern Studies and the South Caroliniana Society of the University of South Carolina, the series is advised by a board of distinguished scholars who suggest titles and editors of individual volumes to the general editor and help establish priorities in publication.

Chronological age alone does not determine a title's designation as a Southern Classic. The criteria also include significance in contributing to a broad understanding of the region, timeliness in relation to events and moments of peculiar interest to the American South, usefulness in the classroom, and suitability for inclusion in personal and institutional collections on the region.

BARBARA L. BELLOWS
JOHN G. SPROAT
General Editors

INTRODUCTION

THIS book is a classic for what it achieved as well as what it made possible for others to achieve.[1] No less is it a classic for the man who wrote it and the challenges he overcame in writing it. That man, Lorenzo Dow Turner, was the first African American with professional training in linguistics. He focused on a people whose language had long been misunderstood, and he lifted a shroud that had obscured the true history of Gullah (also called Geechee and, more recently, Sea Island Creole), the creole language spoken on the coastal islands and adjacent mainland of South Carolina and Georgia.[2] By means of his linguistic training, natural curiosity, and openness to all that he heard and observed, Turner was uniquely suited to reveal the centuries-long linguistic journey of the Gullah people. He studied them without preconceptions, but with the respect and dignity of a kinsman who saw fellow human beings having much to tell. Long suspicious of outsiders but sensing something new and different in this African American researcher, they in turn entrusted him with their stories and memories—indeed, much of their private world and customs—in their own language.

Turner's work as a linguist and an educator demonstrated what an obscure people's language could reveal to us about human adaptation in general and the development of American English in particular. His work opened a way for Gullah people to reclaim and value their past and made possible a new era of learning about the great continent of Africa and the spread of African culture. The first, and still the most important, book on Gullah, Turner's *Africanisms in the Gullah Dialect* is a foundation for much subsequent thinking and writing on the subject and on African elements in American culture. After its publication in 1949, Gullah could never be viewed in the same way again.

In the early twentieth century, most Americans had little if any education about Africa, relying more on myths than factual knowledge for their ideas about that vast continent. Many viewed Africa as a great monolith and rarely differentiated its peoples, languages, cultures, or terrains. In the Sea Islands and mainland coastal areas of South Carolina and Georgia (the "lowcountry"), some believed that African remnants had been retained in the speech and culture of the Gullah people there. But these speculations were based on little hard evidence, and few elsewhere believed that significant Africanisms (elements of African culture) could have survived into twentieth-century America. In the low-country, whites had occasionally commented on Gullah speech and culture and had written stories in Gullah purportedly to "preserve this quaint speech for posterity," but there was no understanding of Gullah as a dynamic, coherent, and distinct language, one with an evolving, adapting, and patterned structure and a complex history of its own. Rather, early commentators had seen Gullah either as a collection of words corrupted from English or as a repository of archaic features preserved from contact with whites and traceable to dialects from the British Isles. In short, they often saw Gullah as a debased form of "Elizabethan English."[3]

Against this backdrop, Lorenzo Dow Turner's work provided, for the first time, concrete, comparable, and measurable correspondences between Gullah and African languages, tangible objects for those wanting to substantiate speculations about the history of this unusual variety of language, which H. L. Mencken characterized as the only type of American speech not intelligible to outsiders.[4] As the first student of Gullah to have modern linguistic training, Turner approached the subject with a fresh mind, one not preoccupied with searching for the sources of Gullah words in earlier English literature and speech. With *Africanisms*, the product of two decades of research and analysis, and with a lifetime of teaching about Africa, Turner provided persuasive evidence that a substantial African inheritance in North America was recoverable after all. In the process he penetrated the mist of popular mythology about the "dark continent" and successfully challenged scholarly belief that African Americans had no linguistic past.

LORENZO DOW TURNER, THE MAN

Lorenzo Dow Turner was named for a famous itinerant evangelist, Lorenzo Dow (1777–1834), who was born in England but spent much of his life on the Southern frontier of the United States. Though of eccentric appearance and habits, Dow's tireless preaching, especially at Methodist camp meetings, inspired countless followers in America and the British Isles. His passionate but controversial ministry later became known as Primitive Methodism.

Lorenzo Dow Turner, the linguist, was born into an educated African American family a century later and was destined to become a missionary with another message and another style.[5] His teaching, beginning with his scholarly investigation of the African element in Gullah, would inspire a devotion in the halls of American academe and the circles of the educated African American elite. Unlike his namesake, Turner had credentials within the higher education establishment. Throughout his career he would deliver his message about African history, culture, and language to African American students, civic groups, and communities hungry to learn of such things. He would inspire devotion to racial pride and combat the ignorance resulting from years of oppression and the legacy of slavery that discouraged African Americans from examining their past. He would minister to the African American national consciousness for four decades.

Turner was born in 1895 in Elizabeth City, North Carolina, to Rooks and Elizabeth Freeman Turner, both strong advocates of higher education for their sons, of whom Lorenzo was the youngest. In 1910 he entered Howard University in Washington, D.C. (his father's alma mater) and worked as, among other things, a waiter and a railroad porter to pay his college expenses and support his mother, who by this time was widowed. At nineteen he completed his A.B. (cum laude) and entered the Masters program in English at Harvard, completing it in 1917. Thereafter he returned to Howard, where he became professor and head of the Department of English. While on the faculty there, Turner used several summers and one year of leave to earn his doctorate in English from the University of Chicago (1926), completing a dissertation titled "Anti-Slavery Sentiment in American Literature Prior to 1865."[6] He left Howard University in 1928 to found a newspaper with his brother, for a year editing the *Washington Sun*. Within months, the newspaper ceased publication, and Turner found a job as professor and head of the Department of English at Fisk University in Nashville—not, however, before going to Orangeburg, South Carolina, to teach summer school at South Carolina State College in 1929. This temporary job, taken to earn extra income for his family, was unexpectedly to open the door to the rest of his career.

It was in Orangeburg, sixty miles northwest of Charleston, that Turner heard Gullah for the first time. He was intrigued by the fact that students from coastal areas sounded so different from other African Americans and sometimes had unusual nicknames (he would later learn that these were "basket names" given at birth), but he lacked the training to analyze what he heard. To learn more about the discipline of dialectology, the scientific study of speech differences, he attended the Linguistic Society of America Summer Institute at New York University in 1930, where he met prominent American linguists. Among these was Hans Kurath, director of the *Linguistic Atlas of the United States and Canada*, a project designed to survey the pronunciation, vocabulary, and grammar of all English-speaking parts of North America systematically by asking a uniform set of questions of each participant. Among the ambitious goals of the atlas project were describing and mapping the major geographical and social dialects on the continent. The focus of attention and excitement at the institute was the testing of the questionnaire for the *Linguistic Atlas of New England*, the first stage of the national project.[7] That summer, Turner studied under Kurath and other members of the atlas team and learned about atlas work.

Later that same year, Kurath asked Turner to collect some of the first atlas data in the South by interviewing Gullah speakers in South Carolina and Georgia. Turner promptly accepted the offer, declaring, ". . . [I like] this kind of work better than any I have ever done" and planning further training in collecting and analyzing dialect data at the LSA Summer Institute at Yale in 1931.[8] In the meantime, he became the first black member of the Linguistic Society of America. He would later join the International Phonetic Association and the American Dialect Society. While on the Fisk faculty, and when not attending a Linguistics Institute, Turner used his summers to teach at other predominantly African American schools in the South, including Alcorn A & M College, Atlanta University, and Tuskegee Institute. In the course of these assignments he was able informally to compare African American speech patterns from South Carolina with others he heard. His gifts as a dialectologist were becoming apparent.

With extensive training in phonetics and having learned a new discipline, Turner was ready for field work. He spent the period from June to December 1932 and the summer of 1933 conducting interviews on the Sea Islands for the *Linguistic Atlas* under the sponsorship of the American Council of Learned Societies.[9] With his lengthy, systematic interviews of Gullah speakers, the first by a linguist, he embarked on an investigation that would become his life's work, leading ultimately to *Africanisms in the Gullah Dialect*, published in 1949. In his initial year of work, Turner interviewed twenty-one Gullah speakers, three in each of seven areas: in South Carolina on Johns, Wadmalaw, Edisto, and St. Helena Islands, and in Georgia on Sapelo and St. Simons Islands and on Harris Neck and Brewer's Neck, parts of a peninsular mainland area. (See map on page 3). In each locality, he chose two speakers over the age of sixty and one between forty and sixty (appendix I, page 291; for a list and short description of these individuals, see pages xlv-xlvi of this introduction). For each speaker he filled a notebook with extensive notations on their pronunciation, vocabulary, and grammar.

In the course of his work Turner made one hundred wire recordings of Gullah speakers, many of which are transcribed in this book's appendix, "Gullah Texts" (pages 256–89), a collection of stories, chants, testimonies, and recollections. He first presented excerpts of these at the American Dialect Society meeting at Yale University on 31 December 1932.[10] As his horizons broadened, he turned his attention to Louisiana, going there in the summer of 1935 to collect data on a French-based creole often known as "Gombo." Many years later, his widow, Mrs. Lois Turner Williams, stated that Turner's observations in these years led him increasingly to believe that the "archaic English dialect" explanation for the origin of Gullah was implausible.[11] He had begun to hear and note things that other investigators had overlooked but that gave him the necessary clues to build a new case and a new theory for the origin and nature of Gullah. He realized that his ideas required him to look elsewhere—to Africa.

By 1935, Turner had decided to study the African languages that he believed crucial to understanding the background of Gullah. With support from the American Council of Learned Societies and the Humanities Institute of Fisk University, he spent the 1936–37 academic year based in England. There, at the School of Oriental and African Studies of the University of London, he studied with scholars of West African cultures, learning five African languages and concentrating on the culture and language of the Krio, Twi, Kimbundu, Efik, Fante, Ewe, Yoruba, and other groups.[12] As he schooled himself on languages different in countless ways from English, he likely began to realize that he had already observed in Gullah many features of plausible African ancestry, features that were to receive attention over a decade later in *Africanisms*. In 1937, while in Paris, he interviewed more than twenty French West Africans, exploring the structure and vocabulary of their languages while constructing word-lists for comparison to Gullah.

In September 1937 Turner returned from abroad to resume his academic post at Fisk and the next year married Lois Morton, a former student there. He was not home long, however; in the fall of 1938 he left for Yale to study Arabic with Edward Sapir. Developing interests in larger issues of African-New World contact, he went to Brazil in 1940–41 to study the persistence of African cultural features, especially folklore and music, in a culture quite unlike that of the Gullah in North America.[13] He had already begun a public career, speaking before civic, church, and educational groups, as well as colleges and universities, often presenting his recordings from Africa and Brazil along with anthropological materials. In 1942, for example, he was invited to lecture the Louisville Pan-Hellenic Council, where he spoke on "Education for Citizenship." There he pointed to the neglect of knowledge about West African contributions to civilization: "If all races," he maintained, "were made aware of the offerings of Africans and their New World descendants, a better world would develop."[14] In this lecture, Turner set about disproving commonly held beliefs that "Negroes [were] naturally a childlike and submissive people; that the American slaves represented the most degraded Africans; that the African culture was a savage culture which, when brought into contact with another one, could not preserve its cultural heritage; and that the Negro race had no past of which to be proud." He contrasted the shame of many North American blacks with the pride of South American blacks who knew their contributions in music, art, dance, and folklore to be among the best, for example, in Brazil. He exhorted his race in the U.S. to become educated about its past, especially the part that originated in Africa, in order to participate proudly in American democracy.

In 1944, while still at Fisk, Turner became lecturer in linguistics and director of the Inter-Departmental Curriculum in African Studies, one of the earliest such programs (if not the first) in the country. It is thus no surprise that, when he left Fisk in 1946 to become professor of English at the newly opened Roosevelt College in Chicago, his reputation preceded him. An editorial in the *Chicago Defender* before his arrival called his appointment "one of the most encouraging signs on the academic horizon."[15] By this time, the editor pointed out, Turner had been invited to present his research at Yale, Columbia, Ohio State, and Northwestern Universities, and with his appointment at Roosevelt he became "the first Negro scholar to be retained on a permanent basis with a full professor status in a white institution of higher learning," others before him holding only temporary posts or visiting professorships. The editor described Turner as "a very quiet, unassuming, mild-mannered man," but went on to say that "beneath is the incandescent fire of a vital searching intellect, nurtured by years of sound scholarship." At Roosevelt, Turner taught African culture as well as English, and he continued to give public lectures, such as one at North Central College, Naperville, Illinois, in which he investigated the liberalism of Walt Whitman in light of the poet's beliefs about slavery. This talk was one of several during that engagement, which also included "Brazil: An Example of Racial Harmony" and "Democracy Comes of Age in an American College" (referring to Roosevelt College). At Roosevelt, Turner taught a wide range of English courses, including Anglo-Saxon and Chaucer. He frequently taught extra courses in the evening and in the summer, including some at the University of Illinois at Chicago Circle, to support his family.[16]

Finally, in 1949, after nearly two decades of painstakingly sifting his data and clarifying and refining his arguments, Turner published *Africanisms in the Gullah Dialect*. His most memorable and influential work, it took approximately four thousand words and names in Gullah and identified their possible or probable African antecedents. *Africanisms* was a model for comparative linguistic study. It became one of the most widely reviewed books of its time in American linguistics and was recognized immediately as ground breaking. One reviewer wrote, "we must now consider the older viewpoint (which considered African influence negligible) as definitely superseded. . . . In the study of American English, Turner's book is not only noteworthy, it is revolutionary."[17] His own institution hailed Turner's accomplishment as "the first authentic study of the contributions and influence of African culture in the Americas."[18] Roosevelt College took pride in the special niche occupied by its undergraduate program in African Studies and in the potential for its graduates to pave new roads for freedom in Africa. The college was particularly pleased to claim Turner on its faculty, as he was well-established as an influential educator and national leader in African studies.[19]

While *Africanisms* was his best-known, most influential, and most enduring work, it was for Turner also a point of departure for the remaining two decades of his career. He held a Fulbright lectureship at University College in Lagos, Nigeria, in 1950–51, at which time he traveled widely in British and French West Africa conducting field work, making extensive recordings, and lecturing. In 1961 he received a grant of $54,579 from the U.S. Department of Health, Education and Welfare to complete a dictionary and grammar of Krio, the first language of the Krio group of Sierra Leone and a second language throughout the rest of that country, a colony which was due shortly thereafter to receive its independence from Great Britain.[20]

In 1963, Turner published *The Krio Language of the Sierra Leone*, based on his fieldwork in that African country.[21] Over the years he had compiled folk tales in Krio and traced the origin of this language to the speech of African slaves from the United States and the West Indies who escaped or were given their freedom and in the 1790s settled in Freetown, the capital of Sierra Leone.[22] The volume was to be studied by trainees for the Peace Corps, as was his *Krio Texts: With Grammatical Notes and Translation in English* (1965). During these years Turner continued to teach English and African culture at Roosevelt, and his public career flourished as he fulfilled one invitation after another to speak about African cultural materials and the importance of building knowledge about African influences in America. Through his interests and contacts, he became involved in the development of the first Peace Corps programs in Africa and served as the Peace Corps faculty coordinator at Roosevelt in the early 1960s. He retired in 1970 and remained Professor Emeritus at Roosevelt until his death in 1972 at the age of seventy-seven.

The foregoing chronicle reveals a full and productive life, but it hardly captures the character of the man or suggests the personal transformation he must have experienced in the course of his work on Gullah language and culture. Already a successful academic before becoming acquainted with the language, he decided in mid-career to master an entirely new discipline and see where it would lead him. As he conducted interviews for the *Linguistic Atlas* on the Sea Islands in the early 1930s and recorded stories, songs, and other texts there, he found himself exploring a world that Gullah people had not previously shared with outsiders. In part because he was a kinsman, but also because he listened so attentively and openly to what they said, he was the first to perceive in their language and culture the rich store of linkages that would return to the Gullah people a part of their history.

THE HISTORICAL IMPACT OF TURNER'S WORK

Before Turner's *Africanisms in the Gullah Dialect*, Gullah was popularly viewed—to the extent that there was any public awareness of it—as broken or debased English. Scholarly opinions were not always more positive or enlightened, though they often purported to give some historical perspective in seeing Gullah as derived largely from earlier English, sometimes preserving it, sometimes modifying it. The African components of both Gullah and American English were unacknowledged because these were undocumented and unsuspected beyond a handful of terms native to Africa such as *banana* and *voodoo*. Indeed, most scholars argued that the African American population had lost all significant trace of its African cultural ancestry.[23]

Turner's realization that Gullah was distinctive was not new. That was a view long and broadly shared in the lowcountry, as well as in the scholarly community (where explanations for that distinctiveness varied). William Gilmore Simms had used Gullah for novelistic purposes as early as 1846 in *The Wigwam and the Cabin*.[24] Also, in *Army Life in a Black Regiment*, the memoir of a Union soldier stationed in South Carolina during the Civil War, Thomas Wentworth Higginson had provided excerpts of Gullah.[25] Toward the end of the nineteenth century local observers had begun to describe Gullah in print.

Perhaps the most authoritative sketch of Gullah before Turner was a small book simply titled *Gullah* and written by Reed Smith.[26] Professor of English at the University of South Carolina, Smith lent his reputation as an expert on folk literature and balladry to his views on Gullah, attributing its distinctiveness to three sources. Most generally, he saw Gullah as a modification of the English learned by Africans from whites in early colonial days.[27] According to Smith, "What the Gullah seemed to have done was to take a sizable part of the English vocabulary as spoken on the coasts by the white inhabitants from about 1700 on . . . and reproduce it changed in tonality, pronunciation, cadence, and grammar to suit their native phonetic tendencies, and their existing needs of expression and communication."[28] He quoted approvingly the views expressed in a personal letter from Yates Snowden, a colleague at the University of South Carolina: "The Africans, plastic as they are by nature, quickly lost their own language, and acquired imperfectly the dialects of the British peasantry among whom they worked, and by whom very generally they were directed."[29] At the same time, Smith argued in his section "Survivals (Archaisms)" that Gullah retained many pronunciations (such as *ax* "ask") and usages ("Coz, cuz, or cuzn" as a form of address) that represented earlier British English and could be found in writings of great Elizabethan and Jacobean authors.[30] These and other elements of Gullah had been preserved by the geographical and social isolation of its speakers.

Only a few vocabulary items, and only those whose source was either obvious or not traceable to any known English term, did Smith consider to be Africanisms:

> There are curiously few survivals of native African words in Gullah, a fact that has struck most students of the language. The commonest are the exclamation ki (or kai) to express wonder or to express emphasis to a statement, and buckra for white man, both, however, being widely found elsewhere. To these may be added nyam, oona, swanga (or swongger), du-du, goober, pinder, okra, geechy, cymbi, backalinga (obsolescent), guffer, penepene, da, da-da.[31]

Smith agreed with the view of George Philip Krapp, the most eminent scholar of American English of the day, that the structure of Gullah owed nothing to an African ancestry: "A few words, such as *voodoo*, *hoodoo*, and *buckra*, may have come into English from some original African dialect, but most of the words commonly supposed to be of Negro origin, e.g. *tote*, *jazz*, and *mosey*, are really derived from ancient English and other European sources . . . it is reasonably safe to say that not a single detail of Negro pronunciation or Negro syntax can be proved to have any other than an English origin."[32] Smith, Krapp, and other scholars, who knew the classics of English literature exceedingly well and were steeped in the history of English and other European languages, did not hesitate to seek antecedents of Gullah features in older stages of British English, even if they had to scour obscure works from Renaissance or medieval times to do so. They could see Gullah only through the prism of English and favored an English source for a Gullah word whenever a possible English candidate could be found.

Krapp actually knew nothing about Gullah firsthand, while Smith and others in South Carolina and Georgia paid attention only to certain of its features. It was for Lorenzo Dow Turner to examine Gullah systematically, to identify its African component, and to provide a plausible explanation of its distinctiveness. He began simply by refusing to accept the views of previous scholars and by considering an African source whenever there was a good reason to do so. In the process he forever changed the understanding of Gullah. Although he dealt with only a minority of the elements of the language, those he considered of likely African ancestry, his list of African-derived vocabulary (pages 190–208) was much longer than that of any previous scholar, and his compilation of personal names (pages 31–189) was staggering. More important, his careful description of aspects of the syntax (pages 209–22), morphology (pages 223–31), word formation (pages 232–39), pronunciation (pages 240–48), and intonation (pages 249–53) marked a turning point in thinking about Gullah. After Turner, African influence on all aspects of Gullah was inarguable.

Turner's work confronted the view that Gullah was "broken English" with little if any structure. Most of its words were English, but because Gullah was so difficult for outsiders to comprehend, its variations seemed random, unpredictable, and undisciplined. The fact that it was spoken but not written (no one was taught to read or write it) gave force to the opinion that it surely could not have a grammar of its own. In showing that Gullah did have grammatical rules (see chapter 4), Turner presented a major challenge to scholarly and popular beliefs about the language and its people.

Earlier accounts had often likened Gullah speech to baby talk. Krapp, in addition to tracing specific words and features to British dialects, suggested that Gullah resulted from slaves' having learned English from white masters who simplified their speech to be understood by newly arrived Africans. He believed that these whites deliberately eliminated tenses of verbs and plural suffixes of nouns and that they modified difficult sounds and the distinctions between pronouns. The belief that Gullah originated from mimicking or modifying the simplified speech of overseers and other whites has persisted until recent times. However, this explanation fails to account for the effect of all the non-simplified language that slaves were sure to have heard whites use with one another. Krapp's view also implied that slaves did not progress towards adult competence in English (though they could hardly have failed to do so unless they were older slaves brought directly from Africa). The "baby talk" idea also failed to account for the grammatical complexity present in Gullah, a complexity first glimpsed in Turner's work (Gullah, for instance, makes verbal distinctions that do not exist in English).

Krapp and other scholars were unaware of sounds in Gullah that were native to West African languages and were, by English standards, difficult to pronounce. In fact, Turner had not identified them before going to the University of London in 1936, where he received advanced training and observed native speakers of African languages using them. Absent from the field notebooks compiled by Turner for the *Linguistic Atlas* in the early 1930s are all the African-derived phonetic features in chapter 7 of *Africanisms*: the labio-velar plosives, nasalized stops, bilabial fricatives, palatal plosives, palatal nasal, etc. Neither trained nor attuned to identify these sounds when he first listened to Gullah, he simply did not realize what he heard until he studied African languages firsthand. After returning from London he had his wire recordings copied onto aluminum disks so that he could replay them repeatedly. It was then that he heard the African-derived sounds of Gullah.

Before Turner, much of what was believed about Gullah outside its communities came from literary dialect writing. Such observers and raconteurs as Caroline Gilman, William Gilmore Simms, Joel Chandler Harris, Rev. John G. Williams, John Bennett, and Ambrose Gonzales (author of four volumes of stories) are among the most notable white writers who developed a literary tradition portraying Gullah.[33] They contributed to our knowledge of Gullah speech and folklore, although it is safe to assume that their works were neither verified nor edited by Gullah speakers and that their intended audiences were white. Some works also contributed to the prevailing reasoning of white supremacy that equated Gullah speech with a limited intellect and primitive mind. What made the stories so appealing to white audiences may have been the paradoxical tension between the low station and frequent comic simplicity of Gullah literary characters on the one hand and the folk wisdom and insights often attributed to them on the other. As long as Gullah literary characters were "in their place" their insight was non-threatening.

Before Turner, the white public and some white scholars routinely explained the divergence of Gullah from educated, standard English—indeed, from American English generally—as not just the preservation of simplified baby talk, but as the product of impoverished learning capacity. Its speakers were alleged to lack the physical and mental capacity to learn or speak educated English. A description in the Foreword of Gonzales's *The Black Border* reveals the bias that characterized many writers before Turner: Africans were said to have taken the English language, "wrapped their clumsy tongues around it" and changed it to suit their tendencies, which included laziness.[34] "Theirs," one observer wrote, "is the worst English in the world."[35]

The literary portrayal of Gullah language had developed a life of its own by the 1920s. Even writers intent on presenting Gullah-speaking characters as fully rounded and dignified relied on established precedent for representing Gullah speech.[36] In the low-country, where the image of Gullah culture was managed and controlled by whites, a tradition of white story tellers and folklorists—usually self-appointed lay people—continued to flourish, producing stereotyped stories with stock characters for the enjoyment of white audiences. Often presented in nostalgic terms, these stories represented efforts to recall and preserve the perception of a social order that had disappeared, where the commodities were the quaintness, beauty and humor of "the good old days." These efforts achieved formal organization, for example, in Charleston's Society for the Preservation of Negro Spirituals.

In raising the idea that Gullah was systematic, patterned speech, Turner's *Africanisms* implied that it was different from, rather than deficient to, the standard. That Gullah had rules as well as a different history was more than just a novel consideration.

It provided a fresh way of looking at any variety of American English and implied that other types that also lacked social status, such as African American English and Appalachian English, might have developed in distinct fashions with their own structures, rules, and histories. These points are now touchstones of modern linguistic thinking and investigation. *Africanisms* in effect challenged a belief system that depended on a hierarchy of races, strictly segregated, and a hierarchy of language varieties resulting from that segregation. While Turner's description of Gullah grammar was incomplete, it offered a way of seeing Gullah and, by extension, other varieties as coherent systems, full-fledged languages.

What must have made this simple idea problematic for some lowcountry whites was that it challenged their opinions about a type of speech so intimately familiar to them. Gullah was not the language of a distant, exotic country that could be viewed with a neutral eye. It was the speech of local black farmers, nannies, fishmongers, "yardboys," maids, and laundresses, few if any of whom were schooled or literate, all of whom were legally segregated away from the best fruits of society. Lowcountry whites had heard Gullah spoken all their lives and had often associated it with ignorance and cheap labor. They had built their own theories why Gullah people were poor, or disenfranchised, or why they deserved to be these things. Gullah speakers were first of all black, descended from Africans and African Americans branded by the institution of slavery, which had relied on a theory of their lesser humanity. They were rural and for the most part uneducated. While their speech was sometimes described with paternalistic affection as "colorful" and "rhythmic," it was popularly viewed as a failed attempt to master English. Even today, its speakers in public schools are more likely to be diagnosed as having speech or learning disabilities.

Turner's *Africanisms* dispelled myths that had arisen about Gullah because of the race of its speakers and the fact that it had no written rules. The book required readers to rethink assumptions about the structure of an unwritten language and the linguistic (hence, cognitive) capacity of persons not literate in the educated standard variety of the language. Widespread literacy, a modern standard of education, is a relatively new development in the history of human languages. Its rise, though invaluable to modern civilization, has often led—erroneously—to equating unwritten spoken dialects with deficient intellect.

Another of Turner's achievements was to pioneer the now familiar Afrocentric approach to academic study. In turning to West African languages to examine them for the sources of Gullah features, he found that Gullah had its own distinct history. His work transformed Gullah in scholarly circles from "broken English" to a subject of academic respectability. *Africanisms* is indispensable to understanding the early development of Afrocentric thinking in this country.

Turner took many careful years to organize his material and to present it with dispassionate thoroughness before publishing it in *Africanisms*. He knew that any imperfections might lead to the dismissal of his work and his professional standing as an African American linguist. To make his case persuasively to his peers, he knew he had to meet the highest technical standards, but also make a clear and decisive break with the past. In retrospect we understand why Turner's book was so long in gestation. Nothing remotely similar had ever been attempted.

By identifying Africanisms in Gullah, Turner made it possible to move beyond a view of African slave descendants as anonymous, interchangeable individuals who had been stripped of culture and memory. Proposing linkages between West African languages and Gullah offered hope for recovering a fuller history in the future and restoring dignity to speakers of Gullah. *Africanisms in the Gullah Dialect*, together with the work of Turner's fellow scholar and colleague Melville J. Herskovits,[37] stimulated scholarly interest in an Afrocentric approach to studying the past of Americans of African descent. Turner did this for the language and culture of the Sea Islands and then Brazil, Herskovits for African elements in cultures throughout the Americas. Indeed, this new orientation advanced by Turner and Herskovits hastened the development of African American culture as an autonomous field of study.

Turner's fresh orientation fleshed out, speculatively in some cases, the bare bones of a people's past which had been practically obliterated by slave-trade attempts to dehumanize its cargo. The practices of this trade, such as renaming captives, mixing speakers of different languages to foil rebellion, selling off family members to different buyers, and sexually exploiting slave women to flaunt control while increasing holdings, had cut deeply into the normal transmission of family and cultural values and language. Turner's new direction in thinking would reveal how Africans had adapted and survived under these conditions.

Turner also gave Gullah the rudiments of a settlement history. His mentor Hans Kurath had as one of the goals of the *Linguistic Atlas* to correlate American speech forms with ones in the British Isles in order to demonstrate colonial emigration and settlement patterns. In similar fashion, Turner sought correlations between West African languages and Gullah. Shipping and other historical records of the slave trade exist in few forms that scholars can use to determine which groups went where, but Turner employed linguistic comparisons to compensate.

It would be a mistake to conclude that Turner's work simply traded the view that Gullah was a static repository of British dialects for one that saw it as a static repository of African ones. Turner demonstrated that Gullah contained both African components and some elements of British-dialect origin.[38]

Turner also revealed Gullah to be a dynamic, changing language, not a museum of linguistic artifacts. Gullah brought together material from African languages with material from various English dialects to create a new creole language and culture. Historical records show that during the first fifty years of the South Carolina colony (1670–1720), Africans often worked alongside nearly equal numbers of whites on small farms; chattel slavery had not yet become an institution. Salikoko Mufwene (1992) argues that Africans were less encumbered in learning English under these circumstances. But when large plantations grew up around 1720 and thereafter as rice production increased, Anglo-Americans came increasingly to see their slaves as chattel, and total segregation became the law, even though slaves with artisan or other skills might be "hired out" to whites in town where they had relative freedom of movement and must have had contact with many varieties of English. After 1720, dramatic increases in the importation of Africans created a majority slave population in the lowcountry and fewer contacts with English speakers. Africans arriving in the eighteenth century must often have learned their English from the African Americans already within the system. To this they contributed African elements and gave birth to what became Gullah.[39]

Turner called Gullah a "creolized form of English" (page v). Today it is considered a creole, a completely functional language developed by the children of a people that had been abruptly displaced and subordinated, and that needed a common form of speech because they spoke different native tongues. In Turner's day the general public understood little about creoles. They were viewed as superficial modifications (and usually as inferior versions) of European languages and were not appreciated as having grammatical systems of their own. Turner realized that Gullah, like similar language varieties in Jamaica and Suriname, had emerged from forced contact between different languages, a European one spoken in the Caribbean originally by the dominant, but usually minority population, and two or more African or American ones spoken by the subordinated population. But at the time of Turner's research, little had been written in English about creole languages (or pidgins, their relatives) as a category of study, and he lacked both the terminology and the concept of what a creole language was.[40]

So it was that Turner helped propel the field of creole studies forward by his work first on Gullah and then on Krio. Specifically, he showed how rich were the linguistic resources that a subjugated colonial people could bring to the formation of a new, mixed language. His work demonstrated that Gullah—and by implication other creoles—was not just a modification of a dominant European language (English, French, Portuguese, etcetera). He further showed that Gullah had words and idioms that superficially appeared to be English but were almost certainly African. Using them for comparison, Turner discovered a phenomenon now universally recognized in creole studies—that many retentions from African languages were indirect and that Gullah sometimes disguised or camouflaged its African origins.[41] (This is seen especially in Turner's fourth chapter, "Syntactical Features"). In short, Turner established that Gullah could be analyzed as a language on its own terms without reference to English. Turner correctly saw that the future of creole studies lay in comparisons of creoles having different European-language bases (e.g., Jamaican English creole, Suriname English creole, and Haitian French creole). He argued (*Africanisms*, page 13) that such comparisons would reveal common, if disguised, similarities and would refute traditional claims that Gullah was derived from British dialects and creoles simply from European languages. Indeed, many structures he identified in Gullah (such as serial verbs; pages 210–12) have also been found in other creoles, regardless of the European language on which they were based; such commonalities have enabled scholars to understand how creole languages originated.

When *Africanisms* appeared in 1949, it had been long anticipated by scholars and the public. Not only had Turner published two excerpts of his material[42], but Herskovits, professor of Anthropology at Northwestern and a professional colleague of Turner's since they were on the Howard faculty together in the 1920s, had relied heavily on Turner's unpublished material to make a case for broad-ranging African retentions in the New World in his landmark volume, *The Myth of the Negro Past* (1941).[43]

In 1940 Turner delivered a paper at the American Council of Learned Societies meeting, one of the first occasions on which he shared the details of his research on Gullah's African connections.[44] He outlined the difficulties for researchers to establish African survivals in the New World and attributed the presumption of no linguistic survivals to ignorance of African languages, the paucity of slave records, the absence of ethnological studies of West African peoples, and the lack of grammars of West African languages.

Turner had originally projected a descriptive grammar of Gullah, a much larger work, but by 1936 had abandoned this goal in favor of the book that became *Africanisms*,[45] which some in his profession considered only a partial fulfillment of his research.[46] He realized that the more important and evolving task was to recover the African past in Gullah.

Turner's partial account of Gullah laid a secure foundation on which others would build. His legacy is shown perhaps most dramatically by the generation of researchers he inspired in the 1970s and 1980s to work on the grammar of Gullah: Irma Cunningham, Patricia Nichols, Ian Hancock, Patricia Jones-Jackson, John Rickford, Salikoko Mufwene, and Tometro Hopkins, among others. With perhaps one or two exceptions, these followers never met Turner; it was his book that motivated them. Others took up the task of identifying Africanisms in other language varieties, including American English in general.[47] The architecture of much later scholarship, linguistic and otherwise, rests on his case in *Africanisms*. For instance, the naming patterns he identified are significant less for the linguistic information they contain than for the implication that such a practice and so many names could have survived into the twentieth century. The patterns have served, like so much of what Turner collected, as a foundation for later researchers.[48]

Using some of the earliest portable recording machinery, Turner recorded dozens of short texts (stories, songs, chants, prayers, etc.). Many of these were published in phonetic transcription in chapter 9, "Gullah Texts." In doing so he followed a model developed by anthropologists working on Amerindian languages. His publication of texts in a linguistic work on an American "dialect" was unprecedented at the time and remains quite rare. One reason for including texts was for accountability: to provide material to be examined and double-checked by other researchers.

Although the texts went unremarked in reviews, their value became apparent in succeeding years. As a permanent, scholarly record of Gullah speech, they permit scholars and others to ask questions and make interpretations for themselves. Indeed, as modern research paradigms relied upon quantitative and statistical analysis, scholars reformulated the data in Turner's texts to compare Gullah with Caribbean creole languages and to measure the contributions of African language families to the vocabulary of Gullah. For instance, Frederic Cassidy analyzed Turner's material and found Congo-Angola elements strongest in the word-lists and Nigerian elements strongest in the texts.[49]

It is important to realize the limitations of Turner's conclusions. He showed that the Africanness of Gullah speech and culture was indisputable. But the Sea Islands do not represent wider African American culture (even in the rural South), and much of what Turner found there was not found elsewhere. Possibly those elements had disappeared in other areas; possibly the Gullah territory was unique and a special case because of the unusually high proportion of Africans to whites. Turner's work was based on material gathered from older speakers in the 1930s and in many ways is not a record of what one would find in the Sea Islands today. The social isolation of the islands has eroded significantly since Turner's day, and the language has changed in many respects.[50]

Turner's book and his career as an educator bore many fruits, not only demonstrating the Africanness of Gullah, but also awakening African Americans to recover their cultural heritage. His work implied that other African American speech varieties had substantial African elements. However, those elements turn out to be less prominent than in Gullah. Most African Americans will not discover in *Africanisms* documentation of their ancestors' speech, but they will find verification that in one part of the U.S. Americans of African descent sustained a vital past that generations of subjugation failed to extinguish. Turner took immense pride in the triumph of reclaiming this legacy. However, he never doubted that English played a predominant role in the formation of Gullah and never stated that its influence on Gullah was only superficial. Indeed, his conclusion about Gullah was characteristically modest: "Gullah is indebted to African sources" (page 254).

In his early work for the *Linguistic Atlas,* Turner found few African elements in Gullah, but within a few years he had identified many of them in every part of the language. The mid 1930s must have been a breathtaking time for him, as suspicious Gullah speakers became his confidants, opening their hidden world to him, and as he explored the African languages that he later chided colleagues for having ignored so completely. How he broke through the barriers of professional prejudice against the existence of Africanisms and undertook a one-man comparison of several dozen African languages with Gullah is one of the most remarkable stories in American scholarship. Turner dispelled once and for all the notion that a substantial African element could not have survived into African American speech. This is a testimony both to the man and to the vitality and endurance of the culture whose language he investigated.

ARCHIVAL COLLECTIONS

Turner kept voluminous records of his research and activities. Thanks to careful organization by his widow, Lois Turner Williams, his papers and materials form a permanent record for scholars who wish to learn more about him or continue his work. On 10 May 1984, the Lorenzo D. Turner Collection, with material spanning the years 1915–1973, officially opened as part of the Melville J. Herskovits Library of African Studies at Northwestern University.

The Turner Collection at Northwestern comprises fifty-two boxes and other containers having a wide variety of personal and research materials, many of which have been microfilmed and are also available for borrowing in that format. These materials include linguistic notes, diagrams of mouth positions for sounds, dictionaries, word lists, and similar materials. Also included are proverbs and folktales that Turner collected, notebooks, newspaper clippings, articles and speeches, programs and bulletins, biographical information, photographs, bibliographies, biographical information, correspondence, teaching materials from his classes at Roosevelt University, and various papers, reports, publications, and writings. His correspondence deals mainly with routine professional matters, but in it he often elaborates and defends his theories of African American speech development. Turner's Gullah recordings are now available on an indexed series of cassette tapes at Northwestern, the original recordings having been sent to Indiana University, Bloomington, to the Archives of Traditional Music. The Turner Collection covers not only the Sea Islands, but it is particularly rich in the extensive materials he collected in Brazil in 1940–41 and in West Africa in 1950–51. It contains nearly seven hundred audio disks and over one hundred twenty-five tape and wire recordings[51], as well as voluminous materials on African languages such as dictionaries and translations of numerous folktales and proverbs that he collected.

Some of Turner's early Gullah material is archived in the collection, viz. his wire recordings of texts from the early 1930s. His interviews with twenty-one Sea Island speakers for the *Linguistic Atlas* in 1932–33, which consist of notebooks of phonetically transcribed responses to survey questions and original field notes, are available in other repositories.[52]

BEYOND TURNER'S AFRICANISMS TO TODAY'S "EBONICS"

Major breakthroughs in thought are usually surrounded by debate and tensions, and the case of Lorenzo Dow Turner's *Africanisms* is no exception. The investigation that Turner launched not only revealed the historical connections of a displaced people but also set the stage for other scholars to study the diversity and dynamics of human language in real-life situations. A language whose beginnings could be partially reconstructed and whose continued use yielded rich opportunities for investigation, Gullah (as other creole languages) became a laboratory for understanding principles of human language acquisition and maintenance under duress, as its speakers sought to survive far from their cultural roots and sustenance.

The focus on low-prestige varieties of language, such as offered by Turner's work, improved understanding of the social dynamics of all languages—for example, between the conflicting motivations to speak the prestige form of a language (such as standard English or, in Great Britain, the Queen's English) or to speak a low-prestige, parochial variety such as one used in the home or neighborhood, or in a geographical region. The assumption that anyone with a choice would prefer the standard variety for its social advantages is challenged by strong motivations for speaking a "stigmatized" variety (such as Southern Drawl, Appalachian, Brooklynese), in order to demonstrate solidarity with and membership in the group that speaks it.

Sociolinguistic study since Turner has led to an understanding that speaking is an act in which individuals project their distinctive identity,[53] reinforcing how they view themselves, but at the same time how outsiders insist on viewing them. Despite occasional put-downs of Southern speech, for example, most Southerners retain their distinctive variety to mark pride in their origins. Beyond the individual's personal speech identity, linguists have learned that in examining speech variation they must take into account the geographic, social, economic, ethnic, gendered and educational segregation of communities that produced their speech varieties and that sets them as a group or community apart from the mainstream. It was this focus on ethnic markers in Gullah (such as basket names) that led Turner to the languages of West Africa instead of English for explanations and linkages to its history. Linguists have also learned, particularly from studies of numerous other creole languages like Gullah, that even the most isolated communities develop a language completely adequate to their needs, whether their speech is standard or non-standard, their language written or only spoken. Turner, to his credit, was open to that possibility as he launched his investigation.

Just as Turner reversed prevailing views of Gullah, later researchers have done the same for other stigmatized varieties such as African American Vernacular English (AAVE). In the United States, research on minority and creole language patterns began in earnest in the mid 1960s, just as sociolinguistic study of AAVE (known then as Black English or Black English Vernacular) gained national attention. Scholarly debate grew around the relationship between Gullah and the more generalized Black English, spurring research on the grammar of both varieties. Black English was easily recognized by the general public because it could be heard from coast to coast in some form (as on television). There was considerable concern about connections between racism, urban poverty and the disenfranchisement of blacks on the one hand, and lagging educational achievement on the other. At the same time, caricatures of Black English speakers appeared in television situational comedies (as well as caricatures of Southern Drawl speakers), integration brought previously separated school children together where they observed each other's speech patterns, and the first large-scale projects to study Black English were launched. But while linguists were establishing the pronunciation and grammar of many African American communities, rural and urban, Black English in the public's mind was (and still is) tantamount to "street slang." Black English appeared to be a problem related to numerous others that needed to be fixed, stigmatized like Gullah. Turner had responded to the stigma and myth surrounding Gullah by uncovering facts about its cultural origins and how speakers adapted their language to the conditions of their lives. Sociolinguists would follow in his footsteps as they examined Black English or AAVE.

Unlike Gullah, AAVE, often referred to as "Ebonics" as of the late 1990s, spans the North American continent. Much research has focused on the relationship between the two varieties as well as on their relationships with English.[54] Researchers in the 1960s and 1970s often took the view that AAVE was once more or less identical to Gullah. Many linguists today believe that AAVE developed separately from Gullah but in a somewhat similar fashion because they share some ingredients (such as a tendency for not marking verb tense). Regardless of their actual lineages, a close historical relation is evident not only in their shared features but also in the obvious fact that their speakers share a similar heritage and common experience of *de facto* segregation.

Turner had the benefit of none of the sociolinguistic knowledge and methods available today. Because of his work, however, assumptions once easy to make from within a dominant cultural perspective became less tenable as research brought a new perspective on Gullah and other marginalized language varieties. Among these were five common assumptions governing reactions to minority language forms, the people speaking them, and teaching strategies.

The first assumption is the dualism that while the target "standard" language in education is desirable, other varieties are bad forms of language and undesirable. This assumption ignores the rich and creative resources that minority dialects have for expression and thought, the fact that they are rule-governed, engaging the human mind as fully as any other variety, and that they reflect a community's history. Dialect speakers need not lose their dialect in order to gain the educated standard—each form of speech has value in proper contexts and both can be maintained.

Indeed, in some cases, what became the standard variety was a dialect whose speakers came into power or one which became widely available and compelling to speakers of different dialects as in the case of Martin Luther's sixteenth-century translations of the Bible from Greek into one form of German vernacular, which then became the standard. A classic example of one language replacing another as the prestige variety is that of French in England following the invasion by William of Normandy in 1066. The Anglo-Saxon language of the defeated natives became the low-prestige variety while the conqueror's French took over as the gold standard, the language of the court and social elite. Generations of English speakers continued to use "high" forms derived from French rather than "low" forms from Anglo-Saxon to make foods sound more appetizing and meals more refined: *mutton*, *veal*, *beef*, *poultry* (from French *mouton*, *veau*, *boeuf*, *poule*) rather than Anglo-Saxon derived *sheep*, *calf*, *cow*, and *fowl*.

A second popular assumption that Turner's work overturned is that social and ethnic dialects are a product of inherent mental or physical incapacity of the individuals using them—limited intelligence, distinctive physical traits such as nose or lip shape (see Turner's first chapter)—rather than a product of external events and social contacts. Turner rejected beliefs about inherent incapacity, replacing myth about nose and lip shape with facts about the complex and differing phonetic systems of African languages on which Gullah speakers drew.

A third assumption brought into relief by Turner's work is that observers from the dominant culture can easily witness a true representation of a local or ethnic dialect like AAVE and assess the speaker's capacity to use language. A phenomenon known in social science research as "the observer's paradox," the mere presence of an observer from the outside is enough to restrict or alter a speaker's performance. This problem confronts all researchers, and yet Turner was able to overcome it, as he acknowledged in chapter 1 of *Africanisms*.[55] Although an educated man from the university, he was also of African descent, and he conveyed sufficient respect for the Gullah people to merit their trust. He thereby gained access to their language, even noting their private basket names (chapter 3, section H).

A fourth frequent assumption is that speakers of marginal varieties are anxious to abandon the language they share with family and friends in order to adopt the prestige variety—for its guaranteed rewards. Although equipping students with mastery of the standard language variety is vital to their educational advancement, the corollary that they must simultaneously abandon their dialect ignores the incentive to remain attached to their home group and also underestimates the power of the very prejudice that established the economic and political segregation of some communities in the first place. To think that a change of language, in other words "upgrading" to the standard, will guarantee underprivileged students upward mobility is perhaps naive. Trading one's native variety for a more prestigious one does not necessarily nullify the prejudice that people endure because of their ethnicity, gender or social class.

A fifth assumption is that speakers of stigmatized dialects cannot be fully competent actors in society. The false equation of dialects with inferior or childlike intellect often reinforces their speakers' exclusion from the privileges of the mainstream. Historically, the infantilization of ethnic minorities, indigenous people, and mainstream women contributed to continued segregation and division of labor for these groups, thus ensuring that they would develop ever more distinctive speech varieties. These varieties were for a long time of little interest to linguists, but modern studies have revealed how creatively and powerfully people, including children, use their particular community dialects to form social networks and to establish their positions within them.

Indeed, speakers of stigmatized dialects such as AAVE or Gullah may act in solidarity with their home group or social network to assert their shared identity, by using the non-prestige variety to the fullest extent.[56] With linguistic virtuosity and educational resources to gain use of a second speech variety, often the prestige variety, they may also choose to shift dialects as needed, thereby assuring that they can always "come home." Or they may focus on social mobility away from their home group into the educated mainstream and shift to regular use of the standard, hoping to break the cycle of segregation and exclusion. To do the last of these things, they must have reason to believe that they can "pass," that is, elude prejudice.

Throughout the world, educated speakers often look down on dialects formed in socially segregated communities near them (take, for example, British views of Cockney or Irish working-class dialects). The more that educated people are familiar with a stigmatized dialect, the more likely they are to harbor feelings of superiority over its speakers, their attitudes informed by the social hierarchies in which they live. Speakers of an educated standard, themselves at the top of the hierarchy, have no way to look at dialects unlike their own except downward.

Turner had to deal with some of the attitudes discussed above, many of which continue into the present day. To a large extent, these issues became involved in public debate following the 1996–97 "Ebonics" controversy in the schools of Oakland, California, just as they had two decades earlier in Ann Arbor, Michigan. When Oakland schools submitted a proposal for a grant to teach English as a second language to some of their native-born African American students on the grounds that they spoke Ebonics, media confusion and a sharp public reaction against the plan ensued. Here the public's views of language converged with their views of class, race and ethnicity.

The power of these views becomes more tangible when one compares attitudes toward "innocent" speakers of non-standard English—internationals—with attitudes about native-born speakers of marginalized English varieties. Internationals may present a blank slate to Americans who have no history with them and no assumptions about their native language. But the Oakland students in question were American speakers of a familiar and stigmatized social dialect, AAVE. These Oakland students' history in America involved a separate existence, outside the circles of education, power and privilege. If, by contrast, Americans know nothing of a certain foreign language, they are not sensitive to the markers that rank or stigmatize its speakers.

Methods for teaching English to internationals are based on certain assumptions about them and their speech. One assumption is that international students are eager to acquire standard English as a key to opportunity. This is quite different from the circumstances that faced the enslaved ancestors of most African Americans who saw no prospects for assimilation. It is also quite different from the circumstances of modern-day Ebonics speakers, whose speech is not understood (perhaps even by its speakers) to be a separate system from that of standard English.

Another assumption is that the first language of non-native speakers is a legitimate one that fills an important role in their lives. It suffices, therefore, to help internationals bridge from the grammar, phonology and vocabulary of their first language to those of English. English language teachers have no mission to eradicate the native language of international students, yet they may feel compelled to do so with a poor child from a ghetto or an Appalachian outpost. Teachers' approaches thus depend on their attitudes and beliefs about students' home language.

The concerns raised in response to the Oakland Ebonics issue revealed a wide-scale misapprehension of linguistic principles by the general public. The intent of the Oakland proposal was, in fact, to train English teachers to recognize linguistic features of Ebonics or AAVE as they would recognize linguistic features of Spanish speakers, in order to use appropriate bilingual strategies to teach Ebonics speakers standard English, thereby improving their educational prospects. But this proposal was unclear and the press reported that Ebonics would be taught, and its speakers in the Oakland schools (for the most part, poor black students) would be permitted to use non-standard dialect rather than being taught the educated standard. Many African American leaders sensed danger in official acknowledgment of an African American vernacular: after all, not all African Americans speak AAVE, and some of those who do, speak it only some of the time. This focus on AAVE, they feared, could paint with a broad stroke all African Americans as less educated, or less educable, than other Americans. The convergence of class-based and race-based sentiments provoked opposition from both the white and African American public. Some critics opposed the notion that black children should be singled out for special language instruction, as if these children suffered language disability. Ebonics critics, black and white, asserted that without standard English, the black children of Oakland would be condemned to educational failure. The question for all was how to get the children to use standard English.

Because language is used to gauge the success of educational efforts, tension remains unresolved in many classrooms where teachers are unprepared to deal with language varieties like Gullah or AAVE. Academic gatekeepers measure achievement against a standard scale. Meanwhile, competing language norms of students' peer groups appear, according to some researchers, increasingly to diverge from standard academic English. How can one acknowledge and value difference while insisting on mastery of the standard? Perhaps the answer lies in investigating how approaches would change if teachers viewed AAVE, Gullah, and other marginal varieties, as valid and valuable parts of a community's life, and as rule-governed dialects from which two-way bridges can be built to the standard variety.

When he set out to investigate Gullah, Turner did not have alternatives to prevailing assumptions and beliefs about it, but as a linguist he was committed to serious inquiry rather than merely to counter one view with another one. His answer was to match ignorance with knowledge and to test assumptions by gathering more data. He set a high standard for cutting through the confusion engendered by prejudice. Until recently "Gullah" in the low-country, and "Black English" more generally, were rarely anything but derogatory labels to educators and to parents seeking social mobility for their children. Today, thanks in part to the ongoing revolution initiated by Turner, some African Americans are reclaiming their heritage of AAVE and Gullah even as they participate fully in the educated mainstream.

In American culture, with its overwhelmingly European-centered set of assumptions, a growing interest in African-centered perspectives and contributions and a fascination with the details of Gullah cultures are positive developments that not only build on, but also are made possible by, what Lorenzo Dow Turner began fifty years ago with *Africanisms in the Gullah Dialect*.

POINTERS FOR THE LAY READER

This book does not tell a story, though an exciting drama of discovery and adventure lies behind it, as detailed earlier. Instead, it presents a technical account by a trained linguist who employed the tools, terminology, and methods of his profession. It is a technical survey of African elements in Gullah, not a general introduction or description of the language, much less a guide to speaking or constructing sentences in Gullah. Turner organized his material according to the conventions of his profession. He was a methodical scholar who laid out his patiently collected evidence, often with little or no commentary and, except in a preliminary chapter in which he sets the stage for his investigation, without conveying a sense of anticipation to the reader. Few linguists can read his book without keen excitement, but few other readers will follow it from beginning to end. It does not build toward a climax. Turner has no chapter titled "Conclusion" or any other section that summarizes his case for the African heritage of Gullah. Nor does he systematically argue a case, as, for example, Herskovits did in his *Myth of the Negro Past*. He comes closest to stating his case in a nutshell in his very first sentence (page 1), saying simply that investigators of Gullah "would do well to acquire some acquaintance" with West African languages. With this understatement to set the tone of his work, Turner presents his evidence and lets it speak for itself.

Africanisms is a reference work that Turner designed for his colleagues in linguistics, a volume that presents—often merely by listing—various elements likely or plausibly to have an African source. For this reason, we have tried in this introduction to place Turner's work and ideas in larger contexts and make them accessible to a readership that is broader than the one he had in mind, but one that his book deserves to have. Because the book reveals next to nothing about the author beyond his careful scholarship and his respect for Gullah culture, we have sketched his life and accomplishments at some length. Turner was far more interested in forefronting his subjects of inquiry—Gullah and its speakers—than his own role in revealing the character of their speech.

In his first chapter Turner introduces the reader to the Sea Islands of South Carolina and Georgia. He outlines their historical role in the slave trade and identifies the principal areas from which Africans were brought to North America in the eighteenth century, providing in the process a rudimentary settlement history for Gullah. He also surveys existing research on Gullah and indicates its shortcomings in failing to identify African elements.

He thereby sets the stage for his own work demonstrating how important it is for investigators to have first-hand acquaintance with African languages.

Turner drew on many African languages for comparison to Gullah. Most of these he studied in London or Paris in 1936–37 by interviewing native speakers and by consulting dictionaries, grammars, and other linguistic works. He lists twenty-one languages (page 2) and situates them on a map of Africa (page 7).[57] He cites eleven other languages, including Arabic, in which he found forms that represented plausible sources for Gullah words (page 43).[58] While he no doubt chose some of them for reasons of convenience (their speakers were available for him to consult), all of Turner's languages were spoken in areas from which West Africans were enslaved in earlier centuries, indicating that his selection was also based on historical research. These thirty-two languages represent members of four large, diverse language families (Niger Congo, Nilo-Saharan, Afro-Asiatic, and Semitic) and several subfamilies spoken from the Upper Guinea Coast (what today is Mali) southward to Angola, a stretch of several thousand miles. Some of them shared structural similarities, but they were rarely, if ever, mutually intelligible. Turner's use of so many African languages for comparison to Gullah remains unprecedented.

In chapter 2, "Phonetic Alphabet and Diacritics," Turner presents the symbols to be used for the sounds of Gullah and African languages in the book. Like linguists of his day (and ours), he employed phonetic notations, called the International Phonetic Alphabet (IPA), that is often quite different from the ones found in most American dictionaries and pronunciation guides.[59] Because it has symbols for all known sounds in the world's languages, the IPA enabled Turner to represent exactly what he heard in Gullah and African languages (many quite different from English) and to compare them directly and precisely. In this chapter he outlines the vowels of Gullah (pages 15–20, quite similar to English), the consonants of Gullah (pages 22–29, often quite different from English), and sounds such as tones (whereby the meanings of two words having the same vowels and consonants are distinguished by different pitch levels given to syllables). Providing the clearest phonetic evidence of African ancestry are consonants, some of which do not exist in English at all and others of which differ subtly from English.

The placement of the second chapter is strategic, because Turner uses phonetics rather than conventional spelling throughout the book to represent both African languages and Gullah. For example, he cites Gullah personal names (pages 43–189) only in phonetics, and he used phonetics to transcribe his texts (presented with English translations in chapter 9). To be sure, phonetic notation showed fellow linguists the details of Gullah pronunciation and facilitated more direct comparison between languages, but there were practical reasons for using it also. Because Gullah was a spoken language without an established written form, Turner had no alphabet or spelling system to guide him. No matter how he might arrange them, English letters could never represent what he heard in Gullah. A reader who wants an idea of how Gullah sounded to Turner or who wants to read the texts in chapter 9 aloud must rely on chapter 2 and must know the IPA.

The third chapter, "West African Words in Gullah" (pages 31–189), is the centerpiece of Turner's book, especially his listing of personal names, also known as basket or pet names that were given at birth and used in the home and among friends and acquaintances. Some terms he listed, including the personal names, were noted from conversations or from stories, songs, and prayers, but the vast majority of them Turner must have gathered through other means. He does not tell us how he got them, much less how he got thousands of them, but he must have questioned Sea Islanders directly about their naming practices. He was not the first to identify the phenomenon of basket names, but his compilation far outranks all others and provides some of the most persuasive evidence for Gullah's African ancestry.[60] Among hundreds of names Turner cites and matches with one another are the Gullah *ade'biyi* (feminine) and Yoruba personal name *adebiyi* meaning "the crown has begotten this" in that language; Gullah *a'fiba* (feminine) and the Ewe personal name *afiba* meaning "name given a girl born on Friday." Turner found that Gullah people sometimes, but not always, knew the original meaning of a name handed down through their communities. More important, he found that Gullah people preserved African methods when giving English nicknames to children, for example, to name them after the weather or their appearance, temperament, or health.

It is important to understand and appreciate the methodology that Turner used for comparing languages. While he wished to establish that many terms he heard in Gullah were almost certainly of African origin, he was also determined to avoid undisciplined speculation. In comparing two languages a linguist employs three general types of evidence to posit a connection: an external one (the historical relations between the speakers of the languages), and two internal ones (the meaning of a term and its form or pronunciation). Turner lays out at the beginning of his book (pages 1–2) an external case for African settlement in South Carolina and Georgia that is brief, but at the same time persuasive and indispensable.[61]

Turner was cautious when comparing meanings and forms for a variety of reasons. He faced a two-hundred-year time gap for African languages. Except for Arabic, few African languages he used had a written form in the eighteenth century, when they were brought by African slaves to North America. Tracing words is a far less exact science than tracing genetic traits. Words can evolve much more quickly, shifting meaning or developing more than one meaning over a short period of time. No matter how conservative a language may be or how "isolated" its speakers, it changes constantly. For the purpose of comparison, Turner had to assume that the items he found in modern African languages were exactly the same as those brought to North America two centuries or more earlier. Because of this passage of time, Turner decided to distinguish two types of Gullah personal names. Those marked with an asterisk were well known as a name in West Africa, those without an asterisk being words not used as names there. This distinction helps us understand some limitations of Turner's work.

After Turner's book was published, some reviewers complained that he did not indicate the currency—which were common and which were rare—or the geographical distribution of the terms he cited (many were undoubtedly used or known only by older speakers or in one local area). Such matters were beyond Turner's overriding purpose: to show the Africanness of Gullah speech and culture.[62] It is also important to realize, as stated earlier, that Turner neither assumed nor showed that the Sea Islands represented a microcosm of all African American culture. Later research has not found elsewhere much of what Turner found there—possibly because what was preserved in Gullah was lost elsewhere, but just as likely because the Sea Islands were always a unique area. It seems clear that in many ways Gullah is a cousin to African American English rather than a parent or grandparent.

Turner's fourth chapter, "Syntactical Features" (pages 209–22) identifies patterns (in this case, of word order) that differed from American English but resembled what could be found in African languages. Gullah, for example, substitutes an active voice for the English passive voice, so that "He was beaten" becomes *Dem beat um* "they beat him." Turner also treats serial or compound verb phrases (pages 209–13), the helping verb *duh* as a verb of "incomplete predication" (usually associated with a progressive verb in English; thus, *duh go* "is/are going"), the comparison of adjectives, the use of verbal adjectives, and word order in sentences. While Turner linked these patterns to African languages, later scholars have found them in much of the Caribbean, suggesting that Jamaican, Guyanese, and other creoles have a common heritage with Gullah. In the 1970s the young field of creole studies and researchers like Ian Hancock, John Rickford, John Holm, and Frederic Cassidy relied on Turner's groundwork to show with precision how English-based creoles had evolved and diversified over the past three-and-one-half centuries.

Chapters 5, "Morphological Features" (pages 223–31), and 6, "Some Word Formations" (pages 232–39) deal with grammatical and other details affecting individual words in Gullah. Turner showed that Gullah often differs from English in that it expresses noun plurality, verb tense, and pronoun case and gender through context rather than by suffixes or a change in form.

In chapter 7 Turner identifies the Gullah forms from chapter 2 that are of African origin by describing and documenting analogous forms in West African languages. When a Gullah sound was not found in English, Turner discovered that in every case it occurred in two or more West African languages. In other instances, the Gullah speakers in Turner's samples used an African sound close to an English one, just as German or French speakers use their own [t, d] to approximate the English "th" sounds (/θ/ and /ð/) and their own [v] for the English [w]. Some of the more striking correspondences Turner found were as follows:

ENGLISH	GULLAH	EXAMPLES
interdental fricatives	alveolar stops	
[θ, ð]	[t, d]	[trot] "throat"; [dɛm] "them"
labiodental fricatives	bilabial fricatives	
[f, v]	[Φ, β]	[Φaɪβ] "five"
palato-alveolar affricatives	palatal plosives	
[ʧ, ʤ]	[c, ɟ]	[cu] "chew"; [ɟak] "Jack"

Consistent with some West African languages, Gullah speakers often add [n] to words beginning with a [y] or palatalize an initial [n], producing [ɲuz] "use" or [ɲu] "new." Turner noted that [l] and [r] alternated in Gullah ([byulo] "bureau" and [bluə] "brewer") and thought this probably related to the fact that languages like Kongo, Umbundu, Bobangi and Tshiluba lack /r/. By the same token Efik, Twi, and Fante lack /l/, while [l] and [r] are interchangeable in many words in Bambara, Malinke, Kru and Mandingo (e.g., in Mandingo the word for "mountain" is *kulu* or *kuru*). He also noted that Gullah favors words ending in vowels and that when it borrows from English, Gullah either adds a vowel or drops a consonant: [hosi] "hoarse," [bɑgə] "baggage." Certain consonant combinations are avoided either by deleting one of the consonants or by inserting a vowel: [pɑlimetə] "palmetto," [mani pis] "mantel piece." Turner found that Gullah favors simplifying consonant combinations and often drops a word-initial [s], as in [te] "stay." All of these patterns Turner documented as phonologically common and natural in such West African languages as Kongo, Mende, Yoruba, and Kimbundu.

In his ninth chapter, "Gullah Texts" (pages 255–89), Turner provides two dozen stories, songs, chants, and prayers that he recorded on disks from Gullah speakers (one text was entirely in Mende). Texts are presented with the recorded version transcribed in phonetics and Turner's English translation in conventional spelling. Many of them are presented only in Gullah, and some apparently have no words from African languages. Turner's texts are among his book's most important material. While invaluable to linguists because they show forms and usages in context (one could write a brief grammar of Gullah using them), they are of no less interest to the lay reader in showing the functions of Gullah in community life and how modern Gullah has blended influences from English and African languages.

TURNER'S SPEAKERS

Turner's Gullah material was collected primarily from fifty-three people, whom he listed in Appendix I (pages 291–92). Twenty-one of these were his principal Gullah informants, interviewed for the *Linguistic Atlas* in 1932–33, but he identifies them only by name and locality. It is appropriate to supplement the information in *Africanisms* by noting their age, sex, level of education, and literacy, all of which were noted by Turner in the note books he completed in his atlas research. None of the twenty-one had much formal education (thirteen had none at all) or literacy, and thirteen of them were over seventy-five years old (meaning that they were born before the Civil War). None had traveled outside their immediate vicinity except for brief periods, and all but one were native, and had parents who were native, to the immediate area in which they lived (one exception was Wallace Quarterman, of Frederika, St. Simons Island, Georgia, who was born in Liberty County, two counties to the north along the coast, and moved to St. Simons at an early age). Although they recalled songs and other texts with extensive Africanisms (especially from Vai and Mende), none retained any knowledge of an African language.

South Carolina Informants

1. Paris Capers, Frogmore, St. Helena Island, Beaufort County S.C., 60 year old male, three to four years schooling, reads Bible and newspaper
2. Anne Scott, Frogmore, St. Helena Island, Beaufort County S.C., 85 year old female, no schooling, illiterate
3. Sam Polite, Frogmore, St. Helena Island, Beaufort County S.C., 89 year old male, no schooling, illiterate
4. Sackie Sweetwine, Martin's Point, Wadmalaw Island, Charleston County S.C., 87 year old female, no schooling, illiterate
5. Prince Smith, Rockville, Wadmalaw Island, Charleston County S.C., 88 year old male, no schooling, taught himself to read Bible
6. Sarah Ross, Rockville, Wadmalaw Island, Charleston County S.C., 50 year old female, four years schooling, reads Bible only
7. Anne Crosby, James Clark Shell House, Edisto Island, Charleston County S.C., 87 year old female, no schooling, illiterate
8. Diana Brown, Seabrook, Edisto Island, Charleston County S.C., 88 year old female, no schooling, illiterate
9. Hester Milligan, Seaside, Edisto Island, Charleston County S.C., 49 year old female, no schooling, illiterate

10. Susan Anne Quall, Sand Hill, Johns Island, Charleston County S.C., 78 year old female, four years schooling, reads Bible and almanac with difficulty
11. Sancho Singleton, Johns Island, Charleston County S.C., 50 year old male, two years schooling, reads Bible and almanac with difficulty
12. Lucy Bailey Capers, Stater White Place, Johns Island, Charleston County S.C., 97 year old female, no schooling, illiterate

Georgia Informants

13. Bristow McIntosh, Townsend, Harris Neck, McIntosh County Ga., 80 year old male, several years schooling, reads Bible
14. James Napoleon Rogers, Townsend, Harris Neck, McIntosh County Ga., 76 year old male, no schooling, illiterate
15. Mrs. Scotia Washington, Townsend, Brewers Neck, McIntosh County Ga., 60 year old female, irregular schooling through fifth grade, reads Bible only
16. Katie Ben Brown, Raccoon Bluff, Sapeloe Island, McIntosh County Ga., 60 year old female, reached fourth or fifth grade, used to read Bible
17. Balaam Walker, Raccoon Bluff, Sapeloe Island, McIntosh County Ga., 59 year old male, two or three years schooling, reads Bible with difficulty
18. Shadrach Hall, Raccoon Bluff, Sapeloe Island, McIntosh County Ga., 85 year old male, no schooling, illiterate
19. Belle Murray, Glynn Harrington, St. Simons Island, Glynn County Ga., 59 year old female, three years school, reads Bible and Sunday School books
20. Wallace Quarterman, Frederika, St. Simons Island, Glynn County Ga., 90 year old male, no schooling, taught himself to read Bible
21. Dave White, South End, St. Simons Island, Glynn County Ga., 76 year old male, no schooling, illiterate

OPPORTUNITIES FOR CULTURAL ENRICHMENT

Turner's *Africanisms* opened a wide door for appreciating Gullah and its African inheritance, but the book had little immediate impact outside scholarly circles. It took a generation for the implications of his work to penetrate the South Carolina/Georgia lowcountry at large. Only in the 1980s was Turner's case for Gullah's lineage extended to other aspects of culture, and African Americans there began awakening to their distinctive heritage. Recent years have witnessed a remarkable growth in Gullah cultural awareness in which the Gullah community has increasingly taken the lead and the responsibility. Because of festivals, publications, television programs, musical and dramatic productions, and other developments presenting Gullah culture, Americans on the Sea Islands and elsewhere are discovering Gullah and the culture that gave it birth. Once considered an inferior and marginalized language whose speakers shunned it in public and often forbade their children to use it, Gullah has enjoyed an extraordinary re-evaluation. Speakers have developed cultural pride as they learn its history. Attention from other Americans, especially African Americans elsewhere seeking the roots of their culture, has exploded. The opportunities available today for exploring Gullah language and culture were all made possible to one degree or another by Turner's work.

Today two community-based cultural festivals are held annually in the heart of the Gullah territory, Beaufort County, South Carolina. The Gullah Festival, held on Memorial Day weekend on the waterfront in Beaufort since 1986, features Gullah and African American music, dance, and storytelling and offers a bazaar of goods and wares for the visitor. On nearby St. Helena Island, the homecoming celebration "Heritage Days" is held in early November at the Penn Center, a school founded in 1862. Originally known as the Penn School because missionaries from Pennsylvania established it to educate freed African Americans, the center has long been a leader in community education and has taken the lead in preserving and reviving Gullah.

During the same period literature for the lay person on Gullah language and culture has increased and improved markedly. Whereas earlier books on the subject were limited almost exclusively to technical works by linguists and nostalgic accounts by lowcountry whites, a far better and wider selection of titles is now available. Some of these are scholarly-based, including Charles W. Joyner's *Down by the Riverside*, Patricia Jones-Jackson's *When Roots Die: Endangered Traditions on the Sea Islands*, Margaret Washington Creel's *A Peculiar People: Slave Religion and Community Culture among the Gullahs*, Mary Twining and Keith Baird's *Sea Island Roots: African Presence in the Carolinas and Georgia*, Marquetta Goodwine's *The Legacy of Ibo Landing: Gullah Roots of African-American Culture*, and most recently, William Pollitzer's *The Gullah People and Their African Heritage*.[61] Each of these recovers a range of Gullah traditions. Books by Virginia

Mixson Geraty of Charleston, South Carolina, have done much to preserve the language and inform the public about it. A well-known local authority, Geraty has compiled a Gullah dictionary and a Gullah cookbook and has translated the Dubose Heyward play *Porgy* into Gullah (1990) for stage production and for public television.[64]

More significant than any other event in the renaissance of Gullah was the publication in 1995 of *De Good Nyews Bout Jedus Christ Wa Luke Write*, a translation of the Gospel of Luke into the language.[65] Beginning in 1979, the Sea Island Literacy and Translation Team—more than a dozen native speakers of Gullah assisted by linguists trained through the Wycliffe Bible Translators—has continued to work painstakingly to complete a dynamic translation of the New Testament for use in lowcountry churches alongside the more traditional King James Version. The greatest significance of the Gullah translation of Luke lies in its being the first written version produced by Gullah speakers.

Millions of Americans were first introduced to Gullah on the "Black on White" episode of the *Story of English* series produced by the British Broadcasting Corporation and broadcast on American public television in 1986.[66] The program examined the use of English in West Africa today and traced the coming of pidgin English, a precursor to Gullah, to the Western Hemisphere through the slave trade in centuries past. It featured a segment filmed on St. Helena Island of individuals having a conversation in Gullah (with subtitles) and part of a church service.

A particularly exciting development has been increased interest in exploring connections with cultures in West Africa and elsewhere in North America that are historically related to the Sea Islands. A watershed event for the recognition of Gullah was the visit in 1988 of President Joseph Momoh and a delegation from Sierra Leone, a small West African country from which a disproportion of Africans were brought to South Carolina in the eighteenth century.[67] The most significant event of their ten days in the U.S. was a visit to Penn Center, where its director Emory Campbell addressed them in Gullah and Momoh responded in Krio. For many speakers of Gullah this was the first time they heard their language on a formal, public occasion; for them Gullah had at long last come out of hiding. Bonds formed at the occasion resulted in a delegation of fourteen Americans visiting Sierra Leone the following year to retrace the paths of some of their ancestors. Their fascinating, but emotionally painful experiences were captured in *Family across the Sea* (1990), a video widely shown on public television that also explores similarities in language, lifestyle, folklore, and art between the Sea Islands and Sierra Leone. A captivating sequel to that program, *The Language You Cry In* (1999), recounted the successful efforts of two American researchers, anthropologist Joseph Opala and ethnomusicologist Cynthia Schmidt, to discover the origin in Sierra Leone of the song (more accurately characterized as a funeral chant) recorded and transcribed by Turner (page 256).

On other fronts, the recovery of the history and language of Gullah people has progressed in exciting ways. In 1981, Ian Hancock, a linguist at the University of Texas, found in Oklahoma and Texas a quite conservative type of Gullah that he called Afro-Seminole, which had been taken in the 1830s to Oklahoma (and later to Texas) by Seminoles who were part descendants of runaway slaves from the Sea Islands. In 1996 Hancock arranged a meeting between representatives of Afro-Seminoles and Sea Islanders, their first contact in more than a century and a half. Bridges have gradually been built between other different Gullah speaking communities.[68] Since 1994 the cable television network Nickelodeon has produced *Gullah Gullah Island*, an award-winning television program for pre-school children. Hosted by Ron and Natalie Daise and their children, the show is set on an imaginary South Carolina island and features a multicultural format with selected Gullah words and culture. The Daises have widely performed *Sea Island Montage*, a program of Gullah song and story. Touring groups such as the Georgia Sea Island Singers, Hallelujah Singers, and Plantation Singers provide cultural enrichment in the form of traditional songs and hymns, stories, chants and rituals, and dramatic presentations re-enacting the life of the Sea Islands. The full-length film *Daughters of the Dust* (1992), shot on St. Helena Island, presented a vivid, lush portrait of the Sea Islands and attracted a wide audience. Set in 1902, it compared the experiences of three generations of women and emphasized the importance of preserving memory from one generation to another. It captured the imagination of many viewers and brought Gullah out of the abstract.

Finally, Gullah speakers themselves have become politically active, mobilizing citizens to protect and preserve the heritage and history of the Sea Islands. One group in the forefront of this effort is the Gullah/Geechee Sea Island Coalition, founded in 1997 and headquartered on St. Helena Island, South Carolina. More than half a century after the publication of Turner's volume, those who follow his legacy continue in many ways to show that Gullah language and culture have much to teach all of us.

NOTES

1. The authors gratefully acknowledge the advice and gracious assistance of Scott Evan Burgess, Christine Corcoran, Anne Marie Hamilton, Ian F. Hancock, Alexander Moore, Salikoko Mufwene, Patricia C. Nichols, Joe Opala, John Singler, Grace Song, Jack Sproat, Margaret Wade-Lewis, and Lois Turner Williams in writing this introduction.

2. Gullah is the only English-based creole known to exist in North America. It was termed "Sea Island Creole" by Irma Aloyce Cunningham in her 1970 dissertation, "A Syntactic Analysis of Sea Island Creole" (University of Michigan), since published (*Publication of the American Dialect Society 75,* Tuscaloosa: University of Alabama Press, 1992). "A creole," according to John Holm (*Pidgins and Creoles,* vol. 1, *Theory and Structure* [Cambridge: Cambridge University Press, 1988]) "has a jargon or pidgin in its ancestry; it is spoken natively by an entire speech community, often one whose ancestors were displaced geographically so that their ties with their original language and sociocultural identity were partly broken" (6–8). Children born to this displaced population are exposed less to their parents' native languages than to the new but incompletely acquired language or pidgin. With this highly variable linguistic input, the children are somehow able to organize the creole, which serves as their native language—one complete with phonological rules and vocabulary to cover all aspects of their life. This expansion and elaboration often reorganizes the grammar to include the creation of a coherent verbal system and even complex phrases and clauses.

3. The best bibliography of writing in and studies of Gullah from the nineteenth century through the early 1970s can be found in John Reinecke et al., eds. "Gullah," *A Bibliography of Pidgin and Creole Languages* (Honolulu: University Press of Hawaii, 1975), 468–80, which lists and annotates 160 items.

4. H. L. Mencken, *The American Language: Supplement Two* (New York: Knopf, 1948), 101.

5. The chief published source on Turner's biography is the work of Margaret Wade-Lewis: "Lorenzo Dow Turner: First African-American Linguist," *Occasional Paper No. 2* (Philadelphia: Temple University Department of African-American Studies, 1988) and "Lorenzo Dow Turner: Pioneer African-American Linguist" *Black Scholar* 21, no. 4 (1991): 10–24 (the latter contains a cumulative bibliography of Turner's publications). Wade-Lewis, on the faculty at the State University of New York at New Paltz, conducted extensive archival research in the Lorenzo Dow Turner Collection at the Melville J. Herskovits Library of African Studies at Northwestern University and interviewed Turner's widow, Mrs. Lois Turner Williams. Our account rests heavily on hers, which contains much more detail than can be provided here. For a number of years Wade-Lewis has been working on a biography of Turner, utilizing the extensive correspondence and other materials in the Turner Collection at Northwestern.

6. This work was published in 1929 by the Association for the Study of Afro-American Life and History in Washington, D.C., and reprinted by Kennikat Press, Port Washington, New York, in 1966.

7. Miles Hanley, "Progress of the Linguistic Atlas and Plans for the Future Work of the Dialect Society," *Dialect Notes* 6 (1931): 91–96.

8. Wade-Lewis, "Lorenzo Dow Turner: First African-American Linguist," 7.

9. Turner was accompanied by Guy S. Lowman, Jr., principal field investigator for the *Linguistic Atlas of the United States and Canada,* who participated in some of Turner's interviews with Gullah speakers. Lowman was a skilled fieldworker and brilliant phonetician, but Turner later related that his presence inhibited some speakers (*Africanisms*, 12). Shortly after the publication of Turner's book, *The Roosevelt Torch* (October 24, 1949) offered a more frank and insightful report: "'Mek oona bring di buckra?' (why did you bring the white man?). This question was consistently asked of Dr. Turner by the natives of the Rice Islands bordering the coast of S.C. Their memories of subjugation by white men, their tales of slavery handed down through the generations, and their hard times illustrated in the latter part of his book explain why even he was treated as an outsider until his friendly manner and expert use of their mother tongue had them accept him as one of them."

10. *New York Herald Tribune*, January 1, 1933.

11. Wade-Lewis, "First African-American Linguist," 7.

12. Ibid., 10. According to Wade-Lewis ("Lorenzo Dow Turner: Pioneer African-American Linguist," 13), Turner had written to Daniel Jones of the University of London that he wanted to "study the phonetic structure of certain West African languages with a view to determine, if possible, the nature and extent of African survivals in Gullah."

13. In northeastern Brazil Turner found several African languages still spoken, including Yoruba, Fon, and Kimbunda, and discovered thriving African religious practices, music and art. See his essay "African Survivals in the New World with Special Emphasis on the Arts," in *Africa Seen by American Negroes*, ed. John A. Davis (Paris: Presence Africaine, 1958), 101–16.

14. *Louisville Defender*, June 6, 1942 (from microfilm of Turner Collection, Northwestern University Library).

15. *Roosevelt Torch*, May 25, 1946.

16. According to Lois Turner Williams, Turner worked for years on three to four hours sleep a night, eventually developing an ulcer and general poor health. During his hospitalization from the ulcer, she taught his African culture course at Roosevelt.

17. Robert A. Hall, "The African Substratum in Negro English," in *American Speech* 25 (1950), 53–54.

18. *Roosevelt Torch*, October 24, 1949.

19. Ibid., January 19, 1953.

20. *Hyde Park Herald*, April, 1961.

21. The full title was *An Anthology of Krio Folklore and Literature with Notes and Interlinear Translation in English* (Chicago: Roosevelt University, 1963).

22. *Hyde Park Herald*, 1961.

23. Among prominent scholars who held this view were sociologists Gunnar Myrdal, *An American Dilemma: The Negro Problem and Modern Democracy* (New York: Harper, 1944) and E. Franklin Frazier, *The Negro in the United States* (New York: Macmillan, 1949).

24. Simms, *The Wigwam and the Cabin* (London: Wiley, 1846).

25. Thomas Wentworth Higginson, *Army Life in a Black Regiment* (Boston: Fields and Osgood, 1870).

26. Reed Smith, *Gullah: Bulletin of the University of South Carolina No. 10* (Columbia: University of South Carolina, 1926).

27. Similarly, other commentators, such as John Bennett, pointed to features shared by Gullah and the English of poor whites and attributed them to the non-standard speech of white British and Irish settlers. Some of these whites were bondsmen, indentured servants, or "redemptioners"; some became overseers who supervised slaves in the field. The slaves could easily have borrowed from the language of these largely Scotch-Irish whites who were nearer their circumstances. See the October 23, 1918 letter from Bennett quoted in Smith, *Gullah*, 25.

28. Smith, *Gullah*, 18

29. Ibid., 21.

30. Ibid., 25.

31. Ibid., 28.

32. George Philip Krapp, "The English of the Negro," *American Mercury* 2 (1924): 190, 193.

33. Caroline Gilman, *Recollections of a Southern Matron* (New York: Harper, 1838); William Gilmore Simms, *The Wigwam and the Cabin* (1846); Joel Chandler Harris, *Nights with Uncle Remus: Myths and Legends of the Old Plantation* (Boston: Osgood, 1881); Rev. John G. Williams, "De Ole Plantation": Elder Coteney's Sermons (Charleston, S.C.: Walker, Evans and Cogswell, 1896); Bennett, "Gullah: A Negro Patois" *South Atlantic Quarterly* 7 (1908): 332–47; 8 (1909): 39–52; Ambrose Gonzales, *The Black Border: Gullah Stories of the South Carolina Coast* (Columbia, S.C.: The State, 1922); Julia Peterkin, *Black April* (Indianapolis, Ind.: Bobbs-Merrill, 1927); Albert H. Stoddard, *Buh Partridge Outhides Buh Rabbit*. (Savannah, Ga.: privately printed, 1939); Stoddard, *Gullah Tales and Anecdotes of South Carolina Sea Islands*. (Savannah, Ga.: privately printed, 1940).

34. Gonzales, *The Black Border*.

35. Smith, *Gullah*, 18 attributes this comment to an unidentified source.

36. For example, writers such as Julia Peterkin.

37. Melville J. Herskovits, *The Myth of the Negro Past* (Boston: Beacon Press, 1941).

38. For an assessment of this issue, see Salikoko Mufwene and Charles Gilman, "How African is Gullah, and Why?" *American Speech* 62 (1987): 120–39.

39. Mufwene, "Africanisms in Gullah: A Re-Examination of the Issues," in *Old English and New: Studies in Language in Honor of Frederic G. Cassidy*, ed. Joan H. Hall, Dick Wringler, and Nick Doane (New York: Garland Press, 1992), 156–82. Mufwene's arguments are based on historical records published by Peter H. Wood, *Black Majority: Negroes in Colonial South Carolina from 1670 through the Stono Rebellion* (New York: Knopf, 1974); and by Margaret Washington Creel, *A Peculiar People: Slave Religion and Community Life among the Gullahs* (New York: New York University Press, 1988), among others.

40. Very little literature on pidgins and creoles was known at the time. Addison Van Name's "Contributions to Creole Grammar" (1869–70) comparing creoles found in the Caribbean may have been the first scientific study of creole languages (Holm, *Pidgins and Creoles,* vol. 1, 24). The few sources that existed were inaccessible to most scholars, e.g., Reinecke's "Marginal Language: A Sociological Survey of the Creole Languages," 2 vols. (Ph.D. diss., Yale University, 1937). Hugo Schuchardt, the foremost creolist at the turn of the twentieth century, wrote in German and published little of his work (for a translation of an important paper in which he linked West African Krio with New World English creoles, including Gullah, see Glenn Gilbert, "Hugo Schuchardt and the Atlantic Creoles: A Newly Discovered Manuscript On the Negro English of West Africa," *American Speech* 60 (1985): 31–63.

41. Herskovits had pioneered this idea with respect to religious and other cultural practices in his *Myth of the Negro Past*. Turner considered it for language. Seeking to explain Gonzales's use of the expression *done fuh* in a

Gullah story. Turner (page 14) saw a possible source in the word *da*^{3}*fa*^{1} "mouth full/fat" (from the African language Vai). Thus, in the Gullah sentence *ooman done fuh fat* "(that) woman is really fat."

42. "Linguistic Research and African Survivals. The Interdisciplinary Aspects of Negro Studies," ed. Melville J. Herskovits, in *American Council of Learned Societies Bulletin* 32 (1941): 68–89; "Notes on the Sounds and Vocabulary of Gullah," *Publication of the American Dialect Society* 3 (1945): 13–26.

43. See chapter 6, "The Contemporary Scene: Language and the Arts" in Herskovits, *The Myth of the Negro Past*. See also Wade-Lewis, "The Impact of the Turner/Herskovits Connection on Anthropology and Linguistics," *Dialectical Anthropology* 17 (1992): 391–412.

44. Turner, "Linguistic Research," 68–69.

45. Wade-Lewis, "First African-American Linguist," 9.

46. See McDavid's review of Turner's book in *Language* 26 (1950): 323–33. To some extent the promise was fulfilled, however, by Cunningham's *A Syntactic Analysis of Sea Island Creole* (1970; reprint 1992 as *Publication of the American Dialect Society*), 75.

47. For example, David Dalby, "The African Element in American English," in *Rappin' and Stylin' Out: Communication in Urban Black America*, ed. Thomas Kochman (Urbana: University of Illinois Press) 170–86; Wade-Lewis, *The African Substratum in American English* (Ph.D. diss., New York University, 1988); Joseph E. Holloway and Winfred K. Vass, *The African Heritage of American English* (Bloomington: Indiana University Press, 1992).

48. Some reviewers (e.g. Morris Swadesh in *Word* 7 (1951), 83–84) discounted the value of Turner's personal names because their bearers did not know their meanings; for a refutation of this view, see Mufwene, "The Linguistic Significance of African Proper Names in Gullah," *New West Indian Guide* 59 (1985): 149–66; Keith E. Baird and Mary A. Twining, "Names and Naming in the Sea Island," in *The Crucible of Carolina: Essays in the Development of Gullah Language and Culture*, ed. Michael Montgomery (Athens: University of Georgia Press, 1994), 23–37.

49. John Holm, "Variability of the Copula in Black English and Its Creole Kin," *American Speech* 59 (1984), 291–309; Frederic G. Cassidy, "Sources of the African Element in Gullah," in *Studies in Caribbean Language*, ed. Lawrence D. Carrington et al. (St. Augustine, Trinidad: Society for Caribbean Linguistics), 75–81; Joko Sengova, "Recollections of African Language Patterns in an American Speech Variety: An Assessment of Mende Influences in Lorenzo Dow Turner's Gullah Data" in *The Crucible of Carolina*, 175–200; and Joe Opala, *The Language You Cry In* (California Newsreel, 1998).

50. For a discussion of why the disappearance of Gullah may be exaggerated, see Mufwene, "Some Reasons why Gullah is not Dying Yet," *English World-Wide* 12 (1991): 215–43; and Katherine Wyly Mille, "A Historical Analysis of Tense-Mood-Aspect in Gullah: A Case of Stable Variation" (Ph.D.

diss., University of South Carolina, 1990). Mufwene expands his discussion in "On Decreolization: The Case of Gullah." in *Language and the Social Construction of Identity in Creole Situations*, ed. Marcyliena Morgan (Los Angeles: Center for Afro-American Studies, 1994) 63–99.

51. The disks in the collection, master recordings that Turner cut in the field while interviewing in Africa, South America, and the United States, require specialized and now obsolete equipment to play. Researchers will need to consult the Library of African Studies staff concerning their use.

52. Raven I. McDavid Jr., William A. Kretzschmar, Jr., and Gail J. Hankins, eds. *Linguistic Atlas of the Middle and South Atlantic States* and Affiliated Projects: Basic Materials. *Microfilm MSS on Cultural Anthropology* 68.360–64, 69.365–69, 71.375–80 (Chicago: Joseph Regenstein Library, University of Chicago, 1982–86). These records, which can be mined for many research purposes (they are the only materials in existence that permit study of geographical variation within Gullah), have been used for only one study to date: Montgomery, "Lorenzo Dow Turner's Early Work on Gullah," in *The Crucible of Carolina*, 158–74.

53. R. B. Le Page, and A. Tabouret-Keller, *Acts of Identity* (Cambridge: Cambridge University Press, 1985).

54. Among the works that compare Gullah and African-American Vernacular English to explore their historical relations are J. L. Dillard, *Black English: Its History and Usage in the United States* (New York: Random House, 1972); John R. Rickford, "The Question of Prior Creolization of Black English," in *Pidgin and Creole Linguistics*, ed. Albert Valdman (Bloomington: Indiana University Press, 1977), 190–221; John Baugh, "A Reexamination of the Black English Copula," in *Locating Language in Time and Space*, ed. William Labov (New York: Academic Press, 1980), 83–106; Holm, "Variability," 291–309; Holm, "The Atlantic Creoles and the Language of the Ex-Slave Recordings," in *The Emergence of Black English: Text and Commentary*, ed. Guy Bailey, Natalie Maynor, and Patricia Cukor-Avila (Philadelphia, Pa.: Benjamins, 1991), 231–48; and Tracey L. Weldon, "Exploring the Gullah-AAVE Connection: A Comparative Study of Copula Variability" (Ph.D. diss., Ohio State University, 1998).

55. See *Africanisms*, 11–13, where Turner attributes the failure of earlier investigators to identify Africanisms in Gullah, especially African personal names, to their inability to overcome the suspicions of Gullah speakers. See also Turner, "Problems Confronting the Investigator of Gullah," *Publication of the American Dialect Society* 9 (1948): 74–84, in which Turner outlines requirements for the valid study of Gullah, including knowledge of the slave trade, acquaintance with African languages, and a close, informal relationship with informants.

56. Patricia C. Nichols, "Black Women in the Rural South: Conservative and Innovative," *International Journal of the Sociology of Language* 17 (1976): 45–54.

57. This map reflects political boundaries of the late 1940s, when much of West Africa was still under the dominion of European colonial powers.

58. In some cases these probably represented words borrowed by African languages from Arabic as Islam spread throughout much of the northern half of Africa, but in other cases these were likely direct borrowings, as some slaves could speak and even read Arabic. From one slave a thirteen-page manuscript in Arabic has survived; see Joseph Greenberg, "The Decipherment of the 'Ben-ali Diary': A Preliminary Statement," *Journal of Negro History* 25 (1940): 372–75; and Harold Courlander, ed. "The Bilali Document," *A Treasury of Afro-American Folklore* (New York: Crown, 1975), 289–90.

59. For further information on phonetic notation, see *The Principles of the International Phonetic Association* (London: International Phonetic Association, 1949).

60. For a different view, see Mufwene, "The Linguistic Significance of African Proper Names in Gullah," 149–66, in which the author compares the pronunciations of Turner's African proper names in Gullah with their proposed African etyma and concludes that they provide limited phonetic evidence supporting Turner's hypothesis that Gullah's phonology was influenced by African phonological systems.

61. Later scholars have worked on the settlement history of the Gullah territory more systematically than Turner was able to do: Wood, *Black Majority*; Daniel C. Littlefield, *Rice and Slaves: Ethnicity and Slavery in Colonial South Carolina* (Baton Rouge: Louisiana State University Press, 1981); James A. Rawley, *The Transatlantic Slave Trade* (New York: Norton, 1981).

62. These questions can be investigated to some extent with the twenty-one records that Turner completed for the *Linguistic Atlas of the Middle and South Atlantic States.*

63. Mervyn C. Alleyne, *Comparative Afro-American: An Historical Comparative Study of English Based Afro-American Dialects of the New World* (Ann Arbor, Mich.: Karoma, 1980); Joyner, *Down by the Riverside*; Jones-Jackson, *When Roots Die*; Creel, *A Peculiar People*; Twining and Baird, ed. *Sea Island Roots*; Mufwene, ed. *Africanisms in Afro-American Language Varieties* (Athens: University of Georgia Press, 1993); Montgomery, ed. *The Crucible of Carolina*; Goodwine, ed. *The Legacy of Ibo Landing*; and Pollitzer, *The Gullah People and Their African Heritage*.

64. Virginia Mixson Geraty, *Porgy: A Gullah Version* (Charleston, S.C.: Wyrick, 1990); *Biddle en' T'ing': Gullah Cooking with Maum Chrish* (Orangeburg, S.C.: Sandlapper, 1992); *Gullah fuh Oonuh: A Guide to the Gullah Language* (Orangeburg, S.C.: Sandlapper, 1997).

65. *De Good Nyews bout Jedus Christ wa Luke Write: The Gospel According to Luke* (New York: American Bible Society, 1995).

66. Robert McCrum, William Cran, and Robert MacNeil. "Black on White," *The Story of English* (New York: Viking), 194–233.

67. See Littlefield, *Rice and Slaves*; Opala, *The Gullah* (Freetown, Sierra Leone: United States Information Service, c 1985).

68. Ian F. Hancock, "On the Classification of Afro-Seminole Creole," in *Language Variety in the South: Perspectives in Black and White*, ed. Michael B. Montgomery and Guy Bailey (University: University of Alabama Press, 1986), 85–101.

PREFACE TO FIRST EDITION

THE distinctiveness of Gullah, the dialect of a large number of Negroes in coastal South Carolina and Georgia, has provoked comment from writers for many years. The assumption on the part of many has been that the peculiarities of the dialect are traceable almost entirely to the British dialects of the seventeenth and eighteenth centuries and to a form of baby-talk adopted by masters of the slaves to facilitate oral communication between themselves and the slaves. Other persons have not been wholly satisfied with this explanation. The present study, by revealing the very considerable influence of several West African languages upon Gullah, will, it is hoped, remove much of the mystery and confusion surrounding this dialect.

Gullah is a creolized form of English revealing survivals from many of the African languages spoken by the slaves who were brought to South Carolina and Georgia during the eighteenth century and the first half of the nineteenth. These survivals are most numerous in the vocabulary of the dialect but can be observed also in its sounds, syntax, morphology, and intonation; and there are many striking similarities between Gullah and the African languages in the methods used to form words. The purpose of this study is to record the most important of these Africanisms and to list their equivalents in the West African languages. One chapter in the volume is devoted to Gullah texts, in phonetic notation, that show varying degrees of indebtedness to African sources.

The present study is the result of an investigation of the dialect that has extended over a period of fifteen years. The communities in coastal South Carolina that furnished the most distinctive specimens of the dialect were Waccamaw (a peninsula near Georgetown) and James, Johns, Wadmalaw, Edisto, St. Helena, and Hilton Head Islands. Those in Georgia were Darien, Harris Neck (a peninsula near Darien), Sapeloe Island, St. Simon Island, and St. Marys. On the mainland of both South Carolina and Georgia many of the communities in which specimens of the dialect were recorded are situated twenty miles or farther from the coast.

In seven of the communities where the dialect was studied, at least three informants were selected, two being above sixty years of age and one between forty and sixty. Both sexes were represented, and with one exception[1] all the informants were natives of their respective communities. Their parents were also natives. In studying the vocabulary of Gullah, however, I consulted a great many additional informants throughout the Gullah area.

Specimens of the dialect were gathered by means of interviews with informants during which work-sheets were used similar to those prepared by the staff of the *Linguistic Atlas of the United States and Canada* but made suitable for use among the Gullahs. In addition, phonograph recordings were made throughout the Gullah area of many varieties of material, including autobiographical sketches of informants, narratives of religious experience, prayers, sermons, religious and secular songs, folk tales, proverbs, superstitions, descriptions of living conditions on the Sea Islands, recollections of slavery, methods of planting and harvesting crops, methods of cooking, systems of counting, etc.

This study has been made possible through the generosity of the American Council of Learned Societies in the form of several grants given at intervals since 1932. These include one grant in 1932, three grants-in-aid in 1933, 1937, and 1940, respectively, and one fellowship in 1938–39. Without such assistance the study could not possibly have been developed into its present form.

To the Humanities Institute of Fisk University I am indebted for a grant-in-aid which was used in connection with the completion of certain details of the investigation.

In addition to the many Gullah and African informants (listed in Appendix I) without whose interested and generous cooperation this work would have been impossible, I wish to acknowledge my gratitude to the following persons:

Four members of the staff of the *Linguistic Atlas of New England*—Dr. Hans Kurath, director and editor; Professor Miles L. Hanley, associate director; Dr. Bernard Bloch, assistant editor; and the late Dr. Guy S. Lowman, Jr., principal field investigator—gave me valuable criticisms and suggestions and manifested a keen interest in the study throughout the period during which it was in preparation. Dr. Lowman accompanied me on one of my field trips and participated in the interviews with my principal Gullah informants. Dr. Kurath, Dr. Robert A. Hall, Jr., of Cornell University, and Dr. M. M. Mathews, of the staff of the *Dictionary of American English,* read the entire work in manuscript and made important suggestions.

On the Sea Islands of Georgia and South Carolina my collection of Gullah material was greatly facilitated by the cooperation of the following persons: on St. Simon Island, Georgia, Mrs. Lydia Parrish; on St. Helena Island, South Carolina, Dr. Y. W. Bailey and the officials of the Penn Normal, Industrial, and Agricultural School, especially Mr. and Mrs. J. P. King; and on Edisto, Wadmalaw, James, and Johns Islands, South Carolina, the Reverend W. L. Metz, Miss Lillian A. Patrick, Mrs. M. Fields, and Miss Lorene Poinsette, respectively.

In connection with my investigation of several West African languages and cultures, I am greatly indebted to still other persons. At the School of Oriental and African Studies of the University of London during the year 1936–37, Dr. Ida C. Ward, who was head of the department of African languages, and under whom I studied five West African languages, gave me very helpful criticisms and suggestions, and at University College, London, Professor Daniel Jones was eager to cooperate. Some measure of my indebtedness to both these scholars is revealed in my many references to their publications. Sir William A. Craigie, editor of the *Oxford Dictionary* and the *Dictionary of American English,* also gave me several useful suggestions; and in Paris during the summer of 1937, Professor Henri Labouret made it possible for me to interview at length more than twenty natives of French West Africa. For the use of many materials relating to the Umbundu language, I am indebted to the Reverend Henry C. McDowell, former missionary at Ngalangi, Angola, and at present pastor of the Dixwell Avenue Congregational Church in New Haven, Connecticut. Dr. Melville J. Herskovits, of Northwestern University, has also made accessible to me numerous materials relating to Africa and has given me encouragement in many other ways. Finally, to my wife I wish to express my gratitude not only for preparing the maps and the diagram of the Yoruba and Gullah vowels but also for generously assisting me in other phases of the investigation.

LORENZO D. TURNER
Roosevelt College
January 1, 1949

AFRICANISMS IN THE GULLAH DIALECT

CHAPTER 1

BACKGROUNDS

PERSONS interested in undertaking the study and interpretation of the speech of uneducated Negroes in the coastal region of South Carolina and Georgia would do well to acquire some acquaintance with several languages spoken in those sections of the West Coast of Africa from which the Negroes were brought to the United States as slaves. The Negro dialect known as Gullah or Geechee[1] is spoken by the ex-slaves and their descendants in that part of this region which extends along the Atlantic coast approximately from Georgetown, South Carolina, to the northern boundary of Florida. It is heard both on the mainland and on the Sea Islands near by.

IMPORTATION OF SLAVES TO SOUTH CAROLINA AND GEORGIA DIRECT FROM AFRICA

If one were to give a conservative estimate of the number of slaves imported direct from Africa to South Carolina and Georgia during the one hundred years prior to 1808, it would be at least 100,000.[2] After January 1, 1808, when the Slave Trade Act became operative, slave-traders continued to bring Negroes direct from Africa, though to do so was illegal.[3] As late as 1858, approximately 420 Negroes direct from Africa were landed near Brunswick, Georgia.[4] Information as to how many of these "new" slaves, i.e., those who had come direct from Africa, remained in coastal South Carolina and Georgia and how many other "new" slaves from Virginia[5] and other colonies joined them there is not available; but if there is any correlation between the number who settled there and the extent to which African customs and speech habits have survived in that area, then the "new" slaves must have constituted a considerable part of the slave population of coastal South Carolina and Georgia.

The slaves brought to South Carolina and Georgia direct from Africa came principally from a section along the West Coast extending from Senegal to Angola. The important areas involved were Senegal, Gambia, Sierra Leone, Liberia, the Gold Coast, Togo, Dahomey, Nigeria, and Angola.[6] Today the vocabulary of Gullah contains words found in the following languages, all of which are spoken in the above-mentioned areas: Wolof, Malinke, Mandinka, Bambara, Fula, Mende, Vai, Twi, Fante, Gã, Ewe, Fon [fɔ̃], Yoruba, Bini, Hausa, Ibo, Ibibio, Efik, Kongo, Umbundu, Kimbundu, and a few others.

Throughout the eighteenth century the number of slaves entering South Carolina who had previously lived in the West Indies was much smaller, and the number of those who came direct from Africa much larger, than many persons have supposed. Legislative enactments in South Carolina during the eighteenth century imposed a much heavier duty on slaves from the West Indies and other places in the New World than on those who came direct from Africa. Slaves from other American colonies, it was said, had frequently been sent to South Carolina because of misconduct. In various places in the New World there had been slave insurrections in which many white persons had been killed. The act of 1721 imposed a duty of £10 on all Negro slaves above ten years of age imported into South Carolina directly from Africa, but on those entering the state from any part of America an additional £30 was imposed for a period of six months after the passage of the act; thereafter £50 had to be paid on such slaves unless the owner, importer, or factor could certify that they were "new" Negroes who had not been on shore six months in any part of America. The law of 1722 continued these provisions with the addition that a duty of £150 was to be imposed on Spanish Negroes entering the state, as they were thought to encourage the South Carolina Negroes to run away.[7] The following quotation from a letter dated June 12, 1755, and written by Henry Laurens of Charleston, South Carolina, to John Yeates, of Jamaica, British West Indies, gives some idea of the difficulty slave dealers in Charleston experienced in disposing of slaves from the West Indies. Yeates had sent, by a Mr. Chapone, two slaves from the West Indies whom Laurens sold in Georgetown, South Carolina, for £570. Laurens wrote: "Altho we shall be always glad to render you our best services in any other matters we must make an absolute objection to the consignment of West India slaves, besides they are subject to a duty of £50 per head which we suppose Mr. Chapone escaped by importing them as his attendants."[8] In 1783 another law was enacted in South Carolina placing a duty of £20 a head on slaves imported from places other than Africa, but on those coming direct from Africa who were over four feet in height only £3 was imposed, and on those under

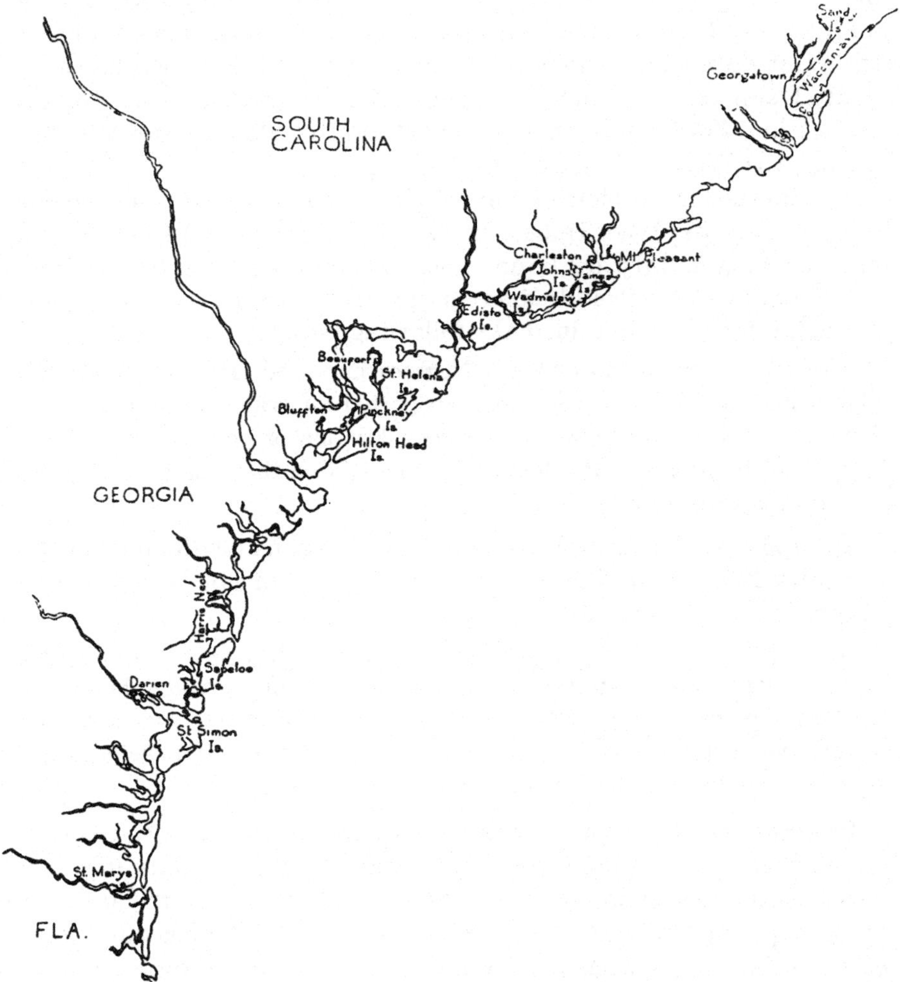

MAP OF THE GULLAH AREA

that height only thirty shillings.[9] The act of 1803 prohibited the importation of all Negroes from the West Indies and those over fifteen years of age from other parts of the United States except under certificate of good character.[10] In 1768 Georgia placed a duty on incoming Negroes who had been more than six months in any of the West India or Continental colonies,[11] and the slave revolution in Santo Domingo is said to have impelled the Georgia legislature to pass an act in 1793 forbidding the importation of slaves from the Bahamas, the West Indies, and Florida.[12]

Virginians also preferred "new" slaves to those who had spent some time in the West Indies. In 1710 during the consideration of a bill imposing a duty on liquor and slaves imported into Virginia, the Virginia Council addressed to the House of Burgesses a communication which contained the following request:

> And forasmuch as most of the Negroes imported from her Majesty's Plantations are either such as are transported for crimes or infected with diseases, the Council submit to the consideration of your house whether it may not be proper that a higher duty be laid on them than on Negroes imported directly from Africa.[13]

In 1733 Governor Burrington of North Carolina complained of the difficulty North Carolinians were experiencing in not being able to obtain "new" slaves:

> Great is the loss this country has sustained in not being supplied by vessels from Guinea with Negroes; in any part of the province the people are able to pay for a ship's load; but as none can come directly from Africa, we are under a necessity to buy the refuse, refractory and distempered Negroes, brought from other governments.[14]

Presumably the slaves coming to South Carolina and Georgia direct from Africa, unlike those who had spent some time in other parts of America or in the West Indies, had, on their arrival, little or no acquaintance with the English language. In the coastal region of these states, especially on the Sea Islands, heat, malaria, and dampness retarded the growth of the white population. The extensive production of rice, indigo, and cotton led to the establishment of plantations on which Negro labor became a necessity. It is said that there were twenty Negro families to every one white family in many sections of coastal South Carolina.[15] On many plantations there were no white overseers. Here the work of the field slaves was directed entirely by Negro drivers. Moreover, there were no bridges connecting the Islands with the mainland. Even as late as 1932 there were Negroes on some of the Sea Islands who had never visited the mainland.

Whereas these facts explain why there was less demand in the Charleston market for slaves from the West Indies than for those who were being brought direct from Africa, they do not warrant the assumption that slaves coming to South Carolina and Georgia who had previously lived in the West Indies had lost their African speech habits. As a matter of fact, the African element in the speech of West Indians is still considerable. These facts do, however, warrant the reasonable assumption that the African speech habits of the earliest Gullahs were being constantly strengthened throughout the eighteenth century and the first half of the nineteenth by contact with the speech of native Africans who were coming direct from Africa and who were sharing with the older Gullahs the isolation of the Sea Islands—a condition which obviously made easier the retention of Africanisms in that area than in places where Negroes had less direct contact with Africa and lived less isolated lives. One should not be surprised, therefore, to find among the Gullahs today numerous African customs and speech habits.

THE BRITISH DIALECTS AND BABY-TALK

Many Americans who have attempted to explain Gullah have greatly underestimated the extent of the African element in this strange dialect. Observing many characteristics that Gullah has in common with certain British dialects of the seventeenth and eighteenth centuries, they have not considered it necessary to acquaint themselves with any of the languages spoken in those sections of West Africa from which the Negroes were brought to the New World as slaves, nor to study the speech of the Negroes in those parts of the New World where English is not spoken; but rather have they taken the position that the British dialects offer a satisfactory solution to all the problems presented by Gullah. They contend also that Gullah is partly a survival of baby-talk which the white people, during the early period of slavery, found it necessary to use in communicating with the slaves. A few quotations from the productions of some of these writers will explain their theory and reveal the unanimity of their views regarding the origin and nature of Gullah.

The late Professor George Philip Krapp, of Columbia University, says:

The assimilation of the language of the Negroes to the language of the whites did not take place all at once. Though the historical evidence is not as full as might be wished, the stages can be followed with some certainty. When the Negroes were first brought to America they could have known no English. Their usefulness as servants, however, required that some means of communication between master and slave should be developed. There is little likelihood that any masters exerted themselves to understand or to acquire the native language of the Negroes in order to communicate with them. On the contrary, from the very beginning the white overlords addressed themselves in English to their black vassals. It is not difficult to imagine the kind of English this would be. It would be a very much simplified English—the kind of English some people employ when they talk to babies. It would probably have no tenses of the verb, no distinctions of case in nouns or pronouns, no marks of singular or plural. Difficult sounds would be eliminated, as they are in baby-talk. Its vocabulary would be reduced to the lowest possible elements. As the Negroes imported into America came from many unrelated tribes, speaking languages so different that one tribe could not understand the language of another, they themselves were driven to the use of this infantile English in speaking to one another.

. . . Very little of the dialect, however, perhaps none of it, is derived from sources other than English. In vocabulary, in syntax, and pronunciation, practically all of the forms of Gullah can be explained on the basis of English, and probably only a little deeper delving would be necessary to account for those characteristics that still seem strange and mysterious.[16]

"Generalizations are always dangerous," writes Professor Krapp in the same article, "but it is reasonably safe to say that not a single detail of Negro pronunciation or Negro syntax can be proved to have any other than an English origin."[17]

A. E. Gonzales, who edited several volumes of Gullah folk tales[18] and whose interpretation of the dialect has been generally accepted as authoritative, writes as follows concerning its origin:

Slovenly and careless of speech, these Gullahs seized upon the peasant English used by some of the early settlers and by the white servants of the wealthier colonists, wrapped their clumsy tongues about it as well as they could, and, enriched with certain expressive African words, it issued through their flat noses and thick lips as so workable a form of speech that it was gradually adopted by the other slaves and became in time the accepted Negro speech of the lower districts of South Carolina and Georgia. . . .

Map of the West Coast of Africa

The words are, of course, not African, for the African brought over or retained only a few words of his jungle-tongue, and even these few are by no means authenticated as part of the original scant baggage of the Negro slaves.

What became of this jungle speech? Why so few words should have survived is a mystery, for, even after freedom, a few native Africans of the later importations were still living on the Carolina coast, and the old family servants often spoke, during and after the war, of native Africans they had known; but while they repeated many tales that came by word of mouth from the Dark Continent . . . they seem to have picked from the mouths of their African brothers not a single jungle-word for the enrichment of their own speech.[19]

Mr. John Bennett, a much earlier interpreter of Gullah than Krapp and Gonzales, says:

At the time of the arrival of these Negroes in the American provinces a considerable proportion of the population was composed of bondsmen, indentured mechanics and "redemptioners," the laborers of the colony, among whom the newly-arrived Negroes learned their English. Their vocabularies were small and very markedly dialectal, in the majority of instances a dialect which had been handed down from father to son for several generations, preserving closely the peculiarities of earliest times, in many cases Elizabethan and Jacobean.

The Africans, plastic as they are by nature, quickly lost their own language, and acquired imperfectly the dialects of the British peasantry among whom they worked, and by whom very generally they were directed. The main reason was, perhaps, that, at the height of the trade, owing to the danger of conspiracy, large groups of Negroes upon great plantations and in any considerable establishments, were generally made up, by preference, of Negroes of different tribes, speaking languages and dialects unknown to one another. They were mostly young, for youth retains no lasting memories and acquires a new language with greater ease.

The new Negroes were parcelled out among the early bond-servants, and, later, among the trained servants, preventing their congregating in a body, hastening their familiarity with their new duties, and more quickly learning the language of their monitors and wardens. This plan was operative from very early days in obliterating the many African dialects and tongues native to the Negro slaves.[20]

Dr. Reed Smith, of the University of South Carolina, says:

What the Gullahs seem to have done was to take a sizeable part of the English vocabulary as spoken on the coast by the white inhabitants from about 1700 on, wrap their tongues around it, and reproduce it changed in tonality, pronunciation, cadence, and grammar to suit their native phonetic tendencies, and their existing needs of expression and communication. The result has been called by one writer "the worst English in the world." It would certainly seem to have a fair claim to that distinction. To understand it requires a trained ear, and at first blush it is equally unintelligible to white people and colored people alike.[21]

Dr. Guy B. Johnson, of the University of North Carolina, has written quite at length regarding the origin and nature of Gullah. He agrees entirely with the writers already quoted:

. . . There are older Negroes in the Sea Islands who speak in such a way that a stranger would have to stay around them several weeks before he could understand them and converse with them to his satisfaction.

But this strange dialect turns out to be little more than the peasant English of two centuries ago. From Midland and Southern England came planters, artisans, shopkeepers, indentured servants, all of whom had more or less contact with the slaves, and the speech of these poorer white folk was so rustic that their more cultured country-men had difficulty in understanding them. From this peasant speech and from the "baby talk" used by masters in addressing them, the Negroes developed that dialect, sometimes known as Gullah, which remains the characteristic feature of the culture of the Negroes of South Carolina and Georgia. . . .

The use of many archaic English words no doubt contributes to the belief held in some quarters that the sea island Negroes use many African words. There are perhaps a hundred of these archaisms, some of which survive only in this dialect, while others are common among the white people in various sections, but especially in the Appalachians and Ozarks. Many of these words are merely outgrown English words, having been used by men like Chaucer, Jonson, and Shakespeare.[22]

Dr. Johnson has discussed the Gullah dialect in more detail in another volume:

The Negro's almost complete loss of African language heritages is startling at first glance, but slavery as practised in the United States made any other outcome impossible. In order to accommodate the slave to the routine of plantation life, as well as in the interest of discipline and order, the planters saw to it that new Negroes were distributed so as to work with seasoned slaves. This broke up tribal bonds and made difficult the survival of Africanisms. The learning of English was a practical necessity. It was the only medium of linguistic exchange. Only thus could the slave understand his overseer, converse with his fellows, and comprehend the interesting things which took place about him. So thorough was the language substitution that there now remains only a handful of words which are indisputably of African origin and which have attained to a respectable degree of diffusion. . . .

. . . As the analysis proceeds it will become more and more apparent that practically every detail of the Gullah grammar and phonology is directly descended from the midland and southern English dialects.[23]

Whereas Stoney and Shelby are less inclined than the writers already quoted to trace practically all of the peculiarities of Gullah to early English, they nevertheless minimize far too greatly the African influence:

What survives of African inheritance in Gullah are: a number of rhymes, games, and systems of counting; tricks of the tongue; and a few words in common usage, most of which, so far as we can identify them, come from the Umbundu dialect of Angola. As a rule these words relate to things of ancient African experience; beliefs that were not derived from and never have been shared with the white man; or plants and animals that the Negro knew as well, or even better than the European. A thorough search of the Low Country would probably yield some twenty or more words of African derivation, of which six or seven are in common use.[24]

The most recent lengthy discussion of Gullah is that of Professor Mason Crum, of Duke University, who in 1940 published a volume describing Negro life in the Carolina Sea Islands. Concerning the speech of the Gullahs he says:

In any discussion of Gullah speech the question of its origin immediately arises. Is it African or English? The answer is very positive: it is almost wholly English—peasant English of the seventeenth and eighteenth centuries, with perhaps a score of African words remaining. Very early the slaves picked up the dialect of the illiterate indentured servants of the Colonies, the "uneducated English." As Bennett continues: . . . "low-bred redemptioners, humble Scotch, Scotch-Irish, and Irish English deportations, the greater part of whom were peasantry, from whose tongue it gathered a wealth of dialectal peculiarities, still traceable to their remote spring in the shires of Britain, where many of them still persist." . . . Gullah speech is conspicuous for its short cuts. Its grammar, which is but an abbreviated and mutilated English grammar, knows no rule except to follow the line of least resistance, violate all rules of logic, and say just that which is natural and to the point. . . .

It is usually thought that the Gullah Negro's confusion of gender is due to his ignorance and primitiveness. It is possible that his abuse of grammar in this respect is due not wholly to his naïvete but to English and Scotch dialectal influence through the unlettered bond servants who came among the slaves.[25]

It will become evident, as this discussion of Gullah proceeds, that the authors of the passages quoted above were not acquainted with the African languages spoken by the Negroes who were being brought to South Carolina and Georgia continually until almost the beginning of the Civil War; nor were they acquainted with the speech of Negroes in other parts of the New World than the United States. It is not surprising, therefore, that they should have entertained such views of Gullah. What is surprising, however, is that they undertook the task of interpreting Gullah, apparently, without feeling the need of acquiring some knowledge of the Negro's African linguistic background.

DIFFICULTIES WHICH HAVE CONFRONTED INVESTIGATORS OF GULLAH

Advocates of the theory that the British dialects and baby-talk constitute the only source of Gullah were handicapped in several respects in their investigation of Gullah.

In the first place, the Gullah Negroes are extremely cautious when talking to strangers. The author of the novel entitled *Porgy* was not at all exaggerating a characteristic of the Gullah Negro in that scene in which officers of the law entered Catfish Row in search of the murderer of Crown, but were unable to get sufficient information from the Negroes to warrant their making an arrest.[26] The Gullahs say that they have fared so badly at the hands of strangers that they are suspicious of anyone whom they do not know very well.

Again, the curiosity always displayed by a stranger on hearing Gullah and frequently his lack of understanding of the temperament of the Gullah Negroes are a source of great annoyance to them and increase their reticence and sensitiveness. A few years ago I invited the late Dr. Guy S. Lowman, Jr., principal field investigator for the

Linguistic Atlas of the United States and Canada, to accompany me on one of my field trips to the Sea Islands. I wanted to see whether the impression Dr. Lowman got of the Gullah sounds, many of which were clearly not English, was similar to my own. On one of the Sea Islands of Georgia, during an interview with one of my informants, Dr. Lowman unintentionally used a tone of voice which the informant resented. Instantly the interview ended. Apologies were of no avail. The informant refused to utter another word. In all the remaining interviews during that trip I talked and Dr. Lowman remained discreetly silent. On my return to the Sea Islands several weeks later, I was confronted on every hand with this question, *mɛk unə fa brɪŋ dɪ bʌkrə?* meaning, 'Why did you bring the white man?'

Moreover, when talking to strangers the Gullah Negro is likely to use speech that is essentially English in vocabulary. When he talks to his friends, however, or to the members of his family, his language is different. My first recordings of the speech of the Gullahs contain fewer African words by far than those made when I was no longer a stranger to them. One striking example of the superficial contact which the writers quoted above had with this dialect, even though some of them believed that they knew the Gullah Negro intimately, is the fact that not one of these writers observed any African personal names among the Gullahs. These names are so numerous, both on the Sea Islands and on the mainland near by, that it is difficult for one to conceive of an investigator's not observing them. It is true that in almost all of their dealings with white people the Gullahs use their English names if they have any. Many, however, have never been given an English name. At school their children are not allowed to use their African names because the teacher, who is usually not a native islander, supposes that they are nonsense words and refuses to record them. If the child has no English name, the teacher will give him one. When the Gullah Negroes write to relatives who no longer live on the Sea Islands, they use their own English names as well as the English names of their relatives. If, therefore, a field-worker does not come in contact with these people in their homes, but merely consults the class-rolls of the teachers or other records, he will assume that they have only English names. Bennett, Gonzales, Krapp, Smith, Johnson, Crum, and others who contend that Gullah is derived solely from English reveal in their writings no knowledge whatsoever of the many thousand African personal names still used by the Gullahs. The following important observation, made by Professor Leonard Bloomfield regarding the difficulty which the investigator of a strange language or a local dialect often encounters because of the diffidence of speakers whose language background is non-standard, is not wholly inapplicable to the experience of these investigators of Gullah:

> Indeed, diffidence as to one's speech is an almost universal trait. The observer who sets out to study a strange language or a local dialect, often gets data from his informants only to find them using entirely different forms when they speak among themselves. They count these latter forms inferior and are ashamed to give them to the observer. An observer may thus record a language entirely unrelated to the one he is looking for.[27]

Another serious handicap that confronted these investigators of Gullah was, as has already been briefly indicated, their lack of acquaintance with the languages and cultures of those sections of West Africa from which the Negroes were brought to the United States as slaves and with the speech of Negroes in the Caribbean, Brazil, and other parts of the New World. They obviously were not aware that the Negroes in those parts of the New World where contact with the British dialects was lacking have the same speech habits as the Gullahs and have retained many of the African words which the Gullahs use. Krapp says that Gullah resembles the Pidgin English of China.[28] A more appropriate comparison would have been that between Gullah and the Negro-French of West Africa, Haiti, Martinique, Guadaloupe, and French Guiana; the Negro-English of Netherlands Guiana; the Negro-Portuguese of Angola and Brazil; and the Negro-Spanish of Latin America, as well as the Negro-English of British West Africa, the British West Indies, and British Guiana.[29] This shortcoming on the part of these writers led to their looking to the British dialects of the seventeenth and eighteenth centuries for the answer to every problem presented by Gullah. When they could not find the answer there, they still contended that if more information had been available regarding these British dialects, then every peculiarity of Gullah would have been explained. The thought that the answer to these unsolved problems might be found in the West African languages did not impress them to the extent that they felt the need of investigating this other important source of Gullah.

The more recent expositors of Gullah have accepted with little or no questioning the interpretation of the dialect as given by Bennett and Gonzales. Assuming that the Gonzales glossary of Gullah, which contains approximately seventeen hundred words, constitutes the entire Gullah vocabulary, they have proceeded to show that with few exceptions the words in this glossary are English and that evidence of the African origin of the exceptions is lacking. As a matter of fact, fewer than a dozen of the words listed by Gonzales are African, and these few he interprets as English, misspelling them and most of the others in his list to indicate the Negro's inability to pronounce them. For example, he lists the English phrase *done for fat* and says that it is used by the Gullahs to mean 'excessively fat,' the obvious inference being that in the judgment of the Gullah Negro when a person is very fat he is done for. But if Gonzales had had sufficient training in phonetics to reproduce accurately what he supposed was the English phrase *done for*, it would have been *'dafa*,[30] which is the Gullah word for 'fat'; and if he had looked into a dictionary of the Vai language, spoken in Liberia and Sierra Leone, or consulted a Vai informant, he would have discovered that the Vai word for 'fat' is da_3fa_1,[31] lit. 'mouth full.' When the Gullah speaker says *'dafa 'fat*, he is merely adding the English equivalent of *'dafa* to make sure that the word will be understood. Other interpretations of Gullah words by the advocates of the baby-talk theory and by others will be discussed later. Smith lists approximately twenty words which he thinks are African in origin, but he cites no parallels in the African languages.[32] Stoney and Shelby believe that a "thorough search of the Low Country would probably yield some twenty or more words of African derivation, of which six or seven are in common use," and they suggest African equivalents for eight Gullah words.[33] The studies of Johnson and that of Crum included no African words that had not previously been given by other writers.

CHAPTER 2

PHONETIC ALPHABET AND DIACRITICS

PHONETIC ALPHABET[1]

THE alphabet used in this study to represent Gullah and African sounds is a slight modification of that recommended by the International Phonetic Association.

A. Vowels

The vowel symbols are [i, ɪ, e, ɛ], *a* [a], [ɒ, ɔ, o, ö, ʊ, u, ʌ, ə, ɐ].

[i]

1. [i]—A high front vowel resembling the English vowel in *meet.* In Gullah, [i] is practically cardinal [i].[2]

In Wolof and Twi, [i] is likewise practically cardinal [i]. In Ewe, Fante, Ibo, Bambara, and Malinke, [i] is slightly below cardinal [i]. In Ewe a subsidiary member of the phoneme, having a somewhat lowered and retracted tongue position, is heard in closed syllables and in the reduplication of polysyllabic words. In Efik the [i]-phoneme consists of two members. The first, a fairly close sound slightly below cardinal [i], is used initially, finally, and before vowels, but never in a closed syllable. The second, having a considerably lowered and retracted tongue position, is always short and is always used in a closed syllable. What appears to be a subsidiary member of the [i]-phoneme occurs in Bambara and Malinke and resembles the vowel in the English *hit.*

[ɪ]

2. [ɪ]—A vowel with a retracted tongue position, approximately the sound of the English vowel in *hit.* In Gullah, as in cultivated English, [ɪ] and [i] belong to separate phonemes. In Gullah there are three subsidiary members of the [ɪ]-phoneme. One, a considerably retracted variety, is heard occasionally when there is an adjacent [k, g, l], or [r]. A shorter variety occurs in the final open syllable of a word, as in [ˈmʌsɪ] 'mercy,' [ˈmelɪ] 'Mary,' etc. A still shorter and less retracted variety is heard in words and phrases of more than two syllables, as in [ˈsatɪde] 'Saturday,' [fətɪˈmɒrə] 'for tomorrow,' etc.

In Fante, [ɪ] and [i] likewise belong to separate phonemes. In this language when [ɪ] is lengthened and when it is final, it resembles somewhat the *a* in the English word *fate* when *a* is pronounced as a pure vowel rather than as a diphthong. When [ɪ] in Fante is followed by [n] or [m] it resembles the English vowel in *foot*.

[e]

3. [e]—A rather close front vowel in Gullah and the African languages included in this study. It resembles *a* in the English word *fate* when *a* is a pure vowel. In Gullah, [e] is slightly above cardinal [e].

In Yoruba and Ibo, [e] is also slightly above cardinal [e]. In Bambara, Malinke, and Efik there appear to be two varieties of [e], one slightly below cardinal [e] and the other more open and more retracted. In Wolof, [e] is above cardinal [e]; in closed syllables it resembes the English vowel in *hit*.

[ɛ]

4. [ɛ]—A front vowel more open than [e]. It resembles the English vowel in *met*. In Gullah, [ɛ] has almost the same tongue position as cardinal [ɛ]. Among many Gullah speakers a more open variety of [ɛ] occurs before nasals.

In Ewe, Yoruba, Fante, Twi, Bambara, and Malinke, [ɛ] is likewise practically cardinal [ɛ]. In Wolof and Efik, [ɛ] is a little above cardinal [ɛ]. A closer variety occurs in Wolof when [ɛ] is short and final.

a [a]

5. [a]—Gullah and most African languages have only one *a*-vowel. In Gullah, [a] is the low front vowel closely resembling the French vowel in *la*. The principal member of the phoneme is practically cardinal [a]. It is the sound used regularly in positions where in General American [æ] and [ɑ] are usually heard. Before [c] and a few other plosives a variety of [a] that is slightly above cardinal is heard in the speech of several Gullah informants, and after [h] a slightly retracted variety of the phoneme is frequently heard. A nasalized variety of Gullah [a] regularly occurs in the word *cã* 'can't.'

In Ewe, Bambara, Malinke, Yoruba, Efik, and Ibo, [a] is slightly less fronted than in Gullah; whereas in Mende, Vai, Kongo, Tshiluba, Kimbundu, and Umbundu it appears to be close to the English *a* in *father*. In Twi, [a] is less fronted than in Gullah, but when occurring as a result of vowel harmony (i.e., the principle which requires that "vowels of neighboring syllables shall have similarity with each

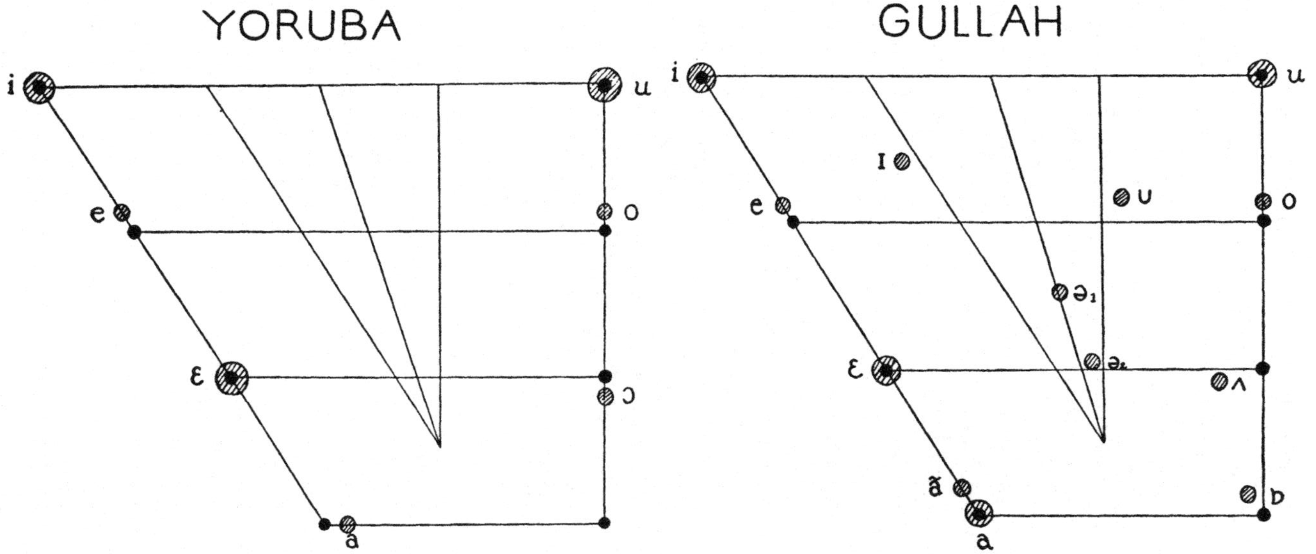

Diagram of the Yoruba and Gullah Vowels

other")[3] it resembles the English vowel in *man.* In Fante there are three (or possibly four) members of the [a]-phoneme. The principal member is a little farther back than Gullah [a] and occurs when the vowel is stressed or long. A second variety is somewhat centralized. It is heard in a final unstressed syllable and resembles the English neutral vowel in *Cuba;* in other unstressed positions it sounds like the English vowel in *but.* The centralized variety of [a] is also heard before a nasal consonant. Another variety of [a] in Fante sounds like [ɑ] in the English *father.* There is also in Fante, as in Twi, an [a] that occurs as a result of vowel harmony and resembles the English vowel in *man.* In Hausa, long [a] resembles the [ɑ] in the English *father;* before the syllable [ki] it has almost the sound of the diphthong [ai]. Short [a] in Hausa resembles the sound of the vowel in the English *sun;* in an unstressed position it resembles the neutral vowel in the English *again.* In Fula, long [a] resembles [ɑ] in the English *father;* short [a], the sound of the English vowel in *run.* In Wolof, long [a] is less retracted than [ɑ] in the English *father* and less fronted than the Gullah [a]. When short or in closed syllables, [a] in Gambian Wolof resembles the English vowel in *but.* In Susu, long [a] resembles the [ɑ] in the English *father;* short [a], the English vowel in *man.* In Temne, long [a] sounds like the [ɑ] in the English *father;* short [a], like the vowel in the German *Mann.*

[ɒ]

6. [ɒ]—A low back vowel having the sound of [ɒ] in the British word *not.* It is pronounced with or without lip-rounding and with the back part of the tongue lower than for [ɔ] in the English word *law* and more retracted than for the [ɑ] in *father.* In Gullah, [ɒ] is heard regularly in such words as *law, all, brought,* etc., as well as in *body, pot, dollar,* etc. Among many Gullahs [ɒ] is heard also in such words as *bundle, ugly, young,* etc., and occurs frequently in positions where in General American the diphthongs [ɑʊ] or [aʊ] would be used, as in *flower, pound, towel,* etc.

[ɔ]

7. [ɔ]—Approximately the sound of *aw* in the English *law.* [ɔ] is seldom heard in Gullah.

In Twi, Bambara, Malinke, and Wolof, [ɔ] is practically cardinal [ɔ]. In some positions [ɔ] in Wolof is above cardinal [ɔ] and resembles [o]. In Ewe, Yoruba, Efik, Ibo, and Fante, [ɔ] is slightly below cardinal [ɔ].

[o]

8. [o]—A rather close, back, rounded vowel resembling the sound of the first vowel of the American English diphthong [ou] in the word *go*. In Gullah and in the African languages included in this study, [o] will represent a pure vowel. In Gullah, [o] is slightly above cardinal [o].

In Ewe, Yoruba, Wolof, and Ibo, [o] is likewise slightly above cardinal [o]. In Ibo when [o] follows a nasal sound it resembles [u]. In Efik the [o]-phoneme has two main members: (1) a centralized [o], a little more open than the first vowel of the British diphthong [ou] (as in *go*) and occurring initially and finally, and (2) a closer variety used in a closed syllable. In Fante, Bambara, and Malinke, [o] is slightly below cardinal [o].

[ö]

9. [ö]—A centralized *o*. In Ibo and Twi, [ö] and [o] belong to separate phonemes. In Ibo, [ö] resembles somewhat the first element of the diphthong heard in Southern England in the word *toe*. It is a pure vowel with a tongue position considerably in advance of and somewhat lower than that for cardinal [o] but nearer to *half-close* than to *half-open*: $\ddot{o}_3s\ddot{o}_3$ 'ribs'; o_3so_3 'bat.' In Twi, [ö] resembles the English vowel in *put*: *so* 'to carry'; *sö* 'to hold.' In Twi words cited in this study, [ö] and [o] will be written *o*.

[u]

10. [u]—A high, back, rounded vowel, slightly closer than the English vowel in *mood*. In Gullah, [u] is cardinal [u]. After an alveolar consonant it is advanced somewhat from a back position.

In Ewe and Yoruba, [u] is likewise cardinal [u]. In Yoruba, as in Gullah, it is somewhat advanced from a back position after an alveolar consonant. In Bambara, Malinke, and Efik, [u] is slightly below cardinal [u]. In Fante, Twi, and Wolof, [u] is a little advanced from a back position. In Ibo it is somewhat advanced and has a lower tongue position than cardinal [u].

[ʊ]

11. [ʊ]—Approximately the sound of the English vowel in *foot*.

[ʌ]

12. [ʌ]—Approximately the sound of the English vowel in *but*. In Gullah, [ʌ] is heard not only in such words as ə'*nʌf* 'enough,'

'*bʌkɪt* 'bucket,' etc., but also in positions where in GA one hears [ɜ], as in *bʌd* 'bird,' *ʌt* 'earth,' etc. Frequently [ʌ] is heard in Gullah in final syllables in which [ə] or [ə̣] would be used in GA: *rɪ*$_1$*wʌ*$_3$ 'river,' *kɒ*$_1$*lʌd*$_3$ 'colored,' *ʃʌ*$_1$*mʌn*$_3$ 'Sherman,' *an*$_1$*sʌ*$_3$ 'answer,' etc. In pronouncing such words, many Gullah speakers use a low level tone on one syllable and a high level one on the other, or a low level or high level tone on both syllables, the hearer not being aware of any difference in stress between the two syllables. Among other words in which [ʌ] is heard in Gullah are *bʌz*$_1$*m*$_1$ 'bosom,' *ʌp*$_3$*m*$_1$ 'open,' etc.

In Gambian Wolof, [ʌ] occurs as the final unstressed vowel of many nouns.[4]

[ə]

13. [ə]—A central vowel resembling the English sound of *a* in *Cuba*. In Gullah the [ə]-phoneme comprises two members: (1) a short variety having a tongue position somewhat above *half-open* and occurring in unstressed syllables, as in ə'*nʌf* 'enough,' and (2) a fairly long variety with tongue position lower than for the first variety but more advanced and higher than for [ʌ]. The second variety occurs in final syllables and is used in the newer type of Gullah to replace [ʌ] by persons who try to distinguish stress, as in '*ansə* 'answer.'

[ə] does not occur in many of the African languages included in this study. Its use in Fante as a member of the [a]-phoneme has already been discussed. In Gambian Wolof the final unstressed vowel of many nouns resembles the English unstressed final vowel of *sofa*. A somewhat high and retracted variety of [ə] occurs in Senegal Wolof in closed syllables as well as in final unstressed syllables.[5] [ə] occurs in Umbundu, but the exact nature of its occurrence has not been determined.[6] In the Anglo dialect of Ewe the sound corresponding to [e] in other dialects is frequently pronounced [ə]. [ə] also occurs in Temne.

[ɐ]

14. [ɐ]—A central vowel slightly below *half-open*. It occurs in Gullah as the first element of the diphthong in such words as *bite*, *bright*, etc., where the diphthong is followed by a voiceless consonant. It occurs frequently also when the diphthong is preceded by the fricative *r*. [ɐ] is heard likewise as the first element of the diphthong in such words as *out*, *house*, etc., where a voiceless consonant follows.

B. Diphthongs

The number of diphthongs occurring in Gullah and in the words from the African languages included in this study is not very large. In Gullah [ɒɪ] and [ɒʊ] are the diphthongs most frequently heard. The first element of [ɒɪ] is usually advanced, frequently to [a], when the diphthong is adjacent to [l] (which in Gullah is clear in all positions), [c], [ɟ], or [ʃ]: *dɒɪ* 'die,' *mɒɪn* 'mine,' *sɒɪd* 'side,' *baɪl* 'boil,' *ɟaɪn* 'join,' *ʃ'ɑɪn* 'shine,' etc. The first element of [ɒɪ] is somewhat advanced and raised to [ɐ] (a central vowel a little below *half-open*) when the diphthong is followed by a voiceless consonant and frequently also when it is preceded by the fricative *r*: *bɐɪt* 'bite,' *brɐɪt* 'bright,' *wɐɪt* 'white,' etc. The Gullah diphthong [ɒʊ] is heard in *kɒʊ* 'cow,' *hɒʊ* 'how,' *plɒʊ* 'plow,' etc. When this diphthong precedes a voiceless consonant, its first element is regularly advanced and raised to [ɐ]: *əbɐʊt* 'about,' *hɐʊs* 'house,' etc.

Several of the African languages discussed in this study, like Gullah, have few diphthongs. In Fula there appear to be no diphthongs.[7] Two diphthongs have been noted in Kongo: [ai] and [au], but frequently the vowels in each of these combinations are pronounced in separate syllables. Sometimes a faint *y* [j] is heard between [a] and [i] and a faint [w] between [a] and [u].[8] There appear to be no diphthongs in Kimbundu, although the vowel combinations [ai, ao, au, ei, eo, oa, oe, oi], and [ou] when pronounced rapidly sound much like diphthongs. Before a vowel in the same syllable Kimbundu [i] and [u] become *y* [j] and [w] respectively.[9] In Ewe and Twi almost every vowel can occur with every other as a diphthong. In Yoruba, [ai, au, ɛi, ɛu, oi], and [ɔi] occur as falling diphthongs, and [ia] and [io], which can also be written *ya* and *yo*, as rising diphthongs. Diphthongs have been noted as follows in other African languages discussed in this study: Hausa: [ai, au, ei]; Bambara and Malinke: [ai, au, ɛi, ou, ɔu, iu]; Temne: [ai, au, oi, ɔi, ui]; Vai: [ai, au, ei, ɛi, ou, ɔu, ui]; Mende: [ae, ai, ao, ei, ɛi, ɪa, oa, oe, ɒɪ, oɪ, ou, ɒʊ, uɪ, uo]; Wolof: [iu, ei, ɛi, ɛu, ɛa, ai, au, ɔi, ɔu, ou, ui, ɔ:u a:u, a:i]; Efik: [ei, ai, ɔi, oi, ui], and the rising diphthongs [ie, ia, iɔ, io, ue, ua, uɔ, uo], which can be written also as *ye, ya, yɔ, yo, we, wa, wɔ, wo*, respectively. In Efik the combinations [ie, ia, io, uɔ], etc., are not always rising diphthongs, however. Some are dissyllabic, as in bi_3a_1 'yam,' $n_1si_1o_3$ 'different,' etc.[10]

C. Consonants

The following are the consonant symbols used in this study: [p, p', b, b', 'b, t, t', d, d', 'd, ḍ, c, ɟ, k, k', kp, gb, g, f, v, Φ, β, x, γ, s, G, z, ʃ, ʃ', ʒ, h, ts, dz, tʃ, dʒ, m, n, ŋ, ɲ, l, r, ʀ, ṛ, hw, w, ϑ], *y*, *tw*, *dw*, [mp, mb, mw, nt, nd, ns, nc, nɟ, ŋg, ŋd, ŋw].

[p]

1. [p]—The voiceless bilabial plosive. In Gullah, [p] is often followed by slight aspiration when it occurs initially before long vowels in very emphatic speech. Many Gullah speakers, however, never aspirate [p]. Others do so only very slightly. Initially in a stressed syllable an ejective (glottalized) *p* [p'] is occasionally heard in Gullah in such words as *p'ɒɪn* 'pine,' *p'ɒt* 'pot,' ʃ'*aɪn* 'shine,' etc. Here the simultaneous glottal stop is rather weak.

Among the West African languages in which [p] is generally unaspirated are Ewe, Malinke, Bambara, and Kimbundu. In Bini, [p] is very slightly aspirated. In Fante, [p] is palatalized before [i, ɪ, e, ɛ], and [r] in several words.

[b]

2. [b]—The voiced bilabial plosive. In some Gullah words an unvoiced variety of [b] was observed initially and finally: *b̥əˈnanə* 'banana,' *kʊb̥* 'coop,' *cub̥* 'tube,' etc.

In Hausa, [b] is often not fully voiced in initial position. In Wolof, [b] is used to replace [p] at the end of a word when the following word begins with a vowel or a voiced consonant. In Bambara and Malinke, intervocalic [b] is sometimes weakened to the voiced bilabial fricative [β]. In Vai, [b] lenis and [b] fortis belong to separate phonemes. The latter will be designated by the symbol [b'].

['b]

3. ['b]—The implosive *b*.[11] This sound is produced with the same lip position as that required for [*b*], but the air is drawn inward rather than expelled. The sound occurs in Hausa, Fula, Ibo, Duala, and several other African languages. Note the Hausa words *ba*:$_3$*be*$_1$ 'a locust' and '*ba*:$_3$'be$_1$ 'to become estranged.'

[t]

4. [t]—The voiceless alveolar plosive. In Gullah [t] occurs regularly in positions where in GA the voiceless inter-dental fricative [θ] is used. Between vowels in Gullah, [t] is usually replaced by the

flapped lingual *r*[ɽ] though occasionally the voiced *t* is heard both between vowels and medially before [l]. In the speech of some Gullahs, [t] is dental in initial position. Many Gullah speakers do not aspirate [t]. Others do so only very slightly. Between vowels a retroflex *t* is sometimes heard in Gullah as a variant of the flapped lingual *r*. As in the case of [p], a weakly glottalized *t* [t'] is sometimes heard at the beginning of a stressed syllable.

In Ewe, Bambara, Malinke, Kikongo, Kimbundu, and in some of the dialects of Ibo, [t] is generally unaspirated. [t] is very slightly aspirated in Hausa and Bini and also in Efik in initial position. In Kikongo and some of the dialects of Twi, [t] is dental. In Ewe, [t] tends to become dental in the combination [tr]. An ejective (glottalized) *t* [t'] occurs in some parts of the Hausa country as a variant of ejective *ts*. In the Owerri area of the Ibo country a retroflex *t* with simultaneous glottal stop is sometimes heard, especially before [o] and [ɔ]. In many words from Gambian Wolof the retroflex *t* occurs finally and between vowels as a variant of the alveolar *t*.

[d]

5. [d]—The voiced alveolar plosive, as in the English word *day*. In Gullah, [d] occurs regularly in positions where in GA the voiced inter-dental fricative is used. Between vowels and medially before [l] in Gullah, [d] is replaced by the retroflex flap [ɽ]. Many Gullahs occasionally used an unvoiced variety of [d] in final position. In the speech of some Gullahs [d] is dental.

In Fante, [d] is dental. In Ewe it tends to become dental in the combination [dr]. [d] is palatalized in Efik in initial position. In some of the dialects of Kimbundu when [d] is followed by [i] or *y* [j] it resembles [l]; in some others, [r].[12] In Hausa, [d] is often not fully voiced in initial position. In Vai, [d] lenis and [d] fortis belong to separate phonemes. The latter will be designted by the symbol [d'].

['d]

6. ['d]—The implosive *d*. This sound occurs in Hausa, Fula, Duala, and other African languages. Note the Hausa words *da:*$_{3-1}$ 'formerly' and *'da*$_3$ 'a son.'

[ḍ]

7. [ḍ]—Retroflex *d*. In Gullah, [ḍ] is occasionally heard between vowels and medially before [l] as a variant of the retroflex flap [ɽ], as in *'maḍə* 'madder,' *'baḍl* 'battle,' etc.

In Ewe and some other African languages [d] and [ḍ] occur as separate phonemes. Note the Ewe words *do*₃ 'to place' and *ḍo*₃ 'to send.' [ḍ] is heard among Gold Coast tribes whose mother-tongue is Guang, but who also speak Twi.

[c]

8. [c]—The voiceless palatal plosive. This sound usually occurs in Gullah in positions where *ch* would be used in GA. [c] occurs in Gullah before front vowels, including [a], as a subsidiary member of the [k]-phoneme. In this position it is sometimes slightly affricated.

Among the African languages in which [c] is found are Twi, Wolof, Mossi, Bambara, the Gɛ̃ dialect of Ewe, Malinke, and others. In Bambara and Malinke, [c] is slightly affricated when followed by the close vowels [i] and [u]. In Wolof it is slightly affricated when followed by [i].

[ɟ]

9. [ɟ]—The voiced palatal plosive. It is the voiced counterpart of [c]. In Gullah it occurs in positions where in GA the voiced palato-alveolar affricate [dʒ] and the voiced palato-alveolar fricative [ʒ] would be used, as in the words *judge* and *measure*, respectively. Before front vowels, including [a], [ɟ] frequently occurs as a subsidiary member of the [g]-phoneme, as in 'ɟ*adn* 'garden.'

Among the African languages in which [ɟ] is found are Twi, Wolof, Bambara, Malinke, the Gɛ̃ dialect of Ewe, Kru, and others. It is slightly affricated in Bambara and Malinke before [i] and [u] and in Wolof before [i].

[k]

10. [k]—The voiceless velar plosive. Many Gullah speakers do not aspirate [k]. Others do so only very slightly. Before front vowels, including [a], a very advanced variety of the [k]-phoneme occurs. Many speakers substitute for [k] in this position the palatal plosive [c], a subsidiary member of the phoneme: *ces* 'case,' '*cɪtn* 'kitten,' etc.

In Ewe, Bambara, Malinke, Kimbundu, and Ibo, [k] is generally unaspirated. In Bini and Hausa it is only slightly aspirated. In Hausa, [k] is palatalized before [i].

[k']

11. [k']—The ejective *k*. An ejective *k* has been observed in Gullah as a variant of [k]: *k'ul* 'cool,' *k'ʌp* 'cup,' etc. In Hausa, [k] and [k'] belong to separate phonemes. Note the Hausa words $ka\!:_1ka\!:_2$ 'harvest,' $k'a\!:_1k'a\!:_1$ 'how'; $ba\!:_1ki\!:_2$ 'mouth,' $ba\!:_1k'i\!:_2$ 'visitors.'[13]

[kp]

12. [kp]—The voiceless labio-velar plosive. In the articulation of the sound the *k* and *p* are exploded simultaneously. In Ibo, [kp] is implosive.

[gb]

13. [gb]—The voiced labio-velar plosive. It is the voiced counterpart of [kp].

[g]

14. [g]—The voiced velar plosive. Before front vowels, including [a], a very advanced variety of the [g]-phoneme occurs. Many speakers use here the voiced palatal plosive [ɟ]. An unvoiced variety of [g] is frequently heard in final position.

In Hausa, [g] is palatalized before [i] and is often not fully voiced in initial position.

[f]

15. [f]—The labio-dental voiceless fricative, as in the English *fun*. In all Gullah words appearing in this study except those listed in connection with the discussion of [Φ] in Chapter 7, the symbol *f* will be used to represent the voiceless bilabial fricative [Φ].

[v]

16. [v]—The labio-dental voiced fricative, as in the English *very*.

[Φ]

17. [Φ]—The bilabial voiceless fricative. In Gullah, [Φ] usually occurs in positions where [f] would be used in GA.

Among the African languages in which [Φ] occurs are Ewe, Hausa, Ibo, and Tshiluba (Buluba-Lulua).[14] In Ewe, [Φ] and [f] belong to different phonemes.

[β]

18. [β]—The voiced bilabial fricative, the voiced counterpart of [Φ]. [β] occurs in Gullah in positions where [v] and [w] would be used in GA. The sound in Gullah is sometimes pronounced with very slight lip-rounding. In all Gullah words appearing in this study except those listed in connection with the discussion of [β] in Chapter 7, the voiced bilabial fricative will be represented by *w*.

[β] occurs also in Ewe, Bini, Ibo, and other African languages. In Bambara and Malinke, intervocalic [b] is sometimes weakened to [β] and intervocalic [w] sounds much like [β].

[x]

19. [x]—The voiceless velar fricative.

[ɣ]

20. [ɣ]—The voiced velar fricative. In Bambara and Malinke, [ɣ] occurs only between vowels, apparently as a weakened form of [k] or [g].

[s]

21. [s]—The voiceless alveolar fricative, as in English *sun*. With some Gullah speakers [s] is fronted a great deal more than with others. This fronting appears to be more marked on the Sea Islands of Georgia than on those of South Carolina. Before [i, ɪ], and [e] many Gullahs substitute for [s] the alveolar palatal fricative [*C*], as in ˈ*Ciəm* 'see them,' ˈ*Cɪʃə* 'sister,' *Celə* 'Sarah,' etc. This sound is articulated near the back of the teeth-ridge with the front of the tongue raised toward the hard palate.

In most of the Ewe dialects, [*C*] occurs before [i] as a subsidiary member of the [s]-phoneme. It is likewise a member of the [s]-phoneme in the Mossi language. Palatalized forms of [s] occur also in Bambara and Bini. In certain areas of the Ibo country [s] occurring before [i] and [e] is pronounced like the English *sh* in *she*. Among Efik speakers during the articulation of [s], a kind of whistle is heard caused by a narrow channel made between the bottom lip and the top front teeth.[15]

[z]

22. [z]—The voiced alveolar fricative, as in English *zinc*. In Gullah an unvoiced variety of the phoneme is frequently heard in final position.

[ʃ]

23. [ʃ]—The voiceless palato-alveolar fricative, like *sh* in English *shame*. In Gullah, [ʃ] is frequently heard in positions where in GA [s] or [z] would be used: *ʃuʃ* 'shoes,' ˈ*ʃoda* 'soda,' ˈ*haʃɪʃ* 'ashes,' etc.

In the Yoruba language [ʃ] before [ɛ] and [a] resembles the alveolar palatal fricative [*C*].

[ʒ]

24. [ʒ]—The voiced palato-alveolar fricative, like the *s* in the English word *measure*. [ʒ] does not occur in Gullah.

[h]

25. [h]—The voiceless glottal fricative, like *h* in English *hand*. In Yoruba and Fante, [*h*] is pronounced with some friction. In Ewe, [h] is voiced.

[ts]

26. [ts]—The voiceless alveolar affricate, like *ts* in the English *hats*. [ts] in Ewe is palatalized before [i]. In some of the dialects it is also palatalized before [ɔ, o], and [u], and in a few before [a] and [e]. In Hausa, [ts] is always ejective.

[dz]

27. [dz]—The voiced alveolar affricate, like *dz* in the English *adz*. [dz] in Ewe is palatalized before [i]. In some of the dialects it is also palatalized before [ɔ, o], and [u], and in a few before [a] and [e].

[tʃ]

28. [tʃ]—The voiceless palato-alveolar affricate, like *ch* in the English *church*. Older Gullah speakers seldom use [tʃ]; they substitute for it the palatal plosive [c].

[dʒ]

29. [dʒ]—The voiced palato-alveolar affricate, like the *j* in the English *judge*. Among the older Gullah speakers [dʒ] is seldom heard; they substitute for it the palatal plosive [ɟ].

[m]

30. [m]—The voiced bilabial nasal, as in English *man*.

[n]

31. [n]—The voiced alveolar nasal, as in English *not*.

[ŋ]

32. [ŋ]—The voiced velar nasal, like *ng* in the English *sing*. In Yoruba, [ŋ] occurs only before [w, k, g, kp, g], and sometimes in final position. It appears to be a subsidiary member of the [n]-phenome.

[ɲ]

33. [ɲ]—The voiced palatal nasal, like *gn* in the French *agneau*. [ɲ] is heard in Gullah in many words in which [n] or *y* [j] would be used in cultivated English, as in *ɲu* 'new,' *ɲuz* 'use,' ɲɒŋ 'young,' etc.

[l]

34. [l]—The voiced alveolar lateral. In Gullah and generally in the African languages [l] is clear in all positions, i.e., it is articulated with the front of the tongue raised in the direction of the hard palate.

In Bambara, Malinke, and Kru, [l] and [r] are interchangeable in many words. There is no [l] in Efik, Twi, and Fante.

[r]

35. [r]—In Gullah words used in this study the symbol *r* will represent a voiced post-alveolar fricative consonant unless there is a note to the contrary. The same symbol, however, will represent the rolled lingual *r* in words from the following African languages: Bambara, Malinke, Mandinka, Wolọf, Twi, Fante, Fula, Ewe, Yoruba, Ibo, Hausa, Efik, and Ibibio.

In Bini, [r] is trilled between vowels and fricative at the beginning of a word.

[R]

36. [R]—The rolled uvular *r*.

[ṛ]

37. [ṛ]—The retroflex flap. This sound is produced by placing the tongue in a retroflex position, i.e., with the tip curled upward near the highest part of the hard palate, and moving it forward and downward quickly so that the underside of the tongue touches the teeth-ridge, making a flapped sound. It occurs in Gullah between vowels and medially before [l] as a subsidiary member of the [d]-phenome. Some Gullah speakers used the retroflex *d* [ḍ] in this position. The occurrence of the retroflex flap in several African languages will be discussed in Chapter 7.

[hw]

38. [hw]—The voiceless *w*, frequently heard in the American English *when*. The sound occurs also in Fante.

[w]

39. [w]—The labio-velar semi-vowel, like *w* in English *way*.

In Twi and Fante the [w]-phoneme has two members—the velar *w*, used before back vowels, and the palatal *w*, used before front vowels.

In Bambara and Malinke intervocalic [w] resembles the bilabial fricative [β].

[ϑ]

40. [ϑ]—The voiced frictionless continuant. Some Gullahs use [ϑ] in positions where others use [β]. [ϑ] was observed more frequently on Edisto Island than in other Gullah communities. In the Vai language, [v], [w], and [ϑ] belong to separate phonemes.

y [j]

41. *y*—The unrounded palatal semi-vowel, like the *y* in English *yes*. In Ewe, *y* before [i] is very weak. In Twi there is a voiceless *y* [ç] usually written *hy* in Twi texts.

tw

42. *tw*—In words from Twi and Fante this symbol will represent the labialized palatal *t*, i.e., the palatal *t* with simultaneous lip-rounding.

dw

43. *dw*—In words from Twi and Fante this symbol will represent the labialized palatal *d*, i.e., the palatal *d* with simultaneous lip-rounding.

[mp, mb, mw, nt, nd, ns, nc, nɟ, ŋg, ŋd, ŋw]

The combination of initial nasal consonant plus another consonant is very common in the African languages and has been observed in the speech of many Gullahs. In this combination the initial nasal may or may not constitute a separate syllable. When such initial nasal is long, or bears any stress, or has a different tone from that of the following vowel, it is usually syllabic.

DIACRITICS

Many of the African languages discussed in this study are tone languages, i.e., languages in which tone or pitch is employed to convey meaning and to show grammatical relationships. In the available dictionaries and grammars of several African tone languages the explanation given of the tones is inadequate. In this study, therefore, I have indicated the tones of the words only when I was able to obtain them from native speakers of the tone languages or from studies by recognized authorities on the tones of these languages. Consequently, in this study the tones will be given only of words from the following languages: Vai, Fante, Gɑ̃, Ewe, Yoruba, Hausa, Bini, Ibo, Efik, and Ibibio.[16]

In many West African languages, however, the employment of tone to distinguish meanings and to show grammatical relationships is greatly restricted. To compensate for such limited use of significant tone other devices are employed, such as accent, quantity or length of sounds, the addition of qualifying words, etc. Bambara, Malinke, and other Mandingo languages appear to fall in this group, and some of the Bantu languages are said to have lost their tones.[17] Wolof is a non-tone language.

Whereas the Gullah dialect does not have significant tone in the sense in which the West African tone languages do, it does have a characteristic intonation and rhythm.[18]

A. Tone Marks

The tones of syllables will be indicated by the following inferior numerals placed after the vowels or syllabic consonants carrying the tones:

$_1$ = a low level tone
$_2$ = a mid level tone
$_3$ = a high level tone
$_{1-3}$ = a tone rising from low to high
$_{1-2}$ = a tone rising from low to mid
$_{2-3}$ = a tone rising from mid to high
$_{3-1}$ = a tone falling from high to low
$_{3-2}$ = a tone falling from high to mid
$_{2-1}$ = a tone falling from mid to low

B. Accent Marks

Accent is indicated by the mark (ˈ) placed before the syllable for the main stress and (ˌ) placed before the syllable for the secondary stress, when it is thought necessary to indicate the secondary stress. Wholly unstressed syllables are unmarked. The accentuation and intonation of Gullah words vary somewhat with individual speakers. Each of the Gullah words listed in Chapter 3 is given the pronunciation used by the particular speaker from whom the word was obtained. In the case of many words of more than one syllable, the syllables differed not so much in stress as in tone. These differences are indicated by the same marks as those used to denote the tones of words from the African tone languages. In the case of non-tone African languages the accentuation of words is given only when there was an opportunity to obtain it from native speakers of the languages.

C. Others

ʼ = glottalization, when used after a voiceless consonant or before a vowel or [h]. After [b] and [d] in words from the Vai language, it represents a sound articulated with very great breath-force (fortis). Before [b] and [d], it indicates an implosive sound.

: = length mark. When placed after a vowel or consonant, it indicates that the sound is long.

˜ = nasalization.

̥ = unvoicing.

CHAPTER 3

WEST AFRICAN WORDS IN GULLAH

THE West African words in Gullah to be listed here will be divided into three groups: (1) personal names; (2) other words used in conversation; (3) words heard only in songs, stories, and prayers.

PERSONAL NAMES

In order that one may comprehend fully the significance of the names the Gullahs have given their children it is desirable first to explain somewhat in detail the methods used by some of the West African tribes in naming their children.

A. THE TWI

Among the Twi people[1] on the Gold Coast one of the names a child receives is that of the day on which he was born. Of other names which he may have, there is a great variety. One name may indicate the place which he occupies among the other children of the same mother. Still another may be given from some religious motive, such as that given in honor of a god. Sometimes the name describes some bodily quality or condition, such as the height, size, or color of the child, or the state of his health. Some names indicate the general or specific occupation of the child's parents. Still others are taken from ancestors or other persons, from towns or countries, and from animals or other objects of nature or of human manufacture. The original meaning of many names used by the Twi people is not known.

B. THE DAHOMEANS

Professor Melville J. Herskovits, of Northwestern University, has written at length concerning the methods employed by the Fon-speaking people of Dahomey in naming their children:

> The names given a person at the time of his birth . . . are particularly important, and it is essential that these be kept secret, for one who might wish to work bad magic against a child when grown would be materially aided in his purpose were he to know the names that had been bestowed at birth. They include a name given by the mother, which is held most secret, the name derived from the deity of the mother, if she has one, and a third

name determined by the deity of the father, if he is a cult initiate. The name of the ancestral spirit whose soul animates the child is given later, while, when a man reaches the age of eighteen or twenty, still another name is added; and to a girl at marriage, her husband gives a new name, while if he or she is initiated as a cult-member, there is still another name.[2]

Furthermore, according to this authority, there is a special name for the child born under one of the following conditions: if he or she is the first born after twins, the second after twins, or the third after twins; if conception occurs before the mother has resumed menstruation, or if he or she is the next child after this; if born feet foremost, or if the next child after one thus born; if born with head presentation and eyes toward the sky, or if the next child after one thus born; if born at noon, or if the next child after one born at noon; if born of a prolonged pregnancy, or if the next child after one thus born; if born with the umbilical cord about the neck, or if the next child after one thus born; if born with a caul but not following the first child after twins, or if the next born after such a child; if born on the road; if born in the market-place.[3] A large variety of names are also given children of the Dahomeans to indicate the exact nature of the religious affiliations of the parents.[4] Moreover, says Professor Herskovits:

> Every exploit in a man's life is signalized by the choice of a new name for himself, and a man's position in a community is enhanced by his resourcefulness in originating for himself ingenious names. When a man who is about to marry is unable to devise a suitable name for his wife, it is possible for him to continue calling her by the name of her village or quarter. This, however, is regarded as inept and as cause for shame, so that a man who cannot think of a clever name for his new wife secretly has recourse to someone in the village, usually a singer who has shown talent in devising names, and this man, for a consideration, supplies him with a suitable name for the girl. At the opportune moment the bridegroom will, to be sure, pronounce it publicly as a name of his own invention.[5]

C. The Mandingo

Among the Mandingo personal names fall into two classes, individual and clan names.[6]

INDIVIDUAL NAMES

The individual name is given by the mother to the child at the time of its birth. Each child receives a name which is determined by its sex and the order of birth with respect to its brothers and sisters on the mother's side. Generally the names thus given are as follows: for the first son, *ŋci, nci, ŋki, nsye:*, or *sye:*; for the second, *nsã, nzã, nsa*, or *sã;* for the third, *ŋgo, ŋko, ŋolo*, or *molo;* for the fourth, *nto, to, ndo*, or *do;* for the fifth, *fye, mfye, pe, mpe*, or *mbe;* for the sixth *ɲa, nso*, or *nzo;* for the seventh, *fa* or *mpa;* for the first daughter, *ŋyele, ŋyere*, or *ŋye;* for the second, *ŋya* or *ya;* for the third, *nzɛle* or *ŋyeleba*. Among the Khassonke and the Foulanke, who have retained many of the customs of their Peul ancestors, one gives often, as among the latter, to the first boy the name *amadu*, to the second, *sãmba*, and to the third, *demba*. Among the Khassonke, *amadu* can be replaced by *sãmbala* and *sãmba* by *dembala*.

This name, given by the mother and determined in reality by the accident of birth, is only temporary. A few days after the birth a ceremony takes place, presided over by the father, the chief of the family, or an influential person, in the course of which the temporary name is either given permanently to the child or is replaced by another. The name thus given is called the true name. Often one changes the name indicating the order of birth because the number of such appelatives being very limited, it may happen that the child has the same name as that of one of his parents. This may cause confusion, and, if the parent is dead, may irritate his soul. In that case one has recourse to the following procedures. Sometimes one gives to a child a name which recalls to mind, without naming him, the person whose birth-name the child is found to have. For example, the child who has the same birth-name as his father will be called *ba:ba* 'dad' or *fatoʀoma* 'homonym of father'; one who has the same name as his paternal uncle will be called *beni* or *bina* 'paternal uncle'; a girl who has the same name as her mother will be called *na* 'mother' or *natoʀoma* 'homonym of mother'; etc. Sometimes, out of regard for an influential person who has rendered service to the father or mother or who by his prayers or his magical power is thought to have facilitated the birth of the child, one gives to the child a name which recalls the title or the quality of this personage, such as, *cɛmɔrɔ* 'notable,' *fode* 'learned in the law,' *maʀã* 'master,' *mo:riba* 'priest,' etc. Sometimes one gives to a child the name of a divinity in order that he may secure the protection of that divinity. Again, the name given a child may reveal some circumstance connected with its birth (generally it is the mother who chooses these kinds of names), such as *bili* 'curvature,' name given a child whose body is bent double at birth; *fili* 'losing one's way,' given the child whose mother gave birth outside the house; *fune* 'twin-born,' given the child born at the same time as his twin; *ala:misa* or *la:misa* 'Thursday,' given the child born on that day; *suŋga:ru* or *suŋka:lu* 'month of the Ramadan' (the ninth month in the Mohammedan year, when strict fasting is practiced), given the child born during this month; etc.

Although the name thus given the child is retained by him, it can happen that in the course of his life some circumstances cause to be added to this name a title (the prop or support of the name) which completes it, such as *ntoɟã*: 'Nto the Great,' or a true surname which ends often by replacing the true name, such as *cɛwule* 'the red man,' *cɛgbɛ* 'the man with clear complexion,' etc.

Some special surnames, expressing nearly always the idea of gratitude to a donor, have been given slaves received as a gift, such as *faŋuma* 'good father,' used for the name of a slave presented to someone by his father; *lamdu* or *lamudu* 'praise to God,' given a slave who has been received as a result of the goodness of God; etc.

The Mohammedan Mandingo give most often to their children names which are borrowed from the Islamic hagiography and which correspond either to persons truly Mohammedan or to those from the Old or the New Testament mentioned in the Koran. They have, however, retained the custom of giving names determined by the order of birth, but they have made a distinction. For the first son, they have chosen one of the names of the Prophet: *amadu, amadi, ma:madu, ma:madi,* etc.; for the second son, the name of his first caliph: *bakari, bokari, kalifa,* etc.; for the third son, the name of the second caliph: *umaru* or *umara;* for the fourth, the name of the third caliph: *tuma:ne* or *ãsuma:na;* for the fifth, the name of the fourth caliph: *ali* or *aliyu.* The Mohammedans who have twins often call one *la:sana* or *alasana* and the other *la:sina* 'the names of the two sons of Ali.' Among other names from the Mohammedan hagiography frequently used in the Mandingo country are the following: for the boys: *haru:na* 'Aaron,' *birama* 'Abraham,' *siya:ka* 'Isaac,' *ayu:ba* 'Job,' *ya:ya* 'John the Baptist,' *isa* 'Jesus,' *bila:li* 'the first muezzin,' *amara* 'a companion of the Prophet,' etc.; for the girls: *maryama* 'Mary,' *ami:nata* 'mother of Mohammed,' *kadi:ɟata* or *hadi:ɟata* 'first wife of Mohammed,' *safiyata* 'another wife of Mohammed,' *fa:timata* or *fa:tumata* 'daughter of Mohammed' and its equivalent *binta* or *bintu,* etc.

CLAN NAMES

The descendants of the founder of an ancient family, even though they are dispersed, form a group known as the clan. Members of the same clan are identified by interdictions or taboos, which can vary with the groups, regions, or periods, and chiefly by the clan name, which is determined by the surname or a device or emblem which the ancestor applied first to himself and afterwards transmitted to his descendants. The clan name is either a true surname, such as *si:se* 'power of descent,' or an allusion to one of the circumstances connected with the foundation of the family, such as *bamba* 'crocodile,' the ancestor having been rescued from a crocodile by the intervention of a cricket; *samakɛ* 'male elephant,' the ancestor having been rescued from a male elephant by the intervention of a female elephant; etc. Thus the clan name can be the name of an animal, but never that of a protecting animal or the taboo of the clan. The clan name is expressed after the name or individual surname in order to establish the complete identity of an individual, such as *nto*, *bamba*, etc. Children bear the clan name of their father in the tribes of masculine descent and that of their mother's brother in the tribes of feminine descent. The wife never takes the clan name of her husband, but retains her own. Serfs, although they have not the right to it in theory, generally borrow the clan name of their lord.

D. THE YORUBA

A rather detailed account of the naming of children among the Yoruba of Nigeria has been given by the Reverend Samuel Johnson.[7] According to this authority there are three classes of names given to children exclusive of the totem or clan name: (1) the $a_1m\tilde{u}_3t\text{ɔ}_1r\tilde{u}_2wa_3$, i.e., the name with which the child is born; (2) the $a_1bi_3s\text{ɔ}_2$, the christening name, also called $o_2ru_3\dot{k}\text{ɔ}_2$; and (3) the $o_2ri_3ki_1$, i.e., the cognomen or attributive name.

The child is said to be "born with a name," lit. "brought from heaven," when the peculiar circumstances of its birth may be expressed by a name which is applicable to all children born under similar circumstances. Twin-births fall in this category. Among other examples are $a_2bi_3\text{ɔ}_3na_1$ 'born by the wayside'; $a_2bi_3\text{ɔ}_3d\tilde{u}_3$ 'born during an annual festival'; $o_2lu_3gbo_3di_2$ 'born with supernumerary digits'; etc.

A child may have two or more christening names or $a_1bi_3s\text{ɔ}_2$ given by the parents or grandparents or by any elderly member of the family. Among these are (*a*) names referring directly to the child or indirectly to the family, such as $a_2yɔ_1de_3le_3$ 'Joy enters the house'; (*b*) names referring directly to the family and indirectly to the child, such as $ku_3r\tilde{u}_2mi_2$ 'Death has impoverished me,' $ɔ_1tɛ_1gbɛ_3yɛ_2$ 'Warfare deprived us of our honors,' etc.; (*c*) names compounded with religious names to show the deity worshipped in the family, such as, $ʃaŋ_1go_3b\tilde{u}_1mi_2$ 'Shango gave me this'; $o_1g\tilde{u}_3di_3kpɛ_1$ 'Ogun consoles me with this'; etc.

Related to the $a_1bi_3sɔ_2$ are the $a_1bi_2ku_3$ names, given to a certain class of children called $a_1bi_2ku_3$ 'born to die.' Johnson says:

> These are supposed to belong to a fraternity of demons living in the woods, especially about and within large $i_1ro_3ko_1$ trees; and each one of them coming into the world would have arranged beforehand the precise time he will return to his company.
>
> Where a woman has lost several children in infancy, especially after a short period of illness, the deaths are attributed to this cause, and means are adopted to thwart the plans of these infants in order that they may stay; for if they can only tide over the pre-arranged date, they may go no more, and thus entirely forget their company.
>
> Besides charms that are usually tied on them and ugly marks they are branded with, in order that their old company may refuse the association of disfigured comrades, . . . certain significant names are also given to them in order to show that their object has been anticipated.

The following are a few of these $a_1bi_2ku_3$ names: $ma_3lɔ_2m\tilde{a}_3$ 'Do not go again'; $ba_3n_2ɟ^8ɔ_3ko_2$ 'Sit down (or stay) with me'; du_3ro_3 $s\tilde{i}_2mi_3$ 'Wait and bury me'; $ti_2ɟu_3\text{-}i_2ku_3$ 'Be ashamed to die'; etc.

The attributive name expresses what the child is or is expected to become. If the child is a male, the name is expressive of something heroic; if a female, it is a term of endearment or of praise. In either case, the name is intended to have a stimulating effect on the child. Among these names are the following: $a_1ɟa_1ni_3$ 'one who possesses (or wins) after a struggle'; $a_1mɔ_1kɛ_3$ 'Whom to know is to pet'; $a_1yɔ_1ka_3$ 'one who causes joy everywhere'; etc.

The number of totems ($o_2ri_3lɛ_1$) among the Yoruba is large, each representing a distinct family. A married woman cannot adopt her husband's totem. Both boys and girls take their father's totem except in rare cases where the father has lost his, or, more usually, when the mother's indicates a higher or nobler rank. Among the totems are $ɔ_1k\tilde{i}_3$ 'the love bird,' a_1gbo_1 'a ram,' $e_2r\tilde{i}_2$ 'the elephant,'

$o_1g\tilde{u}_3$ 'the god of war,' etc. Moslem children among the Yoruba, although named from the Arabic calendar, nevertheless must have their *$o_2ri_3ki_1$* (attributive name) and their *$o_2ri_3l\varepsilon_1$* (totem).

E. The Ibo

G. T. Basden gives the following account of the naming of children among the Ibo, a tribe of Southeastern Nigeria:

> Both boys and girls are given two or more names. The privilege of naming a child (*igu-afa*) is generally the prerogative of the older relatives. The ceremony is observed with feasting and general rejoicing. In due course comes actual bestowal of the names. The first is easy, because it is merely a combination of the word *nwa* 'child' with the name of the day on which it was born. . . . For a girl *mgbɔ* is used instead of *nwa*. The succeeding name (or names) is suggested by some real or fancied peculiarity, or a certain resemblance to a deceased relative. Again, circumstances, or prevailing conditions of the time, may suggest an appropriate name whereby the unusual happenings are kept in remembrance. Some of the names sound rather strangely [*sic*] to European ears, for it should be remembered that all names are capable of translation. Quite a number include the name of the Supreme Being as *Chukuka, Okechuku* and *Nwa-Chuku,* and many have *ɔnwu* 'death' associated in their names. . . . The great majority, however, have to be content to be known by their first name. . . .
>
> In addition to the giving of names of ancestors, some names are influenced by circumstances. For example, a couple who have waited several years for a child will name it *Ogwalu Ony^{9}ekwe* 'He who is told of it will not believe!' (that is, the birth of a child after all these years is almost incredible), or *Ife-yi-nwa* 'There is nothing like a child.'[10]

F. The Northern Tribes of Nigeria

C. K. Meek describes the naming ceremony among several northern tribes of Nigeria as follows:

> A few days after a child's birth a naming festival is held. Among the Igbira this occurs on the fifth day, the child being named by his father, who pours upon the ground a libation of beer to the ancestral spirits, imploring their aid on behalf of his child. The Ngamo, Keri-Keri, and Ngizim custom is for the mother to name the first-born child, all subsequent children being named by the father.
>
> Among the Berom two of the old women who have acted as midwives each select a name for the child, and then repair to crossroads, where they sprinkle corn for the spirits. They then race homewards, and the child

receives the name chosen by the old lady who reaches the compound first. Among the Barke the father chooses the name, generally of some dead relative—not, they say, because of any re-incarnation beliefs, but in order that the family name may be preserved.

Names among the southern tribes are commonly chosen by the divinatory method. Thus, among the Igara, the seer decides whether the child is some re-incarnated relative. Should it appear that he is the father's father re-embodied, he will be given the name of his paternal grandfather, and treated with the utmost respect by his father. Among the Pindiga Jukun a child who cries excessively is taken to the seer, who declares that he is some dead relative, and that if he is given the relative's name the crying will cease.

Where a child is not given the name of one of his ancestors he may be called after the time of day, or season of the year on which he is born. Thus among the Paiemawa and Angas a child is often called *Night* or *Wet Season.* Among these tribes children may also be named after some animal, and are carried by their mothers in satchels made from the skin of the animal after which they are called. The Tangale commonly call their children after some physical feature, plant, animal, or natural phenomenon. Phrases are also commonly used as personal names. Muslims, for example, will call a child *God-will-prevail.* A Bobar father already blessed with several children would call a subsequent child *Many-are-best.*

Twins are given special names. For example, among the Yergum twin boys are called *Tali* and *Bali.* In this tribe also a child with bloodshot eyes would be called *Wuyep* (m.) or *Waiyep* (f.); a child with twelve fingers is called *Jeta* (m.) or *Nate* (f.); if he has a mark on the lobe of his ear he is known as *Meri* (m.) or *Iri* (f.). A Fulani female child born after a succession of sons is called *Dudu.* Common names for Chamba boys are *Livela* 'un-afraid-of-an-arrow,' and for girls *Tirencho* 'remembrance.' An Igara child who is born with a caul is known as *Yabi.*

Among the peoples of Kaiama (Kontagora) a woman who has lost several children will give her next-born some contemptible name. She will treat him with a feigned disdain, and even pretend to offer him for sale in the market-place. The evil spirit that had robbed her of her former children will then be cheated into thinking that the mother does not want her child, and so, to spite her, will allow the child to live. Special dangers surround a first-born child, and it is no doubt for this reason that the Hausa father and mother pretend to be ashamed of and scorn their first-born, and refuse even to give him a name at all. In all the Hausa provinces, when parents have lost several of their children, they shave one side of the heads of their remaining children. When the hair begins to grow the other side is shaved, and this process is continued until the age of six in the case of a girl, and the time of puberty in the case of a boy. A boy thus marked may be known as *Bawa* 'slave,' *Jibji* 'dunghill,' *Sakaina* 'pieces of broken pottery,' or some other disrespectful term.

. . . A man's name among Negro peoples is, in fact, identified with his very soul, and for this reason a child is often (e.g. by the Hausa) given two names —the first a secret name whispered into his ear by his mother, and the second a name for daily use, which is a designation rather than a real name. . . .

It remains to say that names are frequently changed, very often for what appears to be a trivial cause.[11]

G. The Ovimbundu

The methods of naming children employed by the Ovimbundu of Angola have been explained by Wilfred D. Hambly:

If the first child dies, the parents dislike their names; they therefore revert to their original names. . . . A posthumous child is called *Lusati*. A child born after twins is *Kasinda* . . . 'to push.' Twins are called *Lion* and *Elephant*, or *Elephant* and *Hippopotamus*. There are no secret names. The names of the dead must not be mentioned; the deceased is referred to as 'the one who has gone.' Children may change their own names at the age of about sixteen years, and actually do so if their names are distasteful to them. Ngonga's friend, named *Katito* 'little,' changed his name to *Mukayita* (meaning not known). Ngonga's sister, named *Ndumbila* (meaning not known), changed her name to *Cilingohenda* . . . 'It is a pity.' I met a chief near Bailundu who was called *Kandimba* . . . 'the little hare.'

There may be a change of name during sickness. A man now named *Katahali* suffered sickness in addition to other misfortunes. His sickness recurred, so he changed his name from *Kopiongo* to *Katahali*. The meaning of the former name is not known. The new name, *Ka tala ohali*, means 'he who has seen trouble.' . . . Another instance of change of name . . . was that of a man who changed his name from *Lumingo* to *Kaihemba* . . . 'the one who lives by medicine'; because without medicine he would have died. A sick child may receive a bad name, for instance, the name *Pig*. If one or more children have died a subsequent child receives an ugly name with a bad meaning. There is no totemism, but children may be named after animals. A girl is sometimes named *Kambundu* 'a little frog.' Other names for females are *Esenje* 'the rock where corn is pounded' and *Cisengu* 'a small bird with a long tail.' A boy may be *Kangwe* 'the little leopard.'

Names sometimes give an indication of descent. Ngonga's full name is *Ngonga Kalei Liahuka, Ngonga* 'eagle,' *Kalei* 'one who works for the king,' *Liahuka* (the father's surname). . . . The father chooses the names of the three first children whether boys or girls. The mother chooses the name of the fourth child whether male or female. If the child is a boy, the mother probably chooses the name of her brother or of her father's brother. When a first son is born, the father usually gives [him] the name of his father.[12]

H. Personal Names Used by the Gullahs

Most of the Gullah people use two kinds of given names. One is English, and they call it their real or true name and use it at school, in their correspondence, and in their dealings with strangers. The other is the nickname, known also as the pet name or basket name. In their homes and among their friends and acquaintances they use the nickname almost exclusively. In fact, so general is its use that many of the Gullahs have difficulty in recalling their English given-name. The nickname is nearly always a word of African origin. When not African it is likely to be an English word indicating something regarding the nature of the weather at the time of the child's birth (such as *Snow, Snowy, Storm, Rain, Freeze, Hightide*); or the appearance, temperament, or health of the child (such as *Ugly, Egghead, Frogeyes, Badboy, Sick, Laydead, Death, Bigboy, Bigchild, Lookdown, Mamma-sweet, Livefine*); or the time of birth (such as *Harvest, Evening, Night, October, Saturday*); or some particular incident or object with which the child or his parents were associated at the time of the child's birth or later (such as some superstition, or a place, person, animal, or plant). In many instances both the given-name and surname are African words. Some of my ex-slave informants explain this by saying that during slavery they used for their surname (which they called *trimmin'*) the surname of their owner. After slavery, many of them refused to use any longer the name of their former enslavers. Likewise many former slave-holders refused to allow the freedmen to use their names. Thereupon, the former slaves chose their nickname for their surname and gave themselves another nickname. This also is frequently an African word. Many have only one name, which is used both as the given-name and surname.

A study of the following list of words used by the Gullahs as personal names will reveal that they have used the same methods as their African ancestors in naming their children. If these names were classified according to their meanings, they would fall into such groups as the following: names descriptive of the child's physical condition and appearance and of his temperament, character, and mental capacity; names describing the manner in which the child was born; names of family relationships, such as *son*, *daughter*, *mother*, *father*, *uncle*, etc.; animals used as personal names; Mohammedan names and names drawn from African mythology and folklore; names relating to magic, charms, religious festivals, and secret societies; names of the periods of the day, week, and year; names of languages and of tribes, clans, rulers, and other groups of people; names of places; names relating to combat, war, and hunting; names of parts of the body; objects of nature used as personal names; names expressing what the child is expected to become later in life; names of occupations, clothing, ornaments, and musical instruments; greetings, commands, exclamations, and legal terms used as personal names; names describing the condition of the weather; names indicating whether the child is one of twins or triplets or whether he is the first, second, or third born after twins or triplets; names relating to discourse, amusements, etc.

The Gullah names listed below that are accompanied by the asterisk are well known as personal or other proper names among West Africans. Many of them are found in several West African languages with varied meanings, some of which I have indicated. Those Gullah names that are not marked with an asterisk happen not to be known as personal names by my African informants; yet, considering the varied methods described above that the West Africans employ in naming their children, they might well have been used as personal names by the African ancestors of the Gullahs. Even though my Gullah informants do not remember the meanings of these unmarked personal names (nor the precise meanings of most of those that are marked), they continue to use them in naming their children because their older relatives and friends so used them. That they would choose many words whose meanings they do not know is not surprising. As already indicated, even though the Africans attach very great importance to the meanings of the words they use as personal names, they do not follow this practice exclusively. The meanings of many of their names are not known. Like many other peoples, the Africans sometimes choose a name because it is that of some ancestor. Again, the sound of a word may be the sole reason for its being selected; and there are still other reasons apparently not related to the meaning of the word. With a view to indicating possible African sources of these unmarked Gullah names, I have placed opposite them West African words that are phonetically identical with or strikingly similar to them. In addition, I have given several meanings the words have in a number of West African languages. It is not my intention to suggest that any one of the unmarked Gullah names is derived from a particular African language, but rather to emphasize the strong probability that these names are African words. Each of my African informants is certain that every unmarked word from his language which I have placed opposite a phonetically equivalent Gullah name might readily be used as a personal name by the members of his tribe. Even if words from non-African languages could be cited that are phonetically identical with these unmarked Gullah names, it is unlikely that the Gullahs, isolated as they were on the Sea Islands, could have been sufficiently acquainted with such non-African words to use them as personal names. On the other hand, it has been shown in Chapter 1 that the Gullahs were being brought direct from West Africa to South Carolina and Georgia until practically the beginning of the Civil War and were speaking West African languages containing words phonetically identical with these unmarked Gullah names. I originally planned to place these unmarked names in a separate group; but later decided that for the convenience of users of the book, especially those interested primarily in Gullah personal names as such (without reference to their possible African provenience), it would be more desirable to arrange all the names alphabetically in one group.

Approximately three-fourths of all the Gullah personal names I collected in costal Georgia, principally on St. Simon Island, Sapeloe Island, and Harris Neck, and in the vicinity of Darien. The remaining names I collected in coastal South Carolina, chiefly on Edisto, Johns, James, Wadmalaw, St. Helena, and Hilton Head Islands. Many of those which are used in Georgia are likewise heard in South Carolina and vice versa.

The second section of the list that follows contains other African words that are heard daily in the conversation of the Gullahs. In the third section are listed African words that the Gullahs use only in their songs, stories, and prayers. Both these sections are significant for this study not only because of the separate words in them that are of African origin but also because of the interesting combinations of African words that have remained practically unchanged in meaning and pronunciation since the Gullahs were brought to South Carolina and Georgia as slaves.

ABBREVIATIONS

The following abbreviations will be used in the word-list that follows:

adv., adverb
Ar., derived from Arabic[13]
B., Bambara (French West Africa)
Bi., Bini (Southern Nigeria)
Bo., Bobangi (Belgian Congo)
Braz., Brazilian
dat. c., dative case
DAE, *Dictionary of American English*
Dj., Djerma (French West Africa)
E., Ewe (Togo and Dahomey)
Ef., Efik (Southern Nigeria)
Eng., English
F., Fante (Gold Coast)
f., feminine
Fn., Fon (Dahomey)
Fr., French
Fu., Fula (West Coast of Africa)
G., Gã (Gold Coast)
GA, General American
Gb., Gbari (Nigeria)
H., Hausa (Northern Nigeria)
I., Ibo (Southern Nigeria)
Ib., Ibibio (Southern Nigeria)
imp., imperative
K., Kongo (Angola)[14]
Ki., Kikongo (Belgian Congo)
Kim., Kimbundu (Angola)
Kp., Kpelle (Liberia)
lit., literally
M., Mende (Sierra Leone)
m., masculine
Mal., Malinke (French West Africa)
Man., Mandinka (Gambia)
Mand., Mandingo (French West Africa)
N., Nupe (Nigeria)
P., Portuguese
pers. n., personal name
pers. pr., personal pronoun
pl., plural
poss. pr., possessive pronoun
S., Susu (French Guinea)
Sg., Songhay (French West Africa)
sg., singular
T., Twi (Gold Coast)
Tem., Temne (Sierra Leone)
Tl., Tshiluba (Belgian Congo)
U., Umbundu (Angola)
V., Vai (Liberia and Sierra Leone)
W., Wolof (Senegal and Gambia)
Y., Yoruba (Southern Nigeria)

GULLAH PERSONAL NAMES	WEST AFRICAN WORDS
	a [a]
* ˈ*aba* (m.)	F., a_3ba_3 pers. n. f., corresponding to T. *ya*: 'name given a girl born on Thursday'[15]
* *aˈbako* (m.)	T., *abako* 'a kind of shea-tree having brown wood that is used for furniture; the mahogany tree'; Y., pers. n. $a_1gba_3ko_1$ 'an unexpected event'
* *abaˈra* (m.)	Y., $a_1ba_2ra_3$ 'a slap with the palm of the hand'; $a_2gba_3ra_2$ 'power, force'; $a_1gba_1ra_3$ 'torrent'; $a_2gba_1ra_1$ 'barricade'; I., $a_1gba_1ra_1$ 'a fetish'; E., a_1bra_3 'name given a girl born on Tuesday'

GULLAH PERSONAL NAMES	WEST AFRICAN WORDS
aˈbaso (m.)	T., $a_1ba_1so_3$ 'to stand security for'; T., $a_3ba_1so_3$ 'recent'
* *aˈbaʃe* (f.)	Y., $a_1gba_1\text{ʃ}e_2$ pers. n. 'the work of a laborer'
* *aˈbeʃe* (f.)	Y., $a_2be_1\text{ʃ}e_2$ pers. n. 'a worthless person'
* *aˈbɛbɛ* (m.)	Y., $a_2b\varepsilon_1b\varepsilon_1$ ($a_1b\varepsilon_3b\varepsilon_1$) pers. n. 'a fan'; $a_2b\varepsilon_1b\varepsilon_2$ 'advocate, pleader'
* *abiˈɒna* (f.)	Y., a_2bi_3-ɔ_2na_1 pers. n., lit. 'born by the wayside'
aˈbiyas (m.)	Tem., *abias* 'a journey'
* *ˌabitiˈko* (f.)	Y., $a_2bi_2ti_3ko_3$ pers. n.
* *aˈbɒbade* (m.)	Y., $a_2b\text{ɔ}_2ba_2de_3$ pers. n., lit. 'one who comes with the king'
* *aˈbɒlu* (m.)	Y., $a_1b\text{ɔ}_3lu_1$ pers. n. 'the act of feeding together'
ˈabo (m.)	E., a_1bo_1 'suffocation'; a_3bo_1 'a ball for playing'
* *aˈbu* (m.)	T., *abu* 'ruin, overwhelming calamity'; M., *abu* pers. n. m.; Y., a_1bu_3 pers. n. m.
abuˈrika (f.)	Cf. Kim., *burika* 'to be broken'
* *ˈadaba* (m.)	Y., $a_1da_1ba_1$ pers. n. 'the brown dove'
* *aˈdade* (m.)	Fn., *adade* pers. n. 'wife'; 'half'
* *aˈdaɟɒ* (m.)	Y., $a_2da_3\text{ɟɔ}_2$ pers. n. 'a judge'; $a_1da_3\text{ɟɔ}_2$ 'a gathering together'
aˈdaka (f.)	E., $a_1\text{ḍ}a_3ka_1$ 'box, trunk'
* *aˈdamu* (m.)	H., $a\!:_1da_2mu_1$ pers. n. m. 'Adam'; Fu., *adamu* pers n. m.
* *aˈdanse* (m.)	T., *adanse* 'a country situated south of Asante and considered one of the original seats of the Akem nation'
* *aˈdasi* (f.)	Y., $a_1da_3si_2$, pers. n. 'something spared or gleaned'
* *aˈde* (m.)	Y., a_2de_3 pers. n. 'crown'; T., *ade* 'property, possession'; 'duty'; E., a_1de_1 'hunting'; 'any tough or sticky mass'; a_1de_3 'six'
* *adeˈbisi* (m. and f.)	Y., $a_2de_3bi_3si_3$ pers. n., lit. 'My coming causes an increase'
* *adeˈbiyi* (f.)	Y., $a_1de_1bi_3yi_1$ pers. n., lit. 'The crown has begotten this'
* *adeˈkũle* (f.)	Y., $a_2de_3k\tilde{u}_3le_3$ pers. n., lit. 'The crown fills the house'
* *aˈdeniyi* (f)	Y., $a_2de_3ni_3yi_1$ pers. n., lit. 'The crown has honor'
* *aˈdeɲa* (m.)	T., *adeɲã* pers. n. 'the acquisition of wealth'
* *aˈdewale* (m.)	Y., $a_2de_3wa_3le_3$ pers. n., lit. 'A crown comes to the house'

GULLAH PERSONAL NAMES	WEST AFRICAN WORDS
* *a'dɛbɒ* (m.)	Y., *a$_1$dɛ$_3$bɔ$_2$* pers. n. 'an idol-worshipper'; 'one who makes a sacrifice'
* *a$_1$di$_3$* (m.)	Y., *a$_1$dĩ$_3$* 'oil made from the nut in the palm kernel'; T., *adi* 'eating, feasting'; E., *a$_3$ḍi$_1$i$_1$* pers. n.
a'didi (m.)	T., *adidi* 'feasting, a meal'
a'dinɒ (f.)	Fn., *adinɔ̃* 'malignant, poisonous'
* *a'dit* (f.)	Ef., *a$_{1-2}$dil$_{2-1}$* pers. n. f.
* *adi'ti* (m.)	Y., *a$_2$di$_2$ti$_3$* pers. n. 'a deaf person'
* *a'diwe* (m.)	E., *a$_1$ḍi$_1$ve$_3$* pers. n. 'to be busy, industrious'
* *adi'yɛ* (m.)	Y., *a$_2$diɛ$_2$* pers. n. 'a fowl.' Cf. Bi., *a$_3$di$_1$yɛ$_3$* 'a fowl' (borrowed from Yoruba)
* *'adla* (f.)	Fn., *adla* 'name of a Dahomean regiment'
* *'adɒ* (m.)	E., *a$_1$ḍɔ$_1$* pers. n. 'lazy, clumsy'
* *a'dɒna* (m.)	T., *adɔnã* pers. n. 'displeasure, disfavor'
* *a'dɒye* (m.)	T., *adɔe* pers. n. 'kind-heartedness, mercy, affection'
* *a'dodo* (m.)	E., *a$_1$do$_1$do$_1$* pers. n. 'to be obstinate, quarrelsome'; Fn., *adodo* 'a pool, a pond'
* *ado'nowi* (m.)	Fn., *adonovi* 'name of a Dahomean regiment'
* *a'doʃu* (m.)	Y., *a$_2$do$_3$ʃu$_1$* 'one zealously devoted to the *ʃaŋ$_1$go$_3$*[16] mysteries'; 'rank in priesthood of Yoruba cult life'
* *a'du* (m.)	Y., *a$_2$du$_3$* 'one who is very black'; E., *a$_1$ḍu$_1$* 'tooth'; Fn., *adu* 'tooth'; T., *adu* 'a protagonist in Ashanti legend'
* *a'duna* (f.)	Y., *a$_2$du$_1$na$_1$* pers. n. 'a contender'; W., *aduna* 'universe, world'; cf. T., *aduana* 'one of the original families of the Twi people'
a'dunu (m.)	Fn., *adunu* 'food'
a'duwa (m.)	T., *adua* 'fruit'; 'seed, kernel'
* *a'fa* (f.)	E., *a$_1$Φa$_3$* 'a call, a cry for help'; Fn., *afa* 'the genius of wisdom and divination'; 'destiny, chance'; E., *a$_1$fa$_3$* 'Ewe name for the Yoruba deity *Ifa*'
* *a'fara* (f.)	Y., *a$_1$fa$_2$ra$_2$* pers. n. 'sluggishness, slowness'
a'fe (f.)	T., *afe* 'year'
* *a'femu* (m.)	E., *a$_1$Φe$_3$mu$_3$* 'name of a place'
* *a'fene* (f.)	T., *afen:e* pers. n. 'something borrowed'
* *a'fɛ* (f.)	T., *afɛ* pers. n. 'companion'; Y., pers. n. *a$_2$fɛ$_3$* 'pleasure'
* *a'fi* (f.)	T. and E., *a$_1$fi$_3$* 'name used in saluting a person born on Friday'
* *a'fiba* (f.)	E., *a$_1$fi$_3$ba$_3$* 'name given a girl born on Friday'

GULLAH PERSONAL NAMES	WEST AFRICAN WORDS
* *'afɒ* (f.)	I., *a*$_3$*fɔ*$_1$ 'year'; *a*$_1$*fɔ*$_1$ pers. n. 'day of the Ibo week'; *a*$_3$*fɔ*$_3$ 'stomach'; Y., *a*$_1$*fɔ̃*$_2$ 'African breadfruit'; *a*$_1$*fɔ̃*$_1$ 'the baobab tree, the seed of which is poisonous to horses'
* *'afo* (f.)	Fu., *'afo* 'the first-born child'; Y., *a*$_1$*fo*$_2$ 'opportunity, space, vacancy'; Fn., *afo* 'foot, leg'
* *a'fofi* (f.)	T., *afo:fi* 'keeping at home, doing domestic work'; *fo:fie* 'a deity worshipped at Aburi and other places'
* *a'fu* (f.)	E., *a*$_1$*fu*$_3$ pers. n. 'providing food'; *a*$_1$*fu*$_1$ 'mist, fog'
* *a'fura* (f.)	Y., *a*$_2$*fu*$_2$*ra*$_2$ pers. n. 'a suspicious person'
* *a'fuwa* (f.)	T., *afuwa* 'name given a girl born on Friday'; E., *a*$_1$*fu*$_3$*a*
* *a'gali* (f.)	W., *agali* pers. n. 'welcome, greeting'
* *a'gama* (f.)	Fn., *agama* 'a chameleon fetish'
* *agan'ɟu* (m.)	Y., *a*$_2$*gã*$_2$*ɟu*$_3$ per. n. 'the innermost recesses of a king's palace'; *a*$_2$*gã*$_2$*ɟu*$_1$ 'wilderness'
* *a'gawi* (m.)	Fn., *agavi* 'an illegitimate child'
* *ag'baɟa* (m.)	Fn., *agbaɟa* 'the fourth king of Dahomey, who ruled from 1708 to 1729'
* *ag'baka* (m.)	Bi., *a*$_1$*gba*$_3$*ka*$_1$ pers. n. 'crocodile'
'agbi (m.)	Fn., *agbi* 'lightning'
ag'bɒta (f.)	Fn., *agbɔta* 'shoulder-blade'
* *ag'bome* (m.)	Fn., *agbome* 'Abomey, a city in Dahomey'
* *a'gɛmɒ* (f.)	Y., *a*$_2$*gɛ*$_2$*mɔ*$_2$ 'the chameleon, an idol, during the worship of which only the men are allowed to remain standing, while the women kneel with their heads bowed'
* *agɒ'maya* (f.)	Fn., *agɔmaya* pers. n. 'the palm tree'
* *ago'go* (m.)	Y., *a*$_2$*go*$_2$*go*$_2$ pers. n. 'a bell'; 'a clock'; 'a musical instrument made in the shape of a bell'; 'the name of a tree taller than those near it'; 'height, tallness'
* *a'goli* (m.)	Fn., *agoli* 'a tribunal at Whydah'
* *a'gona* (f.)	T., *agona* 'name of a country in the Gold Coast consisting of a southeastern and a northwestern kingdom, the capitals of which are *nsabã:* and *asikuma*'; 'one of the original families of the Twi people'
* *a*$_1$*hi*$_3$ (m.)	T., *ahĩ* pers. n. 'that which causes displeasure'; E., *a*$_1$*hĩ*$_1$ 'to boast'; Fn., *ahi* 'price, value'
a'hɒɟi (m.)	Fn., *ahɔɟi* 'spray, foam'

GULLAH PERSONAL NAMES	WEST AFRICAN WORDS
* *aˈhosi* (m.)	Fn., *ahosi* 'eunuch'; 'wife of the king's son'; E., a$_1$ho$_1$si$_1$ 'widow'
* *ˈahũ* (m.)	Y., a$_2$hũ$_2$ pers. n. 'miser, stinginess'; 'tortoise'; E., a$_1$hũ$_1$ 'dew'
* *ɐɪˈsã* (f.)	Y., ai$_1$sã$_1$ pers. n. 'illness'; ai$_1$sã$_2$ 'want of payment'
* *ˈɐɪto* (m.)	Y., ai$_1$to$_3$ pers. n. 'incompetency'
* *ˈaɟa* (m.)	Y., a$_2$ɟa$_3$ 'dog'; a$_1$ɟa$_1$ 'attic, ceiling'; I., a$_1$dʒa$_1$ 'sacrifice'; a$_3$dʒa$_3$ 'earth, sand, wall'; Fn., *aɟa* 'a province of Western Dahomey'
* *aˈɟagbɒ̃* (m.)	Y., a$_2$ɟa$_2$gbɔ̃$_3$ pers. n. 'one who discovers another's cunning'
* *aɟaˈluma* (m.)	Fn., *aɟaluma* 'the genius who presides over the destinies of the white people'
* *aˈɟana* (f.)	W., *aɟana* pers. n. (*alɟana*) 'heaven, paradise'
* *aˈɟani* (m.)	Y., a$_1$ɟa$_1$ni$_3$ pers. n., lit. 'one who possesses after a struggle'
* *aˈɟaʃɛ* (f.)	Y., a$_1$ɟa$_1$ʃɛ$_3$ 'victorious.' (Among the Yoruba a$_1$ɟa$_1$ʃɛ$_3$ is the word for people from Badagry)
* *aˈɟayi* (m.)	Y., a$_1$ɟa$_1$yi$_3$ pers. n.; a$_2$ɟa$_3$ yi$_2$ 'this dog'
* *ˈaɟe* (m.)	Y., a$_2$ɟe$_3$ 'money, the goddess of money'; a$_2$ɟɛ$_2$ 'trial by ordeal'; Fn., *aɟe* 'shell-fish'
* *aˈɟɛgbe* (m.)	Y., a$_1$ɟɛ$_2$gbe$_3$ pers. n. 'the act of eating without injurious effect anything considered harmful'
* *aˈɟiwa* (m.)	Y., a$_2$ɟi$_3$wa$_3$ pers. n., lit. 'one who wakes to come'
* *aˈɟɒli* (f.)	E., a$_1$ɟɔ$_1$li$_1$ pers. n. 'a singing bird'
* *ˈaɟo* (m.)	T., *adwo* 'the genius of Monday'; 'a title of respect given to chiefs, etc.'; E., a$_1$ɟo$_3$ 'name used in saluting one born on Monday'
* *aˈɟowa* (f.)	E., a$_1$ɟo$_3$wa$_3$ 'name given a girl born on Monday'
* *aˈɟuda* (m.)	Fn., *aɟuda* 'the Portuguese name of Whydah (Dahomey)'
* *aɟudagˈbɛto* (m.)	Fn., *aɟudagbɛto* 'the name given to Creoles of Portuguese or Brazilian origin'
* *aˈkaba* (m.)	Fn., *akaba* 'the third king of Dahomey, who ruled from 1680 to 1708'
* *aˈkala* (m.)	Fn., *akala* pers. n. 'vulture'
* *aˈkaraˌɟɛ* (m.)	Y., a$_1$ka$_1$ra$_1$ ɟɛ$_2$ pers. n. 'to eat a$_1$ka$_1$ra$_1$ (a$_1$ka$_1$ra$_1$ meaning 'bread' or 'cake' or 'a dish consisting of beans, palm oil, pepper, and onions' and ɟɛ$_2$ meaning 'to eat')[17]

GULLAH PERSONAL NAMES	WEST AFRICAN WORDS
ˈ*akasa* (m.)	E., $a_1ka_1sa_1$ 'row line, file'; H., $a_1ka_1sa_1$ 'a dark-bordered white cloth of European manufacture; T., *akasã* 'a beverage prepared from maize.' Cf. P., *acassá* [akaˈsa] 'a mixture of flour, rice, and meal'
* *aˈkãwo* (m.)	Y., $a_1kã_1$-wo_3 ($a_1kã_1$-o_3) 'an attributive name for a boy, expressing strength or bravery'
* *aˈkele* (m.)	Y., $a_1ke{:}_3le_3$ 'name given one who is small but obstinate'; V., $a_1ke_1le_1$ 'Give him (her, it) a name'; $a{:}_3ke_1le_1$ 'He has arrived'
aˈkẽri (m.)	Y., $a_2kẽ{:}_{2-1}ri_3$ 'a plant used for washing,' lit. 'that which removes dirt'
* *akɛgˈbuda* (m.)	Bi., $a_3kɛ_3gbu_3da_1$ 'the name of an $ɔ_3ba_3$, the ruler of Benin, who lives at Benin City'
* *aˈkɛtɛ* (f.)	Y., $a_1kɛ_3tɛ_1$ pers. n. 'a hat'; Fn., *akɛtɛ* 'a large hat (made of palm leaves) which serves as an umbrella'
aˈkɛtɛ-oˈri (m.)	Y., $a_1kɛ_3tɛ_1$ o_2ri_3, lit. 'hat for the head'
* ˈ*aki* (f.)	Y., a_2ki_2 pers. n. 'bravery, a brave person'; K., *aki* 'a prefix applied to the name of a person when he is spoken of and to all who are with him': e.g., *aki-makitu alueke* 'Makitu and his people have come'
* *aˈkiti* (m.)	Man., *akiti* 'a famous hunter in Mandinka folklore who, by conquering the elephant, became king of the bush'; Y., $a_2ki_3ti_1$ 'monkey'
* *akĩˈyɛle* (f.)	Y., $a_2kĩ_3yɛ_2le_3$ pers. n., lit. 'A strong one befits the house'
* *aˈklasu* (m.)	Fn., *aklasu* pers. n. 'vulture'
aˈkluwi (f.)	Fn., *akluvi* 'a drinking cup or bowl'
* ˈ*akɒ* (m.)	Y., $a_1kɔ_1$ 'sheath, scabbard'; $a_2kɔ_2$ pers. n. 'male'
* *aˈkɒdu* (m.)	E., $a_1kɔ_1ḍu_3$ pers. n. 'banana'
* *aˈkɒni* (f.)	Y., $a_2kɔ_2ni_2$ pers. n. 'a brave, strong person'; $a_2kɔ_3ni_2$ 'teacher'; $a_1kɔ_3ni_2$ 'first possessed'
* *aˈkɒ̃rĩ* (f.)	Y., $a_2kɔ̃_2rĩ_2$ pers. n. 'a singer'
* *aˈkɒrɒ* (f.)	Y., $a_1kɔ_3rɔ_1$ pers. n. 'the first rain of the year'
* ˈ*ako* (m.)	Y., a_1ko_3 pers. n. 'genuineness'; a_1ko_2 'branch of the palm tree'; a_2ko_2 'strumpet'; Fn., *ako* 'a straw hat'
* *aˈkotiya* (m).	T., *akotia* 'name of a diety'; 'a plant'
aˈkoto (m.)	Fn. *akoto* 'a snail'
ˌ*akoˈyire* (f.)	Y., a_2ko_2-i_2re_2 'the spurious rubber tree'
akpaˈlode (m).	Bi., $a_1kpa_3lo_3de_1$ 'a leather medicine belt worn as a protection against charms placed on the road with

GULLAH PERSONAL NAMES	WEST AFRICAN WORDS
	the intention of causing such diseases as elephantiasis, leprosy, etc.'[18]
* *ˈakpɛ* (m.)	Y., *a*$_1$*kpɛ*$_3$ pers. n. 'clapping of the hands'; *a*$_2$*kpɛ*$_3$ 'a pot used as saucepan'
**aˈku* (f.)	E., *a*$_1$*ku*$_3$ 'name used in saluting a person born on Friday'; 'name given a male born on Wednesday.' (*Aku* was also a name used by some groups to refer to the Yoruba tribe of Nigeria. See Robert Campbell, *A Pilgrimage to My Motherland* [1861], p. 32) W., *aku* 'to have the hair plaited for the first time'; 'name of a people'
* *aˈkuɟi* (m.)	Y., *a*$_2$*ku*$_3$*ɟi*$_3$ pers. n., lit. 'one who dies and awakes'
* *aˈkukɒ* (m.)	Y., *a*$_1$*ku*$_1$*kɔ*$_2$, pers. n. 'a cock'
* *aˈkwenɒ̃* (m.)	Fn., *akwenɔ̃* pers. n. 'rich'
* *ˈala* (f.)	W., *ala* 'forest, fields'; Y., *a*$_1$*la*$_1$ 'a white cloth'; *a*$_3$*la*$_3$ 'a dream'; E., *a*$_1$*la*$_3$ 'an armlet of ivory'; 'raffia palm'; B. and Mand., *al:a* 'God' (Ar.)
* *aˈlaba* (f.)	Fn., *alaba* 'Arabian, Arabic'
* *ˌalabaˈlaʃɛ* (m.)	Y., *a*$_2$*la*$_3$*ba*$_2$*la*$_2$*ʃɛ*$_2$ 'oracle, the name given to the goddess *ɔ*$_2$*ba*$_1$*ta*$_3$*la*$_3$, who is believed to foretell future events'
* *aˈlabo* (m.)	Y., *a*$_2$*la:*$_3$*bo*$_1$ pers. n. 'defender, protector'
* *aˈlade* (f.)	Y., *a*$_1$*la*$_1$*de*$_3$ 'name given a boy born between girls or after several girls'; *a*$_2$*la*$_3$*de*$_2$ 'one entitled to wear a crown—a prince, a king'
* *alaˈdi* (m.)	Y., *a*$_2$*la*$_1$*di*$_3$ 'an expositor'; Mand., *ala:di* 'Sunday'
* *aˈlafĩ* (f.)	Y., *a*$_2$*la:*$_{2-1}$*fĩ*$_2$ 'king, one who owns the palace'; 'the title of the king of *ɔ*$_1$*yɔ*$_3$'
* *alaˈfiya* (f.)	Y., *a*$_2$*la*$_2$*fia*$_3$ pers. n. 'health, peace'
* *aˈlagba* (f.)	Y., *a*$_2$*la*$_1$*gba*$_1$ 'an elder, one who commands respect'; *a*$_2$*la*$_3$*gba*$_{2-1}$ 'the chief of the *e*$_2$*gũ*$_3$*gũ*$_3$ worship and mystery'
* *aˈlagbe* (m.)	Y., *a*$_2$*la*$_3$*gbe*$_2$ pers. n. 'a beggar'
* *alaˈhadi* (m.)	Man., *al:ahadi* 'Sunday'
* *aˈlaɪku* (m.)	Y., *a*$_2$*lai*$_3$*ku*$_3$ pers. n. 'immortal'
* *aˈlaɪni* (f.)	Y., *a*$_2$*lai*$_3$*ni*$_2$ pers. n. 'a needy person'
* *aˈlaɪye* (f.)	Y., *a*$_2$*lai*$_3$*ye*$_3$ pers. n. 'monarch,' lit. 'owner of the world'
* *aˈlaɪyo* (m.)	Y., *a*$_2$*la*$_3$*-i*$_1$*yo*$_3$ pers. n. 'one who is not satisfied with food'

GULLAH PERSONAL NAMES	WEST AFRICAN WORDS
* *a'laɟe* (m.)	Y., $a_2la_3ɟe_2$ 'one who divines'; 'one who performs trial by ordeal'
* *a'lake* (f.)	Y., $a_2la_3ke_2$ 'the king of Ake [a_1ke_3], the capital of the Egba province'; 'the chief of the Egba kings'
a'lala (f.)	E., $a_1la_1la_1$ 'a slowly flowing stream'; $a_1la_1la_3$ 'quartz'
* *a'lama* (f.)	H., $a_1la{:}_2ma_1$ pers. n. 'a sign' (Ar.)
ala'mari (f.)	Fu., *alamari* 'circumstance, affair' (Ar.)
* *ala'misa* (f.)	B., *alamisa* 'Thursday' (Ar.)
alan'saro (f)	Man., *alansaro* 'three-o'clock prayer time' (Ar.)
* *a'lanu* (f.)	Y., $a_2la{:}_{3-2}nu_3$ pers. n. 'a merciful or gracious person'
a'laŋke (m.)	H., $a_1laŋ_1ke{:}_2$ 'a board used by leather workers'
* *a'lara* (f.)	Y., $a_2la_3ra_1$ pers. n. 'a free person'
* *ala'ranʃe* (f.)	Y., $a_2la_3r\tilde{a}_1ʃe_2$ pers. n. 'a helper'
* *a'laru* (f.)	Y., $a_2la{:}_3ru_{2-1}$ pers. n. 'a carrier of burdens'
* *a'lasa* (f.)	Y., $a_2la_3sa_1$ pers. n. 'a saddler'
* *a'lati* (f.)	Y., $a_1la_2ti_3$ pers. n. 'a kind of pot'
* *ala'waɲo* (m.)	E., $a_1la_1va_1ɲo_1$ 'name of a place in the Ewe country'
* *ala'wiye* (f.)	Y., $a_2la_3wi_2ye_2$ pers. n. 'one who explains a matter clearly'
* *a'lawo* (f)	Y., $a_2la_3wo_2$ 'a priest, one acquainted with the secrets of the gods'
* *a'laya* (f.)	B., *al:aya* pers. n. 'divinity'
* *a'laye* (m.)	Y., $a_2la{:}_1ye_1$ pers. n. 'living, possessing life'
a'layo (m.)	Y., $a_2la_3yo_1$ 'an a_2yo_1 (warry) player'
* *a'layode* (m.)	Y., $a_2la_3yo_2de_3$ pers. n., lit. 'One comes who is physically satisfied'
* *al'faba* (f.)	Tem., *alfaba* 'name of a Temne chief and chiefdom in Sierra Leone'
* a_1li_3 (m. and f.)	Mand., *ali* 'name given the fifth male child'; E., a_1li_1 'hip, loin'; H., a_3li_1 'the first finger'; Fn., *ali* 'road'
* *a'linu* (f.)	E., $a_1li_1nu_1$ pers. n. 'in an erect position'; Fn., *alinu* 'itinerary'; 'a guide'
ali'time (f.)	Fn., *alitime* 'height, size, stature'
a'liya (f.)	Fn., *aliya* 'a ladder staircase'
al'kama (f.)	B., *alkama* 'grain'; H., $al_3ka_3ma_1$ 'wheat, grain' (Ar.)
* *alka'misa* (f.)	Fu., *alkamisa* 'Thursday' (Ar.)
* *al'mudu* (f.)	H., $al_1mu_1du{:}_2$ 'a vendor of anything sold by measure, such as corn'; S., *almudu* 'one of the months of the year'

GULLAH PERSONAL NAMES	WEST AFRICAN WORDS
* *aˈnebi* (f.)	Fu., *'an-ebi* pers. n. 'prophet' (Ar.)
* a_1ni_3-a_1ni_3 (f.)	T., *ani-ani* 'superficially'; Y., a_1ni_3-a_1ni_3 pers. n. 'doubt, uncertainty'
* *aˈnilima* (f.)	Fn., *anilima* 'name of a Dahomean regiment'
* *aˈnima* (f.)	T., $a_1nim{:}_1a_3$ pers. n.; $a_1nim{:}_3a{:}_3$ 'a young or small male animal'
* *aˈnitã* (m.)	Y., $a_1ni_3tã_2$ pers. n. 'perfection, full possession'
* *aˈniya* (f.)	Fu., *'an:iya*, 'intention, resolve' (Ar.); Y., $a_1ni_3ya_1$ pers. n. 'anxiety, attention, generosity'
* *ˈanɒ* (f.)	T., *an:ɔ* pers. n.; I., $a_1nɔ_3$ 'four'
* *aˈnonɒ* (f.)	Fn., *anonɔ̃* pers. n. 'a nurse'
* *ˈanu* (m.)	Tl., *anu* 'only'; Y., $a{:}_2nu_3$ pers. n. 'pity, leniency'
* *anuˈkluyi* (f.)	E., $a_1nu_3klu_1i$ pers. n. 'jealousy'
ˈanwa (m.)	Bi., a_1nwa_3 'tongs'
* *aˈɲadi* (m.)	W., *aɲadi* pers. n. 'to dine'
aˈɲani (f.)	W., *aɲani* 'to beg for a meal'
* *ˈaɲi* (f.)	*aɲi* 'name of an Ivory Coast language'; I., $a_1ɲi_3$ 'we'; $a_3ɲi_3$ 'us, our'
* *aˈɲika* (f.)	V., $a_1ɲi_1ka_3$ pers. n. f., lit. 'She is very beautiful'
aˈɲuɟi (f.)	Fn., *aɲuɟi* 'the epidermis'
ˈaŋgɒ (m.)	E., $a_1ŋɔ_1$ 'paint'; 'a stone containing iron'
* *aŋˈku* (m.)	E., $aŋ_1ku_3$ 'name given a boy born on Wednesday'
ˈapa (f.)	E., a_1pa_1 'an agreement'; T., *apa* 'a scaffold of sticks on which to hang fruits; Y., a_2kpa_2 'a tree used in the construction of drums'; a_1kpa_2 'a wasteful person'; a_2kpa_3 'arm or wing'; a_1kpa_3 'a sign, a scar'
* *aˈpara* (m.)	Y., $a_1kpa_3ra_3$ 'raillery, jest'; $a_1kpa_3ra_1$ pers. n. 'name of a tree'
* *aˈparo* (m.)	Y., $a_1kpa_3ro_1$ pers. n. 'bush-fowl, quail'
* *aˈpenteŋ* (f.)	T., *apenteŋ* pers. n.; cf. T., *mpintĩŋ* 'a kind of tambourine'
aˈpepe (m.)	Y., $a_2kpe_2kpe_2$ 'West African rosewood'
* *aˈpiŋkɛ* (f.)	Y., $a_1kpiŋ_3kɛ_3$ pers. n., lit. 'one in the petting of whom many share'
* *aˈraba* (f.)	B. and Man., *araba* 'Wednesday' (Ar.); Y., $a_1ra_2ba_2$ 'cotton tree.' (Among the Yoruba the chief priest of Ifa is called *Araba*)
* *aˈrɐɪye* (f.)	Y., $a_2rai_3ye_2$ pers. n. 'people, mankind'
* *araˈɟuma* (f.)	Man., *aradʒuma* 'Friday' (Ar.)

GULLAH PERSONAL NAMES	WEST AFRICAN WORDS
* *araˈkana* (m.)	Y., a_2ra_2 $k\tilde{a}_2$ a_3 pers. n. 'His body is sore,' lit. 'The body pains him'
* *aˈrale* (m.)	Y., $a_2ra{:}_{3-2}le_3$ pers. n. 'inmate, one who belongs to a house or family'
* *araˈmisa* (f.)	Man., *aramisa* 'Thursday'
* *arãˈmɒɟu* (m.)	Y., $a_1r\tilde{a}_2m\tilde{ɔ}_2ɟu_3$, pers. n., lit. 'that which shines until the eye is clear'
* *aˈrãʃɒ* (m.)	Y., $a_2r\tilde{a}_3ʃɔ_2$ pers. n. 'a tailor'
* *aˈrɛmɒ* (m.)	Y., $a_1rɛ_1mɔ_2$ 'the eldest child, male or female'
* a_1ri_3 (f.)	Y., a_2ri_3 pers. n. 'We see'
* *aˈriya* (f.)	Y., $a_1ri_3ya_3$ pers. n. 'joy, merriment'
* *ˈaro* (f.)	Y., a_3ro_1 pers. n.; a_1ro_3 'a title of honor among civil authorities'
* *ˈaroko* (m.)	Y., $a_2ro_2ko_2$ pers. n. 'a farmer'
* *aˈrole-ˈɔba* (m.)	Y., $a_1ro_3le_2$ $ɔ_2ba_2$ pers. n., lit. 'heir of the king'
* *aˈrun* (m.)	Y., $a{:}_1r\tilde{u}_3$ 'five'; $a_1r\tilde{u}_1$ pers. n. 'disease, sickness'
* *aˈrupɛ* (f.)	Y., $a_1ru_3kpɛ_1$ pers. n. 'dwarf'
* *ˈasa* (m.)	Y., a_2sa_1 pers. n. 'shield'; E., a_1sa_1 'separated, apart'; a_1sa_{3-1} 'seven'
* *ˈasafo* (m.)	E., $a_1sa_1fo_1$ 'the young men of a community, the warriors; company, association'
asaˈgidi (m.)	Y., $a_2sa_2gi_2di_2$ 'food plant of the African silkworm'
* *aˈsaka* (f.)	W., *asaka* pers. n. 'the first fruit, the beginning'
* *aˈsante* (m. and f.)	T., *asante* 'the country, people, and language of the Asante (Gold Coast)'
aˈsaro (m.)	Y., $a_1sa_2ro_3$ 'pottage'
* *ˈase* (m.)	Y., a_2se_2 'an animal resembling the squirrel'; a_1se_1 'feast'; Fn., *asẽ* 'god of iron'
* *aˈseɟɛ* (f.)	Y., $a_1se_1ɟɛ_2$ pers. n. 'cooked medicine'
* *aˈseni* (m.)	T., *aseni* pers. n. 'descendant, offspring'
* *aˈseti* (f.)	Y., $a_2se_2ti_3$ pers. n. 'a listener'
* *ˈasi* (m. and f.)	E., a_1si_1 pers. n. 'wife, woman, female'; 'market, price'; Fn., *asi* 'wife'; T., *asi* pers. n.
* *ˈasiga* (m.)	E., $a_1si_1g\tilde{a}_3$ pers. n. 'the elder sister of a wife'
* *ˈasigbe* (f.)	E., $a_1si_1gbe_1$ pers. n. 'market day'
* *ˈasɒ* (m.)	Y., $a_2sɔ_1$ 'a quarrel'; E., $a_1sɔ_1$ 'a disease of the feet'; T., *asɔ* pers. n.
* *aˈsɒdũ* (m.)	Y., $a_1sɔ_2d\tilde{u}_1$ pers. n. 'exaggeration'
aˈsɒta (m.)	Y., $a_1sɔ_2ta_1$ 'the business of a professional speaker'
aˈsofi (m.)	Fn., *asofi* 'a flea'

GULLAH PERSONAL NAMES	WEST AFRICAN WORDS
* *aˈlogbo* (f.)	Y., $a_1lo_2gbo_3$ pers. n. 'worn-out, threadbare'
* *aloˈwizɒ* (f.)	Fn., *alovizɔ̃* pers. n. 'inflammation of the fingers or toes'
alˈtelu (m.)	Man., *altelu*[19] 'you' (2d pers. pr. pl.)
* *alˈtine* (f.)	W., *altine* 'Monday' (Ar.)
aˈlura (f.)	H., $al{:}_1u{:}_2ra_1$ 'needle' (Ar.)
aˈluwa (f.)	B., *alua* 'sweets, confectionery'; W., *alua* 'a tablet in wood on which one writes verses of the Koran'
* ˈ*alwi* (m.)	Fn., *alwi*[20] pers. n. 'the fox'
* ˈ*ama* (f.)	E., a_1ma_{1-3} 'name of a girl born on Saturday'; 'naked'; a_1ma_1 'herb, vegetables'; 'a dark-green or dark-blue color'; I., a_3ma_3 'street'; a_1ma_1 'evidence'
* *aˈmadi* (m.)	T., *ama:di* pers. n. m.
amaˈdowa (m.)	E., $a_1ma_1doa_3$ 'a dyer'
* *aˈmamfo* (m.)	G. and T., $a_1mam_1\ f\tilde{o}_3$ pers. n. 'a decayed dwelling or habitation'
* *aˈmanɔ* (m.)	T., *aman:ɔ* pers. n. m.
* *aˈmara* (m.)	Mand., *amara* pers. n. m. 'a companion of the Prophet'; V., $a_3ma_3ra_1$ pers. n. m.
aˈmasi (f.)	Fn., *amasi* 'medicine'; E., $a_1ma_1tsi_1$ 'medicine'
* *aˈme* (f.)	E., a_1me_3 'name used in greeting persons born on Saturday'
* *aˈmεgi* (f.)	E., $a_1m\varepsilon_1\gamma i_{1-3}$ pers. n. 'white man, mulatto, albino'
* *aˈmina* (f.)	Mand., *ami:na* pers. n. f. 'mother of Mohammed'; 'amen, so be it'; B., *amina* 'amen'
* *amiˈnata* (f.)	Mand., *aminata* pers. n. f.
* *aˈmiyi* (m.)	E., $a_1mi_1yi_1$ 'name of a god'
* *aˈmiyɒ* (f.)	Fn., *amiyɔ* pers. n. 'awkward, clumsy, left'
* *aˈmɒkε* (f.)	Y., *a*$_2$*mɔ*$_1$*kε*$_3$ pers. n., lit. 'Whom to know is to pet'
* *aˈmɒna* (f.)	Y., *a*$_2$*mɔ*$_2$*na*$_1$ pers. n. 'a guide, leader'; *a*$_1$*mɔ*$_3$*na*$_1$ 'booty, plunder'
* *aˈmoro* (f.)	Y., $a_2mo_2ro_1$ pers. n. 'a priestess of the o_2ro_1 cult'
* *anaˈbidoŋ* (m.)	Man., *anabidoŋ* pers. n. 'the hymn to the Prophet or the dance for the Prophet'
* *aˈnani* (m.)	E., $a_1na_3ni_3$ 'name given the fourth son'
* *aˈnansa* (m.)	Ef., $a_1nan_3sa_3$ 'name of a god'
* *aˈnanse* (m. and f.)	T., *ananse* pers. n. 'spider'; E., $a_1nan_3se_3$ 'spider'
* ˈ*anaŋ* (m.)	T., *anaŋ* 'name given the fourth child'
* *anˈdafo* (f.)	Ib., $a_1da_1fo_1$ pers. n. 'your friend'
anˈde (m.)	E., an_1de_3 'six'

GULLAH PERSONAL NAMES	WEST AFRICAN WORDS
* ˈ*asonɟɛ* (m.)	Y., *a*$_2$*so*$_2$-*n*$_2$*ɟɛ*$_2$ pers. n. 'a cook'
ˈ*asoso* (m.)	Bi., *a*$_3$*so*$_3$*so*$_3$ 'fruit of the plant called *e*$_1$*biɛ*$_3$*ba*$_2$'
* ˈ*asu* (m. and f.)	Fn., *asu* 'husband, male'; T., *asu* 'a river; any body of water
* *asuˈmana* (m.)	V., *a*$_1$*su*$_1$*ma*$_3$*na*$_1$ 'name of a king of the Gallinas (Sierra Leone)'; cf. T., *asumãn-ne* 'magic arts'
* *aˈsuwa* (f.)	Bi., *a*$_1$*sua*$_3$ 'a harmful charm'
* *aˈsũwɔ̃* (f.)	Y., *a*$_1$*sũ*$_2$*wɔ̃*$_2$ pers. n. 'a medicinal plant used as a laxative'; 'a small bag used as a purse'
* *aˈʃalɛ* (f.)	Y., *a*$_2$*ʃa*$_3$*lɛ*$_1$ pers. n. 'barren land, desert'; *a*$_1$*ʃa*:$_2$*lɛ*$_3$ 'evening'
* *aˈʃante* (f.)	G., *a*$_1$*ʃan*$_1$*te*$_3$ 'a district, people, and language of the Gold Coast'; T., *asante*; F., *a*$_1$*san*$_1$*tsi*$_3$
* ˈ*aʃɛ* (m.)	Y., *a*$_1$*ʃɛ*$_2$ pers. n. 'law, commandment'; *a*$_1$*ʃɛ*$_3$ 'menstruation'; *a*:$_1$*ʃɛ*$_2$ 'amen'
* *aˈʃipa* (m.)	Y., *a*$_1$*ʃi*$_1$*kpa*$_2$ pers. n.; 'accidental murder'
* *aˈʃiri* (f.)	Y., *a*$_1$*ʃi*:$_{1-2}$*ri*$_3$ pers. n. 'a secret'
* ˈ*aʃore* (f.)	Y., *a*$_2$*ʃo*:$_2$*re*$_2$ pers. n. 'benefactor'
* *aˈta* (m. and f.)	T., *ata* 'name given the male of twins'; *ata*: 'the female of twins'; E., *a*$_1$*ta*$_3$ 'twin-child'; 'father'; 'palm-wine'; 'leg'; Y., *a*$_2$*ta*$_2$ 'pepper, anything pungent'; *a*$_1$*ta*$_2$ 'a resinous tree'; *a*$_1$*ta*$_1$ 'the ridge at the top of a house'
* *ataˈmɒra* (f.)	Y., *a*$_2$*ta*$_2$*mɔ̃*$_3$*ra*$_2$ pers. n. 'one who entangles himself with many things'; 'a man fully armed'
* *aˈtanu* (m.)	Y., *a*$_1$*ta*$_2$*nu*$_1$ pers. n. 'useless, rejected'
* *aˈtari* (f.)	Y., *a*$_1$*ta*$_2$*ri*$_3$ pers. n. 'the crown of the head'
* *a*$_1$*ti*$_3$ (f.)	E., *a*$_1$*ti*$_3$ 'tree'; T., *ati* 'name of a deity'
* *aˈtiɟɒ* (m.)	Y., *a*$_1$*ti*$_2$*ɟɔ*$_3$ pers. n. 'long ago'
* *atiˈkuzɛ* (m.)	E., *a*$_1$*ti*$_3$*ku*$_3$*zɛ*$_3$ pers. n. 'mimosa,' lit. 'Tree dies at night'
* ˈ*atila* (m.)	Y., *a*$_1$*ti*$_2$*la*$_1$ pers. n. 'salvation'; 'the act of getting rich'; Fn., *atila* 'branch, stick'
aˈtima (f.)	Fn., *atimã* 'leaf'
* *aˈtini* (m.)	Y., *a*$_1$*ti*$_1$*ni*$_{2-1}$ 'the Mohammedan day of the week corresponding to the Christian Monday'; *a*$_2$*ti*$_2$*ni*$_3$ 'attainment, possession'
aˈtiti (m.)	Fn., *atiti* 'pole, mast (of a vessel)'
* *aˈtiwɒ* (m.)	Cf. Fn., *ativɔdũ* 'the sacred tree, a fetish'
* *aˈtɒwɒ* (f.)	Bi., *a*$_1$*tɔ*$_1$*wɔ*$_1$ pers. n. 'inflammation of the fingers or toes'

GULLAH PERSONAL NAMES	WEST AFRICAN WORDS
aˈtori (m.)	Y., $a_1to_2ri_2$ 'a tree remarkable for its toughness, used for bows, ships, etc.'
* *atˈsufe* (f.)	F., $a_1tsu_3\Phi e_3$ 'the husband's home'; cf. E., $a_1tsu_3\Phi oe_3$ 'name given a girl who is the younger of twins when the older child is a boy'
* *aˈtũbi* (m.)	Y., $a_1t\tilde{u}_3bi_2$ pers. n. 'regeneration'
ˈawa (f.)	Fn., *awa* 'arm, wing'; Y., a_2wa_2 'we'
* *ˈawalɒ* (f.)	Y., $a_2wa_3l\text{ɔ}_2$ pers. n. 'We go'
aˈwane (m.)	Fn., *awane* 'the domestic pigeon'
* *aˈwaɲa* (f.)	E., $a_1\beta a_1\text{ɲ}a_1$ pers. n. 'the cause of war'
aˈweku (m.)	E., $a_1ve_3ka_1$ 'a climber, its fruit being the a_1ve_3 nut'
aˈwĩ (f.)	Y., $a_1w\tilde{i}_3$ 'the velvet tamarind'; $a_1w\tilde{i}_1$ 'buying on credit'
* *aˈwinu* (f.)	E., $a_1vi_3nu_3$ pers. n. 'to speak in a whining voice, to be querulous'
* *awleˈkete* (f.)	Fn., *avlekete* 'the genius of the sea'; 'name of a city'
ˈawɒɟi (f.)	Fn., *aɔ̃ɟi* 'spray, foam'
* *ˈawo* (f.)	E., a_1wo_3 'name used in saluting a male or female born on Thursday'; Y., a_2wo_3 'guinea fowl'; Fn., *awo* 'ten'; *avo* 'linen, cloth'
ˈawodi (m.)	Y., $a_1wo_1di_1$ 'the wedge-tailed kite'
* *ˈawoni* (f.)	Y., $a_2wo_2ni_2$ pers. n. 'visitor'
* *aˈwotã* (m.)	Y., $a_1wo_2t\tilde{a}_3$ pers. n. 'a perfect cure'
ˈawu (m.)	E., a_1wu_1 'dress, garment'; a_1vu_3 'dog'; a_1vu_1 'a marsh'; 'wrestling'; Y., $a_2w\tilde{u}_2$ 'a tortoise'; 'a stingy person'
aˈwulu (m.)	Kim., *avulu* 'much, many'
* *aˈwuna* (f.)	*aˈwuna* 'name of a dialect and tribe in Togo eastward of the mouth of the Volta' (called $a\text{ŋ}_1l\text{ɔ}_1$ by the Ewes and *Awuna* by the English)
* *aˈwuni* (f.)	Fn., *awuni* 'Lagos Island (Nigeria)'
aˈwusa (m.)	Y., $a_2wu_1sa_3$ 'a fruit resembling the walnut'; E., $a_1wu_1sa_3$ 'malagetta pepper'
* *aˈwusi* (f.)	E., $a_1wu_3si_3$ 'name used in saluting persons born on Sunday'
* *ˈaya* (f.)	Y., a_2ya_2 pers. n. 'wife'; E., a_1ya_1 'that section of a farm which belongs to the wife or wives'; T., *aya* 'sacred tree'
* *aˈyanɟɛ* (f.)	Y., $a_1y\tilde{a}_1\text{ɟ}\varepsilon_2$ pers. n. 'cheat, imposition'
* *ˈaye* (f.)	Y., $a{:}_1ye_1$ pers. n. 'alive'; a_1ye_1 'room, space'; E., a_1ye_1 'cunning, slyness'; 'a war-dance of women,

GULLAH PERSONAL NAMES	WEST AFRICAN WORDS
	supposed to support the men who are fighting a battle'
ˈayi (f.)	E., *a*$_1$*yi*$_1$ 'a fishing-net'; *a*$_1$*yi*$_3$ 'bean'; 'skin, hide'
* *aˈyiba* (m.)	Fu., *ayiba* pers. n. 'sin, vice' (Ar.)
* *aˈyisa* (f.)	Fn., *ayisã* 'the genius of metal'
* *ayiˈsata* (f.)	Mand., *ayisata* 'name of the preferred wife of Mohammed'
aˈyiya (f.)	Fn., *ayiya* 'corporal punishment, anguish'
* *aˈyiza* (f.)	Fn., *ayizã* 'the tutelary genius of streets'; 'a fetish belt of palm leaves worn to protect one from fire'
* *ˈayɒ* (m.)	Y., *a*$_2$*yɔ*$_1$ pers. n. 'joy, pleasure'
* *ayɒˈdele* (m.)	Y., *a*$_2$*yɔ*$_1$*de*$_3$*le*$_3$ pers. n., lit. 'Joy enters the house'
* *aˈyɒka* (m.)	Y., *a*$_2$*yɔ*$_1$*ka*$_3$ pers. n., lit. 'one who causes joy everywhere'
* *aˈyɒmɒ* (f.)	Y., *a*$_2$*yɔ*$_1$*mɔ*$_2$ 'the wife of a prince'
* *ˈayo* (m.)	Y., *a:*$_1$*yo*$_1$ pers. n. 'a favorite person or thing'; *a*$_2$*yo*$_1$ 'a game called *warry*'; *a*$_2$*yo*$_2$ 'fullness'; Fn., *ayo* 'the Fon word for *Yoruba*, a people and language of Nigeria'
ˈayu (f.)	U., *ayu* 'garlic.' Cf. P., *alho* [aʎu] 'garlic'
* *aˈyuba* (m.)	Mand., *ayuba* 'Job'
ˈaza (f.)	E., *a*$_1$*za*$_1$ 'a steep declivity'; Fn., *aza* 'a house'
* *aˈzama* (m.)	Bi., *a*$_1$*za*$_3$*ma*$_1$ 'a deity of the *ɔ*$_3$*ba*$_3$, the ruler of Benin'
ˈaze (m.)	Fn., *aze* 'itch, mange'; I., *a*$_3$*ze*$_1$ 'fish'
ˈazɛ (m.)	Bi., *a*$_1$*zɛ*$_1$ 'a fee'
* *aziˈzɒnɒ* (f.)	Fn., *azizɔ̃nɔ̃* pers. n. 'ill, infirm'
* *ˈazɒ* (m.)	Fn., *azɔ̃* pers. n. 'illness'
aˈzɒde (f.)	Fn., *azɔ̃de* 'sometimes'
* *aˈzɒnɒ* (f.)	Fn., *azɔ̃nɔ̃* pers. n. 'illness'

[b]

ba (m. and f.)	Y., *ba*$_3$ 'to meet'; *ba*$_2$ 'to hide'; *ba*$_1$ 'bent'; 'to roost'; E., *ba*$_1$ 'mud'; 'to cheat'; Man., *ba* 'mother'; 'river'; 'big'; cf. Eng., *bar*
* *ˈbaba* (m.)	Y., *ba*$_2$*ba*$_2$ pers. n. 'father'; *ba*$_1$*ba*$_1$ 'guinea corn'; *ba:*$_2$*ba:*$_2$ 'indicating the manner of the hovering of a bird'; H., *ba:*$_1$*ba*$_2$ 'father'; W., *baba* 'grain'; K., *baba* 'to burn'; 'to knock'; Kim., *baba* 'to pat'; E., *ba*$_1$*ba*$_{1-3}$ 'an expression of sympathy'; *ba*$_1$*ba*$_1$ 'termite'; 'a venereal disease'; M., *baba* 'hut, temporary shelter'

GULLAH PERSONAL NAMES	WEST AFRICAN WORDS
* *ba'badu* (m.)	E., $ba_1ba_1ḍu_{1-3}$ pers. n. 'eaten by termites'
* *ba'banla* (m. and f.)	Y., $ba_2ba_2\text{-}n_3la_3$ 'grandfather'
* *baba'lawo* (m.)	Y., $ba_2ba_2la_3wo_2$ 'a priest of Ifa, god of divination'
* *ˌbabalori'ʃa* (m.)	Y., $ba_2ba_2lo_3ri_1ʃa_1$ 'idolatrous priest'
* *ˌbabaluɒɪ'ye* (f.)	Y., $ba_2ba_2lu_3ai_1ye_3$[21] 'the god of smallpox (also called $ɔ_2mɔ_2lu_3$).' See $ɔ_2ba_2o_2lu_3ai_1ye_3$.
baba'ta (m.)	K., *babata* 'to feel one's way'
* *baba'tunde* (m.)	Y., $ba_2ba_2tũ_3de_3$ 'name given a male child born soon after the death of its grandfather,' lit. 'Father comes again.' (The sire is supposed to reappear in the newly-born child.)
* *'babɒɪ* (m.)	H., $ba{:}_3bai_3$ pers. n. (pl. of $ba{:}_1ba{:}_2$) 'eunuchs, impotent men'; V., ba_2bai_1 pers. n. m.
* *'babo* (m.)	B., *babo* 'a kind of spirit that is reputed to eat female goats'
ba'bu (m.)	B., *babu* 'conversation'; K., *babu* 'a spit on which fish are threaded'
* *'bada* (m.)	E., ba_1da_1 'muddy, swampy'; gba_1da_1 'to be out of one's senses'; Y., ba_2da_1 'lieutenant'; gba_2da_2 'a large knife'; Fn., *gbada* 'evening'; cf. H., $ba{:}_3da_1ha_2nya_1$ 'an official title among women in Daura'
* *'bade* (m.)	Y., ba_3de_3 pers. n. 'to be suitable'; ba_2de_1 'to lie in ambush for'; Fn., *gbade* 'walnut'
'badi (m.)	K., *mbadi* 'a cloth of native manufacture made of the fiber of frondlets of the *mpusu* palm'; toughness, firmness'
ba'doro (m.)	B., *badoro* 'name of a plant of the Niger'
* *'badu* (m.)	T., *badu* 'name given the tenth male child of a mother'; Y., ba_3du_1 'to compete with another'; E., $ba_1ḍu_3$ 'name given the tenth son'
* *'bafa* (m.)	Y., ba_3fa_1 'to argue with'; E., ba_1fa_3 pers. n. 'lame from birth'
* *ba'fata* (m.)	Man., *ba fata* pers. n. 'high-tide,' lit. 'The sea or river is full'
* *'bafɛ* (f.)	Y., $gba_3fɛ_3$ pers. n. 'to be fond of show'
* *'bafĩ* (m. and f.)	Y., $ba{:}_1fĩ_2$ ($i_2ba{:}_1fĩ_2$) 'the eunuchs in the palace of the king of the Yoruba (also called $i_1wɛ_1fa_1$)'
'baga (m.)	E., $ba_1ga{:}_1$ 'thin, wavering'
ba'gaya (m.)	B., *bagaya* 'blue'; 'to make blue'
* *'baɟɛ* (m.)	Y., $ba_3ɟɛ_2$ pers. n. 'to eat with'; $ba_1ɟɛ_3$ 'to corrupt'
* $ba_1ɟi_3$ (m.)	Y., $ba_3ɟi_3$ pers. n. 'to wake with'

GULLAH PERSONAL NAMES	WEST AFRICAN WORDS
* ˈ*baɟɒ* (m.)	Y., *ba*$_3$*ɟɔ*$_2$ pers. n. 'agreeable, similar'
ˈ*baka* (f.)	E., *ba*$_{3-1}$*ka*$_1$ 'a bird resembling the canary; *ba*$_1$*ka*:$_1$ 'wide'; *ba*$_1$*ka*$_1$ 'to mix'; Y., *ba*$_3$*ka*$_1$ 'to help to count'; Kim., *baka* 'to keep'; K., *baka* 'to obtain'; 'to tear'; 'to disclose'; 'to charge with'; T., *baka* 'a lake communicating with the sea'; H., *ba*$_1$*ka*:$_2$ 'a bow (weapon)'
baˈkali (m.)	M., *gbakali* (*kpakali*) 'a chair or seat having three legs, made from a three-pronged branch of a tree'
* *baˈkarɪ* (m.)	B., *bakari* pers. n. m. (Ar.) Mand., *bakari* 'name given the second son'
ˈ*baki* (f.)	K., *mbaki* 'ambush, ambuscade'
* ˈ*bala* (m.)	Mand., *bala* 'name given a child by its mother when its birth has been difficult'; E., *ba*$_3$*la*$_3$ 'to be attached to'; 'a river-fish'; K., *bala* 'to grow'; B., *bala* (*bara*) 'xylophone'; 'hunger'
baˈlana (m)	B., *balana* 'accidentally'
* *baˈlaye* (m.)	Y., *gba*$_1$*la*$_3$*ye*$_1$ pers. n. 'to occupy one's room or place'
* ˈ*bale* (m.)	Y., *ba*$_1$*le*$_3$ 'to light upon'; *ba*:$_2$*le*$_3$ pers. n. 'landlord'; M., *mbale* 'a hoop for climbing palm trees'
* *baˈlɛma* (m.)	M., *gbalɛma* pers. n. 'a sore, an ulcer'
* ˈ*bali* (f.)	E., *ba*$_1$*li*$_1$ 'valley'; B., *bali* 'to defend'; Fn., *gbali* 'the native name for *La Baranquere* or *Abanankin*'
baˈlɒɟa (m.)	Y., *gba*$_1$*lɔ*$_3$*ɟa*$_2$ 'to brace, to girdle'
* ˈ*bama* (f.)	Man., *bama* pers. n. 'mother'; K., *bama* 'to scold'; 'to tighten'; T., *bam:a* 'the projecting lower part of the wall in native houses, used as a seat'; 'a strip of country-cloth'; B., *bama* pers. n. 'alligator'
* *baˈmale* (f.)	B., *bamale* pers. n. 'a platform'
* ˈ*bamba* (m. and f.)	V., *ba*$_3$*mba*$_3$ pers. n.; K., *bamba* 'a native broker'; 'to tie well'; *mbamba* 'a district of the old kingdom of Kongo, between San Salvador and the coast'; 'cane'; 'a demijohn'; 'the coronella snake'; I., *ba*$_3$*m*$_1$*ba*$_3$ 'to scold'; Mand., *bamba* 'crocodile'
* ˈ*bambali* (m.)	B., *bambali* pers. n. 'without end, immortal'
bambaˈre (m.)	H., '*bam*$_1$'*ba*$_1$*ṛe*:$_2$ 'to rub off completely'
* ˈ*bambo* (m.)	Man., *bambo* 'crocodile, the totem of a Mandinka noble clan, the Mamburi'
* ˈ*bambuk* (m.)	*bambuk* 'name of a place south of the Senegal'
ˈ*bambula* (m.)	K., *bambula* 'to transfer by witchcraft the property of one person to another'; Ki., *bambula* 'to change'

GULLAH PERSONAL NAMES	WEST AFRICAN WORDS
'bame (m.)	Fn., *gbame* 'a marsh'
ba'medo (f.)	Fn., *gbamedo* 'to betray'
bam'wuka (m.)	K., *bamvuka* 'to crack' (said of the earth)
* *'bana* (f.)	Y., ba_3na_3 'to spend together'; B., *bana* 'illness'; 'silk cotton-tree'; Man., *ba:na* 'the last month of the year'
'banda (m.)	K., *banda* 'to make a choice'; 'to make fast'; 'to climb'; 'a cap'
banda'kana (m.)	K., *bandakana* 'to be piled one on the top of the other'
'bando (f.)	Bo., *mbando* 'the fee given to a doctor'
* *ban'duka* (m.)	K., *banduka* pers. n. 'to be disfigured'
* *'bani* (f.)	B., *bani* 'a small female goat'; 'a small stream'; Fu., *bani* 'bush cows'; Mand., *bani* 'name of a river in the Mandingo country'
* *'banɟa* (m.)	V., $gban_3dʒa_3$ pers. n. m.; Y., $gban_1ɟa_2$ 'a kola nut of only two sections'
ban'ʒiya (m.)	K., *banʒia* 'a lid'
* *ban'ɟɒli* (m.)	W., *banɟɒli* pers. n. 'ostrich'
'bano (m.)	H., $ba{:}_3no{:}_3$ 'an eel'
'bantiya (m.)	T., *abantia* 'a small fort, a prison'
'banza (m.)	K., *banza* 'to think'; Kim., *banza* 'to think'
'baɲa (m.)	V., $gba_1ɲa_1$ 'blacksmith's tongs'; 'to squeeze'
* *'baɲin* (m.)	F., $ba_3ɲin_3$ pers. n. 'a man'
* *'baɲun* (m.)	*baɲun* 'name of a language of the Western Sudanic section, spoken principally in the territory south of Senegal—Southern Portuguese Guinea'
* *baŋ'bala* (m.)	Y., $ba_3\text{-}^{22}ŋ_2gba_3la_1$ pers. n., lit. 'Let us save'
* *baŋbo'ʃe* (m.)	Y., $ba_3\text{-}ŋ_2gbo_3ʃe_3$ pers. n., lit. 'Carry this load with me'
* *'baŋga* (m. and f.)	W., *baŋga* 'pumpkin'; K., *baŋga* 'to search for medicinal barks and roots'; 'a plank house'; Tl., *baŋga* 'to begin'; 'to be betrothed to'; M., *baŋga* 'large'; V., $gba_1ŋga_1$ pers. n. f.
'baŋga'baŋga (m.)	Tl., *baŋgabaŋga* 'long ago'
* *baŋ'gala* (m.)	K., *mbaŋgala* 'the season when the grass is burned (July to October)'; 'a stick'
* *'baŋgi* (m.)	B., *baŋgi* pers. n. 'to give birth to'; K., *mbaŋgi*, 'herbalist'; 'a witness'
* *baŋ'gika* (m.)	K., *baŋgika* pers. n. 'to commit to the torments of hell'; 'to send a person out in a very hot sun'; 'to oppress'; 'oppression'

GULLAH PERSONAL NAMES	WEST AFRICAN WORDS
ˈ*baŋgo* (m.)	H., *baŋ*$_3$*go:*$_3$ 'a wall of any kind whatever'
ˈ*baŋgola* (m.)	Bo., *baŋgola* 'to lift up, to open'; 'to notch'
* ˈ*baŋgu* (m.)	K., *mbaŋgu* pers. n. 'a skillful person'; 'a basket'; 'ridgepole'
ˈ*baŋguˈbaŋgu* (m.)	K., *mbaŋgubaŋgu* 'the bark of the *mbaŋgu* tree, given to patients suffering from *nsaku* (an ailment characterized by pains in the back)'
baŋˈgula (m.)	K., *baŋgula* 'to take to pieces'; 'to divulge'
* *baŋˈgura* (m.)	*baŋgura* 'name of a family in Sierra Leone the members of which at one time are said to have been leaders of the Susu horders in the Egyptian Sudan'
ˈ*baŋka* (m.)	W., *baŋka* 'to clash with'; 'to cause bankruptcy'
ˈ*baŋke* (m.)	H., *baŋ*$_3$*ke*$_1$ 'to collide with and knock over'
* ˈ*baŋkɒ* (m.)	V., *baŋ*$_1$*kɔ*$_{3-1}$ 'name of a district in the Gallinas country (Sierra Leone)'
* *baŋˈkɒle* (m.)	Y., *ba*$_3$*-ŋ*$_2$*kɔ*$_3$*le*$_3$ pers. n., lit. 'With me build a house'
* ˈ*bara* (m.)	Y., *ba*$_2$*ra*$_2$ 'god of mischief'; *ba*$_1$*ra*$_1$ 'a creeper which bears the *e*$_1$*gu*$_2$*si*$_3$ oil seed'; B., *bara* 'calabash'; 'protuberance'; 'work'; 'bravado'; V., *ba*$_3$*ra*$_1$ pers. n. m.
* ˈ*baraka* (f.)	Mand., *ba:raka* pers. n. 'Thanks' (Ar.)
ˈ*baram* (m.)	W., *ba:ram* 'finger'
ˈ*bare* (m.)	T., *bare* 'to cover'; H., *ba:*$_1$*re:*$_2$ 'a stranger'
* ˈ*bari* (m.)	H., *ba*$_3$*ṛi*$_1$ 'to leave off'; Ef., *ba*$_2$*ri*$_2$ pers. n. 'to be dirty'; S., *bari* 'horse'
ˈ*basa* (m.)	Y., *ba*$_3$*sa*$_1$ 'parlor'; *ba*$_3$*sa*$_3$ 'to elope'; E., *ba*$_1$*sa:*$_1$ 'scattered'; B., *basa* 'lizard'; K., *basa* 'a bedstead covered with a mat'; 'to cut'; *mbasa* 'a hunter's whistle'; 'midrib or leaf stem of palm-frond'
* *baˈsalɒ* (m.)	Y., *ba*$_3$*sa*$_3$*lɔ*$_2$ pers. n. 'to elope'
* ˈ*base* (m.)	Man., *ba:se* 'name of a place in the Mandinka country'
* ˈ*basi* (f.)	B., *basi* 'couscous'; 'amulet'; 'of a dark or brown color'; Y., *ba*$_3$*si*$_3$ 'how?'
* ˈ*baso* (m.)	Man., *bas:o* pers. n. 'lizard'
baˈsuka (m.)	K., *basuka* 'to be released, to burst'
ˈ*baʃi* (f.)	K., *baʃi* 'a chip, splinter'; Kim., *mbaʃi* 'a turtle'
* *baʃɒˈrũ* (m.)	Y., *ba*$_2$*ʃɔ*$_1$*rũ*$_2$ 'a privy-counsellor' (also *ɔ*$_2$*ba*$_2$*ʃɔ*$_1$*rũ*$_2$)
ˈ*bata* (f.)	Y., *ba*$_1$*ta*$_3$ 'the drum used by the *ʃaŋ*$_1$*go*$_3$ and the *e*$_2$*gũ*$_3$*gũ*$_3$ worshippers'; *ba*$_3$*ta*$_1$ 'a small can, a snuff-

GULLAH PERSONAL NAMES	WEST AFRICAN WORDS
	box'; ba_1ta_1 'boot or shoe'; E., ba_1ta_1 'to cleave to'; V., gba_1ta_1 'broad, stout'; I., ba_1ta_3 'to enter'
* *baˈtafo* (m.)	T., *batafo* pers. n. 'the wild boar'
baˈtakoto (m.)	Y., $ba_1ta_3ko_2to_2$ 'a kind of drum'
* *ˈbati* (m.)	Y., ba_1ti_1 'to miss one's aim'; ba_2ti_1 'to crouch by the side of one'; M., *bati* pers. n. 'a grassy swamp'
baˈtika (m.)	K., *batika* 'to stick on, to dress (a wound)'; 'to begin'
baˈtɒɪgi (m.)	Y., $ba_1tai_2gi_2$ ($ba_1ta_2gi_2$) 'a wooden shoe'
ˈbato (m.)	E., $gba_1to{:}_1$ 'flat and round'; M., *gbato* 'a leather whip'
ˈbatu (m.)	H., $ba_1tu{:}_2$ 'a conversation'
baˈtumba (m.)	K., *batumba* 'equality'
ˈbawɒla (f.)	K., *bawɔla* 'coffin'
* *ˈbaya* (f.)	E., $ba_1ya{:}_1$ pers. n. 'soft, fleshy'; K., *baya* 'to shine'; B., *baya* 'maternity'; M., *baya* 'treachery'; T., *baya:* 'wide open'
* *baˈyani* (f.)	Y., *ba:*$_2$*yã*$_1$*ni*$_1$ pers. n. 'an object or idol venerated by *ʃaŋ*$_1$*go*$_3$ worshippers'
ˈbayi (f.)	Y., ba_3yi_3 'to make shift with'; T., *bayi* 'witchcraft, sorcery'; W., *bayi* 'to leave'
baˈzula (f.)	K., *bazula* 'to ache (spoken only of the head)'
be (m. and f.)	E., be_1 'to hide'; 'a grass used for thatching'; be_3 'to speak'; 'to cut away'; $be{:}_3$ 'secretly'; Y., gbe_3 'to carry'; M., *gbe* 'to cease'; Mand., *mbe* 'name given the fifth son'; cf. Eng., *bay*
ˈbebe (f.)	E., be_3be_3 'to lay bare'; Y., be_1be_1 'brink, edge'
ˈbede (f.)	Y., gbe_3de_1 'to know a language'; Fn., *gbede* 'a day'
* *ˈbedu* (m.)	T., *bedu* pers. n.; *abedua* 'palm-tree'
* *ˈbega* (f.)	Y., gbe_3ga_2 pers. n. 'to exalt'; Fn., *gbega* 'pot, saucepan'; cf. Eng., *beggar*
* *ˈbegbe* (m.)	M., *gbegbe* (*kpegbe*) pers. n. 'a frog'
beˈhɒme (m.)	Fn., *gbehɔme* 'a grange, barn'
ˈbehu (m.)	T., *behu* 'infant's food prepared from palm-nuts'
* *ˈbeɟi* (m.)	E., *gbe*$_1$*ɟi*$_3$ 'a large, uninhabited bush-country'; Fn., *gbeɟi* 'the genius of the chase'
ˈbeka (f.)	E., be_1ka_{1-3} 'a rope made of grass'; K., *beka* 'to delay'
ˈbeke (f.)	H., $be{:}_3ke_3$ 'a surprise'
* *beˈkelɛ* (m.)	K., *mbekele* 'the nickname given a short person'
beˈkɒla (f.)	K., *bekɔla* 'to turn over'
* *ˈbela* (m.)	K., *bela* 'to perch'; *mbela* 'illness'; 'near at hand'; M., *mbela* pers. n. 'father-in-law'

GULLAH PERSONAL NAMES	WEST AFRICAN WORDS
* ˈ*bele* (m.)	E., be_1le_1 'a skin disease'; $be_{1-3}le_1$ 'a big frog'; M., *gbele* pers. n. 'to become desperate'; 'to forsake'
* *beˈleŋgɒ* (m.)	M., *gbeleŋgɒ* pers. n. 'to be busy'
* ˈ*beli* (f.)	E., $be_{1-3}li_1$ 'weak, sickly'; W., *beli* pers. n. 'to be amiable'
* ˈ*bembɒ* (m.)	K., *mbembɔ* pers. n. 'news, fame'
* ˈ*bena* (m.)	T., *benã* pers. n. 'the genius of Tuesday, used in saluting persons born on that day'; B., *bena* 'the place of the mother's birth'
* *beˈnaze* (m.)	Fn., *gbenazẽ* 'ripe grain'; 'the twelfth king of Dahomey'
ˈ*benda* (m.)	K., *benda* 'to be crooked'; M., *mbenda* 'a small deer'
ˈ*bende* (m.)	K., *mbende* 'a rat'
benˈdesa (f.)	K., *bendesa* 'to make crooked'
* ˈ*bene* (f.)	B., *bene*, pers. n. f. 'the sesame'; W., *bene* 'the sesame'
* ˈ*beni* (m.)	Mand., *beni* 'one who has the same name as that of his maternal uncle'; K., *mbeni* 'opponent, foe'
* *beˈnin* (m.)	*benin* 'name of a city and section of Nigeria'
* ˈ*beɲin* (m.)	F., $be_3ɲin_3$ pers. n. 'a male'
beŋ (m.)	Man., *beŋ* 'to meet'
* ˈ*bera* (f.)	H., $be{:}_3ra_1$ 'a girl whose mammary glands have not yet developed'; T., *bera* 'come' (imp.)
beˈranda (f.)	W., *beranda* 'a long pole used for propelling a boat'
ˈ*bere* (m.)	T., *bere* 'to grow or become red or yellow'; Man., *bere* 'to hail'; 'ravage by hail'
ˈ*berɛ* (m.)	T., *berɛ* 'the leaves of the oil-palm'
* ˈ*bese* (f.)	T., be_1se_1 (be_3se_3) 'a kind of amulet'; Y., be_3se_3 'saddlecloth'; Fn., *gbese* 'frog'; B., *besɛ* 'a male flirt, overnice in dress'
* *beˈsela* (m.)	E., pers. n. $gbe_1se_1la_3$ 'one who is obedient'; 'an interpreter'
* ˈ*bete* (f.)	Man., *be:te* pers. n. 'to be good'; E., be_1te_3 'something attractive'; $be_1te{:}_1$ 'fortunate, blessed'; 'cool'; be_1te_1 'a small dagger'
beˈtela (m.)	K., *betela* 'equality, accord'
* *betˈsiwi* (f.)	E., $gbe_1tsi_1vi_3$ pers. n. 'a bad, mischievous person'
ˈ*bewɒ* (f.)	Y., $gbe_3wɔ_1$ 'to put on'
ˈ*beya* (f.)	I., bea_3 'to come'

GULLAH PERSONAL NAMES	WEST AFRICAN WORDS
* *be'zuyi* (m.)	Fn., *gbezui* pers. n. 'the hare'
'*bɛbɛ* (f.)	Y., $bɛ_2bɛ_2$ 'a feat'
* '*bɛlɛ* (f.)	Bi., $bɛ_1lɛ_3$ 'to wane'; M., *bɛlɛ* 'trousers'; V., $b'ɛ_1lɛ_1$ 'trousers'; $bɛ_3lɛ_1$ 'name given a member of the Poro Society'
* '*bɛlɪma* (m.)	V., $bɛ_3lɪ_3ma_3$ pers. n. m. 'Be good,' lit. 'good on'
* '*bɛndɛ* (f.)	Y., $bɛn_3dɛ_3$ pers. n. 'a blow with the fist'
* '*bɛndu* (m.)	V., $bɛn_1du_1$ pers. n. m. 'name of a place near Cape Mount on Lake Piso (Liberia)'
bɛŋ (m.)	T., $bɛŋ_1$ 'to approach'; $bɛŋ_3$ 'horn'
* '*bɛrɛ* (m.)	Y., $bɛ{:}_2rɛ_2$ 'the harvest home festival (occurring in January) during which the fields are set on fire to indicate that they have been cleared of the fruits'; $bɛ_3rɛ_1$ 'a title of dignity among women'; 'grass used for thatching'; $bɛ_1rɛ_1$ 'to begin'; 'to bend down'; 'flat, low'; $bɛ_1rɛ_3$ 'sloping'; V., $b'ɛ_1rɛ_1$ ($b'ɛ_1lɛ_1$) 'trousers'
* '*bɛri* (m.)	Y., $bɛ_3ri_3$ 'to behead'; 'to give a military salute'; V., $bɛ_3ri_1$ ($bɛ_3li_1$) 'a male youth organization—a branch of the society known as $pɔ_3rɔ_3$ ($pɔ_3lɔ_3$)'; 'a ceremonial rite'; cf. Eng., *Berry*
* '*bɛrimɒ* (m.)	V., $bɛ_3ri_1mɔ_1$ ($bɛ_3li_1mɔ_1$) 'one who has performed the $bɛ_3ri_1$ ($bɛ_3li_1$) rite, a ceremony during which the male receives the national mark on his back and a new name, at the same time being given certain instructions which he keeps strictly secret, for death is threatened if one reveals the $bɛ_3ri_1$ secrets to the uninitiated'
* '*bɛtɛ* (f.)	T., *bɛtɛ:* pers. n. 'soft, weak'; Bi., $bɛ_3tɛ{:}_3$ pers. n. 'very big'
'*bɛyi* (m.)	W., *bɛi* (*mbɛi*) 'a goat'
mbi (*f.*)	K., *mbi* 'evil-doing'
'*biba* (m.)	Y., bi_3ba_2 'a meeting'; 'that which is to be met'; Fn., *biba* 'hat'; K., *biba* 'to strike'
* '*bibi* (m.)	Y., bi_3bi_3 pers. n. 'begotten'; Bi., bi_1bi_3 'to move to and fro'
bi'biri (m.)	T., *bibiri* 'dark-blue cloth'
* '*bida* (m.)	Man., *bida* 'black cobra, the totem of a noble clan of the Gambia'; *bida* 'a Nupe city (Northern Nigeria)'
'*bidi* (m.)	K., *mbidi* 'an abundance'; Fn., *gbidi* 'to wear out'
'*bidi'bidi* (f.)	K., *bidibidi* 'a bird'; E., $bi_1ḍi_1bi_1ḍi_1$ 'smooth, soft'

GULLAH PERSONAL NAMES	WEST AFRICAN WORDS
bigˈbada (m.)	Fn., *gbigbada* 'suspicion'
ˈbigbi (m.)	Fn., *gbigbi* 'cooked, boiled, roasted'
* *ˈbigɒˈbigɒ* (m.)	Cf. Bi., $bi_3gɔ_3bi_1gɔ_1bi_3gɔ_3$ pers. n. 'a term descriptive of something very crooked, e.g., a cripple walking zigzag'
* *ˈbiɟi* (f.)	K., *mbiʒi* 'uncooked meat'; M., *mbidʒi* pers. n. 'cunning, crafty'
* *biˈkira* (f.)	B., *bikira* pers. n. 'a young girl' (Ar.)
ˈbikula (f.)	K., *bikula* 'spasm of wind (spoken of infants only)'; Tl., *bikula* 'to drink voraciously; to supplant'
ˈbila (f.)	Y., bi_1la_1 'to make way'; Man., *bila* 'to draw (such as water)'; Kim., *bila* 'to look after the cattle'; Tl., *bila* 'to boil, to roar'; 'to call'
* *biˈlahi* (m.)	B., *bil:ahi* pers. n. 'by God'
* *bɪˈlali* (m.)	Mand., *bila:li* 'the first muezzin, son of Ali'
* *ˈbili* (m.)	Mand., *bili* 'name given a child born with curvature of the spine'; V., bi_3li_3 pers. n. m.; M., *bili* 'to fire a gun, to throw'; B., *bili* 'the foreground of a house'; 'to cover a house'; 'a bridge over a river'; I., bi_1li_3 'to rise'
biˈlisa (f.)	B., *bilisa* 'bushes, brushwood'
* *ˈbiliwa* (m.)	M., *mbiliwa* (*mbiriwa*) pers. n. m., lit. 'big drum'
ˈbilu (m.)	Y., bi_1lu_2 'to push heavily against another'; H., $bi{:}_3lu{:}_3$ 'a large beer-pot'
biˈluŋgi (m.)	K., *biluŋgɪ* 'hell'
bim (m.)	T., bim_1 'violently'; bim_3 'a term imitative of the sound of beating'
ˈbima (m.)	K., *bima* 'to rest a load on the staff carried by porters'
* *ˈbimba* (m.)	K., *bimba* pers. n. 'to wrestle with'; 'to test'; 'to be clapped to by someone who is about to make a salute'
* *ˈbimbi* (m.)	Fu., *bimbi* pers. n. 'early morning, approximately 5:30 A.M.'
ˈbimɛ (m.)	M., *bimɛ* (*pimɛ*) 'to run'; 'running'
* *ˈbimɒ* (m.)	Y., $bi_3mɔ_2$ pers. n. 'to give birth to a child'
* *ˈbina* (m. and f.)	Mand., *bina* 'one whose name is the same as that of his paternal uncle'; B., *bina* pers. n. m.; V., bi_3na_3 'horn'
ˈbinda (f.)	K., *binda* 'to braid, to bolt'; 'to change'; Kim., *binda* 'to bind in a net'

GULLAH PERSONAL NAMES	WEST AFRICAN WORDS
* ˈbindi (m.)	M., *bindi* pers. n. m.; K., *mbindi* 'one who locks up'; 'a bolt'
* ˈbini (m.)	B., *bini* 'to go to bed'; 'to descend'; V., $b'i_1ni_3$ 'porcupine'; cf. *Bini* 'name of the people and language of the Benin Province (Southern Nigeria)
* ˈbinta (f.)	Mand. and W., *binta* 'daughter of Mohammed'
* ˈbintu (f.)	Mand., *bintu* 'daughter of Mohammed'
ˈbiŋga (m.)	Tl., *biŋga* 'to be acquitted'; K., *biŋga* 'to take up room'
* biˈrahima (m.)	Mand., *bira:hima* 'Abraham'
* biˈrama (m.)	Mand., *birama* 'Abraham'
* ˈbiri (m.)	B., *biri* pers. n. 'a pigeon'; Y., bi_1ri_3 'suddenly'
ˈbiribi (f.)	T., *biribi* 'something'
* ˈbiriti (f.)	Tem., *biriti* pers. n. m.
ˈbisa (f.)	T., *bisa* 'to question'; B., *bǐsa* 'a supple switch for whipping'
ˈbise (f.)	T., *bise* 'kola nut.' Cf. E., bi_1si_3 'kola nut'
* ˈbisi (m.)	Y., bi_3si_2 'to increase'; cf. $ɔ_2la_3bi_3si_3$ pers. n. 'increased honors'; E., bi_1si_3 'kola nut'; $bi_1si{:}_1$ 'whirling'
* biˈsigi (f.)	B., *bisigi* pers. n. 'image, representation'; 'intention'; 'to think'
ˈbiti (f.)	K., *biti* 'a marimba'
ˈbitili (m.)	M., *bitili* 'unbroken, whole'
biˈtoŋga (m.)	Cf. Tl., *bitoŋgatoŋga* 'open, wide, large'
* ˈbitsi (f.)	T., *bitsi* pers. n. 'a swoon, a faint'
ˈbiya (m.)	E., bia_3 'to beg'; $bi\tilde{a}_1$ 'to be red, glowing'; Kim., *bia* 'to burn'
* biˈyɒla (f.)	K., *biɔla* pers. n. 'to learn to speak very early'
* bɒˈakɒɪ (m.)	V., $bɔa_3kai_3$ pers. n. m.
ˈbɒba (m. and f.)	K., *bɔba* 'to pick up with the beak'; 'a woman who has borne children'; *mbɔba* 'basket'
* ˈbɒbi (m.)	E., $bɔ_1bi{:}_1$ pers. n. 'quiet, bashful'
* ˈbɒbɒ (m.)	E., $bɔ_1bɔ_1$ 'to be soft, to be mild'; $bɔ_1bɔ_{1-3}$ 'a food consisting of boiled beans'; K., *bɔbɔ* 'the lip'; V., $bɔ_1bɔ_1$ 'name given a boy when his real name is not known, the corresponding name for a girl being ti_1ti_3'
$bɒ_1bɒ_1bɒ_1$ (m.)	K., *bɔbɔbɔ* 'cruelty'; *mbɔbɔbɔ* 'woodpecker'; Bi., $bɔ_1bɔ_1bɔ_1$ 'gentle drumming'

GULLAH PERSONAL NAMES	WEST AFRICAN WORDS
bɒˈbɒla (m.)	K., *bɔbɔla* 'to make a hollow sound'
ˈ*bɒbɒyɛ* (m.)	E., *bɔ*$_1$*bɔ*$_1$*ɛ*$_3$ 'low, soft'
* *bɒˈdome* (m.)	E., *gbɔ*$_1$*do*$_{1-3}$*me*$_1$ 'town—the town in which the person speaking lives'
* ˈ*bɒfo* (m.)	T., *bɔfo* pers. n. m.; *ɔbɔfo* 'messenger'
* *bɒɪ* (f.)	M., *bɔɪ* 'name given the first female child of the family'; cf. Eng., *boy*
* ˈ*bɒɪdi* (m.)	B., *baidi* 'the popular name of Ahmadou, the ancient king of Ségou'
* ˈ*bɒɪna* (f.)	H., *bai*$_3$*na:*$_3$ pers. n. 'the Senegal rose-colored fire-finch'
* ˈ*bɒɟɒ* (m.)	E., *gbɔ*$_3$*ɟɔ*$_3$ pers. n. 'to be weak, faint, weary'
* ˈ*bɒlɒ* (m.)	K., *mbɔlɔ* 'film, scum'; 'unripe pod or husk'; M., *bɔlɒ* 'cap'; 'a charm or fetish'; *mbɔlɒ* 'a worm'
* ˈ*bɒma* (m.)	K., *bɔma* 'fear'; *mbɔma* pers. n. 'the black python'; 'wall plate'
ˈ*bɒmbɒ* (m.)	K., *bɔmbɔ* 'ball of the heel'; *mbɔmbɔ* 'smoky mist, haze'; 'nose'; Kim., *mbɔmbɔ* 'the manioc or cassava-root after it has been fermented and dried'
ˈ*bɒni* (m.)	Y., *bɔ̃*$_1$*ni*$_3$ 'a species of acacia used in tanning'
* ˈ*bɒnɒ* (m.)	E., *bɔ*$_1$*nɔ*$_1$ 'a river-fish; K., *mbɔnɔ* 'the castor-oil plant'; M., *bɔnɒ* 'to sell all'; *mbɒnɒ* pers. n. 'extravagant'
bɒŋ (m.)	T., *bɔŋ* 'to crow'; 'to penetrate'
ˈ*bɒŋgɒ* (m.)	K., *mbɔŋgɔ* 'kola nuts'; 'cloth, goods, property'; 'general name for vegetables and other things cultivated for food'.
* ˈ*bɒra* (m.)	Y., *bɔ*$_3$*ra*$_2$ pers. n. 'to undress'
bɒˈre (m.)	T., *bɔre* 'to excavate, to search for'
ˈ*bɒsa* (m).	K., *bɔsa* 'to crush'
* ˈ*bɒte* (m.)	K., *mbɔte* pers. n. 'goodness, excellence'
ˈ*bɒtima* (f.)	V., *gbɔ*$_3$*ti*$_3$*ma*$_3$ 'a coarse-grained rice'
bɒˈtɒmba (m.)	K., *bɔtɔmba* 'thickness, density (of liquids)'
ˈ*bɒula* (f.)	K., *baula* 'bark, shell, the wing-case of insects'
ˈ*bɒuli* (m.)	B., *bauli* 'to urinate' (Ar.)
ˈ*bɒza* (m.)	K., *bɔza* 'to puff'
* *bo* (m.)	E., *bo:*$_3$ 'far away, high up'; Man., *bo* 'to go out of'; Y., *bo*$_3$ 'to peel'; *bo*$_1$ 'rich in foliage'; 'to cover'; M., *bo:* 'name of a town in Sierra Leone'; E., *bo*$_1$ 'a farm'; 'the world of the dead'; *bo*$_1$ 'tree-bark';

GULLAH PERSONAL NAMES	WEST AFRICAN WORDS
	'charm'; Fn., *gbo* 'charm'; 'the genius of war'; cf. Eng., *bow*
bo'adi (m.)	Cf. T., *aboadi* 'treating one cruelly'
* *bo'adu* (m.)	T., *boadu* pers. n.
* *'bobo* (m.)	V., bo_3bo_3 pers. n. 'a person who cannot talk'; E., bo_3bo_3 'a call'; bo_1bo_3 'a cloth'; Y., bo_1bo_3 'wild acacia, the fruit of which is used as a cure for whitlow'; Bi., bo_1bo_3 'to move to and fro'
'bobu (m.)	H., bo_3bu_1 'ulceration of the mouth—a variant form of $bu{:}_3bu_1$'
'boda (m.)	Fn., *gboda* 'to play'
* *'bode* (m.)	Y., bo_2de_1 pers. n. 'the town's gate, custom-house'
'bogo (m.)	B., *bogo* 'loamy earth, clay'
* *'boɟan* (m.)	Man., *bodʒan* 'name of a noble clan whose totem is the *kuto* 'turtle'
'boɟe (m.)	Fn., *gboɟe* 'to rest'; 'to breathe'
'boɟi (m.)	Y., $bo_1ɟi_2$ 'shade'; $bo_2ɟi_1$ 'grave, cemetery'
* *bo'kari* (m.)	Mand., *bokari* 'name given the second son'; B., *bokari* pers. n. (Ar.)
* *'bokɒ* (m.)	E., $bo_1kɔ_3$ 'diviner, priest'
* *'boli* (m.)	B., *boli* 'a fetish'; 'to run'; 'to desert'
* *'boloni* (m.)	B., *boloni* pers. n. 'a small hand or arm'
'boma (m.)	B., *boma* 'a syphilitic skin disease'; M., *mboma* 'a hammock'
* *'bombo* (m.)	B., *bombo* (*bomo*) 'chin'; M., *bombo* pers. n. 'smallpox'
* *bom'bobɒ* (m.)	M., *bombogbɒ* pers. n. 'a scar from smallpox'
'bomo (m.)	T., *bom:o* 'a valuable cloth to cover a bed'; B., *bomo* 'chin'
* *'bondo* (f.)	V., bon_1do_1 'the enclosure in which take place the ceremonial rites of the female organization known as san_1de_1'
* *'bone* (m.)	T., *bone* pers. n. 'wicked, evil.' Cf. B., *bonɛ* 'adversity, calamity'
'bono (f.)	B., *bono* 'to lose'; 'to vie with'
'boŋku (m.)	B., *boŋku* 'a black horse'
* *'bori* (m.)	Y., bo_2ri_3 'to cover the head'; 'to surpass'; V., bo_3ri_3 (bo_3li_3) 'medicine'; H., $bo{:}_1ri{:}_2$ 'spirit'
'bɒsa (m.)	K., *bɔsa* 'to break'
'boro (m.)	B., *boro* 'loss, waste'; V., bo_1ro_3 'mud, dirt'; bo_3ro_3 'country'; bo_3ro_3 'arm, hand'

GULLAH PERSONAL NAMES	WEST AFRICAN WORDS
bo'tina (f.)	Fn., *botina* 'boot.' Cf. P., *botina* [butina] 'boot for a lady or child'
bowa'mɒ (m.)	V., *gbo₂wa₂mɔ₁* 'maniac'
'*bowe* (m.)	Fn., *gbowe* 'to tattoo'
* *bo'wele* (m.)	Fn., *gbowele* 'the shark'; 'the cognomen of the Dahomean king Béhanzin'
'*bowɛ* (m.)	Fn., *gbovɛ* 'poison'; 'to employ'
'*boya* (m.)	Tl., *boya* 'to clear away'; Y., *bo₁ya₂* 'perchance'
* '*bozo* (m.)	H., *bo:₁zo:₂* pers. n. 'great cheapness'
* '*braḍa* (m.)	E., *bra₃ḍa₃* 'Tuesday'; 'the name given a child born on that day'
* '*brafo* (m.)	T., *ɔbrafo* pers. n. 'a public executioner'
bram (m.)	T., *bram* (*baram*) 'to overlay'
* '*brima* (m.)	Man., *brima* 'Abraham'
bu (m.)	B., *bu* 'waste, loss'; E., *bu₁* 'to turn upside down'; 'to cover'; 'to meditate'; *bu₃* 'to disappear'; Y., *bu₂* 'to bake under fire'; 'moldy'; *bu₃* 'to abuse'; *bu₁* 'to take off a portion'; I., *bu₃* 'to carry'
* *bu'ala* (f.)	Tl., *buala* pers. n. 'no'
* '*buba* (m.)	B., *buba* pers. n. m.; 'termite'; Y., *bu₁ba₂* 'ambush, hiding'; *bu₁ba₃* 'a short, loose garment terminating at the waist, worn by men and women'; K., *buba* 'to cut grass'; 'to strike'; 'to put down heavily'; Kim., *buba* 'to run out'
* '*bubu* (m.)	K., *bubu* 'gloom'; 'today'; *mbubu* pers. n. 'awe, fear'; V., *b'u₁b'u₁* 'a term imitative of the noise made by a fowl when about to fly'; Fn., *bũbũ* 'insect'; E., *bu₁bu₁* 'dark'; *bu₃bu₃* 'to be lame'; T., *bubu* 'to bend repeatedly'; M., *bubu* 'to fly'; H., *bu:₃bu₁* 'ulceration of the mouth'; 'very small sticks or twigs'
* '*budi* (m.)	K., *budi* 'cat'; 'swamp'; Kim., *mbudi* (*mburi*) pers. n. 'sheep'
'*budisa* (m.)	Ki., *budisa* 'to cause to break'
* '*bugi,kɒɪ* (m.)	V., *b'u₂gi₂kai₁* pers. n. 'something frightful'
'*buɟe* (m.)	Y., *bu₁ɟe₃* 'a plant bearing a round fruit, the juice of which is used in tattooing'
'*buka* (m.)	Y., *bu₃ka₁* 'stall, market-shed'; K., *buka* 'caravan, flock'; 'dead plantain leaf'; 'to cure'; 'to explode'; Ki., *bu:ka* 'to heal'
* *bu'kama* (f.)	K., *bukama* pers. n. 'to be topsy-turvy, to fall forward'
'*bukisa* (f.)	Ki., *bukisa* 'to cause to burst'

GULLAH PERSONAL NAMES	WEST AFRICAN WORDS
* '*bukũ* (m.)	Y., $bu_1k\tilde{u}_3$ pers. n. 'to increase, to bless'
'*bula* (m.)	Y., bu_1la_1 'to mix'; K., *bula* 'size, importance'; 'to split'; 'to strike'; B., *bula* 'indigo in balls'
* *bu'landa* (m.)	*bulanda* 'a language of the Western Sudanic section, spoken mainly in the territory south of Senegal —Southern Portuguese Guinea'
'*bule* (m.)	Y., bu_1le_3 'to impose a fine upon'
'*bulɛ* (m.)	Y., $bu_1l\varepsilon_1$ 'to patch with a piece of cloth'; M., *bulɛ* (*pulɛ*) 'to burst'
'*buli* (m.)	Fn., *gbuli* 'to lose one's way'; M., *buli* 'cave, den'
* '*bulu* (m.)	E., bu_3lu_1 pers. n. 'a foolish person'; Y., bu_1lu_2 'to supply plentifully'; 'to blow upon'; K., *bulu* 'an edible wild animal'; M., *bulu* 'name of the moon corresponding to April'
'*buluŋga* (m.)	K., *buluŋga* 'to stir (a pot)'; Tl., *buluŋga* 'to be spherical'
bum'bama (m.)	K., *bumbama* 'to be raked or poured into a heap'
* '*bumbo* (m.)	V., bum_3bo_3 pers. n. m.
* '*bumbu* (m.)	M., *mbumbu* pers. n. 'to take, to lift'; H., $bum_1bu{:}_2$ 'a gourd from which the pulp has not been removed'
* *bum'bulu* (m.)	K., *bumbulu* pers. n. 'a foolish person'
'*bumi* (m.)	V., $b'u_1mi_1$ 'to drink the gun, i.e., to swear to use the gun until one's object is accomplished, or until one dies or loses the gun in trying'; K., *mbumi* 'a bush bearing a fruit that resembles an orange in size and color'
'*bundi* (m.)	K., *mbundi* 'the commonest variety of the oil palm'; 'a sheath of palm frond'
* '*bundu* (m.)	K., *bundu* pers. n. 'a fruit'; *mbundu* 'slave'; 'heart'; Tl., *bundu* 'modesty'; 'disgrace'
* '*bunɟi* (m.)	K., *mbunʒi* 'a younger brother or sister'; 'a son or daughter of one's maternal aunt younger than one's self'
* '*buno* (m.)	Ef., bu_3no_3 'to be assembled'; Tem., *gbuno* pers. n .m.
* '*buŋga* (m.)	K., *buŋga* 'to waste'; Tl., *buŋga* pers. n. 'to be drowsy'; H., $bu\eta_3ga{:}_3$ 'an article of poor quality'
'*buŋgo* (m.)	Man., *buŋo* 'house'
'*bura* (f.)	Y., bu_3ra_2 'to swear'
'*buri* (m.)	Man., *buri* 'to run'
bu'rila (f.)	Man., *burila* 'running'

GULLAH PERSONAL NAMES	WEST AFRICAN WORDS
bu'rita (m.)	Cf. Man., *a burita* 'He ran'
* *bu'roni* (m.)	T., *oburoni* 'European, white man, mulatto'
* *'buru* (m.)	T., *buru* 'dirtiness'; Y., bu_2ru_3 pers. n. 'wicked'; $bu{:}_3ru_3$ 'the game of hide and seek'; B., *buru* 'a trumpet'; 'bread'; 'to lose'
* *bu'ruta* (m.)	Y., $bu_1ru_3ta_1$ pers. n. 'He is evil; sell him'
* *'busa* (m.)	Y., bu_1sa_1 pers. n. 'to honor'; B., *busa* 'a flexible branch, a switch'; Man., *busa* 'to strike'
bu'tuna (m.)	K., *butuna* 'to cut off'
'buyε'buyε (m.)	Bi., $bu_1y\varepsilon_1bu_1y\varepsilon_1$ 'crumpled' (used in reference to cloth)
* *bu'yima* (m.)	Kim., *buima* pers. n. 'to breathe'
* *'buzu* (m.)	H., $bu{:}_3zu{:}_3$ 'an undressed skin-mat'; 'a loincloth'; 'a serf of the Azben people'
'bwaza (m.)	K., *mbwaza* 'a grain (of corn)'
'bwila (f.)	K., *mbwila* 'the swarming locust'

[d]

* *'daba* (m.)	Y., da_3ba_2 'to venture'; B., *daba*: pers. n. 'creator'; *daba* 'influence, power'; 'to begin'; V., da_3ba_1 pers. n. 'big mouth'
'dabi (m.)	Y., da_1bi_3 'to resemble'; B., *dabi* 'a scout'; 'a large bug'
da'bida (f.)	T., *dabida* 'never, by no means'; E., $ḍa_1bi_3da_1$ 'never'
* *'dabɒ* (m.)	Y., $da_3bɔ_1$ pers. n. 'to cease'
* *'dabo* (m.)	B., *dabo* 'wean'; T., *dabo*: 'smooth, soft'; Man., *dabo* 'a caste clan, a family of petty traders originally of Jula extraction'; Fn., *dabo* 'in silence'
* *'dada* (f.)	E., da_1da_3 pers. n. 'mother'; Fn., *dada* 'king'; 'grandfather'; K., *dada* 'to shake'; 'to struggle and flap the wings'; Bi., da_1da_3 'to carry (heavy things) by hand'
* *'dade* (m.)	T., *dade* 'name of a deity created by God, subordinate to him, and executing his will with regard to man'; *da:de* 'iron'; Fn., *dade* 'moiety'
* *'dado* (f.)	Y., da_3do_3 pers. n. 'to dwell alone, to be isolated'; Fn., *dado* 'a curl of hair'; 'to urinate'; 'to build a nest'; B., *dado* 'to stir up (the fire)'
* *'dadu* (m.)	T., *dadu* pers. n. 'ten days'
* *'dafa* (m.)	B., *dafa* 'to complete, to fill up'; H., da_3fa_1 'to cook'; $da_3fa{:}_3$ 'boiled rice'; V., da_3fa_1 pers. n. 'fat', lit. 'mouth full'; Y., da_3fa_3 'to divine'

GULLAH PERSONAL NAMES	WEST AFRICAN WORDS
ˈ*dafe* (f.)	B., *dafe* 'a white horse'
* ˈ*dafi* (m.)	Man., *dafi* 'name of a Mandinka caste clan, the leather-workers'
* ˈ*daha* (m.)	T., *daha* 'the leaf or leaves of the *adobɛ*, a species of palm-tree used by the natives to cover the roofs'; B., *daha* 'ink' (Ar.); Fn., *daha* pers. n.
daˈhanɪ (m.)	M., *ndahanɪ* 'any kind of edible meat'
* ˈ*dahe* (f.)	E., $da_{1-3}he_{1-3}$ pers. n. 'destitute, poor'; $da{:}_{3}he_{1}$ 'always'
* *dahoˈme* (m.)	*dahome* 'a colony in French West Africa on the Gulf of Guinea'
* ˈ*daɟa* (m.)	Y., $da_{2}ɟa_{1}$ pers. n. 'serenade'; V., $da_{3}dʒa_{3}$ pers. n. 'to take advantage of by annoying,' lit. 'to make another's mouth red'
* ˈ*daɟɛ* (m.)	Y., $da_{3}ɟɛ_{2}$ pers. n. 'to eat alone, to shun company'; B., *daɟɛ* pers. n. 'to be imperfect, to be deformed'; 'the large antelope'
* ˈ*daɟi* (m.)	Y., $da_{3}ɟi_{3}$ pers. n. 'to rise a great while before day, to wake up suddenly'; B., *daɟi* 'saliva'; Tem., *dadʒi* pers. n.
* ˈ*dakɛ* (m. and f.)	Y., $da_{3}kɛ_{2}$ pers. n. 'to be silent'
ˈ*dala* (f.)	B., *dala* 'to put in order'; 'a manufacturer'; 'a pond'; *dala:* 'a bed'; M., *ndala* 'to pull'
* ˈ*daku* (f.)	Y., $da_{3}ku_{3}$ pers. n. 'to faint, to swoon'; E., $da_{1}ku_{3}$ 'a quiver'; K., *ndaku* 'a wooden-tongued rattle'
* ˈ*dalɒ* (m.)	V., $da_{3}lɔ_{3}$ pers. n. 'in the mouth'
* ˈ*dalo* (f.)	M., *ndalo* pers. n. 'to join, to accompany'
* ˈ*daloɟi* (m.)	V., $da_{3}lo_{1}dʒi_{1}$ pers. n. 'to advise,' lit. 'to bring the mouth down'
ˈ*dama* (f.)	W., *dama* 'to break'; B., *dama* 'value, measure'
* *daˈmasi* (m.)	F., $da_{1}ma_{3}si_{1}$ pers. n. 'to give thanks'
* ˈ*damba* (m.)	M., *ndamba* pers. n. 'alligator, crocodile'
* ˈ*dambo* (m.)	V., $ndam_{3}b'o_{3}$ pers. n. 'to stretch'; Bo., *nda:mbo* 'ambush'
daˈmemi (f.)	E., $ɖa_{1}me_{1}mi_{1-3}$ 'oil used in dressing the hair'
* *daˈmiʃi* (m.)	H., $da{:}_{1}mi{:}_{2}ʃi_{1}$ pers. n. 'the leopard'
* ˈ*damɒ* (f.)	M., *ndamɒ* pers. n. 'a talkative person'; Y., $da_{1}mɔ_{3}$ 'to mix together'; $da_{3}mɔ_{3}$ 'to break inside'
* ˈ*damte* (m.)	T., *damte* 'name of a deity'
* ˈ*dana* (f.)	Y., $da_{3}na_{2}$ pers. n. 'to pay a dowry'; $da_{3}na_{3}$ 'to make a fire'; $da_{3}na_{1}$ 'to commit robbery on the highway'; B., *dana* 'faith, confidence'; *ndana* 'a bell'

GULLAH PERSONAL NAMES	WEST AFRICAN WORDS
ˈ*danda* (m.)	Bo., *nda:nda* 'exterior, surface'
* ˈ*danɛ* (m.)	M., *ndanɛ*: pers. n., lit. 'mouth sweet'
* ˈ*dani* (m.)	Y., *da*$_3$*ni*$_3$ pers. n. 'to overcome (in wrestling'); 'to hold'; B., *dani* 'to pardon'; *da:ni* 'a small earthen vase'; cf. Eng., *Danny*
* ˈ*dano* (m.)	Man., *dano* 'hunter'; Fn., *danõ* 'priest of the serpent god *dã*'
* ˈ*danso* (m.)	Man., *danso* 'originally a slave family of weavers'
* ˈ*daɲa* (m.)	V., *d'a*$_3$*ɲa*$_3$ pers. n. 'a bracelet that is not made of metal'
* *daŋˈgɪɲɛ* (m.)	M., *daŋgɪɲɛ* pers. n. 'an insect which causes the itch'
ˈ*daŋgo* (m.)	Fu., *daŋgo* 'thigh'; H., *daŋ*$_3$*go*$_1$ 'handing a person a thing and then drawing back without giving it'
* *daˈpa* (m.)	T., *dapa*: 'name of a boy or girl born on the day preceding any *adae* (*adae* being a festival day that returns every forty-third day)'
* ˈ*dapi* (m.)	M., *ndapɪ* 'to fight'; 'name given a child born during a war'
* ˈ*dara* (f.)	Y., *da*$_3$*ra*$_2$ pers. n. 'beautiful'; *da*$_3$*ra*$_1$ 'to perform feats'; *da*$_2$*ra*$_2$ 'habitual'
* ˈ*daraya* (f.)	Y., *da*$_3$*ra*$_2$*ya*$_3$ pers. n. 'to be cheerful, to perform physical exercise'
* ˈ*dase* (f.)	Y., *da*$_3$*se*$_1$ 'to prepare a meal without another's aid; E., *ḍa*$_1$*se*$_3$ pers. n. 'Thank you'; *ḍa:*$_1$*se*$_3$ 'witness'
* ˈ*dasi* (m.)	Y., *da*$_3$*si*$_2$ pers. n. 'to spare, to reserve'
* *daˈsiya* (m.)	V., *d'a*$_2$*sia*$_1$ pers. n. m.
* ˈ*daʃa* (m.)	Y., *da*$_3$*ʃa*$_1$ pers. n. 'to adopt a new fashion, to dare to do something'
ˈ*data* (f.)	B., *data* 'to begin'
* ˈ*datɛ* (m.)	T., *datɛ* 'name of a deity'
ˈ*dati* (f.)	U., *ndati* 'what, how'
* *daˈwuta* (m.)	T., *dawuta* pers. n. 'a town-crier's bell, consisting of two pieces of iron fixed in a wooden handle'
* ˈ*daya* (f.)	M., *ndaya* pers. n. 'saliva'
ˈ*dayi* (f.)	Fn., *dayi* 'pledge, security; on the ground'
* *daˈyiye* (f.)	T., *da yiye* pers. n. 'Sleep well!'
* ˈ*debi* (m.)	B., *debi* pers. n. 'a night bird'
ˈ*deda* (m.)	K., *deda* 'to peel'
* *deˈdaku* (m.)	T., *dedaku* 'name of a deity'
* ˈ*dede* (f.)	Y., *de:*$_2$*de:*$_2$ pers. n. 'agreeable, exact'; T., *dede* 'name

GULLAH PERSONAL NAMES	WEST AFRICAN WORDS
	of a female said to be the mother of the Gã people'; K., *dede* 'the chigoe'
* ˈ*deɟe* (m.)	Fn., *deɟe* 'a spirit conferring the power to govern'
* ˈ*deɟi* (m.)	K., *ndeʒi* pers. n. 'a nurse'
ˈ*deka* (m.)	B., *deka* 'after that, afterwards'
*de*ˈ*kɒla* (f.)	K., *dekɔla* 'to sip'
ˈ*dele* (f.)	Y., de_3le_3 'to arrive at home'; B., *dele* 'the common fly'; 'a bat'; 'a giraffe'; Kim., *ndele* 'a white bird'
ˈ*deli* (f.)	B., *deli* 'to demand'; 'to use, to habituate'; cf. Eng., *daily*
* ˈ*dema* (f.)	T., *dema* '*ax*'; E., $de_1m\tilde{a}_1$ 'a kind of divination (by water or by the placing of a calabash on the head)'; M., *ndema* 'forgetfulness'; Tem., *dema* pers. n. m.
* ˈ*demba* (m.)	Mand., *demba* 'name given the third son'; W., *demba* pers. n. m.; B., *demba* 'a woman in labor'
* ˈ*dembɒ* (m.)	K., *ndembɔ* 'a secret society having as one of its requirements for membership the feigning of sudden death'
* ˈ*dembu* (m.)	Kim., *ndembu* 'name given a suzerain of many vassals'
* *de*ˈ*miya* (m.)	M., *demia* 'brother-in-law, father-in-law'
ˈ*demo* (m.)	Man., *demo* 'to hunt'
*de*ˈ*nale* (f.)	W., *denale* 'to direct the service at a feast'
* ˈ*dene* (m.)	W., *dene* pers. n. m.; B., *dene* 'a wall'
* ˈ*deni* (m. and f.)	B., *deni* pers. n. 'a small girl'
ˈ*denu* (m.)	Fn., *denu* 'custom-house, tide-waiter'
* *de*ˈ*ɲalo* (f.)	M., *nde ɲalo* pers. n. 'sister'
* ˈ*deŋka* (m.)	*deŋka* 'name of a chief of Falaba, well known in Futa history of the latter eighteenth century'
* ˈ*deŋcɛ* (m.)	Mand., *deŋcɛ* pers. n. 'son'
ˈ*desi* (f.)	Y., de_3si_2 'to come upon, to befall'; Fn., *desi* 'to remove'
*de*ˈ*sɒnɑ* (f.)	K., *desɔna* 'to sprain'
de_1wi_3 (m.)	E., $ḍe_1vi_3$ 'a child as opposed to an old person'; Fn., *devi* 'a domestic, a serf'; cf. Eng., *Davy*
ˈ*dewɒ* (m.)	K., *ndevɔ* 'a curse'
* ˈ*dɛzɒ* (f.)	Fn., *dɛzɔ* 'stammering'; K., *dɛzɔ* 'God.' Cf. P., *Deus*
* ˈ*dɛdɛ* (m.)	T., *dɛdɛ* pers. n. 'agreeable, sweet'; Fn., *dɛdɛ* 'gently'; Y., $dɛ_1dɛ_1$ 'near, at hand'
ˈ*dɛgũ* (f.)	Y., $dɛ_1g\tilde{u}_1$ 'to make a rough seat on a tree, on which to await animals at night'

GULLAH PERSONAL NAMES	WEST AFRICAN WORDS
* '*dɛlɪ* (f.)	M., *ndɛlɪ* pers. n. 'to wet, to cool, to satisfy'
'*dɛlu* (f.)	W., *dɛlu* 'to return'
dɛm (m.)	T., *dɛm* 'injury, blemish, loss'; *dɛm*: 'quiet, calm'
'*dɛne* (m.)	W., *dɛne* 'a small native adz'
* '*dɛntɛ* (m.)	T., *ɔdɛntɛ* pers. n.; 'name of a town or country genius or demon'
* '*dɛtɛ* (f.)	Y., $d\varepsilon_3 t\varepsilon_1$ pers. n. 'to be leprous'
di (f.)	T., *di* 'to take and use'; E., di_1 'a kind of mouse'; di_3 'to look out for'; 'to wish'; 'to project'; Y., di_3 'closed'; 'entangled'; 'to close'; di_2 'to become'; di_1 'to enchant'; B., *di* 'honey'; 'agreeable'; 'to give something to'; 'to shave'; I., di_3 'husband'; M., *ndi* 'the house fly'
* *di'abu* (m.)	Kim., *diabu* 'any bad spirit of the white man's mythology, any wicked person' (P).
di'bala (f.)	K., *dibala* 'a game'
* '*dibi* (m.)	B., *dibi* pers. n. 'darkness'; 'to be obscure'; 'a place for smoking meat'; H., $di{:}_3 bi{:}_3$ 'becoming thick in consistency'
'*dibo* (m.)	Y., $di_3 bo_1$ 'to cast lots'
'*didi* (m.)	T., *didi* 'to eat'; Y., $di_3 di_1$ 'the condition of being tied'; 'congealed'; Fn., *didi* 'faith'; E., $di_1 di_1$ 'to be far away'; $di_3 di_3$ 'to stretch'; K., *ndidi* 'a weeper'
'*didi'didi* (m.)	T., *dididi* 'to feed'; Y., $di_3 di_1 di_3 di_1$ 'congealed'
* '*dido* (m.)	Bi., $di_3 do_1$ 'to be old'; 'to be mighty'; M., *ndido* pers. n. 'patience, courage,' lit. 'The heart stands'
'*difi* (m.)	W., *difi* 'to protect'
'*diga* (m.)	Fn., *diga* 'long; to be long'
'*digbe* (m.)	M., *digbe* 'heel'
'*digbɒ* (m.)	M., *digbɒ* 'completely'
'*digi* (m.)	Y., $di_3 gi_3$ 'a mirror'; B., *digi* 'the torpedo fish'; 'to push'; 'to cause to suffer'; 'to calm'; 'to plait the hair'
* *di'kanu* (m.)	Kim., *dikanu*[23] (*rikanu*) pers. n. 'mouth'
di'kuba (m.)	Tl., *dikuba* 'bundle, large package'
di'kunda (m.)	Kim., *dikunda* 'the back, shoulders, ribs, etc.'
* '*dile* (f.)	M., *ndile* pers. n. 'a boa constrictor'
* '*dilɛlɪ* (f.)	M., *ndilɛlɪ* pers. n. 'peace, contentment'
* *di'lɒlɒ* (f.)	Kim., *dilɔlɔ* 'a lake near the eastern boundary of Angola'

GULLAH PERSONAL NAMES	WEST AFRICAN WORDS
diˈlɒŋga (m.)	Kim., *dilɔŋga* 'a plate, dish, bowl'; Tl., *dilɔŋga*
ˈ*dima* (m.)	Tl., *dima* 'earth used in making pots'; 'to hoe, to cultivate'; cf. Eng., *Redeemer*
* ˈ*dimba* (f.)	Tl., *dimba* pers. n. 'to tell an untruth'; K., *dimba* 'direction (towards)'; *ndimba* 'valley, glen'
* *dimˈbɒɪya* (m.)	Man., *dimbaia* 'family, dependents'
ˈ*dimbu* (m.)	K., *dimbu* 'gum, resin, pitch'
* ˈ*dimi* (m.)	B., *dimi*, pers. n. 'animosity'; 'suffering'; Man., *dimi* pers. n. 'to feel pain'
* *diˈmina* (f.)	B., *dimina* pers. n. 'pain'
* *diˈmindi* (f.)	Man., *dimindi* pers. n. 'to hurt (someone)'
* *diˈmiŋka* (f.)	S., *dimiŋka* pers. n. f.
ˈ*dimɒ* (m.)	Y., *di*$_1$*mɔ*$_3$ 'to grasp'
* ˈ*dimo* (m.)	Fu., *dimo* pers. n. 'free-born, a free man'
ˈ*dina* (f.)	Y., *di*$_3$*na*$_1$ 'to obstruct a passage'; Fu., *dina* 'religion, faith' (Ar.)
* ˈ*dinu* (f.)	K., *dinu* 'tooth, tusk, fang'; Y., *di*$_2$*nu*$_2$ 'to pucker up the mouth'; *di*$_3$*nu*$_2$ 'ill-tempered'; E., *ḍi*$_1$*nu*$_3$ pers. n. 'something dirty'
ˈ*diŋgi* (m.)	H., *diŋ*$_1$*gi*:$_2$ 'a male giraffe'
* *diŋgo* (m.)	H., *diŋ*$_2$*go*:$_2$ 'to set out hither'; Man., *diŋo* pers. n. 'child'
* *diŋˈgola* (f.)	Man., *diŋola* pers. n. 'the child's'
* *diŋgoˈlɛti* (m.)	Cf. Man., *na diŋoleti* pers. n. 'It is my child' (used in answer to the question, 'Whose child is it?')
* *diŋˈgolu* (f.)	Man., *diŋolu* pers. n. 'children'
* ˈ*diŋgu* (m.)	E., *ḍiŋ*$_1$*u*$_{1-3}$ pers. n. 'curse, malediction.' Cf. K., *ndiŋgu a nʃi* 'midnight'
ˈ*diŋka* (m.)	W., *diŋka* 'to recommend, to enjoin'
* ˈ*diŋke* (m.)	Man., *diŋke* pers. n. 'male child'
* *diŋˈketi* (m.)	Man., *diŋketi* pers. n. 'male child' (the form *diŋke* takes when used as a predicate)
diˈɒkɒlɒ (f.)	K., *diɔkɔlɔ* 'a tadpole which has nearly become a frog'
* *diˈrisu* (f.)	Y., *di*$_1$*ri*$_3$*su*$_1$ pers. n. m.
ˈ*disa* (m.)	K., *disa* 'maize'; B., *disa* 'a kind of muffler, serving also for a turban'
* ˈ*diso* (m.)	W., *diso* pers. n. 'to confide'
diˈʃisa (f.)	Kim., *diʃisa* 'a mat'
diˈtemu (f.)	Kim., *ditemu* 'a hoe'

GULLAH PERSONAL NAMES	WEST AFRICAN WORDS
ˈ*dito* (m.)	B., *dito* 'to shave, to pass very close to'
diˈwale (f.)	M., *ndivale* 'a broom'; 'a kind of mushroom'
* ˈ*diwɒ* (m.)	Y., $di_3wɔ_3$ pers. n. 'to occupy one's whole time'; $di_2wɔ_3$ 'to clench the fist'
ˈ*diwo* (m.)	M., *ndivo* 'a boil'; *ndiwo,* 'a kind of grass'
ˈ*diya* (m.)	K., *diya* 'forgetfulness'; a 'mistake'; *dia* 'to eat'; *ndia* 'eating, a manner of eating'; 'intestine'
* *diˈyadi* (m.)	K., *diadi* pers. n. 'this'
diˈyala (f.)	Tl., *diala* 'to wear'; 'a place for throwing rubbish'
diˈyama (m.)	K., *diama* 'to sink'
* *diˈyamɒ* (m.)	M., *ndiamɒ* pers. n. 'friend, lover'
diyuˈkisa (f.)	K., *diukisa* 'to dip into water'
ˈ*dɪgba* (m.)	M., *ndɪgba* 'to squeeze, to press upon from above'
ˈ*dɪkpa* (m.)	M., *ndɪkpa* 'a cross-bow'
ˈ*dɒdɒ* (f.)	K., *dɔdɔ* 'a knock, a rap'; E., $dɔ_1ḍɔ{:}_1$ 'fleshy, plump'
ˈ*dɒfe* (m.)	E., $dɔ_3Φe_3$ 'a sleeping-place'
* *dɒgˈbe* (m.)	M., *ndɔgbe* 'a fetish supposed to cause headache'
* ˈ*dɒɪma* (m.)	H., dai_3ma_1 'the title of one who has authority over the young folk of the town for communal work, games, etc.'
* *dɒˈkunu* (m.)	T., *ɔdɔkunu* pers. n. 'a beloved husband'
* ˈ*dɒlɛ* (f.)	M., *ndɔlɛ* pers. n. 'hunger, need'
ˈ*dɒli* (m.)	E., $ḍɔ_1li_1$ 'to change'
* ˈ*dɒlu* (f.)	Gb. and Kp., *dɔlu* pers. n. 'five'
ˈ*dɒma* (f.)	K., *dɔma* 'to jump'; T., *dɔm:a* 'a weight of gold (the Asante *dɔm:a* being equal in value to 7 shillings 10½ pence)'; M., *ndɔma* 'on the ground'; I., $dɔ_3ma_3$ 'to set down, to place'
* ˈ*dɒmbe* (*nˈdɒmbe*) (m.)	K., *ndɔmbe* pers. n. 'a black man, blackness'
dɒˈmɒna (f.)	K., *dɔmɔna* 'to pull out'
* ˈ*dɒre* (f.)	T., *dɔre* pers. n. 'to become great, to increase'
* *do* (m.)	Mand., *do* 'name given the fourth son'; Man., *do* 'work'; E., do_{1-3} 'name given a boy born after twins'; 'hole, cavern'; do_1 'to become visible'; do_3 'to prepare'; Y., do_3 'to encamp'; 'to cohabit with'; cf. Eng. *dough*
ˈ*doba* (m.)	B., *doba* 'a light-colored horse with some white hair'
* ˈ*dodi* (f.)	Fn., *dodi* pers. n. 'to assist'
* ˈ*dodo* (f.)	Y., do_1do_1 'fried ripe plantain'; do_2do_2 'dangling';

GULLAH PERSONAL NAMES	WEST AFRICAN WORDS
	do:$_2$*do*$_2$ 'empty'; B., *dodo* 'to watch over'; 'a kind of fish'; E., *do*$_3$*do*$_3$ 'a dense forest'; H., *do:*$_3$*do*$_1$ 'a long line or column'; *do:*$_1$*do:*$_2$ 'water spirit'
* '*dodu* (m.)	G., *do*$_1$*du*$_3$ pers. n. m.; F., *do*$_1$*du*$_3$ pers. n.
* '*dofe* (m.)	E., *ḍo*$_1$*fe*$_1$ pers. n. 'a fine for adultery to be paid to the injured husband'
* '*dofi* (m. and f.)	E., *do*$_1$*Φi*$_3$ 'name given a girl born after *do*$_{1-3}$' (*do*$_{1-3}$ being the name given a boy born after twins)
* *dog'be* (m.)	Fn., *dogbe* pers. n. 'to rejoice, to give thanks'
* '*dogli* (m.)	E., *do*$_3$*γli*$_3$ pers. n. 'crying'
'*dogo* (m.)	E., *do*$_1$*go*$_1$ 'a wasp'; *do*$_1$*go:*$_1$ 'blunt, pointless'; Y., *do*$_3$*go*$_1$ 'to dun a debtor until he settles his debt'; B., *dogo* 'small, short'; 'market-place'; 'to steal'
* '*doɫi* (m.)	Fn., *doɫi* pers. n. 'to speak loudly'; 'to admonish'
* '*doko* (f.)	E., *ḍo*$_3$*ko*$_1$ 'poor, destitute'; *do*$_3$*ko*$_{1-3}$ pers. n. 'name-sake'
* '*doli* (m.)	V., *do*$_1$*li*$_1$ pers. n. 'small'
* *dolɪ'ga* (f.)	M., *ndolɪ ga* pers. n. 'to dance'
do'lula (f.)	Man., *dolula* (dat. c.) 'to, for, or at the others'
* '*doma* (m. and f.)	Man., *doma* 'younger brother'; B., *doma* 'a sorcerer'
* *do'maya* (f.)	B., *domaya* 'magic, witchcraft'
'*dome* (m.)	E., *do*$_3$*me*$_1$ 'the site of an abandoned village'; 'inheritance'; *do*$_1$*me*$_1$ 'the space between'; Fn., *dome* 'the ground'
'*doni* (f.)	B., *doni* 'a burden'
do'nita (f.)	B., *donita* 'to carry a burden'
* '*doŋgo* (m.)	W., *ndoŋgo* pers. n. 'a student, a disciple'; Man., *doŋo* 'to dance'
'*doŋke* (f.)	B., *doŋke* 'to dance'
* '*dopo* (m.)	M., *ndopo* pers. n. 'child'
* '*dori* (f.)	V., *do*$_1$*ri*$_1$ (*do*$_1$*li*$_1$) pers. n. 'young, immature'; H., '*do:*$_3$*ɽi*$_1$ 'setting a fracture'; 'an addition'
* *do'rina* (f.)	H., *do:*$_1$*ɽi*$_2$*na:*$_2$ pers. n. 'hippopotamus'
'*doro* (f.)	B., *doro* 'grains of millet which have the property of putting one to sleep and of causing vomiting'
* *dosu'mu* (m.)	Y., *do*$_1$*su*$_1$*mu*$_3$ 'name of a former king of the Yoruba'
'*doto* (f.)	Fn., *doto* 'an author, a contriver'; 'to listen'
'*driɲa* (f.)	E., *driɲa:*$_1$ 'tough, sticky, filthy'
du (f.)	Y., *du*$_3$ 'black'; *du*$_1$ 'to seek along with another'; *du*$_2$ 'to run'; Mal., *du* 'night'; E., *du*$_1$ 'to pull';

GULLAH PERSONAL NAMES	WEST AFRICAN WORDS
	'a village, a chieftainship'; 'a race'; 'a configuration in divination'; $du{:}_1$ 'in great numbers'; $ḍu_1$ 'to eat'; 'powder'; $ḍu_3$ 'to dance'; B., *du* 'a cottage'; 'to eat'; 'to bend'; cf. Eng., *do*
'*duba* (m.)	H., $du{:}_3ba_1$ 'to look for or at something'; T., *dubã:* 'the branch of a tree'
* *du'baŋgɒ* (m.)	M., *ndugbaŋgɒ* pers. n. 'blessed, favored, a blessing'
* '*dudu* (m.)	Y., du_3du_3 pers. n. 'black'; K., *dudu* 'a fool'; E., du_1du_1 'to fall off, to leak'; $ḍu_1du_{1-3}$ 'edible'; $ḍu_3du_3$ 'to whirl'
'*dufa* (m.)	B., *dufa* 'to extinguish'; T., *dufa* 'medicine'
'*dufe* (m.)	V., du_1fe_1 'to extinguish'
'*dufu* (m.)	H., du_3fu_1 (du_3hu_1) 'darkness'
duku (f.)	Fn., *duku* 'napkin, towel'
'*dula* (f.)	M., *ndula* 'to decay'; 'decayed'
* '*dule* (f.)	B., *dule* pers. n. 'artful, tortuous'
'*dulu* (f.)	B., *du:lu* 'five'; M., *ndulu* 'to smoke'; 'a bird with brown feathers'
* *du'maya* (f.)	B., *dumaya* pers. n. 'sorcery'
dum'bele (m.)	M., *dumbele* 'orange, lime'
du'muna (f.)	K., *dumuna* 'to root up'
* '*duɲa* (m.)	V., $du_3ɲa_3$ pers. n. 'the universe'; H., $du_3ɲa{:}_3$ 'the spur-winged goose'; $du{:}_3ni_1ya_1$ 'the world'
* '*duŋga* (m.)	K., *duŋga* pers. n. 'a fool'; *nduŋga* 'a drum'; Tl., *nduŋga* 'a kind of tree'
'*dura* (f.)	T., *dura* 'to cover'
'*duro* (m.)	Y., du_3ro_3 'to stand, to tarry'
* *du'rori* (f.)	Fu., *durori* pers. n. m.
* *duro'sĩmi* (f.)	Y., $du_3ro_3s\tilde{\imath}_2mi_3$ pers. n., lit. 'Wait and bury me'
* '*duwa* (m.)	T., *dua* pers. n.; *dua:* 'a small tree'; H., $du_1wa{:}_2$ 'loamy soil'
du'we (m.)	Fn., dwe^{24} 'a blow, a thrust'
* *du'wɛlɛ* (f.)	M., *duvɛlɛ* pers. n. 'large'

[e]

'*eba* (m.)	K., *eba* 'the oil-palm'
e'beke (f.)	K., *ebeke* 'a jug'
e'beni (m.)	K., *ebeni* 'the breast'
* '*ebi* (m.)	Y., e_3bi_3 pers. n. 'hunger'; 'journey'; $e{:}_2bi_1$ 'to vomit'; Bi., e_1bi_3 'darkness'

GULLAH PERSONAL NAMES	WEST AFRICAN WORDS
* ˈ*ebo* (m.)	Bi., e_3bo_2 'European, white man'; Y., e_1gbo_2 'corn pudding'; e_2gbo_1 'a sore'; 'the root of a tree'
* *eˈbomi* (m.)	Fn., *ebomi* 'name of the eighth king of Dahomey, who ruled only a few days in 1803'[25]
* *eˈbundi* (m.)	K., *ebundi* pers. n. 'the cheek'
* *eˈbunze* (m.)	K., *ebunze* pers. n. 'a charm supposed to cause illness'
* ˈ*edi* (m.)	Y., e_2di_1 pers. n. 'charm, enchantment'
eˈdila (m.)	K., *edila* 'a bag'
ediˈyata (m.)	K., *ediata* 'grass, a toy gun made of grass'
* *eˈdiye* (f.)	Ef., $e_1di_3ye_{1-2}$ pers. n. 'pretty'
ˈ*efi* (f.)	Y., $e\!:_1fi_3$ 'smoke'
* *eˈfiyo* (f.)	U., *efiyo* pers. n. 'fussiness'
* *egˈbere* (m.)	Y., $e_2gbe_3re_2$ 'an evil spirit supposed to wander about at night and to frequent the woods'
* ˈ*egbeˈzaku* (m.)	Fn., *egbe zaku* pers. n. 'this evening'
ˈ*egbu* (m.)	Bi., e_3gbu_3 'a woodpecker with a big head and short beak'
* ˈ*egede* (f.)	Y., $e_1ge_1de_1$ pers. n. 'incantation, magical formula'; $e_1ge_2de_3$ 'only'
ˈ*egeˈdege* (m.)	Bi., $e_1ge_3de_3ge_2$ 'a two-story house'
* *eˈgũgũ* (m.)	Y., $e_1gũ_3gũ_3$ 'the worship of the spirits of the dead'
eˈhaya (m.)	Bi., $e_1ha_3ya_1$ 'hire, rent.' Cf. Eng. *hire*
ˈ*ekã* (m.)	Y., $e\!:_1kã_3$ 'fingernail, paw'
eˈkabita (m.)	Bi., $e_1ka_{1-3}bi_3ta_1$[26] 'a carpenter'
eˈkala (f.)	K., *ekala* 'ashes, charcoal'; U., *ekala* 'a coal'; 'flowing of water at childbirth'
eˈkaya (m.)	U., $e_1ka_2ya_1$ 'the tobacco leaf'
* *eˈkeɟi* (f.)	Y., $e_1ke_2ɟi_1$ pers. n. 'the second'
* *eˈketɒ* (m.)	K., *eketɔ* pers. n. 'anger'
* ˈ*ekiti* (f.)	Y., $e_1ki_1ti_1$ ($e_1ki_2ti_2$) 'name of a district northeast of the Yoruba country'; 'somersault'; 'mound'
eˈkiye (m.)	Y., $e_2ki_2ye_2$ 'roasted leaves used as a cure for the ear-ache'
eˈkɒfi (f.)	K., *ekɔfi* 'a blow with the fist'
* ˈ*ekɒɪ* (m.)	U., *ekai* 'effeminacy'; cf. the *Ekoi* 'a tribe of Southern Nigeria'
eˈkonɟo (f.)	U., *ekondʒo* 'hoof'
* *eˈkuti* (f.)	U., *ekuti* pers. n. 'a large brown pigeon'
eˈkuzo (m.)	Bi., $e_3ku_3zo_1$ 'a shrub'

GULLAH PERSONAL NAMES	WEST AFRICAN WORDS
* *eˈlembe* (f.)	K., *elembe* pers. n. 'pelican'
ˈeli (f.)	Fn., *eli* 'far off'
eˈlimi (f.)	U., *elimi* 'tongue, language'
ˈelɔ (f.)	K., *elɔ* 'yes'; Y., $e{:}_1lɔ_1$ 'grinder, digestive organs'
elo (f.)	Y., e_1lo_3 'how much'
* *eˈlulu* (f.)	U., *elulu* pers. n. 'greediness'; 'a bonfire'
eˈlundu (f.)	K., *elundu* 'nest of the white ant'; 'ham'; 'a hundred thousand'
* *ˈelusa* (f.)	K., *elusa* pers. n. 'greed'; 'a habit of prowling about'
* *emaˈȷa* (f.)	Y., $e_2ma_2ȷa_2$ 'one of the ladies of high rank at the palace of the Yoruba king'; cf. Y., $ye_2ma_2ȷa_2$ 'the goddess of brooks'
eˈmeme (f.)	K., *ememe* 'sheep'
eˈmiya (f.)	K., *emia* 'the short palm having thin midribs'
ˈemɒ (m.)	Y., $e{:}_1mɔ_1$ 'something strange'
* *eˈmole* (f.)	U., *emole* pers. n. 'sloth'
ˈemu (f.)	T., *emu* 'the interior, in the middle'
* *eˈnana* (f.)	K., *enana* pers. n. 'eight'
ˈeni (f.)	Y., $e{:}_2ni_3$ 'dew'; e_1ni_1 'over-measure'; e_1ni_3 'today'; e_2ni_3 'one'
ˈene (f.)	U., *ene* 'you' (2d pers. pr. pl.); E., e_1ne_1 'four'
* *ˈeɲɔ* (m.)	G., $e_3ɲɔ_1$ pers. n. 'two, second'
eˈpapi (m.)	K., *epapi* 'wing (of a bird)'
eˈpata (m.)	U., *epata* 'family, house, household'
* *eˈpene* (f.)	U., *epene* pers. n. 'nakedness'
* *ˌepɛkˈpɛyɛ* (m.)	Bi., $e_1kpɛ_3kpɛ_3yɛ_3$ pers. n. 'a duck.' Cf. Y., $kpɛ_3kpɛ_3yɛ_3$ 'a duck'
eˈpĩ (m.)	Y., $e_2kpĩ_2$ 'ashes sometimes used with the native dye $ɛ_1lu_3$ (West African indigo)'
* *eˈpini* (f.)	U., *epini* pers. n. 'the left hand'
eˈpole (f.)	U., *epõle* 'a hard-shelled fruit resembling the orange'
* *ˈere* (m.)	Y., e_1re_1 'advantage, profit'; e_2re_3 'a game'; e_1re_2 'an idol'; e_2re_1 pers. n. 'a boa constrictor'; $e_2re{:}_{1-2}$ 'a white bean with black eye'
* $e_1re_1lu_3$ (f.)	Y., $e_1re_1lu_3$ 'a title usually given a woman in the Ogboni House, or a leading woman in any community'
* *ˈerĩ* (f.)	Y., $e_2rĩ_2$ pers. n. 'elephant'
* *eˈrinlɛ* (m.)	Y., $e_2rĩ_2lɛ_1$ 'the god of song'; 'elephant'
eˈrugu (m.)	Y., $e_2ru_2gu_2$ 'an ingredient of a_1gbo_3, a vegetable de-

GULLAH PERSONAL NAMES	WEST AFRICAN WORDS
	coction used for washing babies and also given them to drink'
* *eˈruku* (m.)	Cf. Y., $e_1ru_3ku_1ku_1$ pers. n. 'a pigeon'
ˈ*esa* (m.)	U., *esa* 'an ear of corn'
eˈsafi (f.)	K., *esafi* 'a tassel, the bunch of hair at the end of a tail'
* *eˈsalu* (m.)	K., *esalu* pers. n. 'the witch-doctor's bundle of charms'; 'tool'
eˈsami (m.)	K., *esami* 'a stopper, a cork'
* *eˈsanda* (f.)	U., *esanda* pers. n. 'nonsense, a lie'
eˈsanzu (m.)	K., *esanzu* 'booty, plunder'
eˈsaŋgu (f.)	K., *esaŋgu* 'corn'
* ˈ*ese* (f.)	Y., e_2se_3 'a large fish'; e_1se_2 'a cat'; e_1se_1 'provision'; 'dye'; K., *ese* pers. n. 'father'
* *eˈseke* (f.)	K., *eseke* pers. n. 'the whydah bird when not in full plumage'; 'land'
* ˈ*esi* (f.)	Y., e_1si_1 'answer'; e_2si_2 'a fetish for warding off evil from a town'; Bi., e_1si_1 'bush-pig'; 'good'
eˈsinde (f.)	U., *esinde* 'a blade of grass'
* *eˈsisi* (f.)	U., *esisi* pers. n. 'a forest'
* *eˈsiya* (f.)	F., $e_1s\tilde{i}_3\tilde{a}_3$ 'six'; 'name given the sixth child'; T., *esiã* 'a large hardwood tree'
* ˈ*esɒ* (m.)	E., $e_1s\text{ɔ}_1$ 'yesterday'; Ef., $e_1s\text{ɔ}_1$ pers. n. m.
* *eˈsɒfi* (f.)	K., *esɔfi* pers. n. 'a large water antelope'; 'a thorny caterpillar'
eˈsɒle (m.)	K., *esɔle* 'a garden cleared in a wood or forest'
eˈsɒmbɒ (m.)	K., *esɔmbɔ* 'a variety of the oil-palm and its nut'
* ˈ*esu* (f.)	Y., $e\!:_2su_3$ 'skin eruptions'; E., $e_3s\tilde{u}_1$ pers. n. 'It is good'
* *eˈsundi* (m.)	K., *esundi* pers. n. 'an animal that has not given birth'
* *eˈtele* (m.)	K., *etele* pers. n. 'a whale'
eˈsweŋga (m.)	K., *esweŋga* 'unripe groundnut'
eˈʃimu (m.)	K., *eʃimu* 'a beach, the bank of a river'
* ˈ*eʃu* (m.)	Y., $e_1\text{ʃ}u_1$ 'divine trickster'; $e\!:_2\text{ʃ}u_3$ 'a locust'
eˈtamba (m.)	U., *etamba* 'a fragrant-leaved tree'
etaˈmina (f.)	U., *etamina* 'a small basket'
eˈtaya (m.)	K., *etaya* 'a rag'
eˈtenʒi (m.)	K., *etenʒi* 'a small china or pearl button'
* *eˈtino* (f.)	U., *etino* pers. n. 'a quarrel'; 'a severe thrashing'
eˈtɒmbe (m.)	K., *etɔmbe* 'the midrib of the palm'

GULLAH PERSONAL NAMES	WEST AFRICAN WORDS
ˈetu (f.)	U., *etu* 'we'
eˈtumbi (m.)	K., *etumbi* 'a bed raised rather high (as for pumpkins)'; 'a bed of burned roots and earth'
ˈeci (m.)	U., *etʃi* 'when'; 'this'
ewaˈlanti (f.)	K., *evalanti* 'a carpenter'
eˈwata (f.)	K., *evata* 'town, village'
ˈewe (m.)	E., e_1ve_1 'two'; K., *eve* 'the wing of a bird'
eweˈkoko (f.)	Y., $e_2we_2ko_3ko_1$ 'a vegetable with thick green leaves used every seventeenth day in connection with the worship of $ʃaŋ_1go_3$, the god of thunder'
eˈwele (m.)	K., *ewele* 'a thorny creeping plant'
ˈeweta (f.)	K., *eveta* 'a hunt (with dogs)'
* *eˈwiɟi* (f.)	K., *eviʒi* pers. n. 'a pimple (from the sting of an insect)'
* *eˈwina* (f.)	K., *evwina* pers. n. 'thirst'
eˈwiya (m.)	K., *evia* 'a field'
ˈewɒlɒ (f.)	K., *evɔlɔ* 'charcoal, coal'
eˈwɒnzɒ (m.)	K., *ewɔnzɔ* 'a medicine consisting of leaves bruised with chalk and mud and mixed with palm wine'
eˈwɒŋgi (f.)	K., *evɔŋgi* 'the seed capsule of a tree which is pierced and played on the principle of the ocarina'
eˈwula (f.)	K., *evula* 'station, residence'
* *eˈwuninu* (f.)	K., *evuninu* pers. n. 'that about which there is deceit'
eˈwunze (m.)	K., *ewunze* 'a tree that grows in swampy places, the fruit of which yields a red dye'
* *eˈwuta* (m.)	K., *ewuta* pers. n. 'the horned viper'
eˈwuwu (*eˈwuwuwu*) (m.)	K., *evuvu* 'unoccupied space'
* *ˈeya* (m.)	K., *eya* pers. n. 'the palm tree'
* *eˈyakala* (m.)	K., *eyakala* pers. n. 'man, male'
eˈyala (f.)	U., *eyala* 'a refuse heap, ash heap'
* *eˈyaŋgi* (m.)	K., *eyaŋgi* pers. n. 'joy, comfort'
* *ˈeye* (f.)	Ef., e_3ye_{1-2} pers. n. 'It is beautiful'
* *eˈyili* (f.)	K., *eyili* pers. n. 'oyster'
* *eˈyindu* (f.)	K., *eyindu* pers. n. 'lack of skill in hunting'
* *ˈeyu* (m.)	U., *eyu* pers. n. 'tooth'
ˈeyulu (f.)	K., *eulu* 'hole, socket'
* *eˈzandu* (f.)	K., *ezandu* pers. n. 'a market'
ˈezɒ (m.)	Bi., $e_1zɔ_3$ 'a repair'

GULLAH PERSONAL NAMES	WEST AFRICAN WORDS
* ˈezu (m.)	K., ezu pers. n. 'sound, echo'
eˈzunda (f.)	K., ezunda 'one thousand'

[ɛ]

* ˈɛda (m.)	Y., ɛ$_1$da$_3$ pers. n. 'nature, inclination'; 'creature'; ɛ$_2$da$_3$ 'a rat remarkable for fast breeding'; ɛ$_1$da$_1$ 'leucorrhea'; 'coining money by magic means'; T., ɛda 'day'
* ˈɛfũ (f.)	Y., ɛ$_1$fũ$_3$ pers. n. 'enchantment'; ɛ$_2$fũ$_2$ 'chalk, lime'; I., ɛ$_3$fu$_1$ 'empty, vain'
* ɛgˈba (m.)	Y., ɛ$_1$gba$_3$ 'a Yoruba tribe inhabiting the town of Abeokuta [a$_2$bɛ$_3$o$_1$ku$_3$ta$_2$]'
* ɛgˈbɛsi (f.)	Y., ɛ$_1$gbɛ$_1$si$_1$ pers. n. 'the African fig, the African peach'; 'African quinine'
ˈɛgi (f.)	Y., ɛ$_1$gi$_1$ 'a ram's mane, prepared and used as an ornament on a dog's neck'
* ˈɛɟɛ (m.)	Y., ɛ$_1$ɟɛ$_1$ pers. n. 'blood'; ɛ$_1$ɟɛ$_3$ 'a doctor's honorarium'; 'a vow'
* ɛˈɟɛmu (f.)	Y., ɛ$_2$ɟɛ$_2$mũ$_2$ pers. n.
* ɛˈɟina (f.)	K., ɛʒina pers. n.; 'to be burnt'
* ˈɛka (f.)	T., ɛka: pers. n. 'finger ring'
* ɛkˈpɛrɛ (f.)	Bi., ɛ$_1$kpe$_{3-1}$rɛ$_1$ pers. n. 'a musical instrument'
* ɛˈkunosi (f.)	Y., ɛ$_1$kũ$_3$-o$_1$si$_1$ 'one of the ɔ$_1$yɔ$_2$ provinces'
* ɛˈlɛmi (f.)	Y., ɛ$_1$lɛ$_3$mi$_2$ pers. n. 'having life'
* ɛˈlɛgbara (m.)	Y., ɛ$_2$lɛ$_3$gba$_3$ra$_2$ 'the god of mischief'
* ɛˈlɛrĩ (f.)	Y., ɛ$_2$lɛ$_3$rĩ$_1$ pers. n. 'one who laughs frivolously'
* ɛˈlɛsɛ (f.)	Y., ɛ$_2$lɛ$_3$sɛ$_1$ pers. n. 'a footman, one who visits friends'
* ɛˈlɛya (f.)	Y., ɛ$_2$lɛ$_3$ya$_1$ pers. n. 'ridicule, contempt'
ˈɛlu (f.)	Y., ɛ$_1$lu$_3$ 'West African indigo'; I., ɛ$_3$lu$_3$ 'top, a high place'
* ˈɛmba (f.)	W., ɛmba pers. n. 'to be prepared'
* ˈɛna (f.)	T., ɛ:na 'after this'; ɛna pers. n. 'mother'; Y., ɛ$_2$na$_1$ 'the act of transposing letters, syllables, words, or sentences in order to conceal the meaning or to change it'
ˈɛne (m.)	Fn., ɛne 'fair'
* ɛniˈmimɔ̃ (f.)	Y., ɛ$_2$ni$_2$mi$_3$mɔ̃$_3$ pers. n.; 'one who is clean morally and physically'
* ˈɛnira (m.)	Y., ɛ$_2$ni$_2$ra$_1$ pers. n. 'one who buys'
ˈɛnu (f.)	Y., ɛ$_2$nu$_2$ 'mouth, opening'

GULLAH PERSONAL NAMES	WEST AFRICAN WORDS
ˌ*ɛrãyɛˈlɛdɛ* (m.)	Y., ɛ$_2$*rã*$_2$-ɛ$_2$*l*ɛ$_3$*d*ɛ$_1$ 'pork'
ˌ*ɛrãˈyiyɒ* (f.)	Y., ɛ$_2$*rã*$_2$-*i*$_2$*y*ɔ$_1$ (ɛ$_2$*rã*$_2$-*o*$_2$*ni*$_3$*y*ɔ$_1$) 'salt meat'
* ˈ*ɛri* (m.)	Y., ɛ$_1$*ri*$_3$ pers. n. 'witness, token'
* ɛˈ*se* (f.)	Bi., ɛ$_1$*se*$_{3-1}$ pers. n. 'goodness, favor'; ɛ$_1$*se*$_3$ 'well, properly'
ɛˈ*senu* (f.)	W., ɛ*senu* 'to rub against something to relieve itching'
* *ɛsiˈyɛmɒ* (m.)	Ef. ɛ$_3$*si*$_3$ɛ$_3$*m*ɔ$_3$ pers. n. 'his own'
* ɛˈ*sɒrũ* (m.)	Y., ɛ$_3$*s*ɔ$_1$*rũ*$_3$ pers. n., lit. 'You came from the sky'; ɛ$_2$*s*ɔ$_3$*rũ*$_1$ 'an ulcer on the neck'
* ɛˈ*sodi* (m.)	T., ɛ*sodi* pers. n. 'rule, domination'
* ˈɛ*ʃi* (f.)	Y., ɛ$_2$*ʃĩ*$_2$ pers. n. 'a horse'; ɛ$_1$*ʃĩ*$_3$ 'a spear'
* ˈɛʃɔ (m.)	Y., ɛ:$_1$ʃɔ$_3$ pers. n. 'a guard'
* ɛ*taˈoko* (m.)	Y., ɛ:$_2$*ta*$_2$-*o*$_1$*ko*$_1$ pers. n. 'the third of triplets'
ɛˈ*towa* (f.)	T., ɛ*towa* 'a crowbar, lever, hoe'
* ˈɛ*tu* (m.)	Tl., ɛ*tu* pers. n. 'ours'; Y., ɛ$_2$*tu*$_1$ 'guinea fowl'; ɛ$_2$*tu*$_2$ 'antelope'; ɛ$_1$*tu*$_1$ 'medicinal powder'
* ˈɛ*ya* (f.)	Y., ɛ$_2$*ya*$_1$ 'a small leopard'; ɛ$_1$*ya*$_1$ 'tribe, division'
* ˈɛ*y*ɛ (f.)	Y., ɛ$_2$*y*ɛ$_3$ pers. n. 'fitness'; ɛ$_1$*y*ɛ$_2$ 'parrying'
* ˈɛ*y*ɒ (f.)	Y., ɛ$_1$*y*ɔ$_1$ 'a masquerade peculiar to Lagos'

f,[27] [f]

* *fa* (f.)	E., Φ*a*$_1$ 'to snore'; 'to plant seeds'; Φ*a*$_{1-3}$ 'sediment'; Φ*a*$_3$ 'to polish'; *fa*$_1$ 'to envelop'; 'to crush'; 'to utter a sound'; *fa*$_3$ 'to be cool'; Fn., *fa* 'to console'; 'name given the Yoruba deity Ifa'; T., *fa* 'to take'; Mand., *fa* 'father'; 'name given the seventh child'; Man., *fa* 'father'; 'to kill'; Y., *fa*$_3$ 'to shave'; *fa*$_1$ 'to pull'; 'slow'; 'behind'; cf. Eng., *far*
* ˈ*faba* (m. and f.)	Mand., *faba*, pers. n. 'one who has the same name as that of his paternal uncle'
* *faˈber*ɛ (m.)	Mand., *faber*ɛ pers. n., lit. 'a generous father'
* ˈ*fabi* (f.)	W., *fabi* pers. n. 'to surpass'
* ˈ*faf*ɛ (f.)	E., *fa*$_3$*f*ɛ̃$_3$ pers. n. 'tender, young'
ˈ*faɟ*ɛ (m.)	B., *faɟ*ɛ 'a fruit tree'
faˈlasa (f.)	H., *fal*:$_3$*a*$_1$*sa*:$_2$ 'to squander, to waste'
ˈ*fale* (f.)	B., *fale* 'solid'; 'to push'; 'to change'; Y., *fa*$_1$*le*$_2$ 'to draw tight'
* *fa*$_1$*li*$_3$ (m.)	V., *fa*$_1$*li*$_3$ pers. n. 'alligator'
* ˈ*falim*ɒ (m.)	M., *falim*ɒ pers. n. 'a sower'

GULLAH PERSONAL NAMES	WEST AFRICAN WORDS
* '*falo* (m.)	Man. *falo* pers. n. 'donkey'; *falo* 'stick'
* '*fama* (f.)	B., *fama* 'a king, a powerful man'; 'an absence of long duration'; V., fa_1ma_3 pers. n.; M., pers. n. *fama* 'compliments, salutation'; H., $fa{:}_3ma{:}_3$ 'encountering difficulty'
* *fa'mara* (f.)	Man., *famara* pers. n., lit. 'Keep my father's name'
* '*famata* (f.)	V., $fa_3ma_3ta_3$ pers. n. f.
'*fami'fami* (f.)	Y., $fa_2mi_2fa_2mi_2$ 'a wind instrument,' lit. 'something which draws water'
* '*fana* (f.)	B., *fana* pers. n. 'a fish of the Niger with large scales'; 'an indiscreet reporter'; 'food'; 'to give hospitality'; T., *fana* 'to trouble'
* '*fande* (m.)	V., $fan_1d'e_3$ 'cotton'; 'name given a male child born during the cotton season'; M., *fande* 'cotton'; W., *fande* 'to dispense with supper'
* *fa'niya* (f.)	V., fa_1nia_{3-1} 'a lie'; 'name given a child when there is doubt concerning the identity of its father'
* '*faɲa* (f.)	E., $fa_1\text{ɲ}a_1$ pers. n. 'to knead'
* '*faɲɒ* (m.)	E., $fa_3\text{ɲɔ}_3$ pers. n.
'*fari* (f.)	V., fa_1ri_3 (fa_1li_3) 'the cleared place in a forest where the ceremonies of the $b\varepsilon_3ri_1$ and san_1de_1 (youth organizations) are performed'; 'alligator'; Y., fa_3ri_3 'to shave the head'; 'to cheat'
fa'saɪ (m.)	M., *fasaɪ* 'to explain'
fa'sale (f.)	W., *fasale* 'to separate'
* *fa'siya* (f.)	V., fa_1sia_3 pers. n. f.
* '*fatima* (f.)	V., $fa_2ti_1ma_2$ pers. n. f.; Mand., *fa:tima* 'daughter of Mohammed'
* *fati'mata* (f.)	Mand., *fa:timata* pers. n. f., 'daughter of Mohammed'
* '*fatme* (f.)	V., fat_2me_2 pers. n. f.
* *fa'tɒma* (f.)	V., $fa_1t\text{ɔ}_3ma_3$ pers. n. f.
* *fa'tosĩ* (m.)	Y., $fa_1to_3s\tilde{\imath}_1$ pers. n., lit. 'Ifa is worthy to be worshipped' (Ifa [i_2fa_3] being the Yoruba god of divination)
* '*fatu* (f.)	M., *fatu* pers. n. f.
* '*fatuma* (f.)	Man., *fatuma* pers. n. f.
* *fa'yɛmɒ̃* (m.)	Y., $fa_3y\varepsilon_2m\text{ɔ̃}_2$ pers. n., lit. 'Ifa honors the child'
* '*fede* (m.)	Fn., *fede* pers. n. 'delicate, thin'; E., $fe_1\text{ḍ}e_1$ 'thin, narrow'
'*fefe* (m.)	B., *fefe* 'pepper'; E., fe_3fe_3 'a thorny shrub'; 'twisted'; fe_1fe_3 'playing'; Y., fe_3fe_3 'cleanly'

GULLAH PERSONAL NAMES	WEST AFRICAN WORDS
*'*fela* (m.)	H., $fe{:}_3la{:}_3$ 'a kind of cheap matting without any binding'; E., $fe_3l\tilde{a}_1$ 'a leopard'; M., *fela* 'one of twins'
*'*fele* (m.)	B., *fele* pers. n. 'a calabash'; a 'flute'; 'beating the bushes for game; to unbind'; M., *fele* 'two'
'*fena* (f.)	U., *fena* 'to dig'
fe'niya (f.)	K., *fenia* 'to take snuff'
feŋ'golu (m.)	Man., *feŋolu* 'things'
'*fere* (f.)	Y., fe_3re_2 'asthma'; fe_1re_1 'a flute, a trumpet'; T., *fere* 'to fail, to miss'; B., *fere* 'means, expedient, effort'
'*fesre* (m.)	E., fe_3sre_1 'a window'
*'*fewi* (m.)	Fn., *fevi* 'nail, claw, hoof.' Cf. E., $a_1\Phi e_3vi_3$ 'a native of a place; a free-born person'; 'a small hut for storing cowries'
*'*feya* (f.)	T., *fea* 'name given a child who died before any of its brothers or sisters'
'*feyi* (f.)	T., *fei* 'to search, to pick'
**fɛ* (m.)	Y., $f\varepsilon_3$ pers. n. 'to love, to desire'; 'to blow'; $f\varepsilon_1$ 'to enlarge'; 'extensive'; $f\varepsilon_2$ 'with surprise'; M., *fɛ* 'a pot'; I., $f\varepsilon_3$ 'to fly'; $f\varepsilon_1$ 'to cross,' 'to be contagious'
*'*fɛfɛ* (m.)	Y., $f\varepsilon_2f\varepsilon_2$ 'quickly'; $f\varepsilon_3f\varepsilon_2$ 'to seek occasion for fault-finding'; T., *fɛfɛ* pers. n. 'beautiful, amusing'; M., *fɛfɛ* 'air, wind'
*'*fɛlɛ* (m.)	Y., $f\varepsilon_2l\varepsilon_2$ 'thin'; Kim., *fɛlɛ* pers. n. m.
'*feŋka* (m.)	W., *fɛŋka* 'to rise; to lift'
'*fɛtɛl* (m.)	W., *fɛtɛl* 'a gun'
*'*fiba* (f.)	Tl. *fiba* 'to suckle'; K., *fiba* 'to make a sucking noise'; Y., fi_2ba_1 'to touch'; E., $a_1fi_3ba_3$ 'the name given a girl born on Friday'
fi'beya (f.)	T., *fibea* 'source, origin'
*'*fida* (m. and f.)	T., *fida* 'Friday'; E., $fi_3ḍa_3$ 'Friday'
*'*fidi* (m. and f.)	Y., fi_2di_1 'to wrap'; fi_2di_3 'to replace with'; M., *fidi* pers. n. m.
'*fidɒ* (m.)	Fn., *fidɔ̃* 'here and there, up and down'
'*fifini* (f.)	K., *fifini* 'the guns'; 'the back of a knife'
*'*fila* (f.)	Man., *fila* pers. n. 'two'
fi'lare (f.)	Fu., *filare* 'a narrow band of colored beads threaded together so as to make a pattern and worn round a woman's head'
*'*fili* (f.)	Mand., *fili* 'losing one's way'; 'name given a child

GULLAH PERSONAL NAMES	WEST AFRICAN WORDS
	born outside the house'; B., *fili* 'to abandon'; 'to deceive'; 'to throw'; M., *fili* 'tail, mane, tassel'
ˈ*filu* (m.)	K., *mfilu* 'a tree'
ˈ*fimba* (f.)	K., *fimba* 'to search for'; 'to examine'
ˈ*fina* (f.)	U., *fina* 'strife, to strike'; K., *fina* 'to use the influence of black art, to put under a spell'
* *fi*ˈ*nama* (f.)	K., *finama* pers. n. 'to be near'
ˈ*finda* (f.)	K., *finda* 'to kill, to dispatch'; *mfinda* 'a forest'; Tl., *finda* 'to be cloudy'
* ˈ*findi* (f.)	Fu., *findi* pers. n. 'flower, bud'
* ˈ*fini* (f.)	V., fi_1ni_3 pers. n. f.; B., *fini* 'clothing'; 'a variety of plant'
* ˈ*fino* (f.)	Man., *fino* pers. n. 'black'
ˈ*firi* (f.)	Y., fi_3ri_3 'greater than, strongest, oldest'; fi_1ri_3 'at a glance'; V., fi_1ri_1 'to throw away'; 'to leap'; B., *firi* 'a kind of couscous, cooked in boiling water'; 'thickness'; 'to reverse'
* ˈ*firiŋ* (m.)	S., *firiŋ* pers. n. 'two'
ˈ*fisi* (f.)	Y., fi_2si_3 'to add to, to put in'; M., *fisi* 'to dye cloth the second time'
* ˈ*fiʃi* (f.)	K., *mfiʃi* pers. n. 'the itch'
ˈ*fita* (f.)	K., *fita* 'to ascend'
* *fi*ˈ*tama* (f.)	K., *fitama* pers. n. 'to be crumpled'
ˈ*fite* (f.)	K., *mfite* 'the smallest variety of ants'
ˈ*fiti* (f.)	T., *fiti* 'to enter'; Y., fi_2ti_1 'to lean something against, to suspend a matter under discussion'
*fi*ˈ*tila* (f.)	Y., $fi_1ti_3la_1$ 'a lamp'; H., $fi_1ti_2la_1$ 'a lamp'
* *fi*ˈ*tima* (f.)	M., *fiti:ma* pers. n. 'evening, dusk'
* *fi*ˈ*tina* (f.)	Fu., *fitina* 'misfortune, trouble'; Y., $fi_1ti_3na_1$ pers. n. 'trouble'; 'to harass one'
* *fi*ˈ*tini* (f.)	K., *fitini* pers. n. 'a morsel'
* *fi*ˈ*tiro* (m.)	Man., *fitiro* pers. n. 'six o'clock prayer'
*fiya*ˈ*kalu* (f.)	Y., $fi_2\text{-}a_2k\tilde{a}_3lu_1$ 'to strike with agility'
* ˈ*fiya* (m.)	E., Φia_1 'whirling, buzzing'; $\Phi ia{:}_1$ 'long'; fia_1 'a king, a paramount chief'; 'to speak a foreign language'; fia_3 'to teach'; 'an axe'; M., *fia* 'quickly'
*fiya*ˈ*se* (f.)	T., *mfiase* 'the beginning'
*fi*ˈ*yata* (f.)	K., *fiata* 'to be placed together'
ˈ*fiye* (f.)	E., fie_1 'to itch'; 'to boil'; fie_3 'the long-tailed monkey'; $fi_3\text{-}e_1$ 'the tigernut'; 'the Cyperus'

GULLAH PERSONAL NAMES	WEST AFRICAN WORDS
* ˈ*fɒɪma* (f.)	V., $fai_{3}ma_{1}$ 'name of a place in the Vai country'
ˈ*fɒkɒla* (f.)	K., *fɔkɔla* 'to conclude; to fold back'
* *fɒˈkɒmba* (f.)	K., *fɔkɔmba* pers. n. 'a valley'
ˈ*fɒle* (m.)	Y., $fɔ_{2}le_{3}$ 'to scrub the floor of a house'; $fɔ_{3}le_{3}$ 'to break into a house'; M., *fɔle* 'a cane-shaped drum'
fɒˈlɒna (f.)	K., *fɔlɔna* 'oven.' Cf. P., *forno* [fornu] 'oven'
ˈ*fɒŋga* (m.)	K., *fɔŋga* 'to sit'
* *fɒŋˈgɒna* (f.)	K., *fɔŋgɔna* pers. n. 'to speak through the nose'
* *foˈfiye* (m.)	T., *fo:fie* 'name of a fetish or tutelar genius worshipped at Aburi and other places'; 'name of the Friday ten days before the day on which the natives do not work on the plantation, but may do domestic work'
* ˈ*fofo* (m.)	E., $fo_{1}fo_{3}$ pers. n. 'father'
* ˈ*folema* (m.)	M., *folema* pers. n. 'a kind of fish'
* *foli* (m.)	E., $fo_{1}li_{3}$ pers. n.
* *foˈlo* (m.)	M., *folo* pers. n. 'day, sun'
* ˈ*foma* (f.)	M., *foma* pers. n. 'whip'
* ˈ*fome* (f.)	E., $\Phi o_{1}me_{1}$ pers. n. 'abdominal cavity'; 'family, tribe'
* *foˈmona* (f.)	U., *fomona* pers. n. 'to disjoin'
ˈ*fono* (f.)	B., *fono* 'to vomit'; 'a large fish of the Niger'
* ˈ*fotu* (f.)	Sg., *fot:u* pers. n. 'bitterness'
fu (f.)	E., fu_{1} 'trouble'; fu_{3} 'to be directed upwards'; 'to cut'; 'to rub'; 'to blow'; 'hair'; 'fallow-land'; 'foetus'; 'early in the morning'; 'foam'; B., *fu* 'fiber'; 'something futile'; K., *fu* 'defect'; 'manner, custom'; I., fu_{1} 'to lose, to be lost'
ˈ*fufu* (m.)	E., $fu_{1}fu_{1}$ 'yam, cassava'; 'to deceive'; $fu_{3}fu_{3}$ 'blowing, breathing'; $fu_{3}fu_{1-3}$ 'the cotton fibre'; 'mold'; 'dust';[28] Y., $fu_{1}fu_{3}$ 'meal prepared from grated cassava'
ˈ*fuka* (m.)	K., *fuka* 'the formalities which have to be observed in approaching a great chief or in the worship of God'
ˈ*fukula* (f.)	K., *fukula* 'to uncover'
* ˈ*fula* (f.)	*fula* 'name of a West African tribe and language'; Man., *fula* 'two'; K., *mfula* 'working in metals'; Tl., *fula* 'to be submissive'; M., *fula* 'village'
* *fuˈlando* (m.)	Mand., *fulando* 'twins'
* *fuˈlani* (m.)	*fulani* 'name of a West African tribe and language'; B., *fulani* 'twins'
* ˈ*fulbe* (m.)	*fulbe* 'name of a West African tribe'

GULLAH PERSONAL NAMES	WEST AFRICAN WORDS
**fuˈmina* (f.)	K., *fumina* pers. n. 'to be quiet'; 'to be vexed'
*ˈ*fumu* (f.)	K., *mfumu* pers. n. 'chief, nobleman, sovereign'
ˈ*funa* (f.)	Kim., *funa* 'to earn'; K., *funa* 'to increase'; 'a kind of mash'; Tl., *funa* 'to threaten'
funˈdaŋga (m.)	Kim., *fundaŋga* 'gunpowder'; U., *ofundaŋga* 'gunpowder'
ˈ*funɟi* (m.)	Kim., *funʒi* 'cassava mush'
*ˈ*funɒ* (f.)	E., *fu*$_3$*nɔ*$_1$ 'a woman with child'; 'a nickname of the spider'
ˈ*funta* (m.)	K., *funta* 'to shave off the surface of the ground with a hoe or adze'
ˈ*fuŋga* (m.)	K., *fuŋga* 'to be insufficiently cooked'
**fuˈtila* (m.)	K., *mfutila* 'a title of nobility'
fuˈtisa (f.)	K., *futisa* 'to extort'
**fwa* (f.)	K., *fwa* pers. n. 'to die'; 'a corpse'; 'a cripple'
fwaˈlansa (m.)	K., *fwalansa* 'the Kongo speaker's pronunciation of *France*'
fwaˈyeta (f.)	K., *fwayeta* 'a tailor.' Cf. P., *alfaiate* 'tailor'
ˈ*fweŋka* (f.)	K., *fweŋka* 'to cut off close to the ground'
*ˈ*fyene* (f.)	B., *fyene* pers. n. 'struck with blindness'
*ˈ*fyeɲa* (f.)	B., *fyeɲa* pers. n. 'blindness'; 'shame'; 'to relieve'

[g]

**gã* (m.)	Cf. *gã* 'name of a people and language on the Gold Coast'; Fn., *gã* 'chief'; 'metal'
**gaˈdaya* (f.)	B., *gadaya* pers. n. 'the position of servant'
*ˈ*gafa* (m.)	H., *ga*:$_1$*fa*:$_2$ 'a wooden bit put into an animal's mouth to prevent it from eating'; M., *ŋgafa* 'spirit, soul, idol'
*ˈ*gafe* (m.)	E., *ga*$_3$*Φe*$_3$ pers. n. 'the place where one has been cured, i.e., the shrine of a deity'; B., *gafe* 'a manuscript, a book'
ˈ*gala* (f.)	M., *ngala* 'a mat'
ˈ*gale* (m.)	M., *ŋgale* 'to break'
*ˈ*galu* (m.)	M., *ŋgalu* pers. n. 'moon, month'; 'egg'
*ˈ*gama* (m.)	B., *gama* 'a bovine animal with a hump'; M., *ŋgama* pers. n. 'eye, face'
ˈ*gamɒ* (m.)	M., *ŋgamɒ* 'to twist hard, to harden'
**gamˈbiŋgɒ* (m.)	M., *gambiŋgɒ* pers. n. 'to be stripped'
*ˈ*gana* (f.)	E., *ga*$_1$*na*:$_1$ pers. n. 'bent, bowed'; *gã*$_1$*na*$_1$ 'jackal, hyena'; K., *ŋgana* 'fable, proverb, folklore'

GULLAH PERSONAL NAMES	WEST AFRICAN WORDS
*ˈ*ganda* (m.)	K., *ŋganda* 'a name given to San Salvador as the chief city of the Kongo country'; M., *ganda* 'strongly, vigorously'
*ˈ*gane* (f.)	B., *gane* 'deceit, knavery'; Fn., *gane* 'four o'clock'; W., *gane* 'to lodge with someone'; H., *ga:*$_1$*ne:*$_1$ pers. n. m.
*ˈ*gani* (f.)	B., *gani* 'a secret'; H. and Fu., *ga:ni:* pers. n. m.; K., *ŋgani* 'grit which has been taken into the mouth with food'
*ˈ*ganɟi* (f.)	K., *ŋganʒi* pers. n. 'pain'; 'anger'
ˈ*ganu* (f.)	E., *ga*$_1$*nu*$_3$ 'any metal implement, especially tin'; Fn., *gãnu* 'an iron case or box'
garapˈgi (m.)	W., *garap gi* 'the tree'
*ˈ*gasa* (f.)	H., *ga:*$_1$*sa*$_1$ 'an exclamation of astonishment or exasperation'; *ga:*$_1$*sa:*$_2$ 'rivalry'; W., *ŋgasa* 'a ditch, a moat'; M., *ŋgasa* 'to seize, to catch after pursuit'
*ˈ*gasi* (f.)	B., *gasi* pers. n. 'misfortune'
ˈ*gawa* (m.)	H., *ga:*$_3$*wa:*$_3$ 'a corpse'; 'an abundance'; M., *gawa* 'to bend back, to strut'
*ˈ*gaya* (f.)	M., *ŋgaya* pers. n. 'a tear,' lit. 'eye water'
*ˈ*gebu* (m.)	M., *ŋgebu* pers. n. 'under the sky,' i.e., 'in the world'
*ˈ*gela* (f.)	M., *ŋgela* 'to sweep'; Tl., *ŋgela* pers. n. 'a good marksman'
*ˈ*gele* (f.)	M., *ŋgele* pers. n. m.; 'sky, heavens, lightning'
* *geˈleŋgeru* (m.)	Fu., *ŋgeleŋgeru* pers. n. 'crocodile'
*ˈ*geli* (m.)	Fn., *geli* pers. n. 'elephant'
*ˈ*gezo* (m.)	Fn., *gezo* 'the tenth-king of Dahomey, who reigned from 1818 to 1858'
*ˈ*gɛlɛdɛ* (f.)	Y., *gɛ*$_1$*lɛ*$_1$*dɛ*$_3$ 'a kind of masquerade, peculiar to Lagos and its suburbs'
*ˈ*gɛlɛma* (m.)	M., *gɛlɛma* (*kɛlɛma*) pers. n. 'end, termination'
ˈ*gɛnɛ* (m.)	V., *gɛ*$_1$*nɛ*$_3$ 'cricket, a chirping insect'; *gɛ*$_3$*nɛ*$_1$ 'a circle'
ˈ*gɛwɛ* (m)	M., *gɛwɛ* 'different, various'; *gɛvɛ* 'to bury'
*ˈ*gibril* (m.)	Man., *gibril* 'Gabriel'
ˈ*gidi* (m.)	E., *gi*$_1$*di*$_1$ 'violently, with a loud noise'
*ˈ*giɟi* (ˈ*gici*, ˈ*ɟiɟi*, ˈ*ɟici* (f.)	*gidʒi, gitʃi, gitsi, gisi* 'a language and tribe in the Kissy country (Liberia)'; M., *gidʒɪ* 'a country called Kissy'
*ˈ*giza* (m.)	K., *ŋgiza* pers. n. 'a coming, an advent'

GULLAH PERSONAL NAMES	WEST AFRICAN WORDS
* '_gɒɪgɒɪ_ (m.)	Y., _gɔi_$_1$_gɔi_$_1$ pers. n. 'sluggishly'
* '_gɒɪmɒ_ (m.)	M., _ŋgaɪmɒ_ pers. n. 'a blacksmith'
* '_gɒli_ (m.)	M., _gɔli_ (_kɔli_) pers. n. 'leopard'; 'greedy, stingy'
* '_gɒma_ (m.)	K., _ŋgɔma_ pers. n. 'a drum'; M., _gɔma_ 'a crow'
* '_gɒmbɒ_ (m.)	K., _ŋgɔmbɔ_ 'the charm to which the witch-doctor appeals in order that he may discover a witch'
'_gɒme_ (m.)	E., _gɔ_$_1$_me_$_1$ 'foundation, bottom'
* '_gɒni_ (m.)	M., _ŋɔni_ pers. n. 'bird'; 'oyster'
'_gɒnɟi_ (m.)	K., _ŋgɔnʒi_ 'a rope'
* '_gɒɲɒ_ (m.)	M., _gɒɲɔ_ (_kɒɲɔ_) pers. n. 'enemy'
* '_gɒŋ_'_gɒlɒ_ (m.)	K., _ŋgɔŋgɔlɔ_ pers. n. 'the millipede'
'_gɒrɒ_ (f.)	M., _gɔrɒ_ 'a defensive wall'
'_goba_ (m.)	E., _go_$_1$_ba:_$_1$ 'bent, crooked, hollow'
'_golɛ_ (m.)	B., _golɛ_ 'gun, cannon, pipe'
'_goli_ (m.)	B., _goli_ 'to run away'; M., _ŋgoli_ 'ear, tail, mane'
'_golo_ (m.)	E., _go_$_1$_lo_$_1$ 'a pouch made of leaves of the fan palm'; M., _ŋgolo_ 'to break'
'_gomɛ_ (m.)	M., _gomɛ_ 'to meet, to assemble'
* _go_'_nima_ (f.)	B., _gonima_ pers. n. 'hot, ardent'
* '_goŋgolo_ (m.)	M., _goŋgolo_ (_koŋgolo_) 'a cart, a gig'; cf. Fn., _agɔ̃_(ŋ)_gulo_ 'a king of Dahomey'
* '_goro_ (m. and f.)	B., _goro_ 'baboon'; 'button'; M., _ŋgoro_, pers. n. 'an ape'; _goro_ (_golo_) 'to obey'
* '_goru_ (m)	T., _goru_ 'to play'; V., _go_$_3$_ru_$_1$ (_go_$_3$_lu_$_1$) 'the month of May'
* _go_'_yito_ (m.)	Fn., _goyito_ pers. n. 'haughty, proud'
* '_gudi_ (m.)	W., _gudi_ pers. n. 'night'; K., _ŋgudi_ 'mother'; 'one's maternal relatives'
* '_gula_ (m.)	_gula_ 'name of a tribe in Liberia'; M., _gula_ (_kula_) 'to fall, to drop'
* _gu_'_leli_ (f.)	Fu., _gul:eli_ 'the hot season, beginning about March after the conclusion of the harmattan wind'
* '_gumba_ (m.)	M., _gumba_ (_kumba_) pers. n. 'shirt, gown'; _ŋgumba_ 'top, summit'
* '_guŋga_ (m.)	K., _ŋguŋga_ pers. n. 'a bell.' Cf. Bo., _ŋgoŋga_ 'a double bell'
'_guro_ (m.)	H., _gu_$_1$_ro:_$_2$ 'okra'; T., _guro_ 'suddenly'
* _gu_'_cili_ (m.)	Fn., _gucili_ 'a king of Dahomey, brother of Behanzin'
* '_guwu_ (m.)	K., _ŋguvu_ pers. n. 'hippopotamus'

GULLAH PERSONAL NAMES	WEST AFRICAN WORDS
	[h]
ˈ*hadi* (m.)	Man., *hadi* 'yes'; H., $ha'_{3}di_{1}$ 'the wearing of two or more gowns simultaneously'
* *hadiˈɟata* (f.)	Mand., *hadi:ɟata* 'the first wife of Mohammed'
*ˈ*haga* (f.)	M., *haga* pers. n. 'lazy.' See *hawa*
* *haˈɟela* (m.)	E., $ha_{1}\text{ɟ}e_{1}la_{3}$ pers. n. 'a disorderly person'
ˈ*haɟu* (m.)	B., *haɟu* 'affairs, matters' (Ar.)
*ˈ*hala* (*hla*)	Fn., *hala* (*hla*) pers. n. 'the hyena'; W., *hala* 'to disentangle'; 'a bow for throwing arrows'; E., $ha_{1}l\tilde{a}_{1}$ 'pork'; Fu., *hala* 'a discourse'; M., *hala* pers. n. 'first'
*ˈ*hale* (m.)	B., *hale* pers. n. 'to have an air of superiority'; Y., $ha_{3}le_{3}$ 'to repair the roof of a house with thatch'
ˈ*hali* (f.)	E., $ha_{1}li_{1}$ 'to dislocate'; H., $ha{:}_{3}li_{1}$ 'circumstances'; $ha_{3}li{:}_{3}$ 'innate character'; Mal., *hali* 'very much'
*ˈ*hama* (m.)	H., $ha_{3}ma{:}_{3}$ 'a yawning hole'; T., *hãmã* 'a cord, a bond'; M., *hama* 'the rainy season (from May to October)'
ˈ*hani* (m. and f.)	H., $ha_{3}ni_{1}$ 'the act of prohibiting'; Man., *hani* 'no'; M., *hanɪ* 'thing'
ˈ*hanifo* (m.)	Man., *hanifo* 'until'
ˈ*hanɟi* (m.)	Kim., *hanʒi* 'still'
*ˈ*hanu* (f.)	E., $ha_{1}nu_{3}$ pers. n. 'a subject for a song, a great event, a great misfortune'; H., $ha_{3}nu{:}_{3}$ 'either of two varieties of the frankincense tree'
* *haraˈmata* (f.)	T., *haramata* pers. n. 'a dry wind from the interior of Africa which blows in December, January, and February toward the Atlantic Ocean and which is accompanied by a dusty haze'
* *haˈruna* (m. and f.)	Mand., *haru:na* 'Aaron'
* *haˈsana* (f.)	Fu., *hasana* pers. n.
*ˈ*hate* (f.)	B., *hat:e* pers. n. 'Good! Well done!'
*ˈ*hawa* (m. and f.)	M., *hawa* pers. n. f.; 'lazy'; Mand., *hawa* pers. n. f.; 'Eve'
* *haˈwaɲa* (f.)	H., $ha_{3}wa_{3}\text{ɲ}a_{3}$ pers. n. 'a tear'
ˈ*hayi* (f.)	Fn., *hayi* 'to ascend'; *hãyi* 'music'
*ˈ*heke* (m.)	M., *heke* pers. n. 'a large wild animal, a bush cow'
*ˈ*hele* (m.)	M., *hele* pers. n. 'elephant'
* *heˈleŋga* (f.)	M., *heɪleŋga* pers. n. 'the period just after dark (the "sitting together" time)'

GULLAH PERSONAL NAMES	WEST AFRICAN WORDS
*ˈ*hema* (f.)	M., *heɪma* pers. n. 'residence, resting-place'; T., *ɔhem:a*: 'the queen mother'
*ˈ*hembe* (f.)	V., *hem*$_3$*be*$_3$ pers. n. f.; M., *hembe* 'crown, kingdom'
*ˈ*hemɒ* (m.)	M., *heɪmɒ* pers. n. 'a person of means'
ˈ*hemu* (f.)	Fn., *hẽmu* 'to destroy'
*ˈ*hendu* (m.)	Fu., *hendu* pers. n. 'the wind'
*ˈ*hene* (f.)	T., *hene* 'itching, prurient'; *ɔhene* 'king, chief'
*ˈ*heɲɒ* (m.)	M., *heiɲɔ* pers. n. 'neighbor'
*ˈ*heŋga* (m.)	W., *heŋga* pers. n. 'to be deformed, to have a hump on the back'; M., *heŋga* 'to dream'; 'a dream'; *heɪŋga* 'to piece out cloth when it is insufficient for the pattern'
ˈ*hɛkɛ* (m.)	Bi., *hɛ*$_1$*kɛ̃*$_{3-1}$ (<*hɔ*$_1$-*e*$_3$*kɛ̃*$_1$) 'to collect and mix mud'
ˈ*hɛlɛ* (f.)	M., *hɛlɛ* 'to hang'; 'to insult by the use of disrespectful language'
ˈ*higi* (m.)	M., *higi* 'a white-ant hill'
ˈ*hihũ* (m.)	Y., *hi*$_3$*hũ*$_2$ 'a mode of weaving'
*ˈ*hima* (f.)	Kim., *hima* pers. n. 'monkey'; H., *him*:$_3$*a*$_1$ 'energy, attentiveness'; T., *hĩmã* 'to shake; to turn'
*ˈ*hina* (f.)	U., *hina* pers. n. 'to be obstinate, to press'; T., *ahĩna* 'a pot, an earthen vessel'; M., *hĩna* 'male'
ˈ*hinda* (f.)	M., *hĩnda* 'place, thing, circumstance, act'
*ˈ*hindo* (m.)	M., *hĩndo* pers. n. 'man'
* *hin*ˈ*doya* (m. and f.)	M., *hĩndoya* pers. n. 'manhood'
*ˈ*hini* (f.)	T., *hini* 'to close'; M., *hĩni* pers. n. 'husband'
* *hi*ˈ*tɛlo* (f.)	M., *hitɛlo* pers. n. 'an illegitimate child'
*ˈ*hitu* (m.)	Kim., *hitu* 'in Angola folklore, a lion-man, i.e., a man transformed into a lion'
ˈ*hiyɛ* (m.)	I., *hi*$_3$*ɛ*$_3$ 'to prop'; Bi., *hiɛ*$_{1-3}$ 'to deceive'; 'to fail'; *hiɛ*$_{3-1}$ 'to be prosperous'; G., *hĩ*$_1$*ɛ̃*$_1$ 'face'
ˈ*hɒɪma* (f.)	W., *haima* 'to evaluate'; 'estimation'
ˈ*hɒɟi* (m.)	Fn., *hɔ̃ɟi* 'door-sill'
* *hɒ*ˈ*luwa* (f.)	Kim., *hɔlua* pers. n. 'a drunkard.' Cf. U., *oholua* 'a drunkard'
*ˈ*hɒmbɒ* (m.)	Kim., *hɔmbɔ* pers. n. 'goat.' Cf. U., *hombo* 'goat'
ˈ*hɒna* (f.)	M., *hɔna* 'to practice witchcraft'
* *ho*ˈ*bolɪ* (m.)	M., *hobolɪ* pers. n. 'a riddle'
* *ho*ˈ*doto* (m.)	Fn., *hodoto* pers. n. 'an orator'
*hog*ˈ*befe* (m.)	E., *ho*$_1$*gbe*$_1$*Φe*$_3$ 'the old, original home'

GULLAH PERSONAL NAMES	WEST AFRICAN WORDS
* ˈ*hoho* (m.)	E., $ho_1ho{:}_1$ pers. n. 'many-voiced, loud-sounding'; Fn., *hoho* 'the spirit protector of twins'; 'old'
* *hoˈhowi* (m.)	Fn., *hohovi* 'one of twins (the child of Hoho)'
* ˈ*holima* (m.)	M., *holima* pers. n. 'patience'
* hon_1do_3 (f.)	V., hon_3do_3 pers. n. m.
* ˈ*hota* (m.)	M., *hota* pers. n. 'stranger'; 'to visit'
* *hoˈtaya* (f.)	M., *hotaya* pers. n. 'the state of being a stranger'
ˈ*hotse* (f.)	T., *hotse* 'to scatter'
huˈbɪndɪgɒ (m.)	M., *hũgbɪndɪ(ŋ)gɒ* 'to be dark'
* ˈ*hudidi* (m.)	Fn., *hũdidi* pers. n. 'bleeding, blood-letting'
* ˈ*huɟuˌkulu* (f.)	M., *hʊ̃dʒukulʊ* pers. n. 'to waste'
ˈ*hula* (f.)	Fn., *hula* 'to preserve'; 'to ravage'
ˈ*huli* (f.)	Fn., *huli* 'to save, to take care of'; H., $hu{:}_3li_1$ 'the fruit of the $da_3ɲa{:}_3$ tree'
* ˈ*huma* (f.)	M., *hũma* pers. n. 'to steal'; 'theft'
* *huˈmɒlɪ* (m.)	M., *hʊ̃mɔlɪ* pers. n. 'to investigate'
ˈ*hunɛ* (f.)	M., *hʊ̃nɛ* 'to explain plausibly'
* ˈ*huno* (m.)	Cf. Fn., *hunɔ̃* 'priest'
* ˈ*hunu* (f.)	Fn., *hunu* 'a noise, fame, reputation'; H., $hu{:}_3nu{:}_3$ pers. n. 'a fool'
ˈ*hura* (f.)	T., *hura* 'to be covered with'; 'to overgrow'
* ˈ*husu* (f.)	W., *hu:su* 'a ford'; Fn., *hũsu* 'one of twins'
ˈ*huta* (m.)	Kim., *huta* 'food'
* ˈ*huto* (m.)	Fn., *huto* 'the sea coast'; *hũto* pers. n. 'drummer'
ˈ*hutu* (m.)	Kim., *hutu* 'a bag'
* ˈ*huwa* (m.)	Y., hu_1wa_1 'to behave, to conduct one's self'; Fn., *huwã* 'to be jealous'; U., *huva* 'elder brother'
* ˈ*huza* (m.)	Fn., *hũzã* pers. n. 'to lie awake'
ˈ*hũzɒ* (m.)	Fn., *hũzɔ̃* 'anemia'

[i]

* ˈ*iba* (m.)	Ef., i_3ba_{3-1} pers. n. 'a big lizard; i_1ba_1 'two'; i_1ba_2 'bathing trunks'
* *ibaˈʃɒrũ* (m.)	Y., $i_2ba_2ʃɔ_1rũ_3$ 'prime minister'
* *iˈbeɟi* (m.)	Y., $i_1be_2ɟi_1$ 'twins'
* *iˈbibio* (m.)	$i_1bi_3bi_1o_1$ 'name of a Nigerian language and tribe'
* *ibiˈyiŋka* (m.)	Y., $i_1bi_3yi_3$-$ŋ_2ka_3$ pers. n., lit. 'Births surround me'
* *ibˈɒla* (m.)	Y., $i_1bɔ_2la_3$ pers. n. 'the act of paying respect'
iˈbogidi (m.)	Y., $i_2bo_2gi_2di_2$ 'a vine with white, yellow-centered flowers'; 'edible fruit'

GULLAH PERSONAL NAMES	WEST AFRICAN WORDS
* *i'brahima* (m.)	Man. *ibrahima* 'Abraham'
* *'ida* (f.)	Y., i_2da_1 'sword'; i_1da_2 'beeswax'; i_1da_3 'creation'; cf. *Ida* 'a Nigerian tribe'
* *'idi* (f.)	Y., i_2di_1 pers. n. 'eagle'; i_1di_1 'bundle'; i_1di_3 'waist, groin'; 'reason, base'; i_2di_2 'a plant whose roots are used for chewsticks'
* *i'dowu* (m.)	Y., $i_1do_1wu_3$ 'the first child, male or female, born after twins'
* *'ifa* (m.)	Y., i_2fa_3 'the god of divination'; i_1fa_2 'a tool used to remove the pulp of green calabash'; i_1fa_1 'good luck, gain'
'ife (m.)	Y., i_3fe_3 'a cup, a tumbler-shaped gourd'; i_1fe_2 'a small bird'; i_1fe_3 'whistling'
'ifũ (m.)	Y., $i_1fũ_2$ 'intestines'
'igi (f.)	Y., i_2gi_2 'tree, wood, fuel'
* *'igũ* (m.)	Y., $i_2gũ_3$ pers. n. 'vulture'; $i_2gũ_2$ 'leaves pounded and thrown into rivers to stupefy fish'; 'shin'; 'corner, angle'
* *igũ'nuko* (m.)	Y., $i_2gũ_2nũ_2ko_3$, 'god of the forest, the impersonator of whom walks on stilts'; cf. N., *gunoko* pers. n.
* *i'ɟaiye* (m. and f.)	Y., $i_1ɟai_2ye_3$ pers. n. 'enjoyment of luxury or pleasure'
* *'iɟɛʃa* (m.)	Y., $i_1ɟɛ_1ʃa_1$ ($i_2ɟɛ_1ʃa_1$) 'a Yoruba tribe of the Ilesha Province'
* *'iɟɒ* (m.)	*idʒɔ* 'name of a Western Sudanic language in the Niger estuary'; Y., $i_2ɟɔ_3$ 'day'; $i_1ɟɔ_2$ 'assembly'
* *i'kiɟa* (m.)	Y., $i_1ki_2ɟa_1$ 'name of a district of which the king or lord is $a_2la_3ki_2ɟa_1$'
* *'ikɒ* (m.)	Ef., $i_3kɔ_{3-1}$ pers. n. 'word, speech'
i'koko (m.)	Y., $i_1ko_1ko_1$ ($i_1ko_2ko_1$) 'a pot'
* *i'kuyiwu* (f.)	Bi., $i_1xui_{3-1}wu_1$ pers. n. 'hatred'
'ila (f.)	Y., i_2la_1 'tattooing'; circumcision'; i_2la_3 'okra'; i_1la_1 'line, mark'; $i{:}_1la_1$ 'state of salvation, escape from danger'
* *i'laɪya* (m.)	Y., $i_1lai_3ya_1$ pers. n. 'courage, boldness'; $i_1lai_2ya_1$ 'medicine supposed to give courage'
'ilam (m.)	Fu., *'ilam* 'flood'
* *i'lawɒ* (f.)	Y., $i_1la_2wɔ_3$ pers. n. 'generosity'
* *i'le-ori* (f.)	Y., i_1le_3-o_1ri_3 'a place of worship in the Yoruba country—a kind of shrine where o_2ri_3, the god of fate, is worshipped'
* *i'male* (f.)	Y., $i_1ma_1le_2$ 'a Mohammedan'

GULLAH PERSONAL NAMES	WEST AFRICAN WORDS
* *imˈbuwa* (m.)	Kim., *imbua* pers. n. 'dog'
i_1mi_3 (f.)	Y., i_1mi_3 'the act of breathing'; 'strength'; i_2mi_3 'excrement'
* ˈ*ina* (f.)	U., *ina* 'mother'; Y., i_1na_2 'a flogging'; i_2na_3 'fire'; Tl., *ina* 'to immerse'; 'to dye'; H., $in{:}_3a_1$ 'mother of all spirits'
ˈ*inama* (m.)	Kim., *inama* 'legs'; Tl., *inama* 'to stoop'
* *inˈwula* (m.)	Tl., *nvula* pers. n. 'rain'; K., *mvula* 'rain'
* *iŋˈkiʃi* (f.)	K., *ŋkiʃi* pers. n. 'a charm, medicine'
iˈpampa (m.)	Y., i_1kpa_2-$ŋ_2kpa_3$ 'a bargain, agreement between traders'
* *iˈpanda* (f.)	V., i_3 $kpan_3da_3$ pers. n. 'you alone'
* *iˈpete* (m.)	Y., $i_1kpe_2te_2$ 'intention'; cf. T., *opete* 'vulture'; 'deity'
iˈreno (f.)	Y., $i_2re_2no_2$ 'male rubber tree'
ˈ*irɛ* (f.)	Y., $i_2rɛ_3$ 'silk rubber tree'; $i_1rɛ_2$ 'fatigue'; I., $i_3rɛ_3$ 'tongue'; $i_1rɛ_1$ 'potent'
iruˈkɛrɛ (f.)	Y., $i_1ru_1kɛ_1rɛ_1$ 'the cowtail carried about by the priests or kings; a whisk'
* ˈ*isa* (m.)	Y., i_2sa_1 'a tomb, a hold'; i_1sa_1 'honor'; Mand., *isa* 'Jesus'; V., i_2sa_1 pers. n.; i_3sa_1 'Lie down'
* *iˈsala* (f.)	*isala* 'a dialect of Gurunsi spoken in the area between the White and Black Voltas'
* ˈ*isɛ* (f.)	Y., $i_1sɛ_3$ pers. n. 'a denial'; I., $i_1sɛ_3$ 'five'
ˈ*iso* (m.)	U., *iso* 'eye'; Y., i_1so_2 'the state of being tied'; i_2so_3 'discharge of the wind from the anus'
ˈ*isuwa* (f.)	Ef., i_3sua_1 'year'
* ˈ*iʃã* (m.)	*iʃã* 'one of the Western Sudanic languages of the Kwa group'
iˈʃagidi (f.)	Y., $i_2ʃa_2gi_2di_2$ 'cream fruit (poison)'
* ˈ*iʃaɪ* (m.)	Fu., *iʃai* pers. n. 'about 7 o'clock P.M.'
iˈʃawewe (f.)	Y., $i_2ʃa_2we_2we_2$ 'a plant'
* ˈ*iʃi* (f.)	Kim., *iʃi* pers. n. 'earth, ground'; Y., $i_1ʃĩ_3$ 'a small fish'; $i_2ʃĩ_2$ 'a tree with edible fruit'
ˈ*ita* (f.)	Ef. i_1ta_2 'three'; i_1ta_{3-1} 'a torch made from calabash soaked in oil'
iˈtadi (f.)	Kim., *itadi* (*itari*) 'money' (pl. of *kitadi*)
iˈtondi (m.)	Man., *itondi*? 'What is your name?'
* ˈ*iwa* (f.)	Y., i_1wa_1 pers. n. 'conduct, character'
* *iˈwalɛ* (m.)	Y., $i_1wa_2lɛ_1$ 'one who digs' (applied to a male child)
* *iwaˈlula* (f.)	U., *ivalula* pers. n. 'to cause to remember'

GULLAH PERSONAL NAMES	WEST AFRICAN WORDS
* *iˈwapɛlɛ* (m.)	Y., i$_1$wa$_1$kpɛ$_1$lɛ$_3$ pers. n. 'gentleness'
* i$_1$ya$_3$ (f.)	Y., i$_1$ya$_3$ 'mother'; i$_1$ya$_1$ 'affliction'; i$_2$ya$_2$ 'the African balsam'
* *iˈyaba* (f.)	Y., i$_1$ya$_3$-a$_1$gba$_1$ (i$_1$ya:$_{3-1}$gba$_1$) 'matron, elderly woman'; cf. Y., a$_2$ya$_2$ba$_2$ 'queen'
* *iˈyaɟi* (m.)	Cf. Y., ma$_2$ga$_1$ɟi$_1$-i$_1$ya$_3$ɟi$_3$ 'a member of the royal family who serves as an elder brother to the king'
* *iˈyakala* (f.)	Y., i$_1$ya$_3$ka$_3$la$_3$ pers. n.
* *iˈyakekeˈre* (f.)	Y., i$_1$ya$_3$ke$_3$ke$_2$re$_3$ 'name given the second wife by the children of the first'; 'junior, small'
* *iyaˈlemɒlɛ* (f.)	Y., i$_1$ya$_3$le$_3$mɔ̃$_2$lɛ$_1$ 'a Yoruba priestess who has in her keeping the king's Ifa god and who participates in ceremonies which take place when Ifa priests come every fifth day to worship and to consult the Ifa god'
iˈyama (f.)	Bi., i$_1$ya$_{3-1}$ma$_1$ 'a mark of ownership or identification'
* *iˈyami-iˈyami* (m. and f.)	Y., i$_1$ya$_3$mi$_2$!i$_1$ya$_3$mi$_2$! pers. n. 'My mother! my mother!'
* *iyamɒˈnari* (f.)	Y., i$_1$ya$_3$mɔ̃$_1$na$_1$ri$_3$ 'one of the ladies of the king's palace whose duty it is to execute by strangling any ʃaŋ$_1$go$_3$ worshippers condemned to capital punishment, since they are not to die by the sword'
* *iˈyansa* (f.)	Y., i$_1$ya$_3$-n$_3$sã$_3$ 'the wife of ʃaŋ$_1$go$_3$, god of thunder'
* *iyaˈyemaɟa* (f.)	Y., i$_1$ya$_3$ye$_2$ma$_2$ɟa$_2$ 'the mother of the goddess of brooks (ye$_2$ma$_2$ɟa$_2$)'
* *iˈyanaso* (f.)	Y., i$_1$ya$_3$na$_3$so$_2$ 'one of the eight ladies of highest rank at the king's palace'
* *iˈya-ɒtũ* (f.)	Y., i$_1$ya$_3$-ɔ$_1$tũ$_3$ 'one of the ladies of high rank at the king's palace'
* *iˈya-ɒba* (f.)	Y., i$_1$ya$_3$-ɔ$_2$ba$_2$ 'mother of the king'
iˈyɒha (f.)	Bi., i$_1$yɔ$_1$ha$_1$ 'a pawn'
iˈyɒyɒ (f.)	Bi., i$_1$yɔ$_1$yɔ$_1$ 'the bushy end of things'
iˈzabɒ (m.)	Bi., i$_3$za$_3$bɔ$_2$ 'shoulder'
izaˈduma (f.)	Bi., i$_1$za$_1$du$_1$ma$_3$ 'a drum'
ˌizaˈzako (m.)	Bi. i$_1$za$_1$za$_1$ko$_3$ 'a red antelope believed to run continuously on some days and to walk on others'
* *ˌizeˈwudu* (m.)	Bi. i$_1$ze$_1$βu$_1$du$_1$ pers. n. 'obstinacy'
* *ıˈzɒla* (m.)	Bi. i$_3$zɔ$_1$la$_3$ 'the European week'
iˈzobo (m.)	Bi., i$_1$zo$_{3-1}$bo$_3$ 'feeding evil spirits, witches, etc.'[29]

GULLAH PERSONAL NAMES	WEST AFRICAN WORDS
	[ɟ]
ɟa (m.)	Y., *ɟa*$_3$ 'to break'; *ɟa*$_1$ 'to fight'; Man., *dʒa* 'to be dry'; M., *dʒa* 'to touch'; V., *dʒa*$_1$ 'home'; *dʒa*$_3$ 'eye'
'*ɟaba* (m.)	B., *ɟaba* 'onion'; Y., *ɟa*$_2$*gba*$_1$ 'to contest in a wrestling match'; *ɟa*$_3$*gba*$_1$ 'to snatch from'; cf. Eng., *jabber*
* *ɟaba'laɪyɒ* (m.)	Y., *ɟa*$_1$*gba*$_1$*lai*$_3$*yɔ*$_1$ pers. n.
* '*ɟabata* (m.)	Y., *ɟa*$_2$*gba*$_2$*ta*$_2$ 'name of a place in the Yoruba country—the residence of the chief of an army'
'*ɟabi* (m.)	B., *ɟabi* 'to respond'; 'to insult'
* *ɟa'biro* (m.)	Man., *dʒabiro* pers. n. m. 'an answer'
* *ɟag'bandɪ* (m. and f.)	M., *ndʒagbandɪ* (*ndʒakpandɪ*) pers. n. m. 'hot water'
* *ɟag'bema* (m.)	M., *ndʒagbema* 'name of a place near or in sight of the water'
* '*ɟaɪya* (m.)	Y., *ɟai*$_3$*ya*$_1$ 'to be afraid'; V., *dʒai*$_3$*a*$_1$ pers. n. m.
'*ɟaɟo* (f.)	M., *dzadʒo* 'a small tree'
* '*ɟakɛ* (m.)	V., *dʒa*$_3$*kɛ*$_1$ pers. n. 'to prophesy'
* '*ɟala* (m. and f.)	V., *dʒa*$_1$*la*$_3$ pers. n. m. 'lion'; M., *ndʒala* 'the indigo plant and its dye'; B., *ɟala* 'lace'; 'dry'; 'creole, mixed'
* '*ɟalawa* (m. and f.)	V., *dʒa*$_1$*la*$_1$*wa*$_3$ pers. n. m.
* '*ɟalɒ* (f.)	Y., *ɟa*$_3$*lɔ*$_{1-2}$ 'to solve a riddle'; *ɟa*$_3$*lɔ*$_2$ 'to escape from tether'; M., *ndʒalɒ* 'a fabulous water spirit'
* *ɟa'loŋka* (m.)	*dʒaloŋka* 'one of the Western Sudanic languages of the Mande fu group'
* *ɟa'lore* (f.)	Fu., *dʒalore* pers. n. 'laughter'
* '*ɟama* (m.)	B., *ɟama* 'an assembly, company'; 'to travel'; 'to rebel'; M., *dʒama* 'to become independent of labor'; *ndʒama* 'name given a child born by a stream'; Man., *dʒama* 'many'; H., *dʒa:*$_3$*ma:*$_3$ 'great-great grandfather'; Tl., *ʒama* 'to be steadfast'
* '*ɟamba* (m.)	Y., *ɟam*$_1$*ba*$_3$ 'treachery'; V., *dʒam*$_1$*ba*$_3$ 'any kind of leaf'; M., *ndʒamba* 'a skirt of palm fibers'; *dʒamba* 'to give a present to.' Cf. U., *ondʒamba* pers. n. 'elephant'
* '*ɟambi* (m.)	V., *dʒam*$_1$*bi*$_3$ pers. n. 'the wild yam'
* *ɟam'bila* (m.)	K., *ŋgyambila*, pers. n. 'adultery, immorality'
* '*ɟambo* (m.)	Man., *dʒambo* 'leaf'; M., *dʒambo* pers. n. 'to disgrace'

GULLAH PERSONAL NAMES	WEST AFRICAN WORDS
* ˈ*ɟame* (m.)	T., *ɟa:me* 'an amulet'
ˈ*ɟami* (m.)	K., *ʒami* 'cemetery'
ˈ*ɟamɒ* (m.)	Y., *ɟa*$_3$*mɔ*$_3$ 'to be equal in value to'; M., *dʒamɔ* 'light green, pale'
* ˈ*ɟaŋga* (m. and f.)	Tl., *dʒaŋga* 'to be immodestly clad'; V., *dʒaŋ*$_3$*ga*$_3$ pers. n. f.
ˈ*ɟaŋya* (m.)	Man., *dʒaŋya* 'length'
ˈ*ɟare* (m.)	Y., *ɟa*$_1$*re*$_2$ 'to be in the right'; 'a polite term of request equivalent to *please*'; T., *ɟare* 'soap'
ˈ*ɟari* (m.)	Man., *dʒari* 'next year'; H., *dʒa:*$_3$*ri*$_1$ 'capital for trading purposes'; *dʒa*$_1$*ri:*$_2$ 'name of a fish'
* *ɟa*ˈ*rume* (m.)	Fu., *dʒarume* pers. n. m.
* *ɟa*$_1$*sa*$_3$ (m. and f.)	V., *dʒa*$_1$*sa*$_3$ pers. n. f.; M., *dʒasa* 'the palm leaf used for thatching'
* ˈ*ɟase* (m. and f.)	W., *nɟa:se* pers. n. m.
* ˈ*ɟasi* (f.)	Y., *ɟa*$_1$*si*$_3$ pers. n. 'to dispute'; *ɟa*$_3$*si*$_3$ 'to lead to'; B., *ɟasi* 'to scorn'; M., *dʒasi* 'to scorn'
* ˈ*ɟaso* (m. and f.)	V., *dʒa*$_1$*so*$_3$ (*dʒa*$_3$*so*$_3$) pers n. f.; B., *ɟaso* 'to take up a child cleverly in order to place him on the back'; 'long cotton underwear for girls'
* ˈ*ɟato* (m.)	Man., *dʒato* 'lion, the totem of a Mandinka noble clan'; B., *ɟato* 'lazy, cowardly'; cf. H., *dʒa:*$_1$*tau*$_2$ 'a light-skinned native'
* ˈ*ɟatu* (f.)	V., *dʒa*$_3$*tu*$_3$ pers. n. f., lit. 'oily face'
ˈ*ɟawa* (m.)	M., *dʒawa* 'a tree'
* *ɟe* (m.)	B., *ɟe* 'a fetish (the tail of a cow)'; M., *dʒe* 'upright'; *ndʒe* 'a goat'; 'matron'; *ndʒeɪ* 'to descend, to lessen'; Man., *dʒe* 'to see'; E., *ɟe*$_1$ 'to split'; 'to buy'; 'to fit'; 'to be worn out'; 'to rise'; 'salt'; 'a flute'; 'conversation'; *ɟe*$_3$ 'to become visible'; T., *ɟe* 'to take'; cf. Eng. *jay*
ˈ*ɟebi* (m.)	W., *ɟebi* 'to push back (used in reference to the branches of a tree which has been pruned)'
ˈ*ɟede* (m.)	Fn., *ɟede* 'to perspire'
* ˈ*ɟedeka* (m.)	E., *ɟe*$_1$*ḍe*$_1$*ka*$_3$ pers. n. 'handsome, stately'
ˈ*ɟeke* (m.)	E., *ɟe*$_1$*ke*$_1$ 'a windlass, a handscrew'; H., *dʒe:*$_3$*ke:*$_3$ 'a bird'; K., *ʒeke* 'seeds which are often threaded and attached to bundles of charms worn by those who have been initiated into the mysteries of *ndembɔ* (a guild or secret society)'
* ˈ*ɟelɪ* (f.)	M., *dʒelɪ* pers. n. 'to judge'

GULLAH PERSONAL NAMES	WEST AFRICAN WORDS
ˈɟ*elu* (m.)	Man., *dʒelu* 'how many?'; 'how much?'
ˈɟ*ema* (m.)	H., *dʒe:*$_3$*ma*$_1$ 'a scented grass used for thatching and for making toy hoops'; *dʒe:*$_1$*ma*$_2$ 'to be tanned'
ˈɟ*embu* (m.)	M., *ndʒembʊ* 'the part of a river below any given position'
* ˈɟ*emɒ* (f.)	M., *ndzemɒ* 'mother-in-law'
ɟ*e*ˈ*nena* (f.)	K., *ʒenena* 'the bladder'
* ˈɟ*ɛdo* (m.)	B., ɟ*ɛdo*: pers. n. 'to be suitable, to be understood'
ˈɟ*ɛgu* (m.)	Fn., ɟ*ɛgu* 'to revolt'
* ˈɟ*ɛ*ɟ*i* (m.)	Fn. ɟ*ɛ*ɟ*i* 'the native inhabitants of Porto Novo (Dahomey)'; 'to begin'
* ˈɟ*ɛlɛmɒ* (f.)	V., *dʒɛ*$_3$*lɛ*$_3$*mɔ*$_1$ (*dʒɛ*$_3$*rɛ*$_3$*mɔ*$_1$) pers. n. f., lit. 'a bald-headed person'
* ˈɟ*ɛmbɛ* (m.)	M., *dʒɛmbɛ* pers. n. 'to grow, grown up'
* ˈɟ*ɛnɛba* (f.)	V., *dʒɛ*$_3$*nɛ*$_3$*ba*$_1$ pers. n. f.
* ˈɟ*iba* (m.)	Fu., *dʒiba* 'pocket' (Ar.); H., *dʒi*$_3$*'ba:*$_3$ 'a small termite's nest'; *dʒib:*$_3$*a*$_1$ 'a kind of sleeveless gown'; M., *dʒiba* pers. n. m.; Kim., *ʒiba* 'to kill'; Tl., *ʒiba* 'to wink or close one eye'
* ˈɟ*ifa* (m.)	E., ɟ*i*$_1$*fa*$_3$ pers. n.
ˈɟ*iku* (m.)	E., ɟ*i*$_1$*ku*$_3$ 'annoyance, excitement'; H., *dʒi*$_3$*k'u*$_1$ 'to soak'; K., *ʒiku* 'positiveness'
* ˈɟ*iku*ˈɟ*iku* (m.)	E., ɟ*i*$_1$*ku*$_3$ɟ*i*$_1$*ku*$_3$*vi*$_3$ 'a child whose elder brothers and sisters have died'
* ˈɟ*ilo* (f.)	Fn., ɟ*ilo* 'law, justice'; M., *dʒilo* pers. n. f.
* ˈɟ*ima* (m. and f.)	H., *dʒi:*$_3$*ma*$_1$ 'tanning'; *dʒi:*$_1$*ma:*$_2$ 'a matter of doubtful veracity'; *dʒi*$_3$*ma*$_1$ 'to wait'; *dʒi*$_1$*ma:*$_2$ 'quivering with fear, anger or excitement'; *dʒim:*$_3$*a*$_1$ 'name given a girl born on Friday'; B., ɟ*ima* 'liquid, watery'; K., *ʒima* 'to be closed (spoken of the eyes only)'; 'to extinguish'; *nʒima* 'the civit cat'; Tl., *ʒima* 'to extinguish'; 'whole, perfect'
* ˈɟ*imba* (m.)	Kim., *ʒimba* 'to swell'; U., *ondʒimba* pers. n. 'a singer'; 'a hilled row of corn'
ˈɟ*imbu* (m.)	K., *nʒimbu* 'beads, money'
ˈɟ*imbuwa* (m.)	Kim., *ʒimbua* 'dogs'
ˈɟ*imi* (m.)	K., *ʒimi* 'pregnancy'
ɟ*i*ˈ*nisa* (f.)	K., *ʒinisa* 'to burn'
ɟ*i*ˈ*nuwi* (f.)	Fn., ɟ*inũvi* 'to cause a miscarriage'
* ˈɟ*iɲɒ* (f.)	M., *ndʒiɲɔ* pers. n. 'bedfellow, companion'
ɟ*i*ˈ*ɒna* (f.)	K., *ʒiɔna* 'to take by force'

GULLAH PERSONAL NAMES	WEST AFRICAN WORDS
'ɟ*iwa* (f.)	M., *ndʒiva* 'a breast pocket in men's gowns'
* 'ɟ*iya* (f.)	Y., ɟ*i*$_1$*ya*$_1$ 'to suffer'; E., ɟ*i*$_1$*ya:*$_1$ 'an eagle'; 'broad'; ɟ*i*$_3$*ya:*$_1$ 'south wind'; H., *dʒi*$_3$*ya*$_1$ 'yesterday'; M., *ndʒia* pers. n. 'talk, palaver, a case at law'
* ɟ*i'yamɒ* (f.)	M., *dʒiamɒ* pers. n. 'a traveler, a walker'
'ɟ*iyo* (m.)	Man., *dʒio* 'water'; M., *ndʒio* 'finger or toe'
'ɟ*ɒbɒ* (m.)	M., *ndʒɔgbɒ* 'to cause to conform'
'ɟɒɟɒ (m.)	Y., ɟɔ$_1$ɟɔ$_1$ 'wattle'; K., *ʒiɔʒiɔ* 'a tuft of hair'
'ɟɒ*lɒ* (m.)	Y., ɟɔ$_1$*l*ɔ$_1$ 'smooth, even'
* 'ɟɒ*mbɒ* (m.)	V., *dʒɔm*$_1$*bɔ*$_3$ pers. n. 'a cassava field after the rice is removed'
'ɟɒ*mbu* (m.)	M., ɟɔ*mbu* 'a small animal whose bones are celebrated for their magical power'
'ɟɒ*mɒ* (f.)	M., *dʒɔmɒ* 'the craw of birds'
'ɟɒ*na* (m.)	K., *ʒiɔna* 'to snatch away something held by another'
* 'ɟɒ*ndu* (m.)	V., *dʒɔn*$_1$*d'u*$_3$ 'name of a place in the Vai country'
'ɟɒ*ɲa* (m.)	M., *dʒɔɲa* 'to affect with mildew'; 'to refuse to work'
ɟ*o'bali* (m.)	B., ɟ*obali* 'not habitual, not frequent'
'ɟ*ode* (m.)	Fn., ɟ*ode* 'to make free'
'ɟ*o*ɟ*o* (m.)	Y., ɟo$_1$ɟo$_1$ 'brilliant, fine' (applied to cloth); M., *dʒodʒo* (*dʒɪodʒɪo*) 'to hiccough'
'ɟ*ombo* (m.)	M., *ndʒombo* 'feathers'; 'the hair of animals'; 'hair on the human body except that on the head'
ɟ*onɛ'gɛni* (f.)	B., ɟ*onɛgɛni* pers. n. 'an amulet'
ɟ*o'wɛyi* (m.)	M., *ndʒowɛɪ* 'the sweet potato'
* 'ɟ*owo* (m.)	M., *ndʒowo* pers. n. 'sweet potato'
ɟ*u'ana* (f.)	W., ɟ*ua:na* pers. n. f.
* 'ɟ*uba* (f.)	Y., ɟ*u*$_3$*ba*$_1$ 'to acknowledge as superior'; B., ɟ*uba* 'a hen which has young chickens'; W., ɟ*uba* 'a tuft of hair on the head'; V., *dʒu*$_3$*ba*$_3$ pers. n. f.; M., *dʒuba* pers. n. f.
'ɟ*ube* (m.)	B., ɟ*ube* 'a roan horse with black eyes'; Man., *dʒube* 'to look at'
* 'ɟ*ula* (f.)	B., ɟ*ula* 'a merchant'; 'suddenly'; Man., *dʒula* pers. n. 'a petty trader'; Tl., *ʒula* 'to lift'; *ʒu:la* 'to put in danger'; K., *ʒiula* 'to open'
'ɟ*uma* (f.)	V., *dʒu*$_3$*ma*$_3$ 'witchcraft'
ɟ*u'male* (m).	Cf. Man., *dʒumale mu?* 'Who is it?'
* ɟ*u'mare* (f.)	Fu., *dʒumare* 'Friday' (Ar.)
* 'ɟ*umo* (m.)	Man., *dʒumo* 'Friday'

GULLAH PERSONAL NAMES	WEST AFRICAN WORDS
* ˈ*ɟuna* (m.)	Man., *dʒuna* pers. n. 'early'
* *ɟuˈnala* (f.)	Man., *dʒunala* pers. n. 'early'
ˈ*ɟuru* (m.)	B., *ɟuru* 'rope'; V., *dʒu*$_1$*ru*$_3$ (*dʒu*$_1$*lu*$_3$) 'rope, string'
ˈ*ɟuso* (m.)	Man., *dʒuso* 'liver'

[k]

ka (m.)	Y., *ka*$_1$ 'to count'; *ka*$_3$ 'to reap'; E., *ka*$_1$ 'to scatter'; 'upright'; 'firm'; 'a vine, a cord'; *ka*$_3$ 'to say'; 'to wound'; 'to mend'; 'to do a little'; Man., *ka* 'to do'; M., *ka* 'an agreement'; 'waste matter'; B., *ka* 'neck (of an animal)'; 'voice, language'; 'responsibility'; I., *ka*$_3$ 'to surpass'; 'to dry'; *ka*$_1$ 'to tell'; *ka:*$_3$ 'please'; Fn., *ka* 'a calabash'; cf. Eng., *car*
* ˈ*kaba* (f.)	B., *kaba* pers. n. 'maize'; 'to admire'; K., *kaba* 'to eat'; E., *ka*$_3$*ba*$_3$ 'swift'; M., *kaba* 'food consisting of roasted cassava and groundnuts beaten together'; 'without hindrance'; H., *ka*$_3$*ba*$_1$ 'a young dum palm'; *ka:*$_3$*ba*$_1$ 'a weed'; *ka:*$_3$*ba:*$_3$ 'a goat which has borne only once'; *k'a:*$_3$*ba:*$_3$ 'pains felt in various parts of the body'; K., *ŋkaba* 'cassava'
* *kaˈbala* (f.)	B., *kabala* pers. n. 'an admirer'; M., *kabala* 'roasted cassava and groundnuts beaten together'; Tl., *kabala* 'a native wooden sandal'
ˈ*kabi* (f.)	T., *kabi*: 'thick, deep'
* *kaˈbila* (f.)	Tl., *kabila* pers. n. 'to urge on'
ˈ*kabo* (m.)	H., *ka:*$_3$*bo:*$_1$ 'a small calabash'; *ka*$_3$*'bo*$_1$ 'young red-fronted gazelle'; 'a youth'
* *kaˈbokolo* (m.)	U., *kabokolo* pers. n. 'a lascivious person'; 'a species of animal'
* ˈ*kada* (f.)	E., *ka*$_3$*da*$_3$ 'a black, nonpoisonous snake'; Fn., *kada* 'rust, mildew'; H., *ka*$_3$*da*$_1$ pers. n. 'a crocodile'; *ka:*$_3$*da*$_1$ 'to overthrow'; *ka*$_3$*'da*$_1$ 'to beat'; Bi., *ka*$_{3-1}$*da*$_1$ 'a term used by men in giving thanks to the host after a meal'; 'an expression directed to someone who has sneezed'
ˈ*kadan* (m.)	H., *ka*$_1$*'dan*$_2$ 'a few, a small quantity'
* ˈ*kadi* (m. and f.)	Kim., *kadi* (*kayadi, kayari*) pers. n. 'second'; Y., *ka*$_3$*di*$_3$ 'to wind up with'; K., *ŋkadi* 'a demon, a witch'; E., *ka*$_1$*ḍi*$_1$ 'sticky'; 'obstinate'; H., *ka*$_3$*'di*$_1$ 'spinning'; *ka:*$_3$*'di*$_1$ 'throwing'; 'a colliding with'
* *kadiˈɟata* (f.)	Mand., *kadiɟata* 'the first wife of Mohammed'
* *kaˈdiŋgu* (m.)	Kim., *kadiŋgu* pers. n. m.

GULLAH PERSONAL NAMES	WEST AFRICAN WORDS
* '*kado* (f.)	H., *ka*$_3$*do:*$_3$ 'a tree having large leaves'; *ka:*$_3$*'do*$_1$ pers. n. 'an aboriginal'
* '*kafa* (m. and f.)	E., *ka*$_3$*fa*$_3$ 'soft corn-pap'; V., *ka*$_3$*fa*$_1$ pers. n. 'to cheat'; *ka*$_2$*fa*$_2$ 'shoulder'; M., *kafa* 'to cheat'; B., *kafa* 'a weaver's comb'
ka'fi (m.)	H., *ka*$_3$*fi*$_1$ 'a stockade'; Tl., *kafi* 'rectum'; K., *ŋkafi* 'oar, paddle'
* '*kafo* (m.)	Fn., *kafo* 'a fetish of iron carried before the king in the ceremonies'
* '*kafri* ('*kafiri*) (m).	M., *kafri* 'basely degraded, heathen (used by Mohammedans in reference to idol and spirit worshippers)'; H., *ka:*$_3$*fi*$_1$*ri:*$_2$ 'strictly, a non-Moslem provided he is not a Christian, Jew, or Zoroastrian; but, quite commonly, any one who does not follow the tenets of Islam'
* *kag'bɪndɪ* (m.)	M., *kagbɪndɪ* 'name given a child born at night'
* '*kaɟi* (m.)	Fn., *kaɟi* 'corn-pap'; K., *kaʒi* 'inflammation of the bladder'; *ŋkaʒi* pers. n. 'a relative'; 'a remainder'
'*kaɟu* (m.)	Y., *ka*$_3$*ɟu*$_3$ 'to be equivalent to'; *ka*$_2$*ɟu*$_3$ 'cashew nut'; H., *ka*$_3$*ɟu*$_3$ 'conceit'
ka'kela (f.)	Kim., *kakela* 'to cackle'
* *ka'kraba* (m.)	F., *ka*$_1$*kra*$_3$*ba*$_3$ pers. n. 'very small'
'*kala* (f.)	B., *kala* 'any oblong object'; 'to sew'; 'hot'; K., *kala* 'to dwell'; 'to deny'; 'life'; 'denial'; 'dryness'; M., *kala* (*kara*) 'large green or black flies'; Tl., *kala* 'to cut off'; 'to scratch'; 'to strike'; 'a small wire'
* *kala'ba* (m.)	Tl., *kalaba* 'to crawl'; B., *kalaba* 'a tailor'; H., *ka*$_3$*la:*$_1$*ba:*$_2$ 'a curved instrument used in the paring of the interior of calabashes and wooden basins.' Cf. the *Calabar* district, river and estuary of Southern Nigeria.
* '*kalala* (f.)	U., *kalala* 'to gargle'; K., *kalala* 'asparagus'; Tl., *kalala* pers. n. 'deputy, officer'; B., *kalala* 'needles'
* '*kalawa* (f.)	Tem., *kalawa* pers. n.; H., *k'a*$_1$*la:*$_2$*wa*$_1$ 'greed'; 'begging'
'*kale* (m.)	B., *kale* 'a shrub whose dried and pounded branches are used to sweeten a native food called *dɛgɛ*, a kind of porridge'; 'a plant from the shores of the Niger'; 'a white horse with reddish nostrils'; 'sulphur of antimony, serving as a cosmetic and eye-salve'; Tl., *kalɛ* 'long ago'; H., *ka:*$_3$*le:*$_3$ 'a worn-out long-handled hoe'

GULLAH PERSONAL NAMES	WEST AFRICAN WORDS
* ˈ*kalɛ* (f.)	Y., *ka*$_2$*lɛ*$_1$ 'to sit down'; *ka*$_3$*lɛ*$_1$ 'abroad'; *ka*$_2$*lɛ*$_3$ 'until the end of time'; *ka*$_2$*lɛ*$_3$ *o*$_2$ 'Good evening'; *ka*$_3$*lɛ*$_2$ pers. n.; M., *kalɛ* 'seed, bone'; 'a fishing weir'
* ˈ*kalifa* (m.)	Mand., *kalifa* 'name given the second male child'
* ˈ*kaliga* (m.)	Fn., *kãliga* pers. n. 'a wolf'
* *kaˈlima* (f.)	B., *kalima* 'nephew'
kaˈlimu (f.)	B., *kalimu* 'a pen for writing'
* *kaˈliya* (f.)	V., *ka*$_1$*lia*$_{3-1}$ pers. n.
* *kaˈlɪgomɛ* (m.)	M., *kalɪgomɛ* pers. n. m. 'one who collects snakes'
kaˈlɪŋgu (f.)	M., *kalɪŋgu* 'a hoe handle'
ˈ*kalɒ* (m.)	Y., *ka*$_3$*lɔ*$_2$? 'Shall we go?'
* ˈ*kalo* (f.)	B., *kalo* pers. n. 'moon'; 'error, falsehood'; M., *kalo* (*karo*) 'a broad dish, a pan'
kaˈlumbo (m.)	H., *ka*:$_1$*lum*$_1$*bo*:$_2$ 'the name of a small tree'
* *kaˈlundi* (f.)	U., *kalundi* pers. n. 'a species of large hyena'
* *kaˈluŋga* (f.)	U., *kaluŋga* 'the ordinary word of salutation'; *kaluŋga* pers. n. 'the ocean, the abode of the dead (entered through the grave whence spirits issue to do evil on earth)'; K., *kaluŋga* 'sea, ocean'; Kim., *kaluŋga* 'sea'
* ˈ*kama* (m. and f.)	V., *ka*$_1$*ma*$_3$ pers. n.; 'elephant'; M., *kama* 'unusual'; K., *kama* 'to squeeze'; Tl., *kama* 'to squeeze'; 'to abate'; 'a mute'; B., *kama* 'shoulder, wing'; U., *kama* 'to pucker, to wring'
* *kaˈmale* (m., and f.)	B., *kamale* pers. n. 'a young man'; 'vigorous'
* ˈ*kamba* (f.)	V., *kam*$_3$*ba*$_3$ pers. n. 'grave'; M., *kamba* 'grave'
kambaˈlala (m.)	K., *kambalala* 'to pass a hill along its base in order to avoid climbing'
* *kamˈbinda* (m.)	Kim., *kambinda* pers. n. 'a small gourd'
* ˈ*kamɒ* (f.)	Y., *ka*$_3$*mɔ*$_3$ 'to encircle'; *ka*$_1$*mɔ*$_3$ 'to reckon with'; M., *kamɒ* pers. n. 'a paramour'
* *kamˈpuku* (m.)	Tl., *kampuku* pers. n. 'a small rat.' Cf. K., *mpuku* 'rat'
* *kamuˈbika* (f.)	Kim., *kamubika* pers. n. 'a little slave'
kamuˈʃɒʃɒ (m.)	Tl. *kamuʃɔʃɔ*[30] 'a small stick' (*ka-* being the diminutive prefix). Cf. Kim., *kamuʃi* 'a shrub,' lit. 'a small tree'
* ˈ*kana* (f.)	Man., *kana* 'iguana, the totem of a Mandinka noble clan'; K., *kana* 'to plan'; J., *kana* 'name of a city

GULLAH PERSONAL NAMES	WEST AFRICAN WORDS
	in Dahomey' (*Cana*, sometimes called *Calamina*); U., *kana* 'to be severe'; 'to be on the way to'; Bo., *kana* 'to plan, to resolve'
'kanda (f.)	E., $kan_1da{:}_1$ 'rearing, prancing'; $kan_1ḍa{:}_1$ 'lean, thin'; K., *kanda* 'to straighten'; 'the under part of an animal's paw' *ŋkanda* 'skin, covering'; U., *kanda* 'to milk'; 'to forbid'; Tl., *kanda* 'to tie'; 'to forbid'
kan'daɟi (m.)	K., *kandaʒi* 'the under part of a paw.' Cf. *kandaʒi kia kɔkɔ* 'the palm of the hand'
kanda'lala (f.)	K., *kandalala* 'to stretch the arms well backward, throwing out the chest'
* *'kandi* (m).	Y., $k\tilde{a}_1di_3$ 'to be reluctant to move forward'; ka_2-ndi_2 'stumpy'; K., *kandi* 'palm nut'; *ŋkandi* pers. n. 'a rabbit'
* *kan'dimba* (f.)	U., *kandimba* pers. n. 'a small hare'
* *'kane* (f.)	B., *kane* 'to cut stubble'; 'obligatory'; H., $k'a_3ne_1$ 'a younger brother'; T., *kãne* 'stinginess'; 'competition'
'kani (m.)	B., *kani* 'to implore'; M., *kani* 'a cap ornamented with porcupine quills and used by a dancer'; 'a shining metal'
* *ka'nina* (f.)	K., *kanina* pers. n. 'to take leave of, to bid farewell'
* *ka'niya* (m.)	H., $ka{:}_3ni_1ya{:}_2$ 'the perineum'; M., *kaniya* pers. n.
* *kan'ɟama* (m.)	V., *kan*$_2$*dʒa*$_2$*ma*$_2$ pers. n. m.
* *kan'ɟiya* (m.)	M., *kandʒia* pers. n. 'a quarrelsome person'
kan'ɟolo (m.)	M., *kandʒolo* 'at once'
* *'kano* (f.)	Cf. *kano* 'name of a city in Northern Nigeria'
* *'kanu* (m.)	M., *kanu* 'crooked'; 'to wind'; Y., $ka{:}_2nu_3$ 'to be sorry'; Tem., *kanu* 'a family name common in the Temne-speaking area of Sierra Leone'
'kanza (f.)	K., *kanza* 'to snap, to bite'
* *ka'ɲama* (m.)	M., *kaɲama* 'a window'; U., *kaɲama* pers. n. 'to be strong'
* *'kaŋga* (m.)	E., *kaŋ*$_3$*ga*$_1$ 'a vulture'; K., *kaŋga* 'to fry'; M., *kaŋa* 'a box'; *kaŋga* pers. n. 'stubborn'; Tl., *kaŋga* 'to snarl'; 'to roast, to fry'; U., *kaŋga* 'to fry'; B., *kaŋga* 'a small ant which eats termites'; 'to gossip'; 'to foam'
* *'kaŋgo* (m.)	H., *kaŋ*$_3$*go:*$_3$ 'an uninhabited house, compound, or town'; *kaŋ*$_3$*go*$_1$ 'a concentrated decoction of various remedies for sores'; *kaŋ*$_1$*go:*$_2$ pers. n. 'a male water-buck'; Man., *kaŋo* 'neck'

GULLAH PERSONAL NAMES	WEST AFRICAN WORDS
'*kaŋkan* (m.)	Y., $k\tilde{a}_3k\tilde{a}_3$ 'hastily'
* '*karamɒ* (f.)	M., *karamɒ* pers. n. 'a teacher'; cf. H., $ka_1ra{:}_2ma_1$ 'generosity'; 'supposed magic powers'
ka_1ri_3 (m.)	V., ka_1ri_3 pers. n. 'a mild sort of itch'; ka_1ri_1 'to break'; Y., ka_3ri_3 'to go around'
* *ka'riɟɒ* (m.)	Y., ka_1ri_3*ɟɔ*$_2$ pers. n., lit. 'that we may find a gathering of people'
* *kari'kunda* (f.)	Kim., *karikunda* 'a hunchback'
* *ka'riru* (m.)	Y., ka_1ri_3-n_3ru_1 pers. n. 'that we may find something to carry'
ka'risu (m. and f.)	Kim., *karisu* 'the man with the eye'
* '*karo* (f.)	V., ka_1ro_1 (ka_1lo_1) 'Vai'; 'the Vai country'; B., *karo* 'trickery'; 'a woman whose breasts are not developed'
* ka_1*sɒɪ* (f.)	*kasai* 'a river in the Belgian Congo'
* *ka'sanɟi* (f.)	*kasanʒi* 'an Angola tribe between the Tala Mungongo depression and the Kuangu River, east of Malange'
* '*kase* (f.)	W., *kase* 'a Wolof family name'
'*kasi* (f.)	Y., ka_1si_3 'to regard as of some importance'; ka_1si_1 'stale'; B., *kasi* 'the cry of animals'; 'tears'; 'to cry'; E., $ka_1si{:}_1$ 'singed, burned'
* *ka'sike* (m.)	Y., $ka_3si_1ke_3$ pers. n. 'and that we may cry out'
* *ka'siya* (f.)	E., $ka_3sia{:}_3$ pers. n. 'suddenly'
* '*kaso* (f.)	V., ka_3so_3 pers. n. 'the four days following birth during which a male child has to be kept indoors before he is allowed to be carried into the open air'; B., *kaso* 'a dungeon, a prison'
ka'sula (f.)	U., *kasula* 'to strike'
* *kaˌʃinɟeŋ'gele* (f.)	Kim., *kaʃinʒeŋgele* pers. n. 'a squirrel'
'*kata* (f.)	T., *kata* 'to cover'; K., *kata* 'the male genital organ'; 'to extend'; Tl., *kata* 'a venereal disease'; H., ka_3ta_1 'a small calabash used by women hairdressers to hold their paraphernalia'; $ka{:}_3ta{:}_3$ 'a small calabash used by purveyors of butter or honey'; 'section of a kola nut'; 'lumps of salt'; G., ka_1ta_1 'to grasp'
* '*katama* (m.)	E., $ka_1ta_1ma_3$ pers. n. 'a large umbrella used by chiefs'
* *ka'tɛndɛ* (f.)	Tl., *katɛndɛ* pers. n. 'a small yellowish bird'; Kim., *katende* 'a small lizard'

GULLAH PERSONAL NAMES	WEST AFRICAN WORDS
'*kati* (m.)	Y., ka_3ti_1 'to roll aside'; K., *kati* 'the interior'; *ŋkati* 'proboscis'
* *kat'sina* (f.)	*katsina* 'name of a section and city in Northern Nigeria'
ka'tutu (f.)	H., $ka:_1tu:_2tu:_2$ 'abundance (used mainly with reference to debts and poverty)'; $ka_3tu:_3tu:_3$ 'guarding a doorway, preventing ingress or egress'; $ka:_3tu:_3tu:_3$ 'a bird'; Fn., *kãtũtũ* 'tow, oakum'
'*kawu* (m.)	K., *ŋkawu* 'a staff cut from the stem of climbing palm'
* '*kaya* (m.)	E., ka_1ya_1 'useless'; K., *kaya* 'to distribute'; 'to be parched'; 'to collect medicinal leaves'; Tl., *kaya* 'to trouble'; U., *kaya* 'to get well'; 'to scratch'; B., *kaya* 'the scrotum'; Tem., *kaya* 'a Temne family name'
* '*kaya'kaya* (f.)	K., *ŋkayakaya* pers. n. 'the hornbill'
'*kaye* (m.)	Y., ka_1ye_3 'to read to the understanding of another'; ka_2ye_2 'to number, to reckon'; M., *kaye* 'fault'; 'prohibition'; H., $ka:_3ye_1$ 'flooring an opponent'; ka_3ye_1 'to scatter'
'*kayi* (m.)	E., $ka_1yi:_1$ 'empty, flabby'; H., $ka:_3yi_1$ 'shifting a herd of cattle every few days to manure a farm all over'; Fn., *kayi*! 'ah!'; K., *kayi* 'a cutlass'
* '*kayisa* (f.)	K., *kayisa* pers. n. 'to greet'; 'to parch'; 'to cause to distribute'
* *ke'anu* (m.)	Y., $ke_3\ a_1nu_3$ pers. n. 'Cry mercy'
* '*keba* (m. and f.)	Man., *keba* 'a term used as a form of address to a man of middle age';[31] Y., ke_3ba_3 'to approach one for assistance of any kind; K., *keba* 'to take care of'
* '*kebu* (m.)	*kebu* 'a Western Sudanic language of the Central Togo group'
* *ke'diza* (m.)	E., $ke_1ḍi_1zã_3$ 'name of a star'
'*keɟi* (m.)	Fn., *kẽɟi* 'ford, river'
* '*keɟo* (m.)	E., $ke_1ɟo_1$ pers. n. 'lightning'
ke'kare (f.)	T., *kekare* 'to venture'
* *ke'kere* (f.)	Y., $ke_3ke_2re_3$ pers. n. 'small, petty'
* '*kela* (m. and f.)	K., *kela* 'to cut to pieces; 'to filter'; 'cassava peeled and dried in the sun'; U., *kela* pers. n.' to brew'; 'to walk with long strides'
* '*kele* (m.)	E., ke_1le_1 'the second rainy season, autumn'; M., *kele* 'a kind of palm the leaf of which is used for thatching'; 'a drum'; Y., ke_3le_2 'a young lizard'; B., *kele* 'one'; 'jealous'

GULLAH PERSONAL NAMES	WEST AFRICAN WORDS
* *ke'lena* (f.)	B., *kelena* pers. n. 'first'; 'only'
* *'kelifa* (f.)	W., *kelifa* 'chief, head'
* *ke'lili* (m.)	E., $ke_1li_3li_3$ pers. n. 'firmness'
'kelɒ (m.)	K., *ŋkelɔ* 'a funnel'; 'medicine for the eyes which is administered through a funnel'; 'a fountain, a spring'
* *ke'lola* (f.)	Man., *kelola* pers. n. 'to fight'
* *'kelu* (m.)	M., *kelu* pers. n. 'faint'; 'the act of fainting'; H., $ke{:}_1lu_2$ 'sexual excitement'
* *'kema* (f.)	E., ke_3ma_3 'the next'; M., *kema* pers. n. f.; 'a magician'; H., $ke{:}_3ma_1$ 'to complete what one is doing'; 'to go out in search of something'; B., *kema* 'masculine, male'; V., ke_1ma_3 pers. n. f.
* *'kemba* (m.)	Kim., *kemba* 'to decorate'; U., *kemba* pers. n. 'to deceive'; 'to be mistaken'; K., *kemba* 'to put on gaudy clothes and go out merrymaking'
* *'kembela* (f.)	K., *kembela* pers. n. 'to praise'
'keme (f.)	B., *keme* 'eighty'; Mal., *keme* 'one hundred'; H., $k'e{:}_1me{:}_2$ 'staining the teeth and mouth with the pounded thorns of the red silk-cotton tree and other substances to give the appearance of having eaten kola nuts'
'kemi (f.)	Ef., ke_1mi_1 'now'
* *'kemu* (m.)	Man., *kemu*! 'It's a man!' (supposed to be the first words of the proud mother)
* *'kena* (m.)	M., *kena* pers. n. 'man'; 'white spots in the skin caused by destruction of the colored pigment'; T., *kenã* 'a mark'
* *'kene* (m.)	B., *kene* pers. n. 'vigorous'; 'health'; 'a plain surface'; 'clarity'
* *ke'niya* (f.)	K., *kenia* pers. n. 'to grin'
'kenɟa (m.)	U., *kendʒa* 'to strain, to refine'
'kenɟi (m.)	K., *ŋkenʒi* 'a fine for bloodshed paid to the judges'
* *'kenti* (f.)	Tem., *kenti* 'a Temne family name'
'kenza (m.)	K., *kenza* 'to filter'
* *'keɲa* (m.)	M., *keɲa* 'one's mother's brother'; 'the origin of a matter'
keŋ (m.)	G., $keŋ{:}_3$ 'plain, distinct'; E., $keŋ_3$ 'completely'
'keŋgɒ (m.)	Bo., *ŋkeŋgɔ* 'a perforated bowl, a steamer for cooking'

GULLAH PERSONAL NAMES	WEST AFRICAN WORDS
* '*kera* (f.)	Fu., *kera* 'name given by the Fulani to any very dark-skinned woman'; H., *ke:*$_3$*ɽa*$_1$ 'loud lamentation at a death, especially by professional mourners'; *k'e:*$_3$*ɽa*$_1$ 'to work in metal'
* '*kere* (m.)	Y., *ke*$_3$*re*$_3$ 'small'; B., *kere* pers. n. 'a cricket'; 'the disposition to digress'
* '*keriŋ* (m. and f.)	Man., *keriŋ* pers. n. m.; 'small man'
* '*kese* (m.)	E., *ke*$_1$*se*$_3$ pers. n. 'the baboon'; B., *kese* 'grain'
* '*keta* (m.)	B., *keta* 'feasible'; Y., *ke:*$_{1-2}$*ta*$_2$ pers. n. 'animosity'; H., *ke:*$_3$*ta*$_1$ 'to tear'; *k'e:*$_1$*ta:*$_2$ 'mischief'
'*kete* (f.)	E., *ke*$_1$*te*$_1$ 'a flute'; *ke*$_1$*te*$_3$ 'a thick country cloth used as bedcover'; M., *kete* 'a species of brown corn'; K., *ŋkete* 'one skilled in making small things'
'*ketemɒ* (f.)	E., *ke*$_3$*te*$_3$*mɔ*$_3$'the path to Kete'
'*ketete* (m.)	K., *ketete* 'hardness, crispness'
* '*kewu* (m.)	V., *ke*$_1$*wu*$_3$ pers. n. 'tortoise'
* '*keyita* (m.)	B., *keita* pers. n.; Man., *keita* pers. n.
'*keyole* (f.)	Man., *keole* 'the man'
kɛ (m.)	Y., *kɛ*$_3$ 'to indulge'; 'to set (as a trap)' *kɛ*$_1$ 'to grow worse'; M., *kɛ* 'master, teacher'; 'to teach'
* *ke'hinde* (m.)	Y., *kɛ*$_3$*hin*$_1$*de*$_2$ 'the second of twins'; lit. 'the last to come'
* '*kɛkɛ* (f.)	Y., *kɛ*$_3$*kɛ*$_3$ 'the cry of the hen'; 'a peculiar mark'; G., *kɛ*$_1$*kɛ*$_1$ pers. n. 'alone, only'
kɛ$_1$*lɛ*$_3$ (m.)	I., *kɛ*$_1$*lɛ*$_3$ 'to salute'; 'to thank'; M., *kɛlɛ* 'to stop'; 'small'; 'a promise'
* *kɛlɛ'fala* (m.)	V., *kɛ*$_1$*lɛ*$_1$*fa*$_3$*la*$_3$ pers. n. m.; 'death in war'
* *kɛ'nuɟa* (f.)	V., *kɛ*$_1$*nu*$_3$*dza*$_3$ 'name given a child born in a foreign land'
* '*kɛɲɛ* (m. and f.)	M., *kɛɲɛ* 'country, kingdom'; 'to notch'; 'few, small'; 'sand used by the magicians called *kɛɲɛmɒ*'
* '*kɛrɛma* (f.)	V., *kɛ*$_1$*rɛ*$_1$*ma*$_1$ (*kɛ*$_1$*lɛ*$_1$*ma*$_1$) pers. n. 'lately, some time ago'
* *kɛ'sina* (f.)	V., *kɛ*$_1$*si*$_3$*na*$_3$ pers. n.
'*kɛtɛ* (f.)	T., *kɛtɛ* 'a mat'
* *ki'adi* (m.)	K., *kiadi* pers. n. 'compassion'; 'the vagina'
ki'aɟi (m.)	K., *kiaʒi* 'fruit of the oil palm'
ki'ana (m.)	K., *kiana* 'farm, garden'
* *ki'anɪ* (m.)	M., *kianɪ* 'an exclamation denoting surprise or scorn'
ki'anzu (m.)	Kim., *kianzu* 'a nest'

GULLAH PERSONAL NAMES	WEST AFRICAN WORDS
kiˈata (f.)	K., *kiata* 'to form a line, to be drawn up in order'
* ˈ*kiba* (m.)	Kim., *kiba* 'skin'; Bo., *kiba* pers. n. 'to feel restrained, to feel full'; 'to be complete'
kiˈbamba (m.)	K., *kibamba* 'a commission, a payment'
* ˈ*kibi* (f.)	K., *kibi* pers. n. 'It is too bad'; Ef., ki_3bi_3 'to cover'; ki_1bi_1 'to *pluck*'
* ˈ*kidi* (f.)	Man. *kidi* pers. n. 'to be lonely'; Kim., *kidi* 'truth'; K., *ŋkidi* 'gum copal'
ˈ*kididi* (m.)	K., *kididi* 'warmth, tepidity'
kiˈdola (f.)	Man., *kidola* 'a gun'
kidoˈlula (f.)	Man. *kidolula* 'guns'
kiˈelo (m.)	K., *kielo* 'a door, a gate'
* *kiˈese* (f.)	K., *kiese* pers. n. 'joy'
* *kiˈɟera* (m.)	Man., *kidʒera* 'name of a Mandinka caste clan of goldsmiths and blacksmiths'
ˈ*kiɟɛ* (m.)	M., *kidʒɛ* 'ginger'
kiˈɟila (m.)	Kim., *kiʒila* 'fasting precept'
* ˈ*kiki* (m.)	Y., ki_3ki_3 pers. n. 'a salutation'; ki_3ki_1 'compressed'; ki_3ki_2 'thick'; ki_1ki_1 'alone, only'
ˈ*kikɒ* (m.)	Y., $ki_3kɔ_3$ 'teaching'; $ki_3kɔ_2$ 'written'; $ki_3kɔ_1$ 'refusal'
kiˈkula (f.)	K., *kikula* 'to take up and immediately carry away'
* ˌ*kikulaˈkaɟi* (f.)	Kim., *kikulakaʒi* 'an old person'
* ˈ*kilama* (f.)	K., *kilama* pers. n. 'to be still'
* *kiˈlamba* (m.)	Kim., *kilamba* 'name given a vassal chief'
* ˈ*kile* (f.)	Y., ki_3le_1 'to wager, to pledge'; Tem., *kile* pers. n.
kiˈlembe (m.)	Kim., *kilembe* 'a plant said to wither and die simultaneously with the illness and death of the person with whom it is connected'
* *kiˈliya* (f.)	Man., *kiliya* pers. n. 'envy'
* *kiˈlundu* (f.)	Kim., *kilundu* 'a spirit'
* ˈ*kima* (f.)	K., *ŋkima* pers. n. 'a white-faced monkey, an ape'; *kima* 'thing'; Kim., *kima* 'thing'
* ˈ*kimba* (m.)	K., *ŋkimba* pers. n. 'a secret society'
* ˈ*kimbi* (*m.*)	K., *kimbi* pers. n. 'hawk'; 'buzzard'
* *kimˈbiɟi* (f.)	K., *kimbiʒi* pers. n. 'animal nature'
* *kimˈbundu* (m.)	*kimbundu* 'name given the language of the Ambundu tribes of Angola (also called the *Mbundu* language)'[32]
* *kimˈbuŋgu* (m.)	Kim., *kimbuŋgu* pers. n. 'a wolf'
* *kiˈmɒna* (f.)	Kim., *kimɔna* pers. n.

GULLAH PERSONAL NAMES	WEST AFRICAN WORDS
* *kiˈmɒniya* (f.)	Kim., *kimɔnia* pers. n. 'lazy'
* *kiˈmɒyɒ* (f.)	K., *kimɔyɔ* pers. n. 'one living'
* *kimˈpiti* (m.)	K., *kimpiti* pers. n. 'a gazelle-like antelope'
ˈ*kina* (f.)	K., *kina* 'to dance'
* ˈ*kini* (f.)	Y., ki_2ni_3 'first'; ki_3ni_2 'what?' V., ki_1ni_3 pers. n. 'sympathy'; B., *kini* 'a native dish consisting of rice or meal boiled in water'; K., *kini* 'shadow'
* *kinˈlaza* (f.)	K., *kinlaza* 'name of a Kongo clan'
* ˈ*kinsa* (f.)	K., *kinsa* 'Christianity'; Ki., *kinsa* pers. n. 'what I should do'
* *kinˈsaŋga* (f.)	K., *kinsaŋga* pers. n. 'weeping'
kinˈtuba (m.)	K., *kintuba* 'a medium-sized basket'
* *kiˈnuni* (f.)	K., *kinuni* pers. n. 'of the nature of a bird'
* ˈ*kinza* (f.)	K., *ŋkinza* pers. n. 'a mouse which lives in woody places near streams'; 'the water rat'
ˈ*kinzu* (m.)	K., *kinzu* 'an earthen pot, pail'
ˈ*kiŋga* (f.)	K., *kiŋga* 'to delay'; 'charred stubble'; *kiŋga*! 'indeed!'; U., *kiŋga* 'to wait'
* *kiŋˈkuba* (m.)	K., *kiŋkuba* pers. n. 'a small antelope'
kiˈɒla (f.)	K., *kiɔla* 'to tear off'
* *kiri* (f.)	Y., ki_3ri_3 'to roam about'; B., *kiri* 'judgment'; 'to swoon'; 'to draw in the sand'; Fu., *kiri* 'name of a place'
* ˈ*kirifi* (f.)	V., $ki_3ri_3fi_3$ 'ghost'
kiˈrima (f.)	Kim., *kirima* 'a plant'
kiˈriri (f.)	Kim., *kiriri* 'place, position'
ˈ*kisa* (f.)	Y., ki_3sa_1 'a wonder, a feat'; T., *kĩsã* 'to wither, to fade'
kiˈsala (f.)	Kim., *kisala* 'feather'
* *kiˈsama* (m.)	Kim., *kisama* 'name of a tribe in Angola'
kiˈse (f.)	K., *kise* 'fatherhood'; B., *kise* 'ardent'; 'grain'; 'to have grain well developed'
* ˈ*kisi* (f.)	*kisi* 'name of a Western Sudanic language belonging to the Atlantic group'; B., *kisi* 'to save'; E., ki_3si_1 'a rat'; T., *kisi* pers. n.; *okisi* 'a rat'; V., ki_3si_1 'a termite'
* *kiˈsile* (m.)	B., *kisile* pers. n. 'saved, delivered'
* ˈ*kiʃi* (f.)	K., *kiʃi* 'that which pertains to the people of a country'
* *kiˈtanda* (f.)	K., *kitanda* 'the Portuguese language and custom'

GULLAH PERSONAL NAMES	WEST AFRICAN WORDS
ˈ*kiti* (f.)	B., *kiti* 'judgment'; K., *kiti* 'husk, shell, refuse'; *ŋkiti* 'merchant'; E., ki_3ti_1 'a rat'; T., *kiti* 'to gnaw off'; Ki., *ŋkiti* 'a stool'
* *kiˈtimu* (f.)	Man., *kitimu* 'a feast at the end of the month of Ramadan'; 'name given a boy born during the time of the feast'
* *kiˈtuta* (m.)	Kim., *kituta* 'in Angola folklore a demon who rules over the water and who is fond of great trees and hilltops'
* ˈ*kiwula* (f.)	K., *kiwula* pers. n. 'a toad'
* ˈ*kiya* (f.)	K., *kiya* pers. n. 'to take a walk'; 'a journey'
kiˈyadi (m.)	Kim., *kiyadi* (*kiyari*) 'two'
* ˈ*kiyaŋ* (m.)	Man., *kiaŋ* 'name of an ancient African kingdom'
kiwaˈwulu (f.)	K., *kiavulu* 'a door'; Kim., *kiavulu* 'much'
kiyaˈyiba (m.)	Kim., *kiayiba* 'badly'
ˈ*kiyeɟi* (m.)	K., *kieʒi* 'cataract, waterfall'
kiˈyɛlo (m.)	Ki., *kiɛlo* 'a door, a gate'
ˈ*kiyu* (m.)	Bo., *ki:u:* 'wrenched off'
* *kiˈyuŋga* (f.)	K., *kiuŋga* pers. n. 'to whine'
* *kiˈzɒmba* (m.)	Kim., *kizɔmba* pers. n. 'a place for dancing'; 'the dancing party'
ˈ*kizu* (m.)	K., *ŋkizu* 'a kind of bush'
kiˈzuwa (f.)	Kim., *kizu-a* 'day'
kla_1si_3 (f.)	E., kla_1si_3 'chicken pox'
* ˈ*klema* (f.)	Mand., *klema* 'the hot season (from March to May)'
* ˈ*klɒsi* (f.)	E., $xl\tilde{ɔ}_1si_{1-3}$ pers. n. 'weak, sickly'
* *klu* (m.)	E., klu_3 'a male slave'
ˈ*kɒba* (m.)	K., *kɔba* 'to climb a palm tree'
* *kɒˈbena* (m.)	F., $kɔ_2be_3na_3$ 'name given a boy born on Tuesday'
ˈ*kɒbɒ* (m.)	M., *kɒbɒ* 'a large, coarse mat'
kɒˈbɒla (f.)	K., *kɔbɔla* 'to put into'
* ˈ*kɒdɛ* (f.)	M., *kɔdɛ* pers. n. 'to tempt, to deceive'
* ˈ*kɒdɛmɒ* (m.)	M., *kɔdɛmɒ* pers. n. 'a deceiver, a tempter'
ˈ*kɒdi* (m.)	Y., $k\tilde{ɔ}_1di_3$ 'to turn the back toward, to be reluctant'; K., *kɔdi* 'a stick'
* *kɒɪ* (m.)	Y., kai_{3-1}! 'an expression of great wonder'; T., *kai*! 'an expression used in cursing a person'; Man., *kai*! 'ho'!; Tl., *kai?* 'what?' 'which?' 'who?'; H., kai_3 'you' (sing. masc.); kai_{3-1} 'head, crest'; kai_{3-1}! 'Come, come!'; G., kai_{3-2} 'to remember'; kai_{3-1}! 'an expression of great surprise'

GULLAH PERSONAL NAMES	WEST AFRICAN WORDS
* ˈ*kɒɪba* (m.)	V., *kai*$_1$*ba*$_1$ pers. n. 'big man'
* ˈ*kɒɪli* (m.)	V., *kai*$_2$*li*$_1$ pers. n. m.
* ˈ*kɒɪma* (m.)	V., *kai*$_1$*ma*$_3$ pers. n. m.; H., *k'ai*$_3$*ma:*$_3$ 'small sticks or twigs used as firewood'
* ˈ*kɒɪni* (m.)	Tem., *kaini* 'a family name common in the Temne-speaking area of Sierra Leone'
* ˈ*kɒɪra* (f.)	Tem., *kaira* 'a Temne family name'
* *kɒɪˈrabe* (m. and f.)	Man., *kairabeʔ* pers. n. 'Are you at peace?'
ˈ*kɒɪya* (m.)	V., *kai*$_3$*a*$_3$ (*kai*$_3$*ɲa*$_3$) 'a fish-trap made by placing sticks across a creek so that only a small opening is left into which a long cone-shaped basket, made of bamboo sticks from three to six feet long, is inserted in such a way that the fish are forced into it by the strong current of the water'
* ˈ*kɒɟa* (m.)	Y., *kɔ*$_1$*ɟa*$_1$ pers. n. 'to refrain from fighting or wrestling'
* ˈ*kɒɟi* (m.)	V., *kɔ:*$_1$*dʒi*$_3$ pers. n. m. 'salt water'
* *kɒ*$_1$*ɟo*$_3$ (*kʌ*$_1$*ɟo*$_3$) (m.)	E., *kɔ*$_1$*ɟo*$_3$ 'name given a boy born on Monday.' Cf. T., *kwadwo;* G., *ko*$_1$*dʒo*$_3$
* ˈ*kɒkɒ* (m.)	E., *kɔ*$_3$*kɔ*$_3$ pers. n. 'to stammer'; 'high'; *kɔ*$_1$*:kɔ:*$_1$ 'to judge unjustly'; K., *kɔkɔ* 'arm, hand'; 'sleeve (of a coat)'; M., *kɒkɒ* 'a kind of ant'; 'an ant hill'
ˈ*kɒkɒla* (f.)	K., *kɔkɔla* 'to empty'; 'to crow'
ˈ*kɒla* (f.)	Y., *kɔ*$_2$*la*$_1$ 'to be circumcised'; 'to have tribal marks on the face, arms, or back'; K., *kɔla* 'to draw out'; 'to become hard'
ˈ*kɒle* (f.)	K., *kɔle* 'two'; 'hoof'
* ˈ*kɒli* (m.)	M., *kɔli* pers. n. 'leopard'; 'stingy'
kɒˈlinɛ (f.)	M., *kɔlinɛ* 'a plane'
* ˌ*kɒlɒmˈbɒlɒ* (m.)	Kim., *kɔlɔmbɔlɔ* pers. n. 'a rooster'
ˈ*kɒma* (f.)	K., *kɔma* 'to add to'; 'to fasten by nailing'
* ˈ*kɒmbɒ* (m.)	K., *ŋkɔmbɔ* pers. n. 'a goat'; 'a gun with a very long barrel'; Ki., *ŋkombo* 'a goat'
* ˈ*kɒmena* (f.)	K., *kɔmena* pers. n. 'to urge'
* ˈ*kɒmla* (m.)	E., *kɔm*$_1$*la*$_3$ 'name given a boy born on Tuesday'
* ˈ*kɒmɒ* (m.)	M., *kɒmɒ* pers. n. 'a warrior'; K., *kɔmɔ* 'heaviness'
* *kɒˈmɒɪna* (m.)	M., *kɒmɒina* pers. n. 'There is no warrior'
* ˈ*kɒndi* (f.)	K., *ŋkɔndi* 'a title of nobility'
* ˈ*kɒnɛ* (m.)	V., *kɔ*$_1$*nɛ*$_{2-1}$ pers. n. 'a supplication'; M., *kɔnɛ* 'Please, do!'
* ˈ*kɒnɒ* (f.)	K., *kɔnɔ* 'a remainder'; 'the act of snoring'; B., *kɔ*$_1$*nɔ*$_{2-1}$ pers. n. 'a bird'; *kɔ*$_3$*nɔ*$_{3-1}$ 'belly, stomach'[38]

GULLAH PERSONAL NAMES	WEST AFRICAN WORDS
* ˈ*kɒnzɒ* (f.)	K., *kɔnzɔ* 'one of the four days of the Kongo week' (the others being *ŋkeŋge*, *nsɔna*, and *ŋkandu*)
* ˈ*kɒɲa* (f.)	M., *kɒɲa* (<*kɒ* 'war' + *ɲahã* 'woman') pers. n. 'a wartime woman'
* ˈ*kɒɲe* (f.)	E., *xɔ̃*$_{3}$*ɲe*$_{1}$ pers. n. 'my friend'
* ˈ*kɒŋgɒ* (m.)	K., *kɔŋgɔ*! 'a respectful answer to a call'; *kɔŋgɔ* (*ekɔŋgɔ*) 'the Kongo country'
ˈ*kɒŋkɒ* (m.)	E., *kɔŋ*$_{3-1}$*kɔ*$_{3}$ 'glass, tumbler, cup'; K., *kɔŋkɔ* 'prohibition, taboo'; 'an angle, a corner'
* *kɒ*ˈ*rɛka* (m. and f.)	Y., *kɔ*$_{3}$*rɛ*$_{3}$*ka*$_{3}$ pers. n. 'that he may see descendants'
ˈ*kɒriwa* (f.)	Kim., *kɔriwa* 'to become intoxicated'
ˈ*kɒrɒ* (m.)	Y., *kɔ*$_{1}$*rɔ*$_{1}$ 'nook, corner'; 'defiantly'
* *kɒ*ˌ*si*$_{3}$ (m. and f.)	E., *kɔ*$_{1}$*si*$_{3}$ 'name given a boy born on Sunday'; *kɔ*$_{1}$*si*$_{1}$ 'heaped up, crowded'
* *kɒ*ˈ*silɛ* (f.)	Y., *kɔ*$_{1}$*si*$_{3}$*lɛ*$_{1}$ pers. n. 'to leave something undone'
ˈ*kɒta* (f.)	K., *kɔta* 'to enter'; 'to suit'
ˈ*kɒte* (m.)	K., *ŋkɔte* 'No!'
*kɒ*ˈ*tela* (f.)	K., *kɒtela* 'to go in for'; 'to enter with'
ˈ*kɒto* (m.)	E., *kɔ*$_{1}$*to*$_{3}$ 'edge, border'
* ˈ*kɒule* (f.)	Mand., *kã-ule* 'the intermediary season (November),' lit. 'red sky'
*kɒu*ˈ*lula* (f.)	K., *kaulula* 'to give away a portion of what has been received as a gift'
* ˈ*kɒwa* (m.)	M., *kɒwa* pers. n. 'great war'; I., *kɔ*$_{3}$*wa*$_{3}$ 'to explain'
* ˈ*kɒwaɪ* (f.)	M., *kɒwaɪ* pers. n. 'the great war'
ˈ*kɒza* (f.)	K., *kɔza* 'cassava root'; 'to bend, to be bent'
ko (m. and f.)	E., *ko*$_{1}$ 'deficiency, sterility'; *ko*$_{3}$ 'to be bald, to be naked'; 'stomach'; 'an exclamation of disagreeable surprise'; Y., *ko*$_{1}$ 'to meet'; *ko*$_{3}$ 'to gather'; 'to plunder'; 'tough'; M., *ko* 'stomach'; Bi., *ko*$_{3}$ 'to fold'; *ko*$_{1-3}$ 'to gather'
*ko*ˈ*ako* (m.)	V., *ko*$_{1}$*a*$_{3}$*ko*$_{1}$ 'to wash clothes'
ˈ*koba* (m. and f.)	M., *koba* 'a tree having broad, thick leaves'
* ˈ*kobɛ* (m.)	T., *kobɛ* pers. n. f. 'a species of yam'
ˈ*kobi* (m.)	B., *kobi* 'a tree whose fruit yields a bitter oil'
ˈ*kodo* (f.)	Man., *kodo* 'silver'
* *ko*$_{1}$*fi*$_{3}$ (m.)	T., E., F., and G., *ko*$_{1}$*fi*$_{3}$ 'name given a boy born on Friday'
* ˈ*kofo* (m.)	E., *ko*$_{1}$*fo*$_{1}$: pers. n. 'bent, curved'
* *ko*ˈ*hũne* (f.)	M., *kohũnɛ* pers. n. 'joy, gladness'

GULLAH PERSONAL NAMES	WEST AFRICAN WORDS
* *ko$_1$ɟo$_3$* (m.)	G., *ko$_1$dʒo$_3$* 'name given a male child born on Monday'; cf. E., *kɔ$_1$ɟo$_3$* 'name of a male born on Monday'
ˈ*kokoro* (m.)	Y., *ko$_1$ko$_1$ro$_1$* 'worm, fly'
* ˈ*kola* (f.)	E., *ko$_1$la$_3$* pers. n. 'one who laughs, a mocker'; M., *kola* 'cloth'
ˈ*kole* (m.)	Y., *ko$_3$le$_3$* 'to steal, to break into a house'; M., *kole* 'a flute'; 'to clean'; 'pure, just'
ˈ*koleˈkole* (f.)	Y., *ko$_3$le$_3$ko$_3$le$_3$* 'a housebreaker, a burglar'
* ˈ*koli* (f.)	E., *ko$_3$li$_3$* 'a poor person'; 'poverty'; V., *ko$_2$li$_2$* 'leopard'; *ko$_1$li$_1$* 'to move in a circle, to turn something over'; Mand., *koli* pers. n.; Fn., *koli* 'shoulder'
* ˈ*kolifa* (f.)	Tem., *kolifa* 'name of a chiefdom in the Temne country'
ˈ*koliko* (f.)	E., *ko$_1$li$_1$ko$_1$* 'yam or sweet potatoes fried in palm oil'
koˈlisa (f.)	U., *kolisa* 'to intensify'
* *koˈliya* (f.)	Mand., *koliya* pers. n. 'descended from *koli*'
* ˈ*kolo* (m.)	M., *kolo* pers. n. 'the redheaded lizard'; 'cask, barrel'; 'fireplace'
* ˈ*komba* (f.)	V., *kom$_3$ba$_3$* pers. n. f.
* ˈ*kombo* (m.)	M., *kombo* pers. n. m. 'to scratch, to scrape'; 'to increase'; 'a steep bank by the water'
* ˈ*kona* (f.)	Y., *ko$_2$na$_3$* 'to stir the fire'; *ko$_3$na$_3$* 'to spend money unlawfully'; V., *ko$_3$na$_3$* pers. n. f. 'to be bitter'; M., *kona* 'to state the object of a visit, to deliver a message'
* ˈ*koni* (m.)	T., *konĩ:* pers. n. 'speechless, absolutely still'
* ˈ*konɒ* (f.)	E., *ko$_1$nɔ$_1$* 'a woman without children, one who is barren'
* *koˈnondo* (m.)	Mand., *konondo* pers. n. 'nine'
ˈ*konu* (m.)	M., *konu* 'ax'; 'a fishing-weir made of palm leaves'
* ˈ*koɲa* (m.)	E., *ko$_1$ɲa:$_1$* pers. n. 'slow, immovable'
* ˈ*koŋko* (m.)	T., *koŋko* 'to retail'; Y., *koŋ$_3$ko$_3$* 'small'; *koŋ$_2$ko$_2$* 'the sound made from the knock on the back of the hand with the shell of a snail'; Mand., *koŋko* pers. n. 'hunger'
* ˈ*kore* (f.)	Y., *ko$_3$re$_1$* 'to harvest'; V., *ko$_1$re$_3$* pers. n. 'clean, washed'
ˈ*kori* (f.)	B., *ko:ri* 'cotton'; 'a bamboo ring for repairing the roof of a round cabin'

GULLAH PERSONAL NAMES	WEST AFRICAN WORDS
ko'riyo (f.)	H., $ko{:}_{1}ri_{2}yo_{1}$ 'a bottle made of plaited palm leaf and used for the conveyance of liquid food'
* '*koro* (m.)	Y., $ko_{2}ro_{1}$ 'bitter'; $ko_{3}ro_{1}$ 'crucible'; B., *koro* 'old age'; 'signification'; 'a native harp with six strings'; 'a fruit tree'; *ko:ro* pers. n. 'lizard'
* *koro'bali* (f.)	B., *korobali* pers. n. 'young'
* '*koroke* (m. and f.)	B., *koroke* 'elder brother'
* '*korocɛ* (m.)	Mand., *korocɛ* 'elder brother'
'*kosa* (m.)	E., $ko_{1}sa_{1}$ 'to mend superficially'; B., *kosa* 'last, recent'; H., $ko{:}_{3}sa_{1}$ 'a form of chalk obtained by burning a clay of certain marshy places'; $k'o{:}_{3}sa_{1}$ 'to satisfy'; U., *kosa* 'to tread'
* '*kosɛ* (m.)	T., *kosɛ* pers. n. 'an exclamation denoting pity or indignation'; G., $ko_{1}s\varepsilon_{1}$ 'something abhorrent'; 'I am sorry'
* '*kosi* (m.)	E., $ko_{1}si_{1}$ 'a female slave'; M., *kosi* 'trousers reaching to the knee'; Fn., *kosi* 'a prostitute'; Ki., *ŋkosi* 'a lion'
* '*koso* (f.)	Y., $ko_{3}so_{3}$ pers. n. 'a kind of drum'; $ko_{3}so_{2}$ 'to restrain, to control'
* '*koʃi* (f.)	K., *ŋkɔʃi* pers. n. 'a lion.' Cf. Ki., *ŋkosi* 'a lion'
'*koti* (f.)	Y., $ko_{3}ti_{1}$ 'to assail'; 'to pucker'; T., *koti*: 'large, luxuriant'
* *koto* (f.)	Y., $ko_{1}to_{3}$ 'not enough'; $ko_{1}to_{1}$ 'a ditch, a deep vessel'; $ko_{2}to_{2}$ 'a deep calabash'; $ko_{3}to_{3}$ 'hollow, narrow'; M., *koto* 'to bend'; 'retribution from God or from the spirits of deceased relatives upon one who did not mourn for them'; T., *okoto* 'a by-name of *kwadwo*'
* '*kowa* (f.)	M., *kowa* pers. n., lit. 'a large stomach'
'*koya* (f.)	H., $ko{:}_{3}ya_{1}$ 'to teach'; $ko{:}_{1}ya{:}_{2}$ 'to learn'
* '*koyɒ* (f.)	Bi., $ko_{3}y\text{ɔ}_{2}$ 'a form of greeting among the Bini'
* '*krifi* (f.)	Tem., *krifi* pers n. m. 'demon, tutelary spirit'[34]
* '*kristu* (f.)	K., *kristu* 'Christ.' Cf. Ki., *klisto*
* '*kuba* (m.)	E., $ku_{3}ba_{3}$ 'death-mat'; K., *kuba* 'to weave'; 'a well-worn hoe'; H., $ku_{1}ba{:}_{2}$ 'a farm left uncultivated'; $ku_{3}ba_{1}$ 'to repeat'; $ku{:}_{3}ba_{1}$ 'a door lock'; M., *kugba* pers. n. 'a leading warrior'; Tl., *kuba* 'to care for'; 'to await'
'*kube* (m.)	T., *kube* 'the fan palm'; B., *kube* 'an entire edifice in masonry'

GULLAH PERSONAL NAMES	WEST AFRICAN WORDS
* *'kuda* (m.)	E., *ku*$_3$*ḍa*$_3$ 'Wednesday'
ku'dima (f.)	Kim., *kudima* 'hoeing, cultivating'
ku'diya (m.)	Kim., *kudia* (*kuria*) 'food'
ku'dodo (m.)	E., *ku*$_3$*do*$_3$*do*$_3$ 'to wish a person's death'
* *'kudu* (m.)	E., *ku*$_3$*du*$_1$[35] pers. n. 'announcement of a death'
ku'elu (m.)	U., *okuelu* 'a style of hair-dressing'
* *'kufi* (f.)	K., *kufi* pers. n. 'shortness'; Ki., *ŋkufi*
* *'kufiya* (m.)	E., *ku*$_3$*fia*$_{1-3}$ 'the sentence of death'; *ku*$_3$*fia*$_1$ 'king of death (a name for the goddess *so*$_1$*dza*$_1$)'; cf. Kim. *kufua* 'death'
* *'kuɟi* (f.)	E., *ku*$_3$*ɟi*$_{1-3}$ pers. n. 'sudden death'
'kuɟo (m.)	Cf. E., *ku*$_3$*ɟo*$_3$*ɟo*$_{1-3}$ 'sudden death'
ku'kuta (f.)	K., *kukuta* 'to chew'
* *'kula* (f.)	V., *ku*$_3$*la*$_1$ pers. n. f.; K., *kula* 'to frighten, to disperse'; 'to grow'; 'to redeem'; M., *kula* 'to fall'; 'to throw down'; B., *kula* 'an ant'; U., *kula* 'to grow'; Kim., *kula* 'to grow'
'kuli (f.)	B., *kuli* 'a lock of hair'; M., *kuli* 'a circular fish-trap of palings; 'an enclosure for bathing'
* *ku'liya* (f.)	Man., *kuliya* pers. n. 'weight'
* *'kulo* (f.)	M., *kulo* pers. n. 'small'
* *'kulu* (f.)	K., *kulu* 'leg'; 'a wooden frame and door'; 'antiquity'; *ŋkulu* 'an ancestor'; M., *kulu* 'a flock' (as of birds)
* *'kuma* (f.)	K., *kuma* 'daylight, dawn'; 'reason, responsibility'; B., *kuma* 'speech, discourse'; 'having a tail'; U., *kuma* pers. n. 'to annoy'; Tl., *kuma* 'to cover a house'; 'to chastize'
* *'kumba* (f.)	V., *kum*$_3$*ba*$_3$ pers. n. f.; M., *kumba* 'shirt, frock, coat'; U., *kumba* 'to roar'; 'to graze'; K., *kumba* 'to roar'; 'to be amazed'; 'to scandalize'; Bo., *kumba* 'to bend the knees'; W., *kumba* pers. n. f.; Man., *kumba* 'name given a child who cries a great deal'
* *'kumbi* (m.)	K., *ŋkumbi* 'a drum'; 'a slanderer'; 'a subordinate chief, a vassal chief'; 'a large tree'; 'a large rat'; Kim., *kumbi* 'sun'; U., *ekumbi* 'sun'; 'a clock, a watch'
* *ku'mɒna* (f.)	K., *kumɔna* pers. n. 'to see one's self'; Kim., *kumɔna* 'to see'; 'possession'
* *'kuna* (m.)	Y., *ku*$_1$*na*$_1$ 'to fail'; K., *kuna* 'to plant'; M., *kuna* 'in the future'; U., *kuna* pers. n. 'to plant'; 'to be dull'; 'to be disobedient'; Kim., *kuna* 'to plant'; T., *kũnã* 'widowhood'

GULLAH PERSONAL NAMES	WEST AFRICAN WORDS
* ˈ*kuni* (f.)	K., *ŋkuni* 'a planter'; 'firewood'; B., *kuni* pers. n. 'a small head'
* *kuˈnini* (f.)	T., *okũnini* pers. n. 'distinguished, eminent'
* ˈ*kunɒ* (f.)	E., *ŋ*$_1$*ku*$_3$*nɔ*$_1$ pers. n. 'one suffering from a disease of the eye'; 'a blind man'
* *kunˈtiɲo* (f.)	Man., *kuntiɲo* pers. n. 'hair'
ˈ*kunci* (f.)	H., *kun*$_3$*tʃi:*$_3$ 'the side of the face, the cheek'
* ˈ*kunu* (m.)	Y., *ku*$_3$*nu*$_2$ 'to be reticent in asking for a favor'; E., *ku*$_3$*nu*$_3$ 'something dangerous'; V., *ku*$_3$*nu*$_1$ pers. n. 'yesterday'; Mal., *kunu* 'yesterday'; Tl., *kunu* 'here'; B., *kunu* 'a boat'; 'to arouse'; 'to swallow'; 'yesterday'
* ˈ*kunza* (m.)	K., *ŋkunza* pers. n. 'a funeral feast'
ˈ*kuŋgo* (m.)	B., *kuŋgo* 'hysteria'; Man., *kuŋo* 'head'
* ˈ*kupɒru* (f.)	Y., *ku*$_3$*kpɔ*$_1$*rũ*$_3$ pers. n. 'Die to call heaven'
* ˈ*kura* (f.)	W., *kura* pers. n. f.; V., *ku*$_3$*ra*$_1$ pers. n. f. 'green, fresh, uncooked'; E., *ku*$_1$*ra*$_3$ 'all together'; H., *ku:*$_3$*ra:*$_3$ 'the spotted hyena'; 'name given a woman called *a*$_3$*mi:*$_3$*na*$_1$ (*a*$_3$*mi:*$_1$*na:*$_2$)'
* ˈ*kuraŋ* (f.)	Man., *kuraŋ* pers. n. 'to be ill'
* *kuˈrisa* (f.)	Kim., *kurisa* pers. n. 'to grow'
* *kuriˈzɒla* (f.)	Kim., *kurizɔla* pers. n. 'to love one's self'
* *kuˈroma* (f.)	Tem., *kuroma* 'name of a Temne clan'
* *kuˈrumi* (f.)	Y., *ku*$_3$*rũ*$_2$*mi*$_3$ pers. n., lit. 'Death destroys me'
ˈ*kusa* (m.)	Y., *ku*$_2$*sa*$_2$ 'to threaten'; 'effort, attempt'; K., *kusa* 'to rub on'; B., *kusa* 'the stomach of the alligator'
* *kuˈsasi* (m.)	*kusasi* 'a Western Sudanic language of the Gur group'
* *kusoˈluwa* (m.)	Y., *ku*$_3$*so*$_3$*lu*$_3$*wa*$_3$ pers. n. 'Die in the hands of God'
ˈ*kusuˈkusu* (m.)	K., *kusukusu* 'an edible fungus'
ˈ*kuʃa* (m.)	H., *ku*$_3$*ʃa*$_1$ 'a thin cake made from groundnuts'
ˈ*kuʃi* (f.)	K., *ŋkuʃi* 'a breaking of wind'; Kim., *kuʃi* 'how much, how many'
* *kuˈʃila* (f.)	K., *kuʃila* pers. n. 'to shake violently with laughter'
* ˈ*kuta* (f.)	B., *kuta* pers. n. 'the water turtle'; Kim., *kuta* 'to tie'; U., 'to tie'; 'to be satisfied'; Y., *ku*$_3$*ta*$_1$ 'a kind of fish'; *ku*$_1$*ta*$_1$ 'to be unsalable'; E., *ŋ*$_1$*ku*$_3$*ta*$_{1-3}$ 'the region above the eye'; K., *kuta* 'to collect'; 'to assemble' (used in reference to people only); *ŋkuta* 'provisions for a journey'
kuˈtama (m.)	K., *kutama* 'to assemble'

GULLAH PERSONAL NAMES	WEST AFRICAN WORDS
ˈ*kuti* (m.)	K., *ŋkuti* 'a herd of wild pigs'
* ˈ*kuto* (m.)	Man., *kuto* pers. n. 'a salt-water turtle (a totem of some of the noble clans of Gambia)'
ˈ*kutsu* (f.)	E., *ku*$_1$*tsu*$_1$ 'hernia, rupture'
* ˈ*kutu* (f.)	E., *ku*$_3$*tu*$_3$ 'an earthern pot used for cooking soup'; *ku*$_1$*tu*:$_1$ 'crowded'; K., *kutu* 'the ear'; *ŋkutu* 'a scorpion'; M., *kutu* pers. n. 'short, small'
* *kuˈtukudiya* (f.)	K., *kutukudia* pers. n. 'an owl'
* *kuˈcina* (f.)	Kim., *kutʃina* pers. n. 'to fight, to beat'
ˈ*kuwa* (f.)	K., *kuwa* 'to strike with a blunt instrument'
* ˈ*kuwiya* (f.)	E., *ku*$_3$*via*$_3$ pers. n. 'sudden terror'; 'idleness'
* *kuˈwɒnda* (f.)	K., *kuvɔnda* pers. n. 'suicide.' Cf. Ki., *kuiˈvɔnda* 'suicide'
* *kuˈwuna* (f.)	K., *kuvuna* pers. n. 'to pretend'
kwa (m.)	K., *kwa* 'sweet potatoes'; I., *kwa*$_1$ 'to slip off'; 'to miss'; U., *kwa* 'to bark'; 'to halloo in hunting'; B., *kwa* 'salt'; 'the breast'; 'to arrive at maturity'; T., *kwa*: 'the sound of scratching or laughing'; 'to make incisions'; 'joint, juncture'
* ˈ*kwabena* (m.)	T., *kwabenã* 'name given a boy born on Tuesday'
* ˈ*kwabla* (m.)	G., *kwa*$_2$*blã*$_3$ pers. n. 'Tuesday'
* *kwa*$_1$*ɟo*$_3$ (m.)	G., *kwa*$_1$*dʒo*$_3$ 'name given a boy born on Monday.' Cf. T., *kwadwo;* E., *kwa*$_1$*ɟo*$_3$
* *kwa*$_1$*ku*$_3$ (m.)	T. and E., *kwa*$_1$*ku*$_3$ 'name given a boy born on Wednesday'
* *kwaˈkuwa* (f.)	T., *kwakuwa* pers. n.
ˈ*kwama* (m.)	K., *kwama* 'to persist in'; 'to burn'
* ˈ*kwame* (m.)	T., *kwa:me* 'name given a boy born on Saturday.' Cf. E., *kwa*$_3$*mi*$_1$
* *kwam*$_1$*la*$_3$ (m.)	E., *kwa*$_1$*mla*$_3$ (*kwa*$_3$*mla*$_3$) 'name given a boy born on Tuesday'
kwaˈnuka (m.)	K., *kwanuka* 'to be scratched, to have a long scratch across'; 'to be jerked down or along'
ˈ*kwariya* (f.)	H., *k'wa*$_l$ $_3$*ya*$_1$ 'a calabash-basin'
ˈ*kwasa* (m.)	K., *kwasa* 'to cut with one rapid stroke'; 'to rub on'; Ki., *'kwasa* 'to scratch'
* *kwa*$_1$*si*$_3$ (m. and f.)	T. and E., *kwa*$_1$*si*$_3$ 'name given a boy born on Sunday'
ˈ*kwata* (f.)	Kim., *kwata* 'to catch'; K., *kwata* 'to catch'; 'to scratch'; Tl., *kwata* 'to catch'; Bo., *kwata* 'to scratch'
ˈ*kwati* (m.)	T., *kwati* 'to omit, to lay aside'

GULLAH PERSONAL NAMES	WEST AFRICAN WORDS
* kwe_1fi_3 (m.)	F., kwe_1fi_3 (ko_1fi_3) 'name of a boy born on Friday'
* ˈ*kweku* (m.)	F., kwe_3ku_3 'name given a boy born on Wednesday'
ˈ*kwenda* (f.)	K., *kwenda* 'to go'; 'an advancing'
ˈ*kweniya* (f.)	K., *kwenia* 'to pick'
* ˈ*kwenɒ* (f.)	K., *kwenɔ* pers. n. 'yours, your, yourselves'
* ˈ*kweŋga* (f.)	K., *kweŋga* pers. n. 'to be tight'
* kwe_1si_3 (m.)	F., kwe_1si_3 'name given a male born on Sunday'
* *kwiˈate* (m.)	Tem., *kwiate* 'a family name common in the Temne-speaking area of Sierra Leone'
ˈ*kwiɟi* (f.)	K., *kwiʒi* 'a squamous affection, mange'
ˈ*kwiŋga* (f.)	K., *kwiŋga* 'to squeal, to grunt'
ˈ*kwiya* (m.)	K., *kwiya* 'a tree having a rough, hard, sandpaper-like leaf'; 'a plane, sandpaper'
* ˈ*kwiza* (f.)	K., *kwiza* pers. n. 'to come'; 'the coming'
* ˈ*kwora* (f.)	Fu., *kwora* 'name of a river familiar in Fula folklore; T., *kwora* 'the Niger River'

[l]

* *la* (m.)	Y., la_1 'to appear'; 'to split'; 'to escape'; la_3 'to lap'; 'to dream'; I., la_3 'to leak'; 'to return'; E., la_1 'to stir'; la_3 raffia palm'; V., la_2 pers. n. m.; M., *la* 'to rest'; 'to confide in'
* *laˈfiya* (f.)	Fn. *lafiya* pers. n. 'to be in good health'; H., $la{:}_3fi_3ya_1$ 'health, outward prosperity'
* ˈ*laguna* (f.)	Y., $la_3gu_3na_1$ 'a hereditary title of nobility at $ɔ_1yɔ_2$'[36]
* ˈ*lahi* (f.)	M., *lahĩ* (*ndahĩ*) pers. n. 'to advise, to caution'; 'a warning'
* *laˈila* (f.)	Man., *la ila*! 'Oh, God!' (used by the Mandinka and other people of the Gambia, whether Mohammedans or not, to express great astonishment)
* ˈ*laɪnde* (f.)	Fu., *lainde* pers. n. 'forest'
ˈ*laɪsi* (f.)	Y., lai_3si_2 'not existing'
* *lakuˈmuna* (f.)	K., *lakumuna* pers. n. 'to move the tongue'; 'to send forth flames'
* ˈ*lala* (f.)	K., *lala* 'to become reduced in size'; 'to ebb'; 'to sleep'; E., la_1la_1 'to expect'; Y., la_3la_{1-2} 'to dream'; $la{:}_{1-2}la{:}_{1-2}$ pers. n. 'trouble, agitation'; M., *lala* 'paddle, oar'
ˈ*lali* (m.)	Y., $la{:}_{1-2}li{:}_{2-1}$ 'henna, hair dye'
ˈ*lalɒ* (m.)	W., *lalɔ* 'young leaves from the baobab tree which are dried and crushed to be mixed with couscous'

GULLAH PERSONAL NAMES	WEST AFRICAN WORDS
'*lalo* (f.)	E., $la_1lo{:}_1$ 'tasteless, insipid'; M., *lalo* 'a long, cylindrical, iron rattle or bell'; H., $la{:}_3lo_1$ 'one or more varieties of jute used as a pot herb'; 'name of a bird'
'*lalu* (f.)	K., *lalu* 'a raft'; H., $la{:}_1lu_2$ 'the banded catfish'
* '*lalula* (f.)	K., *lalula* pers. n. 'to pick up something or someone floating on the water'
* '*lama* (m.)	U., *lama* 'to salute'; K., *lama* 'to join, to accompany'; 'tenacity'; M., *lama* pers. n. 'talkative'
la'mami (m.)	Fn., *lamami* 'a turban' (Ar.)
'*lambi* (m.)	K., *nlambi* 'a cook'; 'mint' (the herb); H., lam_3bi_3 'the stem which bears the fruit of the dum palm'
la'mika (f.)	K., *lamika* 'to run'; 'to stick'
* *la'mini* (m.)	V., $la_1mi_3ni_3$ pers. n. m.; B., *lamini* 'a circuit; to surround'
'*lamuna* (f.)	K., *lamuna* 'to detach'
'*landa* (f.)	K., *landa* 'to pursue, to escort'
* *lan'daɟi* (m.)	K., *landaʒi* 'a Dutchman.' Cf. P., *Hollanda* [ulanda] 'Holland'
* '*landi* (m.)	Man., *landi* 'to lay something down'; K., *nlandi* pers. n. 'a follower, an escort'
* '*landu* (m.)	K., *nlandu* pers. n. 'affected deafness; disobedience'
* *lani'yɒnu* (m.)	Y., $la_3ni_3y\text{ɔ}_2nu_2$ pers. n., lit. 'Honor has troubles'
* '*lanu* (m.)	Y., la_2nu_2 'to open the mouth'; E., la_1nu_3 pers. n. 'foolishness'; $\tilde{la}_1nu_1$ 'an instrument for cutting'
* '*lapeɟɒ* (m.)	Y., $la_3kpe_3\text{ɟɔ}_2$ pers. n. 'Honors gather'
* '*laraba* (m. and f.)	H., $la{:}_1ra_1ba{:}_2$ 'Wednesday'; 'name given a girl born on Wednesday'
'*lasa* (f.)	Y., la_1sa_1 'to be free to act'; K., *lasa* 'to wander'; H., $la{:}_1sa{:}_2$ 'to lick'; $la{:}_3sa_1$ 'to obtain a small profit'; $la{:}_3sa{:}_3$ 'salt, potash, etc., given to an animal to lick'
'*latsi* (f.)	H., la_3tsi_1 'softness'
* *la'weŋgɒ* (f.)	M., *laveŋgɒ* pers. n. 'full'
* '*laya* (f.)	K., *laya* 'to wink'; B., *laya* 'the sheep which is sacrificed on the day of the *fête du mouton* (the great Mohammedan festival)'; H., $lay{:}_3a_3$ 'the Moslem festival of the tenth day of Muharram'; 'benefit, advantage'; $lay{:}_3a{:}_3$ 'the length of thread between two hands when one unwinds it from a spindle and collects it round the fingers'; $la{:}_3ya_1$ 'a written charm'; 'any folded epistle'

GULLAH PERSONAL NAMES	WEST AFRICAN WORDS
* ˈ*layi* (m.)	H., *la:₃yi₁* ‘a native court’; ‘a market of clay-built booths’; W., *layi* ‘dew’
* *laˈyia* (f.)	M., *layia* pers. n. ‘word,’ lit. ‘mouth word’
ˈ*lazɒ* (f.)	Fn., *lãzɔ̃* ‘tetanus’
le (f.)	Y., le_2 ‘able, powerful’; le_3 ‘to appear; to drive away’; to be more than the number specified or needed’; E., le_1 ‘to wash’; le_3 ‘to seize’; B., *le* ‘the wild bar’; Bi., le_3 ‘to cook’; cf. Eng., *lay*
leˈbela (f.)	K., *lebela* ‘to wave’
* ˈ*leka* (m.)	K., *leka* pers. n. ‘to sleep; ‘to be well’; ‘to set a trap’; ‘to tune an instrument’; ‘to cock a gun’; *nleka* ‘one who is gentle or meek’; U., *leka* ‘to choke’; ‘to draw in the stomach’; ‘to thatch a thin layer’
* *leˈkana* (m.)	K., *lekana* pers. n. ‘to harmonize with’
* ˈ*leke* (f.)	Y., le_3ke_1 pers. n. ‘to be prominent’; E., le_1ke_1 ‘ornament, attire’; K., *leke* ‘a child’
* ˈ*lekeˈleke*(f.)	Y., $le_3ke_2le_3ke_2$ pers. n. ‘a white-feathered bird’
ˈ*lela* (f.)	K., *lela* ‘to nurse’; ‘the breast of the palm rat’; U., *lela* ‘to be easy’
* ˈ*lele* (f.)	E., le_3le_3 pers. n. ‘to cry’; Bi., $'le_1le_3$ ‘to follow’; B., *lele* ‘to neglect’; K., *lele* ‘disinclination to work’; Fn., *lɛle* ‘to revolve’; ‘to ramble’
leleˈmesa (f.)	K., *lelemesa* ‘to lubricate’
* ˈ*lelemi* (f.)	*lelemi* ‘a Western Sudanic language of the Central Togo group’
* ˈ*lema* (m.)	M., *lema* pers. n. ‘to forget’
ˈ*lembɒ* (m.)	K., *lembɔ* ‘a fish-basket’; *nlembɔ* ‘finger, thumb, or toe’
* ˈ*lemɒ* (m.)	V., $le_3mɔ_1$ ‘parent, master’
ˈ*lemu* (m.)	W., *le:mu* ‘to bewitch’; B., *lemu* ‘rudder, helm’
* ˈ*lende* (m.)	M., *lende* pers. n. ‘a small rat or mouse’
* ˈ*lenza* (m.)	K., *lenza* ‘to eat’ (said of animals; an offensive term if used in reference to people)
* ˈ*leŋga* (f.)	K., *leŋga* pers. n. ‘to flatter’; ‘to smear on’; ‘to sharpen’; U., *leŋga* ‘to disregard’; ‘to be at ease’; ‘to ornament’; M., *leŋga* ‘in unison’
* *leŋˈgela* (f.)	K., *leŋgela* pers. n. ‘a hawk’; ‘to hover as a hawk’; ‘to wither, to fade’
* ˈ*leŋgol* (m.)	Fu., *leŋgol* ‘family’
ˈ*lesa* (f.)	U., *lesa* ‘to lick’
ˈ*lewesa* (f.)	K., *levesa* ‘to soften’

GULLAH PERSONAL NAMES	WEST AFRICAN WORDS
*ˈ*lewu* (f.)	Y., $le_{3}wu_{2}$ pers. n. 'dangerous'; Fn., *lewu* (*leu*) 'to bathe; a bath'
ˈ*lezo* (m.)	K., *lezo* 'an edible leaf'
lɛ (m.)	Bi., $lɛ_{1-3}$ 'to run, to flow, to lose color'; Y., $lɛ_{2}$ 'lazy'; $lɛ_{1}$ 'to patch, to fasten'; 'elastic, pliable'; $lɛ_{3}$ 'to transplant'; E., $l\tilde{ɛ}_{1-3}$ 'stupid'; Tl., *lɛ* 'long, tall, deep'; M., *lɛ* 'to condemn'
*ˈ*lɛgba* (m.)	Y., $lɛ_{3}gba_{2}$ 'paralytic'; cf. $ɛ_{3}lɛ_{3}gba_{3}ra_{2}$ 'divine trickster'; see Y., $e_{1}ʃu_{1}$; E., $le_{3}gba_{1-3}$ 'divine trickster'; Fn., *lɛgba* 'divine trickster'
* *lɛˈkula* (f.)	E., $l\tilde{ɛ}_{1}ku_{3}la_{3}$ pers. n. 'a stupid person'
ˈ*lɛlɛma* (f.)	Tl., *lɛlɛma* 'to float'
*ˈ*lɛlu* (f.)	Tl. *lɛlu* pers. n. 'today'
*ˈ*lɛma* (f.)	Tl., *lɛma* pers. n. 'to put on a bowstring, to stretch a skin over a drum'; 'to be crippled'; Ki., *lɛma* 'to glow'
*ˈ*lɛmba* (m.)	Tl., *lɛmba* pers. n. 'to hunt'; 'to swing'; Ki., pers. n. *lɛmba* 'to soothe'
*ˈ*lɛmbɛka* (m.)	Ki., *lɛmbɛka* pers. n. 'to soothe, to make calm'
*ˈ*lɛmɒ* (f.)	Y., $lɛ_{1}mɔ_{3}$ pers. n. 'to cleave to'
*ˈ*lɛʃɛ* (m.)	Y., $lɛ_{2}ʃɛ_{1}$ pers. n. 'sinful'
ˈ*lɛwu* (m.)	Y., $lɛ_{3}wu_{1}$ 'the down of the palm tree used for tinder'
lɛˈwuma (m.)	M., *lɛvuma* 'in a resting-place'
ˈ*lifu* (f.)	E., $li_{1}fu\!:_{1}$ 'dim, dark, sleepy'; $li_{1}fu_{3}$ 'a nonpoisonous brown snake'
*ˈ*lile* (f.)	Fn., *lile* 'to join'; 'to return'; Y., $li_{3}le_{2}$ pers. n. 'solid, strong'; 'durability'; $li_{3}le_{3}$ 'that which is to be driven'
ˈ*lili* (f.)	Y., $li_{2}li_{2}$ 'an animal of the porcupine family which lives under rocks'; E., $li_{1}li_{1}$ 'to smear'; $li_{1}li_{3}$ 'security'; $li_{3}li_{3}$ 'to surprise'; $l\tilde{i}_{1}l\tilde{i}_{1}$ 'concealment'; 'black wasp'; Fn., *lili* 'a delay'
ˈ*lilili* (f.)	E., $li_{1}li_{1}li_{1}$ 'an unpleasant odor.' (Cf. $β\tilde{ɛ}_{1}$ $li_{3}li_{3}li_{3}$ 'to emit an agreeable odor'; $β\tilde{ɛ}_{1}$ $li_{1}li_{1}li_{1}$ 'to emit a disagreeable odor')
ˈ*lilɒ* (f.)	Y., $li_{3}lɔ_{2}$ 'departure'; $li_{3}lɔ_{3}$ 'twisted'; E., $li_{3}lɔ_{3}$ 'fine sand mixed with salt and eaten by pregnant women'
*ˈ*lima* (m.)	U., *lima* 'to cultivate'; M., *lima* pers. n. 'beloved, favorite'

GULLAH PERSONAL NAMES	WEST AFRICAN WORDS
* ˈ*limba* (m.)	*limba* 'a Western Sudanic language of the West Atlantic group, spoken mainly in the territory south of Senegal'; U., *limba* 'to slip the memory, to be forgotten'; Bo., *limba* 'to lose, to forget'
* ˈ*limo* (f.)	H., *lim:*$_3$*o*$_1$ 'name given a girl born on Friday'
* ˈ*lisa* (f.)	Fn., *lisa* 'the genius of the sun'; U., *lisa* 'to feed'; E., *li*$_1$*sa*$_1$ pers. n.
*li*ˈ*sinda* (f.)	U., *lisinda* 'to crowd'
* ˈ*liʃa* (f.)	H., *li:*$_1$*ʃa*$_2$ 'the evening from the beginning of darkness until nearly midnight'; Fu., *liʃa* pers. n. 'about 7:00 P.M.'
*li*ˈ*taɲa* (m.)	U., *litaɲa* 'to entangle'
* ˈ*litsa* (f.)	E., *li*$_1$*tsa*$_1$ pers. n. 'a chameleon'
ˈ*liya* (f.)	U., *lia* 'to eat'
ˈ*liyana* (f.)	U., *liana* 'to brag'
*li*ˈ*yata* (m.)	U., *liata* 'to tread upon'
ˈ*liyo* (m.)	Fn., *liyo* 'soured corn-pap'
* *lɒ*ˈ*anda* (f.)	*lɔanda* 'name of a city in Angola'
* ˈ*lɒka* (m.)	W., *lɔka* pers. n. 'the large antelope'; Tl. *lɔka* 'to rain'
* ˈ*lɒlɛ* (f.)	M., *lɔlɛ* (*ndɔlɛ*) pers. n. 'hunger, need'
* ˈ*lɒlɒ* (f.)	K., *lɔlɔ* 'a bush yielding a yellow edible fruit'; 'a tree whose wood is bright yellow and very bitter'; M., *lɔlɒ* 'a duck'; E., *lɔ*$_1$*lɔ̃*$_1$ pers. n. 'beloved'
ˈ*lɒlu* (f.)	Y., *lɔ*$_3$*lu*$_1$ 'to plait, to entwine'; M., *lɔlu* 'five'
ˈ*lɒmba* (m.)	K., *lɔmba* 'to beg'; 'to become cloudy'
ˈ*lɒnde* (m.)	K., *lɔnde* 'a hill'
* ˈ*lɒnzɒ* (m.)	K., *lɔnzɔ* pers. n. 'inordinate sexual desire'
ˈ*lɒse* (f.)	K., *lɔse* 'forehead, face, presence'
* ˈ*lɒti* (f.)	K., *nlɔti* pers. n. 'a dreamer'
ˈ*lɒtiya* (f.)	K., *lɔtia* 'a skin disease'
* ˈ*lɒtɒɪ* (f.)	W., *lɔtai* pers. n. 'fatigue, lassitude'
* *lɒʊl*ˈ*wila* (m.)	K., *laulwila* pers. n. 'to wink, to raise the eyebrows'
ˈ*lɒwɒ* (f.)	Y., *lɔ*$_2$*wɔ*$_2$ 'at hand, under the influence of'; M., *lɔwɒ* 'a goiter'
* *loko* (m.)	Fn., *loko* 'tree'; 'name of a deity'
* *loko*ˈ*ɪsiya* (f.)	M., *lokoɪsia* pers. n. 'the hands'
ˈ*lolo* (f.)	E., *lo*$_1$*lo*$_1$ 'to be large'; *lo*$_3$*lo*$_3$ 'to dissolve'; M., *lolo* 'a cat of thievish tendencies, a bush cat'; Fn., *lolo* 'to be delirious'

GULLAH PERSONAL NAMES	WEST AFRICAN WORDS
* *lo'maɲɒ* (f.)	M., *lomaɲɔ* pers. n. 'a dear companion'
* *lom'beyɪ* (m.)	M., *lombeɪ* pers. n., lit. 'Stay here'
'*lombo* (m.)	M., *lombo* 'to patch'; 'a patch'; B., *lombo* 'a kind of sandalwood highly perfumed'
* '*lome* (m.)	E., lo_1me_1 'name of a coastal city in the Ewe country'
* '*lometɒ* (m.)	E., $lo_1me_1t\text{ɔ}_3$ 'a man from Lome'
* '*lomɛ* (m.)	M., *lomɛ* pers. n. 'softly, noiselessly'
'*londi* (m.)	Man., *londi* 'to place'; M., *londi* 'a peninsula'
* '*loni* (m.)	Y., lo_3ni_{1-2} pers. n. 'today'
'*loriŋ* (f.)	Man., *loriŋ* 'standing'
'*loyi* (m.)	Y., lo_3yi_1 'dizzy'
lu'aɟi (f.)	K., *luaʒi* 'an ax'
lu'aka (f.)	K., *luaka* 'to arrive'
* *lu'ala* (f.)	K., *luala* pers. n. 'to be cut, wounded'
* *lu'ayi* (f.)	K., *luayi* pers. n. 'the umbilical cord'
* *lu'bambu* (m.)	Kim. *lubambu* pers. n. 'a chain'
* '*ludi* (m.)	K., *ludi* pers. n. 'truth'; 'advice'
'*luga* (m.)	H., $lug{:}_3a_1$ 'learned language, an expression whose meaning is not known by a large number of people'
* '*luha* (f.)	Fu., *luha* 'morning prayer time, between eight and nine o'clock' (Ar.)
lu'ila (f.)	K., *luila* 'an ant's nest'
lu'ina (f.)	K., *luina* 'perspiration'
* *lu'kala* (f.)	*lukala* 'name of a river in Angola'
lu'kata (f.)	K., *lukata* 'box, chest'
lu'kaya (m.)	K., *lukaya* 'the leaf of a tree'; 'a sheet of paper'
* *lu'kubiku* (m.)	K., *lukubiku* pers. n. 'order, arrangement'
lu'kula (f.)	K., *lukula* 'to collect'
'*lukusu* (m.)	K., *lukusu* 'a white discoloration of the skin generally affecting the hands'
'*lulu* (f.)	K., *nlulu* 'an edible plant having a bitter leaf'; Mand., *lu:lu* 'five'
* '*lulule* (f.)	Man., *lulule* pers. n. 'five'
'*luma* (m.)	M., *luma* 'to consent'; K., *luma* 'to emit semen'
'*lumbu* (m.)	K., *lumbu* 'day'; 'stockade'; 'a song'; Kim., *lumbu* 'yard wall'
* *lu'miŋgu* (f.)	K., *lumiŋgu* 'to dress elaborately'; *lumiŋgu* 'Sunday.' Cf. P., *domingo* [*dumĩŋgu*] 'Sunday'

GULLAH PERSONAL NAMES	WEST AFRICAN WORDS
* '*lunza* (m.)	K., *lunza* pers. n. 'to ache'
'*luɲa* (f.)	M., *luɲa* pers. n. 'multitude'; 'very numerous'
luŋ (m.)	Mand., *luŋ* 'a day of twenty-four hours'
* '*luŋgo* (f.)	Man., *luŋo* pers. n. 'day'
* '*luri* (f.)	Mand., *lu:ri* pers. n. five'
* '*lusa* (f.)	K., *lusa* pers. n. 'to prowl about'
* *lu'sala* (f.)	K., *lusala* pers. n. 'plume, feather'
'*luse* (f.)	K., *luse* 'forehead, face, countenance'; cf. Eng. *Lucy*
* *lu'ʃindu* (f.)	K., *luʃindu* pers. n. 'noise, riot'
'*luta* (m.)	K., *luta* 'to excel, to make a profit'
'*lute* (m.)	K., *lute* 'a fishy flavor'
* '*luwa* (f.)	M., *luwa* pers. n. 'to be afraid'; 'to cook vegetables thoroughly'; *luva* 'to remain all day'; U., *luva* 'to manufacture'; 'to beg' (especially for food)
* *lu'wadi* (m.)	K., *luvadi* pers. n. 'a squirrel'
* *lu'waŋga* (f.)	K., *luwaŋga* pers. n. 'a small abscess'; 'a small frog'
* *lu'wesɒ* (f.)	K., *luvezɔ* pers. n. 'disobedience, contempt'
'*luwε'luwε* (f.)	Bi., $lu\varepsilon_1lu\varepsilon_3$ 'to wither'; $lu\varepsilon_{1-3}lu\varepsilon_{1-3}$ 'description of the movement made by the bird $a_3h\tilde{\imath}a_3\tilde{\beta}o_{3-1}sa_1$, which nods with the upper part of its body'
* *lu'wila* (f.)	K., *luvila* 'relationship, family, clan'
lu'zemba (f.)	K., *luzemba* 'the sling upon which an infant is carried'

[m]

GULLAH PERSONAL NAMES	WEST AFRICAN WORDS
* *ma'bibi* (m.)	K., *mabibi* pers. n. 'fatigue, faintness'
* *ma'ḍambo* (m.)	M., *madambo* pers. n. 'to stretch'
* *ma'ḍimba* (f.)	Tl., *madimba* 'a musical instrument made by fastening gourds of different sizes to flat sticks and played by beating on the sticks'; 'xylophone'; Kim., *madimba* (*marimba*) 'name of a place'. Cf. K., *madiumba* 'a native dance to the music of the harmonicon'; 'a harmonicon'
* *ma'ḍina* (f.)	Fn., *madina* 'Medina, a city in Arabia which contains the tomb of Mohammed'
ma'ḍiya (m.)	K., *madia* 'food'
'*madza* (m.)	K., *madza* 'water'
* *maga'riba* (f.)	H., $ma_1ga_1ri_2ba_1$ 'the period between sunset and darkness' (Ar.)
mag'bɪndɪ (f.)	M., *magbɪndɪ* 'to darken'
* '*magεt* (f.)	W., *magεt* pers. n. 'old'

GULLAH PERSONAL NAMES	WEST AFRICAN WORDS
* *ma'gɒɲɛ* (f.)	M., *magɔɲɛ* pers. n. 'to diminish'; 'small, thin, and short'
* *maharo'tɒba* (m.)	Y., ma$_2$ha$_2$ro$_2$tɔ$_3$ba$_2$ 'one of the forty-eight Ilaris, household officers of the Yoruba king'
* *ma'haya* (f.)	M., *mahãya* 'kingship'
* *'maɟɒn* (f.)	V., ma$_2$dʒɔn$_2$ pers. n. f.
* *'maɟo* (f.)	M., *madʒo* 'the leading woman of the Sande, a female society into which nearly all the girls are initiated'
* *ma'kaɲa* (m.)	Tl. and Kim., pers. n. *makaɲa* 'tobacco'
* *'makara* (m.)	Ef. m$_1$ma$_1$ka$_2$ra$_2$ (m$_1$ba$_1$ka$_2$ra$_2$) 'white man, European'; (cf. i$_3$kɔ$_{3-1}$ m$_1$ma$_1$ka$_2$ra$_2$) 'the speech of the white man'); H., ma$_1$ka$_2$ɾa$_1$ 'to be late' ;'a light-brown horse'; ma$_1$ka$_1$ɾa:$_2$ 'a bier'; 'a spider'; cf. ma$_3$k'e:$_3$ɾa:; 'patron spirit of ironworkers'
* *ma'kari* (f.)	H., ma$_3$ka$_3$ɾi:$_3$ 'an antidote'; 'a crease caused by folding'; 'the drift of a speech'; ma$_3$ka:$_3$ɾi:$_3$ 'any kind of protection'; ma$_1$ka$_2$ɾi$_1$ 'a black ox'; 'an evilly disposed person'
* *ma'kaya* (m.)	K., *makaya* 'leaves, foliage'; H., ma$_3$k'a:$_1$ya:$_2$ pers n. 'the porcupine'
ma'kene (m.)	K., *makene* 'an obscene expression'
* *'maki* (m.)	H., ma$_3$k'i$_1$ 'a name given to a male slave'; 'one who refuses'
ma'kinu (m.)	K., *makinu* 'dances'
* *ma'kiʃi* (f.)	Kim., *makiʃi* 'name of a heathen tribe in Angola folklore'
'makɒɪ (m.)	H., ma$_3$kai$_3$ 'any vessel for carrying water'; ma$_1$k'ai$_2$ 'constipation'
* *ma'kɒɪya* (m.)	V., ma$_1$kai$_2$a$_1$ pers. n. m.
* *ma'kɒŋgo* (m.)	K., *makɔŋgɔ* 'persons having some physical deformity'
* *ma'koɲa* (f.)	B., *makoɲa* pers. n. 'service'; 'to serve'
makoyi'rola (f.)	Man., *makoirola* 'for help' (dat. c.)
'maku (f.)	Kim., *maku* 'arms'
ma'kumba (f.)	Kim., *makumba*[37] 'chains, fetters'; 'earrings'
ma'kuna (m.)	K., *makuna* 'to knock over backward'
* *'mala* (f.)	Man., *mala* pers. n. 'shame'; Tl., *mala* 'beer made by brewing corn or millet or cassava'; Y., ma$_1$la$_1$ 'dazzling'; M., *mala* 'to exaggerate'; H., ma$_1$la:$_2$ 'to vanish; 'to be intoxicated'; ma:$_3$la:$_3$ 'a kind of satchel'

GULLAH PERSONAL NAMES	WEST AFRICAN WORDS
* ˈ*malaki* (m.)	Tem., *malaki* pers. n.; H., *ma*$_3$*la*$_3$*k'i*$_3$ 'greedily'; 'extravagant food'
maˈlasa (f.)	B., *malasa* 'rock salt'; 'to ridicule'; H., *ma*$_3$*la:*$_3$*sa:*$_3$ 'usefulness'
* *maˈlawu* (f.)	K., *malavu* pers. n. 'palm-wine, spirit, wine generally'; Ki., *maˈlavu* 'wine'; cf. Tl. *maluvu* 'palm wine'; 'beer made from corn'
* ˈ*male* (m. and f.)	Fn., *male* 'a Mohammedan'; M., *male* 'to meet'; 'an animal of the hippopotamus family'
* *maˈlemba* (m.)	*malemba* 'one of the smaller tribes of Angola'
* ˈ*mali* (m.)	B., *mali* pers. n. 'hippopotamus'
* ˈ*malik* (m.)	W., *malik* pers. n. m.
* *maliŋˈke* (f.)	*maliŋke* 'one of the Mande fu languages of the Western Sudan'
maˈlɒŋga (f.)	Kim., *malɔŋga* 'plates, dishes'
* ˈ*malo* (f.)	B., *malo* 'rice'; 'shame'; 'reason'; Man., *malo* pers. n. 'hippopotamus'
* *maˈlunda* (f.)	Kim., *malunda* 'historical narratives of the Angola'; K., *malunda* 'hunchback'
* *maˈlundi* (f.)	Man., *malundi* pers. n. 'ashamed'
* ˈ*mamada* (f.)	M., *mamada* 'a very old person'; 'a great-grandparent of either sex'
* ˈ*mamadi* (m.)	Mand., *ma:madi* 'name given the first son'
* ˈ*mamadu* (m.)	Mand., *ma:madu* 'name given the first son'
* *maˈmagole* (f.)	M., *mamagole* 'a white woman, an elderly white person'
ˈ*mambu* (m.)	K., *mambu* 'talks, affairs, palavers'
* *mamˈburi* (m.)	Man., *mamburi* 'a Mandinka noble clan whose totem is *bambo* 'the crocodile'
* ˈ*mametu* (f.)	Kim., *mametu* pers. n. 'our mother'
ˈ*mana* (f.)	K., *mana* 'to perfect'; 'to be finished'; 'merchandise'
* ˈ*mande* (f.)	*mande* 'name of a language and a group of languages in the Western Sudan'
* ˈ*mandi* (f.)	B., *mandi* pers. n. 'cherished, privileged'
manˈdoro (f.)	H., *man*$_{3-1}$*'do:*$_2$*ɾo:*$_2$ 'a sweet-tasting gum obtained from the *maɾ*$_3$*ke:*$_3$ tree'
* ˈ*mane* (m.)	H., *ma:*$_3$*ne*$_3$ 'a large red monkey'; Man., *mane* 'a Mandinka noble clan whose totem is *kana* 'the iguana'
* *maˈnelo* (f.)	W., *manelo* pers. n. 'to reconcile'
maˈnene (m.)	K., *manene* 'a much-used path, a highroad'

GULLAH PERSONAL NAMES	WEST AFRICAN WORDS
maˈnesa (f.)	K., *manesa* 'to finish, to dispose of speedily'
maˈnika (f.)	K., *manika* 'to put on, to hang up'
ˈmanɟɛ (f.)	B., *manɟɛ* 'the papaw (fruit)'
* *ˈmanɟi* (*ˈmʌnɟi*)	Tl., *manʒi* pers. n. 'one who kills an adversary in battle'
* *manˈɟiya* (f.)	M., *mandʒia* 'name given a girl born at the time of a great palaver'; 'a talkative woman'
* *maˈnɒni* (f.)	M., *manɒni* 'the custom of taking to *ndʒaye* (the person of highest rank in the Sande Society) cuttings from the nails or hair of a slave so that if the slave runs away, *ndʒaye* may catch and kill him'
* *ˈmansa* (m. and f.)	T., *ma:nsã* 'name given a girl who is the third child of her mother'; E., *man*$_3$*sa*$_3$ (*mã*$_3$*sa*$_3$) 'third daughter'
* *manˈsoti* (m.)	Man., *mansoti* 'the king'
ˈmanzo (m.)	H., *man*$_1$*zo:*$_2$ 'a messenger'
* *ˈmaɲo* (f.)	Man., *maɲo* 'a bride'
* *ˈmara* (f.)	Mand. *mara* 'the region of the Sahel (French West Africa)'; B., *mara* 'protection'; 'economy'; H., *ma:*$_3$*ɾa*$_1$ 'the abdomen'; *ma:*$_3$*ɾa:*$_3$ 'a piece of calabash'; Man., *mara* 'left' (i.e., on the left hand when facing Mecca)
* *ˈmaraka* (m)	Man., *maraka* 'a Sarakolle, a native of the region of Sahel (French West Africa)'
maˈrece (f.)	H., *ma*$_1$*ɾe*$_1$*tʃe:*$_2$ 'the late afternoon, before sunset'
* *maˈrewa* (m.)	T., *marewa* 'the Twi name for Hausa and other countries on and beyond the Niger'
* *mariˈama* (f.)	B., *mariama* 'pers. n. f.; 'Mary'; Man., *mariama* pers. n. f.; Mand., *maryama* 'Mary'
* *mariˈata* (f.)	V., *ma*$_1$*ri*$_1$*a*$_3$*ta*$_1$ pers. n. f.
* *maˈriko* (m.)	Mand., *ma:riko* 'a Mandingo clan name'; lit. 'the case or affair of the hippopotamus' (i.e., an ancestor of *ma:riko* is believed to have been rescued from a hippopotamus by the intervention of a crocodile)
* *mariˈwanu* (f.)	Kim., *mariwanu* pers. n. 'astonishment'
ˈmarũ (m.)	Y., *ma*$_3$*rũ*$_2$ 'five'
* *ˈmasa* (f.)	Kim. and K., *masa* 'corn'; Y., *ma*$_3$*sa*$_1$ 'a kind of pancake'; H., *ma:*$_3$*sa*$_1$ 'a small round cake of flour of guinea-corn, maize, bulrush-millet, or rice'; 'a kind of small fish'; *ma*$_3$*si*$_1$ 'a small plant used as a remedy for guinea-worm'; E., *ma*$_3$*sa*$_3$ 'the rainy season'; *mã*$_3$*sa*$_3$ 'third daughter'; B., *masa* 'king'

GULLAH PERSONAL NAMES	WEST AFRICAN WORDS
* ˈ*masaku* (f.)	K., *masaku* 'a title of nobility'
maˈsale (f.)	W., *masale* 'to equalize, to make level'
maˈsaŋga (m.)	Bo., *masaŋga* 'beer, wine'
ˈ*masi* (f.)	B., *masi* 'tribe, the human race'
* *maˈsina* (f.)	*masina* 'a region in the French Sudan traversed by the Niger'; Fn., *amasina* pers. n. f.
* ˈ*masu* (m.)	B., *masu* 'a chisel'; H., $ma\!:_3su\!:_3$ 'an official position, the holder of which is responsible for the pair of spears which form part of the insignia of the Emir of Kano'
ˈ*matama* (m.)	Kim., *matama* 'faces, cheeks'
* *maˈtaya* (m.)	K., *mataya* pers. n. 'ragged cloth, tatters'
maˈtɪŋga (f.)	M., *matɪŋga* 'curdled milk, butter'
ˈ*mawa* (f.)	M., *mawa* 'a mature palm tree'; 'to reward'; 'a reward'
* *mawaˈkala* (m.)	K., *mavakala* 'a name given to persons being initiated into the *ndembɔ* (a secret society)'
* ˈ*mawu* (f.)	E., ma_3wu_3 (ma_3wu_{1-3}) 'God'; Fn., *mawu* 'God'; *mawũ* (*maũ*) 'genius of the moon'; 'creation'
ˈ*mayɛ* (f.)	T., *mãyɛ* 'fulfilment, fulness'
ˈ*mayi* (f.)	H., ma_3yi_1 'the act of sewing or thatching; ma_1yi_2 'to take the place of another'
* *maˈyɒmbe* (m.)	K., *mayɔmbe* 'a district in the old kingdom of Kongo'
ˈ*mazu* (f.)	K., *mazu* 'noise, commotion'
mbaziˈmene (f.)	K., *mbaʒi mene* 'tomorrow morning'
mˈbila (f.)	K., *mbila* 'a summons'
* *meˈhomi* (f.)	F., $me_1ho_3mi_3$ pers. n. 'I rest'
ˈ*mele* (f.)	Kim., *mele* 'breasts'
meˈlɛntan (m.)	W., *melɛntan* 'a small black ant'
ˈ*mema* (f.)	K., *mema* 'to make the daily cut in the palm for palm wine'
memaˈdoka (m.)	Fn., *memadokã* 'free'
* ˈ*meme* (f.)	Fn., *meme* pers. n. 'delicate'; 'refined'
* ˌ*memeˈneda* (f.)	T., *memeneda* 'Saturday'
ˈ*mena* (f.)	U., *mena* 'to sprout, to spring up'; K., *mena* 'to grow'; 'to cause to grow'; H., $me\!:_3na_1$ 'the Addara gazelle'
* ˈ*mene* (f.)	T., *mene* 'to swallow'; 'the throat'; Fn., *mene* 'nude'; B., *mene* 'to seize'; 'understood'; 'delayed'; K., *mene* pers. n. 'morning'

GULLAH PERSONAL NAMES	WEST AFRICAN WORDS
* ˈ*meneˈmene* (f.)	K., *menemene* pers. n. 'morning.' Cf. Kim., *kamenemene* 'early morning'; B., *menemene* 'greedily'
* *meˈnesa* (f.)	K., *menesa* pers. n. 'to grow'; 'to cause to grow'
* ˈ*mensa* (m.)	E., men_3sa_3 'the third son'; T., *mensã* 'the third son'
ˈ*meɲa* (f.)	Kim., *meɲa* 'water'
meˈɲaɲa (f.)	Fn., *meɲaɲa* 'bad'
ˈ*meɲɒ* (f.)	Fn., *meɲɔ̃* 'good'
* ˈ*meŋga* (m.)	K., *meŋga* pers. n. 'blood'; 'to hate'; 'a frying-pan'
* *meˈriko* (f.)	B., *meriko* 'a Bambara family name'
* ˈ*mesa* (m.)	E., me_3sa_3 'the third son' (a variant of men_3sa_3). H., $me{:}_3sa{:}_1$ 'a python'; 'a water hose'
* *meˈsara* (f.)	W., *mesara* 'Egypt'
ˈ*mete* (f.)	K., *mete* 'saliva'
ˈ*mɛma* (f.)	M., *mɛma* 'Take notice!'
* ˈ*mɛmbu* (f.)	M., *mɛmbu* pers. n. 'a small bird with red head and neck'
* ˈ*mɛmɛ* (f.)	M., *mɛmɛ* pers. n. 'a mirror'
* ˈ*mɛriˈmɛri* (f.)	Y., $m\varepsilon_3r\tilde{\imath}_2m\varepsilon_3r\tilde{\imath}_2$ pers. n. 'four at a time,' 'by fours'
ˈ*mɛsɛri* (f.)	V., $m\varepsilon_3s\varepsilon_1ri_3$ ($m\varepsilon_3s\varepsilon_1li_3$) 'a needle'
* ˈ*mɛsu* (m.)	Tl., *mɛsu* pers. n. 'eyes'
miˈando (m.)	M., *miando* 'there, yonder'
miˈaŋgu (m.)	K., *miaŋgu* 'tumult, bluster'
miˈawa (f.)	E., $mi\tilde{a}_1\beta a_1$ 'the left wing of an army'
ˈ*mika* (m.)	K., *mika* 'wool, fur, hair'
* *miˈkɒlɒ* (f.)	Tl., *mikɔlɔ* 'name given a child whose mother while pregnant wore a charm made of the necks of gourds'; Kim., *mikɔlɔ* 'ropes'
* *miˈlanda* (m. and f.)	Kim., *milanda* pers. n.
ˈ*mile* (f).	G., mi_1le_1 'I know'; mi_3le_{3-1} 'I don't know'
* ˈ*milɒ* (f.)	E., $mi_3l\text{ɔ}_3$ pers. n. 'a small black bird'
* *miˈlɒŋga* (m.)	Kim., *milɔŋga* pers. n. 'cases, disputes'
* ˈ*mimi* (f.)	E., mi_3mi_3 'to press, to push'; 'dumb'; M., *mimi* pers. n. f.; Fn., *mimi* 'delicate, slender'
* ˈ*mimu* (f.)	Y., $m\tilde{\imath}_3m\tilde{u}_3$ pers. n. 'keenness'; 'acute'; $m\tilde{\imath}_3m\tilde{u}_2$ 'that which is to be drunk'
* ˈ*mina* (m. and f.)	V., mi_1na_3 pers. n. m.; Fn., *mina* 'the black native from Elmina or Accra (Gold Coast) and refugee to Popo (Dahomey)'

GULLAH PERSONAL NAMES	WEST AFRICAN WORDS
* ˈ*mini* (f.)	K., *mini* 'a torch'; M., *mini* pers. n. 'heavy'; B., *mini* 'the act of drinking'
ˈ*minto* (m.)	Man., *minto?* 'where?'
ˈ*miŋke* (f.)	B., *miŋke* 'after, when, at the time'
* ˈ*miŋko* (m.)	B., *miŋko* pers. n. 'a tumblerful, a bumper, a prize'; 'a kind of tree'
* ˈ*miraŋ* (f.)	Man., *miraŋ* pers. n. 'calabash'
* ˈ*miri* (f.)	Y., *mi*$_2$*ri*$_3$ 'to shake the head'; B., *miri* pers. n. 'to mediate'; 'a very small fish'
* *miˈrila* (f.)	B., *mirila* pers. n. 'serious'; 'one who reflects'
* ˈ*mise* (f.)	B., *mise* pers. n. 'small, slender'; 'indiscreet, troublesome'
* ˈ*misi* (m.)	B., *misi* pers. n. 'ox, cow'
* *miˈsira* (f.)	B., *misira* 'Egypt'
ˈ*miyɔ* (f.)	E., *miɔ*:$_1$ 'cool, refreshing'
mɒɪ (f.)	V., *mãĩ*$_1$ 'to abuse'; Tl., *mai* 'water'; H., *mai*$_1$ 'the owner or possessor of'; *mai*$_{3-1}$ 'oil, fat'; cf. Eng. *my*
* ˈ*mɒɪde* (f.)	Fu., *maide* pers. n. 'death'
* ˈ*mɒɪma* (f.)	V., *mai*$_3$*ma*$_3$ pers. n. f.; H., *mai*$_3$*ma*:$_3$ 'a deterioration in the appearance of the inside of kola nuts'
* ˈ*mɒɪna* (f.)	V., *mɔi*$_{3-1}$ *na*$_1$ pers. n. 'A person comes'
ˈ*mɐɪso* (m.)	H., *mai*$_3$*so*:$_3$ 'the act of vomiting'; 'a farm which has been left unworked'
* ˈ*mɐɪtɪma* (f.)	M., *maɪtɪma* pers. n. f.
* ˈ*mɒkɒ* (f.)	K., *mɔkɔ* pers. n. 'hands'
* ˈ*mɒkɒɪ* (m.)	W., *mɔkai* pers. n. 'docility'
ˈ*mɒkɒtɒ* (f.)	Bo., *mɒkɔtɔ* 'globular'
* ˈ*mɒle* (m.)	Y., *mɔ*$_2$*le*$_3$ 'to build'; V., *mɔ*$_3$*le*$_1$ (*mɔ*$_3$*re*$_1$) 'a Mohammedan'
* ˈ*mɒmɒ* (f.)	Y., *mɔ̃*$_1$*mɔ̃*$_1$ 'greedily'; *mɔ̃*:$_{1-2}$*mɔ̃*$_{2-1}$ pers. n. 'knowingly'; M., *mɔmɒ* 'a tumor that appears upon the head'; Bi., *mɔ*$_1$*mɔ*$_3$ 'to lend'
* *mɒˈmɒlu* (m.)	M., *mɒmɒlu* pers. n. m.
* ˈ*mɒna* (f.)	Y., *mɔ*$_1$*na*$_1$ 'to know the way'; 'yes, certainly'; Kim., *mɔna* pers. n. 'child'; Tl., *mɔna* 'to see'; K., *mɔna* 'vision, sight'; 'to see'
* *mɒˈnami* (m.)	Kim., *mɔn ami* (*mɔna ami*) pers. n. 'my child'
* *mɒnanˈdeŋge* (f.)	Kim., *mɔnandeŋge* 'the younger child'
* ˈ*mɒnana* (f.)	E., *mɔ*$_3$*na*$_3$*na*$_3$ 'cutting a road'; 'giving permission'; 'leave of absence, vacation'; K., *mɔnana* pers. n. 'to greet, to visit, to interview'

GULLAH PERSONAL NAMES	WEST AFRICAN WORDS
* ˈ*mɒŋgɒ* (m.)	K., *mɔŋgɔ* pers. n. 'a hill, plateau'
* ˈ*mɒre* (m.)	M., *mɔre* 'a Mohammedan'
* *mɒˈrɛmi* (f.)	Y., *mɔ̃*$_3$*rɛ*$_1$*mi*$_2$ 'the wife of a nobleman of *i*$_2$*le*$_3$-*i*$_2$*fɛ*$_1$'
* ˈ*mɒse* (m.)	V., *mɔ*$_3$*se*$_3$ pers. n. m.
* *mɒˈsɛyi* (m.)	V., *mɔ*$_2$*sɛi*$_2$ pers. n. m.
* ˈ*mɒʃi* (m.)	K., *mɔʃi* 'one, identical, equal'; Kim., *mɔʃi* 'one' ([mɔʃi] is a variant pronunciation of *Mossi*, a language of French West Africa)
* ˈ*mɒtɒ* (f.)	E., *mɔ*$_3$*tɔ*$_{1-3}$ pers. n. 'edge, border of the road'
* ˈ*mɒwɒla* (f.)	E., *mɔ̃*$_3$*wɔ*$_1$*la*$_3$ pers. n. 'a liar'
* ˈ*mɒyɒ* (m.)	K., *mɔyɔ* pers. n. 'spirit, life'
* ˈ*mɒzɒwa* (m.)	E., *mɔ*$_3$*zɔ*$_1$*a*$_3$ pers. n. 'a wanderer'
mo (m.)	Man., *mo* 'man'; T., *mo* 'a congratulation, thankful acknowledgment'; E., *mo*$_1$ 'face, front side'; cf. Eng. *mow*
* *moˈdiŋgo* (m.)	Man., *modiŋo* 'the man's child'
* ˈ*mofi* (m.)	Y., *mo*$_1$*fĩ*$_2$ pers. n. 'to know the law'
* ˈ*mole* (f.)	Man., *mole* 'man'
* ˈ*molo* (f.)	Y., *mo*$_3$*lo*$_3$ 'a Hausa guitar'; Mand., *molo* 'name given the third son'
ˈ*molu* (m.)	Man., *molu* 'people'
* ˈ*momo* (f.)	B., *momo* pers. n. 'to pry into'; 'to try'
* *moˈrɛnike* (m. and f.)	Y., *mo*$_2$*rɛ*$_3$*ni*$_2$*kɛ*$_3$ pers. n., lit. 'I have someone to pet'
* ˈ*mori* (m.)	H., *mo:*$_1$*ri:*$_2$ 'a white, hard-grained variety of guinea corn'; *mo:*$_3$*ri*$_1$ 'a stable'; Mand., *mo:ri* 'a priest'
* *moˈriba* (m.)	Mand., *mo:riba* 'a Mohammedan hermit or saint or his shrine'
* *moˈrifi* (m.)	Mand., *mo:rifi* pers. n. m.; 'Mori the Black'
ˈ*mosa* (m. and f.)	T., *mmosã* 'strong drink'
* *mpiˈaza* (f.)	K., *mpiaza* 'the season when the grass is burned (from July to October)'; 'the ground which has been cleared by fire' (a synonym of *mpela*)
mũ (m.)	E., *mũ*$_1$ 'to stagger'; *mũ*$_3$ 'to be intoxicated'; 'to emit a strange odor'; 'fresh, green'; 'a mosquito, a gnat'; Y., *mũ*$_1$ 'to sink'; *mũ*$_2$ 'to drink'; *mũ*$_3$ 'to take'; 'sharp, clean'; B., *mu* 'to do over, to coat'
* *muˈana* (f.)	Tl., *muana* 'child, offspring, seed'; V., *mua*$_3$*na*$_1$ pers. n. m.
* *muˈbidi* (m.)	Kim., *mubidi* pers. n. 'shepherd, herdsman'
* *muˈbika* (f.)	Kim., *mubika* pers. n. 'a slave'

GULLAH PERSONAL NAMES	WEST AFRICAN WORDS
ˈ*muda* (m.)	H., *mu*$_3$'*da*$_1$ 'to reply'
* *muˈhatu* (f.)	Kim., *muhatu* pers. n. 'woman'
* *mukaˈʒina* (f.)	Kim., *mukaʒina* 'the second or third wife of a polygamist'
* *muˈkama* (f.)	V., *mu*$_3$ *ka*:$_1$*ma*$_1$ pers. n. 'Let us get up'; *mu*$_2$ *ka*$_3$*ma*$_1$ 'How many of us?'
* ˈ*mukitɛ* (f.)	V., *mu*$_3$*ki*$_1$*tɛ*$_3$ pers. n. 'We sleep in the middle'
* ˈ*mukɪla* (f.)	V., *mu*$_3$*kɪ*$_1$*la*$_1$ pers. n. 'We become big'
* *muˈkɒŋgɒ* (m.)	Kim., *mukɔŋgɔ* pers. n. 'hunter'
ˈ*muku* (m.)	K., *muku* 'the odor arising with the steam from hot food'
* *muˈlambu* (m.)	Tl., *mulambu* pers. n. 'offering, tax, tribute'
ˈ*mule* (f.)	Y., *mu*$_3$*le*$_2$ 'to harden'; M., *mule* 'soapstone'
* *muˈlɒŋga* (f.)	Tl., *mulɔŋga* 'an edible winged ant'; Kim., *mulɔŋga* pers. n. 'speech, dispute, lawsuit, offense'
* *muˈlulu* (f.)	Kim., *mululu* 'great-grandchild'
muˈluŋga (f.)	Tl., *muluŋga* 'the inside of an egg'
muˈmari (f.)	B., *mumari* 'velvet' (Ar.)
* ˈ*mumo* (f.)	T., *mũmõ* 'name of a month, approximately December'; G., *mũ*$_2$*mõ*$_{2-1}$ 'spirit, breath, life'
* ˈ*mumu* (f.)	E., *mu*$_3$*mu*$_3$ pers. n. 'deaf and dumb'; 'to emit a disagreeable odor'; *mu*$_3$*mu*$_{1-3}$ 'green, unboiled, precocious, priggish'; Fn., *mumu* 'green, uncooked'; T., *mumu* 'deaf and dumb'
* ˈ*muna* (f.)	Y., *mu*$_3$*na*$_3$ pers. n. 'high-spirited'; T., *muna* 'to become dark, to look gloomy'; Tl., *muna* 'to tame, to raise livestock'; U., *muna* 'to be abundant'
* ˈ*munda* (f.)	M., *mʊnda* pers. n. 'our own, ours'
ˈ*muni* (m.)	B., *muni* 'unction, the act of anointing'
* *muniˈmiya* (f.)	V., *mu*$_1$*ni*$_1$ *mĩa*$_3$ pers. n. 'Where to turn?'
* ˈ*munse* (f.)	K., *munse* pers. n. 'sugar cane'
* *muˈɲiɲi* (f.)	Tl., *muɲiɲi* pers. n. 'meat, flesh'
ˈ*muŋgu* (m.)	Kim., *muŋgu* 'tomorrow'
* ˈ*muŋgwa* (m.)	Kim., and K., *muŋgwa* pers. n. 'salt'
* *muˈrimi* (f.)	Kim., *murimi* pers. n. 'a tiller, a cultivator'
* ˈ*musa* (m.)	Mand., *mu:sa* 'Moses'; Man. and S., *musa* 'Moses'; W., *musa* pers. n. m.; Y., *mu*$_3$*sã*$_1$ 'to heal'
* *muˈsaŋgu* (m.)	Tl., *musaŋgu* pers. n. 'a birthmark'; 'a person with a birthmark'; 'time, turn'; 'a long stick with which a boat is pushed along'

GULLAH PERSONAL NAMES	WEST AFRICAN WORDS
muˈsɛki (f.)	Tl., *musɛki* 'a cluster of bananas on the stalk'
muˈsolu (f.)	Man., *musolu* 'women'
* *muˈsondiŋ* (f.)	Man., *musondiŋ* pers. n. 'girl'
* *muˈsoti* (m. and f.)	Man., *musoti* pers. n. 'the woman'
* *ˈmusu* (f.)	V., mu_1su_3 pers. n. 'woman'; W., *musu* pers. n. f.; H., mu_3su_1 'contradiction, denial'
* *muˈʃiba* (f.)	Tl., *muʃiba* 'barrel of a gun, stem of a pipe'; 'a tribe'
* *muˈʃima* (f.)	Kim., *muʃima* pers. n. 'heart'
ˈmuta (f.)	Man., *muta* 'to take'
* *muˈtɒmbɒ* (m.)	Kim., *mutɔmbɔ* pers. n. 'the young of the antelope'
* *muˈtudi* (f.)	Kim., *mutudi* pers. n. 'a widow'; Tl., *mutudi* 'a blacksmith'
* *muˈtumba* (m.)	Tl., *mutumba* pers. n. 'a species of rat'; 'boundary, limit'
ˈmutwe (f.)	Kim., *mutwe* 'head'
* *muˈzumbu* (m.)	Kim., *muzumbu* 'an official in Angola corresponding to the foreign secretary or minister of foreign affairs in European countries'; 'the spokesman of the chief'
* *ˈmwaɲa* (f.)	Kim., *mwaɲa* (*lwaɲa*) pers. n. 'the heat and light of the sun, daylight and noon heat'
ˈmwene (f.)	Kim., *mwene* 'the same'
ˈmwinda (m.)	K., *mwinda* 'a candle'
* *mwiʃiˈkɒŋgɒ* (f.)	K., *mwiʃikɔŋgɔ* 'a person of Kongo'
* *ˈmwula* (m.)	Kim. and K., *mvula* pers. n. 'rain'

[n]

* *naˈgo* (m.)	Fn., *nago* 'the Yoruba language of Southern Nigeria.' Cf. E., $a_1na_1go_3$ 'Yoruba'
* *ˈnali* (f.)	B., *nali* pers. n. 'arrival'; M., *nali* 'a mysterious sound or sight supposed to warn of death'
naˈmara (f.)	V., $na_3ma_3ra_3$ 'slippery'; 'to slip.' Cf. $na_3ma_3ra_3$ $na_3ma_3ra_3$ 'very slippery'
naˈmaya (f.)	B., *namaya* 'the sojourn of a married woman in the house of her father'
naˈmuna (f.)	U., *namuna* 'to seize one who flees'
* *ˈnana* (f.)	Y., $n\tilde{a}_{1-2}n\tilde{a}_{1-2}$ 'name of a female deity'; T., *nãnã* 'a grandparent'; Tl., *nana* 'a grandparent'; 'to stretch'; 'to ask one to pay a debt'; 'glue, paste'; Bo., *na:na* 'to go upstream'; K., *nana* 'eight';

GULLAH PERSONAL NAMES	WEST AFRICAN WORDS
	'to stretch'; B., *nana* 'a species of fish without scales'; 'house-leek'; M., *nana* 'an herb with its spinose seed'; Man., *nana* 'the swallow' (a totem of a Mandinka noble clan)
ˈ*nan*-ˈ*nan* (f.)	Ef., nan_1-nan_1 'blindly'
* ˈ*nanɒ* (m.)	M., *nanɒ* 'the Mende month corresponding to July'
ˈ*nano* (f.)	Fu., *nano* 'the left hand'; T., *nnano* 'recently'
* ˈ*naŋge* (f.)	Fu., *naŋge* pers. n. 'sun, daytime'
na_1sa_3 (f.)	Y., na_1sa_3 'to spread out to dry'
ˈ*natu* (m.)	K., *natu* 'the small present which is always given by those who go for medicine or for a witch doctor'
* ˈ*nawa* (f.)	H., $na{:}_1wa_2$ pers. n. 'mine'
ˈ*nawi* (f.)	M., *navi* 'flexible'
*n*ˈ*dɛda* (m.)	T., *ndɛda* 'yesterday'
* *n*ˈ*dɒkɒ* (f.)	Bo., *ndɔkɔ* pers. n. 'a bewitching which is said to cause illness'; K., *ndɔkɔ* 'a clicking noise'
* *n*ˈ*duŋgu* (m.)	K., *nduŋgu* pers. n. 'pepper'; Bo., *nduŋgu* 'a water-pot'
* *nem*ˈ*paŋgu* (m.)	K., *nempaŋgu* 'a title of nobility'
* ˈ*nena* (f.)	U., *nena* 'to bring'; T., *nẽna* 'grandchild'
* ˈ*nene* (f.)	K., *nene* pers. n. 'greatness, stoutness'; B., *nene* 'cold'; 'to taste'
ˈ*neni* (f.)	B., *neni* 'to abuse, to insult'
nɛ (m.)	E., $nɛ_3$ 'nut'; $nɛ_{3-1}$ 'give him, for him'; M., *nɛ* 'tongue'; Bi., $nɛ_3$ 'to defecate'
* ˈ*nɛgɛ* (f.)	B., *nɛgɛ* pers. n. 'desire, envy'; 'to flatter'; 'a metal (especially iron)'
* ˈ*nɛgɪ* (f.)	M., *nɛgɪ* pers. n. 'sweetness'
* ˈ*nɛma* (f.)	B., *nɛma* pers. n. 'happiness, affluence'
* *nɛ*ˈ*mahʊ̃* (f.)	M., *nɛmahʊ̃* pers. n. 'mind, opinion, reason'
* ˈ*nɛndi* (m.)	M., *nɛndi* pers. n. 'a toothless gum'
* ˈ*nɛnɛ* (f.)	M., *nɛnɛ* 'shadow, spirit, ghost'; Tl., *nɛnɛ* pers. n. 'large, famous'
* ˈ*nɛnɪ* (f.)	M., *nɛnɪ* pers. n. 'sweet, agreeable'; 'to indulge, to sweeten'
ˈ*nɛsi* (m.)	M., *nɛsi* 'a pineapple'
ˈ*nɛtɛ* (f.)	M., *nɛtɛ* 'a door made of bamboo or of boards'; cf. the Dahomean sea-goddess *Naete*
* ˈ*nigli* (f.)	E., ni_1gli_1 pers. n. 'crippled, maimed'

GULLAH PERSONAL NAMES	WEST AFRICAN WORDS
'*nika* (f.)	Y., ni_3ka_1 'cruel'; $ni_1k\tilde{a}_3$ 'alone, single'; K., *nika* 'to crush, to rub and pound in washing'
'*nili* (f.)	M., *nili* 'very dark'; 'completely'
ni'*lɔlɔ* (f.)	Y., $n\tilde{\imath}_3lɔ_2lɔ_2$ 'recently'
'*nima* (m.)	K., *nima* 'back, rear'; 'keel'
* '*nimisa* (f.)	V., $ni_3mi_3sa_3$ pers. n. 'misfortune'
* '*nina* (f.)	Y., ni_3na_1 'a flogging'; 'elastic'; ni_3na_3 'fiery'; M., *nina* 'new'; B., *nina* pers. n. 'a gift'
* '*ninso* (m.)	Man., *ninso* pers. n. 'cow, ox'
'*niso* (f.)	H., $ni{:}_2so{:}_2$ 'to reappear'; 'to flow into a well'
* '*nɒlɪ* (f.)	M., *nɔlɪ* pers. n. 'black.' Cf. *nɔli* 'inactive'
* '*nɒma* (f.)	M., *nɒma* pers. n. 'perseverance'
'*nɒni* (m.)	M., *nɒni* 'a fragment'
'*nɒnɒ* (f.)	K., *nɔnɔ* 'an unctuous exudation from the skin'
* $nɒ_1wi_3$ (f.)	E., $nɔ_1vi_3$ 'brother, sister, a child of the same mother as another'; 'mate, fellow'
* *nɒ*'*wisi* (f.)	E., $nɔ_1vi_3si_3$ pers. n. 'brother's hand.' Cf. na_3 $nɔ_1vi_3si_3$ 'to become reconciled,' lit. 'to give brother's hand'
'*noke* (m.)	U., *noke* 'soon'
'*noko*'*noko* (m.)	G., no_3ko_2, no_3ko_2 'nothing, nothing'
'*noma* (f.)	Man., *noma* 'to sit'; cf. T., *anõmã*: 'bird'
'*nomo* (m.)	Man., *nomo* 'to lie down' (used by a young man in speaking to an old man)
'*noni* (f.)	B., *no:ni* 'the act of swimming'; 'to dilute with water'
'*nono* (f.)	H., $no{:}_3no_1$ 'the mammary gland of the female, and the corresponding structure in the male'; 'the fins below the head of fish'; 'a cluster of fruit'
* '*noŋbo* (f.)	V., $noŋ_3bo_3$ pers. n. f.
'*noro* (f.)	B., *no:ro* 'grain abandoned in a field'
'*nowa* (f.)	H., $no{:}_3wa_1$ 'ulcerative gingivitis'
n'*sɒle* (m.)	K., *nsɔle* 'a large root used for medicinal purposes'
n'*sɒye* (f.)	T., *nsɔe* 'thorn, thornbush'
n'*tama* (f.)	T., *ntãmã* 'cloth, a native dress consisting of one large cloth wrapped around the body in various ways'
n'*telu* (m.)	Man., *ntelu* 'we'
* *n*'*to* (m.)	Mand., *nto* 'name given the fourth son'; I., n_3to_3 'ashes'; 'gunpowder'; cf. K., *ntɔ* 'fountain'; cf. T., *ntɔŋ* 'family group '
* *nubi*'*yala* (f.)	E., $nu_3bia_3la_3$ pers. n. 'a beggar'

GULLAH PERSONAL NAMES	WEST AFRICAN WORDS
ˈnuka (m.)	K., *nuka* 'to emit a bad odor'; 'rottenness'; H., *nu*$_3$*ka*$_1$ 'to ferment'; 'to ripen fruit by storing it'; *nu*$_1$*ka:*$_2$ 'to become ripe by being stored'
nuˈkisa (m.)	K., *nukisa* 'to corrupt, to cause putrescence'
* *ˈnumu* (m.)	V., *nu*$_3$*mu*$_3$ pers. n. 'a small black frog'
* *ˈnuna* (f.)	K., *nuna* pers. n. 'to be old'; 'to grow old'; Tl., *nuna* 'to increase'; Bo., *nu:na* 'to grow old'
* *ˈnunu* (f.)	K., *nunu* 'an aged person'; Tl., *nunu* 'aged'; T., *nũ*$_1$*nũ*$_3$ 'to stir up'; *nũ*$_1$*nũ*$_1$ 'to censure'
* *ˈnuɲa* (f.)	E., *nu*$_3$*ɲa*$_3$ (*nu*$_3$*ɲa*$_1$) pers. n. 'knowledge, discretion'
ˈnuɲi (f.)	E., *nu*$_3$*ɲi*$_3$ 'food, foodstuff'
* *ˈnuŋge* (m.)	K., *nuŋge* pers. n. 'a mouse'
ˈnuŋka (m.)	Tl., *nuŋka* 'to emit an odor'
ˈnwanina (f.)	K., *nwanina* 'to fight for'
* *nˈzala* (f.)	Kim. and K., *nzala* pers. n. 'hunger'; K., *nzala* 'fingernails, claws'
* *nˈzamba* (m.)	K., *nzamba* pers. n. 'elephant'
* *nˈzambi* (f.)	Kim., K., and Tl., *nzambi* 'God'; Bo., *nzambi* 'dowry to a wife's relatives'; 'responsibility for another's debt'; K., *nzambi*! 'a respectful answer to a call'

[ɲ]

* *ɲa* (m.)	E., *ɲa*$_1$ 'speech, palaver'; *ɲa*$_3$ 'to understand, to be capable'; *ɲã*$_1$ 'to knead'; 'to wash'; 'to drive away'; Mand., *ɲa* 'name given the sixth son'; Bi., *ɲa*$_3$ 'to open'; 'to weaken'; 'to be bright'; *ɲa*$_{1-3}$ 'to own'; 'to promise'; 'to spoil a child by the wrong education'
* *ˈɲaba* (f.)	K., *ɲaba* pers. n. 'a swamp'
* *ˈɲaɪle* (f.)	Fu., *ɲaile* pers. n. 'the end of the harvest season'
* *ˈɲalo* (f.)	M., *ɲalo* 'girl, daughter'
* *ɲamaˈnole* (f.)	Man., *ɲamano* 'a euphemism for wife.' Cf. *i ɲamano le?* 'How are your home comforts?' (a euphemistic way of making inquiry concerning a man's wife, after whom inquiries should not be made by the use of her name)[38]
* *ˈɲambe* (f.)	M., *ɲambe* pers. n. 'my own'
ˈɲami (f.)	B., *ɲami* 'to mix'
* *ɲaˈmuna* (f.)	U., *ɲamuna* pers. n. 'to talk nonsense'; 'to rejoice greatly'
ˈɲana (f.)	U., *ɲana* 'to dislike, to repudiate'; 'to steal'; B.,

GULLAH PERSONAL NAMES	WEST AFRICAN WORDS
	ɲana 'a creeper with tubercle resembling the yam but slightly poisonous, a kind of wild yam'
* 'ɲ*anda* (f.)	B., *ɲanda* pers. n. 'a pigeon'
* 'ɲ*ande* (m.)	M., *ɲande* pers. n. 'good, valuable'; 'to beautify, to adorn'
* 'ɲ*ani* (f.)	M., *ɲani* pers. n. 'to spoil, to become impoverished''
* 'ɲ*antɛ* (m.)	T., *ɲantɛ* pers. n. m.
'ɲ*awa* (f.)	T., *nɲawa* 'coals'
* 'ɲ*eda* (f.)	B., *ɲeda* pers. n. 'face, figure'; 'to see, to visit'
'ɲ*ege* (f.)	B., *ɲege* 'to carve, to paint'
* 'ɲ*ele* (f.)	B., *ɲele* pers. n. 'successful, well executed'
* 'ɲ*ɛgɪ* (f.)	M., *ɲɛgɪ* pers. n. 'to mark'; 'marked, scarred'
'ɲ*ɛma* (f.)	Tl., *ɲɛma* 'to run away'
* 'ɲ*ɛta* (f.)	W., *ɲɛta* pers. n. 'three'
* ɲ*i* (f.)	K., *ɲi* 'an ugly person'; M., *ɲi* 'to bite'; E., *ɲi*$_1$ 'to nurse, to educate'; 'to observe a religious prescription'; *ɲi*$_3$ 'elephant'; 'cow, cattle'; 'to melt'; 'to suck'; 'to impose a fine'; *ɲĩ*$_{1-3}$ 'uncle'
* 'ɲ*ibre* (m.)	Fu., *ɲibre* pers. n. 'darkness'
'ɲ*ibu* (m.)	Fn., *ɲibu* 'cow, ox, bull'
* 'ɲ*idi* (f.)	E., *ɲi*$_1$*di*$_1$ pers. n. 'morning'
'ɲ*igi* (m.)	B., *ɲigi* 'disgust'; 'to be envious of'; 'to moisten'
'ɲ*iki* (m.)	Tl., *ɲiki* 'pyorrhea'; Kim., *ɲiki* 'a bee'
* 'ɲ*imbidi* (f.)	K., *ɲimbidi* pers. n. 'a singer'
'ɲ*imɪ* (f.)	M., *ɲimɪ* 'to tread upon, to injure'
'ɲ*ina* (f.)	V., *ɲi*$_1$*na*$_1$ 'to forget'; Man., *ɲina* 'fine'; B., *ɲina* 'this year'; M., *ɲina* 'rat'
* 'ɲ*inɒ* (f.)	E., *ɲi*$_3$*nɔ*$_{1-3}$ pers. n. 'female elephant'; 'a small mouse'
ɲ*iŋ* (m.)	Man., *ɲiŋ* 'this'
* ɲ*i*'*ri* (f.)	E., *ɲrĩ*$_3$ 'uncle (mother's brother)'
'ɲ*iwi* (m.)	E., *ɲi*$_1$*wi*$_3$ 'calf'
* 'ɲ*ɒka* (m.)	Kim. and Tl., *ɲɔka* 'snake'; K., *niɔka* pers. n. 'snake'; 'to be weary physically'
* 'ɲ*ɒmɒ* (m.)	E., *ɲɔ*$_1$*mɔ:*$_1$ pers. n. 'ugly'
* ɲ*o* (m.)	E., *ɲo*$_3$ 'to be good, to be agreeable'; 'brother-in-law, sister-in-law'; *ɲo*$_1$ 'sea cow'
'ɲ*olo* (m.)	B., *ɲo:lo*: 'a thorny bush'
* 'ɲ*ula* (f.)	U., *ɲula* 'to refuse one and accept another'; *ɲũla* pers. n. 'to visit'

GULLAH PERSONAL NAMES	WEST AFRICAN WORDS
* 'ɲ*uri* (m.)	E., *ɲrĩ*$_{1-3}$ 'one's mother's brother, uncle'
* 'ɲ*uwi* (m.)	E., *ɲui*$_3$ pers. n. 'good, pretty'

[ŋ]

* ŋ'*di* (f.)	E., ŋ$_1$*di*$_3$ pers. n. 'morning'
* ŋ'*gaŋga* (m.)	K., ŋ*gaŋga* 'doctor, diviner, priest'; Tl., ŋ*gaŋga* 'doctor, witch doctor'
ŋ'*gɒmbɛ* (m.)	Tl., ŋ*gɔmbɛ* 'ox, cow'
* ŋ'*guzu* (m.)	Kim., ŋ*guzu* pers. n. 'strength'
ŋ'*kidi* (m.)	K., ŋ*kidi* 'gum copal'
* ŋ'*kiʃi* (m.)	K., ŋ*kiʃi* pers. n. 'a charm, medicine'
* ŋ'*kwiza* (f.)	K., ŋ*kwiza* pers. n. 'I come'

[ɒ]

* 'ɒ*ba* (m.)	Y., ɔ$_2$*ba*$_2$ 'king, monarch'; Bi., ɔ$_3$*ba*$_3$ 'the ruler of Benin'
* ɒ*ba*'*lade* (f.)	Y., ɔ$_2$*ba*$_2$*la*$_3$*de*$_3$ pers. n., lit. 'The king has a crown'
* ˌɒ*baluaɪ*'*ye* (f.)	Y., ɔ$_2$*ba*$_2$-*o*$_2$*lu*$_3$*ai*$_1$*ye*$_3$ 'ɔ$_2$*m*ɔ$_2$*lu*$_3$, the god of smallpox'
* ɒ'*baŋku* (m.)	T., ɔ*baŋku* pers. n. 'a food made of ground maize, commonly eaten when yam is scarce'
* ɒ'*ba-ogo* (m.)	Y., ɔ$_2$*ba*$_2$-*o*$_1$*go*$_2$ 'God,' lit. 'King of Glory'
* ɒ*ba*'*siya* (m. and f.)	T., ɔ*basia* 'woman, female'
* ɒ*ba*'*tala* (m. and f.)	Y., ɔ:$_2$*ba*$_1$*ta*:$_3$*la*$_3$ 'the great goddess of the Yoruba, supposed to be the framer of the human body in the womb'
'ɒ*bɛ* (m.)	Y., ɔ$_1$*bɛ*$_2$ 'a knife'; ɔ$_2$*bɛ*$_1$ 'sauce, soup'
* ɒ'*bɛsɛ* (f.)	T., ɔ*bɛsɛ* 'the period extending from the beginning of the rains in October until January'
* ɒ'*bɒfo* (m.)	T., ɔ$_1$*b*ɔ$_3$*fo*$_2$ 'a messenger'; ɔ$_1$*b*ɔ$_3$*fo*$_3$ 'creator'; ɔ$_1$*b*ɔ$_1$*fo*$_3$ 'a hunter'
ɒ*bo*'*daŋ* (m.)	T., ɔ*bodaŋ* 'a stone house, a cave'
* 'ɒ*da* (m.)	T., ɔ$_1$*da*$_1$ 'tar, wax'; ɔ$_1$*da*$_3$ 'need, famine'; 'old wine, strongly fermented'; T., ɔ*da* 'grave, tomb'; ɔ*da* pers. n. 'He sleeps'
'ɒ*dam* (m.)	T., ɔ*dam* 'madness'
ɒ'*daɲa* (m.)	T., ɔ*daɲã* 'a medicinal plant'; G., ɔ$_1$*da*$_3$*ɲã*$_2$ 'a plant'
ɒ'*dasu* (m.)	T., ɔ*dasu* 'a sleep'
* ɒ'*dena* (f.)	T., ɔ*denã* 'Elmina, a city on the Gold Coast'

GULLAH PERSONAL NAMES	WEST AFRICAN WORDS
* ɒdɛ'wale (m.)	Y., ɔ$_2$dɛ$_2$wa$_3$le$_3$ pers. n., lit. ɔ$_2$dɛ$_2$ [a hunter] comes to the house'
* ɒdɒ'fĩ (f.)	Y., ɔ$_2$dɔ$_2$fĩ$_3$ 'an Ogboni [o$_2$gbo$_3$ni$_2$] title' (The Ogboni constitute the town council in the Egba Province.)
* ɒ'ga-ogo (m.)	Y., ɔ$_1$ga$_3$-o$_1$go$_2$ 'illustrious (used only in reference to the Supreme Being)
'ɒɟa (m.)	Y., ɔ$_2$ɟa$_1$ 'a market'; ɔ$_1$ɟa$_3$ 'band, girdle, head-tie'
* ɒɟɛ'biyi (m.)	Y., ɔ$_1$ɟɛ$_1$bi$_3$yi$_2$ 'ɔ$_1$ɟɛ$_1$ (a chief of the e$_2$gũ$_3$gũ$_3$ cult) begot this'
'ɒkĩ (f.)	Y., ɔ$_1$kĩ$_3$ 'a bird whose white feathers are highly valued'
* ɒ'kĩkĩ (f.)	Y., ɔ$_1$kĩ$_3$kĩ$_3$ pers. n. 'a wind instrument resembling the bugle'
ɒk'pɒtɒ (m.)	Y., ɔ$_1$kpɔ$_2$tɔ$_3$ 'fig'
* ɒ'kra (m.)	T., ɔkra pers. n. m. 'soul'
* 'ɒla (f.)	Y., ɔ$_2$la$_3$ pers. n. 'dignity, authority'; ɔ$_2$la$_1$ 'wealth'; ɔ$_1$la$_2$ 'tomorrow'; K., ɔla 'hour' (P. hora [ɔrɐ])
* ɒ'labisi (m.)	Y., ɔ$_2$la$_3$bi$_3$si$_2$ pers. n. 'Honors increase'
* 'ɒlɒf (m.)	W., ɔlɔf 'the Wolof language and people'
* ɒ'lɒrũ (f.)	Y., ɔ$_2$lɔ$_3$rũ$_2$ 'God,' lit. 'the owner of the heavens'
ɒ'lɒʃa (m.)	Y., ɔ$_2$lɔ$_3$ʃa$_1$ 'a burglar'
* ɒ'lɒwɒ (m.)	Y., ɔ$_2$lɔ$_1$wɔ$_1$ pers. n. 'a person who commands respect'
'ɒmɒ (f.)	Y., ɔ$_2$mɔ̃$_2$ 'child, offspring'; ɔ$_1$mɔ̃$_1$ 'a tree of the banyan family having broad leaves'; ɔ$_1$mɔ̃$_2$ 'a builder of walls, an architect'
* ɒmɒ'lara (f.)	Y., ɔ$_2$mɔ̃$_2$la$_2$ra$_3$ pers. n., lit. 'The child has relatives'
* ɒmɒ'lu (m. and f.)	Y., ɔ$_2$mɔ̃$_2$lu$_3$ 'the god of smallpox'
* ɒmɒ-'ɒlɒ (f.)	Y., ɔ$_2$mɔ̃$_2$-ɔ$_3$la$_3$ 'one of the three members of the royal family who instruct the king (especially when he is young), the other two being o$_2$ni$_3$ʃo$_3$kũ$_1$ and ɔ$_1$na$_1$-a$_1$ka$_3$
'ɒna (f.)	Y., ɔ$_2$na$_1$ 'art, workmanship'; ɔ$_1$na$_1$ 'road, path, channel'; Tl., ɔna 'to snore'; 'to cause to wear out'
'ɒno (m.)	I., ɔ$_3$no$_3$ 'mouth, hole'; 'number, price'; 'the stem of young plants'
ɒri'bitu (f.)	Kim., ɔ ribitu 'the door'
'ɒsa (m.)	Y., ɔ$_1$sa$_1$ 'season, interval'; 'a lagoon'; Tl., ɔsa 'to produce'
ɒ'sãni (m.)	T., ɔsãni 'a habitual drunkard'
* ɒ'sãyĩ (f.)	Y., ɔ$_1$sã$_3$yĩ$_1$ 'the god of healing, medicine'

GULLAH PERSONAL NAMES	WEST AFRICAN WORDS
* ɒ'*sɛnɛ* (f.)	T., *ɔsɛn-nɛ* 'a righteous cause'; cf. T., *asẽneɛ* 'one of the original families of the Twi people'
'ɒ*so* (m.)	E., ɔ$_1$*so*$_1$ 'a mountain'
'ɒʃɒ (f.)	Y., ɔ$_1$ʃɔ$_3$ 'elegance'; ɔ$_1$ʃɔ$_2$ 'thorns used in pitfalls'; 'a pickax'
* ɒ'ʃɔ*si* (m.)	Y., ɔ$_1$ʃɔ:$_3$*si*$_1$ 'the god of hunters'; 'the god of the moon'
* ɒʃ*un*'*toki* (m. and f.)	Y., ɔ$_1$ʃ*ũ*$_2$*to*$_3$*ki*$_3$ pers. n., lit. ɔ$_1$ʃ*ũ*$_2$ '(the goddess of rivers) is worthy of honor'
* ɒ'*tunɛfa* (m.)	Y., ɔ$_1$*tũ*$_3$-ɛ$_1$*fa*$_1$ 'one of the three eunuchs or lordlings of the king's palace, the other two being ɔ$_2$*na*$_2$-ɛ$_1$*fa*$_1$, or the chief, and *o*$_1$*si*$_1$-ɛ$_1$*fa*$_1$'
* ɒ'*tunla* (m. and f.)	Y., ɔ$_1$*tũ*$_3$*la*$_2$ 'name given the third child born after twins,' lit. 'day after tomorrow'
ɒ'*waye* (m.)	T., ɔ*wae* 'apostasy, a falling away'
* 'ɒ*ya* (f.)	Y., ɔ$_2$*ya*$_2$ 'the wife of ʃ*a*ŋ$_1$*go*$_3$ (the god of thunder)'
* ɒ'*yabi* (m. and f.)	Y., ɔ$_2$*ya*$_2$*bi*$_3$ 'one of the twelve *kakanfos* in the Yoruba country, a *kakanfo* [ka$_2$ka$_2$-n$_2$fo$_1$] being a kind of field marshal'
* ɒ'*y*ɒ*misi* (m.)	Y., ɔ$_1$*y*ɔ$_3$*mi*$_1$*si*$_1$ 'one of the two classes of noblemen at ɔ$_1$*y*ɔ$_2$, the other being the ɛ$_1$ʃɔ$_3$'

[ɒɪ]

ɒɪ'*fɛ* (m.)	Y., *ai*$_1$*f*ɛ$_3$ 'disagreeableness, unwillingness'
ɒɪ'*m*ɒ (f.)	Y., *ai*$_1$*m*ɔ$_3$ 'unclean, filthy'; *ai*$_1$*m*ɔ$_1$ 'ignorance'
* 'ɒɪ*ye* (f.)	Y., *ai*$_2$*ye*$_3$ pers. n. 'world, earth'; 'time of life'
* ɒɪe'*deru* (m.)	Y., *ai*$_2$*ye*$_3$*de*$_1$*ru*$_3$ pers. n. 'fraud, dishonesty'

[ɒʊ]

'ɒʊ*ma* (f.)	W., *auma* 'to have'
* 'ɒʊ*sa* (m.)	Fn., *ausa* 'Hausa, a people and language of Northern Nigeria'

[o]

'*obada* (m.)	Y., *o*$_2$*ba*$_2$*da*$_2$ 'a rubber tree'
* '*obi* (m.)	Bi., *o*$_3$*bi*$_1$ 'poison'; I., *ö*$_3$*bi*$_1$ 'heart, bosom'; 'dwelling'; 'course of life'; 'fathom of cloth'; *ö*$_1$*bi*$_3$ 'title given to a king'; 'guesthouse'; Y., *o*$_2$*bi*$_1$ 'kola nut'; *o*$_2$*bi*$_3$ 'the female sex'; *o*:$_1$*bi*$_3$ 'parent'; T., *obi* 'person, someone'
* '*obidu* (m.)	Y., *o*$_2$*bi*$_1$*dũ*$_2$ (*a*$_1$*bi*$_1$*dũ*$_2$) pers. n. 'the kola nut'
* '*obobo* (m.)	Bi., *o*$_3$*bo*$_1$*bo*$_3$ pers. n. 'cooked yam mashed with oil'; 'a timber tree'; *o*$_3$*bo*$_{1-3}$*bo*$_1$ 'a flower'

GULLAH PERSONAL NAMES	WEST AFRICAN WORDS
o'boya (m.)	T., *oboya*: 'pig, swine'
* *o'dayi* (f.)	Bi., $o_1da_1yi_3$ 'a young man functioning as the senior of his $ɛ_1gbɛe_{3-1}$ (sib)'
* *odu'duwa* (m.)	Y., $o_2du_1du_3wa_1$ 'creator'
* *o'firi* (f.)	G. and T., $o_1fi_1ri_3$ 'an albino, a mulatto'
o'fiye (f.)	T., *ofie* 'home'
'ogbo (m.)	Y., o_2gbo_2 'latex'
* *og'bomɒʃɒ* (m.)	Y., $o_1gbo_2mɔ_1ʃɔ_2$ (m.) 'name of a city in the $ɔ_1yɔ_2$ Province'; 'a kind of field marshal, a ka_2ka_2-n_2fo_1'
* *og'boni* (m.)	Y., $o_1gbo_2ni_3$ 'name of a Yoruba cult'
* *o'gũ* (m.)	Y., $o_1gũ_3$ 'god of iron and of war'; 'a kind of basket'; $o_2gũ_3$ 'heritage'; 'twenty'; $o_2gũ_2$ 'war, battle'; $o{:}_{1-3}gũ_1$ 'perspiration'; $o{:}_1gũ_1$ 'medicine, poison, charm'
* *o'gũfɛtemi* (m.)	Y., $o_1gũ_3fɛ_3te_2mi_2$ pers. n., lit. '$o_1gũ_3$ likes mine'
o'gugu (m.)	Y., $o_2gu_2gu_2$ 'name of a tree'
* *o'hali* (m.)	U., *ohali* pers. n. 'misfortune'; 'to be unfortunate'
o'hambi (f.)	U., *ohambi* 'loss, lack'
* *ˌohun'dahũ* (m.)	Y., $o_2hũ_1$ $da_3hũ_1$ pers. n. 'A voice answers'
o'huta (m.)	U., *ohuta* 'provisions'
* *o'ɟika* (m.)	Y., $o_1ɟi_1ka_1$ pers. n. 'a sound sleep'
o'ɟiya (m.)	Y., $o_1ɟi_2a_3$ 'gum copal, myrrh'
* $o_1ɟo_3$ (m.)	Y., $o_1ɟo_3$ pers. n.; $o_1ɟo_1$ 'rain'; 'new, fresh'; $o_2ɟo_2$ 'fear'; 'a coward'
'okan (m.)	Y., $o_2kã_2$ 'the African greenheart'
ˌokan'dumba (m.)	U., *okandumba* 'screen, partition'
o'kati (f.)	U., *okati* 'middle, midst'
* *'oke* (m.)	Y., o_1ke_1 pers. n. 'top, hill, mountain'
* *o'keho* (m.)	Y., $o_1ke{:}_2ho_1$ 'name of a kingling in the $ɛ_1kũ_3$-$ɔ_1tũ_3$ Province'
o'kõĩya (m.)	Y., $o{:}_2kã_2$-ai_1ya_1 'bosom, chest'
* *o'kõɲe* (f.)	E., $o_{3-1}xɔ̃_3ɲe_1$ pers. n. 'oh! my friend'
* *'oko* (f.)	Y., o_2ko_2 pers. n. 'farm, plantation'; o_2ko_3 'copulatory organ of the male animal'; o_1ko_1'a stone thrown'
ˌoko-'alɛ (f.)	Y., o_2ko_2-$a_2lɛ_3$ 'an afternoon's farm work
* *o'kuta* (f.)	Y., $o_1ku_3ta_2$ 'stone'; $o_1ku_1ta_1$ 'worthless'; Bi., $o_1ku_3ta_3$ 'stone'
o'kutwi (m.)	U., *okutui* 'ear'
* *'ola* (f.)	Y., $o{:}_1la_1$ pers. n. 'that which saves, that which effects a deliverance'; 'a wedge'; $o{:}_1la_3$ 'the moth'

GULLAH PERSONAL NAMES	WEST AFRICAN WORDS
'ole (f.)	Y., o_2le_1 'thief'; 'theft'
'olɛ (f.)	I., $ö_1lɛ_3$ 'how many?'
o'lodo (m.)	Y., $o_2lo_3do_1$ 'one who owns a well'
o'loŋgo (m.)	Y., $o_2loŋ_2go_2$ 'the red-billed firefinch'
* *o'lowo-o'ri* (m.)	Y., $o_2lo_3wo_2$-o_2ri_3 pers. n., lit. 'a curly-headed child'
* *olu'biyi* (f.)	Y., $o_1lu_3bi_3yi_2$ pers. n., lit. 'A chief has begotten this'
* *o'lugbodi* (m.)	Y., $o_2lu_3gbo_3di_2$ 'name given a child born with supernumerary digits'
* *o'lulu* (f.)	Y., $o_1lu_3lu_2$ ($ɛ_1lu_3lu_2$) pers. n. 'a Senegal lark-heeled cuckoo'
o'lumbi (f.)	U., *olumbi* 'white hair'
o'luŋgu (m.)	U., *oluŋgu* 'vine'
* *olu'sami* (m.)	Y., $o_2lu_3s\tilde{a}_1mi_2$ 'one of the "brothers" to the king'; $o_2lu_3sa_1mi_1$ 'The chief makes a sign'; $o_2lu_3s\tilde{a}_1mi_2$ pers. n. 'The chief rewards me'
o'lusi (f.)	W., *olusi* 'to hasten'; 'to come to the aid of'; U., *olusi* 'fish'
* *o'luwa* (f.)	Y., $o_2lu_3wa_2$ 'lord, master'
* *o'luwo* (f.)	Y., $o_2lu_3wo_2$ 'a title in the Ogboni cult'
* *'oma* (m.)	Bi., o_3ma_1 'a large tree used for lumber'; Man., *omar* pers. n.
* *om'bala* (f.)	U., *ombala* 'residence of the chief, the capital'
* *om'baŋgi* (m.)	U., *ombaŋgi* pers. n. 'an incessant talker'
* *om'bela* (f.)	U., *ombela* pers. n. 'rain'
om'boka (f.)	U., *omboka* 'to loiter'
* *o'meke* (f.)	U., *omeke* pers. n. 'a blind man'
o'meme (f.)	U., *omeme* 'sheep'
* *omi'yale* (m.)	Y., $o_2m\tilde{i}_2ya_2le_3$ pers. n., lit. 'The god of streams visits the house'
o'mɒɪ (f.)	U., *omai* 'foot'
'omo (f.)	G., $o_2m\tilde{o}_3$ 'rice'
* *o'muye* (f.)	Y., $o_2m\tilde{u}_3ye_1$ 'one of the forty-eight Ilaris, household officers of the king'
'ona (f.)	U., *ona* 'a louse'
* *o'nali* (f.)	U., *onali* pers. n. 'a species of small bird'
on'dambo (m.)	U., *ondambo* 'girded clothes'; 'dryness in the mouth and throat from great thirst'
* *on'dumba* (f.)	U., *ondumba* 'a widow'; 'a lion'
* o_1ne_3 (f.)	I., $ö_1ne_3$ pers. n. f.
* *o'nende* (f.)	U., *onende* pers. n. 'a small pigeon'; 'an eye cataract'

GULLAH PERSONAL NAMES	WEST AFRICAN WORDS
onˈgole (m.)	U., *ongole* 'crime'
* ˈ*oni* (f.)	Y., o_1ni_3 'today'; T., *onĩ* 'mother'; 'relative'
* *oniˈabo* (m.)	Y., $o_2ni_3a{:}_1bo_1$ pers. n. 'a defender'
ˌ*onikosiˈlibɛ* (f.)	Y., $o_3ni_3ko_1si_3li_3b\varepsilon_1$ 'He said it was not there'
oˈnima (f.)	U., *onima* 'to pay'; 'payment'
oˈnine (f.)	U., *onine* 'excrement'
oˈnipa (f.)	T., *onipa* 'man, human being'
* *oniˈʃaŋgo* (m.)	Y., $o_2ni_3ʃaŋ_1go_3$ 'a worshipper of $ʃaŋ_1go_3$'
oˈniti (m.)	U., *oniti* 'a firefly'
onˈʒoma (f.)	U., *ondʒoma* 'mashed squash seed' (used as food)
ˈ*ono* (f.)	U., *ono* 'source of a stream, a spring'
ˈ*onu* (f.)	Fn., *onu* 'mouth'
* *oˈnusi* (f.)	U., *onusi* pers. n. 'a large antelope'; 'a mischievous person'
oˈɲime (f.)	U., *oɲime* 'a blanket'
oˈɲimi (f.)	Fn., *oɲimi* 'beeswax'
oˈpepe (m.)	Y., $o_1kpe_2kpe_2$ 'brimstone, wood'
* ˈ*orɛ* (f.)	Y., $o_3r\varepsilon_3$ pers. n. 'He is friendly'
oˈri (f.)	Y., o_2ri_3 'head'; o_2ri_2 'a wild pigeon'; o_1ri_3 'shea butter'; $o{:}_1ri_1$ 'the black plum'
oriˈgele (f.)	Cf. Y., $o_2ri_3ge_2ge_2le_2$ 'the top of the hill'
* *oˈriki* (f.)	Y., $o_2ri_3ki_1$ 'a Yoruba family name'
* ˈ*oriʃa* (m.)	Y., $o_1ri_1ʃa_1$ 'an object of worship, an idol'
* ˌ*oriˈʃa-oko* (m.)	Y., $o_1ri_1ʃa_1$-o_2ko_2 'the god of the fields'; 'name given a child whose family worships this god'
* *oˈritɛ* (f.)	Y., $o_2ri_3t\varepsilon_1$ 'name given the child for whose birth o_2ri_3 (a deity who protects the head) is believed to be responsible'
oˈrobo (m.)	Y., $o_2ro_3gbo_3$ 'the bitter kola nut'
oˈrombo (m.)	Y., $o_1ro_2m_1bo_2$ 'orange,' lit. 'the white man's o_1ro_2' (< o_1ro_2 'a small native fruit resembling the orange' + o_1-$\tilde{ı}_1bo_2$ 'white man, European')
oˈruka (m.)	Y., $o_1ru_1ka_2$ 'a ring'
* *oˈruŋgan* (m.)	Y., o_2ru_3-$ŋ_3g\tilde{a}{:}_1$ pers. n., lit. 'Night is reproaching him'
oˈruru (m.)	Y., $o_2ru_3ru_1$ 'the African tulip tree'
oˈseke (f.)	U., *oseke* 'a small, reddish-brown mushroom'
ˈ*osi* (m.)	Y., o_1si_1 'left'; 'a post'; 'spleen'; U., *osi* 'ground'
* *oˈsilo* (f.)	U., *osilo* 'a charm'; 'that part of a room opposite the door'

GULLAH PERSONAL NAMES	WEST AFRICAN WORDS
oˈsisi (f.)	Bi., $o_3si_3si_3$ 'a gun'
oˈsisimo (f.)	U., *osisimo* 'fine grits'; 'fine grains of salt'
* ˈ*osɒɪ* (m.)	U., *osaɪ* 'moon, month'; T., *osai* pers. n.
ˈ*osu* (f.)	T., o_1su_3 'rain'; o_1su_1 'a species of yam'
* ˌ*oʃaˈla* (m. and f.)	Y., $o_1ʃa_2la_3$[39] 'the great god, the chief of the Yoruba deities'
* ˌ*oʃaluˈfã* (m.)	Y., $o_1ʃa_2lu_3fã_1$ 'god of the city of $i_2fã_1$'
ˈ*oʃe* (m.)	Y., $o_1ʃe_1$ 'baobab tree'; 'sour gourd'; 'cork tree'; $o_2ʃe_3$ 'the club of $ʃaŋ_1go_3$, the god of thunder'
* ˌ*oʃofũˈmikɛ* (f.)	Y., $o_2ʃo_3fũ_3mi_2kɛ_3$ pers. n., lit. '$o_2ʃo_3$ (a sorcerer) gives me for petting'
* ˌ*oʃogiˈyã* (f.)	Y., $o\!:_1ʃo_1gi_2yã_3$ < $o_1ri_1ʃa_1$-$o_1gi_2yã_3$ 'name of a deity (synonymous with $o_1ʃa_2la_3$)'
* *oˈʃonu* (f.)	Y., $o_1ʃo_3nũ_3$ pers. n. 'a person easily enraged,' 'an ill-natured person'
* ˈ*oʃu* (m.)	Y., $o_2ʃu_1$ pers. n. 'new moon, month'; $o_1ʃu_1$ 'tufts of hair left on the head after the remainder has been shaved off'
* ˈ*oʃugbo* (f.)	Y., $o_1ʃu_2gbo_3$ 'the Ogboni cult'
ˈ*oʃuka* (m.)	Y., $o_1ʃu_2ka_3$ 'a pad used for the head when one is carrying a load'
* *oˈʃumare* (f.)	Y., $o_1ʃu_1ma_1re_1$ ($e_1ʃu_1ma_1re_1$) 'the rainbow'; 'the god of the rainbow'
* ˈ*oʃumi* (m.)	Y., $o_2ʃu_1mi_2$ 'my month'
oˈtembo (m.)	U., *otembo* 'generosity'; 'time, opportunity.' Cf. P., *o tempo* [u tẽmpu] 'time'
oˈtili (f.)	Y., $o_1ti_2li_3$ 'a kind of fruit'
* *oˈtiyo* (m. and f.)	Y., o_3 ti_2 yo_3 pers. n. 'He (or she) has become satisfied physically'
* ˈ*otu* (m.)	I., $ö_3tu_3$ 'waterside, shore'; Bi., o_1tu_1 'age-group, generation'; o_3tu_1 'a tree'; T., *otu* 'flying'; pers. n. m.
oˈcenu (f.)	U., *otʃenu* 'a nut resembling the peanut'
oˈcimbo (m.)	U., *otʃimbo* 'a gash' (as in a tree)
* *ociˈtena* (f.)	U., *otʃitena* pers. n. 'power, ability'
oˈcunda (m.)	U., *otʃunda* 'herd, drove'; 'corral, pen'
* *oˈwita* (f.)	U., *ovita* pers. n. 'war'
ˈ*owo* (m.)	Ef. o_3wo_3 'person.' Cf. e_3ren_{3-1} o_1wo_1 'male person, man'; Y., o_2wo_3 'money'; o_1wo_1 'trade'
oˈwusa (m.)	U., *owusa* 'rest, cessation'
* *oyeˈbisi* (m.)	Y., $o_2ye_1bi_3si_2$ pers. n., lit. 'Titles increase'

GULLAH PERSONAL NAMES	WEST AFRICAN WORDS
	[p]
'*pakasa* (m.)	K., *mpakasa* 'a buffalo'
pa'kata (f.)	U., *pakata* 'to carry under the arm'
* *pa'kolo* (m.)	V., $kpa_1ko_1lo_1$ 'name given a male child unusually large'
* '*pala* (f.)	K., *mpala* pers. n. 'a rival'; U., *pala* 'to grind'; Y., kpa_1la_1 'with difficulty'; $kpa{:}_1la_1$ 'to mark the boundary of territory'; M., *kpala* 'to lament'
'*pali* (m.)	E., kpa_1li_1 'to place crosswise'; 'beams laid crosswise'; M., *pali* 'a channel, the deeper part of a river'
pa'lɒti (f.)	Y., $kpa_2lɔ_2ti_3$, pers. n. 'to be drunk; to swell with pride'
* '*pama* (m.)	U., *pama* pers. n. 'to be stout'; M., *pama* 'a large, spotted, amphibious lizard'
'*pambi* (m.)	M., *kpambi* 'line, course'; 'a red handkerchief'
'*pana* (m.)	Y., kpa_2na_3 'to put out the light'; 'to quench a burning fire'; U., *pana* 'distant'
'*panda* (f.)	M., *panda* 'properly, well'; *kpanda* 'half a fathom, a yard'; K., *mpanda* 'crime'; 'divination, a resort to magic'; U., *panda* 'to husk'; 'to approach'
* '*pando* (m.)	E., $kpan_1do_1$ 'name of a city in Togo'
'*pani* (f.)	Y., kpa_2ni_2 'to kill'; B., *pani* 'to leap, to fly'
'*pansa* (f.)	Y., $kpa_3n_3sa_3$ 'dry, uncut calabash'
'*pantu* (m.)	T., *pantu* 'a large bottle'; *mpantũ* 'a species of plantain'
* '*paŋge* (m.)	Kim., *paŋge* pers. n. 'brother'
* '*paŋge-'ami* (m.)	Kim., *paŋge ami* pers. n. 'my brother'
'*paŋgu* (m.)	K., *mpaŋgu* 'those meats or fish which a child is forbidden to eat because they were served at the feast held for his mother shortly before his birth'
pa'payi (m.)	Kim., *papayi* 'father.' Cf. Braz. P., *papai* 'father'
'*pape* (m.)	T., *pape*: 'tight, fast'
para'pandu (m.)	Y., $kpa_2ra_2kp\tilde{a}_2du_1$ 'the pennant-winged nightjar'
pa'rika (m.)	Kim., *parika* 'to peg'
* '*pasi* (f.)	Y., kpa_1si_2 'a coarse grass used for thatching'; V., kpa_1si_1 pers. n. 'to flog'
* '*pasɒka* (m.)	V., $kpa_3\ s\tilde{ɔ}_1ka_1$ pers. n. 'Remove the debt'
* '*paʃi* (f.)	K., *mpaʃi* pers. n. 'pain, misfortune'
'*patamo* (m.)	Man., *patamo* 'a shark'
pa'tana (f.)	U., *patana* 'to doubt'; 'to ridicule'

GULLAH PERSONAL NAMES	WEST AFRICAN WORDS
ˈ*pato* (m.)	E., *pa*$_1$*to:*$_1$ 'broad'; Y., *kpa:*$_1$*to*$_3$ 'to make noise'; *kpa*$_1$*to*$_3$ 'definitely, exactly'
* ˈ*pawo* (f.)	V., *kpa*$_3$*vo*$_1$ pers. n. f.; M., *kpawo* 'a person in single life'; *kpavo* 'to catch with the hand'; 'to toss'; 'to sadden'
* ˈ*paya* (f.)	Tem., *paya* 'the eighth Temne month'; M., *kpaya* 'strength'; 'powerful'
paˈyula (f.)	U., *payula* 'to beckon'
ˈ*pede* (m.)	E., *kpe*$_3$*de*$_3$ 'children'
ˈ*pegli* (m.)	E., *kpe*$_3$*gli*$_1$ 'a stone wall'
* ˈ*pela* (f.)	K., *mpela* 'the season when the grass is burned (from July to October)'; 'the ground which has been cleared by fire'; M., *kpela* 'to mature, to reach puberty' (used of females)
ˈ*pele* (f.)	Y., *kpe*$_3$*le*$_3$ 'tribal marks on the face'; *kpe*$_1$*le*$_3$ 'to put on a second native cloth over the first one'; *kpe*$_2$*le*$_2$ 'to increase, to abound'; M., *pele* 'road, passage'
ˈ*pemba* (m.)	K., *pemba* 'to become white'; U., *pemba* 'to blow the nose'
peˈmuna (f.)	U., *pemuna* 'to trim the hair, to shave'
ˈ*pene* (f.)	T., *pene* 'to pinch'
* ˈ*peni* (m.)	T., *mpeni* 'name of a fetish and a tree at Akropong called *ɔpantɔ̃*, in which the stems and leaves of several climbers are intertwined'; M., *kpeni* 'a small greenish lizard'; 'a cunning person'
ˈ*pepe* (m.)	T., *pepe* 'firm, dense'; *pe:pe:* 'inquiry'
* ˈ*pepi* (m.)	E., *pe*$_3$*pi*$_{1-3}$ pers. n. 'the harmattan wind'
ˈ*pere* (m. and f.)	Y., *kpe*$_2$*re*$_2$ 'only'
* *pereˈwahũ* (m.)	M., *perewahʊ̃* pers. n. 'in the big road'
ˈ*pesi* (m.)	T., *pesi* 'the act of keeping awake'
ˈ*peʃi* (f.)	Kim., *peʃi* 'a pipe'
* ˈ*petu* (m.)	F., *pe*$_1$*tu*$_3$ pers. n. 'an owl'
ˈ*pewi* (m.)	E., *kpe*$_3$*vi*$_3$ 'little children'
* ˈ*peya* (m.)	U., *peya* pers. n. 'to importune'
* ˈ*pegba* (f.)	M., *pegba* 'the Mende month corresponding to January'
* ˈ*pɛnda* (f.)	W., *pɛnda* pers. n. f.
ˈ*pɛndɛ* (f.)	M., *kpɛndɛ* 'to delay'; 'a hardwood tree used for making furniture'
ˈ*pɛnɛ* (m.)	M., *pɛnɛ* 'ringworm'

GULLAH PERSONAL NAMES	WEST AFRICAN WORDS
pɛŋ (m.)	T., *pɛŋ*$_3$ 'accurate'; 'accurately'; 'once'; *pɛŋ*$_1$ 'to watch some one in order to find occasion for ruining him'; M., *pɛŋ* 'first in order'
* ˈ*pɛpɛ* (m.)	Y., *kpɛ*$_3$*kpɛ*$_3$ 'gently'; *kpɛ*$_2$*kpɛ*$_2$ 'altar, shelf'; M., *pɛpɛ* 'continually, often'; *kpɛkpɛ* pers. n. 'to tremble convulsively'; 'to sift'
ˈ*pɛrɛ* (m.)	Y., *kpɛ*$_1$*rɛ*$_3$ 'made to open wide'; B., *pɛrɛ* 'a noise'; 'to cry loudly'
* ˈ*pɛtiti* (m.)	Y., *kpɛ*$_3$*ti*$_3$*ti*$_3$ pers. n. 'to linger'
* ˈ*pidi* (m.)	K., *mpidi* pers. n. 'an adder'
ˈ*pili* (m.)	M., *pili* 'to throw, to shoot'
ˈ*pilu* (m.)	K., *pilu* 'purple'
* *piˈlula* (f.)	U., *pilula* pers. n. 'to consult spirits'; 'to turn (in frying)'
ˈ*pimɛ* (m.)	M., *pimɛ* 'to run'; 'the act of running'
* ˈ*pinda* (*mˈpɪnda*) (f.)	K., *mpinda* 'groundnut'; U., *pinda* 'to influence the character of a child'; 'discipline'; Tl., *mpinda* pers. n. 'a bird resembling the canary'
ˈ*pire* (f.)	T., *mpire* 'a whip cut from the skin of an animal'
piˈreyu (m.)	T., *pireu* 'to roll, to wallow'
ˈ*pita* (m.)	U., *pita* 'to pass'; 'to happen'; Y., *kpi*$_1$*tã*$_2$ 'to give the history of a person or thing'
* ˈ*piti* (m.)	E., *kpi*$_1$*ti*$_1$ 'mange, itch'; K., *mpiti* pers. n. 'a gazelle-like antelope'
* ˈ*pitipa* (m.)	M., *pitipa* 'name given a child born during a rain (the word being imitative of the patter of rain)'
ˈ*pitsi* (m.)	E., *kpi*$_1$*tsi*$_1$ 'leprosy'
* ˈ*piwi* (f.)	K., *mpivi* pers. n. 'an orphan'; cf. Eng., *peewee*
ˈ*pɪkpɪ* (m.)	M., *kpɪkpɪ* 'electric fish'
* ˈ*pɪndɪ* (f.)	M., *kpɪndɪ* pers. n. 'night'; 'to darken'; 'obscure'
ˈ*plimɒ* (m.)	E., *kpli*$_1$*mɔ*:$_1$ 'round, swollen'
pɒɪ (m.)	Cf. E., *pɔe*$_3$ 'a small frog'
* ˈ*pɒɪdo* (m.)	Fu., *paido* pers. n. 'a corpulent man'; 'proud, conceited'
ˈ*pɒɪna* (f.)	M., *kpaɪna* 'a large black ant'
ˈ*pɒɟu* (m.)	M., *pɔdʒu* 'tough, elastic'
ˈ*pɒkɒ* (m.)	Kim., *pɔkɔ* 'a knife'; Y., *kpɔ*:$_1$*kɔ*$_2$ 'a small calabash used as a ladle'
* ˈ*pɒŋgi* (m.)	K., *mpɔŋgi* pers. n. 'a chimpanzee'
* ˈ*pɒŋgɒ* (f.)	K., *mpɔŋgɔ* pers. n. 'fatness'

GULLAH PERSONAL NAMES	WEST AFRICAN WORDS
* ˈ*pɒrɒ* (f.)	M., *pɔrɒ* 'the great secret society of the men'; *kpɔrɒ* 'to overboil'; 'weakened by sickness or wounds'
po (m.)	Y., *kpo*$_1$ 'to knead'; 'to tan leather'; *kpo*$_2$ 'inadequate'; E., *kpo*$_1$ 'a stump'; 'a cluster of fruit'; 'a walking stick'; 'a bag'; 'suddenly'; *kpo*$_3$ 'a hump, a knob'; *kpo*$_{1-3}$ 'an oven'; *kpo*:$_3$ 'quiet'; Fn., *kpo* 'the protecting genius of kings incarnate in the leopard'; M., *po* 'multiplied by natural increase'; *kpo* 'dregs, excrement'; *kpo*: 'an exclamation expressing triumph or admiration'; Bi., *kpo*:$_1$ 'a bright, but not flaming, fire'
* *poˈdumbo* (m.)	V., *po*$_1$*dum*$_1$*bo*$_1$ (*po*$_1$*lum*$_1$*bo*$_1$) pers. n. 'orange'
ˈ*pofiri* (m.)	T., *pofiri* 'a medicinal plant'
* ˈ*pola* (m.)	Y., *kpo*$_1$*la*$_1$ 'the report of a gun'; V., *kpo*$_3$*la*$_3$ pers. n. m.
* ˈ*poli* (m.)	Tem., *poli* 'a family name common in the Temne-speaking area of Sierra Leone'; M., *poli* 'a fresh-water fish'; *kpoli* river, brook'
poˈlila (f.)	M., *kpolila* 'mouth of a river'
ˈ*poma* (f.)	M., *poma* 'corpse'
ˈ*poɲa* (m.)	U., *poɲa* 'to fail'
* ˈ*popo* (m.)	Fn., *popo* a principality in Dahomey'; Y., *kpo*$_3$*kpo*$_2$ 'a thoroughfare'; *kpo*$_1$*kpo*$_1$ 'to be busily engaged'; *kpo*:$_1$*kpo*:$_{1-2}$ 'bamboo sticks'; M., *popo* 'to carry on the back'; *kpokpo* 'a vine'
ˈ*porĩ* (f.)	Y., *kpo*$_2$*rĩ*$_2$ 'to smelt iron'
* ˈ*poro* (m.)	V., *po*:$_1$*ro*$_1$ 'white man'; 'any foreigner'; M., *kporo* 'an oath'
ˈ*posi* (f.)	Y., *kpo*$_3$*si*$_3$ 'coffin'; cf. Fn., *kpɔsi* 'a worshipper of the leopard deity'
ˈ*poso* (m.)	M., *kposo* 'a trap for catching small animals'
ˈ*puɟa* (m.)	M., *pudʒa* 'to dig, to loosen the soil'
ˈ*puɟɛ* (m.)	M., *pudʒɛ* 'pepper'
ˈ*puka* (m.)	T., *puka* 'a string of beads'
pukˈpula (f.)	M., *kpukpula* 'to cause diarrhea'
* ˈ*puku* (*mˈpuku*) (m.)	K., *mpuku* pers. n. 'rat, field mouse'; Tl., *mpuku* 'rat, mouse'
ˈ*pula* (f.)	M., *kpula* 'a calabash, a bottle gourd'; U., *pula* 'to drive off'
* ˈ*puli* (f.)	Tem., *puli* 'a professional storyteller'; Fu., *puli* pers. n. m.

GULLAH PERSONAL NAMES	WEST AFRICAN WORDS
puˈlule (f.)	U., *pulule* (*upulule*) 'open, ajar'
* ˈ*purɒ* (m.)	Y., *kpu$_2$rɔ$_3$* pers. n. 'to tell a lie'
* ˈ*pusa* (m.)	U., *pusa* pers. n. 'to wash the face'; 'to rinse the mouth'
ˈ*pusu* (m.)	K., *mpusu* 'the *mbadi* palm, from the fronds of which native cloth is made'
puˈsula (f.)	U., *pusula* 'to strike with the fist'; 'to strip off'; 'to chew meat'
* ˈ*puyi* (f.)	E., *kpui$_3$* 'short'; W., *pui* 'a Wolof family name'
ˈ*pweɲa* (f.)	U., *pweɲa* 'to wipe'
ˈ*pwita* (f.)	Kim., *pwita* 'a dance'

[r]

GULLAH PERSONAL NAMES	WEST AFRICAN WORDS
rɐɪ (f.)	B., *rai* 'a flag'; H., *ɾai$_{3-1}$* 'life'
ˈ*rɐɪna* (f.)	H., *ɾai$_3$na$_1$* 'to quarrel with, to have contempt for'
ˈ*rami* (m.)	H., *ɾa:$_3$mi$_1$* 'a hole or pit in the earth or in anything built of earth'; 'a town'; 'the term applied to the ditch surrounding a town'
* ˈ*randa* (f.)	W., *randa* pers. n. 'bush, thicket'
* ˈ*rani* (m.)	H., *ɾa:$_3$ni$_3$* pers. n. 'the hot season after the cold harmattan period and immediately preceding the earliest rains'
raˈwaye (f.)	Y., *ra$_2$wa$_2$ye$_2$* 'a plant whose roots yield a yellow dye'
ˈ*rawe* (m.)	W., *rave* 'a species of fish having a dart in its tail'
* ˈ*rere* (f.)	Y., *re$_2$re$_2$* pers. n. 'good, honest'; 'well'; 'welfare'; *re$_3$re$_3$* 'at a great distance'; 'wild coffee plant, all parts of which are used for medicinal purposes'
ˈ*reyi* (m.)	W., *rei* 'big'
* *riˈbiya* (m.)	Kim., *ribia* pers. n. 'a field'
riˈbitu (f.)	Kim. *ribitu* 'door'
reˈkɒkɒ (m.)	Kim., *rikɔkɔ* 'coconut'
* ˈ*rilu* (f.)	Kim., *rilu*, pers. n. 'sky, heaven'
ˈ*rimi* (f.)	Kim., *rimi* 'language, tongue'; H., *ɾi:$_3$mi:$_3$* 'the silk-cotton tree'
ˈ*rindi* (f.)	W., *rindi* 'to sacrifice, to decapitate'
ˈ*rinu* (m.)	H., *ɾi$_1$nu$_2$* 'to dye with indigo'; 'to contaminate'
* ˈ*risa* (f.)	Kim., *risa* pers. n. 'to feed'; 'corn'
* ˈ*risu* (f.)	Kim., *risu* pers. n. 'eye'
riˈtemu (f.)	Kim., *ritemu* 'hoe'

GULLAH PERSONAL NAMES	WEST AFRICAN WORDS
'*riya* (f.)	H., *ri*$_1$*ya*:$_2$ 'hypocrisy'; *ɽi*$_3$*ya*$_1$ 'to intend to'; Kim., *ria* 'to eat'
ri'*yunda* (f.)	Kim., *riunda* 'arrow'
ri'*zaŋga* (f.)	Kim., *rizaŋga* 'a lagoon'
* '*roko* (m.)	Y., *ro*$_2$*ko*$_2$ 'to cultivate a farm'; *i*$_1$*ro*$_3$*ko*$_1$ 'a tree and a spirit sanctuary'
'*roŋgo* (m.)	Fu., *roŋgo* 'to inherit'
'*ruba* (f.)	H., *ru*:$_3$*ba*$_1$ 'the act of boasting'; 'intimidation' (Ar.) *ɽu*$_3$'*ba*$_1$ 'to cause to ferment'; 'to fold up'; 'to exceed'; *ɽu*$_1$'*ba*:$_2$ 'decay'
* '*rubɒ* (m.)	Y., *ru*$_3$*bɔ*$_2$ pers. n. 'to offer a sacrifice'
	[s]
* '*saba* (f.)	Y., *sa*$_3$*ba*$_1$ 'to be accustomed to'; *sa*$_1$*ba*$_2$ 'to incubate'; K., *saba* pers. n. 'a temporary house, a hut'; Bi., *sa*$_1$*ba*$_3$ 'to be able'; B., *sa:ba* 'dangerous'; *saba* 'three'; 'to strike'; W., *saba* pers. n. 'an honest person'; Tl., *saba* 'to play'; 'to ferment'
* *sa*'*bala* (f.)	E., *sa*$_1$*ba*$_3$*la*$_{3-1}$ 'onion'; Bo., *sabala* 'Saturday'
* '*sabi* (m.)	Bo., *sabi* 'a kind of pot-herb'; H., *sa*:$_3$'*bi*$_1$ pers. n. 'wrongdoing'
* *sa*'*biɲa* (f.)	Bo., *sabiɲa* pers. n. 'to forgive'
* '*sabɒ* (m.)	V., *sa*$_3$*bɔ*$_3$ pers. n. 'comrade'
* '*sabo* (m.)	H., *sa*:$_3$*bo*:$_3$ 'new, young'; *sa*:$_1$*bo*:$_2$ 'the act of becoming accustomed to a person or thing'; *sa*:$_1$'*bo*:$_2$ 'blasphemy, adultery, perjury'; 'any heinous sin against God'; V., *sa*$_3$*bo*$_1$ pers. n. m.
'*sabu* (m.)	H., *sa*:$_1$*bu*$_2$ 'to become accustomed to'; M., *sabʊ* 'good conduct, kindness'
sa'*daka* (f.)	H., *sa*:$_1$'*da*$_2$*ka*$_1$ 'a concubine'; *sa*$_3$*da*$_3$*ka*$_1$ 'alms'; Fu., *sadaka* 'alms, almsgiving' (Ar.)
'*sadɛ* (m.)	E., *sa*$_3$*dɛ*$_3$ 'light, agile'
'*sadi* (m.)	Y., *sa*$_3$*di*$_2$ 'to take shelter under one's protection'; K., *sadi* 'a wild yam, the creeping stalk and roots of which are thickly covered with thorns'; 'a workman'; *nsadi* 'a reaper of corn'; H., *sa*$_3$*di*:$_3$ 'a stick used in carrying loads'
sa'*doyi* (m.)	T., *sãdoi* 'habitual drinking'
* '*sadu* (m.)	H., *sa*:$_1$*du*$_2$ 'to meet'; 'to arrive'; Fn., *sadu* pers. n. m.; W., *sadu* 'a native blacksmith's hammer'
* '*safa* (f.)	Y., *sa*$_2$*fa*$_3$ 'to spread over something (such as cream over boiled milk)'; H., *sa*:$_3$*fa*:$_3$ 'leeks, young onions';

GULLAH PERSONAL NAMES	WEST AFRICAN WORDS
	'a simpleton'; $sa{:}_1fa{:}_2$ 'a riding-boot reaching to the knee and having soles of soft leather'; 'a quilted garment worn by warriors'; 'a thimble'; sa_3fa_1 'to increase slightly'; $sa_1fa{:}_2$ 'a mountain at Mecca'
* *sa'fari* (f.)	H., $sa_1fa_1ri_2$ 'a female gadabout who is careless in household matters'
sa'fero (m.)	Man., *safero* 'the act of writing.' Cf. *safero ke* 'to write, to do writing'
* *safi'yata* (f.)	Mand., *safiyata* 'the second wife of Mohammed'
* *'safo* (f.)	Man., *safo* 'the last prayer of the day' (Ar.)
* *sag'buwa* (m.)	Y., $sa_2gbu_1wa_1$ 'one of the sixteen superior captains of the guard in the $\varepsilon_1ʃɔ_3$ sect'; 'name of a former king of Abeokuta [$a_2b\varepsilon_3o_1ku_3ta_2$]'
'sago (m.)	Fu., *sago* 'a sheepskin mat'
* *sa'ɟada* (m.)	H., $sa_1dʒa_2da_1$ ($su_1dʒa_2da_1$) 'the act of prostrating the body in worship'; 'among the Mohammedans the name of a special prayer carpet'
* *'saka* (f.)	Tl., *saka* 'to hoe'; 'to push'; 'to comb the hair'; 'to tune an instrument'; 'to shrug the shoulders'; K., *saka* 'to be too late'; 'to exceed'; 'to cut off'; 'a rattrap'; *nsaka* pers. n. 'amusement'; 'a pipe for smoking'; T., *saka* 'to scatter'; *saka:* 'disorder'; *nsaka:* 'a bracelet, handcuffs'; E., sa_1ka_1 'a climber'
* *'saka'saka* (f.)	T. and G., $sa_1ka_1sa_1ka_1$ pers. n. 'in confusion'
'sakɛ (f.)	E., $sa_1k\varepsilon_1$ 'a climber'; 'a rope used in fishing'
* *'saki* (f.)	K., 'a bunch, a cluster'; *nsaki* 'a reaper'; M., *sakı* 'a dagger'; 'pointed'; H., sa_3ki_1 'a divorce'; 'a small portion thrown in gratis by a seller'; 'the act of becoming slack'; $sa{:}_3k'i_1$ 'a cotton material of black and blue strands woven into a very tiny check'; V., sa_3ki_3 pers. n. m.
'sakli (f.)	E., $tsa_1kli{:}_1$ 'rough, torn'
* *'saku* (f.)	K., *saku* 'a ring of dry plants together with the *ŋguba* "groundnuts" which it encircles'; 'a sack' (P. *saco* [saku]); *nsaku* 'backache'; 'a knife having a large blade'; 'the title of the heir apparent of the throne of Kongo'
sa'kunu (m.)	B., *sakunu* 'plume, tuft'
* *'sala* (f.)	Y., sa_3la_1 'to escape, to flee for safety'; E., sa_1la_1 'soaring, swooping down'; V., sa_1la_3 'Mohammedan prayer'; B., *sala* 'recitation of the exploits of a

GULLAH PERSONAL NAMES	WEST AFRICAN WORDS
	hero or a brigand'; Tl., *sala* 'to tattoo'; 'to mix'; 'to squirm'; K., *sala* 'to work'; 'industry'; 'to reap'; 'a dance characterized by rapid movement of the hips'; 'fin, tail of a fish'
* *sa'lala* (f.)	U., *salala* pers. n. 'to be rich'; Tl., *salala* 'to itch'; H., $sa_1la_1la_1$ 'a thin gruel used medicinally'; $sa{:}_3la{:}_3la{:}_3$ 'a doctored gruel used by elephant hunters'; $sa{:}_1la{:}_1la_2$ 'a tall, thin person'; 'a horse'
* *sa'lama* (m.)	H., $sa_1la{:}_2ma_1$ (Ar.) 'tranquillity, bond of friendship'; $sa_3la_3ma_1$ 'a greeting'; 'taking one's leave'; $sa_1la_2ma_1$ 'an official title and position held by one of the slaves of the Emir of Kano'
* *sa'lamu* (f.)	H., $sa_1la{:}_2mu_1$ (Ar.). Cf. $a_1lai_2ka_1$ $sa_1la{:}_2mu_1$ 'On thee be peace' (a reply to one giving a similar greeting)
'sale (f.)	Y., sa_3le_3 'to run after'; B., *sa:le* 'duty, tax'; *sale* 'a thoroughbred horse'; 'a kind of fish'; M., *sale* 'parable, example, similitude'
* *'sali* (m.)	B., *sali* 'to pray' (Ar.); *sa:li* 'a festival, especially a Mohammedan festival' (Ar.); V., sa_1li_3 pers. n. m. Cf. Eng. *Sally*
* *sa'liba* (f.)	B., *saliba* 'a Mohammedan who makes the salaam'; 'the great festival of the fetish cults'
* *sali'fana* (f.)	Man. and B., *salifana* 'two o'clock (P.M.) prayer'
* *sa'lifu* (m.)	*salifu* 'an eighteenth-century ruler and warrior of Futa'
* *sa'lihu* (m.)	Tem., *salihu* pers. n. m.
'saliwa (m.)	M., *salɪ wa* 'a big joke'
'salo (m.)	Man., *salo* 'a feast'
'salu (f.)	Y., sa_3lu_1 'to intervene in one's interest'; K., *salu* 'toil, industry'; *nsalu* 'land lying waste after a crop has been gathered'; 'earthworm'; 'a sieve'
* *sa'luka* (m.)	K., *saluka* pers. n. 'to be gathered' (used in reference to corn only); 'to recoil'; Tl., 'to be revealed'; 'to be lukewarm'; 'to be mixed'; U., *saluka* 'to be astonished'
sa'lulula (f.)	K., *salulula* 'to repeat a performance several times'
* *'sama* (m.)	E., sa_3ma_3 'to summon'; Man., *sama* 'the rainy season'; Tl., *sama* 'to be ill'; 'to crow'; 'to become invisible'; 'to place the head on a pillow'; 'to cry out excitedly'; T., *sãmã* 'figures made on the head by an uneven cutting of the hair'; *nsama* 'handful'; *nsa:ma* 'handbreadth'; cf. *ɔsãmãŋ* 'an

GULLAH PERSONAL NAMES	WEST AFRICAN WORDS
	ancestral spirit'; M., *sama* 'a person of wealth or power'; 'an agreement by which meat is divided, each purchaser agreeing to pay a definite sum within a specified time'; H., $sa{:}_3ma_1$ 'to give'; $sa{:}_1ma{:}_2$ 'to find'; sa_3ma_1 'the heavens'; B., *sama* 'elephant'; 'a gift of welcome'; 'a fish-crawl'; 'to attract'
saˈmali (f.)	W., *samali* 'to send someone to feed the flock'
* ˈ*samba* (f.)	K., *samba* 'to squall'; 'to pray, to worship'; M., *samba* 'a broad open basket'; 'a leading member of the Sande Society who, dressed in leaves, appears in the town and assembles the girls for initiation'; Tl., *samba* 'to be merciful toward'; 'to jump about'; 'to cackle'; U., *samba* 'to do homage'; Man., *samba* 'an elephant'; W., *samba* pers. n. m.; V., sam_3ba_3 pers. n. m.; Kim., *samba* 'to pray'; B., *samba* 'to beat down'
* ˈ*sambabɛ* (m.)	V., sam_3ba_3 $bɛ_1$ pers. n. 'May Samba live'
* ˈ*sambala* (f.)	B., *sambala* pers. n. 'a syphilitic malady'
ˈ*sambale* (f.)	H., $sam_3ba_3le{:}_3$ 'a dance of youths and maidens'
* ˈ*sambi* (m.)	Tem., *sambi* pers. n. m. K., *nsambi* 'a worshipper'; 'a guitar, a banjo'
* ˈ*sambo* (m.)	H., sam_3bo_1 'name given the second son in a family'; 'name given to anyone called *Muhammadu*'; 'name of a spirit'; M., *sambo* 'to disgrace'; 'to be shameful'; V., sam_3bo_1 pers. n. 'to disgrace'
* ˈ*sambu* (m.)	K., *sambu* pers. n. 'prayer'; 'the squall of a baby'; *nsambu* 'good fortune'
ˈ*same* (m.)	B., *same* 'disgrace, confusion'
* *saˈmɛya* (f.)	S., *samɛia* 'the town of Samo'
sa_1mi_3 (m.)	Y., sa_1mi_1 'to make a sign.'[40] Cf. Eng., *Sammy*
saˈmina (f.)	T., *sãmĩnã* 'soap'
* *saˈmiɲa* (f.)	Mand., *samiɲa* 'the rainy season'
ˈ*samo* (m.)	H., $sa{:}_2mo{:}_2$ 'to obtain'; sa_3mo_1 'dried leaves, especially from the jujube tree'
* *saˈmola* (f.)	Man., *samola* pers. n. 'to the elephant'
* ˈ*sanda* (f.)	Y., $sã_3da_1$ 'to be armed with short swords'; E., $san_1da{:}_1$ 'light, brisk, nimble'; Kim., *sanda* 'to scratch'; Tl., *sanda* 'to commit adultery with'; 'to seek'; U., *sa:nda* 'to look for'; Tem., *sanda* 'name of a chiefdom in the Temne country'; H., san_3da_1 'name given to anyone called *Umaru*';

GULLAH PERSONAL NAMES	WEST AFRICAN WORDS
	san$_1$*da*:$_2$ 'a staff'; 'a measure of length'; 'any kind of European cotton goods'; *san*$_3$*'da*:$_3$ 'the act of stalking'; *san*$_3$*'da*$_1$ 'to rub cloth on a beaten floor to make it glossy'
* '*sande* (f.)	M., *sande* 'the great female society into which nearly all girls are initiated and receive new names'
'*sandɛ* (m.)	E., *san*$_3$*dɛ*$_3$ 'agile, brisk'
* '*sandi* (m.)	V., *san*$_1$*d'i*$_3$ pers. n. m.; H., *san*$_1$*'di*$_2$ 'a worthless person'; 'a deceitful person'
* '*sando* (f.)	V., *san*$_3$*d'o*$_1$ 'name given a girl born after the death of twins'; H., *san*$_3$*'do*:$_3$ 'a small insect having many legs'
* '*sane* (m.)	Man., *sane* 'name of a Mandinka noble clan whose totem is the swallow (*nana*)'; H., *sa*:$_3$*ne*$_1$ 'to steal'; *sa*:$_1$*ne*:$_2$ 'the act of stealing'; *sa*$_1$*ne*:$_2$ 'sagacity'; 'eyeservice'
'*sani* (m.)	V., *sa*$_1$*ni*$_3$ 'a glass container'; B., *sani* 'to purchase'; 'to comb'; 'to give a thrashing to'; H., *sa*$_3$*ni*$_1$ 'to know'; 'knowledge'; *sa*:$_3$*ni*$_1$ 'that from which all goodness or flavor has been extracted'
* *san'ɟano* (m.)	Man., *sandʒano* 'the period after the rains' (from November to December)
* '*sanɟi* (m.)	Kim., *sanʒi* pers. n. 'a hen'; K., *sanʒi* 'a marimba'; U., *osandʒi* 'a hen'
* '*sansa* (f.)	K., *sansa* 'Providence'
* *san'zala* (m.)	Kim., *sanzala* 'a village'; K., *sanzala* 'the lying-in state of a great chief'
'*saɲa* (f.)	U., *saɲa* 'to pick to pieces'; to be fervent'; 'to scatter'
* '*saŋga* (f.)	E., *saŋ*$_1$*ga*$_1$ 'a climber, the fruit of which is used as a vegetable'; *saŋ*$_1$*ga*:$_1$ 'slanting, tottering'; Tl., *saŋga* 'to assemble'; 'to intermingle'; W., *saŋga* pers. n. 'master'; 'to cover'; U., *saŋga* 'to meet'; K., *saŋga* 'to dance'; 'exultation'; 'to mix'; 'an island'; Kim., *saŋga* 'to find'
'*saŋge* (f.)	W., *saŋge* 'to fortify'; 'a barricade'
* '*saŋgo* (m.)	Man., *saŋo* 'sky'; H., *saŋ*$_1$*go*:$_2$ 'a harpoon fired from a gun, or thrown by hand, in elephant-hunting'; 'a Yoruba idol'[41]
* '*saŋko* (m.)	Tem., *saŋko* 'name of a chiefdom in the Temne country'; H., *saŋ*$_3$*k'o*:$_3$ 'baldness'; M., *saŋko* pers. n.
'*sara* (f.)	H., *sa*:$_3$*ɾa*:$_3$ 'a stroke, a blow'; Y., *sa*$_3$*ra*$_2$ 'to avoid'; *sa*$_1$*ra*:$_2$ 'alms'

GULLAH PERSONAL NAMES	WEST AFRICAN WORDS
* *'sari* (m.)	Y., sa_2ri_3 'to rub medicinal powder into the scalp'; $sa{:}_1ri_1$ 'the early meal of the Mohammedans before daybreak during their fast'; B., *sari* 'a food consisting of pounded millet cooked in water'; 'the act of scattering'
'saro (f.)	Fu., *saro* 'a parent'; H., $sa{:}_1ro{:}_2$ 'a long, close-fitting, narrow-sleeved shirt'; $sa{:}_1ro{:}_2$ 'certain kinds of fish dried in the sun for use in soups, etc.'
sa'safe (f.)	H., $sa_3sa{:}_3fe{:}_3$ 'early morning'
* *'sase* (m.)	Y., sa_1se_1 'to make a feast'; T., *asase* 'goddess of the earth'
* *'sata* (f.)	V., $sa{:}_3ta_1$ pers. n. f.; H., $sa{:}_1ta{:}_2$ 'to steal'; $sa{:}_3ta_1$ 'theft' (not applied to pilfering by one of a household from another of the same household)
* *'saci* (m.)	T., *saci* pers. n. m.; H., $sa{:}_1\text{tʃ}i_2$ 'to steal'
* *saci'rifa* (f.)	T., *sacirifa* pers. n. m.
* *'satu* (f.)	K., *nsatu* pers. n. 'hunger'; E., sa_1tu_3 'a knot, a loop'; Tl., *satu* 'three'
'sawa (f.)	U., *sava* 'to be unsavory' H., $sa{:}_3wa{:}_3$ 'respite, mitigation'
* *'sawo* (f.)	Y., sa_3wo_1 $o!_2$ 'behold! lo!'; V., sa_1wo_3 'no'; sao_{3-1} 'name given the first of twins'; H., $sa{:}_2wo{:}_2$ 'to place in'; M., *sao* 'no'
se (m.)	E., se_1 'to understand'; 'to taste'; 'to feel'; 'to smell'; se_3 'to reach'; 'to command'; 'a deity'; 'a flower'; Y., se_3 'to shut'; 'to miss one's aim'; se_1 'to cook'; 'to dye cloth or leather'; I., se_3 'to decide'; 'to say'; T., *se* 'to say, to tell, to command'; M., *se* 'very much'; cf. Eng., *say*
'sebe (f.)	E., se_3be_1 'excrement'; K., *sebe* 'obstinacy'
* *se'biyo* (m.)	E., se_3bio_1 'an interjection expressing disapprobation'
'seda (f.)	W., *seda* 'a portion'; 'to give to someone the portion which falls to him'; Fn. and K., *seda* 'silk'; E., se_3da_1 'silk.' Cf. P., *seda* 'silk'
se'dale (f.)	W., *sedale* 'to divide among many'
* *'sede* (f.)	Mal., *sede* pers. n. 'witness, testimony'
se'diya (f.)	K., *nsedia* 'an infant'
'sedu (m.)	W., *sedu* 'to take one's own share'
* *'sefo* (f.)	Man., *sefo* 'the chief'
'sege (m.)	E., se_1ge_1 'swinging, shaking'; B., *sege* 'a hawk'; 'saltpeter'; 'ashes'

GULLAH PERSONAL NAMES	WEST AFRICAN WORDS
* ˈ*segi* (m.)	Mand., *se:gi* pers. n. 'eight'; B., *segi* 'eight'
ˈ*seɟima* (f.)	K., *seʒima* 'to flash' (said of lightning)
* ˈ*seke* (f.)	E., se_1ke_1 'an anchor'; B., *seke* pers. n. 'an interjection expressing complete satisfaction'
* ˈ*seki* (m.)	Tem., *seki* 'a Temne family name'
ˈ*sela* (f.)	U., *sela* 'to cohabit'
ˈ*sele* (f.)	Y., se_1le_3 'to refine palm oil by extra boiling'; se_3le_2 'to become adamant,' lit. 'to shut hard'; K., *nsele* 'a fringe'; B., *sele* 'tomb, sepulcher'
* ˈ*selɪ* (f.)	M., *selɪ* pers. n. 'a witness'
* ˈ*sema* (f.)	M., *sema* pers. n.; 'a large tree'
ˈ*sembo* (f.)	K., *sembo* 'spur, short nail'
ˈ*semɒ* (f.)	Y., $se_3mɔ_3$ 'to inclose'; K., *nsemɔ* 'brightness, a flash'
* *seˈmuna* (f.)	U., *semuna* pers. n. 'to speak incorrectly, to mispronounce'
ˈ*senda* (f.)	K., *senda* 'to reward for services rendered'
ˈ*seni* (f.)	B., *seni* 'the act of digging'; Man., *seni* 'to cultivate, to plant'
ˈ*sensa* (f.)	K., *sensa* 'to cut into small pieces'
* *seˈreya* (f.)	Mand., *se:reya* pers. n. 'testimony'
* ˈ*seri* (m.)	Mand., *seri* pers. n. m.; B., *seri* 'the act of dispersing'; 'to diffuse'; 'to daub'
* *seˈriya* (f.)	Mand., *seriya* pers. n. 'descending from Seri'
ˈ*sese* (f.)	Y., se_1se_3 'a kind of bean'; Fn., *sẽsẽ* 'to worship'
ˈ*sewa* (f.)	U., *seva* 'to cook'; 'to circumcise'
ˈ*sewe* (f.)	K., *nseve* 'the heel of hoofed animals'
ˈ*seya* (f.)	U., *sea* 'to adjust, to agree upon'
* ˈ*seyi* (f.)	W., *sei* 'to marry'; 'marriage'; E., tse_1yi_1 pers. n.
seˈyila (m.)	Man., *seila* 'to return to'
* ˈ*sɛbɛ* (f.)	T., *sɛbɛ* 'an amulet, a talisman made of leather'
* *sɛˈdiya* (f.)	V., $sɛ_1d'ia_{3-1}$ pers. n. f.
* ˈ*sɛɟɛ* (m.)	M., *sɛdʒɛ* pers. n. 'a small porcupine having long spines upon its tail'
* ˈ*sɛli* (f.)	M., *sɛli* 'a Mohammedan prayer'; Fn., *sɛli* 'a lock'
* ˈ*sɛmbɛ* (f.)	M., *sɛmbɛ* pers. n. 'of medium size'
* *sɛn* (f.)	W., *sɛn* 'name of a Wolof family of whom the rabbit is considered an enemy'
* ˈ*sɛŋga* (f.)	Tl., *sɛŋga* pers. n. 'to mourn some one, mentioning the deceased by name'; 'to shake, to sift'

GULLAH PERSONAL NAMES	WEST AFRICAN WORDS
sɛ'pɛyu (m.)	T., *sɛpɛu* 'to become free from restraint'
* '*sɛri* (m.)	V., *sɛ*$_1$*ri*$_3$ pers. n. m.; Y., *sɛ*$_1$*ri*$_1$ 'to drop dew'
* '*sɛsɛ* (f.)	T., *sɛ*$_3$*sɛ*$_3$ 'a noise'; *sɛ*$_1$*sɛ*$_1$ 'to backstitch'; E., *sɛ*$_3$*sɛ̃*$_3$ (*sɛ*$_3$*sĩ*$_3$) pers. n. 'strong, well'; *sɛ*$_1$*sɛ*$_3$ 'being strong'
* '*sɛsi* (f.)	E., *sɛ*$_3$*sĩ*$_3$ pers. n. 'strong, well.' Cf. *nɔ*$_1$ *a*$_1$*ɲi*$_3$ *sɛ*$_3$*sĩ*$_3$ 'Keep well'
* *sɛ'tilu* (f.)	Y., *sɛ*$_1$*ti*$_1$*lu*$_3$ 'name of a Yoruba chief'
* '*sɛyi* (m.)	V., *sɛi*$_{3-1}$ pers. n. 'to pray'
si (m.)	E., *si*$_1$ 'to put to flight'; 'to smear'; 'to cut off'; 'to press'; Man., *si* 'to sit'; Bi., *si*$_3$ 'to pull'; I., *si*$_3$ 'to cook'; 'to pass'; M., *si* 'a game in which tops are used.' Cf. Eng., *see* and *sea*.
* *si'afa* (m.)	V., *sia*$_1$*fa*$_3$ pers. n. m.
* *si'aka* (m.)	V., *sia*$_3$*ka*$_1$ pers. n. m.
* *si'ana* (f.)	V., *sia*$_3$*na*$_1$ pers. n. f., lit. 'Sit down; she has come'
* '*sibiti* (m.)	Mand., *sibiti* 'Saturday'
* '*sidi* (m.)	Tem., *sidi* pers. n. m.; H., *si:*$_3$*'di*$_1$ 'name given any one who claims descent from Mohammed, and who, it is believed, cannot be harmed by fire'
* *si'ɛkɛ* (f.)	V., *siɛ*$_3$*kɛ*$_1$ pers. n. 'to thank'
'*sifa* (m.)	B., *sifa* 'kind, nature'; H., *si*$_3$*fa*$_1$ 'likeness, model'; 'description'
* *si'fawa* (f.)	Fu., *sifawa* 'name of a place'
'*sigi* (m.)	B., *sigi* 'to establish'; 'to doubt'; 'to be incomplete'; 'fear'
* *si'ikɛ* (f.)	I., *si*$_3$ *i*$_3$*kɛ*$_3$ pers. n. 'to be strong, to be stubborn'
'*sika* (f.)	Fn., *sika* 'gold'; E., *si*$_1$*ka*$_3$ 'gold, money'; *si*$_3$*ka*$_3$ 'to detain'; Bi., *si*$_1$*kã*$_3$ 'to shake each other' (the first phase in wrestling); U., *sika* 'to play an instrument'; T., *sika* 'gold, money'
* '*siki* (m.)	V., *si*$_3$*ki*$_3$ (*si*$_1$*ki*$_3$) pers. n. m.; W., *siki* 'to draw out a splinter'
'*sila* (f.)	V., *si*$_1$*la*$_1$ (*si*$_1$*ra*$_1$) 'to sit with'; Man., *sila* 'sitting'; M., *sila* 'completely'
'*sile* (m.)	B., *sile* 'bruised'; Y., *si*$_2$*le*$_3$ 'to cool,' 'to assuage'
* '*silo* (f.)	M., *silo* pers. n. 'a spider'; Man., *silo* 'road'
* *si'lula* (f.)	U., *silula* pers. n. 'to speak contemptuously'
* '*sima* (m.)	B., *sima* pers. n. 'hairy'; 'prudent'; 'animated'; 'a large, bearded fish larger than the crocodile'
'*simba* (m.)	Bo., *simba* 'to stop in the course of doing'

GULLAH PERSONAL NAMES	WEST AFRICAN WORDS
ˈ*sime* (f.)	E., $si_{1-3}me_1$ 'marshy land'; Fn., *sime* 'outwardly'
ˈ*simfa* (f.)	Man., *simfa* 'foot,' lit. 'full foot' (unit of measurement)
* ˈ*simɒ* (m.)	V., $si_1mɔ_{3-1}$ pers. n. m.
siˈmuna (f.)	U., *simuna* 'to refuse to answer when called, to loiter'
* ˈ*sina* (f.)	M., *sina* 'tomorrow'; 'an indefinite future time'; B., *sina* 'wild, unsociable, spontaneous'; T., *sĩna* 'to pierce, to thread a needle'; V., si_3na_1 pers. n. f.
ˈ*sinda* (f.)	U., *sinda* 'to advance, to push'
ˈ*sini* (m.)	Mal., *sini* 'tomorrow'; B., *sini* 'tomorrow'; 'in the future'; 'about 7 A.M.'
ˈ*siniŋ* (f.)	Man., *siniŋ* 'tomorrow'
* *siˈnola* (m.)	Man., *sinola* pers. n. 'sleeping'
ˈ*siɲa* (f.)	Man., *siɲa* 'times' (as in *siɲa nani* 'four times')
siˈoti (m.)	Man., *sioti* 'a fly'
ˈ*sipi* (m.)	W., *sipi* 'to unload an animal'
* ˈ*sira* (f.)	V., si_1ra_1 (si_1la_1) 'to sit with'; B., *sira* 'road'; 'baobab'; 'brass'; 'to filter honey'; Tem., *sira* pers. n.; W., *sira* pers. n. f.
* ˈ*siriŋ* (f.)	Man., *siriŋ* pers. n. 'remaining'
* *siˈsala* (f.)	*sisala* 'a language of the Western Sudanic section spoken in the area between the White Volta and the Black Volta rivers'
* ˈ*sise* (m.)	Mand., *si:se* 'power of descent'; Tem., *sise* pers. n.; Y., si_3se_1 'the act of cooking'; si_3se_2 'the act of missing'
* ˈ*sisi* (f.)	T., si_3si_3 'a bear'; si_1si_1 'the lower part of the back'; V., si_1si_3 pers. n. 'smoke'; 'rumor'; B., *sisi* 'vapor'; 'to burn'; 'to cook'; 'to become sad'
ˈ*sisifa* (m.)	Man., *sisifa* 'full chest' (unit of measurement)
* ˈ*sisiye* (f.)	T., *sisie* pers. n. 'bear'
* ˈ*sitafa* (m.)	Mand., *sitafa* pers. n. m.
ˈ*site* (f.)	Fn., *site* 'to rise'
* ˈ*sitifa* (m.)	M., *sitifa* pers. n. m.
* *siˈwaya* (f.)	U., *sivaya* pers. n. 'to praise'
ˈ*siya* (f.)	Man., *sia* 'to be plentiful'; E., sia_3 'to expose to the sun or to the air'; 'to polish'; $sia{:}_3$ 'all together'; M., *sia* 'to anoint'; 'to accuse'; U., *sia* 'to leave'
* *siˈyaka* (m.)	Mand., *siya:ka* 'Isaac'

GULLAH PERSONAL NAMES	WEST AFRICAN WORDS
*'*siye* (f.)	V., *sie*$_{3-1}$ pers. n. f. 'one desired'; T., *sie* 'to preserve'; 'to keep one's word'; 'to bury'
* *si'yere* (f.)	B., *syere* pers. n. 'witness'; 'to confess'
*'*siyɛ* (f.)	T., *nsĩyɛ* pers. n. 'diligence, industry'
'*sizi* (f.)	E., *tsi*$_1$*zi*$_{1-3}$ 'darkness, obscurity'
'*sizo* (m.)	Fn., *sizo* 'coffee, tea,' lit. 'firewater'
sɒ'*fale* (f.)	W., *sɔfale* 'to cause to unite'
* sɒɪ (m.)	M., *sai* 'September'; H., *sai*$_3$ 'urine'; 'until'
'sɒ*ika* (f.)	U., *saika* 'to hedge, to cover with boughs'
*'sɒ*ki* (f.)	Y., *sɔ̃*$_3$*ki*$_1$ 'to shrink'; K., *nsɔki* pers. n. 'an inventor, a schemer'
'sɒ*lɛ* (m.)	M., *sɔlɛ* 'noise'; 'to sing loudly'
'sɒ*mb*ɒ (m.)	M., *sɔmb*ɒ 'to assemble'; 'assembled'
*'sɒ*na* (m.)	K., *sɔna* 'to drip'; 'the first few drops of a shower'; *nsɔna* 'one of the four days of the Kongo week' (the other three being *ŋkandu, kɔnzɔ,* and *ŋkeŋge*)
*'sɒ*ni* (m.)	K., *nsɔni* pers. n. 'modesty'; 'a writer'
'sɒ*nʒi* (m.)	K., *nsɔnʒi* 'eels'
'sɒ*n*ɒ (m. and f.)	E., *sɔ*$_3$*nɔ*$_{1-3}$ 'a mare'; *sɔ*$_3$*nɔ*$_1$ 'the mother of a foal'
'sɒ*nsa* (m.)	K., *sɔnsa* 'to drip'
*'sɒ*ŋga* (f.)	K., *sɔŋga* pers. n. 'to be virtuous, to be honest'; Tl., *sɔŋga* 'to carve'; 'to excite'; 'to cohabit with'
*'sɒ*ŋgi* (m.)	K., *sɔŋgi* pers. n. 'a just man'
*'sɒ*ŋg*ɒ (m.)	M., *sɔŋg*ɒ pers. n. 'recompense'
*'sɒ*ŋgu* (m.)	V., *sɔŋ*$_3$*gu*$_3$ pers. n. m.
'sɒsɒ (f.)	V., *sɔ*$_3$*sɔ*$_3$ 'a large worm about four inches in length and two inches in diameter which lives in the palm cabbage and which, when fried or boiled, is considered a delicacy by the natives'
'sɒ*t*ɒ (m.)	E., *sɔ*$_3$*tɔ*$_3$ 'the owner of a horse, a horseman'
'sɒ*wi* (m.)	E., *sɔ*$_3$*vi*$_3$ 'the young of the horse, foal'
* *so* (m.)	E., *so*$_1$ 'the god of thunder and lightning'; 'a species of the fan palm'; Y., *so*$_2$ 'to tie'; 'to produce'; *so*$_3$ 'to emit wind from the stomach'; M., *so* 'horse'; 'cicatrices made in lines or patterns upon the body for beauty'; B., *so*: 'a thief'; 'occasion, proper time'; cf. Eng., *so* and *sow*
*'*soba* (m.)	Fu., *soba* pers. n. 'friend'; H., *so*:$_3$'*ba*$_1$ 'to protrude, to extend beyond'
'*sobe* (m.)	B., *sobe* 'perfectly'

GULLAH PERSONAL NAMES	WEST AFRICAN WORDS
* ˈ*sobo* (m.)	*sobo* 'a language of the Western Sudanic section spoken in Southern Nigeria'; E., so_3bo_3 'calf of the leg'; Fn., *sogbo* 'the god of thunder'
so_1di_3 (m.)	V., so_1di_3 'the heart of a horse'
ˈ*sodo* (m.)	B., *sodo* 'to approach, to be easy of access'
* *so*ˈ*fati* (f.)	E., $so_3fa_{3-1}ti_3$ pers. n. 'the heavy surf prevailing between September and December'
ˈ*sofi* (m.)	E., so_3fi_1 'a spade, a shovel'; cf. Eng., *Sophy*
* *so*ˈ*goma* (f.)	B., *sogoma* pers. n. 'morning'
* ˈ*soɟa* (f.)	E., $so_1ɟa_1$ 'a female deity, the wife of so_1 or $so_1gbl\tilde{a}_1$, god of thunder and lightning'
ˈ*soke* (f.)	Y., so_3ke_1 'loudly'; 'in an upward direction'; E., so_1ke_{1-3} 'basket, bag'
ˈ*sokɪ* (f.)	M., *sokɪ* 'high, lofty'
ˈ*soli* (f.)	E., $so_1l\tilde{i}_1$ 'an herb' (used in smoking meat)
* *so*ˈ*liba* (f.)	B., *soliba* pers. n. 'early, early rising, morning'
* ˈ*solo* (m.)	Man., *solo* pers. n. 'the leopard'; cf. Eng., *solo*
* *so*ˈ*mala* (f.)	Man., *somala* pers. n. 'in the morning'
* *so*ˈ*manda* (f.)	Man., *somanda* pers. n. 'morning, in the morning'
* ˈ*sombo* (f.)	V., som_1bo_1 pers. n. f.; M., *sombo* pers. n. f.
* ˈ*sona* (m.)	Y., so_1na_1 'to hold at bay'; B., *sona* pers. n. 'one who sacrifices'
ˈ*sondu* (m.)	M., *sondu* 'to curse by a fetish'; 'an oath'
* ˈ*soni* (m.)	V., so_1ni_3 pers. n. m.; B., *so:ni* 'an instant'; *soni* 'nail, claw, hoof'; 'a small house'; 'sacrifice'; 'irrigation'; 'to load'
ˈ*soɲa* (m.)	E., $so_1ɲa_3$ 'a euphoria' (an African plant)
* ˈ*soŋgo* (m.)	V., $soŋ_1go_1$ pers. n. m.
* ˈ*soŋko* (m.)	Man., *soŋko* 'name of a Mandinka noble clan of Gambia whose totem is the *kuto* "turtle"'
* ˈ*sori* (m.)	V., so_3ri_3 pers. n. m.; Tem. and M., *sori* pers. n. m.
* ˈ*soso* (m.)	B., *soso* 'to dispute'; 'to fill up'; 'mosquito'; Fn., *soso* 'to cause to fry'; M., *soso* 'Susu country'
* *so*ˈ*tigi* (m.)	Mand., *sotigi* 'chief of the village'
ˈ*sotu* (m.)	T., *nsõtu* 'the taking-up and strewing of the ashes from the fuel used for the fire that is kept during the yam custom'
ˈ*sowi* (m.)	M., *sowi* 'to fear'; E., so_1vi_3 'a small adze'
* ˈ*sudi* (m.)	Fn., *sudi* 'long'; 'large'; H., $su_3'di_1$ pers. n. 'remains of food left in vessel for dependents to partake of'; 'a woman who has no husband'

GULLAH PERSONAL NAMES	WEST AFRICAN WORDS
* ˈ*suki* (f.)	W., *suki* 'to recover someone from the crowd'; M., *suki* pers. n. m.
* ˈ*sukri* (m.)	V., *su*$_1$*kri*$_3$ pers. n. m.
* ˈ*suku* (m.)	V., *su*$_1$*ku*$_3$ pers. n. m. and f.; K., *suku* 'haunch, rump' (of an animal); H., *su*:$_1$*ku*:$_2$ 'a barbless arrow with serrations along the metal shaft'
* *suˈkuta* (m.)	Bo., *sukuta* 'to support the head with the hand in sleep'; Man., *sukuta* pers. n. '8:00 P.M.,' lit. 'night arriving'
* ˈ*sulima* (f.	*sulima* 'name of a city and river in the southeastern part of Sierra Leone'
ˈ*sume* (f.)	K., *nsume* 'an ant'
* ˈ*sunda* (f.)	V., *sun*$_1$*da*$_1$ 'to send'; K., *sunda* pers. n. 'victory'; 'to excel'
* ˈ*suni* (f.)	B., *suni* pers. n. 'fasting, abstinence'
* ˈ*suŋga* (m.)	K., *suŋga* 'to wrap in a shroud'; 'a habit of mind or thought'; Tl., *suŋga* pers. n. 'to mediate'
* *suŋˈgila* (m.)	Kim., *suŋgila* pers. n. 'to visit by night'
suˈole (m.)	Man., *suole* 'horse'
suˈriya (f.)	H., *su*$_1$*ɾi*$_2$*ya*:$_2$ 'a loose-fitting garment'
suruˈru (f.)	H., *su*:$_3$*ɾu*:$_3$*ɾu*$_1$ 'bran obtained from corn ground without being made wet'
* ˈ*suso* (m.)	Man., *suso* 'name of a Mandinka caste clan of drummers and jesters having as their totem the *kana* ''iguana'' '
suˈsuwi (f.)	T., *nsusui* 'measure'; 'thought'
* ˈ*suti* (f.)	Y., *su*$_1$*ti*$_2$ 'a contemptuous pouting of the lips, a hiss'; Man., pers. n. *suti* 'short, small'
* ˈ*suto* (f.)	Man., *suto* pers. n. 'late evening, night'
suˈwana (f.)	H., *su*:$_3$*wa*:$_1$*na*:$_{2-1}$ 'which one's?'
* ˈ*swaŋgɒ* (f.)	M., *suaŋgɒ* pers. n. 'to be proud, evil, lascivious'
* ˈ*sware* (m.)	T., *suare* 'a plot of ground, a beaten path'; 'vestige, mark'; Tem., *suare* 'a family name common in the Temne-speaking area of Sierra Leone'

[ʃ]

* ˈ*ʃaɪtan* (m.)	H., *ʃai*$_1$*t'an*$_{2-1}$ (*ʃai*$_1$*tsan*$_{2-1}$) 'an evil spirit'; 'a cantankerous person'; 'a person skilled in any craft' (Ar.)
* ˈ*ʃaluga* (m.)	Y., *ʃa*$_2$*lu*$_3$*ga*$_{2-1}$ 'title of *a*$_2$*ʤe*$_3$, the goddess of money'
* *ʃaŋ*$_1$*go*$_3$ (m.)	Y., *ʃaŋ*$_1$*go*$_3$ 'the god of thunder'

GULLAH PERSONAL NAMES	WEST AFRICAN WORDS
* ˈʃ*aworo* (f.)	Y., ʃa$_3$wo$_3$ro$_3$ 'small brass bells'; ʃa$_2$wo$_1$ro$_3$ pers. n. 'to be stingy'
ˈʃ*ɛkɛrɛ* (f.)	Y., ʃɛ$_1$kɛ$_1$rɛ$_1$ 'a rattle made from a calabash netted with strings of cowries'
ˈʃ*ibi* (f.)	Y., ʃi$_3$bi$_3$ 'a spoon'
ˈʃ*ibidi* (f.)	K., *nʃibidi* 'a game of odds and evens'
* ʃ*i*ˈ*ele* (f.)	K., *nʃiele* pers. n. 'the whydah bird'
ʃ*i*ˈ*kama* (f.)	Kim., ʃ*ikama* 'to sit down'
ʃ*i*ˈ*kɒla* (f.)	K., ʃ*ikɔla* 'school' (P., *escola* [ɪʃkɔlɐ])
ˈʃ*ima* (f.)	K., ʃ*ima* 'to forbid'; 'a pool, a hole for water'
* ˈʃ*ina* (f.)	K., ʃ*ina* pers. n. 'to be deep'; 'depth'; 'wealth, capital'; 'a wealthy person'; H., ʃi$_3$na$_1$ 'to know'; 'knowledge'
ʃ*i*ˈ*nisa* (f.)	K., ʃ*inisa* 'to deepen'
ˈʃ*inza* (f.)	K., ʃ*inza* 'a stump'; 'to make fresh the cutting in a palm'
ˈʃ*iŋgu* (m.)	Kim., ʃ*iŋgu* 'neck'
ˈʃ*iʃã* (f.)	Y., ʃi$_3$ʃã$_1$ 'watery, flowing'
* ˈʃ*ita* (f.)	K., ʃ*ita* pers. n. 'a barren, impotent person or animal of either sex'; Tl., ʃ*ita* 'to close tightly'
ˈʃ*itu* (f.)	Kim., ʃ*itu* pers. n. 'meat'
* ʃ*i*ˈ*yama* (f.)	K., ʃ*iama* pers. n. 'strength, security'
* ʃ*ɒ*ˈ*pɒna* (f.)	Y., ʃɔ$_1$kpɔ:$_2$na$_3$ pers. n. 'god of smallpox'
* ʃ*o̩*ˈ*kalu* (f.)	Y., ʃo$_3$ka$_3$lu$_2$ pers. n. m.
ˈʃ*oʃo* (m.)	Y., ʃo$_2$ʃo$_2$ 'only'

[t]

ˈ*taba* (m.)	Y., ta:$_2$ba$_1$ 'to clean the under parts of the body'; ta$_3$ba$_1$ 'tobacco' (Fr. *tabac*); Kim., *taba* 'to draw water'; Fn., *taba* 'tobacco'; H., ta:$_1$ba:$_2$ 'dishonest work'; ta$_3$'ba$_1$ 'to touch, to handle'; ta:$_3$ba$_1$ 'tobacco'; B., *taba* 'an edible fruit'; 'a beautiful tree with large leaves'; 'to make a hole in a watermelon to see whether it is ripe'; 'tobacco'; *ta:ba:* 'he who departs'
* ˈ*tabu* (m.)	Y., ta$_1$bu$_3$ 'a splash'; E., a$_1$ta$_3$bu$_3$ 'oath' (ka$_1$ a$_1$ta$_3$bu$_3$ 'to swear an oath'); H., ta$_1$'bu$_2$ 'to be ill'; 'to be affected'; Kim., *tabu* pers. n. 'a landing-place on the edge of a river or lagoon'
ˈ*tadi* (m.)	Y., ta$_2$di$_3$ 'to be irreconcilable'; K., *tadi* 'iron, metal'; 'an article, tool, or instrument made of metal';

GULLAH PERSONAL NAMES	WEST AFRICAN WORDS
	tadi! 'Look!'; *ntadi* 'an onlooker'; M., *tadi* 'citizen'; cf. Eng., *tardy*
'*tafe* (m.)	E., ta_3fe_1 'the bride-piece'; 'the ransom paid in the freeing of a slave'; B., *tafe* 'cotton underwear for girls'; H., $ta{:}_3fe_1$ 'to be destitute'
* '*tafi* (m.)	*tafi* 'a language of the Western Sudanic section belonging to the Central Togo group'
* '*tafo* (m.)	T., *ntafo* 'natives of Nta, a land on the Upper and the White Volta'
ta'hana (f.)	U., *tahana* 'to press, to squeeze'
'*taɟi* (m.)	Y., $ta_2ɟi_3$ 'to wake suddenly from sleep'; Fn., *taɟi* 'summit, top,' lit. 'top of the head'
ta'kula (f.)	B., *takula* 'bread made from the flour or meal of millet'; K., *ntakula* 'a trap for birds'
'*tala* (m.)	Y., ta_3la_1 'bleached calico, white muslin'; Man., *tala* 'half'
* *ta'lata* (f.)	B. and Man., *talata* 'Tuesday'
* '*talo* (f.)	V., ta_1lo_3 'name given a girl who is a member of the Sande Society'; M., *talo* 'grandchild'; Y., ta_1lo_3 'a splash' (such as that caused by the fall of a stone into water)
* '*tama* (f.)	K., *tama* 'to measure distance'; 'space'; 'fathom'; *ntama* 'distance'; B., *tama* 'a spear'; 'cheek'; 'a tambourine'; 'a voyage'; M., *tama* 'deception'; V., ta_1ma_1 pers. n. 'gentle'; T., *tãmã*: 'smooth, soft'; Tl., *tama* 'to be extended'; H., $ta_3ma{:}_3$ 'ore'; 'a cheap kind of sword'; $ta{:}_3ma_1$ 'to assist'
* '*tamba* (m. and f.)	V., tam_1ba_1 'a spear'; K., *tamba* 'to offer, to extend the hand or arm'; U., *tamba* 'to tempt'; Tl., 'to surpass'; H., tam_3ba_1 'name of a grass yielding a seed that is usable as a cereal'; B., *tamba* 'the second daughter of a woman'
'*tambe* (m.)	M., *tambe* 'a thorny rattan'; 'a species of palm'
'*tambi* (m.)	K., *tambi* 'a foot'; *ntambi* 'footmark, track'; Man., *tambi* 'to pass'
'*tambo* (m.)	Man., *tambo* 'spear'; H., tam_3bo_1 'a form of leprosy'; 'a scar'; $tam_1bo{:}_2$ 'name of a fish'
'*tambu* (m.)	K., *ntambu* 'a trap'; 'a lock, a bolt'
'*tame* (m.)	Fn., *tame* 'character, intelligence'; E., ta_3me_1 'intelligence, summit, the interior of the head'
'*tamɒ* (m.)	Y., $tã_1mɔ{:}_{3-1}$ 'to think, to suppose'
* '*tamu* (m.)	V., ta_3mu_1 pers. n. m., lit. 'He belongs to me'; K.,

GULLAH PERSONAL NAMES	WEST AFRICAN WORDS
	ntamu 'a measured distance' (such as a span of the hand or a stride of the legs)
* ˈ*tana* (f.)	Y., $t\tilde{a}_2na_3$ 'to light a lamp'; 'to blossom'; Man., *tana* 'trouble'; Bo., *tana* pers. n. 'to be beautiful'; V., ta_1na_3 'totem'
* ˈ*tani* (m.)	V., ta_1ni_3 'lead' (metal); E., ta_3ni_3 'completely'; Y., ta_2ni_2 'who?'; M., *tani* 'completely'; cf. T., *ɔtani* 'a native of Nta'
taˈnina (f.)	K., *tanina* 'to defend'
* ˈ*tanu* (f.)	Kim., Tl., K., and U., *tanu* 'five'; Y., ta_2nu_1 'to cast out'; ta_2nu_2 'to make fun of'; E., ta_1nu_3 'the morning star'; 'bride price, dowry'; Fn., *tanu* 'Abomey customs'
ˈ*taɲa* (m.)	U., *taɲa* 'to kick'; 'to struggle'; 'to be convulsed'
ˌ*taɲiˈɲika* (f.)	Tl., *taɲiɲika* 'to spread out, to open'
ˈ*taŋga* (f.)	U., *taŋga* 'to read'; W., *taŋga* 'hot'; Kim., *taŋga* 'to read'; M., *taŋga* 'cassava'
ˈ*taŋgu* (m.)	Kim., *taŋgu* 'branch'
ˈ*taŋgwa* (m.)	K., *ntaŋgwa* 'the sun, time, opportunity'
ˈ*taŋka* (m.)	W., *taŋka* 'foot, leg'; H., $ta\eta_3ka_1$ 'to reply'; $ta\eta_1ka{:}_2$ 'a copy'
ˈ*tapo* (m.)	T., *ta:po* 'half a string of cowries, twenty cowries'
* ˈ*tara* (f.)	Y., ta_2ra_2 'to be earnest'; $ta{:}_1ra_1$ 'straight'; Mal., *tara* 'time of the great heat (from March to May)'; B., *ta:ra:* 'a wooden gutter or spout'; *tara* 'a native bed'
* ˈ*tare* (m.)	V., ta_3re_3 (ta_3le_3) pers. n. m.; 'gone'; H., $ta{:}_3\text{ɽ}e_1$ 'to collect'; 'to settle in a new home or in different quarters'; $ta_3\text{ɽ}e_1$ 'to intercept'; $ta_1\text{ɽ}e{:}_2$ 'the act of intercepting'
ˈ*tari* (f.)	Y., $ta{:}_2ri_2$ 'to push violently or headlong'; B., *tari* 'prompt'; 'where?'
* ˈ*taro* (f.)	V., ta_1ro_3 (ta_1lo_3) pers. n. m.; Y., ta_1ro_2 'to estimate'
ˈ*taru* (f.)	Y., ta_2ru_1 'to carry a heavy load on the head'; H., $ta{:}_3\text{ɽ}u{:}_3$ 'a caravan on the outward journey'
ˈ*tasa* (f.)	E., $ta_1sa{:}_1$ 'slanting'
ˈ*tase* (f.)	T., *tase* 'to pick up, to assemble'; Y., ta_1se_3 'to fail'
* ˈ*tasi* (f.)	E., ta_3si_{1-3} pers. n. 'father's sister, aunt'; ta_3si_3 'to desist from, to finish'; Y., ta_2si_3 'to shoot at'; 'to anoint'
ˈ*taʃi* (f.)	K., *taʃi* 'long ago'; H., $ta_3\text{ʃ}i{:}_3$ 'a light'; $ta{:}_3\text{ʃ}i_1$ 'to get

GULLAH PERSONAL NAMES	WEST AFRICAN WORDS
	up'; $ta{:}_1ʃi{:}_2$ 'a pad of bark or grass for a pack animal'; $ta_3ʃi_1$ 'courting'; 'a fiancee'
*ˈ*tata* (f.)	T., *tata* 'a two-edged sword'; *ta:ta*: 'to be filled or swollen with water'; E., ta_1ta_3 'castration'; 'drawing'; 'father'; K. and Kim., *tata* pers. n. 'father'; Bo., *ta:ta* 'father'; *tata* 'to creak'; Tl., *tata* 'to be annoyed'; Man., *a tata* 'He has gone'
*ˈ*tatu* (f.)	K., *tatu* 'a shriek'; 'three'; Tl., *tatu* 'father' (used as a title of respect in addressing a chief, master, or elder')
ˈ*tawa* (m.)	M., *tawa* 'forehead, brow of a hill, gable'; H., $ta{:}_1wa_2$ 'mine' (poss. pr. f.)
taˈwara (f.)	V., $ta_1ϑa_3ra_3$ 'a pipe'
*ˈ*tawɛ* (m.)	V., $ta_1ϑɛ_1$ pers. n. m. and f.; M., *tavɛ* 'a tobacco pipe'
ˈ*taya* (f.)	K., *taya* 'to run away'; Tl., *taya* 'to throw down'; H., $ta{:}_1ya{:}_2$ 'to tear the skin of fowl'; 'to strip off bark'; ta_3ya_1 'to make a tentative offer of a price for something'; 'to provoke'; U., *taya* 'to scratch'; B., *taya* 'domination'
*ˈ*tayɛ* (f.)	V., $ta_3yɛ_1$ pers. n. 'to walk'; 'a walk'
ˈ*tayi* (f.)	E., ta_1yi_1 'a variety of yam'; K., *tayi* 'limb of a tree'
te (m.)	Y., te_1 'to worship, to adorn'; te_3 'on the top'; E., te_1 'to go away'; 'to approach'; 'to remove'; 'to swell'; 'yam'; te_3 'to press'; 'to pull'; 'to surpass'; 'to sting'; 'bottom'; 'millstone'; M., *te* 'a game of skill played with seeds upon a board containing twelve cup-shaped hollows in two parallel rows'
teˈase (f.)	T., *ntease* 'understanding'
ˈ*tebe* (f.)	E., $te_1be{:}_1$ 'flat, brimful'; K., *tebe* 'plantain'
ˈ*tegble* (m.)	E., te_1gble_{1-3} 'a yam farm'
ˈ*tege* (m.)	E., te_3ge_3 (ti_3gi_3) 'to be crowded'; B., *tege* 'the palm of the hand'
ˈ*tela* (f.)	E., $te_1lã_3$ 'the finest yam tubers'; K., *tela* 'to add to'; *ntela* 'height'; 'a climbing fern'
ˈ*telama* (f.)	K., *telama* 'to rise'; 'departure'; 'to put on the fire'; *ntelama* 'attitude'; 'posture'
ˈ*tele* (m.)	Y., te_2le_2 'to gather in chips or in small quantities'; Man., *tele* 'sun, sunshine'; B., *tele* 'sun'
ˈ*teli* (m.)	E., $te_1lĩ_1$ 'a wasp'; B., *teli* 'prompt, alert'
ˈ*telu* (m.)	Man., *ntelu* 'we'
ˈ*tema* (f.)	W., *tema* 'to pause, to remain stationary'

GULLAH PERSONAL NAMES	WEST AFRICAN WORDS
'tembɒ (m.)	K., *ntembɔ* 'the stern of a boat'
*'temi (m.)	Y., te_1mi_2 pers. n. 'mine.' (See ti_2 e_1mi_2)
'temɒ (f.)	K., *temɔ* 'the custom of pooling resources of any kind to achieve some particular result, such as men clubbing together to help one another in house building or women to clear the fields for farming, or a group of persons contributing money on every market day to a fund with the result that each contributor in turn receives the whole of one day's contributions'
*'temuna (f.)	K., *temuna* pers. n. 'to open wide' (used especially in reference to the eyes)
*'tena (f.)	T., *tenã* 'to sit down'; K., *tena* 'to retract the prepuce'; M., *teɪna* pers. n. 'a young woman'
*'tene (m.)	B. and Mand., *tene* 'Monday' (Ar.)
*'teneŋ (m.)	Man., *teneŋ* 'Monday'
*'tenɛw (m.)	W., *tenɛv* pers. n. 'a panther'
'tenteŋ (m.)	T., *tenteŋ* 'long'; 'length'; 'high'; 'height'
*'teŋkuŋ (m.)	Man., *teŋkuŋ* pers. n. 'quiet, to be quiet'
'tere (f.)	Y., te_3re_3 'in small quantities'; T., *tere* 'to flow'
'teta (f.)	E., te_1ta_{1-3} 'small yam tubers used as seedlings'; K., *teta* 'to peel'
'tete (f.)	Y., te_1te_1 'early'; te_2te_2 'quickly'; 'leg'; 'the kick of an animal'; E., te_1te_1 'unimportant'; 'to push aside'; K., *ntete* 'bundle, sheaf'; 'a basket made of woven palm fronds'
tete'tɒwo (f.)	Y., $te_1te_2tɔ_3wo_1$ 'to taste beforehand'
'tezɒ (f.)	K., *tezɔ* 'measure, pattern'; 'distance'
tɛ (m.)	Y., $tɛ_3$ 'to fall into disgrace'; 'to be insipid'; 'to spread'; $tɛ_1$ 'to trample under foot'; 'crooked'; I., $tɛ_3$ 'to rub'; Bi., $tɛ_3$ 'to be contemptible'; $tɛ_{1-3}$ 'to urge by flattery'; M., *tɛ* 'domestic fowl, hen, rooster'
'tɛkpɛ (m.)	M., *tɛkpɛ* 'a basket with its cover'
*'tɛli (m.)	M., *tɛli* pers. n. 'to blacken'; 'black'
'tɛlo (m.)	M., *tɛlo* 'a young chicken'
'tɛmbɛ (m.)	V., $tɛm_1bɛ_1$ 'to stand or place in a line'
'temɒ (m.)	Y., $tɛ_1m\tilde{ɔ}_3$ 'to press upon, to imprint'
*'tɛnɛ (f.)	M., *tɛnɛ* 'a day of the week among the Mende corresponding to the Sabbath'; V., $tɛ_2nɛ_{2-1}$ pers. n. f.

GULLAH PERSONAL NAMES	WEST AFRICAN WORDS
ˈ*tɛre* (f.)	T., *tɛre* 'broad, flat'
ˈ*tɛtɛ* (f.)	Y., *tɛ*$_3$*tɛ*$_3$ 'a game of chance'; *tɛ*$_1$*tɛ*$_1$ 'a kind of herb'; 'spinach'; M., *tɛtɛ* 'to hatch, to crack'
* ˈ*tɛtu* (m.)	Y., *tɛ*$_1$*tu*$_3$ 'an officer of justice, an executioner'
ˈ*tɛwɒ* (f.)	Y., *tɛ*$_3$*wɔ*$_3$ 'to spread the hand'
ˈ*tɛyi* (f.)	W., *tɛ:i* 'to be clear'; *tɛi* 'today'; 'to make plain'
tiˈama (f.)	K., *tiama* 'to fetch'; 'to collect'; U., *tiama* 'to move aside'; Ki., *tiama* 'to cut down'
tiˈaso (f.)	T., *ntiaso* 'a thing to tread upon'
ˈ*tiba* (m.)	K., *tiba* 'banana'; 'the banana tree'; W., *tiba* 'to take hold of'; B., *tiba* 'to break to pieces'
ˈ*tibo* (m.)	T., *ti*$_3$*bo*$_2$ 'price'; *ti*$_1$*bo*$_3$ 'top stone'
ˈ*tibu* (m.)	K., *ntibu* 'bow' (weapon)
tiˈemba (m.)	K., *tiemba* 'to copulate'
* *tiˈemi* (f.)	Y., *ti*$_2$ *e*$_1$*mi*$_2$ pers. n. 'belonging to me, mine'
tiˈɛri (m.)	V., *tiɛ*$_1$*ri*$_3$ (*tiɛ*$_1$*li*$_3$) 'an ax, a hatchet'; 'something that has been cut'
ˈ*tigi* (m.)	E., *ti*$_3$*gi*$_3$ (*te*$_3$*ge*$_3$) 'to be pressed, to be crowded'; B., *tigi* 'owner, proprietor'; 'a fish'; Bi., *ti*$_1$*γi*$_3$ 'to twist'
* ˈ*tihũ* (m.)	M., *tihũ* pers. n. 'on an island'
* *tiˈɟani* (m.)	B., *tiɟani* pers. n. m.; 'a round, tall cap'
* ˈ*tiɟo* (m.)	M., *tidʒo* pers. n. m.; 'a hardwood tree'
* ˌ*tiɟoˈtayo* (m.)	Y., *ti*$_2$*ɟo*$_3$*ta*$_2$*yo*$_1$ 'one of the forty-eight Ilaris, household officers of the crown who are below the eunuchs in rank'
* ˌ*tiɟuˈiku* (m.)	Y., *ti*$_2$*ɟu*$_3$-*i*$_2$*ku*$_3$ pers. n., lit. 'Be ashamed to die'
ˈ*tiki* (m.)	K., *tiki* 'a cloth of native manufacture'
* ˈ*tila* (f.)	Fn., *tila* 'an amulet'; H., *ti*$_3$*la*$_1$ 'to pile up'; *ti*$_1$*la:*$_2$ 'the earth piled up outside its burrow by a rodent, etc.'
ˈ*tile* (f.)	B., *tile* 'the sun'; Bi., *ti*$_3$*le*$_1$ 'to bet'
ˈ*tili* (m.)	V., *ti*$_3$*li*$_3$ 'waist'; Man., *tili* 'day'; Mal., *tili* 'sun'; B., *tili* 'to cover'
* ˈ*tilibo* (m.)	Man., *tilibo* 'name of the country to the east of the Gambia'
* *tiliˈboyi* (m.)	Man., *tiliboi* pers. n. 'sunset'
* *tiliˈbuŋko* (m.)	Man., *tilibuŋko* 'a man from Tilibo'
* ˈ*tiliɟi* (f.)	Man., *tilidʒi* pers. n. 'the setting of the sun'
* ˈ*tilim* (m.)	W., *tilim* pers. n. 'to be dirty'

GULLAH PERSONAL NAMES	WEST AFRICAN WORDS
ˈ*tiliŋ* (m.)	Man., *tiliŋ* 'to be straight'
ˈ*tilo* (f.)	Man., *tilo* 'sun'
ˈ*tima* (f.)	K., *tima* 'to excavate'; *ntima* 'heart, mind, conscience'; Bo., *tima* 'to excavate'
ˈ*timba* (f.)	B., *timba* 'anteater'
ˈ*timbi* (f.)	W., *timbi* 'to return'; 'to float on the surface'
*ˈ*timbo* (m.)	*timbo* 'name of a town in French Guinea'
*ˈ*timɒ* (m.)	Y., *ti*$_3$*mɔ*$_3$ 'closely'; V., *ti*$_1$*mɔ*$_1$ pers. n. 'possessor'
ˈ*tina* (f.)	U., *tina* 'to be hard'; 'to be costly'; K., *tina* 'to flee, to shrink from, to be afraid of'
ˈ*tini* (m.)	K., *tini* 'part of a journey'; 'morsel'; *ntini* 'a fugitive'
*ˈ*tinu* (f.)	W., *tinu* 'to ask pardon'; K., *ntinu* 'flight, speed'; 'chief, emperor'
tiˈrika (m.)	H., *ti*$_3$*rik:*$_1$*a:*$_2$ 'the space in a camp allotted to each member or section of an army or of a caravan'
ˈ*tita* (f.)	Y., *ti*$_3$*ta*$_1$ 'that which is to be sold'; *ti*$_3$*ta*$_2$ 'that which is to be shot'; 'stinging, burning'; K., *tita* 'to shake'
*ˈ*ti*$_1$*ti*$_3$ (m.)	Bi., *ti*$_1$*ti*$_3$ pers. n. 'to be famous'; Y., *ti*$_1$*ti*$_1$ 'violently'; *ti*$_3$*ti*$_3$ 'continually'; *ti*$_3$*ti*$_1$ 'kept under lock and key'; 'public road, thoroughfare'; E., *ti*$_1$*ti*$_1$ 'to stroke'; *ti*$_1$*ti*$_3$ 'rheumatism'; 'gout'; B., *titi* 'many'; K., *titi* 'skin'; 'refuse'; 'name of a game'; V., *ti*$_1$*ti*$_3$ pers. n. 'little girl'
ˈ*tititi* (m.)	E., *ti*$_1$*ti*$_1$*ti*$_1$ 'shaking'; 'for a long time'
*ˈ*tiwɒni* (f.)	T., *ti*$_2$ *wɔ*$_2$ *ni*$_2$ pers. n. 'It is yours'
*ˈ*tiya* (f.)	Y., *ti*$_1$*ya*$_3$ pers. n. 'maternal'; E., *tia*$_1$ 'to choose, to single out'; T., *tia* 'to tread upon'; *tia* 'to unite'; K., *tiya* 'fire, gunpowder'
*ˈ*tiyo* (m.)	Man., *tio* pers. n. 'master'
tiˈyofe (m.)	Man., *tiofe* 'groundnuts'
*ˈ*tiyoˈtiyo* (m.)	Y., *ti*$_3$*yo*$_3$*ti*$_3$*yo*$_3$ (*tio*$_3$*tio*$_3$) pers. n. 'slender'; *tio*$_2$*tio*$_2$ 'the brown singing shrike'
*ˈ*tɪna* (f.)	V., *tɪ*$_1$*na*$_1$ pers. n. 'a rival'
*ˈ*tɪnɪ* (f.)	V., *tɪ*$_1$*nɪ*$_3$ pers. n. f.
*ˈ*tɪtɪli* (m.)	M., *tɪtɪli* pers. n. 'speechless'
tɒ (m.)	Y., *tɔ*$_3$ 'to bring up'; 'to provoke'; 'to be right'; *tɔ*$_1$ 'to follow after'; 'to resort to'; 'to urinate'; *tɔ*$_2$ 'limb, joint, portion of the body'; Tl., *tɔ* 'constantly'; M., *tɔ* 'to increase the acuteness of smell by applying stimulants to a dog's nose'
ˈ*tɒba* (m.)	K., *tɔba* 'to stab'; Tl., *tɔba* 'to be spotted'

GULLAH PERSONAL NAMES	WEST AFRICAN WORDS
* ˈ*tɒfe* (f.)	E., *tɔ*$_3$*fe*$_3$ pers. n. 'the paternal home'
ˈ*tɒɪma* (f.)	U., *taima* 'to shine, to burn'
* ˈ*tɒɪni* (f.)	Y., *ta*$_2$-*i*$_1$*ni*$_3$ pers. n. 'Sell the property'; cf. Eng., *tiny*
ˈ*tɐɪtɒɪ* (f.)	Y., *tai*$_1$*tai*$_2$ 'numbly'; H., *tai*$_3$*tai*$_3$ 'a small circular mat used as a cover for a vessel'; 'a kind of network of rope used for tying up loads'
* ˈ*tɒɪwo* (m. and f.)	Y., *tai*$_3$*wo*$_1$ $<$*tɔ*$_3$+*ai*$_1$*ye*$_3$+*wo*$_1$ 'name given the first of twins,' lit. 'to taste the world'
ˈ*tɒɟi* (m.)	Fn., *tɔɟi* 'an island'
* *tɒkˈpɒmbu* (m.)	M., *tɔkpɒmbʊ* pers. n. 'under the palm tree'
ˈ*tɒkɒ* (m.)	Y., *tɔ*$_1$*kɔ*$_1$ 'to steer a canoe or ship'; T., *tɔkɔ*: 'plentifully'
* ˈ*tɒla* (f.)	K., *tɔla* pers. n. 'to be fat'; M., *tɒla* 'a funnel'
* ˈ*tɒma* (f.)	K., *tɔma* 'to be good, to be pleasant'; 'to taste sweet'; Kim., *tɔma* 'to stick'; V., *tɔ*:$_3$*ma*$_3$ pers. n. m. and f.
* ˈ*tɒmbɛ* (m.)	M., *tɒmbɛ* pers. n. 'a false report of death'
tɒmˈbɒla (m.)	K., *tɔmbɔla* 'to carry'; 'to dish up food'; 'to ascend'
ˈ*tɒmela* (f.)	E., *tɔ*$_1$*me*$_1$*lã*$_1$ 'an animal that lives in water'
* ˈ*tɒnda* (m.)	K., *tɔnda* pers. n. 'to love'; 'affection'; Tl., *tɔnda* 'to dislike'; 'to confess, to reveal'
* ˈ*tɒndi* (m.)	K., *ntɔndi* pers. n. 'a grateful person, one who loves'; 'an eel'
ˈ*tɒnɛ* (f.)	M., *tɔnɛ* 'to tickle'
ˈ*tɒnɟi* (f.)	K., *ntɔnʒi* 'sleeping-sickness'
* ˈ*tɒɲa* (m.)	V., *tɔ*$_1$*ɲa*$_3$ pers. n. 'truth'; 'truthful'; M., *tɔɲa* 'truth'; 'just, right'; Tl., *tɔɲa* 'to bend, to curve'
* *tɒŋ* (m.)	T., *tɔŋ* 'to sell'; *tɔŋ*: 'Togoland'
ˈ*tɒte* (m.)	T., *tɔte* 'the foot of a four-footed animal, paw, hoof'
* ˈ*tɒtela* (m.)	K., *ntɔtela* 'title of the kings of Kongo'
ˈ*tɒtɒ* (m.)	K., *tɔtɔ* 'the sound made from clapping twice; *ntɔtɔ* 'a mongoose'; 'the earth'
ˈ*tɒtɒtɒ* (f.)	E., *tɔ*$_3$*tɔ*$_3$*tɔ*$_3$ 'in great numbers'
ˈ*tɒyɒ* (f.)	K., *tɔyɔ* 'the act of frowning'; *ntɔyɔ* 'a bird known as the blue plantain-eater and supposed to talk a great deal when someone of importance dies'
to (m.)	Y., *to*$_3$ 'sufficient'; *to*$_1$ 'to stand in a line'; *to*:$_1$ 'aloud'; Fn., *to* 'father'; 'country'; E., *to*$_1$ 'to be thick, shriveled'; 'a buffalo'; 'the pulverized bark of a tree, called *to*$_1$*ti*$_3$, that is used in religious ceremonies'; 'an open space within a meeting occupied

GULLAH PERSONAL NAMES	WEST AFRICAN WORDS
	by a speaker or dancer'; to_3 'to say'; 'to grow'; 'to pound' 'to pass through'; 'to be wanting'; 'depth'; 'hill'; 'ear'; 'father-in-law, son-in-law, family'; 'brink'; to_{1-3} 'cavity'; 'shell'; 'mortar'; 'crib'; M., *to* 'a house built over the grave in worship of the dead'; I., $tö_3$ 'to grow'; $tö_1$ 'to praise.' Cf. Eng., *toe* and *tow*
* '*toba* (m.)	E., to_3ba_3 'a broad mat'; B., pers. n. *toba* 'pardoned, acquitted'
'*tobε* (m.)	Fn., *tobε* 'garment, the blouse of the Mohammedan' (Ar.)
* '*tobi* (m.)	Y., to_1bi_3 'an undergarment used by women'; to_3bi_2 'large'; B., *tobi* 'to cook'; W., *tobi* 'to make holes in the earth for planting seed'; V., to_1gbi_3 pers. n. m.; cf. Eng., *Toby*
'*todi* (m.)	T., *ntodi* 'things bought and eaten'; 'expenses' (especially for food)
* '*togbo* (m.)	Fn., *togbo* 'ancestor'
'*toge* (m.)	H., $to{:}_3ge_1$ 'to withdraw'; 'to hesitate through fear'; 'to make exception of'
* '*toli* (m.)	E., to_1li 'a shell'; $to_1li{:}_1$ 'the act of rolling'; Tem., *toli* 'a Temne family name'
* *tolu'fana* (f.)	Man., *ntolufana* pers. n. 'we together, also'
* *to'niyε* (m.)	V., $to_1ni\varepsilon_{3-1}$ pers. n. m. and f., lit. 'Stay here'
* '*toɲa* (f.)	M., *toɲã* < *tolo* + *ɲahã* pers. n. 'jealous woman'
to'sira (f.)	B., *tosira* 'leftover pap'
'*toyi* (f.)	H., $to{:}_1yi{:}_2$ 'burning the forest'; 'the refuse from a farm'
'*traso* (m.)	T., *ntraso* 'that which is beyond the limits, excess'
tu (m.)	E., tu_{1-3} 'birthmark, mole'; tu_1 'to push'; 'to approach'; 'clay'; 'liver'; tu_3 'to be dissolved'; 'to emigrate'; 'to squirt'; 'to be closed'; 'to pay'; 'to be the first to do a thing'; 'to germinate'; 'a gun'; Y., tu_2 'to expectorate'; tu_1 'to soothe'; tu_3 'to loosen'; I., tu_3 'to strap on'; 'to name' (a person). Cf. Eng., *two*
'*tuba* (m.)	Y., $tu{:}_3ba_3$ 'to climb down, to surrender'; K., *tuba* 'to throw'; 'to administer an enema'; H., $tu{:}_3ba{:}_3$ 'to repent'; 'repentance'; $tu{:}_1ba{:}_2$ 'to divest a person of clothing or ornaments'
'*tubu* (m.)	Y., tu_2bu_2 'prison, custody'; H., $tu{:}_1bu{:}_2$ 'the marabou stork'; $tu_1'bu{:}_2$ 'near'

GULLAH PERSONAL NAMES	WEST AFRICAN WORDS
tuˈfina (m.)	Tl. and K., *tufina* 'pus, matter'
tuˈkila (f.)	Tl., *tukila* (*tukidila*) 'to fall into the hands of, to happen upon'
tuˈkuna (f.)	K., *tukuna* 'to press in the hand, to rub'
ˈtula (f.)	Tl., *tula* 'to put down a burden'; 'to forge'; 'to take to pieces'; K., *tula* 'to arrive at'
* *tuˈlante* (m.)	K., *tulante* 'a title of nobility'
ˈtulu (m.)	Tl. and K., *tulu* 'slumber, repose'
tuˈlula (f.)	Tl. and U., *tulula* 'to let down, to take down'
ˈtuma (f.)	Tl., Kim., U., and K., *tuma* 'to send'; K., *tuma* 'to miss'; 'pottery, clay'; M., *tuma* 'a response'
ˈtumba (m.)	K., *tumba* 'to condemn'; 'to correct'; 'to appoint to an office, to initiate into fetish mysteries'; U., *tumba* 'to swell'; Tl., *tumba* 'to be famous'; H., tum_3ba_1 'any sort of heap or pile'
tumbaˈlala (m.)	K., *tumbalala* 'to be made into a heap'
ˈtumbu (m.)	V., tum_1bu_3 'a large brown snake believed by the natives to give birth only once in its life, at which time its young ones are said to issue from every part of its body, causing its death'
ˈtumina (f.)	K., *tumina* 'to send'; Ki., *tumina* 'to give an order'
ˈtumɒ (f.)	Y., $tu_3mɔ_1$ 'to explain, to disclose a secret'
ˈtumo (m.)	Man., *tumo* 'time'
ˈtumpa (m.)	K., *tumpa* 'a throb, a pulsation'; 'to beat'; Tl., *tumpa* 'to parboil, to stew'
ˈtuna (m.)	K., *tuna* 'to skin, to strip without the aid of an instrument'; Tl., *tuna* 'to disobey, to be indifferent'; U., *tuna* 'to strike'; 'to skin'; H., tu_3na_1 'to recall'; $tu_1na\!:_2$ 'fear'; $tu\!:_1na_2$ 'the act of digging up'; $tu\!:_1na\!:_{2-1}$ 'name of a tree'; cf. Eng., *tuna*
* *tuˈniya* (m.)	K., *tunia* pers. n. 'whiteness, cleanness'
ˈtunuka (m.)	K., *tunuka* 'to be peeled off'
* *ˈtunze* (f.)	K., *tunze* pers. n. 'a small bird which nods its head when anyone speaks to it, and in consequence is said to give an affirmative answer to anything, however absurd; hence also a fool who will do or assent to anything'[42]
tuŋ (m.)	Man., *tuŋ* 'again'
* *ˈtuŋga* (m.)	K., *tuŋga* pers. n. 'a fool'; Tl., *tuŋga* 'to sew'; 'to thread, to string'; U., *tuŋga* 'to build'; 'to dwell'; H., $tuŋ_3ga\!:_3$ 'obstinacy'; Kim., *tuŋga* 'to build'

GULLAH PERSONAL NAMES	WEST AFRICAN WORDS
* '*tuŋgi* (f.)	K., *ntuŋgi* pers. n. 'inhabitant, native, founder, builder'
* *tuŋ'kara* (m.)	Man., *tuŋkara* 'name of a Mandinka caste clan of goldsmiths and blacksmiths'
'*tupula* (f.)	K., *tupula* 'to pierce'
* *tu'rawa* (m.)	H., $tu{:}_1ra{:}_1wa{:}_2$ 'white men—Europeans, Arabs'
* '*turi* (m.)	Man., *turi* 'name of a Mandinka noble clan of the Gambia whose totem is *seo* "pig" '
'*tuta* (m.)	U., *tuta* 'to carry'; 'to weave'; 'to be spoiled'; Kim., *tuta* 'to carry'; Tl., *tuta* 'to punish'; 'to return'; Man., *tuta* 'to leave'; T., *ntuta* 'a double-barreled gun'; Y., tu_1ta_1 'to sell oddments'; Man., *tuta* 'to leave'
* '*tutu* (m. and f.)	Y., tu_3tu_1 'cold, meek, calm'; tu_2tu_2 'sad, sulky'; $tu{:}_3tu{:}_3$ 'entirely'; K., *tutu* 'a calabash'; Kim., *tutu* 'a beetle'; Tl., *tutu* 'a title of respect for a brother older than one's self'; Bo., *tutu* 'to cut to pieces'; M., *tutʊ* 'a messenger between lovers'; T., *tutu* 'name of an Akuapem town'; H., $tu{:}_{3-1}tu{:}_2$ 'the blossom of the locust-bean tree'; $tu{:}_3tu_1$ 'human excrement'; 'a moonstone'
'*tuwa* (f.)	Tl., *tuwa* 'to bail out'; M., *tuva* 'to delay a long while'; K., *tua* 'to strike'; B., *tua* 'name, reputation'; *tua*: 'hip'; Bi., tua_{1-3} 'to pull strongly together'; 'to be loud'; 'to swell'; 'to hasten'; U., *tuwa* 'to be accustomed to'
* *tuwa'lala* (f.)	K., *tuvalala* pers. n. 'to be distended'
'*tuyi* (m.)	Y., $t\tilde{u}_3yi_3$ 'to turn over again'
'*twala* (f.)	K., *twala* 'to introduce'; 'to inflict punishment'
twa_1ni_3 (f.)	T., *tuani* 'infantile convulsions, inflammation of the intestines'
'*twedi* (m.)	K., *ntwedi* 'a breeder, one who keeps animals'
'*twela* (m.)	K., *twela* 'to breed animals'
'*twisa* (f.)	K., *twisa* 'to sharpen'

[c]

* *cal* (m.)	W., *cal* 'a Wolof family name'
'*calo* (m.)	Fn., *calo* 'a raft'
* *cam* (m.)	W., *cam* 'a Wolof family name'; Man., *tʃam* 'name of a Mandinka caste clan of goldsmiths and blacksmiths'
'*cama* (f.)	B., *cama* 'numerous, abundant'

GULLAH PERSONAL NAMES	WEST AFRICAN WORDS
* ˈ*cebi* (f.)	G., ce_2bi_2 'name of a town in the Gold Coast'
* ˈ*ceŋku* (m.)	T., *ceŋku* pers. n.
ˈ*cere* (m.)	T., *cere* 'to catch'
* ˈ*cɛba* (m.)	Mand., *cɛba* 'one having the same name as one's parent'
* *cɛ*ˈ*koro* (m.)	Mand., *cɛkoro* 'one having the same name as one's parent' (a synonym of *cɛba*)
ˈ*cɛma* (f.)	B., *cɛma* 'male, masculine'
* *cɛ*ˈ*wule* (m. and f.)	Mand., *cɛwule* pers. n. m., lit. 'the red man'
*ci*ˈ*lombo* (m.)	U., *otʃilombo* 'a camp'
ˈ*cina* (f.)	U., *tʃina* 'to dance'
ˈ*ciɲa* (f.)	Fn., *ciɲa* 'to choose'
ˈ*cici* (f.)	Fn., *cici* 'eyeglasses'

[u]

* ˈ*udi* (m.)	Ef., u_3di_3 'palaver, trouble'; u_1di_1 'grave'; u_3di_1 'a town in Nigeria'; Bi., $u_1d\tilde{\imath}_3$ 'the oil palm'
*u*ˈ*kese* (f.)	U., *ukese* 'mashed mandioc'
* ˈ*ula* (f.)	U., *ula* 'bed'; Tl., *ula* 'to be full'; 'to purchase'; K., *ula* 'to break'; B., *ula* pers. n. 'evening'
* *u*ˈ*lalu* (m.)	Kim., *ulalu* pers. n. 'lounging'
* *u*ˈ*lume* (f.)	U., *ulume* pers. n. 'man, husband, male'
*u*ˈ*lusi* (f.)	B., *ulusi* 'to shell, to husk grain'
ˈ*una* (f.)	U., *una* 'that one'
* *u*ˈ*nene* (f.)	K., *unene* pers. n. 'renown, greatness'
*uni*ˈ*kina* (f.)	K., *unikina* 'to listen'
ˈ*unti* (m.)	K., *unti* 'of the nature of a vegetable'
ˈ*unu* (f.)	I., u_3nu_1 'you' (pl.); K., *unu* 'today'
* *u*ˈ*nunu* (f.)	K., *ununu* pers. n. 'old age'
* *uŋ*ˈ*kete* (f.)	K., *uŋkete* pers. n. 'skill, ingenuity'
ˈ*upa* (m.)	U., *upa* 'to remove'
ˈ*ura* (f.)	H., $u{:}_3ra_1$ 'a brownish goat or sheep'
ˈ*uri* (m.)	W., *uri* 'to play in a game, especially one in which hard globules from a bush called *kuri* are used'
* ˈ*usa* (m.)	Gb., *usa* 'the harvest season' (about November); Bi. u_3sa_1 'secret performances forming part of the worship of the deity $ɔ_1xwa_{1-3}hɛ_1$'
ˈ*usi* (f.)	U., *usi* 'a wooden pestle'; Bi., u_1si_3 'starch obtained from cassava'
* *u*ˈ*suku* (f.)	Kim., *usuku* pers. n. 'night'

GULLAH PERSONAL NAMES	WEST AFRICAN WORDS
* *u'ʃita* (f.)	K., *uʃita* pers. n. 'barrenness' (of persons or animals)
'*uta* (m.)	U. and Kim., *uta* 'a gun'; K., *uta* 'to give birth to'
* *u'zeŋga* (f.)	K., *uzeŋga* pers. n. 'foolishness, stupidity'
* *u'zɛbu* (f.)	Bi., *u*$_1$*zɛ*$_1$*bu*$_3$ 'a dance'; 'the quarters of Chief *ɛ*$_3$*zɔ*$_3$*mɔ*$_3$ at Benin City'

w,[43][w]

* *wa* (f.)	Y., *wa*$_3$ 'to search'; 'to divide'; 'to come'; *wa*$_1$ 'to exist'; 'to dig'; 'to pull oars'; E., *wa:*$_1$ 'rushing'; *va*$_3$ 'to come'; *va:*$_1$ 'broad'; *va*$_1$ 'to tighten'; 'to be arrogant'; I., *wa*$_3$ 'to spread the blood of an animal for juju'; 'to split'; 'to rise'; H., *wa:*$_{3-1}$ 'elder brother'; 'son of the father's elder brother'; 'any male older than one's self'; *wa:*$_3$ 'a tree of the ficus family'; B., *wa* 'a plant'; 'to open'; 'to go'; M., *wa* 'large'; K., *va* 'newness, novelty'; U., *wa* 'good'; 'to fall, to spring'; Bi., *wa*$_{1-3}$ 'to spread'; 'to castrate'
'*wabo* (m.)	E., *va*$_1$*bo:*$_1$ 'broad, wide open'
'*wadi* (m.)	Y., *wa*$_3$*di*$_2$ 'to investigate'; K., *vadi* 'small fish'; *wadi* 'a game of odds and evens played with eight small discs usually cut out of a calabash, each having one side white and the other colored'
* '*wafu* (m.)	Kim., *wafu* pers. n. 'He died (is dead)'
'*wagi* (m.)	Y., *wa*$_3$*gi*$_2$ 'to go into the woods for firewood'; *wa*$_1$*gi*$_2$ 'to take soaked corn out of water for grinding'
* '*wahũ* (m.)	Y., *wa*$_3$*hũ*$_1$ pers. n. 'to trill the voice'
'*waɟi* (m.)	Y., *wa*$_3$*ɟi*$_1$ 'blue, dye'; K., *waʒi* 'a skin disease supposed to be due to the disregard of a taboo, e.g., eating something forbidden'
'*waka* (f.)	U., *vaka* 'to fold'
'*waki* (m.)	Y., *wa*$_1$*ki*$_1$ 'to shrink'
* *wa'kore* (m.)	*wakore* 'name of a town and tribe in the French Sudan'
'*wala* (f.)	Y., *wa*$_1$*la:*$_{1-2}$ 'a board used by Mohammedans in writing'; B., *wala*: 'the small board of Mohammedan students'; U., *wala* 'to wear'; M., *vala* 'to rely upon'; K., *vala* 'a black and red lizard'; 'to scrape, to carve in wood'; G., *wa*$_1$*la*$_1$ 'life'
* *wa'laɪpe* (f.)	Y., *wa*$_3$*lai*$_{3-1}$*kpe*$_1$ pers. n. 'to come uninvited'
* *wa'laɪriʃe* (f.)	Y., *wa*$_1$*lai*$_3$*ri*$_2$*ʃe*$_2$ pers. n. 'to be unemployed'

GULLAH PERSONAL NAMES	WEST AFRICAN WORDS
'walanti (m.)	K., *valanti* 'carpenter'
* wa'laye (f.)	Y., $wa_{1}la{:}_{2}ye_{1}$ pers. n. 'to be alive'
'walɛ (m.)	Y., $wa_{3}l\varepsilon_{1}$ 'to become sober' (said of the eyes)
* 'wali (m.)	B., *wali* 'work, act, deed'; H., $wa{:}_{3}li_{1}$ 'a short walk, usually in the cool part of the afternoon'; 'an official position and title'; $wa_{1}li{:}_{2-1}$ 'a pious man'; 'one who gives a girl in marriage'; 'one who has the right to arrange for the burial of a corpse'; V., $va{:}_{2}li_{2-1}$ pers. n. m.; *vali* 'to go off.' Cf. Eng., *Wally*
* 'walo (m.)	Man., *walo* 'bush-fowl (a totem of a caste clan named *sidibe*)'
'walu (f.)	H., $wa{:}_{1}lu{:}_{2}$ 'cassava in prime condition'
wa'luka (m.)	K., *valuka* 'to go, to put at a distance'
'wama (m.)	K., *vama* 'to strike with' (used only by women)
* wa'mɒɪya (f.)	Y., $wa_{1}mai_{3}ya_{1}$ pers. n. 'to embrace'
'wana (f.)	H., $wa{:}_{1}na{:}_{2}$ 'a food consisting of crushed bulrush-millet fried with onions and butter'; K., *vana* 'to give, to spend'; 'to surrender'; *wana* 'to encounter'; 'children'; Kim., *wana* 'four'
wa'nana (m.)	K., *vanana* 'There is nothing'
* 'wanda (f.)	K., *wanda* 'a net'; 'to strike'; *mwanda* pers. n. 'breath, spirit'; Kim., *wanda* 'a net'
* wan'daɟi (m.)	K., *mwandaʒi* pers. n. 'thunder and lightning'
'wande (m.)	E., $\beta an_{1}de{:}_{1}$ 'filthy'
* 'wandɪ (m.)	V., $van_{1}d\text{ɪ}_{1}$ pers. n. m.
* 'wandu (m.)	K., *wandu* 'a small round bean'; *vandu* pers. n. 'baldness, a bald head'
wa'nɛci (f.)	I., $nwa_{3}n_{3}n\varepsilon_{3}\ \varepsilon_{3}t\text{ʃ}i_{3}$ 'day after tomorrow'
* 'wani (m.)	B., *wani* 'a small native footstool'; 'a sliding knot for catching game'; 'removal'; H., $wa{:}_{3}ni{:}_{3}$ 'disdain'; V., $va_{2}ni_{2-1}$ pers. n. m.
wa'nika (f.)	K., *vankia* 'to put on one's shoulder'
* 'wanina (f.)	K., *vanina* pers. n. 'to give'
'wanɟa (f.)	V., $van_{1}d\text{ʒ}a_{1}$ 'an apron made of beads for small girls'; M., *vandʒa* 'a fringe'
* 'waɲa (f.)	E., $\beta a_{1}\text{ɲ}a_{1}$ 'to move'; $\beta a_{1}\text{ɲ}a{:}_{1}$ pers. n. 'ragged'
* 'waŋga (f.)	U., *owaŋga* 'charm, witchcraft'; K., *mbwaŋga* 'a bundle of aromatic and peppery powder used as a cure for headache'; Kim., *waŋga* 'poison, witchcraft'; M., *vaŋga* pers. n. 'a war drum'

GULLAH PERSONAL NAMES	WEST AFRICAN WORDS
* ˈ*waŋgula* (f.)	K., *vaŋgula* 'to mutilate'; U., *vaŋgula* pers. n. 'to talk'
ˈ*wara* (f.)	Y., *wa*$_3$*ra*$_2$ 'to be in a hurry'; *wa*$_1$*ra*$_1$ 'milk'; H., *wa:*$_3$*ɾa*$_1$ 'the West African sea or river eagle'; *wa:*$_1$*ɾa:*$_2$ 'to set apart'
* *waˈrata* (f.)	Man., *warata* pers. n. 'to be large'
waˈraya (f.)	Man., *waraya* 'size'; B., *waraya* 'unsociableness, wildness'
ˈ*ware* (m.)	T., *ware* 'to be tall'; 'a native game'; H., *wa:*$_3$*ɾe*$_1$ 'to separate'
wari (m.)	Y., *wa*$_{3-1}$*ri*$_1$ 'to do homage to a king or a superior'; H., *wa:*$_3$*ɾi*$_1$ 'one of a pair'; *wa:*$_3$*ɾi*$_3$ 'an odor'; 'an ox which, having been broken for work, has been allowed to lapse to herd'; *wa*$_1$*ri:*$_3$ 'a contemporary'; V., *va*$_1$*ri*$_1$ (*va*$_1$*li*$_1$) 'to go off' (said of a trap)
* *waˈruŋki* (m.)	Y., *wa*$_2$*rũ*$_1$*ki*$_1$ pers. n. 'to be stubborn'; lit. 'to make the neck stiff'
ˈ*wasa* (m.)	E., *wa*$_1$*sa:*$_1$ 'bushy, tufted'; H., *wa:*$_1$*sa:*$_2$ 'any kind of play with or without the accompaniment of drumming'; *wa:*$_3$*sa*$_1$ 'to sharpen a knife, sword, etc.'; 'to quicken a horse's pace'; 'to roughen a millstone'; 'to praise, to flatter'; 'to whip pupils with a view to sharpening their wits'; 'to preach to people, ostensibly for their good, but actually with a view to gain'; *wa*$_1$*sa:*$_2$ 'to find fault with'; B., *wasa* 'to be sufficient'
* ˈ*wasi* (m.)	Y., *wa:*$_{3-1}$*si*$_3$ 'a Mohammedan sermon'
ˈ*waʃi* (f.)	K., *vaʃi* 'a splinter, a chip'
ˈ*watɒ* (m.)	Y., *wa*$_2$*tɔ*$_3$ 'to run at the mouth'
ˈ*wawa* (m.)	H., *wa:*$_3$*wa:*$_3$ 'a fool'; 'a cloth of native make worn round the body and thrown over the shoulder'; *wa:*$_3$*wa*$_1$ 'scrambling to obtain possession of a portion of an animal which has been killed'; K., *vava* 'to wish for'; 'necessity'; E., *βa*$_1$*vã*$_{1-3}$ 'a wasp'
ˈ*wawɒ* (m.)	Y., *wa*$_2$*wɔ*$_3$ 'to cease'
waˈwula (f.)	K., *vavula* 'to separate'
* ˈ*waya* (f.)	U., *waya* 'to sow broadcast'; K., *mwaya* pers. n. 'to yawn'
* *waˈyiba* (m. and f.)	Kim., *wayiba* pers. n. 'bad.' Cf. *eye u mɔna wayiba* 'You are a bad son'
we (m.)	Y., *we*$_3$ 'to twist'; 'to plan'; 'to win a child'; E., *we*$_1$ 'sun'; *we*$_3$ 'dance'; U., *ve* 'husband'; K., *ve* 'eyelash'; *ve*! 'No!' Cf. Eng., *way*

GULLAH PERSONAL NAMES	WEST AFRICAN WORDS
* ˈ*weɟe* (m.)	M., *wedʒe* 'visibly, uncovered'; Fn., *gbweɟe* 'the Dahomean goddess of hunting'
* ˈ*weɟi* (m.)	E., *βe*$_1$*ɟi*$_3$ pers. n. 'a shallow place'
ˈ*wela* (f.)	M., *wela* 'to flee'; K., *wela* 'to hunt'; *vela* 'to gather, to pluck'; U., *vela* 'to be sick'; 'to blame'; 'to exceed'
*we*ˈ*laʃɒ* (m.)	Y., *we*$_3$*la*$_2$*ʃɔ*$_2$ 'to wrap with clothes'
ˈ*wele* (m.)	B., *wele* 'appellation, proclamation'; 'to call'; 'a small bell'; E., *ve*$_3$*le*$_1$ 'waxlight'
*we*ˈ*lela* (f.)	K., *velela* 'to be bright, to be clean'; U., *velela* 'to eat a relish with mush'
ˈ*wele*ˈ*wele* (m.)	Y., *we*$_2$*le*$_2$*we*$_2$*le*$_2$ 'quickly, briskly'
ˈ*weli* (m.)	Fn., *weli* 'potato'
ˈ*wema* (f.)	K., *vema* 'to prowl about'
*we*ˈ*mɒna* (f.)	K., *vemɔna* 'to blow about'
ˈ*wena* (f.)	K., *vena* 'to gird up the loin cloth very tightly'; *vwena* 'to stop temporarily'
*wen*ˈ*desa* (f.)	K., *vendesa* 'to miss the mark'
* *we*ˈ*nɒwi* (m. and f.)	E., *ve*$_1$*nɔ*$_1$*vi*$_3$ 'one of twins'
ˈ*wenza* (m.)	K., *venza* 'to grin'
ˈ*weŋgela* (f.)	K., *veŋgela* 'a small green grasshopper'
ˈ*weŋgula* (f.)	K., *veŋgula* 'to push aside'
ˈ*were* (m.)	Y., *we*$_1$*re*$_2$ 'a foolish person'; *we*$_3$*re*$_2$ 'quickly'
ˈ*wete* (m.)	Y., *we*$_3$*te*$_1$ 'a large-sized canoe'
* ˈ*weti* (m.)	Fu., *weti* pers. n. 'early morning'
ˈ*wetɒna* (m.)	K., *vetɔna* 'to pry into'
* ˈ*wetsi* (f.)	E., *ve*$_1$*tsi*$_1$ pers. n. 'rain'
ˈ*wewela* (f.)	K., *vevela* 'to flutter in the wind'
ˈ*weza* (f.)	K., *veza* 'to neglect'
ˈ*wɛlɛ* (m.)	M., *wɛlɛ* 'to stoop'; 'to cover'; 'to recline'; 'to trust in'
ˈ*wɛlɛ*ˈ*wɛlɛ* (f.)	Y., *wɛ*$_3$*lɛ*$_3$*wɛ*$_3$*lɛ*$_3$ 'with ripples'
ˈ*wɛmɒ* (f.)	Y., *wɛ*$_1$*mɔ*$_3$ 'to make clean'; 'to justify'
*wɛ*ˈ*mɒlɛ* (f.)	Y., *wɛ*$_3$*mɔ*$_3$*lɛ*$_1$ 'to crush'
ˈ*wɛna* (f.)	Cf. T., *wyɛnã* 'discontent'
ˈ*wɛnu* (f.)	Y., *wɛ*$_1$*nu*$_1$ 'to cleanse'
ˈ*wɛsi* (m.)	V., *vɛ*$_1$*si*$_1$ 'to sow, to sprinkle'
ˈ*wɛwɒ* (m.)	Y., *wɛ*$_2$*wɔ*$_3$ 'to wash the hands'
* *wi*ˈ*ala* (f.)	U., *viala* pers. n. 'to govern'

GULLAH PERSONAL NAMES	WEST AFRICAN WORDS
wiˈawo (f.)	E., *via*$_3$*wo*$_3$ 'children'
* ˈ*wida* (f.)	Fn., *wida* 'Whydah, a coastal city in Dahomey'
ˈ*widi* (m.)	K., *vidi* 'a nettle'
ˈ*widiˈwidi* (f.)	K., *widiwidi* 'inattention'
ˈ*wifũ* (m.)	Y., *wi*$_3$*fũ*$_3$ 'to tell'
ˈ*wika* (f.)	K., *vwika* 'to dress, to clothe'
wikuˈmuna (f.)	K., *vikumuna* 'to move rapidly, to whirl'
ˈ*wila* (m.)	K., *wila* 'to listen to'; 'to perceive'; *mwila* 'a creek'; *vila* 'to vanish'; 'to bind securely the edge or rim of a basket'; U., *vila* 'to condemn'; Tl., *vila* 'to deny a charge'
wiˈlama (m. and f.)	K., *vilama* 'to be pregnant'
* *wiˈliki* (f.)	Y., *wi*$_1$*li*$_2$*ki*$_2$ pers. n. 'robust'; 'hairy'
* *wiˈluki* (m.)	K., *mviluki* pers. n. 'a penitent'
ˈ*wilula* (f.)	K., *vilula* 'to reverse'
ˈ*wimba* (m.)	K., *vimba* 'to swell'
ˈ*wina* (f.)	K., *vina* 'to tighten'
ˈ*winda* (m.)	K., *mvinda* 'the rim of a basket'; *mwinda* 'a candle, any light'
* ˈ*wĩnĩˈwĩnĩ* (f.)	Y., *wĩ*$_3$*nĩ*$_3$*wĩ*$_3$*nĩ*$_3$ pers. n. 'in fine showers, finely'; Fn., *winiwini* 'fine, thin'
* ˈ*winɒ* (f.)	E., *vi*$_3$*nɔ*$_1$ 'a mother'
ˈ*winza* (f.)	K., *vinza* 'an excuse'
ˈ*wiriˈwiri* (f.)	Y., *wi*$_3$*ri*$_3$*wi*$_3$*ri*$_3$ 'hastily'
ˈ*wisa* (f.)	K., *wisa* 'authority, mastery'; T., *wyisa* 'a species of pepper'; K., *wisa* 'authority, mastery'
ˈ*wiʃi* (f.)	K., *mwiʃi* 'smoke, vapor'
* ˈ*wita* (f.)	K., *vita* pers. n. 'war'; 'to fight'
ˈ*witiˈwiti* (f.)	Y., *wi*$_1$*ti*$_2$*wi*$_1$*ti*$_2$ 'hurriedly'
ˈ*wiwa* (m.)	Y., *wi*$_3$*wa*$_3$ 'the act of coming'; *wi*$_3$*wa*$_1$ 'the fact of being'; K., *viva* 'to cut down'
ˈ*wiwadi* (m.)	Y., *wi*$_3$*wa*$_3$*di*$_2$ 'scrutiny'
* ˈ*wiwi* (m.)	U., *wi*$_3$*wi*$_1$ 'the act of speaking'; E., *vi*$_1$*vi*$_1$ 'darkness, secrecy'; *vi*$_1$*vi*$_3$ pers. n. 'sweetness, agreeable taste'; 'grandchild'; *vi*$_3$*vi*$_3$ 'to be sweet, to be delightful'; K., *wivi* 'dishonesty, theft'
ˈ*wiwɒ̃* (m.)	Y., *wi*$_3$*wɔ̃*$_3$ 'scarcity'; 'rare'
wiˈwɒra (f.)	Y., *wi*$_3$*wɔ*$_3$*ra*$_2$ 'impressive, weighty'
wɒˈbiya (m.)	Y., *wɔ*$_1$*bia*$_1$ 'greed, lasciviousness'

GULLAH PERSONAL NAMES	WEST AFRICAN WORDS
* *wɒḍi* (m.)	E., *wɔ$_1$ḍi$_3$* 'cold'; *wɔ$_1$ḍi$_{1-3}$* 'something done in advance'; *vɔ̃$_3$ḍi$_3$* pers. n. 'bad, ill-natured'
* *wɒɪ* (f.)	V., *va$_2$-i$_2$* 'name of a language and tribe in Liberia'; Y., *wai$_2$* 'at once'; Man., *wai*! 'an interjection expressing astonishment'
ˈ*wɒɪka* (f.)	K., *vaika* 'to escape'; 'to come into view'
* ˈ*wɒɟa* (m.)	Y., *wɔ$_1$ɟa$_1$* pers. n. 'to be engaged in fighting or wrestling'
* ˈ*wɒɟi* (m.)	Y., *wɔ$_2$ɟi$_1$* pers. n. 'to lose color'
*wɒ*ˈ*ɟunu* (m.)	Y., *wɔ$_3$ɟu$_1$nu$_1$* 'to throw away'
ˈ*wɒku*ˈ*wɒku* (m.)	Y., *wɔ$_3$ku$_2$wɔ$_1$ku$_2$* 'zigzag'
ˈ*wɒla* (f.)	K., *vɔla* 'to become cold'
ˈ*wɒle* (m.)	Y., *wɔ$_2$le$_3$* 'to enter a house'; *wɔ$_2$le$_1$* 'to go into the ground'
ˈ*wɒlesa* (f.)	K., *wɔlesa* 'to decompose'; 'to cause to decompose'
ˈ*wɒli* (m.)	M., *wɔli* 'pewter'; 'a pewter basin'
* ˈ*wɒli*ˈ*wɒli* (f.)	E., *wɔ$_1$li$_1$wɔ$_1$li$_1$* pers. n. 'soft'
*wɒlɒ*ˈ*mɒna* (f.)	K., *wɔlɔmɔna* 'to break'; 'to boil to pieces'
ˈ*wɒmi* (f.)	Y., *wɔ$_3$mi$_2$* 'to go into the water'; 'to fail'
ˈ*wɒmi*ˈ*wɒmi* (f.)	Y., *wɔ$_2$mi$_2$wɔ$_2$mi$_2$* 'a diver'
*wɒ*ˈ*mɒna* (f.)	K., *vɔmɔna* 'to beat with a club'
*wɒn*ˈ*desa* (f.)	K., *vɔndesa* 'to help to kill'
*wɒn*ˈ*titi* (f.)	Y., *wɔ̃$_1$ti$_1$ti$_1$* 'plentifully'
ˈ*wɒnu* (f.)	Y., *wɔ$_2$nu$_3$* 'to enter'; E., *wɔ$_1$nu$_3$* 'fertile, efficient'
* ˈ*wɒŋgɒ* (f.)	M., *wɔŋgɒ* pers. n. 'to worship twins, giving them oil and salt whenever there is a new moon'
ˈ*wɒra* (m.)	Y., *wɔ$_2$ra$_2$* 'to act by force of habit'; 'deeply'
ˈ*wɒsɛ* (m.)	G., *wɔ$_3$sɛː$_1$* 'day after tomorrow, any time in the future,' lit. 'back of tomorrow'
ˈ*wɒsi* (f.)	Y., *wɔ$_3$si$_3$* 'to move away'; *wɔ$_1$si$_3$* 'to lodge at, to stay in'
ˈ*wɒʃɒ* (f.)	Y., *wɔ$_2$ʃɔ$_2$* 'to dress'
ˈ*wɒta* (m.)	K., *vɔta* 'to mash, to knead'
ˈ*wɒtɒna* (f.)	K., *wɔtɔna* 'to make grimaces'
ˈ*wɒtsi* (f.)	E., *wɔ$_3$tsi$_3$* 'flour and water mixed'; 'a beverage'
wɒʊ (m.)	K., *mwau* 'a small pudding consisting of cassava root beaten into flour'; *vau* 'theirs'
ˈ*wɒwɒ* (m.)	Y., *wɔ$_1$wɔ$_2$* 'copious'; E., *wɔ$_1$wɔ$_1$* 'the act of doing'; *vɔ$_{3-1}$vɔ$_1$* 'insipid'; *vɔ$_1$vɔ̃$_1$* 'fear, apprehension'; K., *mvɔvɔ* 'speech, matter under discussion'

GULLAH PERSONAL NAMES	WEST AFRICAN WORDS
ˈ*wɔ̃wɔ̃* (m.)	Y., *wɔ̃*:$_{3-1}$*wɔ̃*:$_{3-1}$ 'a wart'
*wo*ˈ*balɛ* (f.)	Y., *wo*$_3$*ba*$_2$*lɛ*$_1$ 'to break, to pull down'
* *wo*ˈ*du* (m.)	Fn., *vodũ* 'a spirit (good or bad) intermediary between God and man'; 'a deity'; E., *vo*$_1$*du*$_3$ 'tutelary deity, demon'
* *wo*ˈ*dusi* (m.)	E., *vo*$_1$*du*$_3$*si*$_1$ 'a priest of a *vo*$_1$*du*$_3$'
* *wo*ˈ*ele* (f.)	E., *woe*$_1$*le*$_1$ pers. n. 'forenoon'; 'afternoon'
ˈ*wofi* (f.)	H., *wo*:$_1$*fi*:$_2$ 'something useless'; *wo*:$_3$*fi*$_1$ 'conception (in womb)'; Y., *wo*$_1$*fĩ*$_3$ 'to look into closely'
*wo*ˈ*firi* (f.)	Y., *wo*$_1$*fi*$_2$*ri*$_3$ 'to glance over, to see with half an eye'
* *wo*ˈ*ɟina* (f.)	Y., *wo*$_1$*ɟi*$_2$*na*$_3$ pers. n. 'to heal a wound'; *wo*$_1$*ɟi*$_1$*na*$_1$ 'to look afar'
* *woka*ˈ*kiri* (f.)	Y., *wo*$_1$*ka*:$_{2-3}$*ki*$_3$*ri*$_3$ pers. n. 'to look around'
* *wo*ˈ*kɔrɔ* (f.)	Y., *wo*$_1$*kɔ*$_1$*rɔ*$_1$ pers. n. 'to look sullen'
ˈ*wola* (m.)	Fn., *wola* 'a depository'; 'to conserve'; 'to conceal'
* *wo*ˈ*leha* (f.)	Man., *woleha* pers. n. 'one of the divisions of the day (8:00–9:00 A.M.)' (Ar.)
ˌ*woleya*ˈ*tina* (f.)	Man., *woleatina* 'that is why'
* *wo*ˈ*li* (m.)	Y., *wo*$_1$*li*:$_{2-1}$ pers. n. 'a prophet'
ˈ*wolo* (f.)	E., *vo*$_1$*lo*$_1$ 'afterbirth'
ˈ*woni* (m.)	B., *woni* 'a small hole'
ˈ*wora* (f.)	Y., *wo*$_2$*ra*$_2$ 'to cure one's self of a disease'; 'to be a glutton'; T., *wora* 'to hide one's self'; H., *wo*$_1$*ɽa*:$_2$ 'making ridges in a farm for sowing'
* ˈ*wosũ* (m.)	Y., *wo*$_1$*sũ*$_2$ (*wo*$_1$*su*:$_2$) pers. n. 'to be absent-minded'; *wo*$_1$*sũ*$_1$ 'to observe intently'
ˈ*woye* (m.)	Y., *wo*$_1$*ye*$_2$ 'to observe'; T., *awoe*: 'place of childbirth'
wũ (m.)	Y., *wũ*$_2$ 'to weave, to knit'
*wu*ˈ*bika* (f.)	K., *wubika* 'to immerse, to plunge into'; 'to allow one to take a great quantity of something'
* ˈ*wugbɒ* (m.)	Y., *wu*$_3$*gbɔ*$_2$ pers. n. 'to be sullen'
* ˈ*wuɟi* (m.)	Fn., *wuɟi* pers. n. 'astonishment'
* ˈ*wula* (f.)	U., *wula* 'to be shriveled'; 'to follow' (as a slave or vassal); K., *wula* 'to crush'; *vula* 'to strip'; *mvula* pers. n. 'rain'
ˈ*wule* (f.)	M., *wule* 'to sing'
ˈ*wuli* (m.)	B., *wuli* 'to lift'; 'to disperse'; 'to boil'; 'to burst'; E., *βu*$_3$*li*$_1$ 'a rat'; *vu*$_1$*li*$_1$ 'a tobacco plant'; W., *vuli* 'to give a drubbing'

GULLAH PERSONAL NAMES	WEST AFRICAN WORDS
ˈ*wulo* (m.)	Y., wu_3lo_1 ‘useful’
* ˈ*wulula* (f.)	K., *vulula* pers. n. ‘to rescue from great danger to life’
* ˈ*wuluza* (f.)	K., *vuluza* pers. n. ‘to rescue’
ˈ*wumbe* (m.)	E., βum_1be_{1-3} ‘a soup prepared with blood’
ˈ*wumbisa* (m.)	K., *vumbisa* ‘to let out water’
ˈ*wumina* (f.)	K., *vumina* ‘to fear, to respect’
ˈ*wumisa* (f.)	K., *wumisa* ‘to dry’; ‘to cause to dry’; *vumisa* ‘to intimidate’
* ˈ*wumuna* (f.)	K., *vumuna* pers. n. ‘to breathe’
* ˈ*wuna* (f.)	K., *wuna* pers. n. ‘to complain, to groan’; ‘a complaint’
* ˈ*wuni* (f.)	Y., wu_2ni_2 ‘to please’; H., wu_3ni_1 ‘the period from sunrise to sunset’; ‘to spend the day’
* ˈ*wunina* (f.)	K., *vunina* pers. n. ‘to defame’
* ˈ*wunisa* (f.)	K., *vunisa* pers. n. ‘to distrust’
* ˈ*wunɟɒ* (m.)	Y., $w\tilde{u}_2ɟɔ_2$ pers. n. ‘to have wrinkles’
ˈ*wunza* (m.)	K., *wunza* ‘to examine gently something painful or fragile’; *vunza* ‘to forsake’
wuŋˈgisa (m.)	K., *vuŋgisa* ‘to make exceedingly ashamed’; ‘great shame’
wuˈrara (f.)	Cf. Man., *i wurara* ‘good evening’
wuˈruku (m.)	Y., $wu_2ru_2ku_2$ ‘crooked’
ˈ*wusa* (m.)	T., *wusa* ‘Guinea grain’
ˈ*wusĩ* (m.)	Y., $wu_3s\tilde{i}_1$ ‘serviceable’
ˈ*wuta* (m.)	K., *wuta* ‘to give birth to’; ‘to generate’
ˈ*wutulula* (f.)	K., *wutulula* ‘to produce anew, to regenerate’
* ˈ*wuwo* (m.)	Y., wu_3wo_2 pers. n. ‘heavy’
ˈ*wuwu* (m.)	E., $\beta u_1\beta u_1$ ‘brain’; ‘dust’; $\beta u_3\beta u_3$ ‘to be agitated’; ‘to strew’; vu_3vu_3 ‘to be tattered’; ‘to tear’; K., *vuvu* ‘hope, expectation’
ˈ*wuye* (m.)	Y., wu_3ye_1 ‘to perform initial ceremonies on assuming a title’
ˈ*wuza* (m.)	K., *vuza* ‘to root up, to come out, to fall off’

y [j]

* *ya* (f.)	Y., ya_3 ‘ready, early, quick’; ya_1 ‘to separate, to give way’; ya_2 ‘to tear’; Bi., ya_3 ‘to use for a certain purpose’; E., ya_1 ‘to tear’; ‘to strike’; ya_3 ‘to rot’; $ya{:}_1$ ‘insipid’; $ya{:}_3$ ‘air, wind, scent’; Mand., *ya* ‘name given the second daughter’

GULLAH PERSONAL NAMES	WEST AFRICAN WORDS
ˈ*yabi* (m.)	W., *yabi* 'to be infused'
ˈ*yade* (f.)	H., *ya*:$_3$'*de*$_1$ 'to spread over'
* ˈ*yadi* (m.)	Y., *ya*$_2$*di*$_2$ pers. n. 'to be dumb'; *ya*$_3$*di*$_2$ 'to be licentious'
ˈ*yago* (m.)	Y., *ya*$_1$*go*$_1$ 'to avoid'; 'to give way'; H., *ya*:$_2$*go*:$_2$ 'to tear'
*ya*ˈ*kata* (f.)	Y., *ya*$_1$*ka*$_1$*ta*$_1$ 'to bestride'
* ˈ*yakɒ* (m.)	Y., *ya*$_2$*kɔ*$_2$ pers. n. 'to be a male'; 'to be odd'
* ˈ*yakpa* (m.)	Y., *ya*$_1$*kpa*$_1$ pers. n. 'wasteful, prodigal'
*ya*ˈ*kuro* (f.)	Y., *ya*$_1$*ku*$_3$*ro*$_1$ 'to separate from'
ˈ*yala* (f.)	Y., *ya*$_1$*la*$_1$ 'luxuriously'; H., *ya*:$_3$*la*$_1$ 'the skin which adheres to the interior of an eggshell'; K., *yala* 'to spread'; 'to rule'; 'to menstruate'; B., *yala* 'to yawn'; 'to go for a walk'; U., *yala* 'to spread'
* ˈ*yali* (f.)	E., *ya*$_1$*li*$_1$ 'a whirlwind'; *ya*$_1$*li*$_3$ 'frivolous'; M., *yali* 'any person of whom another is a guest'
* *ya*ˈ*limɛ* (f.)	E., *ya*$_1$*li*$_3$*mɛ*$_{1-3}$ pers. n. 'a frivolous person'
*ya*ˈ*lɒfa* (m.)	Y., *ya*$_3$*lɔ*$_3$*fa*$_1$ 'to obtain as a pawn'
*ya*ˈ*lɒtɒ* (m.)	Y., *ya*$_1$*lɔ*$_3$*tɔ*$_1$ 'to set apart, to make a difference between'
*yalu*ˈ*muna* (f.)	K., *yalumuna* 'to spread out'; 'to raise, to put up' (used in reference to an umbrella)
*yambi*ˈ*disa* (m.)	K., *yambidisa* 'to cause to commit adultery'
* ˈ*yambɒ* (m.)	Y., *yã*$_2$*bɔ*$_2$ pers. n. 'hard to please'
ˈ*yãmũ*ˈ*yãmũ* (m.)	Y., *yã*$_1$*mũ*$_1$*yã*$_2$*mũ*$_3$ 'a mosquito'
ˈ*yanda* (m.)	H., *yan*$_1$*da*:$_2$ 'a covering for a doorway made of plaited strings'; U., *yanda* 'to spread'; 'to do good far and wide'; K., *yanda* 'to stretch and fasten the skin on a drum'; 'to spread out to dry'
* ˈ*yande* (m. and f.)	W., *yande* pers. n. f.
ˈ*yandi* (m.)	Y., *yã*$_3$*di*$_2$ 'sensual'; *yã*$_2$*di*$_1$ 'to keep malice'; H., *yan*$_3$*di*$_1$ 'a large ficus tree'
ˈ*yanɟa* (m.)	Y., *yã*$_2$*ɟa*$_2$ 'to dry fish over the fire'
ˈ*yanɟɛ* (m.)	Y., *yã*$_1$*ɟɛ*$_2$ 'to cheat'
*yan*ˈ*ribo* (m.)	Y., *yã*$_3$*ri*$_2$*bo*$_2$ 'a species of beetle'
ˈ*yanrin* (m.)	Y., *yã*$_2$*rĩ*$_1$ 'sand'; *yã*:$_2$*rĩ*$_1$ 'a disease among fowls affecting their mouths'; *yã*$_3$*rĩ*$_2$ 'an edible herb'
ˈ*yanza* (m.)	K., *yanza* 'to tear to pieces with the teeth'
ˈ*yanzu* (m.)	H., *yan*$_1$*zu*:$_2$ 'now, in a very short time'
* ˈ*yaram* (m.)	W., *yaram* 'body'; *ya*:*ram* pers. n. 'a prince'

GULLAH PERSONAL NAMES	WEST AFRICAN WORDS
ˈ*yari* (f.)	Y., ya_2ri_3 'to comb the hair'
ˈ*yaro* (f.)	Y., ya_2ro_3 'to retaliate'
ˈ*yasɛ* (f.)	Y., $ya_3sɛ_1$ 'light-footed'
* ˈ*yate* (m.)	Tem., *yate* 'a Temne family name'
* ˈ*yawa* (f.)	E., ya_3wa_3 (ya_1wa_3) pers. n. 'name given a girl born on Thursday'
yawaˈlala (f.)	K., *yawalala* 'to sprawl'
ˈ*yawɒ* (m.)	Y., $ya_3wɔ_3$ 'to be quick, to be fast'
* ˈ*yawo* (m.)	Y., ya_3wo_3 'to borrow money'; $i_1ya_2wo_3$ 'wife'; E., ya_1wo_3 (ya_3wo_3) 'name given a boy born on Thursday'
* ˈ*yaya* (f.)	Y., ya_1ya_3 'a necklace of beads'; ya_2ya_2 'plentifully'; ya_3ya_3 'vehemently'; U., *yaya* 'to be awkward'; 'to moisten'; Fn., *yaya* 'a baby'; 'simple'; K., *yaya* 'to hiss, to murmur'; 'fame'; 'to be well known'; 'mother'; 'maternal relatives'; 'to bail out'; Tl., *yaya* 'a title of respect for a sister older than one's self'; Mand., *ya:ya* 'John the Baptist'
ˈ*yayɒ* (f.)	Y., $ya_2yɔ_1$ 'to rejoice'
ˈ*yekã* (m.)	Y., $ye_1kã_2$ 'a relative'
yekɒˈlɒla (f.)	K., *yekɔlɔla* 'to reinstate in office'
* ˈ*yela* (f.)	U., *yela* pers. n. 'to be clean, to be pure'; M., *yela* 'one'; K., *yela* 'to be ill'; 'illness'; 'to be guilty, to be overcome'
ˈ*yelesa* (f.)	K., *yelesa* 'to nurse'; 'to defeat, to condemn'
* ˈ*yemaɟa* (f.)	Y., $ye_2ma_2ɟa_2$ 'the goddess of brooks'
* ˈ*yende* (m.)	Fu., *yende* pers. n. 'a storm'
ˈ*yere* (f.)	B., *yere* 'to shine brightly'; 'same'; 'very own'; 'absolutely'; T., *yere* 'to spread, to stretch, to strain'
yeˈrema (m.)	B., *yerema* 'one's self, in one's own right'
* ˈ*yese* (f.)	M., *yese* pers. n. 'first'
* *yeˈtunde* (m.)	Y., $ye_3tũ_3de_3$ 'name given a female child born after the death of its grandmother,' lit. 'Mother comes again.' (See $ba_2ba_2tũ_3de_3$)
* ˈ*yewa* (m.)	K., *yeva* pers. n. 'to be stout'
* ˈ*yeye* (m. and f.)	Y., ye_1ye_3 'mother'
ˈ*yɛɟu* (m.)	Y., $yɛ_2ɟu_3$ 'to avert one's gaze, to withdraw'
* ˈ*yɛlɛ* (m.)	M., *yɛlɛ* pers. n. 'to ridicule'
ˈ*yɛmu* (m.)	Y., $yɛ_3mu_2$ 'to be intoxicated with palm wine'
yɛˈpɛrɛ (m.)	Y., $yɛ_2kpɛ_2rɛ_2$ 'insignificant'

GULLAH PERSONAL NAMES	WEST AFRICAN WORDS
ˈ*yɛra* (f.)	Y., $yɛ_2ra_2$ 'to shun'
ˈ*yɛri* (f.)	Y., $yɛ_2ri_3$ 'to refuse to take responsibility'; $yɛ_1ri_1$ 'a lady's undergarment'
ˈ*yɛri*ˈ*yɛri* (f.)	Y., $yɛ_3ri_3yɛ_3ri_3$ 'brightly'; $yɛ_3ri_2yɛ_3ri_2$ 'having the color of ashes'
*yɛ*ˈ*silɛ* (f.)	Y., $yɛ_1si_3lɛ_1$ 'to avoid'
ˈ*yɛwu* (m.)	Y., $yɛ_1wu_1$ 'the dark part of a room, the private room of a house'
ˈ*yiba* (f.)	K., *yiba* 'to steal'; 'to copulate'
ˈ*yibori* (f.)	Y., $yi_3bo_2ri_3$ 'to cover the head,' lit. 'to pull the head-covering over the head'
ˈ*yidisa* (m.)	K., *yidisa* 'to boil'; 'to cause to boil'
ˈ*yika* (f.)	Y., yi_3ka_2 'to surround'; 'roundabout'; K., *yika* 'to name, to talk about'; 'to add'
*yi*ˈ*kaŋkiri* (f.)	Y., $yi_3ka{:}_{2-1}ki_2ri_2$ 'to surround'
ˈ*yila* (f.)	U., *yila* 'to shut'; K., *yila* 'to boil'; 'to purr'; 'to begin to grow dark'
ˈ*yilo* (f.)	Fn., *yilo* (*yulo*) 'to call, to go for'
ˈ*yima* (f.)	K., *yima* 'to bear fruit'
ˈ*yimbɒ* (m.)	Y., $y\tilde{\imath}_1b\tilde{ɔ}_2$ 'to fire a gun'
*yi*ˈ*misa* (f.)	K., *yimisa* 'to fructify'
ˈ*yina* (f.)	K., *yina* 'to complain'; 'complaint'
*yi*ˈ*nisa* (f.)	K., *yinisa* 'to cause to complain'
*yi*ˈ*pada* (m.)	Y., $yi_3kpa_2da_1$ 'to turn over'
ˈ*yipo* (m.)	Y., yi_3kpo_2 'to turn upside down'
ˈ*yiri* (f.)	Man., *yiri* 'wooden'; T., *yiri* 'to overflow'
ˈ*yiro* (m.)	Man., *yiro* 'a tree'
*ˈ*yiwa* (f.)	K., *yiva* pers. n. 'to grow ugly'
ˈ*yiya* (m.)	Y., yi_3ya_3 'quick'
ˈ*yiyan* (m.)	Y., $yi_3y\tilde{a}_1$ 'choice'; 'preferable'; $yi_3y\tilde{a}_3$ 'neighing'; $yi_3y\tilde{a}_2$ 'the act of boasting'
ˈ*yiyɒ* (m.)	Y., $yi_3yɔ_1$ 'slippery'
yɒ (m.)	Y., $yɔ_3$ 'to melt'; $yɔ_1$ 'to be pleased with'; 'to rejoice'; 'to be slippery'; $yɔ_2$ 'to dismiss'; E., $yɔ_1$ 'to press together'; 'to smoke'; 'to hasten'; $yɔ_3$ 'a grave'; 'a tick'; 'a louse'; 'abdomen'; 'to call'; 'to be full'; 'to fill'; I., $yɔ_3$ 'to return'
*ˈ*yɒbun* (m.)	Y., $yɔ_1b\tilde{u}_1$ pers. n. 'to be untidy'
*ˈ*yɔdɛ* (m.)	Y., $yɔ_1dɛ_1$ pers. n. 'to be of low intelligence'

GULLAH PERSONAL NAMES	WEST AFRICAN WORDS
ˈ*yɒɟu* (m.)	Y., $yɔ_2ɟu_3$ 'to make an appearance'
yɒˈɟusi (m.)	Y., $yɔ_2ɟu_3si_2$ 'to look unto'
ˈ*yɒka* (m.)	K., *yɔka* 'to burn'
ˈ*yɒmba* (m.)	W., *yɔmba* 'pumpkin'
ˈ*yɒmbɒ* (m.)	V., $yɔm_3bɔ_3$ 'dainty, delicious food'
ˈ*yɒnɛ* (f.)	W., *yɔnɛ* 'to send off'
ˈ*yɒni* (f.)	W., *yɔni* 'to send'
ˈ*yɒŋga* (f.)	K., *yɔŋga* 'to copulate'
ˈ*yɒri* (f.)	Y., $yɔ_2ri_3$ 'to be completed'; 'to be successful, to rise higher, to show the head'
* *yɔriˈsɔla* (f.)	Y., $yɔ_2ri_3sɔ_3la_3$ pers. n. 'to achieve honor'; lit. 'to put the head into honor'
* ˈ*yɒtɒˈyɒtɒ* (m.)	Y., $yɔ_1tɔ_2yɔ_1tɔ_2$ pers. n. 'stout, fat'
ˈ*yɒwɒna* (f.)	K., *yɔvɔna* 'to weaken'; 'to tire'
* *yɒʊ* (m.)	T., *yau*[44] 'name given a boy born on Thursday'
* ˈ*yɒʊda* (m.)	T., *yauda*[45] 'Thursday'
ˈ*yɒwo* (m.)	Y., $yɔ_2wo_3$ 'to cause the seller of an article to lower his price'
ˈ*yɒyɛ* (m.)	Y., $yɔ_2yɛ_3$ 'extraordinary'
ˈ*yɒyɒ* (m.)	Y., $yɔ_2yɔ_2$ 'minnows'; 'plentifully'
yo (m.)	Y., yo_3 'to be full, to be satisfied with food or riches'; E., $yo{:}_3$ 'an interjection of assent'; 'a reply to a call'; M., *yo* 'yes'; H., $yo{:}_{3-1}$ 'a reply by villagers to a call'; 'an expression of uncertainty'
ˈ*yoba* (m.)	Y., $yo{:}_{3-1}ba_2$ 'a falsehood'
ˈ*yola* (f.)	U., *yola* 'to laugh'; M., *yola* 'thick and turned back' (used in reference to the lips)
* ˈ*yoŋki* (m.)	Fu., *yoŋki* pers. n. 'life'
ˈ*yoro* (f.)	Y., yo_2ro_2 'to dissolve'
ˈ*yoyo* (f.)	Fn., *yoyo* 'new-fangled'; 'something new'; H., $yo_1yo{:}_2$ 'a leak, a dripping'; E., $a_1yo_1yo_1$ 'a talker, a tattler'; T., *yo:yo:* 'noise, tumult'
* ˈ*yoyoyo* (f.)	E., $yo_1yo_1yo_1$ pers. n. 'dripping.' Cf. e_3le_1 nu_3 Φom_3 $yo_1yo_1yo_1$ 'He is talkative'
yũ (f.)	Y., $yũ_3$ 'pregnant'; 'to scratch'; 'to itch'; $yũ_1$ 'to cut, to saw'
yuˈela (f.)	U., *yuela* 'to gabble, to dispute'
ˈ*yukuta* (m.)	K., *yukuta* 'to be satisfied (especially with reference to food)'

GULLAH PERSONAL NAMES	WEST AFRICAN WORDS
ˈ*yulo* (f.)	Fn., *yulo* (*yilo*) 'to call, to go for'
ˈ*yuna* (f.)	K., *yuna* 'to skin, to flay'
ˈ*yuya* (f.)	K., *yuya* 'to burn with a roar'

[z]

GULLAH PERSONAL NAMES	WEST AFRICAN WORDS
* ˈ*zakama* (m.)	K., *zakama* pers. n. 'to shake, to be agitated'
* ˈ*zala* (f.)	K., *zala* 'to fill, to rise' (as the tide); 'fingernail'; 'to hem'; 'a fringe'; *nzala* 'hunger, appetite'; Kim., *nzala* pers. n. 'hunger'
zaˈlama (f.)	K., *zalama* 'to perch, to settle'
zaˈlela (f.)	Kim., *zalela* 'to stretch'
ˈ*zama* (f.)	K., *zama* 'to settle'; H., *za*$_3$*ma:*$_3$ 'a settling-down'; *za:*$_3$*ma*$_1$ 'good luck'; *za:*$_1$*ma:*$_2$ 'to deprive a person of his proper share'
* ˈ*zambi* (m.)	Kim., *nzambi* 'God'; K., *nzambi* 'God'
ˈ*zambu* (m.)	K., *zambu* 'a branch of one tree that extends to the branches of another, thus affording a climber the means of passing from one tree to another without descending to the ground'; *nzambu* 'a monkey, any animal that climbs a tree or lives in the branches of trees'; 'freight, toll for a bridge or ferry'
* ˈ*zandu* (m.)	K., *nzandu* 'to get into trouble'
ˈ*zanza* (m.)	K., *zanza* 'to cause to fall heavily'; 'to dash to the ground'
ˈ*zaŋga* (m.)	K., *zaŋga* 'to soil'; 'to defecate' (used in reference to babies only)
* ˈ*zawi* (m.)	E., *zã*$_1$*vi*$_3$ 'a free-born person'; 'weeping at night'
zaˈwuna (f.)	K., *zavuna* 'to seize, to take away' (with the hands only)
ˈ*zaya* (f.)	K., *zaya* 'to comprehend'
ˈ*zãzɒzɒ* (m.)	E., *zã*$_3$*zɔ*$_1$*zɔ*$_1$ 'traveling at night, going about at night'
ˈ*zeɟi* (m.)	K., *zeʒi* 'to come'; 'arrival'
ˈ*zekeˈzeke* (m.)	K., *nzekezeke* 'the boring beetle'
ˈ*zela* (f.)	Kim., *zela* 'to be pale'
* *zelolo* (m.)	E., *ze*$_3$*lo*$_1$*lo*$_1$ pers. n.
ˈ*zemba* (f.)	K., *zemba* 'hatred, contempt'
ˈ*zenda* (f.)	K., *zenda* 'to be twisted'
* ˈ*zenza* (f.)	K., *zenza* pers. n. 'to be sweet'; *nzenza* 'a foreigner, a stranger'
ˈ*zeŋgi* (m.)	K., *nzeŋgi* 'a judge'

GULLAH PERSONAL NAMES	WEST AFRICAN WORDS
zi'defo (f.)	Cf. E., $dzi_1de_3fo_1$ 'courage, confidence'
'*zimbu*[46] (m.)	Cf. K., *nʒimbu* 'money, beads'
* '*zina* (f.)	V., zi_1na_1 pers. n. m. and f.; H., $zi{:}_3na_1$ 'any kind of ornamentation'; $zi_1na{:}_2$ 'adultery'
zin'demba (m.)	Cf. Kim., *zindemba* (pl. of *ndemba* 'hair')
'*ziwi* (m.)	Cf. E., $a_1zi_1vi_3$ 'child'
zɒ (m.)	E., $zɔ_1$ 'to walk'; 'base, support'; $zɔ_{1-3}$ 'a large pot for storing water, oil, or palm wine'; K., *zɔ* 'a tuft of grass, plants, or hair'; 'the place on which a single plant grows'
* '*zɒdi* (m.)	K., *nzɔdi* pers. n. 'a lover'
zɒɪ (m.)	K., *zai* 'knowledge, intelligence'
'*zɒka* (m.)	K., *zɔka* 'to bore a hole'; *nzɔka* 'a fathom and a half'; 'two fathoms' (in the dialect of the Bakongo)
* '*zɒla* (f.)	K., *zɔla* pers. n. 'to love, to long for'
* zɒ'*lani* (m.)	K., *nzɔlani* pers. n. 'mutual affection'
* '*zɒleswa* (f.)	K., *zɔleswa* pers. n. 'to have an intense desire for something, thought to be caused by a charm, or, in the case of pregnancy, by that condition'
'*zɒma* (m.)	K., *zɔma* 'to copulate'
'*zɒnda* (m.)	K., *zɔnda* 'to be half-released' (as in the case of the spring of a trap which has caught something)
* '*zɒnɟi* (m.)	K., *nzɔnʒi* pers. n. 'a quarrelsome person'; 'a quarrel'; 'a small scaly fish'; cf. Fn., *zoɟi* 'god of the earth'
* '*zɒnza* (m.)	K., *zɔnza* pers. n. 'to quarrel'; 'strife'; *nzɔnza* 'a quarrel'; 'a pole laid across a stream to serve as a bridge'
'*zɒti* (m.)	E., $zɔ_1ti_3$ 'a walking stick'
'*zɒʊla* (f.)	K., *zaula* 'to take up with a scoop'
'*zɒwa* (m.)	K., *zɔwa* 'to knead, to make a paste of'; 'folly, lunacy'
'*zɒzɒ* (m.)	K., *zɔzɔ* 'bill, beak'
* *zo* (f.)	E., zo_{1-3} (dzo_{1-3}) 'a horn'; V., zo_3 pers. n. f.; zo_2 'the wearer of the mask in the Sande Society'; B., *zo:* 'rust, verdigris'; 'smallpox'
* '*zoru* (m.)	V., zo_2ru_2 pers. n. m.
* '*zozo* (m.)	H., $zo{:}_1zo{:}_2$ 'the cartilage at the base of the nose between the nostrils'; V., zo_3zo_3 pers. n. 'joy, merriment'
* *zu'ana* (f.)	Kim., *nzuana* pers. n. f. Cf. P., *Joana* [ʒuana]

GULLAH PERSONAL NAMES	WEST AFRICAN WORDS
ˈ*zuka* (m.)	K., *zuka* 'to strike'; 'to pay interest'; Bo., *zuka* 'to roar'; *zu:ka* 'to be inflamed'
* ˈ*zumbi* (m.)	K., *zumbi* 'a fetish supposed to bring good luck'
ˈ*zuna* (f.)	K., *zuna* 'to cut off a small portion of something edible'
ˈ*zunta* (m.)	K., *zunta* 'to wring off'; 'to take aim'; 'aim'
ˈ*zunza* (m.)	K., *zunza* 'to smelt, to fuse'
zuŋgaˈnisa (f.)	K., *zuŋganisa* 'to whirl, to brandish'
ˈ*zuŋgu* (m.)	K., *nzuŋgu* 'a curve'; 'difficulty, pain'; 'a cauldron'
ˈ*zura* (f.)	H., $zu{:}_1ra{:}_2$ 'a hoe'; $zu{:}_3ra_1$ 'tyranny'
zuwa (f.)	H., zu_3wa_1 'arrival'; K., *zua* 'to break off by a violent motion'; *nzua* 'the act of frowning'
zuˈzuna (m.)	K., *zuzuna* 'to tear off a piece' (used especially with reference to food)

OTHER WORDS USED IN CONVERSATION

[a]

aˈdobɛ 'a kind of grass used for covering roofs'	T., *adobɛ* 'a species of palm tree, the leaves of which, called *daha*, are used to cover roofs'
agoˈgo 'cowbell'	Y., $a_2go_2go_2$ 'a bell'; 'a metal musical instrument made in the shape of a cowbell'
aˈmin (*aˈmina*) 'amen'	W., *amin* 'amen'; V. and Kp., $a_2mi{:}_2na_2$ 'amen'; B., *amina* 'amen'
ˈ*anduɲu* 'I was not with you'	W., *anduɲu* 'We not unite'

[b]

ban! 'It is done!'	V., ban_1 'to be finished' (a_3 ban_1 'It is finished'); B., *ban* 'to be finished'; 'to finish'; 'the end'
baŋ (ˈ*baŋˌbaŋ*) 'a term imitative of the sound of beating'	V., $gba\eta_3$ ($gba\eta_3gba\eta_3$) 'loudly'; M., *baŋgo-baŋgo* 'noisily'
ˈ*bara* (ˈ*bala*) 'xylophone'	B., *bala* (*bara*) 'xylophone'; Mand., *bala* (*bala:*) 'xylophone'
be 'to clean, to remove debris' (used in the phrase *be dɪ grɒun* 'clean the ground')	W., *bɛi* 'to cultivate, to prepare the ground for planting'
ˈ*beɲto* 'a wooden box in which a dead person is buried'	Tem., *bento* (*bentro*) 'a rafter bier made of sticks on which a corpse is carried'

beŋ 'a rabbit'	Cf. G., *kplẽŋ*$_1$*kplẽ*$_{2-1}$ 'a rabbit'; *kpĩŋ*$_1$ 'a wild guinea pig' (frequently used carelessly for *rabbit*)
ˈ*bɛble* 'to deceive'	E., *be*$_1$*ble*$_1$ 'deceit, untruthfulness'; *be*$_1$-*ble*$_{1-3}$ 'deceived'
ˈ*bɛne* 'benne, the sesame'	W., *bɛne* 'the sesame'; B., *bene* 'the sesame.' Cf. Eng., *benne* (*benny*)
ˈ*bidi*ˈ*bidi* 'a small bird'; 'a small chicken'	K., *bidibidi* 'a bird.' Cf. Eng., *biddy-biddy* 'a small chicken'
bim$_{3-1}$ 'violently'; 'a term imitative of the sound of beating'	T., *bim*$_3$ 'the sound of beating or striking'; *bim*$_1$ 'violently'
ˈ*bɪnda* 'a kite'	V., *bɪn*$_1$*da*$_3$ 'a kite, sail, or anything that is carried by the wind'
ˈ*bɒbɒbɒ* 'a woodpecker'	K., *mbɔbɔbɔ* 'a woodpecker'
ˈ*bɒma* 'a large brownish snake'	K., *mbɔma* 'the black python'
ˈ*bɒndɒ* 'a basket made of palmetto straw or of marsh grass and sewed with palmetto'	K., *mbɔndɔ* 'a large basket'
boɲ 'tooth'	W., *boɲ* 'tooth'
ˈ*bʌkrə* (*bʌ*$_1$*krʌ*$_3$) 'white man'	Ib. and Ef., *m*$_1$*ba*$_1$*ka*$_2$*ra*$_2$ 'white man,' lit. 'he who surrounds or governs'
bu 'dead'	Dj., *bu* 'dead'
ˈ*bubu* 'any insect' (usually one whose sting is poisonous)	V., *b'u*$_1$*b'u*$_1$ 'to fly'; 'the noise made by a fowl when about to fly'; Fu., *mbubu* 'a fly'; K., *mbu* 'mosquito'; Fn., *bũbũ* (*bɔ̃bɔ̃*) 'insect'; B., *buba* 'termite'; H., *bu:*$_3$*bu*$_3$*wa:*$_3$ 'a variety of stingless bee'; M., *bubu* 'to fly, to flutter'; Tl., *dibubu* 'the tsetse fly'
ˈ*budi* 'goat'	Cf. Tl., *mbudi* 'a species of antelope'; Kim., *mbudi* (*mburi*) 'sheep'; K., *budi* 'cat'
ˈ*bumbu* 'to pick up, to carry in the hands'	M., *mbumbu* 'to lift, to take up'

[d]

da (ˈ*dada*) 'mother, nurse, an elderly woman'	E., *da*$_{1-3}$ 'mother'; 'elder sister'; *da*$_1$*da*$_3$ 'mother.' Cf. I., *a*$_1$*da*$_3$ 'eldest daughter'
daf (*dɛf*, ˈ*dɛfu*) 'rice flour, rice cakes'; 'corn cakes'	V., *dɛ*$_1$*fu*$_3$ 'rice flour or any edible grain pounded into a powder'; H., *da*$_3$*fa:*$_3$ 'plain boiled rice'
ˈ*dafa* (ˈ*dãfa*) 'fat'	V., *da*$_3$*fa*$_1$ 'fat,' lit. 'mouth full'; *dã*$_{1-2}$*fa*$_1$ 'to fill to the end'

'*dede* ('*dɛdɛ*) 'correct, exact, exactly'	Y., *de:*$_3$*de:*$_3$ 'accurate, agreeable'; H., *dei*$_3$*dei*$_3$ 'correct, exact'; K., *dedede* 'similarity, correspondence'
'*degati* ɒʊl 'the barn owl'	W., *degati* 'Hear it again' (used among the Wolofs in reference to an owl that hoots frequently near the house)
'*dɛnde* 'oil'	Kim., *ndende* 'palm nuts' (from which oil is made. Cf. Braz. P., *dende*)
dɛt ('*dɛt ren*) 'a heavy rain'	W., *dɛt* 'a heavy rain that lasts several consecutive days'
'*didi* 'two'	Fu., *didi* 'two'
'*didi bʌg* 'a brown bug that lives in the earth'	V., *d'i*$_1$*d'i*$_3$ 'a reddish or black ant.' Cf. B., *dide* 'a bee'; M., *ndindi* 'a small white ant and its columnar nest'
'*dimba* 'valley'	K., *ndimba* 'valley'
'*dɪndĩ* 'a small child' (a term of endearment used by a boy in reference to a girl or vice versa)	V., *dɪn*$_3$ *dɪn*$_1$ 'small child.' Cf. Mand., *dendẽ* 'baby'
di'*ɒkɒlɒ* 'tadpole'	K., *diɔkɔlɔ* 'a tadpole which has nearly become a frog, the legs being well developed'
də 'to, towards,' e.g., *i rɒɪd də calstən* 'He rides to Charleston'	E., *ḍə*$_3$ (*ḍe*$_3$) 'to, towards' (when following a verb of direction), e.g., *ma*$_3$*yi*$_1$ *ḍə*$_3$ (*ḍe*$_3$) *a*$_1$*ve*$_3$ *me*$_3$ 'I shall go to the woods'
də 'to, in order to,' e.g., *unə go də grɒɪn em* 'You go to grind it'	Cf. E., *ḍa*$_1$ 'to, in order to' (when connecting two verbs), e.g, *e*$_3$*yi*$_1$ *ḍa*$_1$ *yɔ*$_3$ *fo*$_1$*foa*$_3$ 'He went to call his father'
də 'to be,' e.g., *də gɒd wʌk* 'It is God's work'	I., *de*$_1$ 'to be,' e.g., *ha*$_3$ *de*$_3$ *i*$_1$*sɛ*$_3$ 'They are five'; E., *ḍi*$_1$ 'to be,' e.g., *ḍi*$_1$ *fɔ*$_3$ 'to be guilty'; W., *di* 'to be, to become,' e.g., *maŋgi di ɟambur* 'I am a free man.' See discussion of *də* in Chapter 4.
do 'child'	M., *ndo* 'child, pupil, the young of animals'
'*duŋgu* 'pepper'	K., *ndunŋgu* 'pepper'

[e]

e'*luke*'*luke* 'a grayish-brown marsh bird on St. Simon Island'	Cf. Bi., *e*$_1$*lu*$_1$*ke*$_3$*lu*$_1$*ke*$_3$ 'the river tortise'
enu '*fole* 'to be pregnant'	E., *Φo*$_1$ *le*$_1$ *e*$_3$*nu*$_1$ 'She is with child'
e'*ria*'*ria* 'a white and brown marsh bird'	Cf., Bi., *e*$_1$*ria*$_{1-3}$*ria*$_1$ 'the sandfly'

[ɛ]

ɛ̃$_{3-1}$ 'yes'	E., ɛ̃$_3$ 'yes'; I., ɛ̃:$_3$ 'yes'

f, [f]

fa 'to take' (used before another verb), e.g., ɒɪ *ẽ no fa go fə no flɒwə* 'I don't intend to go for any flour,' lit. 'I ain't no take go for no flour'	T., *fa* 'to take,' e.g., *fa bera* 'bring,' lit. 'take come'; *kɔ fa bera* 'fetch,' lit. 'go take come'; *fa kɔ* 'take go'; F., *fa*$_1$ 'to take'
fa 'a tree resembling the cedar'	M., *fa* 'a large tree'; 'a large, pod-shaped fruit that bursts with a loud noise'
ˈ*fili* (ˈ*filis*) 'corn, hominy'; 'coarse bread'	Cf. M., *fili* 'tassel, the beard of grain'
ˈ*finda* (ˈ*fɪnda*) 'forest'	K., *mfinda* 'a forest, a wood'
ˈ*fɒfɒ* 'the lungs of an animal'	V., *fɔ*$_3$*fɔ*$_3$ 'lungs'; M., *vɔvɒ* 'lungs'
ˈ*fufla* 'the lungs of an animal'	G., *fu*$_3$*fla*$_1$ 'lungs'
ˈ*fufu* 'the lungs of an animal'	E., *fu*$_3$*fu*$_3$ 'breathing'; *fũ*$_1$*fũ*$_1$*fũ*$_1$ 'panting'; H., *fu*:$_1$*fu*:$_2$ 'lungs'; Fn., *fũfũ* 'breath'; 'breathing'
ˈ*fufu* 'mush'; 'wheat flour made into a thin batter and cooked'	E., *fu*$_1$*fu*$_1$ 'yam, cassava, and coco boiled and pounded'; W., *fufu* 'food made from meal or flour of cassava'; Fn., *fufu* 'food made from maize, fish, and palm oil'; M., *fufu* 'food made of cassava, grated, and fermented'; H., *fu*:$_1$*fu*:$_2$ 'a food made from cassava'
ˈ*fufu dʌs* 'a fine dust used with the intention of bewitching one or causing harm to one'	E., *fu*$_3$*fu*$_{1-3}$ 'dust'; M., *fufule* 'a fine, dry dust'
ˈ*fug*ˈ*fug* (ˈ*fuk*ˈ*fuk*) 'the lungs of an animal'	Y., *fu*$_1$*ku*$_1$*fu*$_2$*ku*$_1$ (*fu*$_1$*ku*$_2$*fu*$_3$*ku*$_1$) 'lungs'
ˌ*fula*ˈ*fafa* 'woodpecker'	M., *fulafafa* 'to bore into a tree' (< *fula* 'to bore into' + *fafa* 'tree')
fut (*fʊt*) 'to be nude'; 'to have sexual intercourse'	W., *fut* 'nude'

[g]

ˈ*gafa* 'evil spirit, devil'	M., *ŋgafa* 'spirit, soul, idol'
ˈ*ganɟa* (ˈ*kanɟa*) 'gingerbread'	H., *sa*$_1$*kan*$_1$*dʒa*$_1$*bir*$_{2-1}$ 'ginger'
ˈ*gembɒ* 'a bat'	K., *ŋgembɔ* 'a bat'

ˈ*giɟi* (ˈ*gici*, ˈ*ɟiɟi*, ˈ*ɟici*) 'the Gullah dialect'; 'one who speaks Gullah'	*gidʒi* (*gitʃi*, *gitsi*, *gisi*), 'a language and tribe in the Kissy country (Liberia)'; M., *gidʒɪ* 'a country called Kissy'
ˈ*gʌla* (ˈ*gola*, ˈ*gula*) 'Gullah, a dialect spoken by Negroes in coastal South Carolina and Georgia'; 'one who speaks Gullah.' See *giɟi*	Cf. *gola* (*gɔla*, *gɔra*, *gula*, *gura*) 'a Liberian tribe and its language.' Cf. also *ŋgɔla* 'a tribe in the Hamba basin of Angola'
ˈ*gʌmbo* 'okra'	Tl., *tʃiŋgɔmbɔ* 'okra'; U., *otʃiŋgɔmbo* 'okra'
ˈ*gɒma* 'a drum'	K., *ŋgɔma* 'a drum'
ˈ*gɒne* 'rat'	K., *ŋgɔne* 'the forest rat, the largest of the rat species'
go 'one'	Fu., *go* 'one'
ˈ*guba* 'peanut'	Kim., *ŋguba* 'peanut'; U., *oluŋgupa* 'peanut'; K., *ŋguba* 'kidney' (used for peanut because of the resemblance between the kidney and the peanut). See *pinda*
ˈ*gulu* 'pig'	K., *ŋgula* 'pig, hog'; U., *oŋgulu* 'pig.' Cf. Tl., *ŋgulubɛ* 'hog, swine'
ˈ*gumbi* 'a weed used for medicinal purposes'	B., *gumbi* 'an herb causing in horses an infectious diarrhoea'; H., *gum*$_3$*bi:*$_3$ 'a thorny plant'

[h]

hɛ̃$_{3-1}$ 'yes'	V., *hɛ̃*$_1$ 'yes, all right'; Y., *hɛ̃*$_2$ 'yes'
ˈ*hihi* (ˈ*higə*ˈ*hi*) 'owl'	V., *hĩ:*$_1$*hĩ*$_1$ 'owl.' Cf. T., *ahĩhĩ* 'speaking with a hoarse and trembling voice'
ˈ*hudu* 'to cause bad luck to'	Cf. H., *hu*$_3$*'du*$_3$*ba*$_1$ 'to arouse resentment in one person against another'
ˈ*hu*ˈ*hu* 'owl'	V., *hũ*$_{3-1}$*hũ*$_{3-1}$ 'owl'

[i]

ˈ*ibi* 'to vomit'	Y., *i*$_1$*bi*$_1$ 'the act of vomiting'; 'a violent push'; *e:*$_2$*bi*$_1$ 'that which has been vomited'
i ˈ*loni* 'He stands'; 'he stood'	M., *i: lo:ni* 'He did not stand'; 'he has not stood'

[ɟ]

ɟa (ˈ*ɟaɟa*) 'to quarrel'	Y., *ɟa*$_1$ 'to fight, to strive'; M., *ndʒia* 'a quarrel, language, palaver'; *ndʒia-ndʒia* 'contentious'

'*ɟabɒ* 'talkative'	Cf. M., *ndʒiamɒ* 'a quarrelsome person'; cf. B., *ɟabi* 'to talk back, to insult'; cf. Eng., *jabber*
'*ɟaɟa* ('*ɟagɟa*, 'ɟɒɟɒ, '*ɟɒgɟɒ*) 'blackbird'	Cf. V., *dʒa$_3$dʒa$_1$lo$_1$* 'blackbird'; lit. 'face ugly'
'*ɟamba* 'elephant'	U., *ondʒamba* 'elephant.' Cf. Kim. and K., *nzamba* 'elephant'
'*ɟambi* 'a reddish sweet potato'	V., *dʒam$_1$bi$_3$* 'wild yam, sweet potato.' See *yam*, *yambi*
ɟe 'five'	Fu., *ɟe* (*ɟuwi*) 'five'
'*ɟedidi* 'seven'	Fu., *ɟedidi* 'seven'
'*ɟego* 'six'	Fu., *ɟego* 'six'
'*ɟenɒɪ* 'nine'	Fu., *ɟenai* 'nine'
'*ɟetatə* 'eight'	Fu., *ɟetati* 'eight'
'*ɟiboli* 'a large fly'	V., *dʒi$_3$bo$_1$li$_1$* 'any insect or animal that is afraid of water'; lit. 'to run from water'
'*ɟiga* ('*ɟika*) 'an insect'; 'a flea'	W., *ɟiga* 'insect'; Y., *ɟi$_1$ga$_3$* 'jigger'; E., *ɟi$_1$ga$_3$* 'a sand flea'; Man., *dʒiga* 'jigger'; H., *dʒi$_1$ga:$_2$* 'jigger'; V., *dʒi$_3$ka$_1$* 'jigger'; M., *dʒikɛ* 'jigger'; cf. Eng., *jigger*
'*ɟɒgal* ('*ɟɒglɒ*) 'to rise' (used in the compound '*ɟɒgal-bod* ('*ɟɒglɒ-bod*) 'rise-up board, seesaw'	W., *ɟɔgal* (*ɟɔglɔ:*, *ɟugal*) 'to rise'; 'to cause to rise'
'*ɟoso* ('*ɟosomɒ*) 'charm, witchcraft'	M., *ndʒoso* 'spirit, magic'; *ndʒosomɒ* 'magician'
ɟug (*ɟuk*) 'infamous, disorderly' (used in the compound *ɟug hɒus* (*ɟuk hɒus*) 'a disorderly house, a house of ill repute'	W., *ɟug* (*ɟɒg*) 'to lead a disorderly life, to misconduct one's self.' Cf. B., *ɟugu* 'wicked, violent'; 'a naughty person.' Cf. Eng., *juke box*
'*ɟuɟu* 'magic, evil spirit'	H., *dʒu:$_1$dʒu:$_2$* 'a fetish, an evil spirit'; cf. Eng., *juju*

[k]

'*kafa* 'a charm'	Cf. H., *kar$_3$fa$_1$* 'a charm used to cause one to be disliked'; *ka$_3$fi$_1$* (*ka$_3$fe$_1$*) 'a charm (usually buried in the ground) to establish the prosperity of a house, town, market, etc.'; Fn., *kafo* 'a fetish in iron carried before the king in the ceremonies'
'*kafa* ('*gafa*) 'rice'	Cf. H., *ʃiŋ$_1$ka:$_2$fa:$_2$* 'rice'; *ka:$_3$fa$_1$* 'a porridge sold wrapped in leaves'

kakaˈtulu 'a large bird'; 'a mockingbird'	V., $ka_1ka_1tu_3lu_3$ 'a large bird'
ˈ*kala* (ˈ*kɒlɒ*) 'rice'	V., $kɔ_1lɔ_3$ 'uncooked rice.' Cf. B., *kala* 'the straw or stalk of a cereal'
kaˈluŋga 'sea'	K. and Kim., *kaluŋga* 'sea'
kambaˈboli (*kambaˈbuli*) 'a gray bird with white breast' (Johns Island, S.C.); 'a brown bird' (St. Simon Island, Ga.); 'a large speckled bird living near the water whose singing when the tide is rising is helpful to fishermen' (Edisto Island, S.C.)	V., $kam_3ba_3bo_1li_1$ 'a long-billed, speckled bird that digs in the earth'; lit. 'to dig a grave'
kan 'to turn'; 'to fall'	Dj., *kan* 'to turn'; 'to be dropped'; 'downfall'; Y., $k\tilde{a}_3$ 'to drop'; 'to break'
ˈ*kandi* 'rabbit'	K., *ŋkandi* 'rabbit'
ˈ*kaŋgɛ* 'an exclamation indicating a shock, unpleasant surprise, provocation'	Cf. B., *kaŋgɛrɛ* 'provocation, incitement'
ˈ*kaŋka* 'a large fish resembling the catfish but larger'	K., *ŋkaŋka* 'a fish'
ˈ*kaŋki* 'boiled corn mashed and served in corn shucks'	Fn. *kãki* 'a porridge made of corn.' Cf. Mand., *ka:ŋga* 'corn'; B., *kaŋaba* 'large corn'; Y., $ka\eta_2gi_1$ 'the corn cake of Gold Coast people'
kaˈpoke 'a green plant that is boiled and used for food'	Cf. U., *okapoke* 'a species of shrub three to five feet high'
ˈ*kela* 'a vase, basin, container made of wood'	K., *ŋkela* (*ŋkele*) 'a box, chest, case'; B., *kela* 'a vase.' Cf. W., *kəla* 'a wooden basin or vase'
keˈlele 'a marsh bird having white and black stripes on its wings'	K., *ŋgelele* 'a guinea fowl'
kiˈlɒmbo 'a black and white bird that frequents the marsh'	Cf. Kim., *kilɔmbelɔmbe* 'the crow'
ˈ*kimbi* 'a hawk'	K., *kimbi* 'a hawk'
kimˈbimbi 'quail'	K., *kimbimbi* 'quail'
kiŋˈkwawi 'partridge'	K., *kiŋkwavi* 'partridge'
$k\text{ɒɪ}_{3-1}$ 'an exclamation indicating great surprise'	Y., kai_{3-1} 'an exclamation of wonder'; Fn., *kayi* 'alas!'; H., kai_{3-1} 'ho!'; T., *kai* 'an expression used in cursing and often followed by the name of the speaker's king or fetish'
ˈ*kɒɪma* 'alligator'	V., $fai_{2-3}kai_{1-2}ma_2$ 'male crocodile'

ˈ*kɒla* 'a round basket made of palmetto or rush'	K., *ŋkɔla* 'a basket'
ˈ*komɛ* 'to assemble'	M., *komɛ* 'to assemble'; 'to surround'; 'an assembly'
ˈ*kulu* 'a blue and white marsh bird'	Cf. M., *kulu* 'a flock' (as of birds)
*ku*ˈ*lula* 'bird trap'	K., *kulula* 'bird trap'
ˈ*kunu* 'boat'	B., *kunu* 'boat'
ˈ*kusu* 'a parrot'	K., and Tl., *ŋkusu* 'a parrot'
kuʃ (ˈ*kuʃkuʃ*) 'corn-meal dough sweetened and fried'	H., $kuʃ_3a_1$ 'a thin cake made from groundnuts'; kus_3kus_1 'a wheaten food'; Ef., kus_1kus_3 'cassava shredded into meal, boiled, and dipped into an oil called $ɛ_3fɛ_3rɛ_3$. Cf. U., *ukusukusu* 'parched meal'
ˈ*kuta* 'tortoise'	B., and Mal., *kuta* 'tortoise'; Ef. i_3kut_3 'tortoise'; Dj., *aŋkura* 'tortoise'; Tl., *ŋkuda* 'tortoise, turtle'
ˈ*kuti* 'a small pig'	Cf. K., *ŋkuti a ŋgulu* 'a herd of wild pigs'
*kwa*ˈ*bena* 'a thorny bush resembling the palmetto'	Cf. T., *kwabenã-ahwi* 'a large tuber or root of various climbing plants of the genus Dioscorea, forming, when roasted or boiled, a wholesome, palatable, and nutritious food, the name being that of the man who first planted this particular variety of the plant'
kwaf (ˈ*kwafa*) 'to scrape'	Cf. H., $kwar_1fa{:}_2$ ($kwal_1fa{:}_2, k'war_1fa_2ta_1$) 'to dip or bail out the last bit of water from a vessel or well'
ˈ*kwasa* 'rope'	K., *ŋkwasa* 'rope, string'

[l]

ˈ*lagən* 'to be superior' (used in the expression *i lagən* 'He is superior')	Cf. W., *la* (*a*) 'a particle rendered in English by 'it is' and placed after the noun, pronoun, or the preposition to which one wishes to draw attention' + *gən* 'to be superior,' e.g., *məm a gən* 'He is superior'; lit. 'He it is who is superior'
ˈ*landu* (*da*ˈ*landu*) 'a striped lizard'	Cf. H., $lan_3do{:}_3$ 'lizard'; Fu., *falandu* 'lizard'; K. and Tl., *ŋgandu* 'crocodile'; U., *oŋgandu* 'crocodile'

laŋ (*laŋk*) 'to remain'	W., *laŋ* (*laŋga*) 'to remain, to be detained'; cf. Eng., *long*
li 'young, small, recently born'	Cf. W., *liːr bu tɔːi* 'a recently born child'
lɒ 'to say'; 'to agree'	V., *lɔ*$_3$ 'to say' (always followed by a quotation, e.g., *i*$_3$ *lɔ*$_3$ 'you say'); E., *lɔ̃*$_1$ 'to agree'; cf. Eng., *allow*

[m]

maˈkaɲa 'tobacco'	Tl. and Kim., *makaɲa* 'tobacco'
maˈlawu[47] 'whiskey'; 'any alcoholic beverage'	K., *malavu* 'palm wine, spirit, wine generally'; Ki., *malavu* 'wine.' Cf. Tl., *maluvu* 'palm wine'; 'beer made from corn'
ˈmalo (*ˈmelo*) 'rice'	B., *malo* 'rice'; Mand., *maːlo* 'rice'; W., *maːlɔ* 'rice'
ˈmeŋga 'blood'	K., *meŋga* 'blood'
ˈmoco 'witchcraft, magic'	Cf. Fu., *moco'o* 'medicine man'
moˈliku 'rice'	Fn., *molikũ* 'rice'
ˈmunse 'sugar cane'	K., *munse* 'sugar cane'
ˈmuŋgwa 'salt taken from the ocean and used for cooking'	Kim. and K., *muŋgwa* 'salt.' Cf. U., *omoŋgwa* 'salt'

[n]

na 'and' (heard in the phrase *mi na unə* 'me and you')	I., *na*$_1$ 'and'; T., *na* 'and'
na (*ˈnana*, *ˈnuna*) 'mother'; 'any elderly woman'	Tem., *na* 'mother'; Nu., *nna* 'mother'; Fu., *ina* 'mother'; Man., *nna* 'my mother' (a term of respect addressed to an aged woman); G., *nã*$_{1-3}$ 'grandmother'; T., *nanã* 'grandparent'; Mand., *na* (*naː*) 'mother.' Cf. K., *nuna* 'to grow old'
ˈnanse (*aˈnanse*) 'spider'; 'a red and black insect, resembling the hornet but not having wings, that lives in the ground'	T., *ananse* 'spider'; E., *a*$_1$*nan*$_3$*se*$_3$ 'spider.' Cf. B., *nansi* 'chameleon'
nˈdɒ 'to know, to understand'	Cf. M., *ndɔ* 'to find out by investigation'
nɒɪ 'four'	Fu., *nai* 'four'
ˈnokoˈnoko 'I'll have nothing to do with you'	G., *no*$_3$*ko*$_2$, *no*$_3$*ko*$_2$ 'nothing, nothing'

[ɲ]

ɲam (ˈ*ɲamɲam*) 'to eat, to eat up'	W., *ɲam* (*ɲamɲam*) 'to eat'; Fu., *ɲama* (*ɲamgo*) 'to eat'; *ɲamdu* 'food'; H., *na:*$_3$*ma*$_1$ 'flesh, meat'; *ɲam*$_1$*ɲam*$_2$ (*yam*$_1$*yam*$_2$) 'a cannibal'; U., *ɲama* 'to suck'; Mand., *ɲama* (*ɲamaɲama*) 'to garble'; Tl., *ɲama* 'animal.' Cf. Ef., *u*$_3$*nam*$_1$ 'flesh'; T., *ɛnãm* 'flesh, meat of any animal'
ˈ*ɲebe* (ˈ*ɲɛbɛ*) 'lima bean'	W., *ɲebe* 'kidney bean'; Fu., *ɲebre* 'bean'; *ɲebi* 'beans'
ˈ*ɲimbidi* 'singer'	K., *ɲimbidi* 'singer'
ˈ*ɲinɪ* (ˈ*ninɪ*, ˈ*nɪnɪ*) 'the female breast'	M., *ɲinɪ* (*ɲɪnɪ*) 'female breast, udder'

[o]

*olu*ˈ*hiso* 'a large, grayish bug'	U., *oluhiso* 'a bedbug.' Cf. Y., *o*$_1$*lu*$_3$ 'the queen of the white ants'

[p]

pat 'silent, silently'	W., *pat* 'to keep silent'
ˈ*pinda* (ˈ*pɪnda*) 'peanut'	K., *mpinda* 'peanut.' Cf. Tl., *kabindi* 'peanut'
ˈ*piŋgi* (ˈ*peŋgi*) 'a pot, vessel'	Cf. U., *otʃipiŋgilo* 'a vessel used to receive the thing asked for'
ˈ*pɒka* 'the horn of a cow, bull, or ox'	K., *mpɔka* 'a horn'
ˈ*poɟo* 'heron'	V., *po*$_3$*dʒo*$_3$ 'heron.' Cf. Eng., *poor Joe*
ˈ*pudi* 'a wide, flat, scaleless salt-water fish having a spotted tail and resembling the sheepshead'	K., *mpudi* 'a fish'
ˈ*puku* (*ka*ˈ*puku*, *m*ˈ*puku*) 'rat'	Tl. and K., *mpuku* 'rat, field mouse'

[s]

sa 'quickly'	V., *sa*$_3$ 'quickly'
ˈ*sadi* 'a sweet potato having a reddish skin'	K., *sadi* 'a wild yam whose creeping stalk and roots are thickly covered with thorns'
ˈ*saka* 'a pipe for smoking'	K., *nsaka* 'a pipe for smoking Indian hemp'
ˈ*saku* 'a crocus bag'	K., *nsaku* 'sack, bag.' Cf. P., *saco* [saku]

saˈkula 'to eat'	K., *sakula* 'to eat'; 'to speak' (used only in reference to a great chief)
ˈ*samba* 'to dance'	Cf. H., *$sam_3ba_3le{:}_3$* 'a dance of youths and maidens'; Tl., *samba* 'to jump about, to be here and there'; 'to cheer'; K., *samba* 'to worship, to entreat'; Kim., *samba* 'to pray'; U., *samba* 'to do homage, to applaud'; Bo., *somba* 'to dance the divination dance'
ˈ*samba* 'to cry'	K., *samba* 'to squall' (as an infant); Tl., *samba* 'to cackle'
ˈ*sambi* 'a guitar'	K., *nsambi* 'a guitar, banjo, or harmonica'
sanˈʒisa 'hen'	Cf. Kim., *sanʒi* 'hen'
ˈ*saŋga* 'a dance'	K., *saŋga* 'to dance'; 'the sword dance'; 'to dance the sword dance (which is done only by a chief on very special occasions, as when someone is to be executed and the chief dances the *saŋga* for a while; then, stopping suddenly, he points the sword at the victim, who is immediately killed)'[48]
ˈ*saŋgalo* 'a wild duck'	M., *saŋgalo* 'a wild duck'
sap 'sweet'	W., *sap* 'savory, delicious'
ˈ*sapə* 'ten'	Fu., *sapo* 'ten'
ˌ*sapəˈdidi* 'twelve'	Fu., *sapo e didi* 'twelve'
ˌ*sapəˈgo* 'eleven'	Fu., *sapo e go* 'eleven'
ˌ*sapəˈɟe* 'fifteen'	Fu., *sapo e ɟe* (*sapo e ɟuwi*) 'fifteen'
ˌ*sapəˈɟedidi* 'seventeen'	Fu., *sapo e ɟedidi* 'seventeen'
ˌ*sapəˈɟego* 'sixteen'	Fu., *sapo e ɟego* 'sixteen'
ˌ*sapəˈɟenɒɪ* 'nineteen'	Fu., *sapo e ɟenai* 'nineteen'
ˌ*sapəˈɟetatə* 'eighteen'	Fu., *sapo e ɟetati* 'eighteen'
ˌ*sapəˈnɑɪ* 'fourteen'	Fu., *sapo e nai* 'fourteen'
ˌ*sapəˈtatə* 'thirteen'	Fu., *sapo e tati* 'thirteen'
ˈ*sari* 'boiled rice pounded'	B., *sari* 'pounded grain or cereal cooked in water'; Sg., *sari* 'eatable grain'; Y., *sa_1ri_1* 'the early meal of the Mohammedans served before daybreak during their fast days.' Cf. Mand., *ma:lo-sa:ri* 'boiled rice'
sarika 'boiled rice pounded and served in leaves'	B., *sarika* 'to cut up or divide pounded grain or cereal'

'*sasa* 'to carve'	K., *sasa* 'to carve'
'*sasi* 'to ridicule'	M., *sasi* 'to treat contemptuously, to ridicule'; cf. Eng., *saucy*
'*saya* 'to bank the earth'	K., *saya* 'a bed of earth'
sa'zuka 'to hurry'	K., *sazuka* 'to hurry'
'*seka* 'pumpkin leaf'; gourd leaf'	K., *nseka* 'pumpkin leaf'
sɛ 'that, saying'	T., *sɛ* 'that, saying'; cf. Eng., *say*
'*sɛnswa* 'calabash'	K., *senswa* 'calabash'
'*sɛsa* 'a straw broom'; 'to sift'	K., *sesa* 'broom'; 'to sift'; Ki., *sɛsa* 'broom'
'*sɛta* 'a black, fuzzy worm'	K., *nseta* 'an intestinal worm'
'*sisi* 'smoke'	V., *si*$_1$*si*$_3$ 'smoke'; 'anything that spreads abroad, rumor'
'*sɪsɪ* 'a yellow fly'	V., sɪ$_3$sɪ$_3$ 'a fly'; 'a gnat'
'*sɒ ɛ a* '*dufe* 'Put wood on the fire'	V., sɔ:$_{3-1}$ ɛ$_1$ *a*$_1$ *du*$_1$*fe*$_1$ 'The wood has been consumed'
'*sɒka* 'to pack'	K., *sɔka* 'to pack full'
'*sɒmbo* 'a red sweet potato'	Kp., *sɔmbo* 'sweet potato'
'*sɒmpa* 'to marry'; 'marriage'	K., *sɔmpa* 'to marry'; *nsɔmpa* 'marriage'
'*sɒya* 'marsh grass'	K., *nsɔya* (*nsɔyɔ*) 'thatching grass'
so! *so*! 'a call to horses'	V., *so*$_2$ 'horse'; M. and Fn., *so* 'horse'
so'kela 'an iron pot'	Cf. B., *kela* 'a vase, a container'
'*sʌbi* ('*sɪbi*) 'lima bean'	W., *səb* 'bean'; *sɛbi ɟɔmbɔr* 'a palm bean with rectangular pod'
'*sudi* 'a bad odor'	K., *nsudi* 'a bad odor'
'*suka* 'the tail of a bird, especially a crane'	K., *suka* 'the tail of a bird'; *nsuka* 'end, extremity'; 'the last child a woman bears'
'*sukwa* 'to be stuck in mud'	K., *sukwa* 'to stick into'; 'to be stuck in something'
'*sumbi* 'a purchaser'	K., *nsumbi* 'a purchaser'
su'miki 'to lose blood'	K., *nsumiki* 'a cupper, one who lets blood.' Cf. K. and Tl., *sumika* 'to draw blood'
su'mikwa 'a goat's horn'	K., *sumikwa* 'a goat's horn used in taking blood'
'*sunda* 'to excel'	K., *sunda* 'to excel'; 'victory'
'*suʃi* 'accident'	K., *suʃi* 'chance, accident'
'*swadi* 'gingham cloth'	K., *nswadi* 'calico'
'*swaŋgɒ* 'to be proud'	M., *suaŋgɒ* 'to be haughty, selfish, evil'; 'to lie in ambush.' Cf. U.,

	suaŋgula 'to gloat, to mock'; *esaŋgi* 'exultation, exuberance which may annoy others'
sweŋ'geɲa 'asthma'	K., *nsweŋgenia* 'asthma'
	[ʃ]
ʃi'ele 'a large blue, white, and black bird that frequents the marsh'	K., *nʃiele* 'whydah bird'
'*ʃiɟi* ('*ɟiɟi*) 'a rat'	K., *nʃiʒi* 'the palm rat'
'*ʃilu* 'a promise'	K., *nʃilu* 'a promise'
'*ʃindu* ('*ʃɪndu*) 'a dance'; 'noise made by the feet'	K., *ʃindu* 'the noise of feet'; cf. Eng., *shindig* and *shindy*
'*ʃiʃi* 'to defame'; 'gossip, rumor'	K., *ʃiʃisa* 'to intimidate by mouth only.' Cf. H., *ʃiʃ:₃i₃gi:₃* 'meddlesomeness'; V., *si₁si₃* 'anything that circulates, rumor'; T., *nsise* 'rumor'; *nsisi* 'imposture, deceit'
ʃɐʊt 'a religious ring dance in which the participants continue to perform until they become exhausted'	Cf. Ar., *ʃaut* 'to move around the Kaaba (the small stone building at Mecca which is the chief object of the pilgrimage of Mohammedans) until exhausted'; *ʃauwata* 'to run until exhausted'
	[t]
'*tabi hɐus* 'a house made of cement and oyster shells with which pieces of brick are frequently mixed'	Cf. Ar., *tabix* 'cement, mortar, brick'; W., *tabax* 'the wall of a house made of sand, lime, mud, etc.'; 'to build of earth'; H., *ta₂'bo:₂* 'mud'; K., *ntaba* 'a muddy place.' Cf. Eng., *tabby* in *DAE*
ta'kula 'to scratch'	K., *takula* 'to scratch' (as a fowl)
'*tambi* 'the foot of anything'	K., *tambi* 'foot, paw, hoof'
'*tanda* 'to grow'	K., *tanda* 'to grow'; 'to get'
tani'anɟi 'a caterpillar'	K., *tanianʒi* 'a caterpillar weaving a cocoon case of sticks'
taŋ'gisa 'to teach'	K., *taŋgisa* 'to teach'; U., *okutaŋgisa* 'to teach'
'*tata* 'father'	Kim. and K., *tata* 'father'
'*tata* 'to cry'; 'an outcry'	K., *tata* 'to utter a cry'; *ntata* 'an outcry, exclamation'
'*tatə* 'three'	Fu., *tati* 'three'
'*tawa* 'to be greedy'	K., *tava* 'to take something greedily'

ˈ*tima* 'to dig'	K., *tima* 'to dig'
ˈ*tintika* 'to tighten'	K., *tintika* 'to tighten'
ˈ*tɒkɒ* 'full, plentiful'; 'plenty'	T., *tɔkɔ*: 'richly, plentifully'; K., *tɔkɔ* 'love of finery'; Bo., *ntakɔ* 'means'; Fn., *tɔgɔ̃gɔ̃* 'growth, overflow'; E., $tɔ_1$ 'to be abundant.' Cf. W., *tɔha* 'to have thickness'
ˈ*tɒmbe* 'darkness'	K., *tɔmbe* 'darkness'
ˈ*tɒmɒ* 'pleasant taste'	K., *ntɔmɔ* 'flavor, taste'
tot (ˈ*totəm*) 'to carry'	Ki., *tota* 'to pick up'; K., *tɔta* 'to pick up.' Cf. E., $Φo_1$ $to_1dzε_3$ 'to lift a load from one's head without help'; M., *tomɒ* 'one who carries a message'; Kim. and U., *tuta* 'to carry'
ˈ*toti* 'frog'	V., to_1ti_3 'frog'; cf. Eng., *toad*
*tukum*ˈ*panda* 'a tall, bluish bird smaller than a heron'	K., *ntukumpanda* 'whydah bird'
ˈ*tumbu* 'calabash'	K., *ntumbu* 'calabash'
ˈ*tuniya* 'very clean'	K., *tunia* (*ntunia*) 'cleanness'
ˈ*tutu* (*tu*) 'excrement'	H., $tu{:}_3tu_1$ 'human excrement.' Cf. Kim., *tuʒi* 'excrement'; Dj., *tosi* 'human excrement'
ˈ*tuwi* 'excrement	K., *tuvi* 'excrement.' Cf. Tl., *tuinvi* 'excrement'
ˈ*tuwiya* 'fire'	K., *tuvia* 'fire'

[c]

ˈ*cika bod* 'a lifting or rising board, a seesaw'	Cf. Mand., *cika* 'to lift'

[u]

ˈ*ula* 'louse, bedbug, insect'	Cf. U., *ola* (*ona*) 'louse'; cf. *ula* 'bed'; Y., $\tilde{o}_1la_3$ 'the moth'
ˈ*unə* (ˈ*hunə*, ˈ*wunə*) 'you'; 'your'	Cf. I., u_3nu_1 'you (pl.)'; 'your (pl.)'

w, [w]

ˈ*wamɐʊt* (ˈ*wɒmɐʊt*) 'catfish,' lit. 'large mouth'	Cf., M., *wa* 'large'
ˈ*wandu* 'a bean which grows on poles'	K., *wandu* 'a small bean which grows on a stem that branches at about three feet from the ground'
ˈ*waŋga* 'charm, witchcraft'	Kim., *waŋga* (*ɔwaŋga*) 'witchcraft'; U., *owaŋga* 'fetish, witchcraft'; K.,

	mbwaŋga 'a bundle of aromatic and peppery powder used as a cure for headache.' Cf. Tem., *awaŋka* 'a protecting charm for a tree or farm'; M., *waŋgwa* 'a small tree having bitter, poisonous leaves, which are used to cause abortion'; Tl., *bwaŋga* 'a charm, fetish'
'*wela* 'pigeon'	K., *mbwela* 'a small wild pigeon'; 'a turtledove'
'*wudu* ('*wodu*) 'witchcraft, sorcery'; 'a sorcerer'	E., vo_1du_3 'a tutelary deity or demon'; $vo_1du_3da_1$ 'a snake which is worshipped'; $vo_1du_3si_1$ 'a priest of a vo_1du_3'; Fn., *vodũ* 'a good or bad spirit'; 'an intermediary between God and man'; 'a deity'; *vodũdoho* 'curse, malediction'; *vodũnɔ̃* 'a priest'; *vodũnu* 'cult, religion'; *vodũxwe* 'a temple'
'*wula* 'a heavy rain'	Kim., and K., *mvula* 'rain'; Tl., *nvula* 'rain'
wulisã'kpãkpã 'woodpecker'	M., *wulisãkpãkpã* 'woodpecker'; lit. 'to pound a tree vigorously'

y [j]

yam ('*yambi*) 'sweet potato'	Cf. M., *yam* (*yambi*) 'the wild yam'; T., *ayamkaude* 'a large edible tuber or root which, when roasted or boiled, constitutes a wholesome, palatable, and nutritious food'; 'a species of yam'; *ɔyamu* 'yam not taken out with the first crop'; G., $ya{:}_1mu_3$ 'a species of yam that is planted early'
yan (*yant*) 'to lie, to be untruthful'	Cf. U., *okuyana* 'to lie'
ye ('*yeye*, '*yɛyi*) 'eye'	B., *ɲe* 'eye'; *ye* 'to see'; Kp., *ɲɛi* 'eye'; Nu., *eye* 'eye'

[z]

'*zundu* 'a hammer'	K., *nzundu* 'anvil'; 'a heavy stone'; 'a sledge hammer'

SOME EXPRESSIONS HEARD ONLY IN STORIES, SONGS, AND PRAYERS[49]

[a]

a 'with, to, at, in'	M., *a* 'with, to, at, in'
a 'you'	M., *a* 'you'
ˌ*awεnayi*ˈ*bina* 'He will come to take you'	V., $a_1\vartheta\varepsilon i_1na{:}_{3-1}i_3$ bi_3na_1 'He will be coming to take you'

[b]

ba 'you'	M., *ba* 'you' (sg.)
ba 'do not'	M., *ba*: 'you not' (imp. sg.)
ba 'at, with'	V., $ba{:}_1 < ba_1la_1$ 'at, with'
*baka*ˈ*leŋga* 'playing instruments in unison'	M., *mbakaleŋga*, 'a group of musicians engaged in playing their instruments,' lit. *mbaka* 'a musical instrument' + *leŋga* 'in unison'
ˈ*bara* 'beads'	V., gba_3ra_3 (gba_3la_3) 'beads'
ˈ*bawalɒ* 'You will come'	M., *bawalɒ* 'You will come'
ˈ*bawo* (ˈ*balo*) 'to get well'	M., *bawo* (*bao, mbao*) 'to heal, to save.' Cf. *ba bao lo* 'You will get well'
bε 'you not'	M., *bε*: 'you not' (sg.)
bi 'you not'	M., *bi*: 'you not' (sg.)
bi 'to take'	V., bi_1 'to take'
ˌ*bisimi*ˈ*laɪ*! 'an exclamation indicating surprise'	B. and Man., *bisimilai*! 'In the name of God' (Ar.)

f, [f]

bɪ 'you'	M., *bɪ* 'you, yours'
*fa*ˈ*lani* 'He died long ago'	V., $fa_1la{:}_{3-1}ni_1 < fa_1la_1$ 'to die' + ni_1 'formerly, long ago'

[g]

ga 'to learn'	M., *ga* (*ka*) 'to learn'; 'to teach'
gbaŋ (*kpaŋ*) 'tightly'	M., *gbaŋ* (*kpaiŋ, kpaŋgbagbaŋ*) 'severely, tightly'
gbla 'near'	M., *gbla* (*gblaŋga*) 'near'

[h]

ha 'to die'; 'death'	M., *ha* 'to die'; 'to tire'; 'death'
ˌ*hola*ˈ*tɪtɪtɪ* 'Hold the door very securely'	Cf. M., *hou la* (*hoʊ nda*) 'Hold the door' + *tɪtɪtɪ* 'an adverb used to in-

	tensify the meaning expressed in the verb'
ˈ*hũma* 'to steal'	M., *hũma* 'to steal'; 'theft'
	[i]
i 'you'	V., *i*$_3$ (*i*:$_3$) 'you'
ikuˈlubiyo 'If you begin now'	V., *i*:$_3$ *ku*$_1$*lu*$_3$*bi*$_1$ *o*$_1$ 'If you begin now'
	[ɟ]
ˈ*ɟamba* 'a gift'	M., *dʒamba* 'a gift'; 'to send a gift to someone absent'
	[k]
ka 'continually'	M., *ka* 'continually'
ka 'to rise'	V., *ka*$_1$ 'to rise'
ˈ*kamba* 'grave'	M., *kamba* 'grave'; V., *kam*$_3$*ba*$_3$ 'grave'
kamˈbɛɪ 'the grave'	M., *kambɛɪ* 'the grave'
ˈ*ka ra* ˈ*bara* 'Rise with the beads'	V., *ka*$_1$ *ra*$_1$ *gba*$_3$*ra*$_1$ (*ka*$_1$ *la*$_1$ *gba*$_3$*la*$_1$) 'Rise with the beads'
kasɪˈtɛ (*kaʃɪˈtɛ*) 'surrounded by rust'	V., *ka*$_1$*sɪ*$_3$*tɛ*$_{3-2}$ lit. *ka*$_1$*sɪ*$_3$ 'rust' + *tɛ*$_{3-2}$ 'in the midst of'
ˈ*komɛ* 'Come together'	M., *komɛ* 'Come together'
ˈ*kpaŋga* 'the remains after a fire or some other destructive force'	M., *kpaŋga* 'a field burnt before clearing'; 'remains'
ku 'to be able'	M., *ku* 'to surpass, to be able'
kuˈhã 'from afar'	M., *kuhã* 'long, distant'
	[l]
la (*nda*) 'mouth, voice, door'	M., *la* (*nda*) 'mouth, doorway, any opening'
la (*ra*) 'with'	V., *la*$_1$ (*ra*$_1$) 'with'
ˈ*lawo* 'to open'	M., *lawo* (*ndawo*) 'to open'
le 'to pass'	M., *le*: 'to pass'
lɛ 'to condemn'; 'to vex'	M., *lɛ* 'to condemn, to convict'; 'to vex'
lɛ 'yet'	M., *lɛ* 'yet'
lɛ 'slowly'	M., *lɛ*: < *lɛlɛ* 'slowly'
lɛɪ 'to cool'; 'to be cool'	M., *lɛ*:ɪ < *lɛlɪ* 'to cool, to appease'
li (*ndi*) 'heart'	M., *li* (*ndi*) 'heart'
lɪ 'to go, to pass'	M., *lɪ* 'to go'
lɒ 'to be'	M., *lɒ* 'to be'
lɒ 'to see, to find'	M., *lɒ* (*dɒ*, *tɒ*) 'to see, to find'

	[m]
mbeɪ 'here'	M., *mbeɪ* 'here, this way'
mbɛ 'to me, for me'	M., *mbɛ* 'to me, for me'
ˈ*mɒnɛ* 'to toil with suffering'	M., *mɔnɛ* 'to toil, to suffer'
mʊ 'we'	M., *mʊ* 'we'
	[n]
na 'to come'	V., na_1 'to come'
na 'that'	M., *na* 'that, which, who'
na 'if'	M., *na* 'if'; 'there' (adv.)
ˈ*nana* 'I have come'	V., $na_3na_1 < n_3la_1na_1$ 'I have come'
nda. See *la*	
ndi. See *li*	
*ndi*ˈ*lewe* 'vexation, anger'	M., *ndilewe* 'anger'; 'angry'
*ndi*ˈ*lɛlɪ* (*ndi*ˈ*lɛ*:ɪ) 'peaceful'	M., *ndilɛlɪ* (*ndilɛ*:ɪ) 'peaceful'; 'contentment'
ni 'formerly, long ago'	V., ni_1 'formerly, long ago'
nu 'there'	V., $nu{:}_3 < nu_3wu_3$ 'there' (adv.)
	[ŋ]
ŋˈ*go* (*wo*) 'to destroy, to break'; 'to open'	M., ŋ*go* (*wo*) 'to open forcibly'; 'to dawn'; 'to break'
ŋˈ*go* 'word'	M., ŋ*go* 'sound, voice, word, report'
	[o]
o 'please' (heard in the expression *o la wo* 'Please, open the door'	M., *o* 'an exclamation indicating surprise or anxiety'
	[p]
pi 'grass'	V., $pi{:}_1$ 'grass'
ˈ*pinɛ*ˈ*pinɛ* 'quickly'	M., *pinɛpinɛ* 'quickly'
pon 'far away'	V., $pon{:}_3$ 'far away'
	[r]
ra. See *la*	
	[s]
sa 'to lie' (heard in the expression sa_1na_1 $pon{:}_3$ 'He is lying far away'	V., sa_1na_1 $pon{:}_3$ lit. sa_1 'to lie' + na_1 (sign of the progressive) + $pon{:}_3$ 'far away'
sa 'to draw' (heard in the expression $sa{:}_1gba_3ra_3$ 'Draw the beads'	V., $sa{:}_1$ gba_3ra_3 ($sa{:}_1$ gba_3la_3) lit. $sa{:}_1 < sa_1ra_1$ (sa_1la_1) 'to draw' + gba_3ra_3 (gba_3la_3) 'beads'

ˈ*sasi* 'boaster, proud one'	M., *sasi* 'boaster'; 'pride'
ˈ*sihã* 'to steal'	M., *sihã* 'to steal, to borrow'; 'to lend'
sɒ 'to receive'	M., *sɔ*: < *sɔlɒ* 'to obtain'; 'receive'
ˈ*sondʊ* 'swearing, oath'; 'crime' heard in the sentence ˈ*sondʊ n*ˈ*di lɛ* 'The crime vexes the heart'	M., *sondʊ ndi lɛ* 'The crime vexes the heart'

[t]

ta 'to go'	V., *ta*:$_3$ 'to go'
ta 'he, she, it'	M., *ta* 'he, she, it'
ˈ*tamɛ* 'cautiously'; 'in quiet'	M., *tamɛ*: 'cautiously'
te 'to remain'	V., *te*:$_1$ < *te*$_1$*le*$_1$ 'to remain'
tɛ 'in the midst of, surrounded by'	V., *tɛ*$_{3-2}$ 'in the midst of'
tɪ 'their'	M., *tɪ* 'they'; 'their'; 'them'
ˈ*tɒmbɛ* 'absolutely, perfectly'	M., *tɒmbɛ* 'absolutely, perfectly'
to 'to send'	M., *to* 'to send'
tu 'to beat'	V., *tu*:$_1$ < *tu*$_1$*lu*$_1$ 'to beat'

w, [w]

wa 'to come'	M., *wa* 'to come'
wɛ 'a particle indicating the future or the habitual'	V., *ϑɛ*$_1$
ˈ*wɒkɒ* 'evening'	M., *wɒkɒ* (*gbɒkɒ*, *kpɒkɒ*) 'evening'; *gbɒkɒlɒ* (*kpɒkɒlɒ*) 'to be aged, to grow old'
wo. See ŋˈ*go*	
ˈ*woŋga* 'kinfolks, relatives'	M., *woŋga* 'family, relatives'
ˈ*wuli* 'tree'	M., *wuli* (*ŋguli*) 'tree'

y [j]

ya 'not'	M., *ya* 'not'
yi 'to sleep'	M., *yi* 'to sleep'
yia 'to speak'	M., *yia* 'to speak'; 'to speak to'

CHAPTER 4

SYNTACTICAL FEATURES

THE most striking similarities in syntactical features between Gullah and the West African languages are revealed in (1) the absence of any distinction of voice; (2) the employment of verb phrases; (3) the use of *də* as a verb of incomplete predication; (4) the comparison of adjectives; (5) the use of verbal adjectives; (6) word order; and (7) the frequent repetition of words and phrases throughout the sentence.

VOICE

In Gullah there is no distinction of voice. The subject of a verb in the passive in English is put in the objective case by the Gullah speaker and the third personal pronoun, *they* or *he*, or some noun is made to serve as subject of the sentence. For example, instead of saying *He was beaten*, the Gullah speaker says, *dɛm bit əm* 'They beat him.'

In a great many of the West African languages, as in Gullah, there is no distinction of voice:

Ewe: *wo*$_3$*tso*$_1$ *ta*$_1$ *le*$_1$ *e*$_3$*nu*$_1$ 'His head was cut off,' lit. 'They cut off his head'

Yoruba: *a*$_1$ *fɛ*$_3$*rã*$_1$ *mi*$_2$ 'I am loved,' lit. 'Someone loves me'
nwɔ̃$_3$ *sɔ*$_2$*fũ*$_3$ *mi*$_2$ 'I am told,' lit. 'They tell me'
a$_2$ *ti*$_2$ *fɛ*$_3$*rã*$_1$ *mi*$_2$ 'I have been loved,' lit. 'Someone has loved me'

Twi: *wɔhwere nõ* 'He is beaten,' lit. 'Men beat him'

Fante: *w'e*$_3$*pi*$_3$*ra*$_3$[1] *ɔ*$_1$*da*$_1$*se*$_1$ *i*$_3$*no*$_3$ 'The man is wounded,' lit. 'They have wounded the man'

Gã: *a*$_1$*hã*$_3$ *lɛ*$_1$ *a*$_1$*ke*$_1$ *kre*$_3$ 'He was given a wreath,' lit. 'People gave him a wreath'

VERB PHRASES

Frequently in Gullah two or more verbs are used to express one idea, one of which performs the same function as a preposition, adverb, conjunction, or participle in English. The Gullah speaker, like the West African, analyzes an action or event by considering its component parts and then using a special verb to describe each part. Hence in his sentences co-ordination is more common than subordination (i.e., parataxis[2] is preferred to hypotaxis), and there are consequently few prepositions, adverbs, conjunctions, and participles as compared with what one finds in cultivated English. Among these verbs which take the place of other parts of speech in English are *də*, *go*, *sɛ*, *tɛk* 'take,' *fa* (also meaning 'to take'), *kʌm* 'come,' and *pas* 'surpass.' The following sentences, together with correspondences from several West African languages, will illustrate their use:

də, following a verb of direction, is best translated by 'toward,' 'to': *i rɒɪd də ɟaksnbʌrə* 'He rides to (or toward) Jacksonboro.'

In the Anglo dialect of Ewe the word *ḍə*$_3$ (pronounced *ḍe*$_3$ in the other Ewe dialects) means 'to reach'; but when it follows a verb of direction, it means 'toward,' 'to': *ma*$_1$*yi*$_1$ *ḍə*$_3$ *a*$_1$*ve*$_3$ *me*$_3$ 'I shall go to the wood,' lit. 'I shall go reach the wood.'

In Gullah when *də* is used between two verbs, it means 'to,' 'in order to,' or 'and': *yu go də grɒɪn əm* 'You go to grind them'; *dat mɛk dɛm də sew dɛ mʌnɪ* 'That causes them to save their money'; *dɛm də ca əm də ɟi əm dɪ pipl wat haw man ən wɐif ən cɪlən də wʌk fə dɛm* 'They are carrying them in order to give them to the people who have man and wife and children to work for them'; *gɒdz gɒɪn in dɛm bɛd də tʌk dɛm ɐut* 'God's going into their bed to take them out.'

Compare with this use of *də* in Gullah that of the Ewe verb *ḍa*$_1$, which is employed to indicate the beginning of an action and is best translated into English as 'to,' 'in order to' when connecting two verbs: *e*$_3$*yi*$_1$ *ḍa*$_1$ *yɔ*$_3$ *fo*$_1$*foa*$_3$ 'He went in order to call his father'; *ma*$_3$*yi*$_1$ *a*$_3$*ḍa*$_1$*Φle*$_1$ *a*$_1$*ti*$_3$*ke*$_1$ 'I am going to buy medicine'; *e*$_3$*yi*$_1$ *ḍa*$_1$ *su*$_3$*bɔ*$_3$*e*$_1$ 'He went to serve him.'

The Gullah verb *go* also means 'to,' 'in order to,' or 'and' when connecting two verbs: ᴅɪ *ẽ gɒɪn go pɪk nʌn dɛ* 'I am not going to pick any there'; *yu bɛtə go hom go si bɐut yo cɪlən* 'You had better go home and (or to) see about your children.'

Compare with this use of *go* that of the Ewe word *he*$_3$, meaning 'to go away,' which, when connecting two verbs, should be translated into English by 'and'; *e*$_3$*xɔ*$_1$*e*$_3$ *le*$_1$ *a*$_1$*si*$_3$*ɲe*$_1$ *he*$_3$*na*$_3$ *nɔ*$_1$*vi*$_3$*ɲe*$_1$ 'He took it from me and gave it to my brother.'

In Fante, *kɔ*$_3$ 'to go' is similarly used in ɔ$_1$*kɔ*$_1$ *ka*$_3$*pra*$_3$ or ɔ$_1$*kɔ*$_1$ *a*$_1$*ka*$_3$*pra*$_3$ 'He goes and sweeps,' lit. 'He goes goes sweeps.' Here *kɔ*$_3$ is written and pronounced *ka*$_3$ in order that its vowel may harmonize with the *a* of *pra*$_3$.

Note the following from Twi: *yɛrekɔ akɔsra yɛŋ na* 'We are going to visit our mother,' lit. 'We are going go visit our mother'; *mɛkɔ akɔpase ɔtʃena* 'I will go and walk tomorrow,' lit. 'I will go go walk tomorrow'; and *ye dunnum yɛŋ akanea kɔda* 'We put out our lamps and sleep,' lit. 'We put out our lamps go sleep.'

Note also from Efik: $m_3mɔ_1$ e_2yom_1 $n_2di_2di_2$ $n_1di_2se_1$ mi_{2-1} 'They want to come to see me,' lit. 'They want to come come see me.'

When following a verb of motion, the Gullah verb *go* often means 'to,' 'toward': *dɛn de tɛk əm go calztən* 'Then they take (or took) them to Charleston.'

Compare with this the Ewe word yi_1 'to go,' which, when following a verb of motion, means 'to,' 'toward': $wo_3tsɔ_3nɛ_1$ yia_1 ke_3ta_3 'One carries him to Keta,' lit. 'One carries him goes Keta.'[3]

The word *sɛ* (also pronounced *se*) is used in Gullah after verbs of saying, thinking, and wishing and introduces objective clauses. It is best rendered in English by the present participle *saying* or the conjunction *that: dɛn dɪ cɪlən dɛ in ɲu yɒk sɛn wʌd sɛ de ẽ gɒɪn gɪt nʌtn* 'Then the children there in New York sent word saying (or that) they were not going to get anything'; *dɪ pipl kʌm hom nekɪd . . . tɛl mi aftə sɛ de cɛc bʌd* 'The people came home naked . . . told me afterward that they caught birds'; *de lɔ sɛ wi tu ol* 'They admit that we are too old.'

This use of *sɛ* or a synonym of it is common in many West African languages. Note the following from Twi: *ne na kã tʃserɛɛ no sɛ:trã ha ara* 'His mother told, showed him saying, "Just stay here" '; *ɛnna o susuwi sɛ ɛyɛ ɔkramaŋ foforo bi*, etc. 'Then he thought that it was some other dog,' etc. Note the following from Ibo: $ö_3tu_1$ $ni_3mɛ_2$ ha_2 jo_1ro_1 se_2, $ö_1lɛɛ_{3-2}$ $ɛ_2bɛ_2$ ha_2 $ga_1a_1gba_2la_2$ 'One of them asked, saying, "What place will they go to?" ' In Ewe the verb used in this way is be_3; in Mende it is *yɛ*.

The verb *to take* in Gullah when used with another verb is often expressed in English by a preposition. It serves to introduce the means necessary for the completion of the action described by the main verb: *i tɛk (s)tɪk kɪl əm* 'He killed them with (by means of) a stick'; *dɛm gɒɪn tɛk əm go bak* 'They are going back in company with them.'

Compare with this a similar construction from Ewe, in which $tsɔ_3$ means 'to take': $e_3tsɔ_3$ $dɔ_1me\gamma_1\gamma e_1\gamma i_3$ yi_1 $a_1\Phi e_3$ 'He took empty belly went home,' i.e., 'He went home without eating.'

Note the following from Twi: *ɔno na ɔde nnuaŋ no ba gua so* 'She takes the food comes market top,' i.e., 'She comes to the market with the food'; *wobɛtɔŋ anum adze ahẽʔ* 'You will sell five take how much?' i.e., 'How much will you take for five?'

Note also from Fante: *me$_1$dze$_1$ se$_3$kã$_3$ me$_3$tʃwa:$_1$no$_1$* 'I take a knife, I cut him,' i.e., 'I cut him with a knife; *me$_1$tɔn$_3$dze$_1$ ta$_1$ku$_1$fa$_3$* 'I sell it take sixpence,' i.e., 'I sell it for sixpence.'

In Gullah, the verb *fa* (pronounced also *fə*) actually means 'to take.' In Twi, one of the verbs meaning 'to take' is *fa*. In Gullah, *fa* is used before another verb and is most accurately rendered in English by 'intend to,' 'choose to,' 'must,' or 'should': ɒɪ *ẽ no fa go fə no flɒwə; dɛm fa brɪŋ əm tu mi* 'I don't intend to go for any flour; they must bring it to me'; ɪ*f* ɒɪ *fa go* ɒ*f tu wɪlyʌm fə dɪ flɒwə, wɪlyʌm g*ɒɪ*n lɒk mi ʌp* 'If I should go off to Williams' for the flour, Williams would lock me up'; *wɛn dɛm* ɟɪ*t dat flɒwə in dɪ* ɒ*təmobil, de fa go r*ɒ*un tu* ɒ*l dɪ ol ledɪ do ən pɪt ɛm dɛ* 'When they get that flour in the automobile, they must go around to all the old ladies' doors and put it there.'

Compare with this the following from Twi: *fa bera* 'Bring,' lit. 'Take come'; *kɔfa bera* 'Fetch,' lit. 'Go take come'; *fakɔ* 'Take it off,' lit. 'Take go.'

From Yoruba note the following: *mũ$_3$ i$_1$we$_3$ rɛ$_2$ wa$_3$* 'Bring your book,' lit. 'Take your book come.'

In Gullah the verb *to come* is frequently used adverbially before another verb in the sense of 'finally': ɒɪ *kʌm n*ɒ*u si tude*, etc., 'Now, after all this time (or finally), I see today,' etc.

Note in the following sentence from Ewe the use of the verb *va$_3$* 'to come,' which is placed before another verb to describe the gradual introduction of a subject: *le$_1$ ŋ$_1$ke$_1$ke$_1$ a$_1$sie$_3$ke$_1$ me$_1$gbe$_3$ la$_3$ wo$_3$va$_3$ va$_3$ gbã$_1$ e$_3$Φe$_3$ xɔ$_1$* 'After nine days they finally went to pull down his house,' lit. 'After nine days they came went to pull down his house.'

Frequently in Gullah in two contiguous clauses, the predicate of the second describes the action expressed in the predicate of the first. The predicate of the second clause is expressed in English by an adjective or adverb: *de be* ɒ*n yu ən de fil k*ɒɪ*n ə hɛwɪ* 'They bear on you somewhat heavily,' lit. 'They bear on you and they feel somewhat heavy.'

Compare with this the following from Ewe: *me$_1$ḍu$_1$ nu$_3$ wo$_1$sɔ$_1$ gbɔ$_1$* 'I have eaten a great deal,' lit. 'I have eaten thing; it was much'; *e$_3$gblɔ$_1$ ɲa$_1$ wo$_1$di$_1$di$_1$* 'He spoke for a long time,' lit. 'He said a word; it was long.'

Sometimes the predicate of the second clause of a Gullah sentence is rendered in English by the present participle: *lʊk ət dat gos; hi trɒɪ tu ske mɪ* 'Look at that ghost trying to scare me,' lit. 'Look at that ghost; he tries to scare me.'

Note from Ewe: *me₁kpɔ₃e₁ wo₁va₃* 'I saw him coming,' lit. 'I saw him; he came.'

də AS A VERB OF INCOMPLETE PREDICATION

In Gullah the verb *də* 'to be' is used in a present, past, or even future sense, dependent upon the context. Most often it can be rendered in English by a present or past tense, and the action to which it refers may or may not be continuous. When *də* is used in a future sense, it is often followed by the progressive form of some other verb. The following sentences illustrate the various ways in which *də* is used as a verb of incomplete prediction. The tense of the verb in each sentence is determined by the context out of which the sentence is taken:

1. *wɛn də delɐɪt, ɒɪ mɛk mɪ lo kʌcɪ* 'When it is daylight, I make my low curtsy'
2. *də gɒd wʌk* 'It is God's work'
3. *dat də dɛbl we de də ɟi yu nɒʊ* 'That is the devil's way they are giving you now'
4. *dɛm dɛ də kəmplen* 'Those there are complaining'
5. *wat dɛm də ɟi yu?* 'What are they giving you?'
6. *ɒɪ də (s)te dɛ* 'I am staying there'
7. *nɒʊ dɪ cɪlən də frɛt* 'Now the children are fretting'
8. *sʌpm də kʌmɪn* 'Something is coming'
9. *dɪ kɒtn də drɒp blɒsm* 'The cotton was dropping its blossom'
10. *hɪm bɒɪ də fɪks fə dɪ solɟə* 'His boy was fixing for the soldiers'
11. *ən də hɪm sew mi* 'And it was he who saved me'
12. *dɪ wʌl də gwɒɪn ʌpsɒɪd dɒʊn* 'The world was going upside down'
13. *ɒɪ no də ɒgəs* 'I know it was August'
14. *de se də gwɒɪn fɒl in ɒn əs* 'They said it was going to fall in on us'
15. *ɛwɪtɪŋ də krɒɪ* 'Everything was crying'
16. *mi də gwɒɪn gɒn* 'I am going to go'
17. *dɛn yu də brag* 'Then you will brag'

də is used redundantly in the following sentences:

1. *ɛnti də kʌmɪn bak?* 'Is it not coming back?'
2. *dɛm ca əm ɟi dɪ ɲɒŋ pipl wat ẽ də wʌk dɛ ɒn dɛm ples* 'They carry them and give them to the young people who are not working there on their place'

In the Anglo dialect of Ewe the verb *də* (pronounced *de* in the other Ewe dialects), meaning 'to go there,' 'to arrive there,' expresses the English perfect *to have been* in the following sentence: *ɲe*$_1$*me*$_3$*də*$_1$ *a*$_1$*fi*$_3$*ma*$_3$ *kpɔ*$_3$ *o*$_1$ 'I have never been there.' If *də* is followed in the same sentence by the ingressive of a verb, it expresses an almost but not quite completed happening: *me*$_1$*də*$_1$ *ku*$_1$*ku*$_3$ *ge*$_3$ 'I almost died,' lit. 'I reached the neighborhood of death.'[4] In the Ewe sentence *a*$_1$*ti*$_3$ *siaa*$_{3-1}$ *a*$_1$*ti*$_3$ *də*$_1$ *a*$_1$*ma*$_1$ *a*$_1$*zɔ*$_1$ 'Every tree is green now,' *də* is equivalent to the present tense of the English verb *to be.*

The uses of the Gullah *də* 'to be' are in many ways similar to those of the Ibo *de*$_1$, a verb of incomplete predication meaning 'to be.' The following are ways in which *de*$_1$ is used in this West African language:

1. When the predicate is completed by adjectives or by nouns used adjectivally:

n$_3$*wa*$_3$ *n*$_3$*wa*$_3$*ɲe*$_1$ *a*$_3$*ho*$_1$ *de*$_1$ *i*$_3$*kɛ*$_3$ *ka*$_1$ *nwö*$_3$*kɛ*$_3$ *m*$_1$*gbɛ*$_1$ *ɔ*$_3$ *de*$_3$ *n*$_3$*do*$_1$ 'That girl was as strong as a man when she was alive'

i$_3$*bu*$_3$ *de*$_1$ *a*$_2$*lɔ*$_2$ 'The load is heavy'

2. Before nouns qualified by an adjective of quantity and before a numeral:

ha$_3$ *de*$_1$ *m*$_3$*ma*$_3$*do*$_1$ *i*$_1$*sɛ*$_3$ 'They are five men'

ha$_3$ *de*$_1$ *i*$_1$*sɛ*$_3$ 'They are five'

3. In questions with or without interrogative adverbs:

nwa$_3$ *ge*$_3$ *ɔ*$_1$ *de*$_1$ *a*$_1$*ŋ*$_3$*aa*$_3$? 'How is your child?'

ɔ$_1$ *de*$_1$ *a*$_3$*ɲa*$_3$? 'Is it far?'

4. In the sense of 'existing,' 'being present,' and 'seeming':

ö$_1$*bö*$_1$*dö*$_1$ *ni*$_3$*lɛ*$_3$ *de*$_3$ *na*$_1$ *a*$_1$*la*$_1$ *i*$_3$*gbö*$_1$ 'All towns which are in the Ibo Territory'

ɔ$_3$ *de*$_1$ *ka*$_1$ *ha*$_3$ *ga*$_1$-*a*$_1$*bea*$_3$ 'It seems that they will come'

5. *de*$_1$ is placed before the verb root with its vowel prefix to make the present progressive form of the verb. This form in Ibo expresses the continuance of the action rather than the actual time of it:

ɔ$_3$ *de*$_1$ *γa*$_1$*dʒo*$_2$ 'He is not asking'

ɔ$_3$ *ga*$_1$ *a*$_1$ *de*$_3$ *n*$_3$*do*$_1$ 'It will be alive'

COMPARISON OF ADJECTIVES

The English verb *pass* (*surpass*) is sometimes used in Gullah to indicate the comparative and superlative degrees of the adjective, though *mo na*[5] 'more than' is used more frequently to indicate the comparative and *dɪ morɪs* 'the most,' the superlative:

i tɒl pas mi 'He is taller than I,' lit. 'He is tall, surpasses me'
i bɪg pas ɒlə unə 'He is the biggest of all,' lit. He is big, surpasses all of you'
i bɪg mo na unə 'He is bigger than you,' lit. 'He is big, more than you'

In many African languages a verb meaning 'to surpass' is used with the adjective to express the comparative and superlative degrees:

Ewe: *sɔ*$_3$ *lo*$_1$*lo*$_1$ *wu*$_3$ *te*$_3$*dzi*$_3$ 'The horse is larger than the donkey,' lit. 'The horse is large, surpasses the donkey'

e$_3$*lo*$_1$*lo*$_1$ *wu*$_3$ *wo*$_3$ *ka*$_3$*tã*$_3$ 'He is the greatest of them all,' lit. 'He is great, surpasses all'

Twi: *wo turo no yɛ fɛ seŋ me de no* 'Your garden is more beautiful than mine,' lit. 'Your garden is beautiful, surpasses mine'

Fante: *ɛ*$_1$*ku*$_1$*tu*$_1$ *yi*$_3$ *yɛ*$_1$ *dɛu*$_3$ *tʃɛn*$_1$ *ɔ*$_3$*no*$_3$ 'This orange is sweeter than that,' lit. 'This orange is sweet, surpasses that'

tam$_3$ *yi*$_3$ *ho*$_1$*a*$_1$ *sen*$_1$ *ɔ*$_3$*no*$_3$ 'This cloth is whiter than that,' lit. 'This cloth is white, surpasses that'

ɛ$_1$*sũ*$_3$ *ɔ*$_1$*sɔ̃*$_3$ *sen*$_1$ *m*$_1$*moa*$_3$ *ɲi*$_1$*na*$_1$: 'The elephant is the largest of all beasts,' lit. 'The elephant is large, surpasses all beasts'

Ibo: *ha*$_3$ *ka*$_1$ *n*$_3$*di*$_3$ *ɔ*$_1$*zɔ*$_3$ *i*$_3$*kɛ*$_3$ 'They are stronger than the others,' lit. 'They surpass other people strength'

ɔ$_3$ *nɔ*$_1$ *na*$_1$ *a*$_1$*la*$_1$ *ɔ*$_3$*ma*$_3$ *ka*$_3$*ra*$_3$ *i*$_3$*bɛ*$_1$ *ya*$_3$ 'It is in better soil than the other,' lit. 'It is in good soil, surpassing its fellow'

a$_3$*na*$_1$ *ha*$_3$ *a*$_1$*ho*$_3$ *na*$_1$ *ö*$_1$*bö*$_1$*dö*$_1$ *a*$_1$ *ka*$_3$*tʃa*$_3$ *ö*$_1$*bö*$_1$*dö*$_1$ *a*$_1$*bo*$_1$*a*$_3$ *n*$_3$*di*$_3$ *ɔ*$_1$*zɔ*$_3$ 'They see that this town is the best of the three,' lit. 'They see that this town completely surpasses the other two'

Kikongo: *kiandu kiaki kisundidi kiokio mu mfunu* 'This chair is more useful than that,' lit. 'This chair surpasses that in usefulness'

yandi uviokɛlɛ awɔnso mu la 'He is the tallest of all,' lit. 'He excels all in height'

Kimbundu: *yu watundu una mu kuwaba* 'This one is more beautiful than that,' lit. 'This one excels that one in beauty'

mutu yu utunda oso mu kuwaba 'This person is the most beautiful of all,' lit. 'This person surpasses all in beauty'

Mandinka: *ɲinnuŋ tiolu siata, a tambita serunti* 'The groundnuts are more plentiful this year than last,' lit. 'This year the groundnuts are plenty, pass last year'

VERBAL ADJECTIVES

Another characteristic common to both Gullah and the West African languages is the very extensive use of verbal adjectives. These words combine adjective and verb into one. They are also called descriptive or adjectival verbs. In the following sentences from Gullah the words *mean* and *tall* signify 'to be mean,' 'to be tall':

i min tɪd dat 'He was mean to do that'; *i tɒl* 'He is tall.' Employment of the verbal adjective results in a type of sentence in which the predicate complement is placed next to the subject without any sign of predication, being similar in structure to the appositional type of sentence widely used in English, especially in colloquial speech, advertisements, in the headlines of newspapers, etc.[6]

The verbal adjective is a common phenomenon in the West African languages. In Ewe it may be made into a real adjective by reduplication or by the suffixing of e_3. When thus made into a real adjective it is generally used attributively only:

a_1ti_3 la_3 $kɔ_3$ 'The tree is high,' la_3 being the word for 'the'; a_1ti_3 $kɔ_3kɔ_3$ 'high tree'

xe_1vi_3 la_3 $ɲo_3$ 'The bird is pretty'; xe_1vi_3 $ɲui_3$ (<$ɲoe_3$) 'pretty bird'

The verbal adjective in Ewe which is already a reduplication is used unchanged as a real adjective:

gli_1 la_3 ke_1ke_1 'The wall is broad'; gli_1 ke_1ke_1 'broad wall'

Examples of the verbal adjective in other West African languages are as follows:

Fante: hwa_3 'to be white'
$dɔ_3$ 'to be deep'
bir_3 'to be black'

Yoruba: $d\tilde{u}_1$ 'to be sweet'
du_3 'to be black'
$f\tilde{u}_3$ 'to be white'

Mandinka: *kidi* 'to be lonely'
toɲa 'to be true,

Kikongo: *kiadi* 'It sad,' i.e., 'It is sad'
kiaki nɛnɛ 'It great,' i.e., 'It is great'
lɛbɛlɛbɛ 'to be flexible'

Kimbundu: *ene makamba* 'They friends,' i.e., 'They are friends'
kusukuka 'to be red,' 'become red'
kubeta 'to be wet'

WORD ORDER

Reference has been made to the fact that the sentences of Gullah and those of the West African languages have many characteristics in common that are not found in the English sentence. These often result in a word order that appears strange to one hearing Gullah for the first time. For example, in Gullah and the West African languages, as already noted, a verb frequently takes the place of an English conjunction, participle, preposition, or adverb with the result that two or more verbs may fall together in a sentence without any other word or words intervening.[7] Moreover, the common practice of both the Gullahs and the West Africans of using a group of words as the equivalent in cultivated English of a noun, a verb, an adverb, or some other part of speech may result in quite a different word order from that of the English sentence.[8] Likewise, their frequent failure to use articles and, in certain constructions, prepositions, pronouns, or other parts of speech that would be required in English contributes greatly to the strangeness of the word order of their sentences.[9]

There are other characteristics that the West African languages and Gullah have in common in regard to word order. Though most, if not all, of these can be found in languages familiar to Americans, the fact that they are of such common occurrence in both the West African languages and in Gullah warrants their being given here.

When the Gullah speaker places the adjective immediately after the noun, it is not always the verbal adjective that he is using; it is sometimes the attributive adjective: e.g., *rol rɒuŋ* 'roll round,' i.e., 'round roll, biscuit'; *de klin brɒd* 'day clean broad,' i.e., 'broad daylight': *prɒɪməs wɒd* 'primary ward,' i.e., 'ward primary'; *ʌtkwek bɪg* 'an earthquake big,' i.e., 'a big earthquake,' etc.

Placing the adjective after the noun it modifies is a common practice among speakers of African languages:

Fante:	*ɲim$_3$pa$_3$ a$_1$tsen$_3$tsen$_3$ du$_2$ no$_2$* 'men tall ten the,' i.e., the ten tall men'
	a$_1$fra$_3$ pa$_3$ 'child good,' i.e., 'good child'
Ewe:	*a$_1$ti$_3$ kɔ$_3$kɔ$_3$* 'tree high,' i.e., 'high tree'
	xɔ$_1$ ɲui$_3$ 'house good,' i.e., 'good house'
Twi:	*ɔsamaŋ pa* 'a ghost good,' i.e., 'a good ghost'
	ɔba bone 'a child bad,' i.e., 'a bad child'
Gã:	*gbe$_3$kẽ$_2$ kpa$_2$kpa$_2$* 'child good,' i.e., 'good child'
Ibo:	*i$_3$hɛ$_3$ ɔ$_3$dʒɔ$_3$ɔ$_3$* 'thing bad,' i.e., 'bad thing'
	ö$_3$ɲɛ$_3$ a$_3$ɲa$_3$ u$_3$ku$_3$ 'person covetous,' i.e., 'covetous person'
Yoruba:	*o$_2$hũ$_2$ bu$_2$bu$_2$ru$_3$* 'thing bad,' i.e., 'bad thing'
Kimbundu:	*muzueri wɔnene* 'the talker great,' i.e., 'the great talker'
	kambinda kɔlulu 'gourd old,' i.e., 'old gourd'
Tshiluba:	*dikɛla dimpe* 'egg good,' i.e., 'good egg'
	mitʃi mile 'sticks long,' i.e., long sticks'
Kikongo:	*nti wambɔtɛ* 'a tree good,' i.e., 'a good tree'

In Gullah the pronoun and noun used in the predicate frequently are placed immediately after the subject without the verb *to be*:[10]

hu hi? 'Who is he?'; *hu dat?* 'Who is that?'; *wɒt it?* 'What is it?'; *hu ɟɒn?* 'Who is John?' etc.

Compare with these the following sentences from the Ewe language: *a$_1$ḍa$_3$ka$_1$e$_3$* 'a box it,' i.e., 'a box it is'; *nu$_3$kae$_1$?* 'What it?' i.e., 'What is it?'; *a$_1$me$_1$kae$_1$?* 'Who it?' i.e., 'Who is it?'; *ga$_1$e$_3$* 'It money,' i.e., 'It is money.'

Among the Gullahs also the practice of opening a sentence with its subject or object and of repeating this subject or object by the use of a personal pronoun is so common as to warrant mention here, though such word order is frequently used for emphasis by speakers of cultivated English.[11] The same variety of word order is quite common also in several West African languages:

Gullah: *tu baskɪt, wɒt ɪt kʌm tu?* 'Two baskets, what do they come to?'
dɪ man ən hi wɒɪf haŋ tu dɪ tri, dɛm lɪk tu pisɪz 'The man and his wife hanging to the tree, they were licked to pieces'
wi wɒt bɪn ɒn dɪ ples, wi sew wʌn ə tu 'We who were on the place, we saved one or two'
rɛbl tɒɪm, wɒt dɛm də ɟi yu? 'Rebel time [slavery], what did it give you?'
ɛn mɪs batn, ən i ɟi yu raʃɪn 'And Miss Barton, and she gave you the ration'
dɛn dɪ wʌn ə wəm hu wek, hil tek ə hanfʊl ə mʌstəd sid ən tro əm ɒndə dɪ bɛd 'Then the one of them who is awake, he'll take a handful of mustard seeds and throw them under the bed'

Yoruba: *i$_1$ya$_3$ mi$_2$, o$_3$ti$_2$ ku$_3$* 'My mother, she has died'
ɛ$_1$gbɔ̃$_3$ mi$_2$, o$_3$ wa$_2$ ni$_3$nũ$_3$ ɛ$_1$gbɛ$_3$ o$_2$gũ$_2$ 'My brother, he is in the Army'

Ewe: *yɛ$_1$vu$_3$wo$_3$ ḍe$_1$ wo$_3$ɲa$_{3-1}$ nu$_3$* 'The Europeans, they know something'
a$_1$fi$_3$ba$_3$ ya$_3$ kpɔ$_3$e$_1$ 'Afiba, she saw it'
kɔm$_1$la$_3$ ya$_3$ me$_3$wɔe$_1$ o$_1$ 'Kɒmla, he did not do it'
a$_1$ti$_3$ ma$_3$ ɲe$_1$me$_3$kpɔe$_3$ o$_1$ 'That tree, I have not seen it'

Kimbundu: *wanda wɔtakula buʃi* 'The net, he throws it down'
mulele, wɔʃi ku me a 'The loincloth, he leaves it at the water'

Kongo: *ɔ madia ma dia ŋge, mau mavidi* 'The food for you to eat, it is ready'

Finally, in interrogative sentences the Gullah speaker usually places the subject before the verb just as he does in declarative sentences, and in both questions and statements he regularly omits the auxiliary *do*.[12] In many instances the question can be distinguished from the statement by the intonation, but not always. In cultivated English when questions requiring *yes* or *no* for an answer involve the element of surprise, the word order is usually that of the declarative sentence, and there is a rising tone on the last stressed syllable: e.g., *You are ill?* The same word order and intonation are used in English when one does not understand a statement and asks for a repetition of it: e.g., *Did you say you were ill?* In Gullah, however, a question requiring *yes* or *no* for an answer usually has the word order of the declarative sentence whether or not the element of surprise is present, and the tone on the last stressed syllable is not always a rising one. It is frequently a level or even a falling tone. Note the following questions and statements:[13]

ˈ*yu*$_3$ *no*$_3$ *wɒt*$_3$ *dɛm*$_3$ ˈ*pe*$_3$ *fə*$_2$ ˈ*bin*$_3$*?* 'You know what they pay for beans?'
ˈɒɪ$_3$ *nɒt*$_3$ ˈʃʌ*m*$_3$ 'I not see him'
ˈ*mi*$_3$ *nə*$_2$ ˈ*gwɒɪn*$_3$ *fə*$_2$ *no*$_2$ ˈ*flɒ*$_2$*wə*$_2$ 'I not going for no flour'
ˈ*wɒt*$_3$ ɪ*t*$_3$ ˈ*kʌm*$_3$ *tu*$_3$*?* 'What it comes to?'
wɒt$_3$ ˈ*dɛm*$_{2-1}$ *də*$_1$ ˈɟ*i*$_2$ *yu*$_2$*?* 'What they are giving you?'
ˈɒɪ$_1$ *gwɒɪn*$_1$ ˈ*lɛf*$_3$ *mɒɪ*$_3$ ˈ*home*$_{3-1}$*?* 'I going leave my home?'

In many African languages the word order in interrogative sentences is the same as that in statements.

In Efik, for example, these two types of sentences have the same word order, but in some forms the tones of the verb in the question are different from those of the statement; in many the intonation is the same; and in a few there is more than one possible intonation.[14]

In the following sentences from the Ewe language, the question is distinguished from the statement only by the addition of an interrogative particle which usually has a low tone:

e$_1$*kpɔe*$_3$*a*$_1$*?* 'You saw him?'; *a*$_1$*ma*$_3$*ḍe*$_3$*ke*$_3$ *me*$_3$*va*$_3$ *oa*$_1$ 'Nobody has come?'; *wo*$_3$*ga*$_1$*le*$_1$ *a*$_1$*fi*$_3$*a*$_1$ 'They still are here?'

In the two following sentences from Gã, only the intonation distinguishes the question from the statement:

o$_2$*ya*$_2$ ŋ*mɛ*$_3$*nɛ*$_{3-2}$*?* 'You are going today?'
o$_1$*ya*$_1$ ŋ*mɛ*$_2$*nɛ*$_2$ 'You are going today'

In Ibo, except when a noun subject is involved, the only difference between a statement and a question without an interrogative word is one of tone:

u$_1$*nu*$_1$ *ma*$_1$*ra*$_1$ *o*$_2$*zɔ*$_1$*?* 'You know the road?'
u$_3$*nu*$_1$ *ma*$_1$*ra*$_1$ *o*$_2$*zɔ*$_1$ 'You know the road'

In the two following sentences from Yoruba, one of which is a question and the other a reply to it, note the similarity between the tonal patterns:

i$_1$*wɔ*$_2$ *ba*$_3$ *mi*$_2$ *sɔ*$_1$*rɒ*$_1$ *ni*$_2$*?* 'You spoke to me?'
bɛ:$_{3-1}$*ni*$_2$ *mo*$_2$ *ba*$_3$ ɔ$_2$ *sɔ*$_1$*rɔ*$_1$ *ni*$_2$ 'Yes, I spoke to you'

Note also the following negative statements from Yoruba:

e$_2$*mi*$_3$ *ko*$_1$ *mɔ̃*$_1$ 'I not know'
ma$_3$ *lɔ*$_2$ 'Not go,' i.e., 'Do not go'

In Kikongo the word order in questions is the same as that in statements. The distinction is revealed in the intonation. Frequently also, but not always, the interrogative sentence ends in the particle ɛ:

wɛti kwɛ:nda wunu? 'You are leaving today?'
wɛti kwɛ:nda wunu 'You are leaving today'

In the question, *kwɛ:nda* receives a high tone on the first syllable and a low one on the second; *wunu* receives a high tone on both syllables. In the statement, *kwɛ:nda* has a low tone on both syllables; *wunu*, a high tone on the first syllable and a low one on the second.

Likewise in the Vai language, distinction between the question and the statement is revealed in the tone rather than in the word order:

a$_3$ *la*$_2$ *na*$_3$ 'He has come?'
a$_3$ *la*$_1$ *na*$_1$ 'He has come'

FREQUENT REPETITION OF WORDS AND PHRASES THROUGHOUT THE SENTENCE

The practice of repeating words and phrases throughout the sentence is general among both the Gullahs and the West Africans, especially in narrative:[15]

Gullah: *mɒɪn cɪlən, mɒɪn cɪlən, mɒɪn cɪlən—rɛbl tɒɪm—mɒɪn cɪlən, mɒɪn cɪlən rɛbl tɒɪm fə dɪ bʌkrə* '[I] mind children . . . during rebel times [slavery] . . . for the white man'

ɒɪ *gɔɪn tɛl dɪ storɪ bɐʊt dɪ—bɐʊt dɪ gos. wʌn de dɪ gos trɒɪ-ɪn tu ske mi. an wɛn dɪ gos trɒɪ tu ske mi, i wəz kʌmɪn pas dɪ hɐʊs; an dɛə* ɪz ə *wɒɪə fɛnc rʌn. an aftə dɪ wɒɪə fɛnc rʌn lɒŋ lɐɪk dat, an* ɒɪ *gɪt tu dɪ wɒɪə fɛnc,* ɒɪ *pɪt mɒɪ han ɒn dɪ wɒɪə; an wɛn* ɒɪ *pɪt* mɒɪ *han ɒn dɪ wɒɪə, i se, 'bu!' etc.* 'I am going to tell the story about the—about the ghost. One day the ghost was trying to scare me. And when the ghost tried to scare, he was coming past the house; and a wire fence ran there. And after the wire fence ran along like that, and I got to the wire fence, I put my hand on the wire; and when I put my hand on the wire, he said, "Booh!" etc.'

ɒɪ *yɛdɪ di hɐʊs krakɪn, yu no, at dɪ bak; yɛdi dɪ hɐʊs krakɪn, krakɪn; an* ɒɪ *lɪsn, kipə lɪsnɪn* 'I heard the house cracking, you know, at the back; heard the house cracking, cracking; and I listened; kept listening'

yu no wɒt dɛm pe fə bin? yu no wɒt dɛm pe fə bin? fɒɪw n wʌn sɛnt. wɛn yu pɪk ʌp dɛm bin—dat laɪmə bin—yu ẽ nɛwə gɒt bət fɒɪw n wʌn sɛnt in tred 'Do you know what they pay for beans? Do you know what they pay for beans? Five and one cents. When you pick those beans—those lima beans—you never have but five and one cents in trade'

ɛnti, ɛnti rɛbl tɒɪm kʌmɪn bak? ɒl hu nɛwə ʃʌm—ɛnti də kʌmɪn bak? 'Is it not, is not rebel time [slavery] coming back? All who never saw it—is it not coming back?'

ɒɪ *ẽ gɒɪn wʌrɪ ə sol;* ɒɪ *satɪfɒɪ wɒt gɒd dʌn fə mi;* ɒɪ *ẽ gɒɪn wʌrɪ ə sol;* ɒɪ *satifɒɪ wɒt i dʌn fə mi; nɒʊ,* ɒɪ *satɪfɒɪ. wɒt i dʌn fə mi* ɒɪ *satɪfɒɪ* 'I am not going to worry a soul; I am satisfied [with] what God has done for me; I am not going to worry a soul; I am satisfied [with] what he has done for me. Now, I am satisfied; [with] what he has done for me I am satisfied'

dɛn de brag, se dɪ nɪgə mɛk dɛm krɒp, mɛk dɛm—mɛk dɛm krɒp ɒf kɒn, kɒn 'Then they brag, saying that the Negro makes their crop, makes their—makes their crop off corn, corn'

dɛn wɛn yu ho kɒn, de ɟi yu twɛl sɛnt fə ho kɒn, twɛl sɛnt 'Then when you hoe corn, they give you twelve cents to hoe corn, twelve cents'

Several examples from one West African language, Yoruba, will be sufficient here to illustrate the extent to which repetitions occur in the sentences of the West African. These passages have been taken from Yoruba narratives, told to me by Brazilian ex-slaves born in Nigeria and by their descendants, which I recorded in Northeastern Brazil during the year 1940–41:

(From ɔ$_2$mɔ̃$_2$bĩ$_1$rĩ$_2$, ɔ$_2$mɔ̃$_2$kũ$_2$rĩ$_2$, a$_1$ti$_2$ ɔ$_2$mɔ̃$_2$wɔ̃$_2$ 'The Young Woman, the Young Man, and Their Son'):

o$_3$ mũ$_3$ i$_2$ʃu$_2$ ti$_2$ e$_2$re$_1$; o$_3$ se$_2$ i$_2$ʃu$_2$ ti$_2$ e$_2$re$_1$;
She took her portion of the yam; she cooked her portion of the yam;

ni$_3$gba$_1$to$_2$ se$_2$ ti$_2$ e$_2$re$_1$, o$_3$ se$_2$ i$_2$ʃu$_2$ e$_2$re$_1$. . . .
when she cooked her portion, she cooked the yam. . . .

ɔ$_2$mɔ̃$_2$de$_3$ nã:$_{3-1}$ bi$_3$nũ$_3$; ɔ$_2$mɔ̃$_2$de$_3$ nã:$_{3-1}$ bi$_3$nũ$_3$, ŋ$_3$kɔ$_3$.
The child became angry; the child became angry, you know.

o$_3$ ni$_3$ o$_1$ũ$_2$ ɔ$_1$ fɛ$_2$ ɟɛ$_2$ yi$_{1-2}$, i$_3$ba$_3$yi$_{1-2}$. . . .
He said he did not like to eat this, this little thing. . . .

ɔ$_2$mɔ̃$_2$de$_3$ nã:$_{3-1}$ bɛ$_1$rɛ$_1$ si$_3$ wɔ$_2$lɛ$_1$; o$_3$ ŋ$_3$ku$_3$lɔ$_2$; o$_3$ ŋ$_3$ku$_3$lɔ$_2$.
The child began to enter the ground; he was dying; he was dying.

(From e$_2$ho$_2$ro$_2$, a$_2$ɟa$_3$, e$_1$wu$_3$rɛ$_3$, a$_1$ti$_2$ ɛ:$_2$dũ$_2$ 'The Rabbit, the Dog, the Goat, and the Chimpanzee')

a$_2$ɟa$_3$ lo$_3$ gbe$_3$ i$_1$lu$_1$ e$_2$ho$_2$ro$_2$ lɔ$_2$;
The dog it was who stole the drum of the rabbit;
a$_2$ɟa$_3$ gbe:$_3$lɔ$_2$; gbo$_2$gbo$_2$ nwɔ̃$_3$ si$_1$ mũ$_3$ a$_2$ɟa$_3$; nwɔ̃$_3$ lu:$_2$;
The dog stole it; and all of them caught the dog; they beat him;
nwɔ̃$_3$ mũ:$_3$ lɔ$_2$ si$_3$ ɛ$_1$wɔ̃$_1$; nwɔ̃$_3$ si$_1$ lu:$_2$ kpa$_2$.
they took him to prison; they beat him and killed him.

(From o$_2$lo$_3$ko$_2$, e$_2$re$_1$, a$_1$ti$_2$ o$_2$le$_1$ 'The Farmer, the Snake, and the Thief')

e$_2$ɟo$_1$ n$_3$la$_3$ kã$_2$ ni$_2$ nwɔ̃$_3$ kpe$_1$ni$_2$ e$_2$re$_1$, e$_2$ɟo$_1$ n$_3$la$_3$,
A big snake it was they called *ere*, big snake,
to$_3$ gbe$_3$ e$_1$ni$_1$yã$_1$ mi$_1$, to$_3$ gbe$_3$ ma$_1$lu:$_{3-2}$ mi$_1$,
which swallowed a person, [and] which swallowed a cow,
o$_1$ũ$_2$ ni$_2$ nwɔ̃$_3$ ŋ$_3$kpe$_1$ ni$_3$ e$_2$re$_1$. . . .
he it was they were calling by the name of *ere*. . . .
ɔ$_2$ba$_2$ yio$_3$ da$_3$wo$_3$ fũ$_3$ ɔ$_2$; da$_3$wo$_3$ fũ$_3$ ɔ$_2$. . . .
The king will provide money for you; provide money for you. . . .
o$_2$le$_1$ wi$_3$kpe$_3$, o$_2$le$_1$ wi$_3$kpe$_3$, 'a:$_{2-1}$! e$_2$ɟo$_1$ n$_3$la$_3$ ba$_3$yi$_{1-2}$,
The thief said, the thief said, 'Ah! a big snake like this,
a$_1$bi$_3$ e$_1$ni$_1$yã$_1$ lo$_3$ gbe$_3$ mi$_1$.' . . .
perhaps it was a person that he swallowed.' . . .
a$_2$ra$_2$ fu$_2$ o$_2$lo$_3$ko$_2$; gba$_1$ti$_3$ a$_2$ra$_2$ fu$_2$ o$_2$lo$_3$ko$_2$,
The farmer was suspicious; when the farmer was suspicious,
o$_3$ wi$_3$fũ$_3$ ba:$_2$lɛ$_1$.
he told the governor.

(From ɔ$_2$mɔ̃$_2$nã:$_{3-1}$ ɟɛ$_2$ a$_1$ɟɛ$_2$ɟu$_1$ 'The Child Eats Too Much')

bo$_3$ ti$_3$ le$_1$ ɟɛ$_2$ũ$_2$ to$_3$, ɟɛ$_2$ũ$_2$ kpa$_2$ra$_2$, o$_3$ ni$_3$
Because he [the child] could eat much, eat too much, he said,
i$_1$ya$_3$ ɛ$_1$, o$_3$ ra$_2$ ɛ$_2$rã$_2$ si$_3$lɛ$_1$ ko$_3$ fi$_2$ kɔ$_2$ka$_1$ ɟɛ$_2$
his mother, she bought meat [and] left [it] with which he should eat
ɔ$_2$ka$_1$.
cooked yam flour.
ba$_2$ba$_2$ rɛ$_2$ɟa$_2$ si$_3$lɛ$_1$ o$_3$ ni$_3$, ko$_3$ fi$_2$ kɔ̃$_2$bɛ$_1$
The father bought fish [and] left [it], he said, with which he should
ɟɛ$_2$. . . .
eat soup. . . .
ba$_2$ba$_2$ fɛ$_2$ɟa$_2$ si$_3$lɛ$_1$, o$_3$ ni$_3$, ko$_3$ fi$_2$ kɔ̃$_2$bɛ$_1$ ɟɛ$_2$. . . .
The father left fish, he said, with which he should eat soup. . . .
o$_3$ fɛ$_2$rã$_2$ ɟɛ$_2$ o$_3$ si$_1$ ko$_3$ ɛ$_2$ɟa$_2$ na:$_{3-1}$ gbo$_2$gbo$_2$ gbo$_2$gbo$_2$ ɛ$_1$,
He [the child] ate the meat and he took all the fish, all of it, in the
ba$_3$kã$_2$nã:$_{3-1}$, lo$_3$ ko$_2$ ɟɛ$_2$.
same way, so that he took it to eat.

CHAPTER 5

MORPHOLOGICAL FEATURES

THE many similarities in form between the nouns, pronouns, and verbs of Gullah and those of the West African languages will be considered under the categories of number, tense, case, and gender.

NUMBER

A. Nouns

Practically all Gullah nouns have the same form in the plural as in the singular.[1] Distinction is made by the use of a qualifying demonstrative pronoun or a numeral adjective: e.g., *dɛm bɒɪ* 'those boys,' *fɒɪw dɒg* 'five dogs.'

There is precedent for this practice in many West African languages.

In Ibo the singular form of a noun is the same as the plural. When it is necessary to make a distinction, one method is to prefix a word to the noun to indicate the plural: e.g., $nwö_3kɛ_3$ 'man,' n_3di_3 $nwö_3kɛ_3$ 'men' (n_3di_3 meaning 'those' or 'people'). A less common method is to use a reduplicated form of the singular.

In Ewe the plural of nouns is formed by adding to the singular the third personal pronoun wo_3 'they': e.g., $xɔ_1$ 'house,' $xɔ_1wo_3$ 'houses'; a_1me_1 'human being,' $a_1me_1wo_3$ 'human beings'; a_1ti_3 'tree,' $a_1ti_3wo_3$ 'trees.'

One method of forming the plural of nouns in Gã is to add to the singular form the word $mẽĩ_1$ 'people': e.g., $nun_3tʃɔ_2$ 'master,' $nun_3tʃɔ_2$-$mẽĩ_1$ 'masters.' Another method is to add to the singular form the word $bi:_{3-2}$ 'children': e.g., $tʃa_1tʃu_2$ 'ant,' $tʃa_1tʃu_2bi:_{3-2}$ 'ants,' lit. 'the children of the ant.'[2]

In Yoruba the plural of nouns is formed (1) by placing the third personal pronoun $a_1wɔ̃_2$ 'they' before the noun, or (2) by placing $a_1wɔ̃_2$ before the noun and the demonstrative pronoun $wɔ̃_1yi_3$ 'these' or $wɔ̃:_2ni_1$ 'those' after it, or (3) by placing the numeral adjective after the noun: e.g., $ɔ_2mɔ̃_2de_3$ 'child,' $a_1wɔ̃_2$ $ɔ_2mɔ̃_2de_3$ 'children'; $ɔ_2kɔ̃_2rĩ_2$ 'man,' $a_1wɔ̃_2$ $ɔ_2kɔ̃_2rĩ_2$ $wɔ̃_1yi_3$ 'these men'; ki_2ni_3 'thing,' $a_1wɔ̃_2$ ki_2ni_3 $wɔ̃:_2ni_1$ 'those things'; $o_2bĩ_1rĩ_2$ 'woman,' $o_2bĩ_1rĩ_2$ $me_3ɟi_1$

'two women.' The Yoruba word *ɔ$_2$mɔ̃$_2$de$_3$* 'child' has another plural form, *ma$_1$ɟe$_1$ʃi$_3$*, less frequently heard than *a$_1$wɔ̃$_2$ ɔ$_2$mɔ̃$_2$de$_3$*.

In Kongo nouns of Classes 2, 4, 6, and 12, the forms of the singular and the plural are the same: e.g., *nzɔ* 'house' or 'houses,' *niɔka* 'snake' or 'snakes,' *nti* 'tree' or 'trees,' *kwa* 'potato' or 'potatoes,' *wivwa* 'mushroom' or 'mushrooms.'

In Tshiluba nouns of Class 3, there is no distinction in form between the singular and the plural: e.g., *nʃila* 'path' or 'paths,' *nsuba* 'house' or 'houses,' *mpuku* 'rat' or 'rats.'

Most Efik nouns have the same form in the plural as in the singular. Distinction is frequently made by the use of adjectives: e.g., *e$_1$kpat$_1$* 'bag,' *e$_1$di$_3$wak$_1$ e$_2$kpat$_1$* 'many bags'; *i$_3$kɔ$_{3-1}$* 'word,' *e$_1$di$_3$wak$_1$ i$_2$kɔ$_1$* 'many words.' The plural of some nouns, however, is indicated by inflection: e.g., *ɔf$_3$n$_1$* 'slave,' *if$_3$n$_1$* 'slaves.'

B. Verbs

There is no distinction in form between the singular and plural of the Gullah verb. Both are uninflected: *mi go, unə go, i go, wi go, unə go, dɛm go* 'I go,' 'you go,' 'he goes,' 'we go,' 'you go,' 'they go.'

This phenomenon of the verb form remaining unchanged throughout the singular and plural is common in the African languages:

Ewe:	*yi$_1$* 'to go':	
	me$_1$ yi$_1$ 'I go'	*mie$_3$ yi$_1$* 'we go'
	e$_1$ yi$_1$ 'you go'	*mie$_1$ yi$_1$* 'you go'
	e$_3$ yi$_1$ 'he goes'	*wo$_3$ yi$_1$* 'they go'
Fante:	*bɛn$_1$* 'to approach':	
	me$_3$ bɛn$_1$ 'I approach'	*yɛ$_3$ bɛn$_1$* 'we approach'
	e$_3$ bɛn$_1$ 'you approach'	*hom$_3$ bɛn$_1$* 'you approach'
	ɔ$_3$ bɛn$_1$ 'he approaches'	*wɔ$_3$ bɛn$_1$* 'they approach'
Yoruba:	*wa$_1$* 'to be':	
	e$_2$mi$_3$ wa$_1$ 'I am'	*a$_2$wa$_2$ wa$_1$* 'we are'
	i$_1$wɔ$_2$ wa$_1$ 'you are'	*ɛ$_2$yĩ$_3$ wa$_1$* 'you are'
	o$_1$ũ$_2$ wa$_1$ 'he is'	*nwɔ̃$_3$ wa$_1$* 'they are'
	fɛ$_3$rã$_1$ 'to love':	
	e$_2$mi$_3$ fɛ$_3$rã$_1$ 'I love'	*a$_2$wa$_2$ fɛ$_3$rã$_1$* 'we love'
	i$_1$wɔ$_2$ fɛ$_3$rã$_1$ 'you love'	*ɛ$_2$yĩ$_3$ fɛ$_3$rã$_1$* 'you love'
	o$_1$ũ$_2$ fɛ$_3$rã$_1$ 'he loves'	*nwɔ̃$_3$ fɛ$_3$rã$_1$* 'they love'
Gã:	*le$_1$* 'to know':	
	mi$_2$ le$_1$ 'I know'	*wɔ$_2$ le$_1$* 'we know'
	o$_2$ le$_1$ 'you know'	*ɲẽ$_2$ le$_1$* 'you know'
	e$_2$ le$_1$ 'he knows'	*a$_2$mɛ̃$_2$ le$_1$* 'they know'

TENSE

In Gullah little importance is attached to the actual time when an event takes place. It may be the manner of the action (mood), or the character of it (aspect), or possibly both as they impress the Gullah speaker at the moment that are important. Accordingly, the form of the verb used to refer to present time is frequently the same as that used in reference to the past, and often there is no change in form when the future is intended. Likewise, there is usually no special form to indicate whether or not the action is continuous. The practice of the Gullah speaker is to select the simplest form of the verb, before which he may or may not place the word *də*: ɒɪ *go* or ɒɪ *də go* may mean any of the following: 'I go,' 'I went,' 'I am going,' 'I was going,' 'I shall go,' or even 'I had gone.' Usually, however, the future is indicated by prefixing the word *going* to the verb *go* without *to*. In Gullah also, *bɪnə* 'been' placed before a verb may be expressed in English by the past, perfect, or pluperfect tense and the action may or may not be continuous: *wɒt unə binə du?* means 'What did you do?' or 'What were you doing?' or 'What have you done?' or 'What have you been doing?' or 'What had you done?' or 'What had you been doing?'

This practice of using a certain form of the verb with very general application as to the exact time of an action is common in many of the West African languages, though these languages employ a great many more forms of the verb than Gullah.

In the Ewe language, for example, the verb is unchangeable. Tense and mood forms are made by a combination of several verbs or of verbs and nouns, and it is difficult to distinguish between tense and mood. One verb form, designated by many grammarians as the aorist, does not indicate any particular time but can represent the present, past, or even future, according to the context. For example, me_1yi_1 can be translated 'I go,' 'I went,' or 'I am going'; $e_3\Phi om_1$ may mean 'He strikes me' or 'He struck me.'

In Mandinka the actual time when an action takes place is of less importance than the nature of the action as regards its completeness or incompleteness. Accordingly, there are three aspects of the verb: the first represents an action without reference to its completeness or incompleteness; the second describes an action which is being continued; and the third describes one which has been completed. In each of these aspects are found varying degrees of time—present, past, and future. The simple past form of transitive verbs is employed to refer to present, past, and future time; whereas the past form of intransitive verbs refers only to the past. There is no form in Mandinka which corresponds to the English present tense. Either the simple past or the continuous present is used instead. The continuous present is also used in a future sense: *m be burila* can mean either 'I am running' or 'I am going to run.'[3]

In Ibo the past form under certain conditions is used to express an action in either present or past time, dependent upon the context: *ö*$_3$ *gwu*$_1$*ru*$_1$ *dʒi*$_3$ means 'He digs yams' when the statement is made without qualification or doubt; whereas the same statement means 'He dug yams' when the words used with it refer to the past or when it is made in answer to a question referring to the past. On the other hand, the present form in the expression *ö*$_3$ *gwu*$_1$*ro*$_3$ *dʒi*$_3$ may in a certain context refer to past action. Similarly, the present progressive form may refer to continuous action in the past.

In Fante the past form of a verb can be distinguished from the present by a change in tone or by the prefixing of *n*$_3$*na*$_1$ 'then' or *n*$_1$*tʃɛ*$_1$ 'sometime ago' to the present:

PRESENT

me$_3$ *bɛn*$_1$ 'I approach'	*yɛ*$_3$ *bɛn*$_1$ 'we approach'
e$_3$ *bɛn*$_1$ 'you approach'	*hom*$_3$ *bɛn*$_1$ 'you approach'
ɔ$_3$ *bɛn*$_1$ 'he approaches'	*wɔ*$_3$ *bɛn*$_1$ 'they approach'

PAST

me$_1$ *bɛn*$_3$ 'I approached'	*yɛ*$_1$ *bɛn*$_3$ 'we approached'
e$_1$ *bɛn*$_3$ 'you approached'	*hom*$_1$ *bɛn*$_3$ 'you approached'
ɔ$_1$ *bɛn*$_3$ 'he approached'	*wɔ*$_1$ *bɛn*$_3$ 'they approached'

Examples of the second method of distinguishing the past from the present in Fante are the following: *ɔ*$_3$*hor*$_1$ 'He washes,' *n*$_3$*na*$_1$ *ɔ*$_1$*hor*$_1$ 'Then he washes,' i.e., 'He washed'; *n*$_1$*tʃɛ*$_1$ *wɔ*$_3$*hor*$_1$ 'Sometime ago they wash,' i.e., 'They used to wash.'

This latter method of indicating a past event by prefixing to the present tense of the verb a word or phrase referring to the past, such as *then, sometime ago,* etc., is frequently used in Gullah.

In Yoruba the present and past indefinite tenses are alike in form: *mo*$_2$*lɔ*$_2$ 'I go' or 'I went'; *a*$_2$*wa*$_2$ *de*$_3$ 'We return' or 'We returned'; *o*$_3$ *sũ*$_1$ 'He sleeps' or 'He slept.' If necessary for clearness the Yoruba speaker may add a statement specifying the time intended: *o*$_3$ *sũ*$_1$ *la*$_3$*na*$_2$ 'Yesterday he slept.'

In Kongo the indicative mood has no future tense. Whenever future time is spoken of, the time or circumstance of the action is distinctly mentioned, and the action is represented as being then present. Instead of saying: *I will come,* Kongo speakers say: ɔ *mbaʒi ŋkwiza* 'Tomorrow I am coming.'[4]

In Kimbundu the simple present tense expresses a universal truth, something that is always a fact, that is habitual. This tense often has the force of a future.[5]

CASE

A. Pronouns

In Gullah the nominative or subjective forms of the personal pronoun are practically the same as the objective forms and the forms of the possessive.

NOMINATIVE

Singular	Plura
mi (sometimes ɒɪ) 'I'	*wi* 'we'
'*unə* 'you'	'*unə* 'you'
i, hɪm 'he'	*dɛm* (sometimes *de*) 'they'

OBJECTIVE

mi 'me'	*wi* 'us'
'*unə* 'you'	'*unə* 'you'
hɪm, əm 'him'	*dɛm* 'them'
ʃi 'her'	

POSSESSIVE

mi, mɒɪ 'my'	*wi* 'our'
'*unə* 'your'	'*unə* 'your'
hɪm 'his'	*dɛm, dɛm on* 'their'
ʃi 'her'	

A glance at the declension of personal and possessive pronouns in several of the West African languages will reveal practically the same situation as exists in Gullah.

Ibo:

PERSONAL

NOMINATIVE

Singular	Plural
m_3, mu_3 'I'	$a_1ɲi_3$ 'we'
ge_3, gi_3, i_3, e_3 'you'	u_3nu_1 'you'
ya_3, $ö_3$, $ɔ_3$ 'he'	ha_3 'they'

OBJECTIVE

m_3 'me'	$a_3ɲi_3$ 'us'
ge_3 'you'	u_3nu_1 'you'
ya_3 'him,' 'her,' 'it'	ha_3 'them'

POSSESSIVE

m_3 'my'	$a_3ɲi_3$ 'our'
ge_3 'your'	u_3nu_1 'your'
ya_3 'his,' 'her,' 'its'	ha_3 'their'

Gã:

PERSONAL

NOMINATIVE

Singular	Plural
mi$_2$ 'I'	*wɔ*$_2$ 'we'
o$_2$, *bo*$_2$ 'you'	*ɲẽ*$_2$ 'you'
lɛ$_2$, *e*$_2$ 'he,' 'she,' 'it'	*a*$_2$*mɛ̃*$_2$ 'they'

OBJECTIVE

mi$_2$ 'me'	*wɔ*$_2$ 'us'
o$_2$, *bo*$_2$ 'thee'	*ɲẽ*$_2$ 'you'
lɛ$_2$ 'him,' 'her,' 'it'	*a*$_2$*mɛ̃*$_2$ 'them'

POSSESSIVE

mi$_2$ 'my'	*wɔ*$_2$ 'our'
o$_3$ 'your'	*ɲẽ*$_2$ 'your'
e$_2$ 'his,' 'her,' 'its'	*a*$_2$*mɛ̃*$_2$ 'their'

Yoruba:

PERSONAL

NOMINATIVE

e$_1$*mi*$_2$, *mo*$_2$ 'I'	*a*$_2$*wa*$_2$ 'we'
i$_1$*wɔ*$_2$ 'you'	*ɛ*$_2$*yĩ*$_3$ 'you'
o$_1$*ũ*$_2$ 'he,' 'she,' 'it'	*a*$_1$*wɔ̃*$_2$, *nwɔ̃*$_3$ 'they'

OBJECTIVE

mi$_2$ 'me'	*wa*$_2$ 'us'
rɛ$_2$ 'you'	*yĩ*$_3$ 'you'
rɛ$_1$ 'him,' 'her,' 'it'	*wɔ̃*$_2$ 'them'

POSSESSIVE

mi$_2$ 'my'	*wa*$_2$ 'our'
rɛ$_2$ 'your'	*yĩ*$_3$ 'your'
rɛ$_1$ 'his,' 'her,' 'its'	*wɔ̃*$_2$ 'their'

Ewe:

PERSONAL

NOMINATIVE AND OBJECTIVE (ABSOLUTE FORMS)

ɲe$_1$ 'I,' 'me'	*mia*$_3$*wo*$_3$ 'we,' 'us'
wo$_1$ 'you'	*mia*$_1$*wo*$_3$ 'you'
e$_3$*ya*$_3$, *ye*$_3$ 'he,' 'she,' 'it,' 'him,' 'her'	*woa*$_3$*wo*$_3$ 'they,' 'them'

NOMINATIVE (CONNECTED FORMS)

me$_1$ (*ye*$_1$, *m*$_1$, *ŋ*$_1$) 'I'	*mie*$_3$, *mi*$_3$ (*ye*$_1$*wo*$_3$) 'we'
e$_1$ (*ne*$_1$, *wo*$_1$) 'you'	*mie*$_1$, *mi*$_1$ 'you'
e$_3$ (*wo*$_1$) 'he,' 'she,' 'it'	*wo*$_3$ 'they'

OBJECTIVE (CONNECTED FORMS)

Singular	Plural
m_1 (ye_1) 'me'	mi_3 (ye_1wo_3) 'us'
wo_1 'you'	mi_1 'you'
e_1 'him,' 'her,' 'it'	wo_3 'they'

POSSESSIVE

$ɲe_1$ (ye_1, $ye_1Φe_3$) 'my'	mia_3, $mia_3Φe_3$ (ye_1wo_3, $ye_1wo_3Φe_3$) 'our'
wo_1 'your'	mia_1, $mia_1Φe_3$ 'your'
e_3 ($e_3Φe_3$) 'his,' 'her'	wo_3, $wo_3Φe_3$ 'their'

In Tshiluba the objective forms of the personal pronouns when used absolutely are the same as the subjective forms.

In Kongo the subjective forms of the personal pronouns of Class 1 are the same as the objective forms of that class.

B. Nouns

Gullah nouns have the same form in all cases. They are uninflected: *di cif mʌṛə* 'the chief's mother,' *di faṛə brɛṛə* 'the father's brother.'[6]

In Ewe in names of relationship, the genitive is similarly uninflected: e.g., fia_1 da_1da_3 'the chief's mother,' fo_1foa_3 $nɔ_1vi_3$ 'the father's brother.'

In Ibo only its position in the sentence can show the case of a noun. For the genitive case, one form of $ŋ_1kɛ_1$ 'of' is sometimes used, especially when the possessor is a person; but it may be omitted.[7]

In Gã the possessive singular of nouns is indicated solely by its position, i.e., the possessor precedes the thing possessed: ko_1fi_3 wo_1lo_1 $lɛ_2$ 'Kofi's book,' lit. 'Kofi book the,' i.e., 'the book of Kofi.' If the possessor is a plural noun, the thing possessed takes *a* before it, a contraction of $a_2mɛ_2$ 'their': $lo_{1-2}f\tilde{o}_1dʒ\tilde{ı}_1$ $a_1f\tilde{ı}_1dʒ\tilde{ı}_1$ 'birds their wings,' i.e., 'birds' wings.'

In Twi the possessive precedes its governing noun: *ɔhene abaŋ* 'the king's palace.' In rare instances the possessive and its governing noun are connected by the possessive pronoun *ne* 'his,' 'her,' 'its,' 'their': *ata ne nã* 'Ata his mother,' i.e., 'Ata's mother.' In certain combinations with *kwa* 'slave,' the possessive stands after the governing noun: *kwatiemo* 'slave of Atiemo.'

The following phrases from Yoruba illustrate the use of the genitive of nouns in that language: $a{:}_1f\tilde{ı}_2$ $ɔ_2ba_2$ 'the palace king,' i.e., 'the king's palace': $ɔ_2ba_2\ a{:}_1ʃĩ_2$ 'the king palace,' i.e., 'the king of the palace'; $i_1ya_3\ o_2lu_3$ 'mother Olu,' i.e., 'Olu's mother'; $a_1wɔ̃_2\ i_1yɛ_3\ ɛ_2yɛ_2$[8] 'the feathers bird,' i.e., 'the bird's feathers.'

GENDER

In Gullah one very common method of indicating the gender of a noun, especially of an animal, is by prefixing to the noun the word *woman* or *man:* ʊmə *caɪl* 'woman child,' i.e., 'girl'; ʊmə *hɒs* 'mare'; ʊmə *cɪkɪn* 'hen'; *man cɪkɪn* 'rooster'; ʊmə *hɒg* 'sow.' Whereas many speakers of Southern American English frequently employ the same method in the case of certain words, especially when it is felt desirable to avoid the use of a taboo word, the use in Gullah is so common as to warrant mention here.

This method of indicating gender is common in many of the West African languages.

In Mandinka the suffix *-muso* 'woman' or *-ke* 'man' is attached to the word meaning 'child' to distinguish between the sexes: *diŋmuso* 'female child'; *diŋke* 'male child.'

In Gã the masculine and feminine genders of many nouns are indicated by prefixing or suffixing, respectively, $yo{:}_1$ 'woman' and $nu{:}_1$ 'man': $yo{:}_1gbɛ_1ʃã_1lɔ_{2-1}$ 'woman traveler,' $nu{:}_1gbɛ_1ʃã_1lɔ_{2-1}$ 'man traveler,' $wu_1ɔ_2nũ_1$ 'cock,' $wu_1ɔ_2yo_1{:}$ 'hen,' etc.

In Fante $ba_3ɲin_3$ or $be_3ɲin_3$ 'man' when attached to $nu_1ã_3$ 'mother's child' means 'brother'—$nu_1ã_3ba_3ɲin_3$; $nu_1ã_3ba_1si_3a_3$ or $nu_1ã_3be_1si_3a_3$, lit. 'mother's child woman,' means 'sister.'

In Ewe $nɔ_1vi_3ŋu_3tsu_1$, lit. 'mother's child man,' means 'brother'; $nɔ_1vi_3ɲɔ_3nu_1$, lit. 'mother's child woman,' means 'sister.'

Note also the Ibo expressions $nwa_3n_3nɛ_3$-$nwö_3kɛ_3$ 'brother' and $nwa_3n_3nɛ_3$-$nwa_3ɲe_1$ 'sister,' in which $nwö_3kɛ_3$ = 'man,' $nwa_3ɲe_1$ = 'woman,' and $nwa_3n_3nɛ_3$ = 'blood relation.'

In Yoruba one of the two ways of denoting gender is by adding to the noun the word $ɔ_2kũ_2rĩ_2$ or $ɔ_2kɔ̃_2rĩ_2$ 'man' for the masculine and $o_2bĩ_1rĩ_2$ 'woman' for the feminine, or by prefixing $a_2kɔ_2$ for the male and a_2bo_2 for the female: e.g., $ɔ_2mɔ̃_2kũ_2rĩ_2$ 'son' or 'young man,' $ɔ_2mɔ̃_2bĩ_1rĩ_2$ 'daughter' or 'young woman,' $a_2kɔ_2$-$ɛ_2ʃĩ_2$ 'male horse,' a_2bo_2-$ɛ_2ʃĩ_2$ 'mare.'

In Kimbundu the word *muhatu* 'woman' and the preposition *a*, with its proper concordance, are added to many nouns to express the feminine gender. The masculine is expressed by the addition of *diyala* and the preposition *a*: e.g., *mɔna wa muhatu* 'girl,' 'young woman'; *mɔna wa diyala* 'boy,' 'young man.' In the case of words referring to animals or a class of animals, *ndumbe* is attached to the generic term for the animals (except the small antelopes) to express the masculine of that class, and *dikɔlɔmbɔlɔ* is added to the generic term for any class of birds to express the masculine of that class: e.g., *hɔmbɔ ya ndumbe* 'the male goat,' *sanʒi ya dikɔlɔmbɔlɔ* 'the rooster.' The generic feminine term *mukaʒi* (for all animals and birds) is added to the particular generic name of a class of animals (except the small antelopes), or birds, to form the feminine of that class: e.g., *hɔmbɔ ya mukaʒi* 'female goat,' *sanʒi ya mukaʒi* 'the hen.'[9]

CHAPTER 6

SOME WORD-FORMATIONS

THE Gullahs make extensive use of certain methods of forming words that are not so generally employed in English but that are of common occurrence in the African languages. Among these are (1) the employment of groups of words for nouns, verbs, adverbs, adjectives, or other parts of speech; (2) the use of reduplicated forms; and (3) the frequent employment of onomatopoetic expressions. The following examples will be sufficient to illustrate each of these methods:

THE USE OF GROUPS OF WORDS FOR PARTS OF SPEECH[1]

Very often instead of using a single word for a person or thing, the Gullah speaker will employ a group of words in which some distinguishing characteristic of the person or thing is expressed:

ə *bit* ɒ*n* ɒɪə*n* 'a mechanic,' lit. 'a-beat-on-iron'

*wa m*ɐʊ*t* 'catfish,' lit. 'wide mouth,' *wa* being the word for 'large' or 'wide' in the Mende language, spoken in Sierra Leone and Liberia.

de klin 'dawn,' i.e., 'day clean,' being a translation of the Wolof expression *bər bu sɛt* 'dawn,' lit. 'the day clean'

ˌ*fulaˈfafa* 'woodpecker,' being the Mende term *fulafafa* 'woodpecker,' lit. 'to bore into a tree'

dɛgati ɒʊ*l* 'the barn owl,' *dɛgati* being a Wolof expression meaning 'listen to it again.' It is used among the Wolof in reference to the owl whose cry or hoot is frequently heard near their homes.

*trut m*ɐʊ*t* 'truth'; 'a truthful person,' i.e., 'truth mouth.' Cf. the Twi expression *anokware* 'truth,' lit. 'the mouth true'

*br*ʌʃ *m*ɐʊ*t* 'a drink of whiskey,' i.e., 'brush mouth'

*h*ʌʃ *m*ɐʊ*t* 'a drink of whiskey,' i.e., 'hush mouth'

ʃ*o dɛd* 'cemetery,' i.e., 'sure dead.' Cf. the Yoruba $i_2sa_1o_1ku_3$ 'cemetery,' i.e., 'the abode of the dead'

*lo w*ʌ*l g*ɒ*d* 'parent,' i.e., 'low-world god'

tebl tapa 'preacher,' i.e., 'one who taps on the table'

yad aks 'preacher,' i.e., 'yard ax'

Frequently the Gullah speaker will employ a group of words to describe the nature of an action rather than use a single verb to express the action:

tɒɪ unə mɐʊt 'Hush, stop talking,' i.e., 'Tie your mouth,' being a translation of the Mende sentence *bi lei yili* 'Stop talking,' lit. 'Your mouth tie'[2]

i tʌn i hɛd 'He changed his mind,' lit. 'He turned his head,' being a translation of the Twi sentence *wa daŋ neti* 'He has changed his mind,' lit. 'He has turned his head'

krak tit 'to speak,' i.e., 'to crack the teeth'

swit mɐʊt 'to flatter,' i.e., 'to sweet mouth'; *i swit mɐʊt* 'He is a flatterer.' Cf. the Twi sentence *no ano yɛdɛ* 'He is a flatterer,' lit. 'His mouth is sweet'[3]

bad mɐʊt 'to curse,' 'to put a spell on,' i.e., 'to bad mouth.' Cf. the Vai expression da_3 $ɲa_3ma_3$ 'a curse,' lit. 'a bad mouth'

i han ʃɒt peʃən 'He steals,' i.e., 'His hand is short of patience'

Groups of words are used in Gullah also for adjectives, adverbs, and prepositions:

enu 'fole 'pregnant.' Cf. the Ewe sentence $Φo_1le_1$ e_3nu_1 'She is with child'

bɪg ɒɪ 'covetous,' i.e., 'big eye,' being a translation of the Ibo expression $a_3ɲa_3$ u_3ku_3 'covetous,' lit. 'eye big.' Cf. the Yoruba expression $lo_3ʃu_3$ $ko_1ko_1ro_1$ 'covetous,' lit. 'to have the eye of a worm'

'anduɲu 'to be away from (someone),' being a translation of the Wolof expression *anduɲu* 'We not unite'

i ɒn ʃi fʊt 'She is pregnant,' i.e., 'She is on her foot'

tɪŋk mʌc 'to be annoyed,' i.e., 'to think much.' Cf. the Ibo expression $u_3tʃɛ_1$ $tʃɛ_1$ 'to be worried,' lit. $u_3tʃɛ_1$ 'thought, mind' + $tʃɛ_1$ 'to think'

mɛk trak 'to be in good health,' i.e., 'to make track'

dat mʌnt wɒt ə kʌmɪn pe 'next month's wages,' lit. 'that month-that-is-coming pay.' Cf. the Yoruba $o_1ʃu_1$ ti_2 $m_3bɔ_1$ 'next month,' lit. 'the month that is coming.' Cf. also the Kikongo *ŋgɔnda yɛti kwiza* 'next month,' lit. 'the month that is coming'[4]

mɛk so? 'why?' i.e., 'make so?' Cf. the Ibo expression ge_3ne_3 $mɛ_1rɛ_1$? 'why?' lit. 'what makes?'

we sɒɪ i də? 'Where is he?' lit. 'What side he is?'

pən tɒp 'on,' i.e., 'upon the top,' used in such a sentence as, *He has five fingers upon the top of* (i.e., *on*) *his hand.* Cf. the Yoruba expression li_3 o_2ri_3 'on,' lit. 'upon the top'

Examples of the use of a group of words or a sentence which is equivalent in English to a noun, verb, adjective, adverb, or some other part of speech are numerous in the African languages:

Ewe: $gbe_3me_1lã_1$ 'a wild beast,' lit. 'bush-inside-animal'
$nu_3ŋɔ_3nu_3$ 'gimlet,' lit. 'thing-bore-thing'
$nu_3ŋlɔ_1kpe_3$ 'slate,' lit. 'thing-write-stone'
$dɔ_1wua_1me_1$ 'starvation,' lit. 'hunger which kills man'
$a_1deɛ_1me_3ɖui_1e_1$ 'spleen,' lit. 'The hunter does not eat it'

ḍua$_1$*me*$_1$*wo*$_1$*a*$_3$*dze*$_3$*kpoe*$_3$ 'scorpion,' lit. 'bites man, he will go mad'

dzi$_1$*ka*$_1$*tso*$_1$*fo*$_{1-3}$ 'fear,' lit. 'heart artery which tears in the belly'

a$_1$*ti*$_3$*ku*$_3$*zẽ*$_3$ 'mimosa,' lit. 'The tree dies at night'

te$_1$ *nu*$_3$ *kpɔ*$_3$ 'to prove,' lit. 'pull thing see'

Yoruba: *i*$_2$*ye*$_1$*me*$_3$*ɟi*$_1$ 'doubt,' lit. 'two minds'

i$_2$*yɔ*$_1$*-o*$_1$*yĩ*$_2$*bo*$_3$ 'sugar,' lit. 'white man's salt'

a$_2$*ba*$_3$*ta*$_2$ 'park,' 'public square,' lit. 'that which meets the street'

a$_1$*ya*$_2$*fo*$_{3-2}$ 'to fear,' lit. 'Courage flies away'

dɛ$_2$*ti*$_3$ 'to listen,' lit. 'to loosen the ear'

de$_3$*bi*$_3$*kpa*$_2$ 'to starve,' lit. 'to make hunger kill''

fɛ$_2$*nu*$_2$*ko*$_2$*nu*$_2$ 'to kiss,' lit. 'to place mouth to meet mouth'

fi$_1$*di*$_3$*ba*$_2$*lɛ*$_1$ 'to sit down,' lit. 'to place one's bottom to touch the ground'

fo$_1$*ri*$_3$*ba*$_2$*lɛ*$_1$ 'to worship,' lit. 'to place head to meet the ground'

sɔ$_1$*rɔ*$_1$*lɛ*$_3$*hĩ*$_1$ 'to calumniate,' lit. 'to tell word in back'

lo$_3$*ri*$_3$ 'on,' 'upon,' lit. 'on the head, on top'

Ibo: *a*$_3$*ŋa*$_3$*-m*$_3$*mi*$_3$*ri*$_3$ 'tear,' lit. 'eye water'

ɔ$_3$*no*$_3$*-m*$_3$*mi*$_3$*ri*$_3$ 'spittle,' lit. 'mouth water'

a$_3$*fɔ*$_3$ *n*$_3$*ri*$_2$ 'greedy,' lit. 'stomach for food'

ö$_3$*bi*$_1$ *de*$_1$ *m*$_3$ *ɛ*$_3$*zi*$_3$ *m*$_3$ *ma*$_3$ 'I am very glad,' lit. 'My heart is true good'

m$_3$*mi*$_3$*ri*$_3$ *de*$_3$ *ɔ*$_3$*kö*$_3$ 'hot water,' lit. 'water which is fire'

sɛ$_1$ *ö*$_3$*kwu*$_3$ 'to quarrel,' lit. 'to draw word'

tʃö$_3$ *a*$_3$*nö*$_3$ 'to hunt,' lit. 'to chase animal'

ma$_3$ *a*$_3$*ka*$_3$ 'to bet,' lit. 'to slap hand'

i$_1$*ku*$_1$*ku*$_1$ *de*$_3$ *ö*$_3$*yi*$_3$ 'cold air,' lit. 'air which is coolness'

na$_1$*zo*$_3$ 'behind,' lit. 'in the back'

no$_{1-3}$*sɔ*$_3$ 'beside,' lit. 'in the extremity'

a$_3$*nwo*$_1$*la*$_1$ 'Thank you,' lit. 'Do not die'

fɔ$_3$*kɔ*$_3$ 'to store up,' lit. 'to move and place'

da$_1$*ga*$_1$ 'until,' lit. 'falls, passes'

kɛ$_1$ *m*$_1$*gbɛ*$_1$ 'since,' lit. 'passing from time'

Mende: *kɔlɔgɔ:mɒ* 'an educated person,' lit. 'book-know person'

pɛlɛkpamɒ 'carpenter,' lit. 'one who hammers a house'

ndʒia wotemɒ 'interpreter,' lit. 'one who turns word'

ndilɛ 'anger,' lit. 'heart cut'

ndilɛlɪ 'peace,' 'comfort,' lit. 'heart wet'

kpandɛ wilimɒ 'hunter,' lit. 'one who throws a gun'

kahũ gbia 'health,' lit. 'bone inside comes out'

Gã: *mi*$_3$*hĩ*$_3$*ẽ*$_1$ *ŋ*$_1$*gbo*$_3$ 'I am shy,' lit. 'My face is dying'

ni$_2$*ne*$_2$ *ʃɛ*$_2$ *nɔ̃*$_1$ 'receive,' lit. 'hand reaches on'

mi$_3$*ya*$_3$*ba*$_3$ 'goodbye' (on leaving a place), lit. 'I go, come'

mi$_3$*ya*$_3$*wɔ*$_2$ 'goodnight,' lit. 'I go sleep'

Vai: *da*$_3$*fa*$_1$ 'fat,' lit. 'mouth full'

ka$_1$*la*$_1$*kɪŋ*$_{2-1}$ 'school,' lit. 'learn-house'

te$_3$*le*$_3$*bi*$_3$*la*$_3$ 'umbrella,' lit. 'sun-catch'

dʒi$_2$*mi*$_3$*ke*$_1$*le*$_1$ 'thirst,' lit. 'Water to drink call'

Bini: *u*$_1$*γe*$_1$*gbe*$_1$ 'mirror,' lit. 'look body'
u$_1$*γɛ*$_1$*dɛ*$_1$ 'clock,' 'watch,' lit. 'day-looker'
mu$_1$-*a*$_1$*ɾo*$_{1-3}$ *da*$_{1-3}$ 'to face,' lit. 'to carry eye toward'
mu$_1$-*i*$_1$*do*$_1$*bo*$_{1-3}$ *yi*$_3$ 'to hinder,' lit. 'to put obstacle to body'

Kikongo: *kaŋga ntima* 'to be adamant,' lit. 'to tie the heart'
nsatu a maza 'thirst,' lit. 'hunger for water'
nsatu a ndɔmbɛ 'brown' or 'gray,' lit. 'hunger for black'
nsatu a mbwaki 'pink' or 'orange,' lit. 'hunger for red'

REDUPLICATED FORMS

The largest number of reduplicated forms in Gullah are personal names. Among these are the following:[5]

ˈbaba	*ˈmeme*	*ˈtɛtɛ*	*ˈmɛriˈmɛri*
ˈbɛbɛ	*ˈmɛmɛ*	*ˈtiti*[7]	*ˈsakaˈsaka*
ˈbɔbɔ	*ˈmimi*	*ˈtɒtɒ*	*ˈtiyoˈtiyo*
ˈbobo	*ˈmumu*	*ˈtutu*	*ˈweleˈwele*
ˈbubu	*ˈnene*	*ˈcici*	*ˈwĩnĩˈwĩnĩ*
ˈdɛdɛ	*ˈnunu*	*ˈwiwi*	*ˈwiriˈwiri*
ˈdidi	*ˈpɛpɛ*	*ˈwuwu*	*ˈwitiˈwiti*
ˈdudu	*ˈpopo*	*ˈzozo*	*ˈwɒkuˈwɒku*
ˈfofo	*ˈsese*	*ˈbaŋguˈbaŋgu*	*ˈwɒmiˈwɒmi*
ˈfufu	*ˈsɛsɛ*	*ˈbuyɛˈbuyɛ*	*ˈzekeˈzeke*
ˈhoho	*ˈsisi*	*ˈdidiˈdidi*	*ˈtititi*
ˈkɒkɒ[6]	*ˈsɒsɒ*	*ˈfamiˈfami*	*ˈtɒtɒtɒ*
ˈlala	*ˈsoso*	*iˈyami-iˈyami*	*ˈyoyoyo*
ˈlele	*ˈtɛŋtɛŋ*	*ˈkusuˈkusu*	
ˈlulu	*ˈtete*	*ˈleleˈleke*	

There are many reduplicated forms in Gullah which are used to intensify the meanings of words. The following are examples of these:

baŋ 'a loud noise,' *ˈbaŋˈbaŋ* 'a very loud noise'
dɛ 'there,' *ˈdɛdɛ* 'exactly there'; 'correct'
ɛ! ɛ! 'an expression of very great surprise'
ˈfɪlfɪl ('fill fill') 'to fill entirely'
ɲam 'to eat,' *ˈɲamɲam* 'to eat' or 'to devour'
ˈʃoʃo ('sure sure') 'very sure'
ʃo nʌf ʃo ('sure enough sure') 'very sure'
ˈtrutru ('true true') 'very true'
ˈwɐɪtwɐɪt ('white white') 'very white'

In the African languages reduplicated forms have a great variety of uses, as the words that follow will illustrate:

Kongo: *benda* 'to be crooked,' *bendabenda* 'to prevaricate,' 'to be unreliable'
fuku 'night,' *fukufuku* 'early morning, just at dawn'
luŋga 'to take care of,' *luŋgaluŋga* 'to take good care of'
suka 'to ache,' *sukasuka* 'rheumatism'

Kikongo: *malɛ:mbɛ* 'slowly, carefully,' *malɛ:mbɛmalɛ:mbɛ* 'very slowly, very carefully'
nswalu 'quickly,' *nswalunswalu* 'very quickly'

Yoruba: du_3 'to be black,' du_3du_3[8] 'black'; 'blackness'
$f\tilde{u}_3$ 'to be white,' $f\tilde{u}_3f\tilde{u}_3$[9] 'white'; 'whiteness'
n_3la_3 'large,' $n_3la_3n_3la_3$ 'very large'
$kpɛ_2ɟa_2$ 'to fish,' $kpɛ_2ɟa_2kpɛ_2ɟa_2$ 'a fisherman'
$m\tilde{u}_2ti_3$ 'to drink any intoxicant,' $m\tilde{u}_2ti_3m\tilde{u}_2ti_3$ 'a drunkard'
$ʃi_2ʃɛ_3$ 'to labor,' $ʃi_2ʃɛ_3ʃi_2ʃɛ_3$ 'a laborer'
$ɔ_2ɟɔ_3$ 'day,' $ɔ_2ɟɔ_3$-$ɔ_2ɟɔ_3$ 'day after day'

Bini: $γɛ_{1-3}$ 'to look,' $γɛ_{1-3}γɛ_{1-3}$ 'to see unexpectedly'
$ɲa_3$ 'to open (mouth),' $ɲa_3ɲa_3$ 'to yawn'
nwa_{1-3} 'to be bright,' $nwa_1nwa_1nwa_1$ 'shining'

Hausa: $to{:}_3fe_1$ 'to expectorate,' $to{:}_1fe_3to{:}_1fe_2$ 'expectorating repeatedly'
$ta{:}_3ɾi_1$ 'many,' 'a collection'; $ta{:}_3ɾi_1ta{:}_2ɾi_1$ 'in heaps'
$ɾa_3ge_1$ 'to shorten,' $ɾa_1ge_3ɾa_1ge{:}_2$ 'repeated acts of diminishing'
$mu_3sa{:}_1ye{:}_2$ 'to exchange,' $mu_1sa{:}_1ye{:}_3mu_1sa{:}_1ye{:}_2$ 'exchanging repeatedly'
$ge_3wa_1ye{:}_2$ 'to surround,' $ge_1wa_1ye{:}_1ge_2wa_2ye{:}_2$ 'beating about the bush'

Bambara: *maga* 'to agitate, *magamaga* 'to make a disturbance'
mugu 'a pulverized substance,' *mugumugu* 'to consume entirely,' 'to reduce to power'
tama 'a voyage,' 'a journey'; *tamatama* 'to go and return'

Ewe: $ḍe_3$ 'one,' $ḍe_3ḍe_3$ 'only'
$ŋu_3s\tilde{ɛ}_3$ 'strength,' $ŋu_1s\tilde{ɛ}_3ŋu_1s\tilde{ɛ}_3$ 'strongly'
$ḍu_1$ 'to eat,' $ḍu_1ḍu_{1-3}$ 'edible'
$tsɛ_3$ 'younger brother,' $tsɛ_1tsɛ_3$ 'second younger brother'

Twi: *ani* 'face,' 'surface'; *aniani* 'superficially'
ɲĩ̃ɲã 'a trailing plant, the sour leaves of which are used against fever,' *ɲĩ̃ɲãɲĩ̃ɲã* 'sour'
pɛ 'alike,' *pɛpɛ* 'exactly,' 'precisely'
pem 'to push,' *pempem* 'to push back and forth'
pĩa 'to grow firm,' *pĩapĩa* 'to command'

ONOMATOPOETIC EXPRESSIONS

The following are a few of the many onomatopoetic expressions heard in Gullah:

'*bagəlag* 'a loud noise'

baŋ, '*baŋ*'*baŋ* 'to pound' (imitative of the sound of beating) *'bidi'bidi* 'a small bird'; 'a small chicken.' Cf. the Kongo word *bididi* 'a bird'

bim$_{3-1}$ 'violently'

'blʌdɪnɒŋ 'a large frog'

'bɒbɒbɒ 'woodpecker.' Cf. the Kongo word *mbɔbɔbɔ* 'woodpecker'

'fug'fug 'the lungs of an animal.' Cf. the Mende words *fugfug* and *fukfuk* 'lungs'

fukfuk 'the lungs of an animal.' Cf. the Yoruba word *fu*$_1$*ku*$_1$*fu*$_2$*ku*$_1$ 'lungs'

'higə'hi 'owl'

'hihi 'owl.' Cf. the Vai *hĩ:*$_1$*hĩ*$_1$ 'owl'

'huhu 'owl'

'ɟaɟa 'to quarrel.' Cf. the Yoruba word *ɟa*$_1$ 'to quarrel,' 'to fight'

'ɲamɲam 'to eat,' 'to devour'

paŋ 'noisily.' Cf. the Twi word *paŋ* 'boldly' (imitative of the sound of firm, heavy steps)

'pak'pak'pak 'to knock' (imitative of the sound of knocking). Cf. the Yoruba word *kpa*$_2$*ka*$_1$*kpa*$_2$*ka*$_1$ 'a corn thresher'

'swɪŋ'swaŋ 'a swing'

wulisã'kpãkpã 'woodpecker,' being the Mende term *wulisãkpãkpã* 'woodpecker,' lit. 'to pound the tree quickly'

The African languages are especially rich in onomatopoetic expressions:

Ewe:[10]
- *gbu*$_1$*du*$_1$ *gbu*$_1$*du*$_1$ 'suggesting the sound of drums'
- *gblu*$_1$ *gblu*$_1$ *gblu*$_1$ 'stepping' or 'galloping'
- *bi*$_1$*ḍi*$_1$*bi*$_1$*ḍi*$_1$ 'giving the impression of softness'
- *bɔ*$_1$*ɲɔ*$_1$*bɔ*$_1$*ɲɔ*$_1$ 'suggestive of softness'
- *hɔ*$_1$*lɔ*$_1$*hɔ*$_1$*lɔ*$_1$ 'suggestive of a speaker's indistinct utterance
- *zɔ*$_1$ *ba*$_3$*fo*$_3$*ba*$_3$*fo*$_3$ 'descriptive of the walk of a small man moving briskly'
- *zɔ*$_1$ *bɔ*$_1$*hɔ*$_1$*bɔ*$_1$*hɔ*$_1$ 'the heavy walk of a fat man'
- *zɔ*$_1$ *dzia*$_1$*dzia*$_1$ 'energetic walking'
- *zɔ*$_1$ *bu*$_3$*la*$_3$*bu*$_3$*la*$_3$ 'walking without looking where one is going'
- *zɔ*$_1$ *ta*$_1$*ka*$_1$*ta*$_1$*ka*$_1$ 'to walk without care'
- *zɔ*$_1$ *wu*$_3$*dɔ*$_3$*wu*$_3$*dɔ*$_3$ 'the weary walk of stately persons, especially women'

Twi:
- *hababaha* 'unintelligible chattering'
- *kɔkɔtekɔ* 'hiccough'
- *mpatabiribiri* 'commotion'
- *nturuturuwi* 'small particles flying out with a crackling noise'
- *patabubu* 'boisterousness,' 'noise'
- *tamtam* 'walking gravely or resolutely'
- *taradada* 'imitative of the sound of water being poured'
- *tekɔtekɔ* 'hiccough'

*torododod*o 'imitative of the sound of a fluid being poured into a vessel or upon the ground'
tutututu 'boiling water'
wakawaka 'in a shaking manner'
wesawesa 'to murmur'
wɔsowɔso 'gradually'
yayaya 'to confound'

Bini:
$a_1kwa_3\gamma a_2\gamma a_2$ 'tree bear,' so called from its cry: $kwa_3\gamma a_1\gamma a_1$-$\gamma a_1\gamma a_1nwa_3nwa_2nwa_1nwa_1nwa_1$
am_{3-1} am_{3-1} am_{3-1} 'descriptive of the cry of monkeys'
$a_1tai_1kp\tilde{\imath}_1$ 'in imitation of the boa, a large snake having a very hard skin'
$bi_3gɔ_3bi_1gɔ_1bi_3gɔ_3$ 'descriptive of something very crooked, such as a cripple walking zigzag'
boa_1boa_1 'suggestive of the walk of a large man who is in a hurry'
$bɔ_1bɔ_1bɔ_1$ 'in imitation of gentle drumming'
$go_2ba_2go_1ba_1go_3ba_3$ 'descriptive of the walk of a cripple whose feet are bent to one side, the boot behind moving sideways'
$gy\tilde{a}_3r\tilde{a}_1r\tilde{a}_1r\tilde{a}_1r\tilde{a}_1r\tilde{a}_1$ 'loud' (in imitation of the crying of an infant)
$\gamma ɛ_2rɛ_2\gamma ɛ_1rɛ_1\gamma ɛ_3rɛ_3$ 'descriptive of the way in which a spy walks, with varying speed and frequent looking around.' Cf. $ɔ_1xia_3$ $\gamma ɛ_2rɛ_2\gamma ɛ_1rɛ_1\gamma ɛ_3rɛ_3$ 'He walks like a spy'
$\gamma i_1ri_1\gamma i_1ri_1$ 'descriptive of a blazing fire.' Cf. $er_1h\tilde{ɛ}_1$ ba_{3-1} $\gamma i_1ri_1\gamma i_1ri_1$ 'The fire blazes up'
$ti_3ti_3ti_3ti_3ti_3ti_3$ 'imitative of the sound produced by a small drum'

Hausa:
ba_1lau_1 ba_1lau_1 'flutteringly' (used in reference to a garment in the wind)
$fun_1dʒum_1fun_2dʒum_2$ 'a learner's efforts at swimming' (in imitation of the beating of the surface of the water with the feet)
fus_3 'the sound of bursting'; also 'energy, endeavor'
$ga_1ras_1ga_1ras_1$ 'a manner of eating' (in imitation of the crunching sound heard when one is eating such food as cassava, raw onions, etc.)
ga_1yan_3-ga_1yan_2 'the sound made by ill-mannered persons when eating'
$gi_3riŋ_3gi_3rin_3$ 'the sound made by the strings of a large three-stringed musical instrument called the $ga_1ra{:}_2ya{:}_2$'

Yoruba:
$fu_1kɛ_1fu_1kɛ_1$ (used with $n_3ɟo_3$ to describe the increased action of the heart produced by running): ai_1ya_1 mi_2 $n_3ɟo_3$ $fu_1kɛ_1fu_1kɛ_1$ 'My heart is palpitating'
$fu_1ku_1fu_2ku_1$ 'lungs'

fu₁tɛ₁fu₁tɛ₁ 'easily' (used to describe the ease with which any fragile texture is torn): *a₂ʃɔ₂ n₃ʃa₃ fu₁tɛ₁fu₁tɛ₁* 'The cloth tears very easily'

gba₁ 'loudly' (used to describe the sound produced by slamming a door): *mo₂ sɛ₃ i₂lɛ₁kũ₁ o₃ ro₃ gba₁* 'The door slammed when I shut it'

gu₁du₁gu₁du₁ 'a small drum which produces a tenor sound'

ma₂hu₂ru₂ma₂hu₂ru₂ 'the cry of a beast of prey'

Kongo: *ʃikuʃiku* 'hiccough'

ʃiɔʃia 'to splutter in cooking'

yayala 'to flow softly, making a murmuring sound'

mbɔbɔbɔ 'woodpecker'

ŋkeʃia 'to sneeze'

zakazaka 'shaking,' 'trembling'

Kikongo: *mɛ:mɛ* 'sheep'

potopoto 'soft,' 'mushy'

sɛkisa 'to sharpen an implement'

tukutuku 'motorcycle' or 'motorboat'

Kimbundu: *haha* 'to pant'

kakela 'to cackle'

kakɔhɔkɔhɔ 'a cough'

kiʃukuʃuku 'hiccough'

kɔkɔla 'to crow'

ŋgaʃaʃa 'to sneeze'

Vai: *ta₁ma:₁ta₁ma:₁* 'suggestive of slow, gentle action'

goŋ₁go₁lo:₁goŋ₁go₁lo:₁goŋ₁go₁lo₁ 'suggestive of something large, immense, ponderous'

CHAPTER 7

SOUNDS

THE sounds of Gullah show many striking resemblances to those of several West African languages. When the African came to the United States and encountered in English certain sounds not present in his native language, he did what any other person to whom English was a foreign language would have done under similar circumstances—he substituted sounds from his own language which appeared to him to resemble most closely those English sounds which were unfamiliar to him. The American in learning to speak French does this when he substitutes the English alveolar *t* for the French dental *t* or the English [ɑ] for the French [a], and the Frenchman and German in learning English do so when they substitute *d* or *t* for the English *th*. It is reasonable to suppose that the African sounds would remain much longer in the speech of the Gullah Negroes than foreign sounds in the speech of other persons coming to America because of the Gullah's comparative isolation on the Sea Islands and peninsulas of South Carolina and Georgia. Some of the more striking resemblances between the sounds of Gullah and those of several West African languages follow:

CONSONANTS

A. The Ejectives [p', t', k', ʃ']

Frequently in Gullah and likewise in many African languages a special type of plosive called ejective is heard when the mouth closure and glottis are released practically simultaneously, the former being generally released a fraction of a second before the latter. In Gullah this sound is unaspirated. It can be heard in such words as *t'ɛk* 'take,' *p'ɒt* 'pot,' *k'ʌp* 'cup,' etc. The ejective [ʃ'] also occurs occasionally in Gullah: e.g., *ʃ'ɑɪn* 'shine' *ʃ'ew* 'shave,' etc.

The ejective occurs in many African languages. Note, for example, the Hausa words *k'a:₁k'a:₁* 'how' and *ka:₁ka:₂* 'harvest,' *ba:₁k'i:₂* 'visitors' and *ba:₁ki:₂* 'mouth.' In some African languages not only [t', p'], and [k'] occur but also [s', y', ts', tl'], and other consonants. In the Ndau group of languages (Southern Rhodesia) the unaspirated plosives are ejective. In Zulu the unaspirated *p* and *t* and the voiceless affricates are ejective.[1]

B. [mb, mp, mw, nd, ns, nt, ŋd, ŋg, ŋk]

The combination of initial nasal plus another consonant is heard fairly frequently in Gullah. Examples of these combinations, most of which consist of homorganic nasal plus plosive, are the following:

m'bila (personal name)
m'puku 'rat'
n'dɒmbe (personal name)
n'tama (personal name)
ŋ'*di* (personal name)
ŋ'*gaŋga* (personal name)

Such consonant combinations constitute one of the peculiarities of African languages as compared with European languages. The following are the equivalents of the Gullah words listed above:

Kongo: *mbila* 'a summons, a call'
mpuku 'rat'
ndɔmbe 'blackness'
ŋgaŋga 'doctor'
Ewe: $ŋ_1di_3$ 'morning'
Twi: *ntãmã* 'a dress'

C. The Labio-velar Plosives [gb] and [kp]

[gb] and [kp], each articulated as one sound, are sometimes heard in the Gullah speaker's pronunciation of African words containing these sounds:

gbaŋ (*kpaŋ*) 'tightly'	M., *gbaŋ* (*kpaiŋ*) 'tightly,' 'severely'
gbla 'near'	M., *gbla* (*gblaŋga*) 'near'
'*kpaŋga* 'the remains after some destructive force'	M., *kpaŋga* 'a field burned before clearing'; 'remains'
wulisã'kpãkpã 'woodpecker'	M., *wulisãkpãkpã* 'woodpecker,' lit. 'to pound a tree vigorously'

D. The Bilabial Fricatives [Φ] and [β]

The Gullah speaker seldom uses the labio-dental voiceless and voiced fricatives [f] and [v] and the voiced labio-velar semivowel [w], but substitutes for [f] the voiceless bilabial fricative [Φ] and for [v] and [w] the voiced bilabial fricative [β] or the voiced frictionless continuant [ϑ]: Φɒl 'fall,' ΦɪΦ'*tin* 'fifteen,' Φɒɪβ (Φɒɪϑ) 'five,' βeβ 'wave,' βɐɪt 'white,' βɒɪl 'while.'

The bilabial fricative is foreign to English, but is found in several West African languages spoken in those areas from which the Gullahs were brought to the United States as slaves. In some of these languages the bilabial sounds occur, but the labio-dentals [f] and [v] do not. In others, however, the bilabial fricatives occur side by side with the labio-dentals. In Yoruba, Hausa, Efik, and Twi, there is no [v]. In Ewe both the bilabial fricatives [Φ] and [β] and the labio-dentals [f] and [v] occur as distinctive sounds: e.g., *Φu*₃ 'bone,' *fu*₃ 'feather,' *vɔ*₁ 'to be finished,' *βɔ*₁ 'python.' In Ibo the voiceless labio-dental [f], the voiceless bilabial [Φ], the voiced bilabial [β], and the labio-velar semivowel [w] occur, but the voiced labio-dental [v] is seldom heard.[2] In Bini the labio-dentals [f] and [v] and the voiced bilabial fricative [β] occur: e.g., *fe*₃ 'to be rich,' *ve*₃ 'to offer a price for something and to argue about it,' *βe*₃ 'and.' In Hausa [f] and [v] do not occur, but the voiceless bilabial fricative [Φ] does.

E. Palatal Plosives [c] and [ɟ]

The voiceless and voiced palatal plosives [c] and [ɟ] occur in Gullah as substitutes for the English palato-alveolar affricates [tʃ] and [dʒ] and for the voiced palato-alveolar fricative [ʒ]: e.g., *cu* 'chew,' *ɟak* Jack,' '*plɛɟə* 'pleasure.'

In Twi and Wolof, the palatal plosives occur rather than the palato-alveolar affricates [tʃ] and [dʒ]. The palatal plosives are also found in Malinke, Kru, Yoruba, and Gɛ̃, a dialect of Ewe. The voiced palato-alveolar fricative [ʒ] likewise does not occur in Yoruba, Gã, Efik, in some of the dialects of Ewe, and in many other West African languages. In Ibo it is heard only as a dialectal substitute for [z]. In Kongo and Kimbundu, however, it appears to be common.

F. [l] and [r]

In Gullah the voiced alveolar lateral is usually very clear in all positions, i.e., it is articulated with the front of the tongue raised toward the hard palate: e.g., *Φɒl̹* 'fall,' *mɪl̹k* 'milk,' *l̹ɒŋ* 'long,' etc.

In the West African languages the *l* sounds are generally clear. This is true also of French, but not of English unless the *l* is followed by a vowel. In the speech of many Americans the dark *l* is heard in all positions, the *l* before a vowel being less dark than that before a consonant or at the end of a word.

In the pronunciation of a great many words, some Gullah speakers substitute an [l] for the English *r*. For example, on Harris Neck, a peninsula on the coast of Georgia, one frequently hears '*melɪ* 'Mary,' '*byulo* 'bureau,' *bluə* 'Brewer,' etc. This substitution may be due to the fact that in many African languages, including Kongo, Umbundu, Bobangi, Tshiluba, and others, from the vocabularies of which many Gullahs use a large number of words, [r] does not occur at all. In some other African languages [l] and [r] are interchangeable. In the Mandingo languages, for example, the word for 'mountain' is *kulu* or *kuru*. In the Kru language the word for 'knee' is *kulu* or *kuru*, and both *blable* and *brabre* are used for 'sheep.'

G. The Palatal Nasal [ɲ]

The palatal nasal [ɲ] (not to be confused with *n* + *y*) is very common in Gullah. It is heard in many words in which *y* and *n* would be used in cultivated English: e.g., *ɲuz* 'use,' *ɲɒŋ* 'young,' *ɲu'nɒɪtɪd* 'united,' *ɲu* 'new,' etc.

In Yoruba, Twi, Gã, Wolof, Efik, Ewe, Kongo, and many other West African languages, the palatal nasal occurs, especially in initial and medial position. It is less common in both Gullah and the African languages at the end of a word:

Ewe:	*ɲa*$_3$ 'to know,' *ɲa*$_1$ 'word'
	ɲe$_3$ 'to be,' *ɲe*$_1$ 'my'
	ɲo$_3$ 'to be good,' *ɲo*$_1$ 'sea cow'
Efik:	*e*$_1$*ɲe*$_2$ 'he,' *ɲe*$_3$*ne*$_3$ 'to have'
Gã:	*ɲẽ*$_1$ 'yesterday,' *ɲo:ŋ*$_1$ 'night,' *ɲẽ*$_3$*ba:*$_1$ 'you come'
Nupe:	*ɲa* 'to dance,' *ɲaɲaɲaɲayi* 'sparkingly'
Wolof:	*boɲ* 'tooth'

In some African languages the palatal nasal and *ny* [nj] occur as separate phonemes:

Karanga (S. Rhodesia): *kuɲara* 'to be tired,' *kunyara* 'to be ashamed'
Bari (Anglo-Egyptian Sudan): *kɛɲa* 'branch of a tree,' *kɛnya* 'to be torn'

Wright points out[3] that in the various British dialects there are a large number of words which have an initial inorganic *n*. In many words this sound has arisen partly from the *n* of the indefinite article *an*, and partly from the *n* of the possessive pronoun *mine*. He makes no reference, however, to [ɲ] as having been observed in these cases. In his *English Dialect Dictionary*[4] approximately fifty words are listed which begin with *ny*. Most of these have a variant spelling beginning with *n*. Two words in the list—*nyam* (or *nyum*) and *nyim*—have a variant spelling which begins with *y*. In no instance is any indication given that *ny* represents [ɲ]. On the other hand, the pronunciation of the *ny* in seven of these words, including *nyum* and *nyim* is given in phonetic symbols as [nj], i.e., English *n* + *y*. It is very probable, therefore, that the *ny* in the spelling of all these words represents the same combination rather than the palatal nasal.

H. The Retroflex Flap[5] [ɽ]

Among the Gullahs the retroflex flap occurs between vowels and medially before [l] as a substitute for the English alveolar *d* and the English voiced *th* [ð]. In the speech of some Gullahs the retroflex *d* [ḍ] occurs in this position. Examples:

brɒɽə 'brother,' *faɽə* 'father,' *mɪɽl* 'middle,' *pɒɽl* 'puddle,' *maḍə* 'madder,' *saḍl* 'saddle,' etc.

The retroflex flap occurs in several West African languages, including Bambara, Malinke, Hausa, Bini, Ewe, Kru, Twi, Ibo, and Mossi (French West Africa). In some of these languages [l], [r], and the flapped sound are members of one phoneme. This appears to be the case in Kru.[6] In certain dialects of Ibo the flapped sound is a member of the [r]-phoneme. In these dialects a rolled *r* is used between all vowels except [i] and [e], where the flapped sound occurs. The flapped sound appears to be the only *r* sound in the Mossi language, spoken in French West Africa. In Chuana (South Africa) the flapped sound is a member of the [l]-phoneme, occurring only before [i] and [u]. In Hausa the sound appears to belong to a different phoneme from [r] and from [l]: e.g., *ba*$_3$*ra*$_1$ 'begging,' *ba*$_3$*ɽa*$_1$ 'servant.' In Ewe the retroflex *d* [ḍ] belongs to a different phoneme from the alveolar *d*: e.g., *e*$_1$*de*$_3$ 'palm,' *e*$_1$*ḍe*$_3$ 'one.' When the retroflex *d* in Ewe occurs between vowels, it is indistinguishable from the retroflex flap.[7]

Wright points out that medial *d* has become *r* in South-Mid Lancashire, South Cheshire, and West Somersetshire in *anibri* 'anybody,' *nobri* 'nobody,' *sumbri* 'somebody,' and a few other words.[8] This *r* is very probably the flapped lingual *r* rather than the retroflex flap.

I. Nonaspiration of Voiceless Plosives

Many Gullah speakers do not aspirate the voiceless plosives [p, t, k] when they occur at the beginning of a stressed syllable. Others do so only very slightly.

Unaspirated voiceless plosives occur in many African languages, among which are Ewe, Wolof, Malinke, Bambara, Kimbundu, Suto (South Africa), and others. In Bini voiceless plosives are very slightly aspirated. In the Ndau group of languages (Southern Rhodesia) the unaspirated plosives are ejective: e.g., *k'amba* 'to be a magician,' *khamba* 'leopard,' *p'anda* 'perhaps,' *phanda* 'to scratch.' In Zulu not all unaspirated *k* sounds are ejective, but unaspirated *p* and *t* are: e.g., *t'eŋga* 'to wave about,' *theŋga* 'to barter.'

J. The Inter-dental Fricatives [θ] and [ð]

The English inter-dental fricative *th* does not exist in Gullah nor in the West African languages included in this study. In pronouncing English words containing this sound, both the Gullah speaker and the West African substitute [d] and [t], respectively, for the voiced and voiceless varieties of it.

Advocates of the theory that Gullah is derived solely from English, ignoring the presence of any African influence in the Gullah Negro's articulation of the English voiceless and voiced *th* sounds as [t] and [d], respectively, point to the fact that many Englishmen in the Shetland and Orkney Isles, Pembroke, Kent, and Sussex pronounced such words as *this*, *that*, and *them*, as *dis*, *dat*, and *dem*. But even if evidence could be produced to the effect that the Gullahs, isolated as they were on the Sea Islands with a minimum of contact with white people, actually did have contact with Englishmen who used [t] and [d] as substitutes for the *th* sounds—but so far no evidence of such contact has been produced—one still would not be justified in assuming that the Gullah's African speech habits did not contribute importantly to his use of these substitutes. Whenever the native West African today first encounters the English *th* sounds, whether in the United States, the Caribbean, West Africa, or elsewhere, he at first substitutes for them [t] and [d], with which he is thoroughly familiar and which he considers closer to the English *th* than any of the other sounds of his language. This is true whether he is literate or illiterate. All of my African informants who have recently learned to speak English use these substitutes, and it is reasonable to suppose that their ancestors who came to South Carolina and Georgia direct from Africa as slaves reacted similarly to the English *th* sounds when encountering them for the first time.

K. [s, ʃ], and [ɕ]

The practice of substituting [ʃ] for the English *s* is fairly common among the Gullahs: e.g., *ʃʌm* 'see them,' *'ʃoḍa* 'soda,' *ʃup* 'soup,' etc. This substitution occurred also in several of the British dialects.[9] The same observation might be made here that was made with respect to the occurrence of [t] and [d] in both Gullah and the British dialects as substitutes for the voiceless and voiced varieties of the English *th*. Even though records were available showing that the Gullahs had contact with Englishmen who used [ʃ] as a substitute for [s], many Gullahs would have made the substitution anyway without such contact, because in some of the African languages spoken by many of the slaves [s] did not occur. In one part of the Yoruba country, for example, [ʃ] occurred but [s] did not. Yoruba speakers today from the non-[s] section invariably substitute [ʃ] for [s] when learning to speak English. In certain areas of the Ibo country, [ʃ], rather than [s], always occurs before [i] and [e].[10]

There is also heard in Gullah as a variant of [s] the alveolar-palatal fricative [ɕ], which is acoustically between [s] and [ʃ]. In the articulation of this sound the front of the tongue is raised toward the hard palate, the friction occurring near the back of the teeth-ridge and the hard palate. Many Gullahs use this sound before [i], [ɪ], and [e]: e.g., 'owəɕiə 'overseer,' 'ɕi əm 'see them,' 'ɕiḍə 'cedar,' 'ɕiʃə 'sister,' 'ɕelə 'Sarah,' etc.

In most of the Ewe dialects this sound occurs before [i]: e.g., $a_1ɕi_1$ 'market,' $a_1mɛ_1ɕi_1$ 'he who,' etc. In these dialects it is a member of the [s]-phoneme, the normal alveolar *s* occurring before all other vowels. The sound is likewise a member of the [s]-phoneme in Mossi and Zande (Anglo-Egyptian Sudan and the Belgian Congo.[11]

VOWELS

The most striking resemblances between the vowels of Gullah and those of the West African languages are found in the quality of the vowels. These similarities include the following:

1. The English central vowel [ɜ] does not occur in Gullah. For this sound the Gullahs substitute [ʌ, ɒ], or [a]. West Africans usually substitute [ɔ] or [a] for [ɜ] when pronouncing English words containing that sound.

2. In Gullah, as in several African languages, including Yoruba and Twi, [i] is very close—practically cardinal [i].

3. Like many West African languages, Gullah has only one *a*-vowel, which is [a], the English [æ] and [ɑ] being absent.

4. [u] in Gullah, as in Yoruba and Ewe, is very close—practically cardinal [u].

5. [e] in Gullah is above cardinal, as in Ibo and Yoruba.
6. [o] in Gullah is likewise above cardinal, as in Efik, Ibo, Yoruba, Twi, and Ewe.

This practice on the part of the Gullahs of using a simplified vowel system based on African models reveals one of the significant influences of the African languages on Gullah.

The diagram on page 17 shows the approximate tongue positions for the vowels of Gullah and for those of one West African language, Yoruba, from which probably more words have survived in Gullah than from any other West African language with the possible exception of Kongo.

Another speech habit of the Gullahs involving the use of vowels is revealed in the fact that they are inclined when pronouncing English words or syllables that end in a consonant either to add a vowel or to drop the consonant. There is also the tendency to avoid certain consonant combinations either by inserting a vowel between the consonants or, more frequently, by dropping one of them. This practice of simplifying English words, together with the rather marked tendency to speak rapidly with an intonation in many respects unlike that of English,[12] contributes greatly to the stranger's difficulty in comprehending the speech of the Gullahs. The following pronunciations of English words and phrases are common among them:

ˈ*bagə* 'baggage'
ˈ*bakə* 'black'
ˈ*bʌmələ bi* 'bumblebee'
εn$_3$*ti*$_1$ʔ 'ain't it?'
ˈ*flɪkɪlɪ* 'afflicted'
*gɪ*ˈ*zaki* 'gizzard'
ˈ*hosi* 'hoarse'
*ɟu*ˈ*zapə* 'jew's harp'
ˈ*krʊkɪtɪ* 'crooked'
ˈ*mani pis* 'mantle piece'
mʌnz 'mumps'
ˈ*nekɪtɪ* 'naked'
ˈ*nibo* 'kneebone'
*pali*ˈ*metə* 'palmetto'
ˈ*pεgənə* 'pregnant'
ˈ*pogəm* 'program'
ˈ*Gɪʃə* 'sister'
ʃʌm 'see them'
te 'stay'
traps 'strap'
ˈ*tεnə* 'tenant'
ˈ*tɪtə* 'sister'
ˈ*wɪkɪtɪ* 'wicked'
ˈ*yεrɪ* 'hear it'

In many African languages, including Kongo, Mende, Yoruba, and Kimbundu, every syllable ends in a vowel, and the tendency among Africans to avoid certain consonant clusters familiar to speakers of English is very marked. The pronunciations given of the English words in the several groups that follow are those of native speakers of the following West African languages:

Bini:

- a$_3$se$_3$za$_1$ 'soldier'
- e$_1$sɔ$_{3-1}$si$_1$ 'church'
- e$_1$ga$_1$la$_{3-1}$hi$_1$ 'glass'
- e$_1$te$_3$bu$_1$ru$_1$ 'table'
- e$_1$sɔ$_3$ki$_1$si$_1$ 'socks'
- i$_3$bi$_3$ri$_3$ki$_1$ 'brick'

Ewe:

- bu$_1$ku$_1$ 'book'
- kla$_1$te$_1$ 'cutlass'
- ka$_1$pi$_1$si$_1$ 'caps'
- me$_1$li$_1$ 'mail'
- ki$_1$ki$_1$ 'kick'
- su$_1$ku$_1$ 'school'

Hausa:

- bir$_3$ki$_1$ 'brick'
- taŋ$_3$ga$_1$ra:$_2$hu$_1$ 'telegraph'
- iŋ$_1$gi$_1$li$_2$ʃi$_1$ 'English'
- ti:$_3$ti$_3$ 'street'

Yoruba:

- ʃu$_1$ku$_3$lu$_1$ 'school'
- te$_3$ʃɔ$_1$ni$_1$ 'station'
- su$_1$pu$_3$nu$_1$ 'spoon'

Twi:

- ba$_3$re$_1$ 'barrel'
- si$_1$ri$_3$ci 'silk'

Ibo:

- n$_3$dʒa$_1$ 'India'
- si$_1$lɛ$_1$ 'shilling'

Kongo:

- buku 'book'
- miliki 'milk'
- bɔta 'boat'

CHAPTER 8

INTONATION

PROBABLY no characteristic of the Gullah Negro's speech appears so strange to one who hears this dialect for the first time as its intonation. To understand fully the intonation of Gullah one will have to turn to those West African tone languages spoken by the slaves who were being brought to South Carolina and Georgia continually until practically the beginning of the Civil War. Among these tone languages are Mende, Vai, Twi, Fante, Gā, Ewe, Yoruba, Ibo, Bini, Efik, and a few others. In the discussion that will follow, an effort has been made merely to reveal some of the more striking similarities between certain tonal patterns of Gullah and those of a few of the West African tone languages.

So far as my own observation is concerned, features of tone in Gullah are not used as primary phonemes, i.e., the tones of Gullah words do not distinguish meanings as do tones in the African tone languages. There are in Gullah, however, several intonation patterns, used in sentences, phrases, and words, that are quite common in the African languages but are not used in cultivated English under similar conditions. These tonal patterns will be grouped under eight headings.

A. The Use of a High or Mid Tone at the End of a Declarative Sentence

In an English declarative sentence in which no implication or special meaning is intended, the final syllable takes a falling tone if it is stressed and a low tone if it is unstressed. In a similar Gullah declarative sentence, however, the final syllable frequently takes a high or mid tone, and the syllable may be stressed heavily, or weakly, or not at all:[1]

de$_2$ ˈ*tɒk*$_3$ *ɒn*$_2$ *hɒʊ*$_2$ *hi*$_2$ ˈ*kʌs*$_3$ *dɛm*$_2$ 'They talked about how he cursed them'
də$_1$ ˈ*gɒd*$_3$ ˈ*wʌk*$_2$ 'It is God's work'

In many West African languages the final syllable of a declarative sentence frequently takes a high or mid tone when no implication or special meaning is intended:

Ewe: $o_1ve_1\ ko_1\ me_1kpɔ_3$ 'No, I saw only two'
$ḍe_1vi_3\ la_3va_3$ 'The child came'
$e_3tsɔ_{3-1}\ tu_3$ 'He took the gun'

Ibo: $ɔ_3\ de_1\ n_1sö_3$ 'It is near'
$ɔ_3\ de_1\ n_2sɔ_2$ 'It is forbidden'

Yoruba: $mo_2ro_3hũ_2ke_3ɟi_1\ lo_2ru_3kɔ_2\ mi_2$ '$mo_2ro_3hũ_2ke_3\ ɟi_1$ is my name'
$mo_2\ sɔ_2\ ɔ_2$ 'I told it'
$nwɔ̃_3\ wa_3\ ni_3\ ɔ_2mɔ̃_2de_3$ 'They came as children'
$o_3\ da{:}_2$ 'It is good'

B. The Use of a Rising Tone at the End of a Declarative Sentence

On the final stressed syllable of an English declarative sentence, as already indicated, only a falling tone would be used unless some special meaning is intended. In Gullah, on the other hand, as in several West African languages, the rising tone is common in this position:

Gullah: $ɒɪ_1\ ˈtɛl_3\ əm_3\ ˈso_{1-3}$ 'I tell them so'
$ˈdat_1\ ˈflat_2\ ˈflɒʊ_{2-3}$ 'That's flat flour'
$ˈman_3\ n_1\ ˈwɐɪf_3\ n_1\ ˈcɪl_3ən_1\ də_1\ ˈwʌk_3\ fə_1\ ˈdɛm_{2-3}$ '[The] man and wife and children are working for them'

Ewe: $e_3kpɔ_3\ ho_{1-3}$ 'He possesses money,' lit. 'He saw, received money'
$gɛ{:}_{1-3}$ 'It is money'
$et_3sɔ_3\ a_1ti_3\ ḍe_3\ a_1bɔ_3ta_{1-3}$ 'He carries a tree on his shoulder'

Efik: e_3fe_{1-3} 'It flies'
e_3be_{1-3} 'He passes'
$a_1mi_1\ ŋ_3ka_{1-3}$ 'I go'

Yoruba: $mo_2\ mɔ̃{:}_{1-2}$ 'I knew her'

C. The Use of Level Tones—Mid, High, or Low—throughout a Statement

Gullah: $yu_2\ ˈgo_3\ dɛ_3\ ən_3\ ˈmit_3\ səm_3\ ˈman_3\ ˈbrʌk_2$ 'You go there and meet some man broken'
$ˈol_3\ ˈle_3rɪ_3,\ yu_2\ ˈbɛ_3tə_3\ go_3\ ˈhom_3\ go_3\ ˈsi_3\ bɐʊ_3co_3\ ˈcɪl_3ən_2$ 'Old lady, you'd better go home and see about your children'
$ˈdɛm_3\ ˈgal_3\ ˈkʌm_3\ ˈhom_3;\ ˈde_3\ ˈtɒk_3\ ɒn_2\ hɒʊ_2\ hi_2\ ˈkʌs_3\ dɛm_2$ 'Those girls came home; they talked about how he cursed them'

The occurrence of many level tones in words, phrases, and sentences is a common phenomenon in West African languages.

Ibo: $ö_3nyɛ_3\ a_3nya_3\ u_3ku_3$ 'covetous person'
$ö_3gö_3nö_3gö_3\ ö_3si_3si_3$ 'tall tree'
$a_3kwa_2la_2\ a_2kwa_2$ 'Do not cry'

e$_{3}$kwu$_{2}$ze$_{2}$na$_{2}$ ö$_{2}$kwu$_{2}$ 'Stop speaking'
mu$_{3}$ lɛ$_{3}$ma$_{3}$ a$_{3}$ɲa$_{3}$ 'Let me be looking'
mu$_{1}$fan$_{1}$ mi$_{1}$, n$_{1}$ɲin$_{1}$ i$_{1}$sa$_{3}$ŋa$_{1}$ ɔ$_{1}$tɔ$_{1}$ kiet$_{1}$ 'My friend, let us walk together'

Yoruba: ba$_{2}$ba$_{2}$ ba$_{2}$ba$_{2}$ mi$_{2}$ 'my grandfather,' lit. 'the father of my father'
mo$_{2}$ mɔ̃$_{2}$ ba$_{2}$ba$_{2}$ rɛ$_{2}$ 'I knew your father'
kai$_{3}$ye$_{3}$ o$_{3}$ gũ$_{3}$ 'May the world be straight'

Ewe: nu$_{3}$ la$_{3}$ tsɔ$_{3}$tsɔ$_{3}$ 'the carrying of the thing'
to$_{3}$ḍo$_{3}$ḍo$_{3}$ nu$_{3}$fi$_{3}$a$_{3}$la$_{3}$ 'obedience to the teacher'
me$_{1}$ga$_{1}$yi$_{1}$ 'I went again'

Vai: goŋ$_{1}$go$_{1}$lo:$_{1}$goŋ$_{1}$go$_{1}$lo:$_{1}$goŋ$_{1}$go$_{1}$lo$_{1}$ 'anything very large or ponderous'

D. The Alternation of Low and Mid or Low and High Tones throughout a Statement

Gullah: 'de$_{3}$ nə$_{2}$ 'en$_{2}$ 'nʌn$_{2}$ ə$_{2}$ dɛm$_{2}$ 'bɪn$_{3}$ dɛ$_{2}$ 'tɒk$_{3}$ 'lɒŋ$_{2}$ 'tɒɪm$_{2}$ 'There haven't been any of them there to talk in a long time'
'tʌk$_{1}$ 'ca$_{1}$ ə$_{1}$ 'mɒɪ$_{3}$ 'hɐʊs$_{1}$ 'wɒɪls$_{3}$ 'ɒɪ$_{1}$ 'liw$_{2-3-1}$ 'Take care of my house while I leave'
'dɛm$_{2}$ də$_{1}$ 'ca$_{2}$ əm$_{1}$ də$_{1}$ 'ɟi$_{2}$ əm$_{1}$ dɪ$_{1}$ 'pi$_{2}$pl$_{1}$ wɒt$_{1}$ haw$_{1}$ 'man$_{2}$ n$_{1}$ 'wɐɪf$_{2}$ n$_{1}$ 'cɪl$_{3}$ən$_{1}$ də$_{1}$ 'wʌk$_{3}$ fə$_{1}$ 'dɛm$_{2-3}$ 'They carry them and give them to the people who have man and wife and children to work for them'

Ibo: ɔ$_{3}$kɔ$_{1}$ ɛ$_{2}$dɛ$_{1}$ 'He planted coco yam'
ɛ$_{3}$ bum$_{1}$ a$_{1}$kwa$_{2}$ na$_{1}$ dʒi$_{2}$ 'I have brought eggs and yam'

Efik: n$_{3}$sin$_{1}$ i$_{2}$sɔŋ$_{1}$ 'I am laying the floor'
e$_{1}$di$_{3}$wak$_{1}$ o$_{2}$wo$_{1}$ 'a crowd of people'

Ewe: a$_{1}$ti$_{3}$zɔ$_{1}$ti$_{3}$ 'walking-stick'
e$_{3}$ḍe$_{1}$ e$_{3}$me$_{1}$ 'He took its inside out'
a$_{1}$ti$_{3}$ la$_{1}$ kɔ$_{3}$ 'The tree is high'

Yoruba: i$_{1}$ya$_{3}$ mi$_{2}$ n$_{3}$ɟɛ$_{3}$ ʃaŋ$_{1}$go$_{3}$bũ$_{1}$mi$_{2}$ 'My mother had the name of ʃaŋ$_{1}$go$_{3}$bũ$_{1}$mi$_{2}$'
ni$_{3}$gba$_{1}$ti$_{3}$ nwɔ̃$_{3}$ si$_{1}$ de$_{3}$ ɔ$_{1}$hũ$_{3}$ nwɔ̃$_{3}$ ʃe$_{1}$re$_{3}$ kpu$_{3}$kpɔ$_{1}$ 'When they arrived there, they played a great deal'

E. The Use of Tones That Fall from High to Mid

Gullah: ɒɪ$_{2}$ gɒn$_{2}$ dɛ$_{2}$, gɒɪn$_{1}$ 'wɪz$_{2}$ɪt$_{2}$ 'hɪm$_{3-2}$ 'I went there to visit him'
i$_{1}$ 'bʌnt$_{2}$ 'ʌm$_{3-2}$ 'He burned them'
'ʌ$_{2}$'ɲʌn$_{3-2}$ 'onion'

Efik: a$_{1}$ma$_{3-2}$ ɔ$_{2}$fɔn$_{2}$, ɲe$_{2}$kop$_{2}$ 'If it is good, I will consider it'

Ibo: ɛ$_{1}$bɛ:$_{3-2}$ ka$_{1}$ i$_{2}$ dʒɛ$_{1}$kɔ$_{1}$ 'Where are you going?'

Yoruba: o$_{1}$ũ$_{2}$ da:$_{3-2}$ 'He is good'
o$_{2}$ ba:$_{3-2}$ lai$_{3}$ye$_{1}$? 'You met her alive?'

F. The Use of Tones That Rise from Low or Mid to High or from Low to Mid

In English this tone might occur when some special meaning is implied, or it might occur at the end of an unfinished tonal group—for example, at the end of a subordinate clause that does not end the sentence; but it does not occur under such conditions as obtain in the following Gullah sentences:

de$_1$ 'aks$_3$ 'ples$_2$ fə$_2$ sɪt$_2$ 'dɒʊn$_{2-1}$ 'af$_3$tə$_2$ u$_2$nə$_2$ 'gɒn$_{2-3}$ 'They asked for a place to sit down after you left'

di$_1$ ol$_1$ le$_1$dɪ$_1$ 'dɒɪ$_{1-3}$ nɒʊ$_1$ 'The old lady is dead now'

Efik: e$_1$ɲe$_3$ a$_3$ka$_{1-2}$ i$_1$ŋwaŋ$_2$ 'He goes to the farm'
a$_1$mi$_1$ ŋ$_3$ka$_{1-3}$ 'I go'

Ewe: ɲa$_{1-3}$ti$_3$ 'my tree'
a$_1$ŋu$_1$ti$_3$ gbo$_3$gbo$_{1-3}$ 'unripe lime'

Yoruba: mo$_2$ mɔ̃:$_{1-2}$ 'I knew her'
ɔ$_1$rɔ$_1$ kpu$_3$kpɔ$_1$ ki:$_{1-2}$ kũ$_3$ a$_2$gbɔ̃$_1$ 'Many words do not fill a basket'

G. The Use of Non-English Tones in Gullah Words and Short Phrases

Gullah: bʌ$_1$krʌ$_3$ 'white man'
hʌz$_1$bʌn$_3$ 'husband'
o$_1$kra$_3$ 'okra'
be$_1$bi$_3$ 'baby'
bʌnt$_2$ ʌm$_{3-2}$ 'Burn them'

Ibo: a$_1$la$_1$ 'ground'
n$_1$nɛ$_3$ 'mother'
u$_1$do$_3$ o$_3$bi$_1$ 'peace of heart'

Efik: u$_1$di$_1$ 'grave'
u$_3$di$_1$ 'a town in Nigeria'
e$_1$fe$_2$ 'shed'
e$_3$fe$_1$ 'which'?
o$_3$du$_3$du$_3$ 'hole'

Twi: ɔ$_1$kra$_3$ 'soul'

Ewe: ka$_1$ 'to scatter'
ka$_3$ 'to touch'
a$_1$tsu$_3$ 'male'

Yoruba: i$_1$fe$_2$ 'a small bird'
i$_1$fe$_3$ 'whistling'
i$_2$fe$_2$ 'cup'

H. The Use of a Level Tone at the End of a Question

In English at the end of a question when no special meaning is implied, a rising tone is the usual one if *yes* or *no* is required for an answer, and a falling tone if it is not. In Gullah, on the other hand, a level tone is quite common at the end of a question whether or not *yes* or *no* is required for an answer.

Gullah: *wɒt*$_3$ ˈ*dɛm*$_{2-1}$ *də*$_1$ ˈ*ɟi*$_2$ *yu*$_2$ 'What do they give you?'
ˈ*yu*$_3$ *no*$_3$ *wɒt*$_3$ *dɛm*$_3$ ˈ*pe*$_3$ fə$_2$ ˈ*bin*$_3$? 'Do you know what they pay for beans?'
ˈ*ɛn*$_2$*ti*$_3$ ˈ*rɛ*$_2$*bl*$_2$ *tɒɪm*$_2$ *kʌm*$_2$*ɪn*$_2$ ˈ*bak*$_2$? 'Isn't slavery coming back?'

In the West African languages a level tone is frequently heard at the conclusion of both types of questions.

Efik: *m*$_1$*mɔ*$_3$*ŋɔ*$_1$ *e*$_1$*nye*$_2$ *ɔ*$_2$*kpɔ*$_2$*bɔ*$_1$? 'Do you think he would have taken it?'
n$_1$*si*$_3$*di*$_3$ *n*$_3$*tak*$_3$ *m*$_3$*mɔ*$_1$ *i*$_1$*mi*$_{3-1}$ *ka*$_1$ *ha*$_2$ *e*$_2$*kɔŋ*$_2$? 'Why didn't they go to war?'

Ibo: *kɛ*$_1$*do*$_3$ *ö*$_3$*tu*$_3$ *ö*$_3$ *si*$_1$ *ti*$_3$ *ge*$_2$? 'How did he hit you?'

Yoruba: *ta*$_2$*lo*$_3$*kɔ*$_2$ *ku*$_3$, *i*$_1$*ya*$_3$ *rɛ*$_2$ *ta*$_1$*bi*$_3$ *ba*$_2$*ba*$_2$ *rɛ*$_2$? 'Who was it that died first, your mother or your father?'
kpɛ$_1$*lu*$_3$ *ta*$_2$*ni*$_2$? 'With whom?'
o$_3$ *ŋ*$_3$*gbe*$_3$ *kpɛ*$_1$*lu*$_3$ *rɛ*$_2$? 'He is living with you?'

Ewe: *mi*$_1$*a*$_3$*va*$_3$*a*$_1$? 'Are you coming?'
ma$_3$*kpe*$_3$ *ḍe*$_3$ *ŋu*$_1$*wo*$_3$*a*$_1$? 'Am I to help you?'

CHAPTER 9

GULLAH TEXTS

THESE texts, all of which I recorded on phonograph disks and later transcribed in phonetic notation, constitute only a small percentage of the materials I collected among the Gullahs; but they are sufficient, it is hoped, to indicate in connected discourse many of the ways in which Gullah is indebted to African sources.

As regards numerals, I interviewed several older Gullahs, each of whom could count from one to ten in a different African language. A few in Georgia could count from one to nineteen in the Fula language. Usually the Gullahs did not know the name of the language in which they counted, but said that they learned the numerals from older relatives or friends. A few, unknowingly, would draw upon two or more African languages in counting from one to ten. In many instances the pronunciation of the numerals had changed somewhat from that of the original African, but not to such an extent that I could not identify the language. There were other cases in which identification was impossible. The Gullahs' pronunciation of the Fula numerals which I have listed below is almost identical with that of my Fula informant, Sayid Ibrahim, of Sierra Leone.[1]

Such recreational forms among the Gullahs as singing (frequently accompanied by dancing and hand-clapping) and story-telling often reveal significant African survivals. I recorded a few songs all the words of which are African. One such song is given below. At least two versions of this song are well known on Harris Neck, Georgia; and in both versions the words are from the Mende language. The singers of the song (Amelia Dawley and James Rogers) had known it all their lives, but did not know the name of the language in which they sang it nor the exact meaning of the words. In a large number of Gullah songs, English and African words occur side by side.[2] In some songs the English words and phrases are literal or free translations of the African; that is, an African word or phrase is followed in the same line or in the next by its English equivalent.

In other songs no such translation accompanies the African portions. Of the four songs below in which English and African words occur, two contain Mende and two Vai words. The English translation of the African words of all five songs is my own, but in each case my translation has been carefully checked and verified by native Mende and Vai informants.

A great many Gullah stories also contain African words, phrases, and sentences. As in the case of the songs, the African portions are frequently followed by explanations in English. In the three stories below, however, no English explanations occur. The translation of the African portions of the stories is my own. In the third section of chapter 3, I have listed the African words, together with their meaning, that occur only in Gullah songs, stories, and prayers.

Even though the African element in the remaining Gullah texts is not so obvious to the casual reader as that in the numerals, the songs, and the stories, it is present nevertheless. For example, it manifests itself linguistically in syntactical and morphological features, in vowel and consonant sounds, in the manner in which words are formed, and especially in intonation.[3] These remaining texts also contain a few African words.

NUMERALS (1–19)

(Recorded near Darien, Georgia)

	1	2	3	4
Gullah	*go*	*ˈdidi*	*ˈtatə*	*nᴅɪ*
Fula	*go*	*didi*	*tati*	*nai*
	5	6	7	8
Gullah	*ɟe*	*ˈɟego*	*ˈɟedidi*	*ˈɟeta'ə*
Fula	*ɟe* (*ɟuwi*)	*ɟego*	*ɟedidi*	*ɟetati*
	9	10	11	12
Gullah	*ˈɟenᴅɪ*	*ˈsapə*	*ˌsapəˈgo*	*ˌsapəˈdidi*
Fula	*ɟenai*	*sapo*	*sapo e go*	*sapo e didi*
	13	14	15	16
Gullah	*ˌsapəˈtatə*	*ˌsapəˈnᴅɪ*	*ˌsapəˈɟe*	*ˌsapəˈɟego*
Fula	*sapo e tati*	*sapo e nai*	*sapo e ɟe* (*sapo e ɟuwi*)	*sapo e ɟego*
	17	18	19	
Gullah	*ˌsapəˈɟedidi*	*ˌsapəˈɟetatə*	*ˌsapəˈɟenᴅɪ*	
Fula	*sapo e ɟedidi*	*sapo e ɟetati*	*sapo e ɟenai*	

SONGS

A. A Mende Song[4]

(*Sung by* Amelia Dawley, *Harris Neck, Georgia*)

a wɒkɒ mʊ mɔnɛ; kambɛɪ ya lɛ; li, lɛ:ɪ tɒmbɛ.
In the evening[5] we suffer; the grave not yet; heart, be cool perfectly.
a wɒkɒ mʊ mɔnɛ; kambɛɪ ya lɛ; li, lɛ:ɪ ka.
In the evening we suffer; the grave not yet; heart, be cool continually.
ha sa wuli ŋgo, sihã; kpaŋga lɪ lɛ:;
Death quickly the tree destroys, steals [it]; the remains disappear slowly;
ha sa wuli ŋgo; ndɛlɪ, ndi, ka.
Death quickly the tree destroys; be at rest, heart, continually.
ha sa wuli ŋgo, sihã; kpaŋga lɪ lɛ:;
Death quickly the tree destroys, steals [it]; the remains disappear slowly;
ha sa wuli ŋgo; ndɛlɪ, ndi, ka.
Death quickly the tree destroys; be at rest, heart, continually.
a wɒkɒ mʊ mɔnɛ; kambɛɪ ya lɛ; li, lɛ:ɪ tɒmbɛ.
In the evening we suffer; the grave not yet; heart, be cool perfectly.
a wɒkɒ mʊ mɔnɛ; kambɛɪ ya lɛ; li, lɛ:ɪ ka.
In the evening we suffer; the grave not yet; heart, be cool continually.
ha sa wuli ŋgo, sihã; kuhã nda yia;
Death quickly the tree destroys, steals [it]; from afar a voice speaks;
ha sa wuli ŋgo; ndɛlɪ, ndi, ka.
Death quickly the tree destroys; be at rest, heart, continually.

B. A Mende-Gullah Song

(*Sung by* Lavinia Capers Quarterman, *Darien, Georgia, and accompanied by dancing and hand-clapping*)

le mbeɪ, ɟal, le mbeɪ;
Pass this way, girl, pass this way;
wa, ɟal, wa.
Come, girl, come.

C. A Mende-Gullah Song

(*Sung by* Emma Hall, *Darien, Georgia*)

a wɒkɒ bɪ lɪ a, ba wa lɒ
In the evening when you go, you will come
ɒl rɒʊŋ dɪ kʌntrɪ.
All around the country.
tɪ bɪ bawo.
You will be healed.
Its ə wɛrɪ fɒɪn ledɪ
It's a very fine lady
bɪ bawo.
[who] will heal you.

D. A Vai–Gullah Song

(*Sung by* Julia Armstrong, *St. Simon Island, Georgia*)

ɲu rɐɪs n okra
New rice and okra
na$_3$*na*$_1$, *na*$_3$*na*$_1$.
I've come, I've come.
it sʌm n liw sʌm,
Eat some and leave some,
na$_3$*na*$_1$, *na*$_3$*na*$_1$.
I've come, I've come.
bit rɐɪs, tu:$_1$, *gbaŋ*$_3$, *gbaŋ*$_3$,
Beat rice, beat, bang, bang,
na$_3$*na*$_1$, *na*$_3$*na*$_1$.
I've come, I've come.

E. A Vai–Gullah Song

(*Sung by* Eugenia Hutchinson, *Edisto Island, South Carolina*)

dɪ sadl n brɐɪdl ɪz ɒn dɪ ʃɛf;
The saddle and bridle is on the shelf;
sa$_1$ *na*$_1$ *pon*:$_3$.
He is lying far away.
dɪ sadl n brɐɪdl ɪz ɒn dɪ ʃɛf;
The saddle and bridle is on the shelf;
sa$_1$ *na*$_1$ *pon*:$_3$.
He is lying far away.
dɪ sadl n brɐɪdl ɪz ɒn dɪ ʃɛf;
The saddle and bridle is on the shelf;
ɪf yu wɒn ɪnɪ mo, yu cɪn ɟɪt ɪt yosɛf.
If you want any more, you can get it yourself.
sa$_1$ *na*$_1$ *pon*:$_3$; *sa*$_1$ *na*$_1$ *pi*:$_1$*tɛ*$_{3-2}$.
He is lying far away; he is lying in the midst of the grass.
fa$_1$*la*:$_{3-1}$ *ni*$_1$; *ka*$_1$*sɪ*$_3$ *tɛ*$_{3-2}$, *sa*$_1$ *na*$_1$ *pon*:$_3$.
He died long ago; surrounded by rust, he lies far away.

SOME MENDE EXPRESSIONS OCCURRING IN GULLAH STORIES

A. From *dɪ lɛpəd an dɪ ɲɒŋ ledɪ* 'The Leopard and the Young Lady'

In this story the leopard transformed himself into a man and married a young lady who had boasted that she would never marry a man with spots on his back. After marrying her, he took her into a swamp and left her there, instructing a fly to guard her and to report to him any intrusion on the part of her friends. An old man, Sambo, went into the swamp and informed the lady that she was married not to a man but to a leopard. This the fly promptly reported to the leopard, who became so enraged that he rushed into the swamp and, seeing Sambo and the lady together, cried out:

"*woŋga! woŋga! woŋga! lɒ!*
"Kinsfolk! kinsfolk! kinsfolk! Look!
nda hoʊ mbeɪ. na ta sondʊ ndi lɛ."
Wait here. That crime, it afflicts the heart."

Whereupon, Sambo replied:

"*komɛ! sɔ mbɛ. na tia sondʊ ndi lɛ,*
"Gather around! Take it from me. If the crime afflicts the heart,
ndi lawo."
open the heart" (i.e., tell the truth about the whole affair).

Thereupon, the leopard promised never to molest the lady again and confessed that he had deceived her in order to prove to her that she was not so clever as she imagined herself to be when she boasted that she would never marry a man with spots on his back.

B. From *dɪ kuta an dɪ dɛə* 'The Tortoise and the Deer'

This is the story of a ten-mile race between the tortoise and the deer for the hand of a young lady who had promised to marry the one who reached her door first. The tortoise, by placing a member of his family at each of the ten mile-posts—the tenth being the door of the lady, where he himself was stationed—was able to convince the deer as he passed each mile-post that he, the tortoise, was not only still in the race but was able to reach the lady's door ahead of the deer. As the deer approached the lady's door, he said:

"*sasi, bɛ: ku gbla nda.*"
"Boaster, you cannot be near the door."

The tortoise, however, was able to reply:

"to *ŋgo a ku gbla nda.*"
"Send word that he [the tortoise] *can* be near the door."

C. From *dɪ wʊf, dɪ rabɪt, an dɪ wel eg* 'The Wolf, the Rabbit, and the Whale's Eggs'

In this story the wolf persuaded the rabbit to explain to him the rabbit's method of entering the house of the whale to steal eggs and of leaving without being caught. The rabbit instructed him to say on entering:

"*o: nda wo! o: nda wo!*"
"Please, open the door! Please, open the door!"

When ready to leave, the wolf was to say:

"*hoʊ nda tɪtɪtɪ!*"
"Hold the door very tightly!"

The wolf, accordingly, followed these instructions. He gained admittance to the house of the whale and obtained the eggs; but finding it impossible to escape, he was caught by the whale and killed.

had tɒɪm ɒn ɛdɪsto

(*By* DIANA BROWN, *Edisto Island, South Carolina*)

unə pɪk ə bascɪt ə bin fə fɒɪw n wʌn sɛnt. tu bascɪt—wɒt ɪt kʌm tu? ɒɪ wʊdn go dɛ tɪde; nɒt mi! ɒɪl it dɪ bin, bʌt ɒɪ ẽ gɒɪn go pɪk nʌn dɛ. wɛn dɛm pipl kʌm lɒŋ dɛ, de ɟi mi ə hanful, bət mi ẽ gwɒɪn dɛ. ɒɪ yɛɽɪ sɛ harɪsən dadɪ—harɪsɛn plant dɛ, yʊ no. sɛ i pa kʌm dɛ, rʌn dɪ pipl ɒf dɪ ples, cɪk dɪ pipl, kʌs ʌp dɪ pipl; dɪ pipl nə gɒn bak. de bɪn dɛ fə hɛp fɪnɪʃ pɪk. i min tɪd dat. i sɛ i ha no yus fə nɪgə. yɛ:, i ca fə mɛn; ẽ gɒt no yus fə nɪgə. i kʌs ʌp dɪ pipl. dɛm ɟal kʌm hom. de tɒk hɒʊ i kʌs dɛm. de ẽ gɒn bak. dɛm mɛn go fɛc dɪ ol pipl hom fə dɛm pɪk dɛm bin; kʌs dɪ pipl ʌp in dɪ fil. sɛ—dɪ pipl sɛ dat man ɪz dɪ minɪs man wʌ. mi nə gwɒɪn dɛ. de ha no bʌkrə—ɪf yu kʌs mi, mi na yu fɐɪt. yɛ:, ɒɪ ẽ no fə kʌs, yu no. ɒɪ rʌɽə yu nɒk mi. me z wɛl tɛl dɪ trut. si? ɒɪ cã pas no bad wʌd. wɛn ɒɪ bɪn kʌmɪn dɒʊŋ dɪ lɒɪn an ɟɪt in dɪ cʌc, man, ɒɪ wʌsə. wɛn ɒɪ had—mɒɪ hʌzbʌn bɪnə mɒɪ liɽə; an wʌsə, ɒɪ had tu stɪk; bət dats mɒɪ liɽə. yɛs, mam! mi nə gwɒɪn gɒn, fə mi na dat bʌkrə fɐɪt. ɒɪ lɪk dɛm hɛd. ɒɪ tɛl dɛm plen yɛs—ɒɪ sɛ, "ɪf ɒɪ fa go ɒf tʊ wɪlyəmz fə dɪ flɒwə,[6] wɪlyəm gwɒɪn lɒk mi ʌp; an dat ɲɒŋ man ha fə lɒk mi ʌp. si?" ɒɪ gwɒɪn kʌs əm, yu no. ɒɪ gwɒɪn tɛl əm—tɛl əm bɐʊt dɪ nɛʃən. ɒɪ gwɒɪn tɛl əm: "yu rɛd dɛwəl! yu z ə rɛd dɛwəl!" ɒɪ sɛ, "gɒdz gɒɪn pɪk yu ʌp"; an ɒɪ sɛ, "yul nɛwə fɛc ʌntɪl mɪstə mɪcɪ sibrʊk brɪŋ yu ɒn dɪ ples fə owəGiə. dɛn yu də brag, bət gɒd gɒɪn pɪk yu ʌp an yu. . . ." ɒɪ tɛl əm so. mi nə gwɒɪn dɛ; nɒt mi! mi nə gwɒɪn fə no flɒwə. de ha fə sɛt dat flɒwə hom. dɪ mel man tɛl mi tɪde, sɛ wɛn dɛm ɟɪt dat flɒwə in dɪ ɒtəmobil, de fa go rɒʊŋ tʊ ɒl dɪ ol leɽɪ do n pɪt əm dɛ. yɛ:, mɪstə belɪ tɛl mi dat tɪde.

ɒɪ ẽ no fa go fə no flɒwə. dɛm fa brɪŋ əm tʊ mi. yu si? nɒʊ, hɒʊ ɒɪ gɒɪn lɛf mɒɪ hom, gwɒɪn yɒndə tu ɔ fɒɪw mɒɪl frəm mɒɪ hɐʊs n go fə flɒwə? an dɛn, yu si, en dɛ no sɛf-rɐɪzɪn. dat flat flɒwə. ɒɪ ha fə bɒɪ ʃoda; ɒɪ ha fə bɒɪ lad. yu si? ɒɪ ha fə bɒɪ ʃʊgə, fɛ ɪf ɒɪ had dɪ flɒwə, ɒɪ had tʊ pe. yu cã plant—yu cã kʊk dɐʊt sɒlt. dɛm pipl wɒt go dɛ ha fə də bɒɪ ɒl dɛm tɪŋ. yu si? won de? en ɒɪ gɒɪn kʊk əm frɛʃ? 'hũ! ɒɪ kʊk əm frɛʃ, ɒl rɐɪt. yɛs, mam!

HARD TIMES ON EDISTO

(*By* Diana Brown, *Edisto Island, South Carolina*)

You pick a basket of bean for five and one cent. Two basket—what it come to? I wouldn't go there today; not me! I'll eat the bean, but I ain't going go pick none there. When them people come along there, they give me a handful, but me ain't going there. I hear that Harrison daddy—Harrison plant there, you know. [They] say he pa come there, run the people off the place, kick the people, curse up the people; the people not gone back. They been there to help finish pick. He [was] mean to do that. He say he has no use for nigger. Yes, he care for men; ain't got no use for nigger. He curse up the people. Them girl come home. They talk how he curse them. They ain't gone back. Them men go fetch the old people home for them [to] pick them bean; [they] curse the people up in the field. [They] say—the people say that man is the meanest man was. Me not going there. They have no white man. If you curse me, me and you fight. Yes, I ain't no [one] to be cursed, you know. I rather you knock me. [I] may as well tell the truth. See? I can't pass no bad word. When I been coming down the line and get in the church, man, I worse. When I had—My husband been my leader; and [what was] worse, I had to stick; but that's my leader. Yes, mam! Me not going go, for me and that white man [will] fight. I lick them head. I tell them plain yes—I say, "If I take go off to Williams' for the flour,[6] Williams going lock me up; and that young man have to lock me up. See?" I going curse him, you know. I going tell him—tell him about the nation. I going tell him: "You red devil! You is a red devil!" I say, "God's going pick you up"; and I say, "You'll never fetch until Mr. Mitchie Seabrook bring you on the place as overseer. Then you will brag, but God going pick you up and you. . . ." I tell him so. Me not going there; not me! Me not going for no flour. They [will] have to set that flour home. The mail man tell me today that when them get that flour in the automobile, they take [it] go around to all the old lady door and put it there. Yes, Mr. Bailey tell me that today.

I don't intend to go for no flour. Them take [it] bring it to me. You see? Now, how I going [to] leave my home [and] go yonder two or five mile from my house and go for flour? And then, you see, ain't there no self-rising. That flat flour. I['d] have to buy soda; I['d] have to buy lard. You see? I['d] have to buy sugar; for if I had the flour, I['d] have to pay. You can't plant—you can't cook without salt. Them people what go there have for to buy all them thing. You see? Won't they? Ain't I going cook them fresh? Huh! I [will] cook them fresh, all right. Yes, mam!

so ɒɪ *ẽ gɒɪn wʌrɪ ə sol.* ɒɪ *satɪsfɒɪ wɒt gɒd dʌn fə mi.*
ɒɪ *ẽ gɒɪn wʌrɪ ə sol.* ɒɪ *satɪsfɒɪ wɒt i dʌn fə mi. nɒu!*
ɒɪ *satɪsfɒɪ. wɒt i dʌn fə mi* ɒɪ *satɪsfɒɪ.* ɒɪ *no i cã du no*
mo, nə bɪt mo. ɒɪ *no* ɒɪ *satisfɒɪ wɒt ɪm dʌn fə mi.*
yɛs! ɒɪ *satɪsfɒɪ. wen de tɛl mi sɛt dɒʊŋ bɒɪ fɒɪə n sɪŋ prez*
mi gɒd—wɛn ɒɪ *dʌn prez mi gɒd, tɛl mi prez,* ɒɪ *gɒn tu bɛd. kʌm!*
ɟizəs, kʌm! ɒɪ *gwɒɪn əɟɛn. wɛn də delɐɪt,* ɒɪ *mɛk mi lo kʌcɪ,*
"taŋk gɒd, ɒɪ *si tʌzdɪ." wɛn dɪ sʌn dɒʊŋ,* ɒɪ *gwɒɪn mi rum,*
mɛk kʌcɪ. ɒɪ *sɛ, "taŋkɪ ɟizəs! mama! mɒsə! ɪf* ɒɪ *ẽ lɪw fə si*
dɪ mɒnɪn, tɛk cɛ ə di sol." dats mɒɪ wʌd: "tɛk cɛ dɪ sol;
ɒɪ *ẽ mɒɪn bɐʊt dɪ bɒɾɪ." dɛn* ɒɪ *sɛ: "*ɒɪ *ẽ gwɒɪn tu dɪ dɛwəl,*
fə i bit mi; i wɛrɪ planɪ." an ɒɪ *aks ɟizəs fə bi wɪd*
mi. ɒɪ *gɒt mɐɪsɛf gɒn ɒn hɛwm; mi wɒn tʊ ɟit dɛ.*

---

bʌkrə ɟi dɪ pipl kɒn—kʌləd pipl kɒn fə mɛk krɒp.
ɛnti bʌkrə wɒt brag, sɛ dɪ nɪgə mɛk im krɒp ɒf
grɐɪn kɒn? ɟi yu dɪ barɪl ə kɒn n dɪ sak. yu go də grɐɪn
əm. dats ɒl. de ẽ pe no mʌnɪ. dat ẽ nə du nɒʊ. bət mi
nɛwə gɒt dɪ wʌn. no, ɒɪ *satɪsfɒɪ; an* ɒɪ *kʊk əm n it əm.*
nɒt ə bag in dɪ stebəl; an de ɟɪt tʊɟɛɾə tʊ dat hɒl. sɛ
de mɛk dɪ krɒp ɒf dɪ nɪgə—dɪ kɒn. nɒʊ de sɛ de had ə
ɐɪʃ pətetə kʌl an dɪ pipl ha fə pɪk əm in. dɛn de ɟɪt ɪt
fərəm. pɪk dat kɒtn in fə dɪ ɐɪʃ tetə.
ɛnti?—ɛnti rɛbəl tɒɪm kʌmɪn bak? ɒl hu nɛwə ʃʌm—ɛnti də
kʌmɪn bak? ɒɪ *sɛ, "taŋk gɒd de ẽ gɒt mi han, cɛ* ɒɪ *cɪn*
sɪt dɒʊŋ n krɒs mɒɪ fit." nobɒɾɪ ẽ wʌrɪ wɛ dɒɪanə bɪn, cɛ
mɒɪ tɒɪm dʌn kʌm tru. ɒɪ *dʌn bɪn tru dat. nɒʊ dɪ cɪlən*
də frɛt. ɒɪ *sɛ dɛm bʌkrə gɒt dɛm ɲɒŋ cɪlən fə wʌk fə*
dɛm—dɛm on. yu si? hɛ̃! yu en nɛwə gɒɪn ɟit no ol pipl.
ɒl dɪ ol pipl dʌn gɒn. dat mɛk dɛm də sew dɛ mʌnɪ. tʌk
dɛm kɒn dɪCiə; had ə bɪg krɒp. kɒtn mos rɛɾɪ fə
pɪk. dɛn go tʊ dɪ sto tru dat hɒl. dɛn de brag sɛ
dɪ nɪgə mɛk dɛm krɒp—mɛk dɛm krɒp ɒf kɒn—kɒn. an nɒʊ
de gɒɪn pɪk. de go dɛ n ɟɪt dat kʌl tetə. dɛn yu
pɪk in dɪ kɒtn fə dɛm. nɒʊ dat də sʌpm! yu ə dɛ ɛdɪsto,
yu no. ɒɪ *kʌm si tɪde;* ɒɪ *bɪn ʌp tʊ sɪstə caməl hɐʊs, an*
ɒɪ *pil sʌm pətetə; pʊt ɒn dɪ do.* ɒɪ *sɛ, "sɪstə caməl,"* ɒɪ
sɛ, "yu ɛwə si cat it rɒ tetə scɪn?"
sɪstə caməl sɛ, "sɪstə, sʌpm də kʌmɪn; ɪt ɪz staweʃən dɛ,
bət dɛm pipl nə no."

So I ain't going worry a soul. I satisfied [with] what God done for me. I ain't going worry a soul. I satisfied [with] what he done for me. Now! I satisfied. [With] what he done for me I satisfied. I know he can't do no more, not [a] bit more. I know I satisfied [with] what him done for me. Yes! I satisfied. When they tell me sit down by fire and sing praise [to] me God—when I done praise me god, tell me praise, I gone to bed. Come! Jesus, come! I going again. When it is daylight, I make me low curtsy, "Thank God, I see Thursday." When the sun down, I go [to] me room, make curtsy. I say, "Thank you Jesus! mama! master! If I ain't live to see the morning, take care the soul." That's my word: "Take care the soul; I ain't mind about the body." Then I say: "I ain't going to the devil, because he [will] beat me. He very resourceful." And I ask Jesus to be with me. I got myself gone on heaven; me want to get there.

The white man give the people corn—colored people corn to make crop. Ain't it the white man what brag that the nigger make crop for him off ground corn? [He] give you the barrel of corn and the sack. You go to grind it. That's all. They ain't pay no money. That ain't not do now. But me never got the [first] one. No, I satisfied; and I cook it and eat it. [There's] not a bag in the stable; and they get together to that hall. [They] say they make the crop off the nigger—the corn. Now they say they had culled Irish potato and the people have to pick it [cotton] in. Then they get it [culled potatoes] for them. [They] pick that cotton in for the Irish potato. Ain't it?—Ain't slavery coming back? All who never saw it—ain't it coming back? I say, "Thank God they ain't got me hand, because I can sit down and cross my feet." Nobody ain't worry where Diana is, because my time done come through. I done been through that. Now the children are fretting. I say them white people got them young children to work for them—themselves. You see? huh! You ain't never going to get no old people. All the old people done gone. That permits them to save their money. Take their corn this year; [they] had a big crop. [The] cotton almost ready to pick. Then [they] go to the store through that hall. Then they brag that the nigger make them crop—make them crop off corn—corn. And now they going to pick. They go there and get that culled potato. Then you pick the cotton for them. Now that is something! You are there [in] Edisto, you know. I come [to] see today; I been up to Sister Campbell house, and I peal some potato; put [them] on the door. I say, "Sister Campbell," I say, "you ever see cat eat raw potato skin?"

Sister Campbell say, "Sister, something is coming; it is starvation there, but them people not know."

ɒɪ sɛ: "*dɛm bʌkrə sɛn fid yɛ fə fid wi,*
an dɛm ca əm ʝi dɪ
ɲɒŋ pipl wɒt də wʌk dɛ ɒn dɛm ples. de en də ʝi əm no wɪdo. dɛm də ca əm də ʝi əm dɪ pipl wɒt haw man n wɐɪf n cɪlən də wʌk fə dɛm."

de ẽ ʝi wi nʌn. de lɒ sɛ wi tu ol. wi cã wʌk fə dɛm. yɛs, mam! nɒʊ də fɒɪw ə wi ol pipl dɛ ẽ ʝit "taŋkɪ." si? fɒɪw! ẽ ʝit "taŋkɪ." si? dɛm dɛ də kəmplen. ɒɪ *tɛl əm* ɒɪ *dõ kəmplen.* ɒɪ *lɛf ɒl tɪŋ in gɒd han.* ɒɪ *sɛ: "sistə ʝenɪ,"* ɒɪ *sɛ, "gɒdz gɒɪn mɛk diz bʌkrə ʝʌmp ʌp ɒn ɛdɪsto."* ɒɪ *sɛ, "gɒdz gɒɪn in dɛm bɛd n tʌk dɛm ɐʊt."* ɒɪ *tɛl əm so. de ẽ—nʌn əw əm—bɪn dɛ tɒk lɒŋ tɒɪm. wɛn de si mi, de aks ples fə sɪt dɒʊŋ aftə unə gɒn.*

ɒɪ *gɒn dɛ gɒɪn wɪzɪt əm.* ɒɪ *sɛ, "ẽ gɒt ə tɪŋ, bət ha fə dɪs sɛn fə ɐɪʃ tetə wɪd tri hɛd ə cɪlən." yu si? dɛn dɪ cɪlən dɛ in ɲu yɒk sɛn wʌd sɛ de ẽ gɒɪn ʝɪt nʌtn. si? nɒʊ, ɛncu no sɛ kʌmɪn bak rɛbəl tɒɪm? bʌkrə ẽ gɒɪn ʝi yu nʌtn ɪf yu wɒk dat rod tɪl yu krezɪ an du wɒcu wɪl.*

yu no wɒt dɛm pe fə bin? yu no wɒt dɛm pe fə bin? fɒɪw n wʌn sɛnt fə—wɛn yu pɪk ʌp dɛm bin—dat lɒɪmə bin—yu ẽ nɛwə gɒt bət fɒɪw n wʌn sɛnt in tred. tu kret kʌm tu—ẽ nʌf fə bɒɪ mɒɪ bakə. dat dɪ dɛwəl we de də ʝi yu nɒʊ. dɛn yu nɒk ɒf wɛn sʌn hɒt. dɛn yu go bak in fil. dɛn wɛn yu ho kɒn, de ʝi yu twɛlw sɛnt fə ho kɒn—twɛlw sɛnt—twɛlw sɛnt—ɒl de. wɛn de kɒl bak fə go bak, yu go rɐɪt bak in dɪ sem sʌn. mi ẽ kʌmɪn bak in dat bʌkrə fil an du dat tɪŋ. nɒt mi! no! nɒt dɪʃɛ dɒɪanə. dɒɪanə dʌn bɪn tru so mʌc tɪŋ in rɛbəl tɒɪm: tɛk wɒtə, pɪʝɪn, n ɒl dɛm tɪŋ.

dɪ ʌtkwek [1886]

(*By* Diana Brown, *Edisto Island, South Carolina*)

wɛn dat fʌs stɒm bɪn yɛ, wɛn dat fʌs stɒm bɪn yɛ, yu— ɒɪ *don tɪŋk yu bɪn bɒn. an dat fʌs stɒm—yu no bɐʊt* ʌtkwek*? yu no bɐʊt dak nɐɪt?* ɒɪ *ẽ fyed bɐʊt ə dak nɐɪt nɒʊ in ɒgəs. wɛl, wɛn dat—wɛn dat fʌs stɒm bɪn yɛ,* ɒɪ *had sɛwm hɛd ə cɪlən in mɒɪ hɐʊs. an mɪs batn—an i ʝi yʊ raʃən. an i ʝi mi tʊ ɛwɪ hɛd. dat wəz ə ʊmən. i ʝi mi tu kwɒt ə grɪts fə dɪ bebɪ an tri kwɒt fə dɪ smɒlɪs*

I say: "Them white people [the Red Cross] send feed here to feed we, and them [the white people on Edisto Island] carry it [and] give [it to] the young people what work there on them place. They ain't give it [to] no widow. Them carry it and give it [to] the people what have man and wife and children to work for them."

They ain't give we none. They say that we too old. We can't work for them. Yes, mam! Now there are five of we old people there [who] ain't get [a] "thank you." See? Five! Ain't get [a] "thank you." See? Them there [the old people] are complaining. I tell them I don't complain. I leave all thing in God hand. I say: "Sister Janie," I say, "God's going make these white people jump up on Edisto." I say, "God's going in them bed and take them out." I tell them so. They ain't—none of them—been there talk [in a] long time. When they see me, they ask place to sit down after you gone.

I gone there going visit them. I say, "[I] ain't got a thing, but have to just send for Irish potato with three head of children." You see? Then the children there in New York send word that they ain't going get nothing. See? Now, ain't you know that coming back slavery? The white people ain't going to give you nothing if you walk that road till you crazy and do what you will.

You know what them pay for bean? You know what them pay for bean? Five and one cent for—when you pick up them bean—that lima bean—you ain't never got but five and one cent in trade. Two crate come to—ain't enough to buy my tobacco. That [is] the devil way they are giving you now. Then you knock off when sun hot. Then you go back in field. Then when you hoe corn, they give you twelve cent to hoe corn—twelve cent—twelve cent—all day. When they call [you] back to go back, you go right back in the same sun. Me ain't coming back in that white man field and do that thing. Not me! No! Not this here Diana. Diana done been through so much thing in slavery: take water, piggin, and all them thing.

THE EARTHQUAKE [1886]

(*By* DIANA BROWN, *Edisto Island, South Carolina*)

When that first storm been here, when that first storm been here, you—I don't think you been born. And that first storm—you know about earthquake? You know about dark night? I ain't afraid about a dark night now in August. Well, when that—when that first storm been here, I had seven head of children in my house. And Miss Barton—and she give you ration. And she give me [some] for every head. That was a woman. She give me two quart of grits for the baby and three quart for the smallest *wʌn; fo kwɒt fə dɪ laɟɪs wʌn; fɒɪw kwɒt fə dɪ bɪɟɪs wʌn. dɛn i ɟi mi n dɪ ol man wʌn sak—ə lɪtl sak ə flɒwə, an dɪ kɒfɪ an dɪ ʃʊgə. an dat stɒm—ɒl dɪ pipl wɒt bɪn wid mi ɒn dɪ ɒɪlən—ɛwɪ gɒd wʌn gɒn. gɒd dɪs sew mi n mɒɪ hɐʊs n cɪlən. yɛs, mam! dɪs sew mi an—dɪs sʌkə yɛ kʌmɪn lɒŋ: dat tɒɪd. ca dɪ pipl rɐɪt dɒʊŋ in dɪ krɪk. sʌm dɛd ɒn dɪ ples. yʊ go dɛ n mit sʌm man brʌk. dɪ man an i wɐɪf haŋ tʊ dɪ tri. dɛm lɪk tʊ pisɪz. man, sʌmə ʃɒkɪn tɒɪm bɪn yɛ. lɪk tʊ pisɪz! an aftə dɛm stɒm, dɛm wɒt ɟɪt we fəm dɪ tɒɪd slip in ʊd. wi dat—wi wɒt bɪn ɒn dɪ ples—wi sew wʌn ə tu. wi haw tʊ ba ʌp dɪ hɐʊs. dɪ pipl kɒmɪ hom necɪd; kʌm hom necɪd! tɛl mi aftə sɛ de kɛc bʌdz. lɒd! lɒd! kɛc bʌdz fə it əm rɒ fə ɟɪt hom. dɪ tɒɪd ca dɛm ɐʊt. dɪ ʊmən drɒʊŋ wid dɪ bebɪ in dɪ han, lɒŋ ɐʊtsɒɪd dɪ hɐʊs. sʌm tɒɪm bɪn dɛ; an ɒɪ sɛ wɛn ɒɪ—tɪde wɛn ɒɪ luk, wən dɪ stɒm də kʌm, ɒɪ sɛ ɒɪ dõ ca fə fridəm. wɛn də kʌm dɒʊŋ las wik, ɒɪ sɛ, "ɒɪ ẽ ca fə fridəm, ke ɒɪ dʌn bɪn tru əm." ɒɪ sɛ, "bɪn fə dɪs gɒd, ɒɪ wʊdn ə bɪn yɛ." an də hɪm sew mi. ɒɪ sɛ ɒɪ had fɒɪw hɛd—smɒl cɪlən. wɛn dɪ ʌtkwek bɪn yɛ, wi gɒn tʊ mitn; wi gɒn tʊ mitn. an wɛn dat ʌtkwek stat tʊ ʃɛk, ɒɪ bɪn bɐʊt ə mɒɪl frəm mɒɪ hɐʊs—mi n mi ol man. wɛn dɪ ol man sɛ, "ol leɾɪ. yu bɛtə go hom go si bɐʊco cɪlən," ɒɪ kudn ɟɪt hom. ɒɪ ha fə wɒk ɒn mɒɪ han n ni, ke dɪ wʌl gwɒɪn ʌpsɒɪd dɒʊŋ; dɪ wʌl də gwɒɪn ʌpsɒɪd dɒʊŋ. an wɛn ɒɪ ɟɪt hom, ɛwɪtɪŋ fɒl dɒʊŋ. "faɾə!"—ɒɪ mʌs taŋk gɒd ɪt nɛwə sɛt dɪ hɐʊs fɒɪə. ɒɪ tʌk ʌp mi cɪlən an rʌn tʊ mi mamɪ. mamɪ sɛ: "o, dɒɪanə," i sɛ, "dõ rʌn; də gɒd wʌk." i sɛ, "pʊt dɪ cɪlən—pʊt dɪ cɪlən in dɪ bɛd an lɛf əm dɛ; dɛn go bak tʊ dɪ mitn."*

ɒɪ sɛ, "ɒɪ cã go tʊ mitn, ke ɒɪ nɛwə si sɪc tɪŋ sɪns ɒɪ bɒn."

yu si? kʌmɪn dɒʊŋ dɪ laɪn—dak nɐɪt! twɛlw əklɒk in dat mʌnt wɒt ə kʌmɪn nɒʊ (i.e., 'next month'). *wi had tu tʌk ʌp dɪ ho go hom. ɒl dɪ hɒs gɒn; an ɒl dɪ fɒʊl gɒn bɛd. dɪ rustə də kro. ɒɪ had tʊ gɒn bɛd. wɛn gɒd kriet dat mɪdlnɐɪt, gɒd ʌpm ɛm bak. si dɪʃɛ gɒd? dɪʃɛ gɒd wɒt pipl donə pre tu? 'hʊ̃! ɒɪ bɪn tru ɒl dɛm tɪŋ. yu si? rɛbəl tɒɪm, wɒt dɛm də ɟi yu? ɟi yʊ pɪɟɪn[7] fə it n ɐɪstə ʃɛl, pɪɟɪn n ɐɪstə ʃɛl. ɒɪ dʌn sɛ, "no!" ɒɪ dʌn tɛl dɛm ɲɒŋ wʌn nɒʊ, "kʌmɪn bak rɛbəl tɒɪm." aɪ dʌn tɛl dɛm.*

one; four quart for the largest one; five quart for the biggest one. Then she give me and the old man one sack—a little sack of flour, and the coffee and the sugar. And that storm—all the people what been with me on the island, every God one gone. God just save me and my house and children. Yes, mam! Just save me and—just such like here coming along: that tide. [It] carry the people right down in the creek. Some dead on the place. You go there and meet some man broken. The man and he wife hang to the tree. Them lick to pieces. Man, some shocking time been here. Lick to pieces! And after them storm, them what get away from the tide sleep in wood. We that—we what been on the place, we save one or two. We had to bar up the house. The people come home naked; come home naked! [They] tell me afterwards that they catch birds. Lord! Lord! Catch birds to eat them raw to get home. The tide carry them out. The woman drown with the baby in the hand, along outside the house. Some time [I] been there; and I say when I—today when I look, when the storm is coming, I say I don't care for freedom. When [it] was coming down last week, I say, "I ain't care for freedom, because I done been through it." I say, "[If it hadn't] been for this God, I wouldn't have been here." And [it] was him save me. I say I had five head—small children. When the earthquake been here, we gone to meeting; we gone to meeting. And when that earthquake start to shake, I been about a mile from my house—me and me old man. When the old man said, "Old lady, you better go home go see about your children," I couldn't get home. I had to walk on my hand and knee, because the world going upside down; the world was going upside down. And when I get home, everything fall down. "Father!"—I must thank God it never set the house afire. I took up me children and run to me mammy. Mammy say: "Oh, Diana," she say, "don't run; it is God work." She say, "Put the children—put the children in the bed and leave them there; then go back to the meeting."

I say, "I can't go to meeting, because I never see such thing since I born."

You see? Coming down the line—dark night! Twelve o'clock in that month what coming now. We had to take up the hoe [and] go home. All the horse gone; all the fowl gone bed. The rooster was crowing. I had to gone bed. When God create that midnight, God open them back. See this here God? this here God what people don't pray to? Huh! I been through all them thing. You see? Slavery, what it give you? give you piggin[7] to eat and oyster shell, piggin and oyster shell. I done say, "No!" I done tell them young one now, "Coming back slavery." I done tell them.

dɪ ʌtkwek [1886]

(*By* Rosina Cohen, *Edisto Island, South Carolina*)

an dɪ ʌtkwek? yu aks mi ɪf ɒɪ *no bɐʊt dɪ ʌtkwek? lɒd, haw mʌsɪ! wɛn dɪ ʌtkwek, mɒɪ* sʌn, *kalwəri kʊdn hol dɪ pipl. yu yɛrɪ dɪ pipl hɒlərɪn* ɒl *rɒʊŋ an hɒlə so mɔnfəl: "o, lɒd! o, lɒd! dɪ wʌl gwɒɪn tʊ ɛn." sɛ wi də gwɒɪn sa.*

tɛl—diʃɛ sem man wɛ ɒɪ *də ste dɛ nɒʊ—hɪm granfaɾə sɛ, "unə stan stɪl"; sɛ, "*ɒɪ *si—*ɒɪ *si ʌtkwek fo tɪde."*

dat wəz ə nɐɪt in ɒ*gəs.* ɒɪ *dõ no dɪ det.* ɒɪ *cã tɛl yu* ɒɪ *no dɪ det, ke* ɒɪ *ẽ no dɪ det.* ɒɪ *wõ lɑɪ, sɛ* ɒɪ *no dɪ det; bət* ɒɪ *no də* ɒ*gəs. an de—ɪt dɪs ə go ʌp n kʌm dɒʊŋ. an ɪf yu haw wɒtə, yu—ɪf yu haw wɒtə in yo pel, ɛwɪ bɪt—ɛwɪ bɪt tʌn əm owə. an ɪt mɛk ə bɪg—wɛn dɪ ʌtkwek sɒt ə lɪtl sis an yu go in dɪ fil, ɪt ʝi yu—ɪt mɛk ə bɪg, wɐɪt—bɪg, wɐɪt hol, lɐɪk ə grew; lɐɪk ə grew. an dɪ san wɐɪt! nɒʊ wi fyed, ke de sɛ de gwɒɪn fɒl in* ɒ*n əs. dat dɛ ɪz dɪ ʌtkwek naʊ. dats dɪ ʌtkwek. an yu nɛwə—dɛm bʌkrə had tʊ mɛk wi ʃʌt ʌp dat hol. dat ɪz dɪ ʌtkwek—wɛ dɪ ʌtkwek bɪg. yu* ɒ*ndəstan?—ʌtkwek bɪg dɛ, bɪg dɛ. o, yɛs! ʌtkwek bɪg dɛ. u:! ʌtkwek! bɪg ʌtkwek! u:!*

mɒɪ cɪlən ɒ*l bɪn bɪg wʌnz. o, yɛs! de* ɒ*l bɪn bɪg wʌnz. de* ɒ*l had dɛ sɛns. de* ɒ*l dɪs ə krɐɪ. wɒɪ, də* ɒ*l rɒʊŋ dɪs sɛkʃən kʊd* ɒɪ *yɛ dɪ hupɪn n hɒlə—*ɒ*l rɒʊŋ, an so mɔnfəl. an kalwəri kʊdn hol dɪ pipl. dɪ cʌc insɒɪd dɪs ɪz tɪk; ɐʊtsɒɪd ɛwɪtɪŋ də krɐɪ: "o, lɒd! o, lɒd! wi dʌn! wi ẽ no wɒɪ tɪz." ɛdwəd welɪ sɛ: "no!" sɛ, "*ɒɪ *si diʃɛ ẽ gɒɪn kɪl yu, bət ɪt ɪz dɪ ʌtkwek."*

dɛn ɪt fʌs sɒt ə lɪtl nʌl ə lɪtl bɪt—sɒt ə lɪtl nʌl, ke ɛwɪtɪŋ də nɒʊ gɒɪn sɪŋk dɒʊŋ, yu no. so ɪt dɒɪ so—dɪ ʌtkwek. sɛ de gwɒɪn dat ə we. ɒɪ *tɛl yu,* ɒ*l rɐɪt.*

ə preə

(*By* Diana Brown, *Edisto Island, South Carolina*)

ɒʊə *faɾə, hu at in hɛwm, halowɛd bi dɒɪ nem, dɒɪ kɪŋdəm kʌm, dɒɪ wɪl bi dʌn* ɒ*n ʌt az ɪt dʌn in hɛwm. ʝiw əs dɪs de* ɒʊə *delɪ brɛd, an fəʝiw doz trʌspəs əʝɛns əs. lid əs nɒt intʊ tɛmteʃən, bət dɪlɪwə əs fəm* ɒ*l tɪŋ lɐɪk iwəl. dɒɪn dɪ kɪŋdəm, pɒwə, an dɒɪ glorɪ.*

THE EARTHQUAKE [1886]

(*By* Rosina Cohen, *Edisto Island, South Carolina*)

And the earthquake? You ask me if I know about the earthquake? Lord, have mercy! When the earthquake, my son, Calvary couldn't hold the people. You hear the people holloing all around and hollo so mournful: "Oh, Lord! oh, Lord! the world going to end." [They] say we are going quickly.

[He] say—this here same man where I am staying there now—him grandfather say, "You stand still;" say, "I see—I see earthquake before today."

That was a night in August. I don't know the date. I can't tell you I know the date because I ain't know the date. I won't lie, say I know the date; but I know it was August. And they—it just go up and come down. And if you have water, you—if you have water in your pail, every bit—every bit turn over. And it make a big—when the earthquake sort of little cease and you go in the field, it give you—it make a big, white—big, white hole, like a grave; like a grave. And the sand white! Now we afraid, because they say it going fall in on us. That there is the earthquake now. That's the earthquake. And you never—them white men had to make we shut up that hole. That is the earthquake—where the earthquake big. You understand?—earthquake big there, big there. Oh, yes! earthquake big there. Oo! Earthquake! Big earthquake! Oo!

My children all been big ones. Oh, yes! They all been big ones. They all had their sense. They all just cry. Why, all around this section could I hear the whooping and holloing—all around, and so mournful. And Calvary couldn't hold the people. The church inside just as thick; outside everything was crying: "Oh, Lord! oh, Lord! We done! We ain't know why 'tis." Edward Whaley say: "No!" say, "I see this here ain't going to kill you, but it is the earthquake."

Then it first sort of little lull a little bit—sort of little lull, because everything was now going sink down, you know. So it die so—the earthquake. [They] say it was going that way. I tell you, all right.

A PRAYER

(*By* Diana Brown, *Edisto Island, South Carolina*)

Our Father, who art in heaven, hallowed be thy name, thy kindgom come, thy will be done on earth as it done in heaven. Give us this day our daily bread, and forgive those trespass against us. Lead us not into temptation, but deliver us from all thing like evil. Thine the kingdom, power, and thy glory.

o gɒd! ɒɪ haw ə cans fə ənʌɾə ɟulaɪ mit mi yʌ. stagə ʌp ən dɒʊŋ hɪlz n mɒʊntɪnz; bət ɒɪ aks yʊ, ɟizəs, fə tɛk cɛ ə mi an tɛk cɛ ə dɪs sol; fə dɪ las mɒnɪn wɛn ɒɪ kʌm dɒʊŋ tʊ dɒɪ, ɒɪ wɒncʊ, mɒsə, fə bi tʊ dɪ hɛd an wʌn bi tʊ dɪ fʊt fə dɪ las mɒnɪn. o! stan tʊ di bɛdsɒɪd, o, gɒd! dɪs mɒnɪn. an, lɒd, wɛn yu si dɒɪana dʌn nɒk fəm sɒɪd tʊ sɒɪd ɒn ɛdɪsto—no mʌɾə, no faɾə, no brʌɾə, no sɪstə—ɒɪ aks yu, ɟizəs, fə bi mi mʌɾə an bi mi faɾə fə dɪ las mɒnɪn. o, gɒd! stan tʊ mi ɪz mɒɪ hiə tu mɒɪ hɛd, ke yu ɪz dɪ onlɪ wʌn ɒɪ cɪn lʊk əpʌn ɪf ɒɪ kɒl yʊ. an yu z mi mʌɾə; yu z mi faɾə; yu z ɒl n ɒl ɒɪ gɒt fə pɛn pʌn. o, gɒd! an tʌk caɟ ə mi wʌns mo tɒɪm—ɒn dɪ rod, ɐʊt in dɪ fil, ʌp tʊ dɪ fɒɪəsɒɪd; o, gɒd! tʊ dɪ wɛl. lɒd, ɒɪ aks yʊ tʊnɐɪt, tʌk caɟ ə mɒɪ hɐʊs wɒɪls ɒɪ liw. frɛnlɪ mɒsə, mɛk pis an lʌw tɪl ɒɪ kʌm bak tʊ hom. an ɒɪ aks yʊ, ɟizəs, o, gɒd! bi wɪd mi wʌns mo tɒɪm; so wɛn ɒɪ kʌm dɒʊŋ tʊ ɟʌdn, o, lɒd, ɒɪ wɒn tʊ krɒs owə ɟʌdn fə misɛf an nɒt fər ənʌɾə. o, gɒd! dɪs iwnɪn, lɒd, ɒɪ dɪdn spɛk fə bɪn dɪs sɒɪd tɪl nɒʊ; bət yu z—yu z ə gʊd kaptɪn. yu holz tʊ dɪ hɛləm. o! ɒɪ aks yʊ, lɒd, wɛn yu si mi dʌn nɒk bɐʊt ɒn ɛdisto fəm cʌc tʊ cʌc, fəm klas tʊ klas, o, gɒd! lɛ mi dɒɪ wɪd mi rɐɪt mɒɪn, fə misɛf an nɒt fər ənʌɾə.

NARRATIVES OF RELIGIOUS EXPERIENCE

A. *sikɪn*

(*By* Hester Milligan, *Edisto Island, South Carolina*)

mɒɪ mɒsə ʃo mi ɒl kɒɪn ə tɪŋ. ɒɪ tɪŋk ɪt bɪn ə frɐɪdɪ, in ɟulaɪ. i ʃo mi hɛl; i ʃo mi hɛwm; i ʃo mi hɒʊ tʊ ɟɪt rɪlɪɟən. an wɛn i ɟɪt tru, i ʌpm ə bɪg bɒɪbl; an dɛn i blɛs mɒɪ sol. dɛn i tɛl mi—i sɛ: "go in pis n sɪn no mo. unə sol də sɛt fri." an aftə wɒɪl ɒɪ kʌm ɐʊt dɛ, an ɒl werəs tɪŋ ɒɪ si. dɪ morɪs ɒɪ si bɪn ə ɲɒŋ manz, n ə ɟal, n cɪlən, n mɒɪ faɾə, n pipl —ɒl ʌp in ə bɒndl. de bɪn wʌk had. dɛn ɒɪ si ə ɟadn n flɒwəz wɪd ə fɛɲc rɒʊŋ. ɒɪ si fɒɪw kɒʊ n ə caf, sɒɪd ə pɒdl ə wɒtə. de də ɲam fɒɾə. dɛn ɒɪ si hɛl; ɒɪ si hɛwm; ɒɪ si ɒl kɒɪn ə tɪŋ.

dɛn dɪ mɒsə ca mi ʌp ə hɒɪ hɪl; an wɛn ɒɪ ɟɪt ʌp, dɛ bɪn ə gret, bɪg wɐɪt hɐʊs; an wɛn ɒɪ ɟɪt in, ɒɪ si tu—wʌn enɟəl ɒn dɪs sɒɪd, an ɒɪ si wʌn ɒn dat sɒɪd. an i ʃo mi—i flɪŋ ʌpm ə bɪg bɒɪbl. an wɛn i flɪŋ ʌpm dɪ bɪg bɒɪbl, ɒɪ bɪn rɐɪt dɛ, standɪn owə dɪ bɪg bɒɪbl. an ɒɪ yɛɾi bʌkrə sɛ, "hɛstə," i sɛ, "unə sol də sɛt fri an unə sɪn fəɟɪwm."

Oh, God! I have a chance for another July meet me here. [I] stagger up and down hills and mountains; but I ask you, Jesus, to take care of me and take care of this soul; for the last morning when I come down to die, I want you, Master, to be to the head and one be to the foot for the last morning. Oh! stand to the bedside, oh, God! this morning. And, Lord, when you see Diana done knock from side to side on Edisto—no mother, no father, no brother, no sister—I ask you, Jesus, to be me mother and be me father for the last morning. Oh, God! stand to me as my hair to my head, because you is the only one I can look upon if I call you. And you is me mother; you is me father; you is all and all I got to depend upon. Oh, God! and take charge of me once more time—on the road, out in the field, up to the fireside; oh, God! to the well. Lord, I ask you tonight, take charge of my house whilst I leave. Friendly Master, make peace and love till I come back to home. And I ask you, Jesus, oh, God! be with me once more time; so when I come down to Jordan, oh, Lord, I want to cross over Jordan for meself and not for another. Oh, God! this evening, Lord, I didn't expect to be [on] this side till now; but you is—you is a good captain. You hold to the helm. Oh! I ask you, Lord, when you see me done knock about on Edisto from church to church, from class to class, oh, God! let me die with me right mind, for meself and not for another.

NARRATIVES OF RELIGIOUS EXPERIENCE

A. Seeking Religion

(*By* Hester Milligan, *Edisto Island, South Carolina*)

My Master show me all kind of thing. I think it been a Friday, in July. He show me hell; he show me heaven; he show me how to get religion. And when he get through, he open a big Bible; and then he bless my soul. Then he tell me—he say: "Go in peace and sin no more. Your soul is set free." And after while I come out there, and all various thing I see. The most I see been a young mans, and a girl, and children, and my father, and people—all up in a bundle. They been work hard. Then I see a garden and flowers with a fence around. I see five cow and a calf, beside a puddle of water. They were eating fodder. Then I see hell; I see heaven; I see all kind of thing.

Then the Master carry me up a high hill; and when I get up, there been a great, big white house; and when I get in, I see two—one angel on this side, and I see one on that side. And he show me—he fling open a big Bible. And when he fling open the big Bible, I been right there, standing over the big Bible. And I hear a white man say, "Hester," he say, "your soul is set free and your sin forgiven."

an wɛn ɒɪ *kʌm dɒʊŋ, m*ɒɪ *liɾə, brʌɾə ɟɛŋkinz, bɪn rɐɪt dɛ. fʌs,* ɒɪ *ẽ ʃʌm. dɛn wɛn* ɒɪ *kʌm dɒʊŋ klos,* ɒɪ *ʃʌm ɒl rɐɪt. dɛn dɪ nɛks tɪŋ* ɒɪ *si*—ɒɪ *si dɪ dɛwəl, dɪ dɛwəl. i gɒt wʌn fɒk ɒn dɪs s*ɒɪ*d an wʌn ɒn dat s*ɒɪ*d. wɛn* ɒɪ *ɟɪt in, dɪ bʌkrə bɪn standɪn ɒn dɪ rɐɪt-han s*ɒɪ*d; an i bɪn ɒl drɛs ʌp in ə ɲu bran sut. an wɛn* ɒɪ *ɟɪt dɛ, i tɛl mi—i sɛ: "dɪ dɛwəl gɒɪn pʊʃ unə in ə bɪg blez ə fɒɪə n bʌn unə tʊ aʃiʃ. mɛk unə dõ kʌm owə tʊ dɪs s*ɒɪ*d? mɛk es. unə nə blɒŋ tʊ dat s*ɒɪ*d—dɪ lɛf-han s*ɒɪ*d; mi na unə blɒŋ tʊ dɪs rɐɪt-han s*ɒɪ*d; an kʌm owə yʌ tʊ mi." an* ɒɪ *gɒn owə tʊ dɪ bʌkrə; an wɛn* ɒɪ *gɒn tʊ dɪ bʌkrə, i ca mi ɒl tru ə gret bɪg hɐʊs. It lʊk lɐɪk ɪt bɪn gol ɒl rɒʊŋ— gol ɒl rɐʊŋ in dɪ bɪg hɐʊs. an* ɒɪ *kʌm ɐʊt əɟɛn; an dɪ las tɪŋ* ɒɪ *si bɪn ə bʌkrə. i sɛ, "ɟi əm dɪ bɪg bɒndl." an wɛn* ɒɪ *tɛk dɪ bɒndl,* ɒɪ *si a gret bɪg gʌtə, lɐɪk ə krɪk; lɐɪk ə rɪwə. an dɪ rɪwəs*ɒɪ*d bɪn so pʊtɪ! dɪ wɒtə bɪn cam. an wɛn* ɒɪ *tɛk dɪ bɪg wɐɪt bɒndl, i də sɛ, "unə go nɒʊ n cas dɪ bɪg wɐɪt bɒndl dɪs ɪz fʌ ɪz unə cɪn ɟɪt əm." an* ɒɪ *gɒn an* ɒɪ *cas əm owə dɪ rɪwəs*ɒɪ*d; an i sɛ: "o!" i sɛ, "dɒtə!" i sɛ, "unə sol də sɛt fri nɒʊ, ɛnti?" an* ɒɪ *sɛ, "taŋk gɒd." an dɛn i də ca mi fə zamɪn mi. an wɛn i ca mi fə zamɪn mi, dɛn i aks mi ɒl werəs tɪŋ. an* ɒɪ *tɛl əm hɒʊ* ɒɪ *ɲus tə bɪfotɒɪm bɪn in tɒmɛnt n kʌm ɐʊt ə dɛ. an i tɛl mi—i sɛ, "ɒl rɐɪt."*

an wɛn ɒɪ *kʌm ɐʊt dɛ, dɪ bʌkrə ca mi owə tʊ ənʌɾə bɪg wɐɪt rum; an ɪt dɪs ɪz pʊtɪ! an ɒl dɪ gol bɪn rɒʊŋ dɛ fəm tɒp tʊ bɒtəm; an ɒl dɪ lɪtl enɟəl sɛtn rɒʊŋ. an* ɒɪ *kʌm ɐʊt; an ɪt lʊk lɐɪk ɪt bɪn ə gret hɒɪ hɪl; an de bɪn lidn mi rɒʊŋ n rɒʊŋ.*

B. *sikɪn*

(*By* Hanna Jenkins, *Waccamaw, South Carolina*)

an ɒɪ *gɒn ɐʊt in dɪ wɪldənɪs, an* ɒɪ *bɛg dɪ lɒd tʊ fəɟɪ mɪ fə mɪ sɪn. an* ɒɪ *haw pas tru mɛnɪ denɟə; haw pas tru mɛnɪ denɟə fo* ɒɪ *kəmɛns tʊ si gʊd. an ɒl dɪ sɪn we* ɒɪ *haw dʌn in dɪs wʌl wɛn* ɒɪ *wəz ə dansə,* ɒɪ *had dat lod tʊ pas fo* ɒɪ *kʊd si gʊdnɪs. an* ɒɪ *bɛg dɪ lɒd tʊ fəɟɪ mɪ n haw mʌsɪ əpʌn mɪ fə krɐɪs sek. an i ca mɪ rɐɪt tru ə pɒʊŋgɪn mil—gɒn tru dat pɒʊŋgɪn mɪl. an ɪt pye lɐɪk* ɒɪ *we ɒn ə scel. yu si? an wɛn* ɒɪ *fʌs kʌm tru bɪfo de dat mɒnɪn,* ɒɪ *kʌm əʃɐʊtɪn.*

an dɛn ɪt pye lɐɪk ɒɪ *rɐɪz, n* ɒɪ *rɐɪz ɐʊt m*ɒɪ *slʌmbə. It pye lɐɪk* ɒɪ *rɐɪz ɒn ə ʃɪp lodɪd wɪd pipl gwɒɪn tʊ dɪ si. an de ɟɪ mɪ ə*

And when I come down, my leader, Brother Jenkins, been right there. First, I ain't see him. Then when I come down close, I see him all right. Then the next thing I see—I see the devil, the devil. He got one fork on this side and one on that side. When I get in, the white man been standing on the right-hand side; and he been all dress up in a new brand suit. And when I get there, he tell me—he say: "The devil going push you in a big blaze of fire and burn you to ashes. Why don't you come over to this side? Make haste. You not belong to that side—the left-hand side; me and you belong to this right-hand side; and come over here to me." And I gone over to the white man; and when I gone to the white man, he carry me all through a great big house. It look like it been gold all around—gold all around in the big house. And I come out again; and the last thing I see been a white man. He say, "Give her the big bundle." And when I take the bundle, I see a great big gutter, like a creek; like a river. And the riverside been so pretty! The water been calm. And when I take the big white bundle, he say, "You go now and cast the big white bundle just as far as you can get it." And I gone and I cast it over the riverside; and he say: "Oh!" he say, "daughter!" he say, "your soul is set free now, ain't it?" And I say, "Thank God." And then he carry me to examine me. And when he carry me to examine me, then he ask me all various thing. And I tell him how I used to formerly been in torment and come out of there. And he tell me—he say, "All right."

And when I come out there, the white man carry me over to another big white room; and it just as pretty! And all the gold been around there from top to bottom; and all the little angel sitting around. And I come out; and it look like it been a great high hill; and they been leading me round and round.

B. Seeking Religion

(*By* Hanna Jenkins, *Waccamaw, South Carolina*)

And I gone out in the wilderness, and I beg the Lord to forgive me for me sin. And I have pass through many danger; have pass through many danger before I commence to see good. And all the sin what I have done in this world when I was a dancer, I had that load to pass before I could see goodness. And I beg the Lord to forgive me and have mercy upon me for Christ's sake. And he carry me right through a pounding mill—gone through that pounding mill. And it appear like I weigh on a scale. You see? And when I first come through before day that morning, I come ashouting.

And then it appear like I rise, and I rise out my slumber. It appear like I rise on a ship loaded with people going to the sea. And they give me a *tɪn bʌcɪt. atə* ɒɪ *gɒn* ɐʊ*t ə kʌpl ə n*ɐɪ*t, ɪt pye l*ɐ*ɪk dɪ bʌcɪt cʌŋk dɒʊŋ in ə blak pɪt; an* ɒɪ *haf tʊ gɒn dɒʊŋ in dɛ n ɟɪt əm* ɐʊ*t; an* ɒɪ *haf tʊ* sɪŋ*k dɒʊŋ. an wɛn* ɒɪ *dɒɪw dɒʊŋ n r*ɐɪz, ɒɪ *r*ɐɪz *wɪd dɪ tɪn bʌcɪt in mɪ han. de tɛl mɪ,* sə, ɒɪ *mʌs ca əm tʊ ol ledɪ hɛndər-*ɪsən*; an i mʌs tɛl mɪ wɒt fə du wɪd əm. si? an dɛn i tɛl mɪ,* *yu no,* sə, ɒɪ *mʌs kip* ɒn. sɛ ɒɪ *mʌs kip* ɒ*n; an* ɛwɪ ʌɾə *n*ɐɪ*t* ɒɪ *si tɪŋ—n* ɛwɪ ʌɾə *n*ɐɪ*t* ɒɪ *si tɪŋ. dɛn* ɒɪ *haf tʊ go tʊ əm də mɒnɪn. si?—l*ɐ*ɪk ɔ dat. ən i zamɪn mɪ. mɪ on sɪn we* ɒɪ *had in dɪs wʌl, dat we mɪ dɒʊŋ fo* ɒɪ *kəmɛns tʊ si g*ʊ*dnɪs.* ɒɪ *had tʊ pʌnɪʃ tru dɪ walɪ fo* ɒɪ *kʊd si l*ɐɪ*t.*

C. *sikɪn*

(*By* Rosina Cohen, *Edisto Island, South Carolina*)

ɒɪ *gɒn* ɐʊ*t in dɪ wɪldənɪs; an wɛn gɒd haz blɛs mɒɪ sol* ɒ*n ə satə-de mɒnɪn,* ɒɪ *gɒn tʊ mɒɪ liɾə an* ɒɪ *tol əm. dat wəz* ʌ*p dɪ kʌntrɪ aftə fridəm—*ʌ*p dɪ kʌntrɪ aftə fridəm, yu* ɒ*ndəstan.*

ɪ*f yu sik rɪliɟən, y*ʊ *kəmpɛl tʊ si dat bebɪ. an wɒt* ɪz *dɪ bebɪ? yo sol—yo sol* ɪz *dɪ bebɪ, yu* ɒ*ndəstan. an yu go tʊ əm an aks, "lɒd,* ɒɪ *ẽ si mɒɪ bebɪ dɪs mʌnt." an yu bɛg əm n bɛg əm; an at las wɛn i ɟi y*ʊ, *y*ʊ *wɒʃ əm* ɒ*f n*ɐɪ*s n klin.* *o, lɒd!* ɒɪ *so glad tʊ haw ə bebɪ. o,* ɒɪ *rʌn rɒʊŋ, ca əm tʊ mɒɪ liɾə; tɛl əm.*

i sɛ: "dats yo sol; dats yo sol. dɪ bebɪ ɪz *yo sol. dõ lɛ nobɒɾɪ ful yu; dɪ bebɪ* ɪz *yo sol."*

*wɛn y*ʊ *si dɪ bebɪ, yu bi* ɒ*n g*ʊ*d fel—*ɒ*n ə g*ʊ*d fɒ*ʊ*ndeʃən. dɛn* ɒɪ *kʌm tru fə baptɒɪz. yɛ! bət dɛn yu k*ʊ*dn baptɒɪz. de had* sɪ*kstin ə wi, an de k*ʊ*dn baptɒɪz bɪkɒz no pricə wz* ʌ*p dɪ kʌntrɪ, yu* ɒ*ndəstan. an wi had tʊ wet tɪl de kʌm* ɒ*n* ʌ*p. dɛn wɛn* ɒɪ *ɟɪt mɒɪ wʌk, dɛn* ɒɪ *wʌk an* ɒɪ *stʌdɪ. an wɛn gɒd blɛs mɒɪ sol,* ɒɪ *wɛl no dat. ha!* ɒɪ *wɛl no dat.*

dɪ hag

(*By* Sanko Singleton, *Johns Island, South Carolina*)

de ɲus tʊ bi kʌmɪn in dɪ rum in yo slip; an dak; an be ɒ*n y*ʊ, *an de fil kɒɪn ə hɛwɪ.* sɛ *dɪ hol pʌsən* ɪz *le wet əpʌn yu in dɪ bɛd. dɛn y*ʊ *cã wek. dɛn dɪ pʌsən hu tɛl* sɛ *dɪ hag ɲus tə r*ɐɪ*d əm, l*ɐ*ɪk di tu ə wi in dɪ h*ɐʊ*s, yul bi wek dat tɒɪm. an wɛn dɪ hag wɪl r*ɐɪ*d yu, yul gron. dɛn y*ʊ*—dɛn dɪ wʌn əw əm hu wek, del tɛk ə hanful ə mʌstəd* tin bucket. After I gone out a couple of night, it appear like the bucket chunk down in a black pit; and I have to gone down in there and get it out; and I have to sink down. And when I dive down and rise, I rise with the tin bucket in me hand. They tell me, sir, I must carry it to old lady Henderson; and she must tell me what to do with it. See? And then she tell me, you know, sir, I must keep on. [She] say I must keep on; and every other night I see thing; and every other night I see thing. Then I have to go to her [in] the morning. See?—like that. And she examine me. Me own sin what I had in this world, that weigh me down before I commence to see goodness. I had to punish through the valley before I could see light.

C. Seeking Religion

(*By* Rosina Cohen, *Edisto Island, South Carolina*)

I gone out in the wilderness; and when God has bless my soul on a Saturday morning, I gone to my leader and I told him. That was up the country after freedom; up the country after freedom, you understand.

If you seek religion, you compel to see that baby. And what is the baby? Your soul, your soul is the baby, you understand. And you go to him and ask, "Lord, I ain't see my baby this month." And you beg him and beg him; and at last when he give [it to] you, you wash it off nice and clean. Oh, Lord! I so glad to have a baby. Oh, I run around, carry it to my leader; tell him.

He say: "That's your soul; that's your soul. The baby is your soul. Don't let nobody fool you; the baby is your soul."

When you see the baby, you be on good faith—on a good foundation. Then I come through to baptize. Yes! But then you couldn't baptize. They had sixteen of we, and they couldn't baptize because no preacher was up the country, you understand. And we had to wait till they come on up. Then when I get my work, then I work and I study. And when God bless my soul, I well know that. Ha! I well know that.

THE HAG

(*By* Sanko Singleton, *Johns Island, South Carolina*)

They used to be coming in the room in your sleep; and [it was] dark; and [they] bear on you, and they feel kind of heavy. [They] say the whole person is lay weight upon you in the bed. Then you can't wake. Then the person who tell that the hag used to ride him, like the two of we in the house, you'll be awake that time. And when the hag will ride you, you'll groan. Then you—then the one of them who wake, they'll take a handful of mustard *sid an tro əm* ɒ*ndə d*ɪ *bɛd. dɛn i wek d*ɪ *p*ʌ*sən hu d*ɪ *hag də r*ɐɪ*d. an wɛn i wek* ɪ*m, dɛn i wek* ʌ*p; dɛn d*ɪ *h*ɐʊ*s krak. an wɛn d*ɪ *h*ɐʊ*s krak, d*ɪ *hag cã go. dɛn d*ɪ *hag g*ɒ*t t*ʊ *p*ɪ*k* ʌ*p* ɛ*w*ɪ *gren ə dat m*ʌ*stəd sid an—*ɛ*w*ɪ *gren—an p*ɪ*t əm in ə l*ɪ*tl k*ʌ*p b*ɪ*fo i k*ʌ*m* ɐʊ*t dɛ. dɛn i kɛc d*ɪ *hag. an wɛn i kɛc d*ɪ *hag, i d*ɪ*dn si d*ɪ *hag. de l*ɒ *i g*ɒ*t əm. wɛl,* ɒ*l r*ɐɪ*t! de klin br*ɒ*d. ə ol led*ɪ *w*ɪ*l k*ʌ*m l*ɒŋ *n*ɒ*k t*ʊ *d*ɪ *do, sɛ, "s*ʌ*n;" sɛ, "pliz"—d*ɪ *wɛr*ɪ *w*ʌ*n hu d*ɪ *hag r*ɐɪ*d n*ɒʊ*—sɛ, "*ɟɪ *m*ɪ *ə dr*ɪŋ*k ə w*ɒ*tə." an dat* ɪ*z d*ɪ *wɛr*ɪ *ol led*ɪ *r*ɐɪ*d dat p*ʌ*sən dat n*ɐɪ*t. an* ɪ*f yu* ɟɪ *əm ə dr*ɪŋ*k ə w*ɒ*tə, dɛn hil go; an* ɪ*f yu dõ* ɟɪ *əm no w*ɒ*tə fə dr*ɪŋ*k, dɛn, kos, hil bi* ɒ*n dɛ* ɒ*l de. k*ʌ*m bak: "*ɟɪ *m*ɪ *s*ʌ*m m*ɪ*lk;* ɟɪ *m*ɪ *s*ʌ*m mo fə dr*ɪŋ*k."*

*s*ʌ*mb*ɒ*d*ɪ *in d*ɪ *nebəh*ʊ*d w*ɪ*l sɛ, "l*ʊ*k ə hyɛ, wɛ dat hag at—ol led*ɪ *wag ar*ɒʊŋ *hyɛ so, kip ə bɛg*ɪ*n fə s*ʌ*mt*ɪŋ *dat ə we?"*

*"wɛl, a hag r*ɐɪ*d mi las n*ɐɪ*t, an* ɒɪ *dõ no we s*ɒ*id i r*ɐɪ*d. i r*ɐɪ*d m*ɪ *in d*ɪ *h*ɐʊ*s an fil hɛw*ɪ ɒ*n mi; an aftə dat sem ol led*ɪ*."*

i sɛ, "yɛs!" i sɛ: "wɛl, ɪ*f yu* ɟɪ *dat ol led*ɪ ɔ *pis ə m*ɪ*lk ə* ɟɪ *əm ə pisə f*ɒɪ*ə, dat ol led*ɪ ɪ*z go fəm hyɛ, b*ɪ*k*ɒ*z hil tɛk h*ɪ*sɛf bak."*

*wɛl, d*ɪ *ol led*ɪ *b*ɪ*n r*ɒʊŋ *dɛ, wz ha*ŋ *d*ɒʊŋ*, swag d*ɒʊŋ *fə tri l*ɒŋ *dez. d*ɪ*dn it n*ʌ*tn; kip ə bɛg*ɪ*n fə ə pis ə brɛd; bɛg*ɪ*n fə ə mac*ɪ*z. an* ɪ*t dõ matə hu* ɟɪ *əm; bət y*ʊ *h*ɑ*f fə* ɟɪ *əm s*ʌ*mt*ɪŋ *wid yo on han—d*ɪ *w*ʌ*n hu d*ɪ *hag r*ɐɪ*d.* ɪ*f y*ʊ *dõ* ɟ*i əm, hil d*ɒɪ*. dɛn, i kip ə w*ʌ*ndər*ɪ*n r*ɒʊŋ*, w*ʌ*ndər*ɪ*n r*ɒʊŋ *fə tri ə fo dez. aftə i f*ɒɪ*n nob*ɒɾɪ *w*ʊ*dn* ɟɪ *əm n*ʌ*tn, i t*ʊ*k s*ɪ*k. dɛn d*ɪ *pipl wɛnt fəm dɛ an aks əm, sɛ, "l*ʊ*k ə hyɛ!" sɛ, "m*ɒ*sə, w*ɒ*ts d*ɪ *matə w*ɪɟ*u?"*

*i sɛ, "*ɒɪ*m tu s*ɪ*k."*

*sɛ: "w*ɒɪ *yu* ɒ*lwez go r*ɒʊŋ *n aks dat man n dat w*ʊ*mən tu* ɟ*i yu ə mac*ɪ*z, ə* ɟ*i yu ə pis ə brɛd, ə* ɟɪ *yu ə pis ə f*ɒɪ*ə, ə s*ʌ*pm l*ɐɪ*k ə dat? w*ɒɪ *yu w*ʌɾɪ*n dat s*ʌ*tn p*ʌ*sən so fə?"*

*i sɛ, "wɛl"; sɛ, "*ɒɪ *w*ɒ*nt s*ʌ*pm t*ʊ *it."*

*"wɛl, poz d*ɪ *nɛks nebə ə d*ɪ *nɛks man* ɟɪ *yu s*ʌ*mt*ɪŋ *t*ʊ *it."*

i sɛ, "no, ɒɪ *m*ʌ*c r*ʌɾ*ə haw* ɪ*t fəm dat man."*

*sɛ, "n*ɒʊ*,* ɪ*f yu tɛl d*ɪ *trut, n*ɒʊ*, wi w*ɪ*l* ɟ*i—mɛk dat* seed and throw it under the bed. Then he wake the person who the hag is riding. And when he wake him, then he wake up; then the house crack. And when the house crack, the hag can't go. Then the hag got to pick up every grain of that mustard seed and—every grain—and put it in a little cup before she come out there. Then he catch the hag. And when he catch the hag, he didn't see the hag. They thought he [had] got her. Well, all right! Broad daylight. An old lady will come along [and] knock to the door, saying, "Son;" saying, "Please"—[speaking to] the very one who the hag ride, now—saying, "Give me a drink of water." And that is the very old lady ride that person that night. And if you give her a drink of water, then she'll go; and if you don't give her no water to drink, then, [of] course, she'll be on there all day. [She'll] come back: "Give me some milk; give me some more to drink."

Somebody in the neighborhood will say, "Look here, where that had at—[that] old lady wag around here so, keep abegging for something that way?"

"Well, a hag ride me last night, and I don't know what side she ride. She ride me in the house and feel heavy on me; and afterwards that same old lady [came here]."

He say, "Yes!" He say: "Well, if you give that old lady a piece of milk or give her a piece of fire, that old lady is go from here, because she'll take herself back."

Well, the old lady been around there, was hang down, swag down for three long days. [She] didn't eat nothing; keep abegging for a piece of bread; begging for a matches. And it don't matter who give her; but you have to give her something with your own hand—the one who the hag ride. If you don't give her, she'll die. Then she keep awandering around, wandering around for three or four days. After she find nobody wouldn't give her nothing, she took sick. Then the people went from there and ask her, saying, "Look here!" saying, "Master, what's the matter with you?"

She say, "I'm too sick."

[They] say: "Why you always go around and ask that man and that woman to give you a matches, or give you a piece of bread, or give you a piece of fire, or something like that. Why you worrying that certain person so for?"

She say, "Well;" [she] say, "I want something to eat."

"Well, suppose the next neighbor or the next man give you something to eat."

She say, "No, I much rather have it from that man."

[They] say, "Now, if you tell the truth, now, we will give—make that man ɟɪ yu dɪ macɪz ə dɪ fɒɪə, wɪcsəmɛwə yu aks əm fə, bəl ẽcu ɪz ə hag?"

i sɛ, "no!"

"wɛl, ɒl rɐɪt! yu ste rɐɪt dɛ n pʌnɪʃ."

an i ste dɛ fə ənʌɾə tu dez; wɛnt bak dɛ əgɛn; i sɛnt fərəm.

sɛ, "ɒɪ wɪlɪn tʊ tɛl yʊ, kɒz ɒɪ fil lɐɪk ɒɪ gɒɪn tʊ dɒɪ." i sɛ, "yɛs, ɒɪm ə hag an ɒɪ raɪdz əm."

i wz so wik i kʊdn wɒk; an dɛ tɛk əm tʊ dɪ man hɐʊs, an dɪ man han əm ə macɪz. dɛn i spɛrɪt kʌm bak tu ɪm an i gɒn əwe.

dɪ gos

(By Mary Smalls, James Island, South Carolina)

ɒɪ gɒɪn tɛl dɪ storɪ nɒʊ bɐʊt dɪ—bɐʊt dɪ gos. wʌn de dɪ gos trɐɪ-ɪn tʊ sce mi. an wɛn dɪ gos trɐɪ tʊ sce mi, hi wəz kʌmɪn pas dɪ hɐʊs, an dɛ ɪz ə wɒɪə fɛɲc rʌn. an aftə dɪ wɒɪə fɛɲc rʌn lɒŋ lɐɪk dat, an ɒɪ ɟɪt tʊ dɪ wɒɪə fɛɲc, ɒɪ pɪt mɒɪ han ɒn dɪ wɒɪə; an wɛn ɒɪ pɪt mɒɪ han ɒn dɪ wɒɪə, i sɛ, "bu!"—in dɪ spɛrɪt, in mɒɪ slip.

an ɒɪ sɛ, "o, no!" ɒɪ sɛ: "lʊk at dat gos trɐɪ tʊ sce mi. ɒɪ tɪŋk ɒɪl wɒk di nɛks pat."

an wɛn ɒɪ ɟɪt rɒʊŋ dɛ, i sɛ tʊ mi—sɛ, "yɛs, yu wɒk fəm dat sɒɪd dɛ, bat ɒɪ ʃo gɒɪn sce yu əɟɛn."

an ɒɪ sɛ: "o, no! yu cã bi scerɪn mi ɒl dɪ tɒɪm lɐɪk dat. ɒɪ tɪŋk ɒɪd bɛtə go ɐʊt in dɪ wɪldənɪs n pre sʌm mo, an dɪ lɒd ɪz ɟɪwm mi fɛt fə stan."

an dɛn ɒɪ gɒn an ɒɪ pre; an aftə ɒɪ pre, dɛn i kʌm bak ənʌɾə nɐɪt n stat tʊ sce mi. i pɪt ɒn ə lɒŋ, ol wɐɪt—wɐɪt gɒʊn. wɛn i pɪt ɒn ə lɒŋ wɐɪt gɒʊn—tɒɪm ɒɪ ɟɪt tʊ dɪ do, i sɛ, "miɒʊ:!"

an wɛn i sɛ, "miɒʊ:!" ɒɪ sɛ, "o, dat ẽ nʌtn bət ə cat."

an wɛn i trɐɪ tʊ sce mi lɐɪk dat, ɒɪ sɛ: "o, yu go we fəm dɪs do. ɒɪ bɪliwz in ɟizəs; yu cã du nʌtn tʊ mi. ɒɪ dõ fred."

i sɛ, "wɛl, dats ɒl rɐɪt; ɒɪ kʌm in əɟɛn."

an wɛn i kʌm əɟɛn, i kʌm lɐɪk i wɒn ə rasəl wɪd mi. wɛn i kʌm lɐɪk i wɒn ə rasəl wɪd mi, ɒɪ sɛ: "o, man, go in dɪ krɪk. dõ wʌrɪ rɒʊŋ mi. ɒɪ dõ wɒn ə haw no pat wɪɟu. du yu no dat ɟizəs krɐɪs"—aɪ sɛ: "ɪf yu bɪliw an trʌs in hɪm, nobɒɾɪ cã ham yu. ɒɪ bɪliwz an trʌs in ɟizəs krɐɪs, an nobɒɾɪ cã ham mi."

man give you the matches or the fire, whichsoever you ask him for, but ain't you is a hag?"

She say, "No!"

"Well, all right! you stay right there and punish."

And she stay there for another two days; went back there again; she sent for them.

[She] say, "I willing to tell you, because I feel like I going to die." She say, "Yes, I'm a hag and I rides him."

She was so weak she couldn't walk; and they take her to the man house, and the man hand her a matches. Then her spirit come back to her and she gone away.

THE GHOST

(*By* Mary Smalls, *James Island, South Carolina*)

I going tell the story now about the—about the ghost. One day the ghost trying to scare me. And when the ghost try to scare me, he was coming past the house, and there is a wire fence run. And after the wire fence run along like that, and I get to the wire fence, I put my hand on the wire; and when I put my hand on the wire, he say, "Booh!"—in the spirit, in my sleep.

And I say, "Oh, no!" I say: "Look at that ghost try to scare me. I think I'll walk the next path."

And when I get around there, he say to me—[he] say, "Yes, you walk from that side there, but I sure going scare you again."

And I say: "Oh, no! You can't be scaring me all the time like that. I think I'd better go out in the wilderness and pray some more, and the Lord has given me faith to stand."

And then I gone and I pray; and after I pray, then he come back another night and start to scare me. He put on a long, old white—white gown. When he put on a long white gown—time I get to the door, he say, "Meeow!"

And when he say, "Meeow!" I say, "Oh, that ain't nothing but a cat."

And when he try to scare me like that, I say: "Oh, you go away from this door. I believes in Jesus; you can't do nothing to me. I don't afraid."

He say, "Well, that's all right; I come in again."

And when he come again, he come like he want to wrestle with me. When he come like he want to wrestle with me, I say: "Oh, man, go in the creek. Don't worry around me. I don't want to have no part with you. Do you know that Jesus Christ"—I say: "If you believe and trust in him, nobody can't harm you. I believe and trust in Jesus Christ, and nobody can't harm me."

i sɛ, "yɛs!" i sɛ, "ɪf yu bɪliw in ɟizəs krɐɪs, ɒɪl kʌm bak əɟɛn; an ɒɪl trɐɪ yʊ in anʌɾə fɒm."

wʌn tɒɪm i kʌm az ə blak snek; an i bɪɟan tʊ stan ʌp. an wɛn i stan ʌp, i sɛ, "miɒʊ:!"

ɒɪ sɛ, "o, ʃʌ! dats dɪ sem cat."

so, wɛn ɒɪ sɛ so, i sɛ, "dats ɒl rɐɪt dɛn; ɒɪl kʌm az ə bʌɪd."

ɒɪ sɛ, "wɛl, ɪf yʊ kʌm az ə bʌɪd, ɒl yu gɒt tʊ du ɪz sɪŋ swit sɒŋ, an ɒɪ wɪl no hu yu ɪz."

so, i sɛ, "lʊk ə mi hyʌ."

ɒɪ sɛ: "hu ɪz dat? dats nʌtn bət ə bʌɪd."

"yɛ, ɒɪ kʌm tʊ sɪŋ mɒnɪn sɒŋ tʊ yu. ɒɪ hop yu wɪl bi glad wɛn ɒɪ kʌm."

dɛn i bɪɟan tʊ sɪŋ; an i sɪŋ. so, wɛn i dʌn sɪŋ, i sɛ: "ɒl cɪlrən mʌs bi hapɪ; kɒz," i sɛ: "fot ə ɟulaɪ kʌm wʌns ə yiə an ɛwɪbɒɾɪ haw dɛ ʃɪə. so wi wɪl drɛs n go ɐʊt tʊ dɪ patɪ; an wɪl haw dɪ drʌm an dɪ bes, an ɒl ple fə wi."

an de bɪɟɪn tʊ wɒlts rɐʊŋ. an wɛn de wɒlts rɐʊŋ, de sɛ, "hɛlo, bɒɪz n ɟalz." de sɛ: "dɪs ɪz dɪ we wi ɟɒɪz wisɛlwz in dɪ sʌmə tɒɪm. ha! ha! ha! ha!"

RECOLLECTIONS OF SLAVERY

A. *dɪ yaŋkɪ*

(*By* Rosina Cohen, *Edisto Island, South Carolina*)

wɛn dɪ yaŋkɪ kʌm tru, ɒɪ bɪn ʌp dɪ kʌntrɪ. an i ɟɪt dɪ fɒɪə n sɛt dɪ hɐʊs fɒɪə—sɛt dɪ bɪg hɐʊs əfɒɪə. an i tʌk ɐʊt ɛwɪtɪŋ ɐʊt dɪ hɐʊs. i dʌn ɪt; dɪ yaŋkɪ dʌn ɪt—tʌk ɐʊt ɛwɪtɪŋ ɐʊt dɪ hɐʊs, n ca əm owə dɪ ʌɾə sɒɪd ɒn dɪ strit n ɟi əm sʌmbɒɾɪ dɛ. bət i sɛt dɪ hɐʊs əfɒɪə. an dɛn ɪf yu kɒl, "yɛs, sʌ; yɛs, mɒsə," i sɛ: "hu ɪz yu kɒlɪn mɒsə? tʊ gɒt no mɒsə. ɒɪ kʌm tu fri yu, an doncu lɛ mi—lɒŋ ɪz ɒɪ yɛ, dõ lɛ mi yɛ yu kɒl əm mɒsə."

no, yʊ kʊdn kɒl əm mɒsə dɛn; yʊ haf tʊ wet tɪl i pas. bət mɒsə ẽ bɪn dɛ. mɒsə bɪn in dɪ amɪ. mɒsə bɪn in dɪ amɪ. mɒsə ẽ bɪn dɛ. mɒsə sɛ i don əlɒʊ. dat wɒt i sɛ—i don əlɒʊ.

mi an dɪ ʌɾə sɪstə ol dɛn mi hɛp mɒɪn mɒsə cɪlən—wɒʃ, pac, hɛp kʊk fə dɛm, fid dɛm. ɒl lɐɪk ə dat, yʊ no, ɪz trenɪn yu, yu no—lɪtl smɒl cɪlən, yʊ no. mɒɪ mamɪ lɛf sɛwm cɪlən. de dɒɪ nɒʊ. n aftə fridəm ɒɪ had tʊ wʌk mɛnɪ ə tas ə

He say, "Yes!" He say, "If you believe in Jesus Christ, I'll come back again; and I'll try you in another form."

One time he come as a black snake; and he began to stand up. And when he stand up, he say, "Meeow!"

I say, "Oh, pshaw! that's the same cat."

So, when I say so, he say, "That's all right then; I'll come as a bird."

I say, "Well, if you come as a bird, all you got to do is sing sweet song, and I will know who you is."

So, he says, "Look at me here."

I say: "Who is that? That's nothing but a bird."

"Yes, I come to sing morning song to you. I hope you will be glad when I come."

Then he began to sing; and he sing. So, when he done sing, he say: "All children must be happy; because," he say, "[the] Fourth of July come once a year and everybody have their share. So, we will dress and go out to the party; and we'll have the drum and the bass, and all play for we."

And they begin to waltz around. And when they waltz around, they say, "Hello, boys and girls." They say: "This is the way we enjoys weselves in the summer time. Ha! ha! ha! ha!"

RECOLLECTIONS OF SLAVERY

A. The Yankee

(*By* Rosina Cohen, *Edisto Island, South Carolina*)

When the Yankee come through, I been up the country. And he get the fire and set the house afire—set the big house afire. And he took out everything out the house. He done it; the Yankee done it—took out everything out the house and carry it over [to] the other side on the street and give it [to] somebody there. But he set the house afire. And then if you call, "Yes, sir; yes, master," he say: "Who is you calling master? You got no master. I come to free you, and don't you let me—long as I here, don't let me hear you call him master."

No, you couldn't call him master then; you have to wait till he pass. But master ain't been there. Master been in the army. Master been in the army. Master ain't been there. Master say he don't allow [it]. That what he say—he don't allow [it].

Me and the other sister older than me help mind master children—wash, patch, help cook for them, feed them. All like that, you know, is training you, you know—little small children, you know. My mammy left seven children. They die now. And after freedom I had to work many a task of *de lebə. an* ɒɪ *pe fɪftin dɒləz ə yiə fə dɪ hɐʊs. yɛs, mam! wɒcu tɒkɪn bɐʊt?*

B. *famɪn ɒn wɒdməlɒ in rɛbəl tɒɪm*

(*By* PRINCE SMITH, *Wadmalaw Island, South Carolina*)

wɛn tɒɪm kʌm tʊ sɛt ɐʊt tʊ wʌk, yʊ lɪs grɒʊn. fəm tɒp ə dɪ bɛd yu brɪŋ dɪ gras ɒl dɒʊŋ tʊ dɪ alɪ tɪl ɒl dɪ lan dʌn fɪks dat we. nɒʊ wɛn tɒɪm tʊ baŋk dɪ grɒʊn, yu wɪl tɛk yo ho in yo han əɟɛn n nɒʊ baŋk dat lan ɒl rɒʊŋ. dɛ ent ɛnɪ plɒʊ. wɛn yʊ ɟɪt tru wɪd ɒl dat, n ɛwɪtɪŋ stretn ʌp, n tɒɪm kʌm tʊ plant, dɛn yu trɛɲc ɒn tɒp ə dɪ bɛd n pʊt dɪ sid in n kʌwə ʌp.

de haw tri clas: hol han, ən tri kwɒtə, an haf han. dɪ tas-ro lɛnt ɪz tʌtɪ-fɒɪw fit lɒŋ. dats tʌtɪ-fɒɪw fit lɒŋ—tas-ro lɛnt. dɪ brɛt ə dɪ tas—dat dɪ wɒɪdɪs ə dɪ tas krɒs n krɒs—ɪz twɛntɪ-fo bɛd. dɪs ca twɛl ro ic sɒɪd. kɒl dat wʌn tas. nɒʊ, diz hol han haf tʊ du tu tas ə dat wʌn de fə dez wʌk. dats dɪ hol han, nɒʊ. nɒt ə ro mʌs lɛf. dɪ tri-kwɒtə han mʌs du wʌn ə doz hol tas an ə haf. dats hɪz dez wʌk. dɪ haf han ʃal du wʌn ə doz hol tas, n dat ɪz hɪz dez wʌk. dat wz dɪ we de had əm fɪks.

an wɛn tɒɪm krɒp dʌn plant n kɒtn kʌm ʌp, dɪ fʌs ho-ɪn ə dɪ kɒtn yu ẽ had tʊ pɪk no gras fəm dɪ kɒtn hɪl dɛn. ɪt tu ɲɒŋ; i cã be pʊlɪn ʌp; dɪ gras pʊl əm ʌp tu. bət dɪ sɛkən ho-ɪn, yu cã pʊt ə ho ɒn dat bɛd bɪfo yʊ go tru dat haf ə nekə də lan n pɪk ɐʊt ɛwɪ gras fəm ɛwɪ hɪl ə dɪ kɒtn. dɛn yu tʌn ərɒʊŋ; dɛn yu tɛk yo ho an yu wɪl go, an ɪt tɛk yu tɛl sʌndɒʊŋ fə ho ɐʊt dɛm tas. wɛl, aftə tru dat, yu gɒt doz gras tʊ pɪk ʌp ɐʊt ə dɪ alɪ an bɒndl ʌp n tot əm, ɪf ə kwɒtə mɒɪl tʊ dɪ ʊd ə dɪ krɪk, bɪfo yo dez wʌk ɪz dʌn; an grɐɪn ə pɛk ə kɒn ɛwɪ sɛwm dez fə yu tʊ fid ɒf fə ə wik. ɛwɪbɒɾɪ had hɪz kɒn tʊ grɐɪn. aftə ɒl dat lebə, yu gɒt yo pɛk ə kɒn tʊ grɐɪn tʊ ɟɪt yo fud tʊ it. an dɪ drɐɪwə wəz minɪ n bɒsɪ.

C. *pʌnɪʃɪn dɪ slewz ɒn wɒdməlɒ*

(*By* PRINCE SMITH, *Wadmalaw Island, South Carolina*)

dɛn de had dɪ rɒ laʃ—kɒʊ hɒɪd yʊ no, sə—flat. de dõ ɟi yʊ ə kʌt ɒn yo kloz; yu necɪd. de kʌt yʊ sʌm ples an dɪ blʌd drin dɒʊŋ ɒn yʊ. had wʌk in had, tɐɪt tɒɪm! sʌmtɒɪm de drɒ ɐʊt dɪ tresɪz fəm dɪ bʌɟɪ—drɒ ɐʊt dat tresɪz fəm dat day labor. And I pay fifteen dollars a year for the house. Yes, mam! What you talking about?

B. Farming on Wadmalaw during Slavery

(*By* Prince Smith, *Wadmalaw Island, South Carolina*)

When time come to set out to work, you list ground. From top of the bed you bring the grass all down to the alley till all the land done fix that way. Now when time to bank the ground, you will take your hoe in your hand again and now bank that land all around. There ain't any plow. When you get through with all that, and everything straighten up, and time come to plant, then you trench on top of the bed and put the seed in and cover up.

They have three class: whole hand, and three-quarter, and half hand. The task-row length is thirty-five feet long. That's thirty-five feet long—task-row length. The breadth of the task—that the widest of the task cross and cross—is twenty-four bed. This carry twelve row each side. [They] call that one task. Now, these whole hand have to do two task of that one day for day's work. That's the whole hand, now. Not a row must [be] left. The three-quarter hand must do one of those whole task and a half. That's his day's work. The half hand shall do one of those whole task, and that is his day's work. That was the way they had them fix.

And when time crop done plant and cotton come up, the first hoeing of the cotton you ain't had to pick no grass from the cotton hill then. It too young; it can't bear pulling up; the grass pull it up too. But the second hoeing, you can't put a hoe on that bed before you go through that half an acre [of] the land and pick out every grass from every hill of the cotton. Then you turn around; then you take your hoe and you will go, and it take you till sundown to hoe out them task. Well, after through that, you got those grass to pick up out of the alley and bundle up and tote it, [even] if [it is] a quarter mile to the wood or the creek, before your day's work is done; and [you] grind a peck of corn every seven days for you to feed off for a week. Everybody had his corn to grind. After all that labor, you got your peck of corn to grind to get your food to eat. And the driver was mean and bossy.

C. Punishing the Slaves on Wadmalaw

(*By* Prince Smith, *Wadmalaw Island, South Carolina*)

Then they had the raw lash—cow hide, you know, sir—flat. They don't give you a cut on your clothes; you naked. They cut you some place and the blood drain down on you. Hard work in hard, tight time! Sometimes they draw out the traces from the buggy—draw out that traces from that *bʌɟɪ n ɟi yʊ tɛn ə fɪftin laʃ. sʌmtɒɪm de pʊcʊ in ə ples de kɒl stɒk. de tɛk ə pis ə plaŋk bɐʊt so wɒɪd an hyu əm ɐʊt dat de cɪn pʊt yo nɛk in, yʊ no; an wʌn han hyɛ n wʌn han dɛ; an de wʌk əm ɐʊt so de fɪco han. an dɪ sem tɪŋ fə dɪ tu fʊt; an laʃ əm dɒʊŋ; n yʊ ste dɛ ɒl nɐɪt tʊnɐɪt n tʊmɒrə. wɛn dɪ bɒs kʌm tʊmɒrə—de gɒcʊ we ʌp steəz, yʊ no—an wɛn dɪ bɒs kʌm tʊmɒrə, de go ʌp dɛ n tɛk yʊ ɐʊt n ɟi yʊ tɛn ə fɪftin, n pʊcʊ bak.*

dʌn wɪd dat, de had ə bɒks. de tʌk əm ɐʊt in dɪ rod an de wɛt dat bɒks n kɒl əm swɛt bɒks. had tri sɒɪd an de lɛf ə do. an de pʊʃ yu in dɛ n ʃɛt dɪ do ɒn yo bak dɛ n lɒk yu ʌp in dɛ in dɪ hɒt tɒɪm ə dɪ sʌn; an dɪ sʌn brɐɪlɪn owə yo hɛd. an yu bi in dɛ tu ɒʊəz. de pʌnɪʃ yu. sʌmtɒɪm ʌp tʊ tri ɒʊəz yu in dat cɛɟ—swɛt bɒks. an wɛn de ʌpm dat do at yo bak fə yu tu kʌm ɐʊt dɛ, sʌmbɒɾɪ haf tʊ hol yʊ, bɪkɒz ɪf de dõ, yu fɒl bakədz; fə yu kʌm ɐʊt ə dɛ wɪdɐʊt wʌn pis ə drɐɪ ɟamən ɒn yʊ—nɒt ə pis ə drɐɪ ɟamən ɒn yʊ wɛn yu kʌm ɐʊt ə dɛ. pʌnɪʃ yu! dats wɒt de dʌn tʊ yʊ ɪf yʊ kudn dʌn tas. an dɪ bɒs ʌp dɪ rɪwə haf drʌŋk. wɛn i kʌm ɒn dɪ planteʃən, dɪ pipl ɒl rʌn in dɪ ud, bət de haf tʊ kʌm bak.

wɛl, de kɒt ə man wʌn de n lɪk əm. an de haŋ əm bɒɪ ə rop tɪl i dɛd fə trut. dɛn de pʊt əm in ə bɒks, an wi tot əm tʊ di grewyad. nʌtn wi cɪn sɛ. ɛnɪbɒɾɪ dɛd ɒn dɪ planteʃən wi tot əm ɒn dɪ hɛd dat nɐɪt—lɐɪt in dɪ midl, lɐɪt bɪfo, lɐɪt in dɪ bak tʊ si dɪ we tʊ go tʊ dɪ yad[8] *n bɛrɪ dat bɒɾɪ dat nɐɪt n kʌm bak hom. dat slewrɪ trʌbl dat wi pas tru.*

mɛkɪn miɲu ɒn sn tɛlɪnə ɒɪlən

(*By* Samuel Polite,[9] *St. Helena Island, South Carolina*)

nɒʊ ɒɪ kʌm tʊ dɪ miɲu. ɒɪ pɪt sewm lod ə traʃ rɐɪt in dɪ bɒtəm. dɛn ɒɪ pɪt tri kɒd ə maʃ strɒ. dɛn ɒɪ pɪt ə lod ə traʃ ɒn əm əɟɛn—so mʌc traʃ ɒn əm eɟɛn. dɛn ɒɪ pɪt əbɐʊt et lod ə san-mʌd krɒs əm—brɒdcas əm krɒs əm—traʃ, maʃ, mʌd. an ɒɪ kip ɒn wɪd dat n kip ɒn wɪd dat ʌntel—yu si hɒʊ mɒɪn stan dɛ nɒʊ? ɒɪ kip ɒn wɪd dat, an wɛn dɪs ren dʌn wɪd dat miɲu, ɒɪ dɪs cɪn tʌk əm n brɒdcas əm. ɒɪ tro mɒɪn dɪs we: ɒɪ tro wʌn fʌrə dat we an ɒɪ tro wʌn dɪs we.

dɛn wɛn ɒɪ gɒɪn plant dɪ kɒn, ɒɪ drɒp dɪ kɒn rɐɪt in yʌ. ɒɪ drɒp

buggy and give you ten or fifteen lash. Sometimes they put you in a place they call stock. They take a piece of plank about so wide and hew it out [so] that they can put your neck in, you know; and one hand here and one hand there; and they work them out so they fit your hand. And the same thing for the two foot; and [they] lash them down; and you stay there all night tonight and tomorrow. When the boss come tomorrow—they got you way up stairs, you know—and when the boss come tomorrow, they go up there and take you out and give you ten or fifteen [lashes], and put you back.

Done with that, they had a box. They took it out in the road and they wet that box and call it sweat box. [It] had three sides and they left a door. And they push you in there and shut the door on your back there and lock you up in there in the hot time of the sun; and the sun broiling over your head. And you be in there two hours. They punish you. Sometimes up to three hours you in that cage—sweat box. And when they open that door at your back for you to come out there, somebody have to hold you, because if they don't, you fall backwards; for you come out of there without one piece of dry garment on you—not a piece of dry garment on you when you come out of there. [They] punish you. That's what they done to you if you couldn't done task. And the boss up the river half drunk. When he come on the plantation, the people all run in the wood, but they have to come back.

Well, they caught a man one day and lick him. And they hang him by a rope till he dead for truth. Then they put him in a box, and we tote him to the grave yard. Nothing we can say. Anybody dead on the plantation we tote him on the head that night—light in the middle, light before, light in the back to see the way to go to the yard[8] and bury that body that night and come back home. That slavery trouble that we pass through.

MAKING MANURE ON ST. HELENA ISLAND

(*By* Samuel Polite,[9] *St. Helena Island, South Carolina*)

Now I come to the manure. I put seven load of trash right in the bottom. Then I put three cord of marsh straw. Then I put a load of trash on it again—so much trash on it again. Then I put about eight load of sand-mud across it—broadcast it across it—trash, marsh, mud. And I keep on with that and keep on with that until—you see how mine stand there now? I keep on with that; and when this rain done with that manure, I just can take it and broadcast it. I throw mine this way: I throw one furrow that way and I throw one this way.

Then when I going plant the corn, I drop the corn right in here. I drop *dɪ kɒn lɐɪk dɪs—wɒc mi gud nɒʊ: si? ɒɪ go ɒn. dɛn wɛn ɒɪ dʌn dat ro, ɒɪ tʌn di krɪtə rɐɪt in dat ro wɪd dɪ kʌltɪwetə nɒʊ. tʌk ʌp dɪ bak fit n lɛt dɪ tu frʌnt fit go dɪs we, n dɛm tu frʌnt fit kʌwə ʌp dat kɒn kəmplitlɪ.*

dɛn wɛn ɒɪ dʌn kʌwə dat kɒn, ɒɪ lod ʌp dɪ cat an hɒl dɪ mɪɲu. dɛn ɒɪ gɪt mɒɪ fɒk n ɒɪ brɒdcas mɒɪ miɲu rɐɪt ɒn dɛ. dɛn ɒɪ lɛt dat kɒn kʌm ʌp tru dat mɪɲu. yʊ si? an ɪz lɒŋ ɪz dat kɒn kʌmɪn ʌp, ɪz lɒŋ ɪz dat mɪɲu wɪl bi ɒn dɪ kɒn rut, dɪ kɒn rut cã kʌm ɐʊt owərəm; n dat mɪɲu wɪl ste ɒn dat kɒn rut, sə, n yu wɪl si krɒp. wɛn dat kɒn kʌm ɐʊt dɛ, wɛn dat kɒn kʌm ʌp, ɪt gɒt tʊ kʌm tru dat mɪɲu, ɛnti? an dat mɪɲu wɪl stɛdɪ le ɒn dat kɒn rut; an dɪ mo dɪ kɒn gro, dɪ blakə ɪt ɟɪt.

bət ɟanu—ɒɪ wʊdn ɟi yʊ tɛn sɛnt fə ɒl dɪ bag yu cɪn brɪŋ tʊ mi. ɪf yʊ wɒn tʊ si dat mɪɲu—yu wɪl bi kʌmɪn in dɪ fɒl—yu kʌm dɒʊŋ n tɛl mi.

dɪ cif ə dɪ stiwɪdo

(*By* Samuel Polite, *St. Helena Island, South Carolina*)

an ɒɪ wəz ə stiwɪdo dɛə. an ɒɪ had wʌn krɒʊd—had əbɐʊt fɒtɪ dɒʊŋ tʊ dɪ ʃɪp. an ɒɪ haw əbɐʊt fɪftɪ ɒn ʃo—lod lɐɪtə. gɒt so mʌc tʊ dɪ maʃlɒ; gɒt so mʌc tʊ wɪlmən ɒɪlən. an ɒɪ haw ɒl dɪ to-ɪn tʊ du. nɒʊ hɒʊ ɒɪ manɪɟ wɪd ɪt? ɒɪ ẽ had no ɛdɪceʃən. hɒʊ ɒɪ manɪɟ wɪd ɪt? ɒɪ tɛl yu:

ɒɪ pɪt yu in dɪs ɟaŋ n ɒɪ pɪt dat man tʊ bi hɛdə. kip ɪt in mɒɪn, nɒʊ. yu kip ɒl yo manz rɐɪt tʊ wʌk. an wɛn ɒɪ nɒk ɒf n kʌm rɒʊŋ tʊ ɛwɪ hɛdə, ɒɪ wɒn tʊ no wɒt de han du. If yu tɛl mi, "wɛl, ʃɪʃə wʌn solɟə ɒn əs tʊde," ɒɪ sɛ,

"dat so?"

"yɛs."

wɛl, ɒɪ wɒk rɐɪt ʌp tʊ yu; ɒɪ sɛ, "dɪ hɛdə tɛl mi yu solɟə ɒn əm, n aɪ dɒk yu ə dɒlə."

o, de wɪl kʌs n rew; bət wɛn tɒɪm fə pe ɒf, aɪ kɒl dɪ hɛdə: "wɛl, yu sɛ ʃɪʃə wʌn solɟə ɒn unə. hyɛz ə dɒlə ɒɪ dɒk ɪm. nɒʊ yu tʌk dɪs dɒlə n yu ɟi ɛwɪ man in yo krɒʊd tɛn sɛnt an yu tʌk twɛntɪ sɛnt."

an ɒɪ bɛcʊ ɐʊt ə dɛm fɒɪw hʌndəd hɛd ə man dat ɒɪ bɪn ca-ɪn ɒn fə abɐʊt fɪftin yɛəz, ɒɪ bɛcʊ yʊ kudn fɒɪn wʌn tʊde pɒɪnt de han n haw dɪ rɐɪt tʊ sɛ ɒɪ cɪt əm ɐʊt ə wʌn sɛnt. an ɒɪ pe dɛm the corn like this—watch me good now: See? I go on. Then when I done that row, I turn the creature right in that row with the cultivator, now. [I] take up the back feet and let the two front feet go this way, and them two front feet cover up that corn completely.

Then when I done cover that corn, I load up the cart and haul the manure. Then I get my fork and I broadcast my manure right on there. Then I let that corn come up through that manure. You see? And as long as that corn coming up, as long as that manure will be on the corn root, the corn root can't come out over it; and that manure will stay on that corn root, sir, and you will see crop. When that corn come out there, when that corn come up, it got to come through that manure, ain't it? And that manure will steady lay on that corn root; and the more the corn grow, the blacker it get.

But guano—I wouldn't give you ten cent for all the bag you can bring to me. If you want to see that manure—you will be coming in the fall—you come down and tell me.

THE CHIEF OF THE STEVEDORES

(*By* Samuel Polite, *St. Helena Island*, *South Carolina*)

And I was a stevedore there. And I had one crowd—had about forty down to the ship. And I have about fifty on shore—load lighter. Got so much to the Marshlaw; got so much to Williman Island. And I have all the towing to do. Now how I manage with it? I ain't had no education. How I manage with it? I tell you:

I put you in this gang and I put that man to be header. Keep it in mind, now. You keep all your mans right to work. And when I knock off and come around to see every header, I want to know what their hand do. If you tell me, "Well, such a one soldier on us today," I say,

"That so?"

"Yes."

Well, I walk right up to you; I say, "The header tell me you soldier on him, and I dock you a dollar."

Oh, they will curse and rave; but when time to pay off, I call the header: "Well, you say such a one soldier on you. Here's a dollar I dock him. Now you take this dollar and you give every man in your crowd ten cent and you take twenty cent."

And I bet you out of them five hundred head of man that I been carrying on for about fifteen years, I bet you couldn't find one today point their hand and have the right to say I cheat him out of one cent. And I pay them *ɒf tu. ɪf ɒɪ sɛ, "nʌmbə wʌn krɒʊd, kʌm!"—wɛn ɒɪ kɒl fə nʌmbə wʌn krɒʊd, de tɛn man kʌmɪn, ɛnti? ɒɪ kɒl fə dɪ nɛks krɒʊd, "nʌmbə tu!" ɒɪ haw dɛm nʌmbə, yu no. an fas ɪz de kʌm: "nɒʊ, bɒɪz, lɛ mi tɛl yʊ, ɒɪ hawm gɒt ɛnɪ ɛdɪceʃən. an ɪf ɒɪ mɛk ə mɪstek in pe-ɪn yu, dɪs don sɛ nʌtn tʊ mi tɛl mʌndɪ yu kʌm bak. an wɛn yu kʌm bak mʌndɪ, n yu kʌm tʊ mi n tɛl mi so n so, ɒɪl mɛk ɪt ɒl rɐɪt wɒt ɒi dʌn tʊ yu."*

an dɛm fɒɪw hʌndəd hɛd ə man fəm ɒl əbɐʊt—fəɟɪŋə, ɟɒɟə, n ɛwɪ wɪc n we—an wʌn wʊdn sɛ, "yu ɪz ə ful."

off too. If I say, "Number one crowd, come!"—when I call for Number one crowd, there [are] ten man coming, ain't it? I call for the next crowd, "Number two!" I have them number, you know. And fast as they come: "Now, boys, let me tell you, I haven't got any education. And if I make a mistake in paying you, just don't say nothing to me till Monday you come back. And when you come back Monday, and you come to me and tell me so and so, I'll make it all right what I done to you."

And them five hundred head of man from all about—Virginia, Georgia, and every which and way—and one wouldn't say, "You is a fool."

APPENDIX I

INFORMANTS

PRINCIPAL GULLAH INFORMANTS

SOUTH CAROLINA

Edisto Island:
DIANA BROWN
ANNE CROSBY
HESTER MILLIGAN

Johns Island:
LUCY CAPERS
SUSAN QUALL
SANKO SINGLETON

St. Helena Island:
PARIS CAPERS
SAMUEL POLITE
ANNE SCOTT

Wadmalaw Island:
SARAH ROSS
PRINCE SMITH
SAKI SWEETWINE

GEORGIA

Harris Neck and Brewer's Neck:
BRISTOW MCINTOSH
JAMES ROGERS
SCOTIA WASHINGTON

Sapeloe Island:
KATIE BROWN
SHAD HALL
BALAAM WALKER

St. Simon Island:
BELLE MURRAY
WALLACE QUARTERMAN
DAVID WHITE

OTHER GULLAH INFORMANTS

SOUTH CAROLINA

Bluffton:
BRISCOE BROWN

Cordesville:
HOPE LLOYD
FRANK ROPER

Edisto Island:
JULY C. BROWN
ROSINA COHEN
LARRY GREENE
S. EUGENIE HUTCHINSON

Georgetown:
TONY ALSTON

Hilton Head Island:
REUBEN CHISOM
RUFUS SINGLETON
LOUIS WRIGHT

James Island:
HESTER FLUDD
HAROLD RICHARDSON
MARY SMALLS
HAGAR DRAYTON WHITE

Johns Island:
MORRIS HAMILTON

Mount Pleasant:
ISAAC SMALLS

Pinckney Island:
CUMBERLAND GRANT

Sandy Island:
ELLA ROBINSON

Waccamaw:
HANNA JENKINS

Wadmalaw Island:
CAESAR ROPER

GEORGIA

Darien:
EMMA HALL
LAVINIA CAPERS QUARTERMAN

Harris Neck:
AMELIA DAWLEY
ADELINE ROGERS
NANCY THORPE

St. Marys:
DANIEL ROBERTS

St. Simon Island:
JULIA ARMSTRONG

Sapeloe Island:
JOHN DUNHAM
CHARLES HALL
TOM LEMON

White Bluff:
LAWRENCE W. JONES

AFRICAN INFORMANTS

Bambara (French West Africa):
MAMALU KEITA

Efik (Southern Nigeria):
E. I. EKPENYON
ASUQUO UDO IDIONG

Ewe (Togo and Dahomey):
W. B. VAN LARE

Fante (Gold Coast):
KWEKU ATA GARDINER
KOBINA MBURA

Fula (Sierra Leone):
SAYID IBRAHIM

Gã (Gold Coast):
AKO ADJEI
D. HYDE

Ibibio (Southern Nigeria):
IBANGA UDO AKPABIO
UDO U. EKAM
ASUQUO UDO IDIONG

Ibo (Southern Nigeria):
O. IKEJIANI
L. N. MBANEFO

Kikongo (Belgian Congo):
ELAINE J. ENGWALL[1]

Mende (Sierra Leone and Liberia):
C. M. ALLENEY
SOLOMON B. CAULKER

Twi (Gold Coast):
AKUFO ADDO

Umbundu (Angola):
EDWARD COLES[2]

Vai (Liberia):
FATIMA MASSAQUOI

Wolof (Gambia):
ELLIMAN W. BAH

Wolof (Senegal):
FRANÇOIS DIENG
OUSMANE DIOUF

Yoruba (Southern Nigeria):
A. ADEBIYI ADU
J. TANIMOLA AYORINDE
ABDUL K. DISU
N. A. FADIKPE

APPENDIX II

BIBLIOGRAPHY

A. GRAMMARS AND DICTIONARIES OF AFRICAN LANGUAGES

ADAMS, R. F. G. *A Modern Ibo Grammar*. London, 1932.

ADAMS, R. F. G., and WARD, IDA C. "The Arochuku Dialect of Ibo: Phonetic Analysis and Suggested Orthography," *Africa* (London), January, 1929, pp. 57–70.

AGINSKY, ETHEL G. *A Grammar of the Mende Language*. Philadelphia: Linguistic Society of America (University of Pennsylvania Press), 1935.

BALMER, W. T., and GRANT, F. C. F. *A Grammar of the Fante-Akan Language*. London, 1929.

BARGERY, G. P. *A Hausa-English Dictionary and English-Hausa Vocabulary*. London, 1934.

BAZIN, H. *Dictionnaire Bambara-Français*. Paris, 1906.

BENTLEY, W. HOLMAN. *Dictionary and Grammar of the Kongo Language*. London, 1887.

BOILAT, M. L'ABBÉ. *Grammaire de la langue woloffe*. Paris, 1858.

BURSSENS, AMAAT. "Le Tshiluba, langue à intonation," *Africa*, XII, No. 3 (July, 1939), 267–84.

CANNECATTIM, FR. BERNARDO MARIA DE. *Collecção de observações grammaticaes sobre a lingua bunda ou angolense e diccionario abreviado da lingua congueza*. 2d ed. Lisboa, 1859.

CHATELAIN, HELI. *Grammatica elementar do Kimbundu ou lingua de Angola*. Genebra, 1888–89.

CHRISTALLER, J. G. *Dictionary of the Asante and Fante Language Called Tshi (Twi)*. Basel, 1933.

CROWTHER, SAMUEL. *A Grammar and Vocabulary of the Yoruba Language*. London, 1852.

DARD, M. J. *Dictionnaíre Français-Wolof et Français-Bambara, suivi du dictionnaire Wolof-Français*. Paris, 1825.

DELAFOSSE, MAURICE. *Manuel dahomeen*. Paris, 1894.

———. *Vocabulaires comparatifs de plus de 60 langues ou dialectes parlés à la Côte d'Ivoire*. Paris, 1904.

———. *La Langue mandingue*. Paris, 1929.

Dictionary of the Yoruba Language (Part I: English-Yoruba; Part II: Yoruba-English). 2 vols. Lagos, Nigeria: C.M.S. Bookshop, 1931.

DUPORT, J. H. *Outlines of a Grammar of the Susu Language*. London, n.d.

Eaton, M. *A Dictionary of the Mende Language*. Freetown, Sierra Leone: Albert Academy Press, n.d.
Fligelman, Frieda. *The Richness of African Negro Languages*. Paris, 1931.
Gaye, J. A., de, and Beecroft, W. S. *Yoruba Grammar*. London and Lagos, Nigeria, 1923.
Goldie, Hugh. *Dictionary of the Efik Language*. Edinburgh, 1900.
Guy-Grand, R. P. V.-J. *Dictionnaire Français-Volof, précédé d'un abrégé de la grammaire volofe*. Nouvelle Édition revue par le R. P. O. Abiven. Dakar, 1923.
Hamlyn, W. T. *A Short Study of the Western Mandinka Language*. London, 1935.
Hava, J. G. *Arabic-English Dictionary*. Beirut, [1915].
Jeffreys, M. D. W. *Old Calabar and Notes on the Ibibio Language*. Calabar, Nigeria, 1935.
Johnson, Amandus. *Mbundu (Kimbundu)–English–Portuguese Dictionary with Grammar and Syntax*. Philadelphia, 1930.
Johnson, Henry, and Christaller, J. *Vocabularies of the Niger and Gold Coast, West Africa*. London, 1886.
Kobes, Mgr. *Dictionnaire Volof-Français*. Revue et considérablement augmentée par le R. P. O. Abiven. Dakar (Sénégal), 1923.
Koelle, S. W. *Outlines of a Grammar of the Vei (Vai) Language, Together with a Vei-English Vocabulary*. London, 1851.
Labouret, H. *Les Manding et leur langue*. Paris, 1934.
Labouret, Henri, and Ward, Ida C. "Quelques observations sur la langue mandingue," *Africa*, VI, No. 1 (1933), 38–50.
Leith-Ross, Sylvia. *Fulani Grammar*. Lagos, Nigeria, n.d.
Marie, E. *Vocabulaire Français-Djerma et Djerma-Français*. Paris, 1914.
Meinhof, Carl. *Die Sprache der Duala in Kamerun*. Berlin, 1912.
Melzian, Hans. *A Concise Dictionary of the Bini Language of Southern Nigeria*. London, 1937.
Mende-English Vocabulary. Good Hope, 1874.
Migeod, F. W. H. *The Mende Language*. London, 1908.
———. *The Languages of West Africa*. 2 vols. London, 1911, 1913.
Morrison, W. M. *Grammar and Dictionary of the Buluba-Lulua Language*. New York: American Tract Society, 1906.
———. *Grammar of the Buluba-Lulua Language*. Rev. ed. Luebo, Belgian, Congo, 1930.
———. *Dictionary of the Tshiluba Language, Sometimes Known as the Buluba-Lulua, or Luba-Lulua*. Revised and Enlarged by a Committee of the American Presbyterian Congo Mission. Luebo, Belgian Congo, 1939.
Picq, Ardant du. *La Langue songhay (dialecte dyerma)*. Paris, 1933.
Practical Orthography of African Languages: Memorandum I. Rev. ed.

London: International Institute of African Languages and Cultures, 1930.

RAMBAUD, J.-B. *La Langue wolof*. Paris, 1903.

RAPP, E. L. *An Introduction to Twi*. Basel, 1936.

ROBINSON, CHARLES HENRY. *Dictionary of the Hausa Language*, Vol. I. Cambridge, 1913.

———. *Hausa Grammar*. London, 1930.

SANDERS, W. H.; FAY, W. E.; *et al. Vocabulary of the Umbundu Language*. Boston, 1885.

SCHLENKER, C. F. A. *Collection of Temne Traditions, Fables and Proverbs, to Which Is Appended a Temne-English Vocabulary*. London, 1861.

———. *An English-Temne Dictionary*. London, 1880.

SEIDEL, A. *Die Duala-Sprache in Kamerun*. Heidelberg, 1904.

SPENCER, J. *An Elementary Grammar of the Ibo Language*. Revised by T. J. DENNIS. London, 1924.

STAPLETON, WALTER HENRY. *Comparative Handbook of Congo Languages*. Yakusu, Stanley Falls, Congo Independent State, 1903.

STOVER, WESLEY M. *Observations upon the Grammatical Structure and Use of the Umbundu or the Language of the Inhabitants of Bailundu and Bihe, and Other Countries of West Central Africa*. Boston, 1885.

SUMNER, A. T. *A Hand-Book of the Mende Language*. Freetown, Sierra Leone, 1917.

TAYLOR, F. W. *A Fulani-Hausa Phrase-Book*. Oxford, 1926.

———. *A Fulani-Hausa Vocabulary*. Oxford, 1927.

Vocabulary of the Umbundu Language, Comprising Umbundu-English and English-Umbundu. West Central African Mission. A.B.C.F.M. N.p., 1911.

WADDELL, H. M. *A Vocabulary of the Efik or Old Calabar Language*. Edinburgh, 1849.

WARD, IDA C. *The Phonetic and Tonal Structure of Efik*. Cambridge, 1933.

———. *An Introduction to the Ibo Language*. Cambridge, 1936.

———. *Tones and Grammar in West African Languages*. Reprinted from the *Philological Society's Transactions 1936*, pp. 43–53.

———. *Practical Suggestions for the Learning of an African Language in the Field*. Supplement to *Africa*, Vol. X, No. 2 (1937).

———. "A Short Phonetic Study of Wolof (Jolof) as Spoken in the Gambia and in Senegal," *Africa*, XII, No. 3 (July, 1939), 320–34.

WERNER, A. *The Language-Families of Africa*. London, 1925.

WESTERMANN, DIEDRICH. *Die Gola-Sprache in Liberia*. Hamburg, 1921.

———. *Ewe-English Dictionary*. Berlin, 1928.

———. *A Study of the Ewe Language*. London, 1930.

WHITEHEAD, JOHN. *Grammar and Dictionary of the Bobangi Language*. London, 1899.

WILKIE, M. B. *Gã Grammar Notes and Exercises*. London, 1930.

WILSON, RALPH L. *Dicionario prático: Português-Umbundu*. Dondi, Bela Vista, 1935.

B. OTHER WORKS ON AFRICA

BASDEN, G. T. *Niger Ibos*. London, 1938.

CAMPBELL, ROBERT. *A Pilgrimage to My Motherland*. New York and Philadelphia, 1861.

CHATELAIN, HELI. *Folk-Tales of Angola*. Boston and New York, 1894.

DELAFOSSE, MAURICE. *The Negroes of Africa*. Translated from the French by F. FLIGELMAN. Washington, D.C., 1931.

ELLIS, ALFRED BURDON. *The Tshi-speaking Peoples of the Gold Coast of West Africa*. London, 1887.

———. *The Ewe-speaking Peoples of the Slave Coast of West Africa*. London, 1890.

———. *The Yoruba-speaking Peoples of the Slave Coast of West Africa*. London, 1894.

GREENBERG, JOSEPH. *The Influence of Islam on a Sudanese Religion*. New York, 1946.

HAMBLY, WILFRID D. *The Ovimbundu of Angola*. Chicago, 1934.

HERSKOVITS, MELVILLE J. *Dahomey*. 2 vols. New York, 1938.

JOHNSON, SAMUEL. *The History of the Yorubas*. Edited by DR. OBADIAH JOHNSON. London, 1921.

MEEK, C. K. *The Northern Tribes of Nigeria*. 2 vols. London, 1935.

RATTRAY, R. S. *The Tribes of the Ashanti Hinterland*. 2 vols. Oxford, 1932.

REEVE, HENRY FENWICK. *The Gambia*. London, 1912.

SAYERS, E. F. *Notes on the Clan or Family Names Common in the Area Inhabited by Temne-speaking People*. ("Sierra Leone Studies," ed. H. C. LUKE.) Freetown, Sierra Leone, 1927.

SIBLEY, JAMES L., and WESTERMANN, D. *Liberia Old and New*. New York, 1928.

SPIETH, JAKOB. *Die Ewe-Stämme*. Berlin, 1906.

WESTERMANN, DIEDRICH. *Die Glidyi-Ewe in Togo*. ("Mitteilungen des Seminars für Orientalische Sprachen an der Universität," Vol. 38.) Berlin, 1935.

WIESCHHOFF, H. A. "The Social Significance of Names among the Ibo of Nigeria," *American Anthropologist*, April–June, 1941.

WOODSON, CARTER G. *The African Background Outlined*. Washington, D.C., 1936.

C. STUDIES RELATING TO THE SLAVE TRADE

BANCROFT, FREDERIC. *Slave-trading in the Old South*. Baltimore, 1931.

DONNAN, ELIZABETH. *Documents Illustrative of the History of the Slave Trade to America*, Vol. IV. Washington, D.C., 1935.

Du Bois, W. E. Burghardt. *The Suppression of the African Slave-Trade to the United States of America, 1638–1870.* New York, London, and Bombay, 1896.

Flanders, Ralph Betts. *Plantation Slavery in Georgia.* Chapel Hill, N.C., 1933.

Herskovits, Melville J. "The Social History of the Negro," in *A Handbook of Social Psychology*, ed. Carl Murchison. Worcester, Mass., 1935.

———. "The Significance of West Africa for Negro Research," *Journal of Negro History*, January, 1936, pp. 15–30.

———. "The Ancestry of the American Negro," *American Scholar*, winter, 1938–39, pp. 84–94.

Phillips, Ulrich Bonnell. *The Slave Labor Problem in the Charleston District.* Reprinted from *Political Science Quarterly*, Vol. XXII, No. 3. Boston, 1907.

D. WORKS RELATING TO THE GULLAHS AND THEIR DIALECT

Ballanta-(Taylor), Nicholas George Julius. *Saint Helena Island Spirituals.* New York, 1925.

Bascom, William R. "Acculturation among the Gullah Negroes," *American Anthropologist* (N.S.), January–March, 1941, pp. 43–50.

Bennett, John. "Gullah: A Negro Patois," *South Atlantic Quarterly*, October, 1908, and January, 1909.

Cooley, Rossa B. *School Acres: An Adventure in Rural Education.* New Haven, 1930.

Crum, Mason. *Gullah: Negro Life in the Carolina Sea Islands.* Durham, N.C., 1940.

Drums and Shadows: Survival Studies among the Georgia Coastal Negroes. Savannah Unit, Georgia Writers' Project, Work Projects Administration. Athens, Ga., 1940.

Gonzales, Ambrose E. *The Black Border.* Columbia, S.C., 1922.

Herskovits, Melville J. *The Myth of the Negro Past*, chap. viii. New York, 1941.

Heyward, Du Bose. *Porgy.* New York, 1925.

Johnson, Guy B. *Folk Culture on St. Helena Island, South Carolina.* Chapel Hill, N.C., 1930.

———. "St. Helena Songs and Stories," pp. 48–81 in T. J. Woofter, Jr., *Black Yeomanry.* New York, 1930.

Jones, Charles C. *Negro Myths from the Georgia Coast.* Columbia, S.C., 1925.

Krapp, George P. "The English of the Negro," *American Mercury*, June, 1924.

———. *The English Language in America*, Vol. I. New York, 1925.

MATHEWS, M. M. *Some Sources of Southernisms.* University, Ala., 1948.

MENCKEN, H. L. *The American Language: Supplement II.* New York, 1948.

PARRISH, LYDIA. *Slave Songs of the Georgia Sea Islands.* New York, 1942.

PARSONS, ELSIE CLEWS. *Folk-Lore of the Sea Islands, South Carolina.* Cambridge, Mass., and New York, 1923.

SMITH, REED. *Gullah (Bulletin of the University of South Carolina).* Columbia, S.C., 1926.

STONEY, SAMUEL G., and SHELBY, GERTRUDE M. *Black Genesis.* New York, 1930.

TURNER, LORENZO D. "Linguistic Research and African Survivals," *American Council of Learned Societies, Bulletin No. 32* (1941), pp. 68–89.

———. "Notes on the Sounds and Vocabulary of Gullah," *Publication of the American Dialect Society, No.* 3, May, 1945.

———. "Problems Confronting the Investigator of Gullah," *Publication of the American Dialect Society, No. 9,* April, 1948.

E. WORKS ON LANGUAGE

BLOOMFIELD, LEONARD. *Language.* New York, 1933.

CURME, GEORGE O. *Syntax.* Boston, 1931.

———. *Parts of Speech and Accidence.* Boston, 1935.

JONES, DANIEL. *An Outline of English Phonetics.* New York, 1932.

NOËL-ARMFIELD, G. *General Phonetics.* Cambridge, 1931.

WESTERMANN, D., and WARD, IDA C. *Practical Phonetics for Students of African Languages.* London, 1933.

WRIGHT, JOSEPH. *The English Dialect Dictionary.* 6 vols. Oxford, 1898–1905.

———. *The English Dialect Grammar.* Oxford, 1905.

F. WORKS RELATING TO AFRICANISMS IN LATIN AMERICA AND THE CARIBBEAN

BELTRÁN, G. AGUIRRE. "Tribal Origins of Slaves in Mexico," *Journal of Negro History,* July, 1946.

———. *La Población negra de México (1519–1810).* Mexico City, 1946.

CARNEIRO, EDISON. *Religiões negras.* Rio de Janeiro, 1936.

———. *Negros bantus.* Rio de Janeiro, 1937.

COMHAIRE-SYLVAIN, SUZANNE. "Creole Tales from Haiti," *Journal of American Folk-Lore,* July–September, 1937, and July–September, 1938. *See also* SYLVAIN, SUZANNE.

Estudos afro-brasileiros. Trabalhos apresentados ao 1° Congresso Afro-Brasileiro reunido no Recife en 1934. Vol. 1. Rio de Janeiro, 1935.

FREYRE, GILBERTO. *Sobrados e mucambos.* São Paulo, 1936.

———. *Casa-grande e senzala.* 3d ed. Rio de Janeiro, 1938. (Translated into English by SAMUEL PUTNAM as *Masters and the Slaves.* New York, 1946.)

HERSKOVITS, MELVILLE J. "Drums and Drummers in Afro-Brazilian Cult Life," *Musical Quarterly*, October, 1944.

HERSKOVITS, MELVILLE J. and FRANCES S. *Suriname Folk-Lore*. New York, 1936.

———. *Trinidad Village*. New York, 1947.

JOHNSTON, SIR HARRY H. *The Negro in the New World*. London, 1910.

LACHATAÑERE, ROMULO. *Manual santeria*. Havana, 1942.

LAYTANO, DANTE DE. *Os Africanismos do dialecto gaucho*. Porto Alegre, 1936.

MAGALHÃES, BASILIO DE. *O Folclore do Brasil*. Rio de Janeiro, 1939.

MENDONÇA, RENATO. *A Influência africana no Português do Brasil*. São Paulo, 1935.

Novos estudos afro-brasileiros. Trabalhos apresentados ao 1° Congresso Afro-Brasileiro do Recife. Vol. 2. Rio de Janeiro, 1937.

O Negro no Brasil. Trabalhos apresentados ao 2° Congresso Afro-Brasileiro da Bahia. Rio de Janeiro, 1940.

ORTIZ, FERNANDO. *Los Negros brujos*. Madrid, 1917.

———. "La Música sagrada de los Negros yorubá en Cuba," *Estudios afro-cubanos*, II (1938), 89–104.

PARSONS, ELSIE CLEWS. *Folk-Tales of Andros Island, Bahamas*. Lancaster, Pa., and New York, 1918.

———. *Folk-Lore of the Antilles, French and English*, Parts I, II, and III. New York, 1933, 1936, and 1943.

PIERSON, DONALD. *Negroes in Brazil*. Chicago, 1942.

QUERINO, MANUEL. *Costumes africanos no Brasil*. Rio de Janeiro, 1935.

RAIMUNDO, JACQUES. *O Elemento afro-negro na lingua portuguesa*. Rio de Janeiro, 1933.

———. *O Negro brasileiro*. Rio de Janeiro, 1936.

RAMOS, ARTHUR. *O Folk-lore negro do Brasil*. Rio de Janeiro, 1935.

———. *As Culturas negras no Novo Mundo*. Rio de Janeiro, 1937.

———. *The Negro in Brazil*. Translated from the Portuguese by RICHARD PATTEE. Washington, D.C., 1939.

———. *O Negro brasileiro*. São Paulo, 1940.

RIBEIRO, JOÃO. *O Elemento negro*. Rio de Janeiro, n.d.

ROBERTS, HELEN H. "Possible Survivals of African Song in Jamaica," *Musical Quarterly*, July, 1926.

RODRIGUES, NINA, *Os Africanos no Brasil*. São Paulo, 1932.

———. *O animismo fetichista dos negros bahianos*. Rio de Janeiro, 1935.

SENNA, NELSON DE. *Africanos no Brasil*. Bello Horizonte, 1938.

SYLVAIN, SUZANNE. *Le Créole haïtien*. Port-au-Prince, 1936.

TURNER, LORENZO D. "Some Contacts of Brazilian Ex-Slaves with Nigeria, West Africa," *Journal of Negro History*, January, 1942.

NOTES

PREFACE

1. One informant, Wallace Quarterman, of St. Simon Island, Georgia, was born in Liberty County, Georgia, and when quite young moved to St. Simon Island, where, until his death recently, he lived more than seventy years.

CHAPTER 1

1. For a probable African origin of the words *Gullah* and *Geechee* see Chapter 3. See p. 3 for a map of the Gullah area.

2. See Elizabeth Donnan, *Documents Illustrative of the History of the Slave Trade to America* (1935), IV, 274–587.

3. See W. E. Burghardt Du Bois, *The Suppression of the African Slave Trade to the United States of America* (1896), pp. 108–50.

4. See Frederic Bancroft, *Slave-trading in the Old South* (1931), pp. 359–60.

5. Between 1710 and 1769 more than forty thousand slaves were imported to Virginia direct from Africa (Donnan, *op. cit.*, pp. 172–234).

6. See p. 7 for a map of the West Coast of Africa.

7. Donnan, *op. cit.*, p. 267 n.

8. *Ibid.*, p. 321.

9. *Ibid.*, p. 472 n.

10. Du Bois, *op. cit.*, p. 240.

11. Donnan, *op. cit.*, p. 624.

12. Du Bois, *op. cit.*, pp. 70–71; Ralph Betts Flanders, *Plantation Slavery in Georgia* (1933), p. 182.

13. Donnan, *op. cit.*, pp. 91–92.

14. *Ibid.*, p. 236.

15. Ulrich B. Phillips, *The Slave Labor Problem in the Charleston District* (1907), p. 418.

16. "The English of the Negro," *American Mercury*, June, 1924, pp. 192–93.

17. *Ibid.*, p. 191.

18. *The Black Border, Gullah Stories of the Carolina Coast* (1922); *With Aesop along the Black Border* (1924); *The Captain, Stories of the Black Border* (1924); *Laguerre, a Gascon of the Black Border* (1924).

19. *The Black Border*, pp. 10, 17–18.

20. Personal letter to Professor Yates Snowden, of the University of South Carolina, January 23, 1918, quoted in Reed Smith, *Gullah* (1926), p. 25 n. For a more detailed account of Bennett's views on Gullah see his "Gullah: A Negro Patois," *South Atlantic Quarterly*, October, 1908, and January, 1909.

21. *Gullah*, p. 22.

22. "St. Helena Songs and Stories," in T. J. Woofter, Jr., *Black Yeomanry* (1930), pp. 49, 53.

23. *Folk Culture on St. Helena Island, South Carolina* (1930), pp. 10, 17.

24. Samuel G. Stoney and Gertrude M. Shelby, *Black Genesis* (1930), p. xv.

25. *Gullah: Negro Life in the Carolina Sea Islands* (1940), pp. 111, 121, 123.

26. Du Bose Heyward, *Porgy* (1925), pp. 174–83.

27. *Language* (1933), p. 497.

28. *Op. cit.*, p. 193.

29. I have recently collected among the ex-slaves and their descendants in the northeastern part of Brazil several thousand African words, a large number of which are used by the Gullahs. The speech of these Brazilians and that of the Gullahs show striking resemblances also in syntax, morphology, sounds, and intonation. Many Brazilian writers, including Arthur Ramos, Gilberto Freyre, Manuel Querino, Jacques Raimundo, Nelson de Senna, Edison Carneiro, Nina Rodrigues, João Ribeiro, Renato Mendonça, and others, have emphasized the large number of African cultural survivals in Brazil. See Appendix II for the titles of many of these Brazilian studies.

There have been still other writers who have pointed out striking similarities between the culture of the New World Negro and that of West Africans. Chief among these in the United States are Elsie Clews Parsons and Melville J. and Frances S. Herskovits. See especially Parsons, *Folk-Tales of Andros Island, Bahamas* (1918), *Folk-Lore of the Sea Islands, South Carolina* (1923), *Folk-Lore of the Antilles, French and English*, Part I (1933), Part II (1936), Part III (1943); M. J. and F. S. Herskovits, *Suriname Folk-Lore* (1936), pp. 117–35, where the authors point out linguistic similarities between Taki-taki of Dutch Guiana and the Negro English of Jamaica, Andros Island (Bahamas), and the Sea Islands of South Carolina, as well as resemblances between the Negro speech of these areas and that of certain sections of West Africa; and M. J. Herskovits, *The Myth of the Negro Past* (1941), pp. 280–91. For an excellent account of the African element in the morphology and syntax of Haitian Creole, see Suzanne Sylvain, *Le Créole haïtien* (1936). For still other studies of African survivals in the New World see Appendix II.

30. Usually pronounced *'daΦa* (*'dãΦa*) by the Gullahs. See Chapter 2 for an explanation of the phonetic symbols used in this study.

31. Another Vai word, $dã_{1-2}fa_1$, means 'to fill up, to fill to the end.'

32. *Op. cit.*, p. 32.

33. *Op. cit.*, pp. xv–xvii.

CHAPTER 2

1. For an analysis of the phonemes of Gullah see my "Notes on the Sounds and Vocabulary of Gullah," *Publication of the American Dialect Society*, May, 1945.

2. The cardinal vowels are "a set of fixed vowel sounds having known acoustic qualities and known tongue and lip positions." They are selected, without regard to any particular language, to serve as a scale or measure with which one can compare the vowels of any language. This method of describing vowel sounds was devised by Professor Daniel Jones, University College, London. For a detailed description of the cardinal vowels see Daniel Jones, *An Outline of English Phonetics* (1932), pp. 28, 31–36. See also D. Westermann and Ida C. Ward, *Practical Phonetics for Students of African Languages* (1933), pp. 22–25, and G. Noël-Armfield, *General Phonetics* (1931), pp. 10–19. See p. 17 for a diagram of the approximate tongue positions for the vowels of Gullah.

3. For an explanation of vowel harmony in African languages see Westermann and Ward, *op. cit.*, pp. 127–29.

4. For a discussion of the occurrence of [ʌ] in Gambian Wolof see Ida C. Ward, "A Short Phonetic Study of Wolof (Jolof) as Spoken in the Gambia and in Senegal," *Africa*, XII (July, 1929), 323–24.

5. For a discussion of [ə] in Gambian and Senegal Wolof see *ibid.*, pp. 323, 324, 328, 329.

6. See W. D. Hambly, *The Ovimbundu of Angola* (1924), p. 238.

7. See Sylvia Leith-Ross, *Fulani Grammar* (n.d.), p. 10.

8. See W. Holman Bentley, *Dictionary and Grammar of the Kongo Language* (1887), p. 518.

9. See Heli Chatelain, *Kimbundu Grammar* (1889), pp. xxi–xxii, and Amandus Johnson, *Mbundu (Kimbundu)–English–Portuguese Dictionary with Grammar and Syntax* (1930), p. 17.

10. See Ida C. Ward, *The Phonetic and Tonal Structure of Efik* (1933), p. 22.

11. For an explanation of the use of implosive consonants in African languages see Westermann and Ward, *op. cit.*, pp. 58–59, 92–96.

12. For a description of [d] in this position in Kimbundu, see H. Chatelain, *Folk-Tales of Angola* (1894), p. 22, and Johnson, *op. cit.*, pp. 18–19.

13. For an account of ejective consonants in African languages see Westermann and Ward, *op. cit.*, pp. 96–97.

14. See W. M. Morrison, *Grammar of the Buluba-Lulua Language* (1930), p. 3, where a sound represented by the symbol *h* is described as follows: "*H* is arbitrarily used to represent a peculiar breathing sound which is not found in English. It is near of kin to *f* and *p*, though clearly distinct from each. . . . To produce this sound, as in the word *luhehele*, place the lips as preparing to whistle, not protruding them too much, and being careful not to press the lower lip up against the teeth, then expel the breath, uttering the sound, allowing the lips to fall apart." See also Amaat Burssens, "Le Tshiluba, langue à intonation," *Africa*, July, 1939, pp. 267–84, esp. pp. 272, 278.

15. See Ward, *The Phonetic and Tonal Structure of Efik*, p. 15.

16. Mende, spoken in Sierra Leone, is a tone language, but inasmuch as I have not been able to make contact with a native Mende informant since most of the Mende words found in Gullah were collected, I have not given the tones of any words cited from this language. The tones of many of the Mende words listed below, however, are given in A. T. Sumner, *A Hand-Book of the Mende Language* (1917) and in Ethel G. Aginsky, *A Grammar of the Mende Language* (1935). In the latter work four tone levels are indicated for Mende words. For a treatment of the tones of Twi, an important tone language spoken in the Gold Coast, the reader is referred to J. G. Christaller, *Dictionary of the Asante and Fante Language Called Tshi (Twi)* (1933), and E. L. Rapp, *An Introduction to Twi* (1936).

17. See Westermann and Ward, *op. cit.*, pp. 139–40.

18. See Chapter 8.

CHAPTER 3

1. See J. G. Christaller, *Dictionary of the Asante and Fante Language Called Tshi (Twi)* (1933), pp. 601–3.

2. *Dahomey* (1938), I, 263–64.

3. *Ibid.*, pp. 264–65.

4. *Ibid.*, pp. 265–66.

5. *Ibid.*, p. 151. For an account of Ewe names see D. Westermann, *Die Glidyi-Ewe in Togo* (1935), pp. 18–27, and *A Study of the Ewe Language* (1930), pp. 43–47.

6. See Maurice Delafosse, *La Langue mandingue* (1929), I, 305–11.

7. See his *History of the Yorubas* (1921), pp. 79–87:

8. In Yoruba texts this sound is represented by *j*. D. Westermann and Ida C. Ward (*Practical Phonetics for Students of African Languages* [1933], p. 168) describe the sound as follows: "*j* . . . is somewhat palatalized and is very weak: it has little friction, and resembles *dy* [ɟ] particularly before [i, e, ɛ]; before [a, ɔ, o] it is like a weak English *j* in *ridge*." I have chosen the symbol [ɟ] rather than [*d*ʒ], which in this study represents the affricate, because in the speech of my Yoruba informant, J. T. Ayorinde, of Abeokuta, Nigeria, the sound in all positions is a plosive rather than an affricate.

9. *ny* = [ɲ].

10. *Niger Ibos* (n.d.), pp. 174–75.

11. *The Northern Tribes of Nigeria* (1925), II, 79–82. For a treatment of Hausa naming customs see Joseph Greenberg, *The Influence of Islam on a Sudanese Religion* (1946), pp. 22–23.

12. *The Ovimbundu of Angola* (1934), pp. 188–89.

13. No attempt has been made to specify every word of Arabic derivation.

14. All references in this study to Kongo are to the language as spoken in Angola and as treated by W. Holman Bentley in his *Dictionary and Grammar of the Kongo Language* (1887).

15. Among the Twi and Fante of the Gold Coast, derivatives of the names of the seven days of the week are given to children to indicate the day of their birth. The Ewe of Dahomey and Togo have borrowed the custom from the Twi people and use the same names with slight changes in pronunciation. The following are the Twi words for the seven days, together with the drivatives given the boys and those given the girls:

Name of the Day		Name Given a Boy	Name Given a Girl
Sunday	*kwasida*	*kwasi*	*akosua*
Monday	*dwoda*	*kwadwo*	*adwowa*
Tuesday	*benada*	*kwabena*	*abena*
Wednesday	*wukuda*	*kwaku*	*akua*
Thursday	*yauda*	*yau*	*ya:*
Friday	*fida*	*kofi*	*afuwa*
Saturday	*memeneda*	*kwame*	*amma*

The seven days of the week are named after the following seven personal beings or genii: *ayisi*, *adwo*, *bena*, *wuku*, *yau*, *afi*, and *ameŋ* (Christaller, *op. cit.*, pp. 599–600).

16. ʃaŋ$_1$go$_3$ is the Yoruba god of thunder. Among the Yoruba a priest or priestess of ʃaŋ$_1$go$_3$ is called a$_2$do$_3$ʃu$_1$ ʃaŋ$_1$go$_3$.

17. In Brazil both *aka'ra* and *akara'*ʒɛ are words for a dish consisting of beans cooked with African palm oil.

18. See Hans Melzian, *A Concise Dictionary of the Bini Language of Southern Nigeria* (1937), p. 8.

19. On St. Simon Island, Georgia, *al'telu* 'you' and *n'telu* 'we' are brothers, both names being Mandinka words.

20. *w* here is the palatal rounded semivowel [ɥ].

21. *ba*$_2$*ba*$_2$*lu*$_3$*ai*$_1$*ye*$_3$ occurs in a current popular song played by Latin-American orchestras.

22. In *ba*$_3$-ŋ$_2$*gba*$_3$*la*$_1$, *ba*$_3$-ŋ$_2$*gbo*$_3$*ʃe*$_3$, and *ba*$_3$-ŋ$_2$*kɔ*$_3$*le*$_3$, [ŋ] is syllabic. It has the mid-tone.

23. For a discussion of the pronunciation of [d] before [i] in Kimbundu, see Amandus Johnson, *Mbundu (Kimbundu)–English–Portuguese Dictionary with Grammar and Syntax* (1930), p. 18.

24. *w* here is the palatal rounded semivowel [ɥ].

25. See Delafosse, *Manuel dahomeen* (1894), pp. 175, 377.

26. Apparently the Bini speaker's pronunciation of the English word *carpenter*. Another word in Bini for 'carpenter' is *on*$_3$*wi*$_1$*na*$_3$.

27. The symbol *f* used in Gullah words represents the voiceless bilabial fricative [Φ].

28. For the meanings of *fufu* in other West African languages see below, p. 193.

29. "The *i*$_1$*zo*$_{3-1}$*bo*$_3$ may be given as a measure of defence as well as in order to injure somebody. . . . It is done at the junction of roads, . . . in one's own backyard, or in still other places. The food is prepared at home and by private individuals; there is no slaughtering as in a real sacrifice; only a chicken may be given and that is killed at home" (Melzian, *op. cit.*, p. 108).

30. Among the ex-slaves of Bahia, Brazil, this word is pronounced *kamu*'ʃɔʃɔ.

31. "Where the use of proper names can conveniently be avoided the Mandinkos prefer some other method of attracting attention or of indicating to whom they are speaking. This is probably due to the fear of magic, that an evilly disposed person on hearing the personal names of the speakers would be able to bewitch them, but that if he did not know the names he would be unable to harm them" (W. T. Hamlyn, *A Short History of the Western Mankinka Language* [1935], p. 80).

32. See Heli Chatelain, *Grammatica elementar do Kimbundu ou lingua de Angola* (1888–89), pp. xi–xii, and Amandus Johnson, *op. cit.*, pp. 13–15.

33. *kɔ*$_1$*nɔ*$_{2-1}$ and *kɔ*$_3$*nɔ*$_{3-1}$ are among those words in the Mandingo languages which are still distinguished by tone.

34. "A being of an intermediate order between God and men, a sort of demigod, and in the opinion of the Temnes an object worthy of adoration. . . . The religion of the Temnes consists properly in the worship of the krifis" (C. F. Schlenker, *Temne Traditions, Fables and Proverbs* [1861], p. 193).

35. On St. Simon Island, Georgia, in the Hunter family, '*kudu* and '*kuɟi* are brother and sister, respectively. Both words are found in the Ewe language.

36. The two classes of noblemen at ɔ$_1$*y*ɔ$_2$ are the ɔ$_1$*y*ɔ$_3$*mi*$_1$*si*$_1$ and the ɛ$_1$ʃɔ$_3$. One of the seven ɔ$_1$*y*ɔ$_3$*mi*$_1$*si*$_1$ is called *la*$_3$*gu*$_3$*na*$_1$.

37. In Rio de Janeiro the African fetish cults are called the *ma*'*kumba;* in Bahia, Brazil, they are known as the ˌ*kandəm*'*blɛ*.

38. See Hamlyn, *op. cit.*, pp. 68, 81.

39. In the Yoruba cult houses of Bahia, Brazil, where most of the worshipers of Yoruba deities are also members of the Catholic church, several of the minor deities are identified with Catholic saints; *o*$_1$*ʃa*$_2$*la*$_3$, however, is identified with Christ (*o Senhor do Bomfim*).

40. In the Yoruba country the Roman Catholics and the Episcopalians use

sa_1mi_1 to mean 'baptize'; whereas the Baptists use $tɛ_1bɔ_2mi_2$, lit. 'to dip into the water.' In biblical translations $bap_2ti_2si_3$ and $i_1bap_2ti_2si_3$ occur, respectively, for 'baptize' and 'baptism.'

41. Apparently the Yoruba god of thunder, $ʃaŋ_1go_3$.

42. Bentley, *op. cit.*, p. 437.

43. The symbol *w* used in Gullah words usually represents the voiced bilabial fricative [β]; in a few instances it represents the voiced frictionless continuant [ϑ].

44. In Twi texts, written *yaw*.

45. In Twi texts, written *yawda*.

46. In his *Collecção de observações grammaticaes sobre a lingua bunda ou angolense* (1859), p. 151, Fr. Bernardo Maria de Cannecattim defines *zimbu* as 'coin, money.'

47. Several lists of Gullah words include *malafee* 'whiskey.' Dr. Guy B. Johnson (*Folk Culture on St. Helena Island, South Carolina* [1930], p. 56) says that "*malafee* could be an English dialectal pronunciation of *malvesie* and might have entered this country with the English. . . . At any rate," he continues, "this word affords an excellent illustration of the need for caution in the study of strange words found in American Negro speech." None of my Gullah informants were acquainted with *malafee*, but most of them knew *ma'lawu*, i.e. [*ma'la*β*u*] ([*ma'lu*ϑ*u*]). The word *malavu* 'wine' is found in the Kongo language, spoken in Angola and the Belgian Congo, the very areas from which thousands of the slaves were being brought direct to South Carolina throughout the eighteenth century and the first half of the nineteenth. Since Kongo has supplied Gullah with several hundred other words, it is not at all unreasonable to suppose that this word got into Gullah in a similar manner. In Tshiluba, also spoken in the Belgian Congo, the word for 'palm wine' and for 'beer made from corn' is *maluvu*.

48. Bentley, *op. cit.*, p. 414.

49. This section is especially important from the point of view of the nature of the linguistic retentions which it reveals. See Chapter 9 for a discussion of the songs and stories containing many of the words and combinations of words listed here.

CHAPTER 4

1. $w'e_3pi_3ra_3 = wɔ_3\ e_3pi_3ra_3$.

2. For varieties of parataxis in English and other languages see Leonard Bloomfield, *Language* (1933), pp. 171, 176–77, 185–86, 254, 259, 263. See also George O. Curme, *Syntax* (1931), pp. 170–73.

3. For a similar construction in Fante see W. T. Balmer and F. C. F. Grant, *A Grammar of the Fante-Akan Language* (1929), p. 120.

4. For other examples see D. Westermann, *A Study of the Ewe Language* (1930), p. 95.

5. In several of the British dialects, *na* 'than' frequently occurs as a variant of *nor*. See Joseph Wright, *The English Dialect Dictionary* (1905), IV, 296–97.

6. See Curme, *op. cit.*, pp. 28–30.

7. See above, pp. 209–12, 215–16.

8. See Chapter 6.

9. See Chapter 9. See also p. 229, where it is shown that the position alone of a noun in the sentence determines whether the noun is the possessor or the thing possessed.

10. For examples of this practice in English see Curme, *op. cit.*, pp. 28–29.

11. For examples see *ibid.*, pp. 3–4.

12. For a discussion of the word order and the *do*-form in interrogative sentences in early and modern English see *ibid.*, pp. 13, 22–26, 352, 353.

13. See Chapter 8.

14. See Ida C. Ward, *The Phonetic and Tonal Structure of Efik* (1933), pp. 132–39.

15. For additional examples see Chapter 9.

CHAPTER 5

1. Among the few exceptions are *'cɪlən* 'children' and *manz* 'men'; but the singular form of each of these is also used as a plural.

2. Another method of forming plurals in Gã is to add *i* to words ending in *lɔ*$_1$ 'one who': e.g., *la*$_3$*lɔ*$_2$ 'a singer, one who sings'; *la*$_3$*lɔ*$_1$*-i*$_1$ 'singers.'

3. See W. T. Hamlyn, *A Short Study of the Western Mandinka Language* (1935), pp. 11–12.

4. W. Holman Bentley, *Dictionary and Grammar of the Kongo Language* (1887), p. 649.

5. See Amandus Johnson, *Mbundu (Kimbundu)–English–Portuguese Dictionary with Grammar and Syntax* (1930), p. 69.

6. A syntactical feature is involved here. The position alone of the noun determines whether it is the possessor or the thing possessed.

7. See R. F. G. Adams, *A Modern Ibo Grammar* (1932), pp. 23–24.

8. Usually written *ɛi*$_2$*yɛ*$_2$ in Yoruba texts.

9. See Johnson, *op. cit.*, pp. 26–27.

CHAPTER 6

1. For a treatment of group words in early and modern English see George O. Curme, *Syntax* (1931), pp. 572–75. For varieties of compounds in English and other languages see Leonard Bloomfield, *Language* (1933), pp. 227–37.

2. Cf. a similar expression from Vai: *i*$_3$ *da*$_3$ *ma*$_1$ *ki*$_1$*li*$_1$ 'Stop talking,' lit. 'Your mouth on tie.'

3. Cf. similar expressions from the following African languages: Gã: *nã*$_1$ *ŋɔ̃*$_3$*lɔ̃*$_2$ 'flattery,' lit. 'one who has a sweet mouth'; Yoruba: *ɛ*$_1$*nũ*$_1$ *di*$_3$*dũ*$_1$ 'persuasiveness,' lit. 'mouth sweet'; Vai: *da*$_3$ *ki*$_3$*ɲa*$_3$ 'flattery,' lit. 'mouth sweet.'

4. Cf. also the Portuguese expression *o mês que vem* 'next month,' lit. 'the month that is coming.'

5. For the meanings of these words in the African languages see Chapter 3.

6. *'kɔkɔ* is also a place-name in coastal South Carolina.

7. *'titi* is also a place-name in coastal South Carolina. There are other place-names in the Gullah area that may be African words. Among these are the following: *Coosaw* (a river and an island), *Okatee* (a river), *Peedee* (a river), *Tybee* (an island and a creek), *Wahoo* (a river and an island), *Wando* (a river), and *Wassaw* (a sound and an island). Cf., respectively, the following African words: Dj., *kusɔ* 'dusty'; U., *okati* 'middle, interior'; K., *mpidi* 'a species of viper'; H., *tai*$_3$*bi*$_3$ 'an especially fertile, low-lying farmland'; Y., *wa*$_3$*hũ*$_1$, 'to trill the voice'; H., *wan*$_1$*do*$_2$ 'trousers'; T., *wasau* 'a district, tribe, and dialect of the Gold Coast' (written *wasaw* in Twi texts).

8. du_3 is used only predicatively; du_3du_3, when an adjective, may be used attributively or predicatively.

9. $f\tilde{u}_3$ is used only predicatively; $f\tilde{u}_3f\tilde{u}_3$, when an adjective, may be used attributively or predicatively.

10. For additional examples of onomatopoetic expressions in Ewe see D. Westermann, *A Study of the Ewe Language* (1930), pp. 107–9, 188–89.

CHAPTER 7

1. See D. Westermann and Ida C. Ward, *Practical Phonetics for Students of African Languages* (1933), pp. 89, 96–97.
2. See R. F. G. Adams, *A Modern Ibo Grammar* (1932), pp. 3–4.
3. Joseph Wright, *The English Dialect Grammar* (1905), p. 221.
4. IV, 314.
5. For a description of [ɽ] see Chapter 2.
6. See Westermann and Ward, *op. cit.*, pp. 89, 96–97.
7. D. Westermann, *A Study of the Ewe Language* (1930), pp. 15, 19.
8. *Op. cit.*, p. 232.
9. *Ibid.*, pp. 241–42.
10. See Adams, *op. cit.*, p. 5.
11. For an account of the occurrence of this sound in several African languages see Westermann and Ward, *op. cit.*, p. 82.
12. See Chapter 8.

CHAPTER 8

1. Such words and phrases in cultivated English would be pronounced with a falling tone on the last stressed syllable.

CHAPTER 9

1. Dr. Ben Gray Lumpkin, of the University of Colorado, has called my attention to a quotation from Joseph B. Cobb's *Mississippi Scenes* (Philadelphia, 1851), p. 176, in which Cobb says that a slave, a native African, taught him the following African numerals from one to ten: "Kelleh, fullah, subah, nanni, lolo, waulo, oolulah, suggah, conontah, tah." Although Cobb's spelling is not strictly phonetic, the numerals which he learned from the slave are very probably from a Mandingo language. The following numerals from one to ten, which bear a striking resemblance to those quoted by Cobb, are from Malinke, Kankanka, Jalunka, and Mandinka—all belonging to the Mandingo group:

Malinke: *kiliŋ, fula, saba, nani, lulu, woro, worõ-ula, segi, konõto, tã*
Kankanka: *keleŋ, fila, saba, nani, lolu, wɔrɔ, woroŋla, segi, konondo, taŋ*
Jalunka: *keleŋ, fila, sawa, nani, lolu, wɔrɔ, woroŋla, sagiŋ, konondo, taŋ*
Mandinka: *kil:iŋ, fula, sab:a, nani, lulu, woro, worowula, sei, kononto, taŋ.*

2. For several of these songs see Lydia Parrish, *Slave Songs of the Georgia Sea Islands* (1942).

3. See Chapters 4, 5, 6, 7, and 8, where many of the Gullah examples are drawn from these texts and where also is demonstrated the way in which these examples reveal the influence of certain West African languages.

4. For the melody of this song, see *Slave Songs of the Georgia Sea Islands*, p. 49, by Lydia Parrish, for whom I recorded this and other Gullah songs.

5. That is, in old age.

6. Flour had been provided by the American Red Cross for needy islanders, but those persons on Edisto Island in charge of the distribution of it apparently had not delivered to Diana Brown her share.

7. That is, coarse food which the piggin contained.

8. Graveyard.

9. Samuel Polite died in the summer of 1944 at the age of one hundred. His death resulted from a burn he received when his pipe fell into his bosom while he was working on his farm on St. Helena Island.

APPENDIX I

1. Elaine J. Engwall, the daughter of missionaries, was taken to the Belgian Congo in 1924 before she was two years of age and lived there until 1940, learning Kikongo and English simultaneously. She speaks both languages equally well.

2. Edward Coles, the son of Americans, was born and reared in Angola and learned Umbundu, Portuguese, and English simultaneously. His father, Mr. Samuel B. Coles, was for several years an agriculturist at Ngalangi, Angola.

INDEX

CPSIA information can be obtained
at www.ICGtesting.com
Printed in the USA
BVOW06s0559161116
468023BV00002B/5/P

9 781570 034527